Essays on the Rhetoric of the Western World

Edited by
Edward P. J. Corbett
James L. Golden
Goodwin F. Berquist
Ohio State University

KENDALL/HUNT PUBLISHING COMPANY
2460 Kerper Boulevard   P.O. Box 539   Dubuque, Iowa 52004-0539

Copyright © 1990 by Kendall/Hunt Publishing Company

Library of Congress Catalog Card Number: 90–60066

ISBN 0–8493–5660–9

All rights reserved. No part of this publication may be reproduced,
stored in a retrieval system, or transmitted, in any form or by any
means, electronic, mechanical, photocopying, recording, or otherwise,
without the prior written permission of the copyright owner.

Printed in the United States of America
10 9 8 7 6 5 4 3 2 1

Contents

Preface

A number of collections of essays on rhetoric have been published over the last sixty-five years or so. One kind of such collections is the festschrift in honor of some noted or influential teacher. The essays in those festschrifts are usually commissioned, many of them being written by former students who have themselves become noted or influential teachers. The life of these celebratory volumes is usually very short. Within two or three years after publication, they go out of print, and then they are available to the general public only in university and college libraries. Perhaps the best of these festschrifts are the four that were published in honor of the first generation of distinguished teachers in the Speech and Drama Department at Cornell University during the first half of the twentieth century: *Studies in Rhetoric and Public Speaking in Honor of James Albert Winans.* New York: The Century Co. 1925; *Studies in Speech and Drama in Honor of Alexander M. Drummond.* Ithaca, NY: Cornell University Press, 1944; *The Rhetorical Idiom: Essays in Rhetoric, Oratory, Language, and Drama Presented to Herbert August Wichelns.* Ed. Donald C. Bryant. Ithaca, NY: Cornell University Press, 1958; *Historical Studies of Rhetoric and Rhetoricians* [in honor of Everett Lee Hunt]. Ed. Raymond F. Howes. Ithaca, NY: Cornell University Press, 1961.

The other kind of collection of essays on rhetoric is the anthology published by a commercial publisher and designed primarily for the undergraduate and graduate classroom. Teachers of seminars in the history of rhetoric, for instance, often require students to read articles that are pertinent to the lecture being given or to the primary text that the class is reading. Usually these articles are available in the library only in bound volumes of professional journals. Even when placed on the reserved shelves in the library, these bound volumes are not readily available to *all* of the students, even in small seminars of 10–15 students. So some professors have been able to convince commercial publishers that there is a market for collections of essays most commonly assigned in college classes. And many teachers have made one or other of these collections a required supplementary text for the course.

One of the best of these collections was put together by two professors of Speech: Lionel B. Crocker and Paul A. Carmack, eds. *Readings in Rhetoric.* Springfield, IL: Charles C. Thomas, 1965. Unquestionably the best of the anthologies put together by professors of English was *The Province of Rhetoric.* Ed. Joseph Schwartz and John Rycenga. New York: Ronald Press, 1965. Although both of these collections remained on the publishers' lists for a number of years, they are now out of print. They are prized possessions of those fortunate enough to have a copy in their private libraries.

We have assembled this collection of essays on the rhetoric of the Western world partly for the convenience of those scholars who want to have in their own library a copy of classic essays on various aspects of rhetoric but mainly for the convenience and edification of students. With a collection like this one available to them, students enrolled in a rhetoric course will not have to register their name in the reading room of the college library on a waiting list for particular volumes of professional journals.

Many of the essays in this collection are firmly established as classics in their field; others are on their way to becoming classics. They are written by people from a variety of disciplines— Speech, Philosophy, English, History,

Classics. We think that all of the periods of rhetoric and all of the major figures in rhetoric in the Western world are covered by the essays in this volume. The footnotes in these articles are so rich in references to other books and articles on rhetoric that we did not feel the need to provide a Bibliography at the end of the volume. In a few instances, we have presented a condensed version of an essay and sometimes have abbreviated long footnotes. At the bottom of the first page of each essay, we have indicated the original source of the selection.

We hope that the readings presented in this volume will prove interesting to many readers. We know that the readings are solid and illuminating. We are confident that the readings will provide helpful overviews of the rhetorical developments of particular periods and insightful introductions to the work of particular rhetoricians. Read and enjoy and profit.

Edward P. J. Corbett
James L. Golden
Goodwin F. Berquist

William Riley Parker

Where Do English Departments Come From?

◊ *William Riley Parker's article should be required reading for anyone choosing English as a field of study. It should be required because it tells us where English departments came from and because it is always healthy for children—to use Parker's domestic metaphor—to know something about their ancestry. We learn that English departments became official administrative units only a little over a hundred years ago in American universities and even more recently in British universities. As Parker points out, the Regius Professorship of Rhetoric at Edinburgh University in the eighteenth century and the Boylston Professorship of Rhetoric at Harvard University in the nineteenth century were "harbingers of things to come." Once English departments drifted from their roots in rhetoric and philology, they assumed responsibility for the teaching of a potpourri of academic subjects, so that today it is difficult for anyone to state precisely just what the mission of English departments is.* ◊

My topic question—Where do English departments come from?—is not intended to be funny, but my answer may strike you as at least ironic. I shall try to answer with something clearer and more illuminating than "Out of the everywhere into the here." I shall try, in fact, to be very definite, and I want you to know at the outset my purpose. If this were a sermon instead of a history-lesson, I would take my text from Cicero, who said, you will remember, "Not to know what happened before one was born is always to be a child." He said

this, of course, in Latin, which is the language in which English studies began and, to some extent, long continued, and which is still a language that all serious students of English literature had better know, despite the fact that we are now allowing it to disappear from our public schools. But that is a sermon for another occasion. Cicero's dictum points up my purpose on this one. Even if history does not truly repeat itself, knowledge of it may, at least sometimes, give current problems a familiar, less formidable look. Moreover,

From College English, 28 February 1967, "Where Do English Departments Come From?" by William Riley Parker. Copyright 1967 by the National Council of Teachers of English. Reprinted with permission.

neglect of experience, personal *or recorded*, condemns us to repeating its follies. To live intellectually only in one's own time is as provincial and misleading as to live intellectually only in one's own culture. These truisms, if you will accept as well as forgive them, apply to the history of the teaching of English as much as they apply to the history of other matters. And they apply to the recent as well as the distant past. It can be most useful to know with certainty how raw and how new some of our problems really are. So let us begin with recognition of a simple fact: the teaching of English, as a constituent of college or university education, is only about 100 years old, and *departments* of English are younger still. Let me underline this by defining "English." A recent dictionary will tell you, not to your great surprise, that it can mean "English language, literature, or composition when a subject of study." It may surprise you, however, to know that you will *not* find this definition or anything like it in the 1925 Webster's unabridged dictionary or in the thirteen-volume *Oxford English Dictionary*. Its absence from these is significant. Its absence from the new Random House dictionary is shocking.

Since I am myself an English teacher, I cannot resist answering my question about the origins of English teaching, first with a flourish of rhetoric, and finally with what I hope will be a full and clear explication. If I may begin by twisting a tired Shakespearean adage, it is a wise child that knows his own parents. "English" as a recognized academic subject was not self-begotten, nor did it spring fully armed from the forehead of ancient rhetoric. It is a normal and legitimate child. It is not a foundling. Present-day professors and graduate students of English should be more aware, therefore, of its once proud parents, both of whom are still very much alive—though living apart. The child, grown to vigorous manhood, is today somewhat ashamed of both, and sees as little of them as possible. Proud of its own accomplishments, confident in its present prestige, it would like to forget its origins. A little more than fifty years ago, after neglecting its mother for some time, it became alienated from her, and became more than ever its father's son. Then, exactly ten years later, it broke with its father. Since increased maturity and a sense of maturity sometimes carry the promise of reconciliation in such domestic tragedies, there is still the possibility, of course, that the child will some day not only feel proud of its parents but even be willing to learn something from them.

As I have said, English was born about 100 years ago. Its mother, the eldest daughter of Rhetoric, was Oratory—or what we now prefer to call public speaking or, simply, speech. Its father was Philology or what we now call linguistics. Their marriage, as I have suggested, was shortlived, and English is therefore the child of a broken home. This unhappy fact accounts, perhaps, for its early feeling of independence and its later bitterness toward both parents. I date the break with the mother, however, not from the disgraceful affair she had with Elocution, but rather from the founding of the Speech Association of America in 1914, which brought, as was hoped, the creation of many departments of speech. I date the break with the father, not from his happy marriage to Anthropology, but from the foundings of the Linguistic Society of America in 1924, and the developing hostility of literary scholars to nonprescriptive grammar, new terminology, and the rigors of language study. Splinter groups form when their founders feel their interests neglected, and English teachers, absorbed in what they considered more important business, were indeed neglecting speech by 1914 and losing all vital concern with linguistics by 1924.

I might go on to speak of the unfortunate divorce of linguistics and speech, who, in my unromantic opinion, were obviously "meant for each other." Optimists like me can hope for an eventual family reunion, but pessimists will, of course, point out that this is impossible because, with the passage of time, the parents have actually forgotten each other and the child has almost forgotten the parents. Because there is an element of truth in this charge, I choose to begin by telling (or reminding) you of the family history; reconciliation requires *remembrance* along with wisdom and good will.

But now I must drop this domestic metaphor, and turn to the prosaic details of the history of English studies and of the teaching and eventual departmentalization of English language and literature.

To prevent some potential confusion, let us recall that English *studies*—or serious scholarship or criticism devoted to English language or literature—are much older than any *teaching* of English. English studies date from Tudor times, and are a fruit of the English Renaissance and Reformation. Let me hammer this point home

with some illustrations; if in every instance I have not yet found the very first example of a now familiar phenomenon of our field, I very much hope that you will correct me. Serious linguistic scholarship on English begins in the 1560's with the work of Laurence Nowell, John Josselin, William Lambarde, and Archbishop Matthew Parker on Anglo-Saxon. Serious biographical and bibliographical scholarship on English literature begins even earlier, in the 1540's, with the impressive Latin catalogues of John Leland and Bishop John Bale. Important lexicographical scholarship also dates from the sixteenth century, though the first really English dictionary was Robert Cawdrey's, as late as 1604. Unless you choose to begin with Caxton or, perhaps, Polydore Vergil, serious editing of important English authors is inaugurated by Thomas Speght's Chaucer in 1598, which, in a prefatory life, also gives us, to the best of my knowledge, the first separate biography of an English literary figure written because he was a literary figure. Francis Thynne's prompt review of Speght's edition is probably our first example of scholarly reviewing; as you may recall, it greatly influenced Speght's second, revised edition of 1602. The first publication of variant readings of a single work was in 1640, by John Spelman. T. S. Eliot was not the first poet to annotate his own work (in *The Waste Land,* 1922); Thomas Watson did this for his *Hekatompathia* in 1582. Perhaps the first annotation of separate works begins with the notes by "E. K." on Spenser's *Shepheardes Calendar* of 1579 and John Selden's notes on Drayton's *Poly-Olbion* of 1613. The first whole volume to be devoted to annotation of a single literary work was Patrick Hume's 321 closely printed pages on *Paradise Lost* in 1695. Recognizable criticism of English literature dates from the sixteenth century, and the collection of critical opinion on authors begins with Sir Thomas Pope Blount in 1690 and 1694. Source study of English drama begins with Langbaine in 1691. Perhaps the first truly scholarly biography, with ample footnotes and indication of sources, was Thomas Birch's life of Milton in 1738.

One could easily go on; it is fun to collect "firsts"; but perhaps I have said enough to remind you that there was a considerable and venerable tradition of serious scholarship and criticism on English language and literature long before there was any continuous teaching of these subjects. I have to put it this way, carefully, because Archbishop Ussher and the Spelmans, father and son, tried hard to have it otherwise: a chair of Anglo-Saxon was actually established at Cambridge in the 1640's, but the English civil war and the deaths of both the Spelmans and the first and only holder of the chair, Abraham Wheloc, aborted this experiment, and Cambridge did not have another professor of Anglo-Saxon until 1878, and did not have a professor of English literature until 1911. It is interesting to speculate on what the history of our profession might have been like had the academic study of English actually begun in 1640, two years after Harvard College opened. But Harvard was not to have a professor of English until 1876, when, ironically, it granted its first Ph.D in English to a man who never entered the teaching profession. Oxford had a professorship of poetry as early as 1708, but this was to mean classical poetry only, until long after the teaching of English literature had otherwise established itself as an academic subject. Even Matthew Arnold, who in 1857 broke all traditions by lecturing in English instead of in Latin, never thought of himself as a professor of English. Oxford did not have a university chair of English literature until 1904. When the Modern Language Association of America was founded in 1883—only eighty-three years ago— twenty leading institutions were represented at the organizational meeting in New York, and at all twenty of these institutions there were only thirty-nine faculty members in English.

I stress these dates in order to remind you that the teaching of English is a Johnny-come-lately—a fact that has some relevance to any answer given the question "Why can't Johnny read?" Our research and criticism are old; our jobs are new. Our profession as scholars demonstrates richly the lessons learned from four centuries of experience; our profession as teachers is still wrestling strenuously and confusedly with initial problems that mass education has suddenly and greatly aggravated. As scholars we have matured; as teachers we—the same people—are still children in our ignorance or innocence, still fumbling and faddish and lacking well-defined goals. These, I realize, are strong statements, and I mean to explain and support them before I finish. Meanwhile, however, let me say that I *think* I am talking to you about one of the central problems of our profession—and one which, in my experience, is almost never discussed.

When, where, and by whom the formal teaching of English began at any level of education is not, I believe, known, and probably will never be known. From very early times it inevitably formed some part of the "petties" (or primary, elementary education as conducted in the parish, or under private tutors, or however). Exactly when it extended upward into secondary education, in private day or boarding schools, is only approximately known; "grammar schools" were originally designed to teach *Latin* grammar; but in the second half of the eighteenth century a slowly increasing number of such schools in English were professing what was called an "English education," in contrast to the usual classical education preparatory to a university, as their aim. This term is now potentially misleading; it embraced considerably more than English language, literature, or composition, but it normally included composition or "rhetoric" in the mother tongue. On this side of the Atlantic, when Benjamin Franklin published in 1750 his *Idea of an English School,* he had in mind a very radical idea indeed—a utilitarian education for citizenship conducted entirely in the English language. Naturally, it was never tried, but a compromise was attempted. An academy in Philadelphia opened in 1751 with a so-called "English School," and when the academy became a college in 1755 (later to be called the University of Pennsylvania), the second head of its English School, Ebenezer Kinnersley, was given the title Professor of the English Tongue and Oratory. Significantly, he was both a Baptist clergyman and a scientist; his experiments in electricity were second

in importance only to those of his friend Franklin. Even more significantly, the title given to Kinnersley, who was probably our first college professor of English in any sense, contained the word "Oratory." Oratory, you may remember, I have called the mother of "English." We shall see in a moment how this happened, but meanwhile let us notice that when Kinnersley resigned in 1773, his successor at Pennsylvania, the lawyer James Wilson, actually gave some lectures on English literature.

In order to understand this momentous development we must turn, not to England, but to Scotland. During the four decades from, roughly, 1742 to 1783, George Campbell, Henry Home (Lord Kames), the philosopher-historian David Hume, the political economist Adam Smith, and other influential Scotsmen agreed on the importance of the arts of public speaking and reading, not only for prospective clergymen, but also for educated citizens in general. As a young man, Adam Smith lectured on rhetoric and literature at Kirkcaldy in 1748–51. Another member of this "Scottish school of rhetoric," the popular Edinburgh preacher Hugh Blair, began to read lectures on composition in the University late in 1759, and the following year the town council made him professor of rhetoric. The experiment was given both significance and permanence in April 1762 with the founding of a regius professorship of rhetoric and belles-lettres, to which Blair was appointed. Rhetoric was, of course, one of the oldest subjects in university education, but something now happened to it. Blair held this post until 1783, and, unlike the Oxford Professor of Poetry, who had a similar opportunity, he chose to lecture in English on English literature. Moreover, when he resigned in 1783 he published his lectures and thus gave other institutions a popular textbook, which Yale adopted in 1785, Harvard in 1788, and Dartmouth in 1822. Blair's was not the only textbook available, however, and the titles of some other influential ones may help me to make the point I am now concerned with. There were, for example, John Ward's two-volume *System of Oratory* (1759) and Thomas Sheridan's *Lectures on Elocution* (1763); and William Enfield's *The Speaker* (1774) quickly became, and long remained, the authoritative anthology of "recitations" from Shakespeare, Sterne, Pope, and more recent writers.

In an age that produced Charles Fox and Edmund Burke in England and Patrick Henry and James Otis in America, the atmosphere was right for a mushrooming of popular interest in oratory and "elocution." What had caused this, I suspect, was the dramatic development of parliaments in the eighteenth century, and the emergence of great orators who were not clergymen. In the second half of the eighteenth century the idea caught on quickly in America, inside, and even more outside, classrooms. The coming century was to witness the fame of Henry Ward Beecher, John Calhoun, Henry Clay, Stephen Douglas, Robert Ingersoll, Wendell Phillips, Daniel Webster, and others—to say nothing of a short, simple address delivered at a place called Gettysburg. Early teachers of "English" were also, usually, teachers of speech. As in ancient Greece

and Rome, the art of "rhetoric" once again embraced non-clerical oratory.

In 1806 the Boylston professorship of rhetoric and oratory was founded at Harvard, and the first appointee was John Quincy Adams, who later became President of the United States, thus setting a provocative precedent for all future teachers of English! Adams' lectures, published in 1810, were the first attempt by an American to reunite rhetorical theory with classical doctrines. The Boylston professor from 1819 to 1851 was Edward Tyrrel Channing, teacher of Dana, Emerson, Holmes, and Thoreau. The first half of the nineteenth century in the new republic was a time of many public lectures, of lyceums and other popular societies for literary and liberal education, of literary and debating societies on college campuses, and, in general, of much amateurish and informal attention to both rhetoric and belles-lettres. Although Emerson's famous "American scholar" address was delivered in 1837, it is important to remember that this was *not* a time that produced in America any literary or linguistic scholarship of real substance, and the professor of English language and literature did not immediately emerge. In the United States before 1860 only a very few colleges ventured to mention English literature as a subject in their catalogues or announcements. Dartmouth dared to do so in 1822. In 1827 Amherst offered "Lectures in English and American Literature" as part of a bravely projected modern course of study to parallel the traditional one for the ancient language and literatures, but the offering was soon withdrawn. Another American pioneer was Middlebury, whose 1848–49 catalogue announced "Critiques on the British and American Classics" as a course in the third term of the junior year, and this offering survived for some decades. On the other hand, Oberlin College considered Shakespeare unsuitable for mixed classes until 1864. The regius professorship at Edinburgh and the Boylston professorship at Harvard were harbingers of things to come, but were not, essentially, first steps in the development of an academic discipline that could demand, and get, equal recognition with the classical languages. For such a revolutionary change in established patterns of education some other factors were necessary—among them, a new, scientific linguistics, a new and rigorous methodology adaptable to literary studies, and a new concept of liberal education. These three factors were all to emerge during the last three quarters of the nineteenth century, but their impacts and results were to be different in the United States from what they were in England.

There were only seven universities in the entire British Isles from 1591 to 1828, a period in which more than *seventy* colleges or universities were founded in America, to survive down to our own day. In 1828, however, what is now University College, London, opened as the University of London, and during the remainder of the nineteenth century the number of British universities *doubled*. This "red-brick" explosion of higher education in England, which tardily reflects a similar phenomenon in the United States, is complex in its origin, but one of the factors was popular reaction against exclusiveness and traditionalism in the curriculum, es-

pecially the domination of the classical languages. It is not, therefore, mere coincidence that the sudden proliferation of universities in England produced formal instruction in the modern languages, including English, and even in English literature. Nor is it coincidence that both Oxford and Cambridge were the last universities in the entire English-speaking world to establish professorships in English language and literature. Even after they had reduced to meaningless formalities the medieval exercises in the Schools, the narrow system of written final examinations which succeeded, in 1780 and 1800, prevented the growth of any new kind of learning. The entrenched classical curriculum was not only reconfirmed in the venerable universities which had been looked up to as models by Harvard, Yale, and other institutions; effective means had been found to discourage any possible competition. Moreover, until as late as 1871 graduates of Cambridge and Oxford still had to subscribe to the Thirty-nine Articles, proving their adherence to the Church of England. This fact accounts for the growth during the eighteenth century of the many nonconformist academies, which served as theological seminaries for non-Anglicans, and often, not incidentally, were receptive to ideas of an "English" education. Although it soon added an Anglican college, King's, the new University of London began as a *non-sectarian* institution, and it is not surprising, therefore, that when it opened its doors on Gower Street in 1828, it had a professor of English language and literature. His name was Thomas Dale; he was a popular preacher in London and an old-fashioned high church evangelical; in his first year as professor he wrote and published *An Introductory Lecture to a Course upon the Principles and Practice of English Composition*. Dale was the author of seventy some other works, including some minor poetry, a translation of Sophocles, and an edition of the poems of William Cowper. We need not be ashamed of England's first English professor. We shall meet many other clergymen as English professors in the decades to follow, in both Great Britain and the United States. The fact is significant; until another new university, the Johns Hopkins, insisted that English professors needed a special kind of preparation, the literacy and oratorical skills and genteel acquaintance with literature that clergymen presumably had were considered preparation enough. What eventually made that preparation seem inadequate was the development of a new scientific linguistics and a new historical criticism.

For my personal edification I have tried to trace the growth of teaching of English in many dozens of institutions in Great Britain, the United States, Canada, and elsewhere, and I wish there were time to give you some of the more interesting details, and to name some of the more interesting people. One other phenomenon, however, I must not fail to mention, for it is important to what I shall later want to say about the departmentalization of our subject. Unlike Thomas Dale of London, many early professors of English were simultaneously professors of modern *history*. This was the case at Cornell, Toronto, Manchester, Queen's University (Belfast), Queen's College (Cork), the University colleges at Cardiff and Liv-

erpool, and elsewhere. On the other hand, one year after Springhill College, Birmingham, opened in 1838, it appointed the *Edinburgh* reviewer Henry Rogers as its professor of English literature and language, mathematics, and mental philosophy. By the time of the commencement of the American Civil War, the embryonic or new universities of England had made English a familiar if not yet wholly acceptable part of the curriculum, and the ancient Scottish and Irish universities then followed suit in their own way. Aberdeen, founded in 1494, in 1860 led the way with the appointment of Alexander Bain as professor of logic and English. This was not an unnatural combination; logic as an academic subject used to be associated with rhetoric, and argumentative composition was even thought of as a branch of logic. In any case, logic and English were not separated at Aberdeen until 1894. At St. Andrews the early professorship embraced logic, metaphysics, and English literature. Dublin University, which had been founded in 1591, in 1855 finally attached to the normal duties of its professor of oratory the obligation to give instruction in English literature, but when this man gave up the post in 1866 to become professor of Greek, Dublin appointed Edward Dowden as its first professor of English, a post he held until his death in 1913.

These titular details, with their suggestions of compromise and uncertainty about the sufficient substance of English as an academic subject, make a revealing background for the stubborn unwillingness of the two most ancient universities to get on the bandwagon of modernity. But in 1873

English was finally admitted into the Oxford "pass" examination for the final Schools—the tacit assumption being that students not bright enough to try for honors in the classics could somehow obtain adequate instruction in English from their college tutors. In 1877 an attempt was made to extend this gain by establishing an honors school of modern literature, including English, but it of course failed.

From 1854 to 1868 Friedrich Max Müller had been the second Taylorian professor of modern European languages at Oxford, but this new post, so widely unwelcome in the University, was abolished when he abandoned it to take the new chair of comparative philology. Here was the shape of things to come. The English Philological Society had been founded in 1842; the Cambridge and Oxford Philological Societies, in 1868 and 1870, respectively. Max Müller, who probably did more than any other man to popularize Germanic philology or linguistics in England, had published his two-volume *Science of Language* in 1861–63. When Oxford finally acquired a Merton Professor of English language and literature, he was to be another eminent philologist (A. S. Napier)—unhappily, as critics immediately complained, an expert on early English *language* with little or no interest in literature. In the United States the first professor of the English language comparative philology was the scholarly Francis Andrew March, who was given this title by Lafayette College in 1857 and held it until 1906. The title was highly significant; it spelled out the new field of linguistics that was eventually to give English studies solidity and respectability and

influence at even the old, established universities. At Harvard, for example, that fine scholar, Francis James Child, who had been Boylston professor of rhetoric and oratory since 1851, and had actually been lecturing on English language and literature since about 1854, in 1876 became the first professor of English literature. English was now moving toward a new "image" or identity.

We need occasionally to remind ourselves of what English amounted to only eighty-three years ago, when a few leaders in the emerging profession felt it necessary to organize a *Modern* Language Association, joining forces with French and German to challenge the entrenched classical curriculum. In most of the colleges that had pioneered in teaching it, the place of English was still quite subordinate, both as to time allotted and results expected. The usual offering consisted of an hour or two of lectures for ten or twelve weeks by the professor of belles-lettres, who also taught such courses as history, logic, evidences of Christianity, moral philosophy, rhetoric, and oratory. The professor who taught *only* English was still a great rarity. The typical survey course was likely to be historical, biographical, and esthetic, with Chaucer, Spenser, and Shakespeare the most important figures. There was rarely any attempt to study the language historically or comparatively, for almost no English teachers had been trained to do this. The simple truth is that by 1883 almost no English teachers had been trained (period). The typical professor, as we have seen, was a doctor of divinity who spoke and wrote the mother tongue grammatically, had a general "society knowledge" of the literature, and had not specialized in this or any other academic subject.

But graduate education was, as everyone now knows, vigorously launched in the United States when the Johns Hopkins University opened in 1876, frankly setting out to import European (particularly German) ideals and methodology. It meant to naturalize, if possible, the spirit of specialization, the concept of the teacher as investigator and producing scholar, and, for our field, the "scientific" approach to literary and linguistic research. The fame of Paris and of the German universities had spread in this country for many decades, and so the stimulating example of Johns Hopkins was soon followed enthusiastically as other graduate schools sprang up in the institutions that could afford them. A new standard of post-baccalaureate work had been set. It was almost a symbolic act when English and German were combined into a single department at Johns Hopkins in 1882–83, with a future professor of German as head. Linguistically speaking, of course, this was not a strange marriage. Nor was it practically speaking, for if the young graduate student or recent Ph.D. in English had something to publish (as was now expected of him), the logical place to send it before 1884 was either the *Englische Studien* or *Anglia,* both published in Germany and both devoted to English philology. No publication in any English-speaking country was yet exclusively devoted to the study of any of the modern languages.

Graduate work in English on the Johns Hopkins pattern meant rigorous training in linguistics and textual analysis. It also meant that little or nothing beyond seventeenth-century English literature was worthy of serious attention in graduate instruction; after all, there was the practical problem of time; with the now accepted need of mastering Anglo-Saxon, Middle English, old and modern French, old and modern German, and, preferably, several other Germanic languages or dialects, how could one possibly take graduate courses in recent English or American literature, even if they were offered? The linguistic emphasis of graduate training at Johns Hopkins—and subsequently at Harvard, Yale, and elsewhere—was to produce, during the next fifty years in America, a completely new kind of English professor, later to be rendered obsolete by the same educational revolution which had created him.

I must now repeat what I have had occasion to write elsewhere: the main objectives for which the MLA was founded would have been achieved during the next few decades whether or not the MLA had ever existed. From about 1883 onward, the classics declined in power and prestige, and the star of the modern languages rose. At least four factors in the decline and fall of the prescribed, classical curriculum are now quite clear. There were the impact of science, the American spirit of utilitarianism or pragmatism, and the exciting, new dream of democratic, popular education, an assumed corollary of which was the free elective system. A fourth factor may be described as a widespread mood of questioning and experimentation in education, a practical, revisionary spirit that challenged all traditions and accepted practices. Ironically, this attitude was later, in the third and fourth decades of the twentieth century, to disperse *all* foreign language study, but meanwhile it suffered the modern foreign languages to compete on equal terms with, and almost to supplant, the classical languages. English, on the other hand, was not to encounter the same reverses in favor; as we have seen, it was almost providentially prepared by recent events to be "scientific" and difficult in the most approved Germanic manner, but it was also, when provided with the means soon after 1883, quite willing to be utilitarian and popular. Since we still live with this paradox, and enjoy its precarious benefits, we had better understand it. It was the teaching of freshman composition that quickly entrenched English departments in the college and university structure—so much so that no one seemed to mind when professors of English, once freed from this slave land, became as remote from everyday affairs as the classicists had ever been. To the best of my knowledge, no one has ever shown why it is more "useful" to know Anglo-Saxon than to know Latin, or educationally more valuable to know English literature than to know Greek literature; and, in my considered judgment, either would be a very difficult case to make. But no one needs to persuade the American public that freshman composition is essential, despite the fact that it rarely accomplishes any of its announced objectives.

Surprising as the idea may first appear to you, there was, of course, no compelling reason at the outset why the teaching of *composition* should have been entrusted to teachers of the English language and literature.

Teaching the language meant teaching it historically and comparatively, according to the latest methods of scientific philology. It was a far cry from this to freshman themes. As everyone knew in 1883, composition was a branch of rhetoric, a subject which had been a basic part of the college curriculum since medieval times. As everyone also knew in 1883, composition involved oratory in addition to writing intended only for silent reading. Another relevant fact was a matter of recent history: composition was now permitted in the mother tongue. But these facts do *not* add up to the conclusion that the professor of rhetoric and oratory should disappear, to be supplanted by the teacher of English language and literature. In 1876, when Francis Child became Harvard's first professor of English, his post as professor of rhetoric and oratory was immediately filled by someone else. And naturally so.

Chronology is the key to what finally happened; if "English" had been somewhat *later* in gaining academic recognition and respectability in the United States (as it actually was at Cambridge and Oxford, for example), it would probably never have been so strongly affected by the educational events of the 1880's and 1890's which we must now consider. This was a period in which the whole *structure* of higher education in America underwent profound changes, yielding to the pressures of new learning, the elective system, increased specialization, acceptance of the idea that practical or useful courses had a place in higher education, and, not least in importance, the actual *doubling* of college enrollments during the last quarter of the century. So long as there had been a narrow, prescribed curriculum and not too many students, departments of instruction had little or no administrative significance, and although the word "department" was sometimes used earlier, it was not really until the 1890's (at Harvard, for example, not until 1891; at my own university, not until 1893) that departments became important administrative units, pigeonholes into which one dropped all the elements of a rapidly expanding curriculum. Delegating responsibility, college officials looked to the various departments to judge the suitability of course offerings, the relationships of courses, prerequisites, and programs for majors and minors; to make recommendations for appointments, promotions, and salary increases; and to seek money or equipment or both. Perhaps inevitably, departments soon became competitive and ambitious, looking anxiously at any unoccupied territory between themselves and neighboring departments.

It was in this atmosphere that "English" in the United States, very recently became an accepted subject, grew to maturity, over-reached itself, and planted deeply the seeds of most of its subsequent troubles as an academic discipline. Early chairmen and early professors of English *literature* were willing if not eager to increase the prestige of their subject and the numbers of their students and course offerings by embracing, not only *linguistics* (including English grammar and the history of the language and even, whenever possible, comparative philology), but also *rhetoric*, which normally included, of course, oratory, elocution, and all forms of written composition. How

this latter coup was possible I shall explain in a moment, but first let us remind ourselves of the full scope of the aggressiveness (some would say acquisitiveness) exhibited by departments of "English." They were later to embrace, just as greedily, journalism, business writing, creative writing, writing for engineers, play-writing, drama and theater, and American literature, and were eventually to be offering courses in contemporary literature, comparative literature, the Bible and world classics in translation, American civilization, the humanities, and "English for foreigners." In sum, English departments became the catchall for the work of teachers of extremely diverse interests and training, united theoretically but not actually by their common use of the mother tongue. Disintegration was therefore inevitable. Since there was no diminishing of the various forces that caused the original creation of departmental structure in colleges of arts and sciences, splintering of departments eventually ensued, often with great bitterness and an unhealthy increase in competitive spirit.

Let us pause a moment to recognize the practical implications of what I have been saying. Thanks first to its academic origins, and then to the spirit of competition and aggressiveness engendered by departmentalization, *"English" has never really defined itself as a discipline.* Before 1883, as we have seen, it was associated chaotically with rhetoric, logic, history, and many another definable subject. In 1885 Professor John McElroy of Pennsylvania was boasting to his MLA colleagues: "Today English is no longer, as it once was, every modern subject of the course except itself." *He* was a Professor of Rhetoric and the English Language, and his self-congratulations came just on the eve of history repeating itself. The typical English teacher in the 1890s and later no longer had a multi-title, but he belonged to a department that had multi-purposes, and normally his graduate training had almost nothing to do with what he found himself doing in the classroom. Having recently mastered Anglo-Saxon and the techniques of textual analysis, he began by teaching composition or speech, with perhaps an occasional survey course to lessen the pain. Much later, if he survived, he might be allowed to teach his specialty to graduate students who, in turn, would begin by teaching freshman composition.

How did it happen that newly created departments of English, with some variety of titles, were able at the close of the nineteenth century to preempt instruction in the skills of writing and speaking, to assume administrative control over the teaching of composition in any form? (This was not, to be sure, universal; at some few institutions, departments of rhetoric, oratory, or elocution developed alongside departments of English; but the prevailing administrative practice was to lump all these subjects under the rubric of "English.") As we have seen, historically the academic study of English literature was a protégé of the study of one of the oldest subjects in the curriculum, rhetoric, which during the later eighteenth and early nineteenth centuries, particularly in the Scottish universities, became increasingly identified with belles-lettres and literacy criticism. But

the Scottish school of rhetoric had also associated rhetoric with secular oratory. What probably changed this in the first half of the nineteenth century, and caused rhetoric to be more and more associated with belles-lettres, was the shift in attention from the written word to the voice and body control involved in the increasingly popular study of "elocution." Although taught in a number of American colleges during the nineteenth century, and required at some, elocution not only failed to achieve academic respectability; it caused a flight of teachers from oratory to imaginative literature (e.g., Hiram Corson at Cornell, or Bliss Perry at a later period), and it seriously damaged the once great prestige and importance of speech training. Elocution in the colleges was taught for the most part by specially trained itinerant teachers rather than by regular faculty members. In 1873 it ceased to be a required subject at Harvard. By 1900 the new School of Oratory at the University of Texas was carefully explaining that its purpose was *not* training in elocution. When the Speech Association of America was founded in 1914, it disdainfully dissociated itself from the "elocutionists" of the private schools. Perhaps in the hope of gaining academic respectability, elocution at the close of the nineteenth century associated itself more and more with literary criticism and appreciation, but this simply caused it to be swallowed up the more easily by English departments, which could then conveniently de-emphasize it.

To sum up: the ancient subject of rhetoric, which at first showed signs of adapting itself to changing times while preserving both its integrity and its vitality, in the nineteenth century lost both integrity and independent vitality by dispersing itself to academic thinness. It permitted oratory to become identified with elocution, and, as for written composition, it allowed this to become chiefly identified with that dismal, unflowering desert, freshman theme-writing. It is little wonder that speech and composition were readily accepted by administrators as appendices of English literature, especially when various events conspired to tie the knot tightly. In 1888, for example, the New England Commission for Colleges set a list of *books for reading* as preparation for college entrance examinations in English *composition*. In 1892 the "Committee of Ten" of the National Education Association formally recommended that literature and composition be unified in the high school course. That did it. Increasingly, thereafter, college entrance exams linked composition with literature, and, not unnaturally, linked high school work in "English" with beginning college work in composition. Speech training, once so important in education (as, indeed, it still is or should be), tended to get left out of this convenient combination, with results that should have been predictable.

And you know the sequel. Little by little English departments lost journalism, speech, and theater, and recently we have seen the development of separate undergraduate departments of comparative literature and linguistics. There have been polylingual grumblings from foreign language departments about the English department monopoly of courses in world litera-

ture. For a time there was a real threat of separate departments of "communication" (e.g., at Michigan State University), but "English" has somehow managed to hold on stubbornly to all written composition not intended for oral delivery—a subject which has always had a most tenuous connection with the academic study of language and literature, but which, not incidentally, from the outset has been a great secret of strength for "English" with both administrators and public, and latterly has made possible the frugal subsidizing of countless graduate students who cannot wait to escape it. Should our graduate students some day be subsidized instead by the Federal Government (as seems to me likely to happen eventually), it remains to be seen whether or not the nineteenth-century union of literature and composition was a true marriage or merely a marriage of convenience.

I have been tracing for you some not very ancient history, and I should like, finally, to draw some personal conclusions from it. They are rather drastic, and you may not be able to accept any of them. History teaches different things to different people, and some people believe that nothing can be learned from it. As I stated initially, I believe that we can learn a great deal. You may think me unfitted to be a chairman when I say, now, that the history of our profession inspires in me very little respect for departments of English; their story is one of acquisitiveness, expediency, and incredible stupidity. I care a lot about liberal education, and I care a lot about the study of literature in English, but it seems to me that English departments have cared much less about liberal education and their own integrity than they have about their administrative power and prosperity.

We cannot turn back the clock and bring speech back into English departments, but this realistic fact seems to me no justification for English abandoning all training in speech and oral composition for its majors—especially for those who intend to become teachers at any level of education, including the graduate level. English needs still to learn something from its mother.

And even more from its father. It strikes me as ironic and more than slightly ridiculous that we increasingly want "English" to mean the close reading of words while we steadily increase our ignorance of the nature and history of language in general and the English language in particular. Study of literature without more than casual or amateurish knowledge of language is destined, in my considered judgment, to share the fate of elocution. The penalty most fitting this crime would be to make us a sub-department of linguistics.

It also strikes me as ironic and more than slightly ludicrous that we take it on ourselves to teach, not only literature in English, but also world literature, in a monolingual vacuum. Our early associations with the classical languages and the modern foreign languages were meaningful and valuable; we have abandoned them at a high cost to our integrity and our common sense.

The history I have sketched for you shows "English" changing its character many times in the brief century of its academic existence, and these changes have of course continued in the past four decades, about which I have said nothing but am tempted to say a great deal, since they are the period in which I have been an active, conscious member of the profession. Let me say only that, so far as I know, few if any of the many changes have come about as a result of deliberate, long-range planning on the national level, despite the existence of the MLA and the NCTE. And that suggests my final thought: there will certainly be further changes in the years to come, but are we not now mature enough as a profession, and "hep" enough as historians, to frame our own future history, not for the benefit of English departments, but for the welfare of the young and the benefit of American education? I believe that we are, and I care about where English departments come from *only* because I care very deeply indeed about where they are going. Let me urge you to strike while the irony is hot.

Notes

1. C. H. Woolbert's *Fundamentals of Speech,* pp. 1–2.

2. Readers of "What Teachers of Speech May Learn from the Theory and Practice of the Greeks" by Paul Shorey, *Quarterly Journal of Speech,* VIII (April, 1922), already have a better view of rhetoric in the classical period than I can hope to suggest here.

Hoyt H. Hudson

The Field of Rhetoric

◊ *The theme of this essay is that the field of rhetoric deserves a "central position" in academic study. In the manner of the* Oxford English Dictionary, *Hudson reveals diverse meanings for the term "rhetoric" from both oral and written tradition. He suggests that the distinction between theory and practice in this field is artificial, that "the practice of persuasion is essentially one." Oral rhetoric focuses on the wielders of public opinion while literary rhetoric emphasizes aesthetic analysis. Like the architect, the rhetorician is a borrower from many fields "with considerable disregard for the airtight partitions sometimes put up between college departments." Written over sixty-five years ago, Hudson's insights are surprisingly timely and readable.* ◊

When Bishop Whately published his *Elements of Rhetoric,* he confessed in his preface that he had hesitated to use the word "rhetoric" in his title, because, he said, it is "apt to suggest to many minds an associated idea of empty declamation, or of dishonest artifice; or at best, a mere dissertation on Tropes and Figures of speech." We can appreciate the good bishop's hesitancy. For "rhetoric" is one of those words which has been so unfortunate as to lose most of its good connections and to be known by the bad company it has sometimes kept. There are five or six meanings given for "rhetoric" in the dictionary; but we are prone to think of only one, and that is "artificial elegance of language, or declamation without conviction or earnest feeling." Thus we are likely to speak of certain pieces of writing or speaking as "mere rhetoric"; or of a writer or speaker as "indulging in meaningless displays of rhetoric." It suggests an inflation of style to cover weakness of thought, or, in our American phrasing, something spread-eagle, or highfaluting—and, as I have suggested, only for display.

Yet some respectable connotations have managed to cling to "rhetoric" through the centuries. Walking along a city street not long ago, I passed a building marked "School of Expression," with a sort of menu-card posted by the door showing the subjects that were taught in this school. Very lowest on the list, which included two or three kinds of dancing, elocution, dramatics, public speaking, and oratory, there was offered "rhetoric." I was reminded of Charles Lamb's answer to the saying

Hoyt H. Hudson, "The Field of Rhetoric," *Quarterly Journal of Speech Education,* 9(April 1923): 167–180. Reprinted with permission of Speech Communication Association.

that a pun is the lowest form of wit: it is the lowest, Lamb insists, only because it is the foundation of all. And if this school of expression had included in its list courses in salesmanship and personal efficiency, as do some similar schools, it would be very much like the schools of the sophists in ancient Athens, wherein rhetoric was the foundation for a training in all the accomplishments and graces necessary to business and social success.

We are more familiar with the word "rhetoric" in the titles of textbooks on writing, of which many published within the past two or three decades have been named "Composition and Rhetoric"; though I am tempted to believe that if you asked the authors of some of these books to tell you which pages were composition and which were rhetoric, they would be at a loss. Some books named "Rhetoric" alone strikingly resemble others named "Composition and Rhetoric" or still others named "Composition" alone. Yet careful writers have maintained a distinction here, one which will throw light on what I have to say a little later about rhetoric in ancient times. Turning to one of the best secondary school texts I know of, Clippinger's *Composition and Rhetoric,* I find these sentences:

> Rhetoric and composition are not always distinguished, because they are usually studied together; however the difference between them should be understood. Composition *produces* discourse; rhetoric *analyzes* discourse to determine its structure.

In other words, speaking roughly, a distinction is here being made between the pure science (rhetoric) and the applied science (composition); or, if we prefer, between the science of discourse (rhetoric) and the art of discourse (composition). A product of composition might be an essay; a product of rhetoric, in this sense, would be an outline or analysis of an essay, perhaps with a list of forms of arrangement and figures of speech employed in it. A similar distinction must have been in the minds of those who used to teach rhetoric and oratory; rhetoric was the theory, oratory was the practice. And yet there have been some, and the author of the definition in the *New International Dictionary* is among them, who have overlooked this distinction and have made rhetoric mean "the art of discourse"—the theory and the practice. It is all very confusing; and I trust you are ready to turn back, with me, to another meaning of the word "rhetoric," one which, with whatever incrustations of additional meanings it may have gathered, the word has held for some students and writers and speakers in every generation for nearly twenty-five centuries.

Wherever we approach the subject of rhetoric, or the subject of oratory or eloquence, we do not go far without meeting finger-posts that point us to the work of Aristotle. Welldon, the translator of Aristotle, refers to his *Rhetoric* as being "perhaps the solitary instance of a book which not only begins a science, but completes it." Welldon says a little too much. A better statement is that of Hugh Blair, the Scottish preacher whose lectures on rhetoric formed the standard text-book both in England and America for fifty years. Blair wrote in 1759:

> Aristotle laid the foundation for all that was afterwards written on the subject. That amazing and comprehensive genius . . .

has investigated the principles of rhetoric with great penetration. Aristotle appears to have been the first who took rhetoric out of the hands of the sophists, and introduced reasoning and good sense into the art. Some of the profoundest things that have been written on the passions and manners of men, are to be found in his Treatise on Rhetoric.

Sears includes in his *History of Oratory* a chapter on "Aristotle, the Rhetorician," from which I shall quote two sentences:

He must be recognized as the father of rhetorical science, and as the man who in an age of orators compassed the whole scale of their practice. It has been observed that in the most perfect example of persuasive oratory on record—the creation of the greatest genius among the English-speaking race—Shakespeare's speech of Mark Antony—the rationale of it all had been set forth by the great Greek scientist eighteen centuries before.

In Henry Peacham's *Compleat Gentleman*, a popular work on polite accomplishments which was first published in 1622, Aristotle's *Rhetoric* is said to have been deemed by some as "being sufficient . . . to make both a Scholler and an honest man." The study of rhetoric, it is needless to say, has not always been credited with such effects.

At any rate, we do well to begin with Aristotle in building up our concept of rhetoric. With him rhetoric is a useful art, the art of persuasion, based upon a pure science. It is a useful art, because it supplements rather than imitates nature; it supplements nature, in that it helps truth and justice maintain their natural superiority. In his book Aristotle begins with the subject as a science, for he defines rhetoric not as the art of persuasion, but as "the faculty of finding, in any subject, all the available means of persuasion." That is, he makes the rhetorician a sort of diagnostician and leaves it to others to be the practitioners; the rhetorician is the strategist of persuasion, and other men execute his plans and do the fighting. In practice, however, and in any study of the subject, this distinction can hardly be maintained, since the person who determines the available means of persuasion in regard to a given subject must also be, in most cases, the one to apply those means in persuasive speech and writing. In passing I might suggest, however, that if anywhere, either in the profession of law or in advertising or in any sort of publicity work, you know a person who spends his time in analyzing subjects given him and deciding how they can best be presented, what appeals can be based upon them, yet who does not himself present the subjects or make the appeals, there you come near to having the pure rhetorician, in the narrow Aristotelian sense.

But in ancient as in modern times (as we have noted in the case of "Composition and Rhetoric") it was found impossible to divorce theory from practice. The rhetorician and the orator were one; and if not in Aristotle himself, at least in the Aristotelian school and tradition, rhetoric is the whole art of persuasion. It does not satisfy itself alone with the finding of means of persuasion; it also includes the persuasive arrangement and presentation of the speaker's material. A product of rhetoric, in this sense, then, is neither an analysis of some speech already made, with a list of figures and tropes, nor an analysis of a subject upon which a speech is to be made, showing what means of persuasion can be employed. Rather it is a speech, or some piece of persuasive discourse, persuasively presented.

I know of no statement of this meaning more simple than the earliest one to be found in any English publication: it is taken from Caxton's translation of *The Mirrour of the World,* published by himself in 1481. Caxton worded it thus: "Rhethoryke is a scyence to cause another man by speche or by wrytynge to beleue or to do that thynge whyche thou woldest haue hym for to do." This identification of rhetoric with persuasion is frequently met with in English literature throughout the sixteenth and seventeenth centuries. Thus Samuel Daniel has a line,

Sweet, silent rhetoric of persuading eyes.

Nowadays we have a proverb, "Money talks," meaning usually, "Money is the most powerful means of persuasion." A seventeenth century writer of epigrams wrote a couplet embodying the same idea; he called his epigram, "New Rhetorique," and it runs,

Good arguments without coyn, will not stick;
    To pay and not to say's best Rhetorick.

Obviously, such an epigram would be understandable only among readers who were accustomed to think of rhetoric as persuasion. In this sense, plainly, the man who speaks most persuasively uses the most, or certainly the best, rhetoric; and the man whom we censure for inflation of style and strained effects is suffering not from too much rhetoric, but from a lack of it.

Let us proceed with this meaning in mind. We recognize that in ancient times persuasion was carried on almost entirely by the spoken word. We know the great place held by public speaking in Greece and Rome, at least in their democratic phases. We know also of the place of preaching in the early church: "How shall they believe in him of whom they have not heard?" asks St. Paul. "And how shall they hear without a preacher?" After the invention of the printing-press we find persuasion carried on more and more by writing, through the pamphlet and the journal, until in our own day if we run over the principal manifestations of the persuasive art we find as many of them in type as in the spoken word. Editorial writing, pamphleteering, the immense business of advertising and the still more immense business of propaganda,—these are occupations which modern rhetoricians may follow. Yet there are also open to them the occupations calling for public speech, those of preaching, of law, of politics, the lecture and chautauqua platform, business and culture clubs. In commerce, corresponding to advertising, there is the great field of salesmanship, carried on for the most part by speaking. We expect of our publicist that he shall both write and speak.

Yet in spite of our habit of thinking of writing and speaking as separate processes, the practice of persuasion is essentially one, in that the same principles apply everywhere in the field. A writer on public speaking at the present time would hesitate to call his work "Rhetoric," because the word is now usually applied to written discourse. But less than a hundred years ago the case was exactly reversed. Bishop Whately, in the preface already cited, gives as another reason against the use of the title, "Rhetoric," that "it is rather the more commonly employed with reference to public speaking alone." E. L. Godkin, the great American editor, wrote ninety years ago: "The art of rhetoric differs from some others in having arrived long ago at perfection. The rules are the same today as they were in the days of Quintilian and Demosthenes. The art, however, has now two distinct branches, writing and oratory." A writer in "The Nation," reviewing Donelly's *The Art of Interesting,* has said: The author "is a sound classical scholar. He has done us the service of showing conclusively that the underlying principles of classical rhetoric are fundamentally valid today—that Aristotle, Cicero, and Quintilian knew not only how to make speeches, but how to preach sermons, write editorials, and sell groceries."

Then, too, in spite of the great bulk of printed material in the modern world, public speaking and eloquence have by no means lost their potency; and to consider the subject of persuasion apart from speech would be indeed to play Hamlet with the prince left out. The printed word can be passed by or laid aside; the persuasive speaker wins willing and continuous attention. "What is read is accepted inertly, or, if questioned for authenticity, affords no easy measures for resolving doubt. When man listens to speaking, however, he has a definite guide for his reaction: he can look the speaker in the eye, study his face, watch his actions and bearing, analyze his voice, penetrate into the man himself, and then

know whether or not he finds him worthy of credence. This is the reason why, when men really care, when an issue is deeply at stake, when the crisis impends, they resort not so much to the writer as to the speaker."[1] We may say further that speaking is still the *norm* of writing; the writer tests his article by reading it aloud "to see how it sounds," and the would-be persuasive writer can do no better than to write as a good speaker would speak.

We might now glance over the field historically, with a view to estimating the body of tradition which has grown up in the study of rhetoric. Greek rhetoric is a large field in itself, too large to be plotted here. Besides Aristotle the other great master of rhetorical theory in Greece was Isocrates, a successful teacher, who gave to his work a more immediately practical turn than Aristotle; the pupils of Isocrates were the great orators, generals, and statesmen of their time. It seems that Isocrates not only taught the form and means of persuasion, but also offered a certain content or body of doctrine which was to provide the subject-matter of his pupils' persuasive efforts. I suppose that when, at the present time, we combine work in Americanization or studies in patriotism with Public Speaking, preparing students to speak on principles of Americanism, we are doing somewhat as Isocrates did in his time. In Rome, Cicero and Quintilian are the great names, though by no means the only ones.[2] St. Augustine was a teacher of rhetoric, and it was as a connoisseur going to hear a great artist that Augustine went to listen to the preaching of St. Ambrose, whose persuasion led to his conversion. Rhetoric was one of the seven liberal arts of the medieval curriculum—and in that statement we are summing up many centuries of rhetorical pedagogy and practice, with some changes which we shall note later. Among the Humanists we find Melanchthon writing a treatise on rhetoric, while Erasmus wrote widely in rhetorical subjects; the *De Copia Verborum* of Erasmus was used as a school text in rhetoric for many years. Coxe and Wilson, two of the English Humanists, wrote the first works on rhetoric in our language.

It is interesting to find how many men who became eminent for other reasons made, at some time in their lives, researches in the field of rhetoric. Sir Francis Bacon tried to recall scholars in his day to the classical view of the subject, and also found time, in the midst of his other pursuits, to become a great speaker,—in the opinion of Ben Jonson the best speaker of his generation. One of the works of Thomas Hobbes is an abridgement of the *Rhetoric* of Aristotle, with an appended treatise of his own on the same subject. Isaac Barrow, Vice-Chancellor of Cambridge University and Head of Trinity College, who was famous both as a preacher and as a mathematician second only to Newton in Newton's time, was in his early days a teacher of rhetoric and gave a year's lectures on the *Rhetoric* of Aristotle. Adam Smith, author of *The Wealth of Nations*, lectured on rhetoric for several years. John Quincy Adams was the first to hold the Boylston Chair of Rhetoric and Oratory at Harvard, and his lectures form one of the principal American contributions to the tradition of the subject. Bishop Whately, great as

a logician, and Alexander Bain, great as a psychologist, were the principal British writers on rhetoric in the nineteenth century.

But in addition to writers on the theory of rhetoric, the student of the subject must take into his account the practitioners,—the men who have gone to the rostrum or the senate-house, to the pulpit or the hustings, and have attempted to influence men by persuasive speech. The names of the great orators comprise too long a list to be enumerated here. It should be noted, however, that the student of rhetoric investigates eloquence, not for its graces and ornaments, and not with regard to its effect upon him as he reads it; our admiration may be excited by a splendid figure in Burke or Canning; we may gain considerable pleasure from perceiving the skill with which words have been joined euphoniously and rhythmically,—but such admiration and pleasure are incidental and are shared by the student of literature or the general reader. The student of rhetoric looks upon each oration as an effort in persuasion; he must learn what he can of the audience to which it was addressed; he takes note of the appeals that are made, with reference to the motives that are touched, the emotions that are aroused. He must know the character and reputation of the speaker at the time when the speech was made; for a speech otherwise persuasive may fail of effect because the speaker lacks a persuasive *ethos*; whereas at times one sentence from a man of great ethical weight is sufficient to perform a difficult task of persuasion. It is true that we must also take into account matters of style and ornament and delivery; but these, too, are to be estimated with reference to their persuasive effect. Figures and tropes, neat turns of speech and well-drawn pictures, are used to feather the arrow of argument and appeal; but they can also impede its flight.

It is true that there are passages in oratory where the orator seems to throw off the bonds of rhetoric as a useful art and to enter the realm of the fine arts. The end of persuasion is for the moment forgotten in sheer delight at beauty of conception and expression. It is as if a stone-cutter, carving out a figure for some public building, should be touched by inspiration and become a sculptor, making of his figure a statue worthy of standing alone, and more important as art than the whole of the building. Mr. Logan Pearsall Smith, whose work as an anthologist of beautiful passages of prose is well known, says in the introduction to his volume of *Selected Passages from Donne's Sermons:*

> It is in the sermon, therefore, that we find some of the highest achievements of English prose—in the sermon, or in prophetic or didactic or even political eloquence written with the same high impulse and inspiration. For great prose needs a great subject-matter, needs great themes and a high spectacular point of vision, and solemn and clear and steadfast conception of life and its meaning.

Such passages we can share with the student of literature, asking him, however, to acknowledge the credit due to the rhetorical discipline and practice which brought the orator to such a measure of perfection, and also taking into account the persuasive task which provided the occasion.

For the most part the student of rhetoric is dealing with broader effects. Goldwin Smith speaks of John Pym as the "first great wielder of public opinion in England." It is the *wielder of public opinion* that the student of rhetoric is interested in. What are the secrets of his power? The rhetorical element in statesmanship is a whole field of study in itself. How many a good policy has been beaten or postponed for want of proper presentation! How many a just and able man has suffered because of an unpersuasive announcement of his purposes! The defeat of Blaine in 1884 is laid, as we know, at the door of his campaigner who untactfully launched against the Democrats the charge of "Rum, Romanism, and Rebellion" phrased with such perverse effectiveness. I shall not enlarge upon the wielding of public opinion which was carried on by Theodore Roosevelt and Woodrow Wilson in later times, by means of their powers of presentation. Enough if I have suggested that in political life a man must be something other than a pure statesman on the one hand or a literary artist on the other; he must know and use rhetoric as a technique of power.

In recent times also we have seen a unique example of the wielding of power through propaganda in the case of the Russian revolution. I recall from John Reed's *Ten Days that Shook the World* a story of how in the first days of the Bolshevik revolution, when the forces of Kerensky were within a few miles of Petrograd and threatening to retake the city, a courier from the battleline came in haste to the city for aid. "Do you want more soldiers?" he was asked. "No, we want orators!'' he said. And a truckload of orators was mobilized and hurried to the scene of conflict. Many have wondered how the Bolsheviki, representing the opinion of only a small fraction of the Russian people, have been able to hold power, conduct military operations, and even extend their sovereignty over new territory. Their use of rhetoric as a technique of power helps answer the question. General C. Birdwood-Thompson of the English Army, writing in the *Manchester Guardian,* relates a conversation held with Trotsky, in which General Thompson asked about the ''new form of war'' carried on by Russia, in which the territory to be conquered was ''leavened by political agents'' and then easily occupied by a small military force. He goes on:

> Trotsky's reply was curious. He said: ''War by propaganda is not the invention of a Russian, but rather of an Englishman.'' And then by way of explanation he added: ''Do you remember the story of Oliver Cromwell, who refused to punish one of his subordinates 'because,' he said, 'this man is a good preacher.'?''

Some question is sure to arise concerning the relation of rhetoric, in our sense, to other fields of study. It is undeniable that rhetoric draws on other fields with considerable disregard for the airtight partitions sometimes put up between college departments. A student of architecture, whose aim is to learn to design buildings, cannot study that subject alone. Without becoming an engineer, he must draw on the special field of engineering for a knowledge of materials and construction. Without becoming a painter or sculptor he must know freehand drawing, color, and

relief. He does well to learn something of surveying and landscape gardening. If he expects not only to design buildings but also to superintend their construction, there are a great many other subjects he must know; yet at the end of it all, he is an architect. The case with the rhetorician is analogous. He must learn much from the psychologist, especially with regard to the subjects of attention and emotion. From the social psychologist he draws what knowledge he can of the crowd-mind and the formation of public opinion. There are certain fundamental problems of society which a publicist is continually going to deal with, usually in relation to political questions. Aristotle, in discussing deliberative rhetoric, says that the subjects embraced are finance, war and peace, defence of the country, imports and exports, and legislation. Yet the rhetorician does not necessarily become an expert in those fields. He attempts to learn the authorities and sources of information in each, and to develop a method which he can apply to specific problems as they arise. He learns, in any given situation, what questions to ask—and to answer. The peculiar contribution of the rhetorician is the discovery and use, to the common good, of those things which move men to action—intangible, obscure, mystic, even as these things may be; yet you and I and our communities find them intertwined with every problem of life.

The question of the relation of rhetoric to the work of the department of English is too involved for me to attempt an answer. From what we have already seen of the field of rhetoric, however, I think one or two suggestions might be drawn. The work of departments of English is already very broad, ranging from courses in Old English and Middle English to those in short-story writing, dramatic structure, biographical studies of authors, and historical studies of literary tendencies. If the department of English absorbs, in addition, the work in rhetoric, at least it should do so with complete knowledge of the breadth and importance of it, and aware of the distinction between rhetoric and other forms of literature. So far as English is the study of language, philology, it is not very closely related to rhetoric; so far as it is a study of literature it deals with a fine art; whereas we have seen that rhetoric is to be classed with the useful arts. Aristotle intended his *Poetics* to treat of discourse designed to delight; he wrote his *Rhetoric* to treat of discourse designed to persuade. We can cite John Milton as a man great in both fields. The student of literature will be especially interested in Milton's poetry. To the student of rhetoric, however, the most important part of Milton's life is the twenty years when, after having written "Lycidas" and "Comus" and other poems, he turned to writing controversial prose for the influencing of public opinion.

The writer in pure literature has his eye on his subject; his subject has filled his mind and engaged his interest, and he must tell about it; his task is expression; his form and style are organic with his subject. The writer of rhetorical discourse has his eye upon the audience and occasion; his task is persuasion; his form and style are organic with the oc-

casion. As for showing this distinction in our curricula, might it not be possible to put all study of exposition and argumentation into a course or group of courses together with other work in rhetoric and public speaking; while the teaching of narration and description, or of such literary forms as the short-story, the familiar essay, and the play, might be kept in closer relation to the courses in literature and in distinction from the forms of writing and speaking as a useful art. There is surely a closer kinship between writing a piece of argumentation and the delivery of an argumentative speech than between the writing of the same piece of argumentation and the reading of Tennyson's poems. Surely it is not asking too much to have this fact somehow recognized.

We may wonder, if the foregoing is a true description of the field of rhetoric, how it has come about that rhetoric usually includes, in present-day usage, only matters of style and ornament. A modern discussion of rhetoric will often consist of chapters on diction, figures of speech, and forms of arrangement, such as antithesis, periodicity, and balance. The identification of rhetoric with persuasion seems to have vanished. This has come about through a process of substituting a part for the whole or of losing sight of the end in the means. For example, in the Middle Ages, there were centuries when there was not a great deal of public speaking, and what was done was in a formal way upon certain conventional themes. At such times, the chief care of the speaker was in the phrasing of his material. His subject-matter was always old—probably dictated down to minute details by the conventions of the occasion; his skill was to be shown in his diction and embellishment. So rhetoric came to be the study of embellishment, and is so defined in some mediaeval and Renaissance rhetorics. At such times, the identification of rhetoric with display is quite warranted; and we can see the ground for the prevalent meaning we noted at the beginning of the paper.

This degradation of rhetoric can be traced quite clearly. The Roman rhetoricians divided the subject into five parts; to quote Cicero's statement, the orator "ought first to find what he should say (*inventio*), next to dispose and arrange his matter, not only in a certain order, but with a sort of power and judgment (*dispositio*), then to clothe and deck his thought with language (*elocutio*); then to secure them in his memory (*memoria*); and lastly to deliver them with dignity and grace (*pronuntiatio*)." Aristotle devotes practically all of his first two books to the subject of invention; in the third he treats of disposition, elocution or style, and very briefly of delivery, omitting the subject of memorizing. But it is plain that in any period when subject-matter was conventionalized, the consideration of invention would be neglected. Disposition would require only the slightest attention, whereas stylistic embellishment, memorizing, and delivery would constitute the orator's task. Some teachers of rhetoric, indeed, by the plan of having students use only the works of others, reduce the study entirely to that of the last two of the five parts—memorizing and delivery.

As we are aware, not in the Middle Ages alone has rhetoric thus been narrowed. In any and all times the tendency is present—the tendency to depend upon tradition or convention for material and devote oneself wholly to style in writing and delivery in speaking; so that rhetoric becomes a study of how to vary a phrase, how to turn a compliment, write certain kinds of letters and formal addresses, how to declaim great orations, or how to deliver a set speech suitable to a certain occasion. Order of words, with regard to emphasis and balance, beauty of figures, dignity and sonorousness become the matters of highest concern. Rhetoric is then an affair of the court and the chamber—or the parlor; and is brought back to its true self only when some divisive issue, a revolution or a great national danger, calls men to sterner tasks of discussion and persuasion. In these times of stress, oratorical power grows out of the subject-matter, eloquence is organic and not an embellishment or flourish added from without. Such eloquence, imbued with great earnestness of persuasive effort, has a simplicity of diction and style which, like poetry in its great periods, lies very close to the common speech of men, and yet at the same time exercises an exalting and purifying influence upon the language. Might it not be possible that in matters of purity and strength of speech the orators, the speaking men— such as Bunyan, Jeremy Taylor, Pitt, Fox, Burke, and Lincoln—have exerted as great an influence upon the language as the poets and essayists? Yet the speakers are too often overlooked when investigations are made upon these points.

But it occurs to me, as I glance back, that my subject is too large to cover even in a paper of such inordinate length as this one is about to assume. I shall attempt no formal summary, hoping that as we have travelled about this field, some of its contours have become clearer and its boundary-lines more definite. I have tried to show that in the field of persuasive discourse, which traditionally and still to a great extent practically is to be identified with oratory and public address, we have a rather definite body of theory and practice, with an honorable history and an excellent academic pedigree. I have mentioned some distinctions that set off rhetorical discourses from all other forms, whether oral or written; notably, that in rhetoric a study of the audience is fundamental; and the essence of it is adaptation to the end of influencing hearers. Rhetoric does not include all the work done by our present departments of public speaking: it does not include the oral interpretation of literature, nor dramatics, nor studies designed to improve the pronunciation and diction of ordinary conversation. But estimated historically and by its influence upon the affairs of the world, rhetorical discourse seems the most important subject with which we have to do. In addition to all we inherit from the past, with modern researches in psychology to draw upon, with modern wielders of publicity to observe, and with the increasing use of a method for sending human speech broadcast, so that a speaker may address thousands where he once addressed scores, the significance of persuasive discourse is continually being enhanced. Surely it would be a mistake to overlook this significance, and in proportioning our emphasis I do not see how we can give any but a central position to rhetorical study.

Donald C. Bryant

Rhetoric: Its Function and Scope

◊ *Thirty years after Hudson, Donald Bryant took a fresh look at the field of rhetoric.*

He first set about to devise a more workable definition of the term. Convinced that Aristotle's classical approach was too narrow and Kenneth Burke's symbolic approach was too broad, Bryant described rhetoric as "the rationale of informative and suasory discourse." Thereby he added exposition to persuasion, embraced both oral and written messages, and excluded such non-language forms of influence as pictures, colors, and design.

Then Bryant turned to the special mission of rhetoric: the adjustment of ideas to people and people to ideas.

Bryant concluded his assessment by assigning four roles to the field: that of practical tool in everyday decision-making; a useful form of literary study encompassing linguistics, critical theory and semantics; a philosophical study involving investigation and inquiry; and a social study devoted to a major behavioral force in society. ◊

When a certain not always ingenuous radio spokesman for one of our large industrial concerns some years ago sought to reassure his audience on the troublesome matter of propaganda, his comfort ran thus: Propaganda, after all, is only a word for anything one says for or against anything. Either everything, therefore, is propaganda, or nothing is propaganda; so why worry?

The more seriously I take this assignment from the Editor to reexplore for the *Quarterly Journal of Speech* (1953), the ground surveyed by Hudson and Wichelns thirty years ago, and since crossed and recrossed by many another, including myself,[1] the nearer I come to a position like our friend's conclusion on propaganda. When I remember Quintilian's *Institutes* at one extreme of time, and lose myself in Kenneth Burke's "new rhetoric" at the other, I am almost forced to the position that whatever we do or say or write, or even think, in explanation of anything, or in support, or in extenuation, or in

Donald C. Bryant, "Rhetoric: Its Function and Its Scope," *Quarterly Journal of Speech*, 39 (December 1953): 401–424. Reprinted with permission of Speech Communication Association.

despite of anything, evinces rhetorical symptoms. Hence, either everything worth mentioning is rhetorical, or nothing is; so let's talk about something encompassable—say logic, or semantics, or persuasion, or linguistics, or scientific method, or poetics, or social psychology, or advertising, or salesmanship, or public relations, or pedagogy, or politics, or psychiatry, or symbolics—or propaganda.

But that is not the assignment. Others have dealt with those subjects, and have given us such illuminating definitive essays as "Speech as a Science" by Clarence Simon,[2] "The Spoken Word and the Great Unsaid" by Wendell Johnson,[3] "General Semantics[1952]" by Irving Lee,[4] and many other interpretive essays and *apologiae* for the various branches of our curricula and for the multiform captions in our departmental catalogues and organization charts. Among these, "Rhetoric and Public Address" can hardly be thought neglected over the years, at least in the *Quarterly Journal of Speech* and *Speech Monographs*. But perhaps we have assumed too quickly that rhetoric is now at last well understood. On the other hand, Hudson's "The Field of Rhetoric" may be inaccessible or out of date, and Burke's "new rhetoric" too cumbersome or recondite in statement, even after Marie Hochmuth's admirable exposition of it.[5] Even if all this be true, however, one can hardly hope to clarify here what may remain obscure in the work of thirty years—or twenty centuries; but in proper humility, no doubt one can try. At least, common practice seems to presume a restatement of most

complex ideas about once in a generation.

I shall not undertake to summarize Hudson's or Wichelns' pioneer essays, relevant as they are to the central problem. They and certain others like Hunt's "Plato and Aristotle on Rhetoric"[6] are by now woven into the fabric of our scholarship. Nor shall I try to duplicate the coverage of my two papers on "Aspects of the Rhetorical Tradition." They can be easily reread by anyone interested.

One further limitation upon the scope of this essay seems necessary: I shall not try to present a digest of rhetoric or even an explanation of the main principles of rhetorical method. Those are also easily available, from Aristotle's *Rhetoric* to the newest textbook in persuasion. Furthermore, I intend to discuss no particular system of rhetoric, but the functions and scope which any system will embrace.

Confusion in Meaning of "Rhetoric"

Very bothersome problems arise as soon as one attempts to define rhetoric, problems that lead so quickly to hairsplitting on the one hand or cosmic inclusiveness on the other, and to ethical or moral controversy, that the attempt usually ends in trifling with logomachies, gloss on Aristotle, or flat frustration. *Rhetoric* is a word in common parlance, as well as in technical use in the SAA and the Chicago school of literary critics. Hence we may presume it to have meanings which must be reckoned with, however vague, various, and disparate; for a word means what responsible users make it mean. Various as the meanings are, however, one occasionally encounters uses which seem little short of perverse, in persons who ought to know better. Not long since, a doctoral candidate in the classics, who had written as his dissertation a "rhetorical" analysis of one of St. Paul's sermons, was asked how Aristotle had defined rhetoric. Though the question, it would appear, was relevant, the candidate was unable to answer satisfactorily. Whereupon the questioner was taken firmly to task by one of his fellow examiners and was told that after all rhetoric could be adequately defined as a *way of saying something*. Now of course rhetoric may be so defined, as poetic may be defined as a way of making something; but there is little intellectual profit in either definition.

Rhetoric also enjoys several other meanings which, though more common and less perverse, serve to make analysis of it difficult. In general these are the same meanings which Hudson reviewed thirty years ago: bombast; high-sounding words without content; oratorical falsification to hide meaning; sophistry; ornamentation and the study of figures of speech; most commonly among academic folk, Freshman English; and finally, least commonly of all, the whole art of spoken discourse, especially persuasive discourse. This last meaning has gained somewhat in currency in thirty years, especially among scholars in speech and renaissance literature.[7] During the same period the use of the term *rhetoric* (or the combinations *composition and*

rhetoric and *grammar and rhetoric*) to label courses and textbooks in Freshman English has somewhat declined, and simultaneously the "rhetorical" content of them has declined also. The tendency now is to prefer just *Composition* or *English Composition*, or to resort to such loaded names as *Basic Writing, Effective Writing, Problems in Writing, Writing with a Purpose,* or *Communication and Analysis.*

In one of his early speeches, President Eisenhower declared that we want action from the Russians, not rhetoric, as evidence of their desire for peaceful settlement. Here is the common use of *rhetoric* to mean empty language, or language used to deceive, without honest intention behind it. Without question this use is in harmony with the current climate of meaning where what our opponents say is rhetoric, and what we say is something else. Hence our attempt to define rhetoric leads almost at once into questions of morals and ethics.

Rhetoric as figures of speech or artificial elegance of language is also a healthy perennial, nurtured in literary scholarship and criticism as well as lay comment. Hence the second of the two meanings of *rhetorical* in *Webster's New Collegiate Dictionary* is "emphasizing style, often at the expense of thought." Here we encounter a second obscuring or limiting factor in our attempt at definition. We are to describe rhetoric in terms of those *elements* of a verbal composition for which it is to be held responsible. This mode of procedure has always been attractive. It can produce interesting and plausible conclusions, and it can be defended as schematically satisfying and pedagogically convenient. Thus it proved in the *trivium* of the middle ages and renaissance. If grammar has charge of the correctness of discourse, and if logic has charge of the intellectual content, then it is natural to assign to rhetoric the management of the language of discourse (or the *elocutio*), and if we do not include poetic in our system, the imaginative and emotional content also.

Another definition in the *New Collegiate Dictionary* points to the identification of rhetoric not with the elements of verbal composition but with the *forms* or *genres:* "The art of expressive speech or of discourse, orig. of oratory, now esp. of literary composition; esp., the art of writing well in prose, as disting. from versification and elocution." This approach is promising and on the whole the most popular through the ages. "Originally of oratory, now especially the art of writing well in prose—" this phrase does well enough as a general description of the scope of rhetoric in ancient Greece, as Baldwin has pointed out, when prose itself was virtually defined as oratory and history, and when even history was composed largely in the spirit of oratory. That is, rhetoric could be the art of prose when prose was predominantly concerned with the intentional, directional energizing of truth, of finding in any given situation all the available means of persuasion, and of using as many of them as good sense dictated.

Even then, however, the weakness of genres as the basis for constructing theories or writing handbooks was ev-

ident. What is the art of Plato's dialogues, which are in prose? or of Sappho's compositions, which are poems? Neither poetic nor rhetoric is adequate to either. The difficulty multiplies as variety in the kinds of compositions increases in Roman, renaissance, and modern times, and as print supplements—and often supplants—speech as the medium of verbal communication. As *poetic*, the art of imitation in language, became crystallized in Roman and renaissance learning as the theory and practice of the drama (especially tragedy) and the epic, so *rhetoric*, in Quintilian's and Cicero's theory the whole operative philosophy of civil leadership, showed in practice as the art of making winning speeches in the law courts, or later in public exhibitions. The very doctrine in rhetoric of the epideictic or ceremonial speech, as I shall show later, is excellent evidence of the weakness of the types or *genres* as the basis for definition.

All these meanings of rhetoric, in spite of their limitations, contribute something to the exposition of our subject, and the pursuit of each has yielded lucrative insights into the subject, or at least into the problem. Some of them, especially rhetoric as bombast, as excessive ornamentation, and as deceit, are evidence of the falling off of rhetoricians from time to time from the broad philosophy of the art which they inherited from the founders. For a redefinition, therefore, I know no better way of beginning than to return to that broad philosophy.

Working Definition of Rhetoric

First of all and primarily, therefore, I take rhetoric to be the *rationale of informative and suasory discourse*. All its other meanings are partial or morally-colored derivatives from that primary meaning. This rhetoric has been, at least since Aristotle; and at least since Aristotle there has existed a comprehensive, fundamental codification of its principles. It would be idolatrous to suggest that Aristotle uttered the first and last authentic words on rhetoric, or that his system is still adequate, or that it was completely satisfactory even for the Greeks of his day. Like his poetic theory, however, it enjoys unequalled scientific eminence in its field though it has sustained many additions and modifications through the centuries. Its limitations are historical rather than philosophical. Like the limitations of his poetic, the limitations of his rhetoric derive mainly from his failure to consider phenomena which had not yet occurred and to make use of learnings which had not yet been developed.

Now as then, therefore, what Aristotle said of the nature and principles of public address, of the discovery of all the available means of persuasion in any given case, must stand as the broad background for any sensible rhetorical system. Much of Aristotle's formulation, even in detail, survives ungainsaid and can only be rearranged and paraphrased by subsequent writers. Again to cite a parallel with his poetic: though the relative importance of plot in drama has shifted radically since Aristotle, when good plots are made their

excellences will still be best discovered by the application of Aristotle's criteria. Similarly, though modern psychology is very different from that of the Greeks, and doubtless more scientific, modern enlightenment has produced no new method of analyzing an audience which can replace Aristotle's.

Aristotle, however, identified rhetoric with persuasion. His chief interests lay in the speaking to popular audiences in the law court and in the legislative assembly, and his system of classification and analysis obviously was framed with those types of speaking as its principal object. Some means of persuasion, however, in spite of Aristotle's comprehensive definition, are not within the scope of rhetoric. Gold and guns, for example, are certainly persuasive, and the basic motives which make them persuasive, profit and self-preservation, may enter the field of rhetoric; but applied directly to the persons to be persuaded, guns and gold belong to commerce or coercion, not to rhetoric.

No more shall we admit the persuasive use of all symbols as belonging to rhetoric. Undoubtedly the persuasive force of pictures, colors, designs, non-language sounds such as fog horns and fire alarms, and all such devices of symbolic significance is great and useful. Traffic lights, however, are not normally agents of rhetorical influence. No more, in themselves, are elephants, donkeys, lions, illuminated bottles of whiskey, or animated packs of cigarettes. Their use has a kinship to rhetoric, and when they are organized in a matrix of verbal discourse, they become what Aristotle called the extrinsic or non-artistic means of persuasion. They are instruments of the wielder of public opinion, and they are staples of two techniques which must be recognized as strongly rhetorical—advertising and propaganda. Unless we are to claim practically all interhuman activity as the field of rhetoric, however, some limits must be admitted, even within the field of persuasion. True, in the "new rhetoric" of Kenneth Burke, where the utmost extension rather than practical limit-setting is the aim, any manifestation of "identification," conscious or unconscious, is within rhetoric. Though the classic limitations of rhetoric are too narrow, others are too broad. Therefore I am assuming the traditional limitation to discourse.

Let us look now at Aristotle's apparent failure to include exposition as well as persuasion within rhetoric. Ancillary to persuasion, of course, exposition is clearly included. The idea of *demonstration*, the characteristic result of the logical mode, implies the most perfect exposition for audiences susceptible of reasoned instruction. Furthermore, another aspect of Aristotle's system admits exposition to independent status. At the expense of a slight venture into heresy (though I believe only a benign heresy) I suggest that any systematic construction of human phenomena, even Aristotle's, will either leave out something important and significant, or will include a category, however named, which is, in effect, "miscellaneous." That I think Aristotle did in discussing the rhetoric of the ceremonial or epideictic speech. The success of his categories, even so, is remarkable. The extension and effective application to the ceremonial

speech in general of the principles of the persuasive speech whose end is active decision, provide very plausible coverage of that somewhat anomalous form. The three-fold, tripartite classification of speeches was too nearly perfect to abandon:

Forensic (time, past; ends, justice and injustice; means, accusation and defense.)
Epideictic (time, present; ends, honor and dishonor; means, praise and blame.)
Deliberative (time, future; ends, the expedient and inexpedient; means, exhortation and dehortation.)

When the problems of what to do with time-present in the system, and with Pericles' funeral oration among the observed phenomena had to be solved, the coincidence was too attractive to be resisted. It provided for a piece of practical realism which no system should be allowed to defeat. Through that adjustment Aristotle admitted within the scope of rhetoric the predominantly literary performance on the one hand and gave an opening on the other for the primarily informative and instructional as well as the demonstrative and exhibitionistic. Through this third category rhetoric embraces, in a persuasion-centered system, the *docere* and *delectare*, the teach and delight, of the Roman and renaissance rhetoric-poetic and permits them an independent status outside their strictly ancillary or instrumental functions in persuasion.

Aristotle's system, therefore, and his rationale of effective speaking comprehend with very little violence the art of the good man skilled in speaking of Cicero and Quintilian, or Baldwin's equation of rhetoric to the art of prose whose end is giving effectiveness to truth[8]—effectiveness considered in terms of what happens to an audience, usually a popular or lay audience as distinguished from the specialized or technical audience of the scientific or dialectical demonstration. This distinction, strictly speaking, is a practical rather than a logical limitation, a limitation of degree rather than kind. No matter what the audience, when the speaker evinces skill in getting into their minds, he evinces rhetorical skill.

If the breadth of scope which I have assigned to rhetoric is implicit in Aristotle's system, the basic delimitation of that scope finds early and explicit statement there. Rhetoric is not confined in application to any specific subjects which are exclusively its own. Rhetoric is method, not subject. But if it has no special subjects, neither are all subjects within its province. In its suasory phase, at least, rhetoric is concerned, said Aristotle, only with those questions about which men dispute, that is, with the contingent—that which is dependent in part upon factors which cannot be known for certain, that which can be otherwise. Men do not dispute about what is known or certainly knowable by them. Hence the characteristic concern of rhetoric is broadly with question of justice and injustice, of the expedient and the inexpedient (of the desirable and undesirable, of the good and the bad), of praise and blame, or honor and dishonor.

To questions such as these and their almost finite subsidiary questions, vital and perennial as they are in the practical operation of human society, the best answers can never be certain but only more or less probable. In reasoning about them, men at best must usually proceed from probable premise to probable conclusion, seldom from universal to universal. Hence Aristotle described the basic instrument of rhetoric, the enthymeme, as a kind of syllogism based on probabilities and signs.

Rhetoric, therefore, is distinguished from the other instrumental studies in its preoccupation with informed opinion rather than with scientific demonstration. It is the counterpart, said Aristotle, of dialectic. Strictly speaking, dialectic also may be said to attain only probability, not scientific certainty, like physics (and, perhaps, theology). The methodology, however, is the methodology of formal logic and it deals in universals. Hence it arrives at a very high degree of probability, for it admits the debatable only in the assumption of its premises. Rhetoric, however, because it normally deals with matters of uncertainty for the benefit of popular audiences, must admit probability not only in its premises but in its method also. This is the ground upon which Plato first, and hundreds of critics since, have attacked rhetoric—that it deals with opinion rather than knowledge. This is the ground also from which certain scholars have argued,[9] after some of the mediaeval fathers, that rhetoric really deals, characteristically, not with genuine probability but only with adumbration and suggestion. It is, they say, distinguished from dialectic in *degree* of probability—dialectic very high, and rhetoric very low.

The epistemological question is interesting, and in a world or philosophers where only certain knowledge was ever called upon to decide questions of human behavior, it would be the central question. Rhetoric exists, however, because a world of certainty is not the world of human affairs. It exists because the world of human affairs is a world where there must be an alternative to certain knowledge on the one hand and pure chance or whimsey on the other. The alternative is informed opinion, the nearest approach to knowledge which the circumstances of decision in any given case will permit. The art, or science, or method whose realm this is, is rhetoric. Rhetoric, therefore, is the method, the strategy, the organon of the principles for deciding best the undecidable questions, for arriving at solutions of the unsolvable problems, for instituting method in those vital phases of human activity where no method is inherent in the total subject-matter of decision. The resolving of such problems is the province of the "Good man skilled in speaking." It always has been, and it is still. Of that there can be little question. And the comprehensive rationale of the functioning of that good man so far as he is skilled in speaking, so far as he is a wielder of public opinion, is rhetoric.

The Problems of Vocabulary in This Essay

Traditionally *rhetoric* and *oratory* have been the standard terms for the theory and the product. The *rhetor* was the speaker, the addresser of the public, or the teacher of speaking; the *rhetorician*, the teacher of rhetoric or the formulator of the principles of rhetoric. Hence the special bias of the terms as I use them has been and probably still is oral. That is a practical bias and is not carelessly to be thrown away. From the beginning of publication in writing, however, essentially rhetorical performances, whether already spoken or to be spoken, have been committed to paper and circulated to be read rather than heard—from Isocrates' *Panathenaicus* or Christ's *Sermon on the Mount* to Eisenhower's message on the state of the nation. Furthermore, for centuries now, especially since the invention and cheapening of the art of printing, the agitator, the teacher, the preacher, the wielder of public opinion has used the press quite independently of the platform. Hence, obviously, rhetoric must be understood to be the rationale of informative and suasory discourse both spoken and written: of Milton's *Aeropagitica* as well as Cromwell's Address to the Rump Parliament; of John Wilkes' *North Briton* as well as Chatham's speech on the repeal of the Stamp Act; of Tom Paine's *Common Sense* as much as Patrick Henry's Address to the Virginia Assembly; of Swift's pamphlet on the *Conduct of the Allies* as well as Dr. Sacheverell's sermon on Passive Obedience; of George Sokolsky's syndicated columns in the press equally with Edward R. Murrow's radio commentaries or Kenneth McFarland's appearances before conventions of the Chambers of Commerce. I will use *rhetoric* and *rhetorical* with that breadth of scope.

Furthermore, the terms *orator* and *oratory* have taken on, like *rhetoric* itself, rather limited or distorted meanings, not entirely undeserved perhaps, which make them no longer suitable for the designation of even the normal *oral* rhetorical performance. *Practitioner of public address*, or some such hyphenated monstrosity as *speaker-writer*, might be used as a generic term for the product of rhetoric, but the disadvantages of such manipulations of vocabulary are obvious. I am using the terms *speech* and *speaker* for both written and oral performance and written and oral performer, unless the particular circumstances obviously imply one or the other. Likewise, in place of such a formula as *listener-reader*, I shall use *audience*, a usage not uncommon anyway.

One must face still another problem of vocabulary, that of the term *rhetoric* in the three distinguishable senses in which I use it: (1) as the rationale of informative and suasory discourse, a body of principle and precept for the creation and analysis of speeches; (2) as a quality which characterizes that kind of discourse and distinguishes it from other kinds; (3) as a study of the phenomenon of informative and suasory discourse in the social context. Similarly, I fear, the term *rhetorician* will sometimes mean the formulator and philosopher of rhetorical theory; sometimes the teacher of the technique of discourse; sometimes the speaker with rhetorical intention; and finally the student or scholar whose concern is the literary or social or behavioral study of rhetoric. I have been tempted to invent terms to avoid certain of these ambiguities, such as *logology,* or even *rhetoristic* (parallel with *sophistic*), but the game would probably not be worth the candle.

In summary, rhetoric is the rationale of informative and suasory discourse, it operates chiefly in the areas of the contingent, its aim is the attainment of maximum probability as a basis for public decision, it is the organizing and animating principle of all subject-matters which have a relevant bearing on that decision. Now let us turn to the question of the subject-matters in which rhetoric most characteristically functions and of the relations it bears to special subject-matters.

Subjects of Rhetorical Discourse

Wrote Aristotle, "The most important subjects of general deliberation . . . are practically five, viz. finance, war and peace, the defense of the country, imports and exports, and legislation." This is still the basic list, though legislation now would be far more generally inclusive than it was to the Athenian assembly. In addition, within the scope of rhetorical discourse fall the subjects of forensic address—crime and its punishment and all the concerns of justice and injustice. Furthermore, the concerns of teaching, preaching—moral, intellectual, practical, and spiritual instruction and exhortation—and commercial exploitation, wherever the problems of adaptation of ideas and information to the group mind are concerned, depend upon rhetorical skill for their fruition. Thus we are brought again to the position that the rhetorical factor is pervasive in the operative aspects of society.

Does this mean that the speaker must be a specialist in all subjects, as well as in rhetorical method? Cicero seemed willing to carry the demands thus far, at least in establishing his ideal orator; and this implication has been ridiculed from Plato onwards for the purpose of discrediting first the claims of the sophists and then all men "skilled in speaking." Plainly, in practice and in plausible human situations, the suggestion is absurd. Does the public speaker or the columnist or the agitator have to be a military specialist in order rightly to urge peace or war? Does the citizen have to be a dentist and a chemist and a pathologist intelligently to advocate the use of fluorine in the municipal water supply? He does not become a specialist in these fields, of course, any more than the head of an industrial plant is the technical master of the specialties of all the men who serve under him. "He attempts to learn the authorities and sources of information in each, and to develop a method which he can apply to specific problems as they arise. He learns, in any given situation, what questions to ask and to answer. The peculiar contribution of the rhetorician is the discovery and use, to the common good, of those things which move men to [understanding and] action."[10] Looked at another way, the relation of rhetoric to the subject-matters of economics, or public health, or theology, or chemistry, or agriculture is like the relation of hydraulic engineering to water, under the specific circumstances in which the engineer is to construct his dam or his pumping station or his sewage system, and in view of the specific results he is to obtain. He develops a method for determining what questions to ask and answer from all that which can be known about water. If he is a good hydraulics engineer, he will see to it that his relevant knowledge is sound, as the good speaker will see to it that his relevant knowledge of hydraulic engineering is the best obtainable if he is to urge or oppose the building of a dam in the St. Lawrence River. If either is ignorant, or careless,

or dishonest, he is culpable as a man and as a rhetorician or hydraulics engineer.

It was not the scientific chronologist, the astronomer Lord Macclesfield, who secured the adoption in England of the Gregorian calendar, thoroughly as he understood the subject in all its mathematical, astronomical, and chronometrical aspects. It was the Earl of Chesterfield, learning from the chronologist all that was essential to the particular situation, and knowing rhetoric and the British Parliament, who was able to impress upon his fellows not necessarily the validity of the calculations but the desirability and the feasibility of making a change. If the truth of scientific knowledge had been left to its own inherent force with Parliament, we would doubtless be many more days out of phase with the sun than England was in 1751. As Aristotle observed in his brief and basic justification of rhetoric, truth itself has a tendency to prevail over error; but in competition with error, where skillful men have an interest in making error prevail, truth needs the help of as attractive and revealing a setting as possible. In the Kingdom of Heaven, truth may be its own sole advocate, but it needs mighty help if it is to survive in health among the nations on earth. As Fielding wrote of prudence in *Tom Jones:* "It is not enough that your designs, nay, that your actions, are intrinsically good; you must take care that they shall appear so. If your inside be never so beautiful, you must preserve a fair outside also. This must be constantly looked to."[11]

In this sense even honest rhetoric is fundamentally concerned with appearances, not to the disregard of realities as Plato and his successors have industriously charged, but to the enforcement of realities. Rhetoric at the command of honest men strives that what is desirable shall appear desirable, that what is vicious shall appear vicious. It intends that the true or probably true shall seem so, that the false or doubtful shall be vividly realized for what it is. A bridge or an automobile or a clothes-line must not only *be* strong but must *appear* to be so. This fact has been an obstacle to the use of many new structural materials. Accustomed to an older kind, we have been reluctant to accept the adequacy of a new, more fragile-seeming substance. Hence one important reason for surrounding steel columns with stone pillars is the necessity of making them seem as strong as their predecessors. Appearances, then, must be the concern of the wielder of public opinion, the rhetorician. Through ignorance or malice, to be sure, skill in establishing appearances may be applied to deceive. This is a grave peril which must be the concern of all men of good will. Knowledge of the devices of sophistry will always be acquired by those whose purposes are bad; ignorance of them will provide no defense for the rest. No great force can be used without hazard, or ignored without hazard. The force understood, rather than the force not understood, is likely to be the force controlled. That understanding is provided by rhetoric, the technique of discourse addressed to the enlightenment and persuasion of the generality of mankind—the basic instrument for the creation of informed public opinion and the consequent expedient public action.

Occasions of Rhetorical Discourse

Whether we will or no, we cannot escape rhetoric, either the doing or the being done to. We require it. As Edmund Burke wrote, "Men want reasons to reconcile their minds to what is done, as well as motives originally to act right."[12] Whether we seek advice or give it, the nature of our talk, as being "addressed," and of the talk of which we are the audience, as being addressed to us, necessitates speaking the language of the audience or we had as well not speak at all. That process is the core of rhetoric. It goes on as genuinely, and is often managed as skillfully, over the frozen-meats counter of the local supermarket as in the halls of Congress; on the benches in front of the Boone County Court House on Saturday afternoon before election as below the benches of the Supreme Court the next Wednesday morning; around the table where a new labor contract is being negotiated as in the pulpit of Sainte-Marie de Chaillot where Bossuet is pronouncing the funeral oration upon Henriette d'Angleterre; in the Petition from Yorkshire to King George III for redress of grievances as in the Communist Manifesto or the Declaration of Independence.

As we are teachers, and as we are taught, we are involved with rhetoric. The success of the venture depends on a deliberate or instinctive adjustment of idea-through-speaker-to-audience-in-a-particular-situation. Pedagogy is the rhetoric of teaching, whether formally in the classroom or the book, or informally in the many incidental situations of our days and nights. The psychological principle, for example, that we learn through association becomes a rhetorical principle when we use it to connect one day's lesson with what has gone before. It is the same principle by which Burke attempted to establish in the minds of the House of Commons the rights of American colonists when he identified the colonists with Englishmen, whose rights were known.

As we are readers of newspapers and magazines and all such information-giving and opinion-forming publications, and as we write for them, we are receiving or initiating rhetorical discourse, bad or good, effective or ineffective. The obligations of the journalists as investigator of the facts, as thinker about the facts, as discoverer of ideas and analyst and critic of ideas, are fundamental. They demand all the knowledge and skill that the political, scientific, and technical studies can provide. The journalist's distinctive job, however, is writing for his audience the highest grade of informative and suasory discourse that the conditions of his medium will permit. Whether editorial writer, commentator, or plain newswriter, reaching into his audience's mind is his problem. If the people who buy the paper miss the import, the paper might as well not be published. Call it *journalism* if you choose; it is the rhetoric of the press: "it is always public opinion that the press seeks to change, one way or another, directly or indirectly."[13] Seldom can the journalist wait for the solution of a problem before getting into the fray, whether the question be a more efficient way of handling municipal finances or independence for India. He must know the right questions to ask and the bases for answering them with greatest probability for his audience now. That is his rhetorical knowledge.

The same is true of the radio and television news reporter, news analyst, and commentator. He must have rhetorical skill to survive in his occupation, and he must have knowledge and integrity if his effect is to be beneficial rather than destructive to informed public opinion. His staple, also, whether good or bad, is rhetoric. His efforts are aimed at the public mind and are significant only as they affect the public mind. If he is an honest rhetorician, he does not imply of most things, "It is so because," but only "I believe so because"; or "I recommend so because it seems probable where I cannot be sure." If he is tempted into exploiting the force of extravagant and authoritative assertion, his morals rather than his rhetoric have gone awry. Whether the use be honest or dishonest, the instrument is rhetoric.

It is obvious and commonplace that the agitator, the political speaker, the pamphleteer, the advocate, the preacher, the polemicist and apologist, the adviser of kings and princes, the teacher of statesmen, the reformer and counter-reformer, the fanatic in religion, diet, or economics, the mountebank and messiah, have enhanced the stature of a noble discourse or have exploited a degraded, shallow, and dishonest discourse. It matters not that we resort to exalted names for the one—eloquence, genius, philosophy, logic, discourse of reason; and for the other, labels of reproach and contempt—sophistry, glibness, demagoguery, chicanery, "rhetoric." That naming process itself is one of the most familiar techniques of rhetoric. The fact is that in their characteristic preoccupation with manipulating the public mind, they are one. They must not all be approved or emulated, but they must all be studied as highly significant social phenomena, lest we be ignorant of them, and hence powerless before them, for good or for ill.

Similarly, though perhaps not so easily acceptable into rhetoric, we must recognize most of what we know as advertising, salesmanship, propaganda, "public relations," and commercial, political, and national "information" services. I shall have some special consideration to give to these later. At present I merely cite them as great users of rhetoric. In this day of press, radio, and television perhaps their rhetoric is that most continuously and ubiquitously at work on the public.

Relations of Rhetoric to Other Learnings

These, then, are fundamental rhetorical situations. In them human beings are so organizing language as to effect a change in the knowledge, the understanding, the ideas, the attitudes, or the behavior of other human beings. Furthermore, they are so organizing that language as to make the change as agreeable, as easy, as active, and as secure as possible—as the Roman rhetoric had it, to teach, to delight, and to move (or to bend). What makes a situation rhetorical is the focus upon accomplishing something predetermined and directional with an audience. To that end many knowledges and sciences, concerning both what is external to audiences and what applies to audiences themselves, may be involved, many of which I have discussed in a previous essay.[14] These knowledges, however, have to be organized, managed, given places in strategy and tactics, set into coordinated and harmonious movement towards the listener as the end, towards what happens to him and in him. In short, they have to be *put to use,* for, as Bacon said, studies themselves "teach not their own use; but that is a wisdom without them, and above them, won by observation." "Studies themselves do give forth directions too much at large, except they be bounded in by experience."[15] Rhetoric teaches their use towards a particular end. It is that "observation," that "experience" codified, given a rationale. Other learnings are chiefly concerned with the discovery of ideas and phenomena and of their relations to each other within more or less homogeneous and closed systems. Rhetoric is primarily concerned with the relations of ideas to the thoughts, feelings, motives, and behavior of men. Rhetoric as distinct from the learnings which it uses is dynamic; it is concerned with movement. It *does* rather than *is*. It is method rather than matter. It is chiefly involved with bringing about a condition, rather than discovering or testing a condition. Even psychology, which is more nearly the special province of rhetoric than is any other study, is descriptive of conditions, but not of the uses of those conditions.

So far as it is method, rhetoric is like the established procedures of experimental science and like logic. As the method for solving problems of human action in the areas of the contingent and the probable, however, it does not enjoy a privilege which is at the same time the great virtue and the great limitation of science and logic—it cannot choose its problems in accordance with the current capacities of its method, or defer them until method is equal to the task. Rhetoric will postpone decision as long as feasible; indeed one of its most valuable uses in the hands of good men, is to prevent hasty and premature formulation of lines of conduct and decision. In this it is one with science—and good sense. But in human affairs, where the whole is usually greater than the most complete collection of the parts, decisions—making up of the mind—cannot always wait until the contingencies have been removed and solutions to problems have been tested in advance. Rhetoric, therefore, must take undemonstrable problems and do its best with them when decision is required. We must decide when the blockage is imposed whether to withdraw from Berlin or to undertake the air lift, not some time later when perhaps some of the contingencies may have been removed. And the making of the choice forever precludes trying out and testing the other possibilities under the circumstances which would have prevailed had we chosen differently at first. Likewise we must make a choice on the first Tuesday in November, whether we are scientifically sure or not. In each case, rhetoric, good or bad, must be the strategy of enlightening opinion for that choice.

To restate our central idea still another way: rhetoric, or the rhetorical, is the function in human affairs which governs and gives direction to that creative activity, that process of critical analysis, that branch of learning, which address themselves to the whole phenomenon of the designed use of langauge for the promulgation of information, ideas, and attitudes. Though it is instrumental in the discovery of ideas and information, its characteristic function is the publication, the publicizing, the humanizing, the animating of them for a realized and usually specific audience. At its best it seeks the "energizing of truth," in order to make "reason and the will of God prevail." But except in science, and no doubt theology, the promulgation of *truth*, sure or demonstrable, is out of the question. Normally the rhetorical function serves as high a degree of probability as the combination of subject, audience, speaker, and occasion admits. Rhetoric may or may not be involved (though the speaker-writer must be) in the determination of the validity of the ideas being promulgated. Such determination will be the province in any given situation of philosophy, ethics, physics, ecoomics, politics, eugenics, medicine, hydraulics, or bucolics. To rhetoric, however, and to no other rationale, belongs the efficiency—the validity if you will—of the relations in the idea-audience-speaker situation.

Functioning of Rhetoric

We are ready now, perhaps, if we have not been ready much sooner, to proceed to the question of how rhetoric works, what it accomplishes in an audience. Speaking generally, we may say that the rhetorical function is the *function of adjusting ideas to people and of people to ideas.* This process may be thought of as a continuum from the complete modification or accommodation of ideas to audiences (as is sometimes said, "telling people only what they want to hear") at the one extreme, to complete regeneration at the other (such perfect illumination that the "facts speak for themselves"). This continuum may, therefore, be said to have complete flattery (to use Plato's unflattering epithet) at one end and the Kingdom of Heaven at the other! Good rhetoric usually functions somewhere well in from the extremes. There, difficult and strange ideas have to be modified without being distorted or invalidated; and audiences have to be prepared through the mitigation of their prejudices, ignorance, and irrelevant sets of mind without being dispossessed of their judgments. The adjustment of ideas to people, for example, was being undertaken by the Earl of Chatham in his speech for the repeal of the Stamp Act, when he agreed that Parliament had legislative supremacy over the Colonies but that legislative supremacy did not include the right to tax without representation. And when Booker T. Washington assured the Southern white folk that they and the Negroes could be as separate as the fingers in social affairs and as united as the hand in economic, he was adjusting people to the idea of real freedom for his race.

The moral disturbances which rhetoric and rhetorical activity seem to breed do not usually result from this process of mutual accommodation itself. Most of them arise when the speaker tries so to adjust ideas to people that the ideas are basically falsified, or when he attempts so to adjust the people to ideas as to deform or anesthetize the people. Report has it that after Senator Hiram Johnson had campaigned through rural New England charging that England would have three votes to one for the United States in the League of Nations, he was taxed by a critic with misrepresenting the nature of the British Empire. One could not assume, so Johnson's critic declared, that Canada and South Africa would vote with England as a single bloc. "That may be," Johnson is said to have replied, "but New England farmers do not know the nature of the British Empire, and they do know common arithmetic." That is adjusting ideas to people so far as to falsify the basic idea. In the other direction, stimulating the "Red-menace-in-the-air-we-breathe" terror in order to adjust people to the idea of giving up their right of dissent is an effort to dispossess people of their judgments.

In terms of the old, but still convenient, faculty psychology, the terms in which rhetoric is most frequently attacked—reason, imagination, passions (emotions), judgment, will—rhetoric may still be described as the method of applying "reason to imagination for the better moving of the will." To complete our broad idea of the scope of rhetoric we should add "and the better clarification of the understanding." That is Francis Bacon's succinct statement of how rhetoric functions in the audience,[16] and it is still a good one. It establishes rhetoric squarely as an

instrumental learning which manages
the creative powers of the whole
logical-psychological man toward a
single dynamic end.

Rhetoric, therefore, has the greatest
possible involvement with the logical
and psychological studies. These learnings must be the core of the speaker's
equipment. They are the *sine qua non*
in the knowledge through which rhetoric must function. In the good rhetoric
which Plato described in the *Phaedrus,*
after knowledge of the truth, he saw the
equipment of the rhetorically skilled
man to consist in knowledge of the various possible kinds of arguments,
knowledge of the various kinds of souls,
and knowledge of which kinds of souls
will be affected by which kinds of arguments—that is, knowledge of the
mutual adaptation of these processes to
audiences. Furthermore, in the great
counter-Platonic *Rhetoric* of Aristotle,
the first Book is devoted chiefly to the
rational processes of rhetoric, and the
next Book is the first extant comprehensive treatise on individual and group
psychology. Likewise, in one of the best
of the recent books on liberal education, which is, therefore, something like
a basic statement on rhetoric, Hoyt
Hudson sees the fundamental equipment of the liberally educated man to
require three parts: the Arm of Information, the Arm of Operative Logic, and
the Arm of Imagination.[17] Of these, in
practical affairs, rhetoric is based on the
second and third, and the first must be
the starting place of the speaker in each
particular situation.

Where in this pattern, then, does
emotion come in, that famous rough-
neck who is said to spoil the rational life
and vitiate the logic of behavior? As

Hudson and many others have observed, and as Bacon knew well, emotion is a derivative of both reason and
imagination. Love of truth and of the
good life must be the results of any genuinely rational functioning, that is, of
operative logic; and vivid realization of
experience, which is imagination, can
hardly occur without those strong emotional accompaniments which, in practice, have given rise to the identifying of
emotion with imagination. This point
seems hardly to need laboring over
again. Hudson's book gives it adequate
coverage, and I have summarized the
traditional position of rhetoric and
rhetoricians on it in the essay already
mentioned.[18] The position is that a
complete rhetoric, and that is the kind
of rhetoric which we are discussing,
knows the whole man and seeks to
bring to bear the whole man in
achieving its ends—what he is and
what he thinks he is, what he believes
and what he thinks he believes, what
he wants and what he tells himself he
wants. Towards its special ends, rhetoric recognizes the primacy of rational
processes, their primacy in time as well
as in importance, as Bacon's definition
implies—applying reason to the imagination. Just so poetry recognizes the
primacy for its purpose of the imagination. But rhetoric has always been
akin to poetry—for long periods of history it has in fact annexed poetry—in
its recognition of the honest and highly
important power of imagination and of
that emotion which does not supplant
but supports reason, and sometimes
even transcends it. Thus Sir Philip
Sidney and most literary theorists of the
renaissance attributed to poetry the
distinctly rhetorical function of using

imagination to create what might be called historical fictions to give power and life to ideas. Rhetoric recognizes the strength of the fictions men live by, as well as those they live under;[19] and it aims to fortify the one and explode the other. Rhetoric aims at what is *worth* doing, what is *worth* trying. It is concerned with *values*, and values are established with the aid of imaginative realization, not through rational determination alone; and they gain their force through emotional animation.

We have observed that psychology, human nature, has been a staple of rhetorical learning through the ages. No doubt, therefore, scientific psychology will have more and more to contribute to modern rhetoric. The first notable attempt to ground rhetoric in a systematic modern psychology was made by George Campbell in his *Philosophy of Rhetoric* (1776), in which he stated as his purpose

to exhibit . . . a tolerable sketch of the human mind; and, aided by the lights which the poet and the orator so amply furnish, to disclose its secret movements, tracing its principal channels of perception and action, as near as possible, to their source: and, on the other hand, from the science of human nature, to ascertain with greater precision, the radical principles of that art, whose object it is, by the use of language, to operate on the soul of the hearer, in the way of informing, convincing, pleasing, moving, or persuading.[20]

That same purpose governs our contemporary writers of treatises and textbooks on public speaking, argumentation, and persuasion, and most of them include as up-to-date a statement as possible of the psychological and the rational bases of rhetoric. It is a commonplace that of the studies re-

cently come to new and promising maturity, psychology, especially social psychology, and cultural anthropology have much to teach modern rhetoric and to correct or reinterpret in traditional rhetoric. The same may be said of the various new ventures into the study of meaning, under the general head of semantics. How language *means* is obviously important to the rationale of informative and suasory discourse. Nevertheless, in spite of I. A. Richards' book,[21] the theory of meaning is not *the* philosophy of rhetoric, any more than is the psychology of perception. Rhetoric is the organizer of all such for the wielding of public opinion.

Advertising, Salesmanship, and Propaganda

Now that we have sketched the rhetorical process functioning at its best for the exposition and dissemination of ideas in the wielding of public opinion, with the ethical and pathetic modes of proof in ancillary relation to the logical, with the imagination aiding and reenforcing the rational, let us turn to some of the partial, incomplete, perhaps misused, rhetorics which I have already mentioned briefly.

It is axiomatic that men do not live by reason alone or even predominantly, though reason is such a highly prized commodity and stands in so high a repute even among the unreasoning and unreasonable, that men prefer to tell themselves and to be told that they make up their minds and determine their choices from reason and the facts. Intellectual activity, both learning and thinking, is so difficult that man tends to avoid it wherever possible. Hence education has almost always put its first efforts into cultivating the reasonable portion of the mind rather than the imaginative or emotional. Furthermore, the strength and accessibility of imaginative and emotional responses is so great in spite of education that though men seldom make effective reasonable decisions without the help of emotion, they often make, or appear to make, effective emotional decisions without the help of rational processes or the modification of reasonable consideration. Inevitably, therefore, the available reason in rhetorical situations will vary tremendously, and the assistance which imagination must provide towards the moving of the will must vary accordingly. Except in Swift's unexciting land of the Houyhnhnms, however, imagination will always be there.

Ever since men first began to weave the web of words to charm their fellows, they have known that some men can impose their wills on others through language in despite of reason. Almost as long, other men have deplored and feared this talent. If the talent were wholly a matter of divine gift and were wholly unexplainable, the only alternative to succumbing to the orator would be to kill him. In time it appeared, however, that this skill could be learned, in part at least, and could be analyzed. Thus if it were good, men could learn to develop it further; and if it were bad, they could be armed in some measure against it. Hence rhetoric, and hence the partial rhetoric of anti-reason and pseudo-reason. And hence the appeal of such rhetorical eruptions as Aldous Huxley's total condemnation of

oratory in *The Devils of Loudon*.[22] His indictment of public speakers is indeed skillful, and ought to be taken seriously. If the talent of his golden-voiced Grandiers be indeed magic, then we will have to agree that the fate of man before such wizards is hopeless. Rhetoric teaches, however, that the method and the power of this kind of discourse can be analyzed, at least in large part, and if its subtleties cannot be wholly *learned* by every ambitious speaker, the characteristics of its operation can be understood, and if understood, then controlled, for better or for worse.[23]

The oratory which Huxley would extirpate presents a rewarding approach to the rhetoric of advertising and propaganda, of which it is the historic prototype. In them the techniques of suggestion, reiteration, imaginative substitution, verbal irrelevance and indirection, and emotional and pseudological bullying have been developed beyond, one might hazard a guess, the fondest dreams of the sophists and the historic demagogues. This development does not represent a change in intention from them to our contemporaries, but an advance in knowledge and opportunity and media.

If you have a soap or a cigarette or a social order for quick, profitable sale, you do not neglect any method within your ethical system of making that sale. That is the paramount problem of the advertiser and the propagandist, and their solutions are very much alike. They are rhetorical solutions, at their best very carefully gauged to the mass audience, adapted to special audiences, and varying basically only as the initial sale or the permanent customer is the principal object. What advertising is in commerce, propaganda is in politics, especially international politics. Neither scorns reason or the likeness of reason, the rhetoric of information and logical argument, if the message and the audience seem to make that the best or only means to the sale. Neither, on the other hand, prefers that method to the shorter, quicker ways to unconsidered action. They concentrate—forcibly where possible, rhetorically where necessary—on the exclusion of competing ideas, on the short-circuiting or bypassing of informed judgment. By preference they do not seek to balance or overbalance alternative ideas or courses of action; they seek to obliterate them, to circumvent or subvert the rational processes which tend to make men weigh and consider. As Adlai Stevenson said, slogans, the common staple of advertising and propaganda, "are normally designed to get action without reflection."

That advertising should enjoy a happier reputation than propaganda in a competitive, commercial-industrial nation such as the United States, which is only just now learning the term *psychological warfare,* is not to be wondered at. We do not have a public service institution for the defensive analysis of advertising, like the Institute of Propaganda Analysis, which assumed that propaganda is something from which we must learn to protect ourselves. The ethical superiority of our advertising is no doubt a compliment to our dominant business code—and to our laws. Still, if one wishes to know what the ungoverned rhetoric of advertising can be, he may get a suggestion by listening to some of what is beamed to us from certain radio stations south of the border.

The kinship of advertising and salesmanship, and their somewhat denatured relatives "public relations" and "promotion," to conventional public address, the established vehicle of rhetoric, may be embarrassing at times, but it must be acknowledged. The family resemblance is too strong to be ignored and too important to be denied. The omnipresence of the rhetoric of advertising, as I have suggested, gives it a standing which must be reckoned with, no matter what opinion the student of public address may hold of it. The rhetoric of public address, in this country at least, must function, whether or no, in a public mind which is steeped in the rhetoric of advertising, a rhetoric whose dominating principles must be recognized as adaptations of a portion of the fundamentals of any rhetoric. One need only compare a textbook or handbook of advertising methods with standard, conventional rhetorics—textbooks in public speaking and persuasion—especially in the handling of such topics as interest, suggestion, and motivation, to be convinced of the coincidence of method if not of philosophic outlook. Many times in adult evening classes in public speaking, have I heard speeches on the secrets of successful salesmanship, and as often have I found myself being offered a more or a less competent parody of certain portions of our textbook, which for some reason the student had omitted to read. Not by mere chance, one must confess, does the non-academic public take great interest in the four "miracle" courses to be found among the offerings of many universities—advertising, salesmanship, psychology, and effective speaking. Nor is it remarkable, though one may think it deplorable, that appearances of the officers of our national government before the mass audience of the citizens are characteristic products of the country's leading advertising agencies.

Likewise propaganda and its brother "information" borrow and refine upon certain portions of rhetoric. No doubt it serves a useful purpose to identify propaganda with the vicious forces in the modern world, with the German Government of World War I and with the Nazi and Soviet totalitarianisms of the present time. At the same time, however, it would be the better part of wisdom to recognize that most of the major techniques of this propaganda are long known rhetorical techniques gone wrong, that propaganda is not a new invention which we have no ready equipment for combatting, let alone fumigating and using for our honorable ends. The understanding of propaganda will be founded in the understanding of rhetoric first of all, whatever else may be necessary.[24] Both Ross Scanlan and Kenneth Burke have demonstrated the enlightenment which can come from the application of rhetorical criticism to both the internal and external propaganda of the Nazis,[25] and two articles by Scanlan and Henry C. Youngerman in the first issue of *Today's Speech* (April, 1953) are grounded on the assumption of a close kinship between rhetoric (or its corollary, "public address") and propaganda.[26] In fact, one of Scanlan's concluding statements indirectly makes both the identification and the basic distinction: "Today it is to be hoped that America will find means to match enemy propaganda in effectiveness without sacrificing the standards of morality and intellect that distinguish democracy from the totalitarian order."

Rhetoric as a Method of Inquiry

More than once in the preceding pages I have in passing assigned to rhetoric a secondary function of the discovery of ideas, contributory to its prime function of the popularizing of ideas. That is the consequence of the division of *inventio*, the term applied in Roman rhetoric to the systematic investigative procedures by which rhetoric sought to turn up all the relevant arguments or consideration in any given situation. As part of *inventio*, for example, the elaborate doctrine of *status* was developed, through which by the application of analytical criteria it was possible to determine just what was the core, the central issue in any given case, just what had to be proved as a *sine qua non*, and where the lines of argument for proving it would lie if they were available. In general the division of *inventio* constituted a codification of the *topoi* or *places where arguments are to be found;* for instance, in *fact past, fact future, more and less, etc.* Rhetoric, thus, as we have said, provides scientific assistance to the speaker in discovering what questions to ask and how to go about answering them. It serves the speaker as laboratory procedures for analysis serve the chemist—by systematic inventory it enables him to determine with reasonable completeness what is present and what is absent in any given case.

We need not be surprised, therefore, that so useful a method tended to be incorporated into other arts and sciences where its original provenience was often forgotten. Historically, some of the studies to profit greatly from his borrowing from rhetoric have been the law, theology, logic, and poetic.[27] The Polandizing of rhetoric, one of the characteristic phenomena of its history, accounts in large part for the splinter meanings and the distortions which we have seen as typical of its current and historic significance. It has been the fate of rhetoric, the residual term, to be applied to the less intellectual segments of itself, while its central operating division, *inventio*, has been appropriated by the studies and sciences which rhetoric serves.

The functions of a complete rhetoric, however, have usually been operative under whatever temporary auspices as the whole art of discourse, even as they were in the renaissance tripartite grammar-logic-rhetoric. This splintering may go so far towards specialism, however, that the investigative function of rhetoric, the method of *inventio*, may be diverted from that to which it most properly applies. This diversion may very well be the tendency today, where a complete rhetoric hardly exists as a formal discipline except in those classically oriented courses in public speaking, debate, group discussion, argumentation, and persuasion whose central focus is on *inventio*—the investigation and discovery of lines of argument and basic issues. Mostly rhetoric today survives, as we have seen, under other names and special applications in those specialties which contribute to it or draw upon it or appropriate selectively from its store of method—psychology, advertising, salesmanship, propaganda analysis, public opinion and social control, semantics, and that which is loosely called "research" in common parlance.

May I attempt in summary of this matter to bring rhetoric back to its essential investigative function, its function of discovery, by quoting from Isocrates, the Athenian politico-rhetorical philosopher, and from Edmund Burke, the eighteenth-century British statesman-orator? Wrote Isocrates in the *Antidosis*, "With this faculty we both contend against others on matters that are open to dispute and seek light for ourselves on things which are unknown; for the same arguments which we use in persuading others when we speak in public, we employ when we deliberate in our thoughts."[28] Twenty-two centuries later, the young Burke included in his notebook digest of the topics of rhetoric, which he headed "How to Argue," the following succinct, Baconian statement about the functions of *inventio*:

To invent Arguments without a thorough knowledge of the Subject is clearly impossible. But the Art of Invention does two things—
1. It suggests to us more readily those Parts of our actual knowledge which may help towards illustrating the matter before us, &
2. It suggests to us heads of Examination which may lead, if pursued with effect into a knowledge of the Subject.

So that the Art of Invention may properly be considered as the method of calling up what we do know, and investigating that of which we are ignorant.[29]

Rhetoric in Education

If the burden of the preceding pages is not misplaced, the importance of rhetoric in the equipment of the well-educated member of society can hardly be in doubt. I am not inclined, therefore, especially in this journal, to offer to demonstrate the desirability of speech as an academic study. Our conventions and our journals have been full of such demonstration for, lo, these thirty years.[30] If enlightened and responsible leaders with rhetorical knowledge and skill are not trained and nurtured, irresponsible demagogues will monopolize the power of rhetoric, will have things to themselves. If talk rather than take is to settle the course of our society, if ballots instead of bullets are to effect our choice of governors, if discourse rather than coercion is to prevail in the conduct of human affairs, it would seem like arrant folly to trust to chance that the right people shall be equipped offensively and defensively with a sound rationale of informative and suasory discourse.

In general education, especially, rhetoric would appear to deserve a place of uncommon importance. That is the burden of a recent article by Dean Hunt of Swarthmore. Rhetoric is the organon of the liberal studies, the formulation of the principles through which the educated man, the possessor of many specialties, attains effectiveness in society.[31] A complete rhetoric is a structure for the wholeness of the effective man, the aim of general education. But, as Dean Hunt concludes, the rhetorician himself must not become a technical specialist:

He will keep his wholeness if he comes back again and again to Aristotle, but he must supplement those conceptions with what modern scientists have added to the mirror for man; he must illuminate the classical rhetoric with psychology, cultural anthropology, linguistics and semantics, special disciplines, perhaps, but disciplines in which he can lean heavily on interpreters who speak to others than their professional colleagues. Departments of speech which have emphasized training in rhetoric have a new opportunity to establish their place in general education. Their very claim to wholeness has been a source of distrust in an atmosphere of specialism. If now they can relate themselves to newer conceptions in the sciences, social sciences, and humanities, they can show that the ideal of the good man skilled in speaking is like the sea, ever changing and ever the same.[32]

So much for rhetoric in education as a study directed at the creation and at the analysis and criticism of informative and suasory discourse—at the ability, on the one hand, "to summon thought quickly and use it forcibly,"[33] and on the other to listen or read critically with the maximum application of analytical judgment.

Rhetoric would appear thus to be in certain senses a literary study, or as Wichelns wrote, at least "its tools are those of literature." It is a literary study as it is involved in the creative arts of language, of informing ideas. It is a literary study also as it contributes substantially to literary scholarship. Not only have literature and literary theory been persistently rhetorical for long periods—during much of the renaissance, for example, the seventeenth and eighteenth centuries in England, and for most of the short history of American literature—but writers and readers until fairly recently had been so generally educated in rhetoric that it provided the vocabulary and many of the concepts in terms of which much literature was both written and read. Clark's *Milton at St.Paul's School* may be cited as one conclusive demonstration of the importance of rhetoric in renaissance education and its importance in renaissance literature. This importance is now being recognized by literary scholars, and rhetoric is taking on considerable proportions in their studies, especially among those who are studying the renaissance. Myrick's study of Sir Philip Sidney as a literary craftsman,[34] for example, demonstrates how thoroughly Sidney was schooled in rhetoric and how carefully he constructed his defense of poetry on familiar rhetorical principles. If Myrick has been in error in his construction of the specific genealogy of Sidney's rhetoric, the fact of Sidney's rhetorical system is nevertheless in no doubt.

The plain truth is that whatever the inadequacies in specific cases of the analytical method ingrained in our educated ancestors, they *had* method, the method of formal rhetoric; whereas a general characteristic of our contemporary education is that it inculcates *no* method beyond a rather uncertain grammar and a few rules of paragraphing and bibliography. Rigidity of method is doubtless a grievous obstacle to the greatest fulfillment of genius in either belles lettres or public address; but the widespread impotence and ineptitude even of our best-educated fellows when faced with the problem of constructing or analyzing any but the most rudimentary expository or argumentative discourse, much less a com-

plicated literary work, are surely worse. Rhetoric supplies the equipment for such practical endeavor in the promulgation of ideas, and twenty centuries have learned to use it to supplement and perfect chance and natural instinct.

That such method has at times become sterile or mechanical, that at other times it has been put to uses for which it was least adapted is amusing, perhaps lamentable, but not surprising. The remote uses to which rhetorical methods of analysis and description have been put, in the absence of a more appropriate method, are well illustrated by the following passage from Sir John Hawkins' *History of Music*, first published in the late eighteenth century:

The art of invention is made one of the heads among the precepts of rhetoric, to which music in this and sundry instances bears a near resemblance; the end of persuasion, or affecting the passions being common to both. This faculty consists in the enumeration of common places, which are revolved over in the mind, and requires both an ample store of knowledge in the subject upon which it is exercised, and a power of applying that knowledge as occasion may require. It differs from memory in this respect, that whereas memory does but recall to the mind the images or remembrance of things as they were first perceived, the faculty of invention divides complex ideas into those whereof they are composed, and recommends them again after different fashions, thereby creating variety of new objects and conceptions. Now, the greater the fund of knowledge above spoken of is, the greater is the source from whence the invention of the artist or composer is supplied; and the benefits thereof are seen in new combinations and phrases, capable of variety and permutation without end.[35]

From its lapses and wanderings, however, rhetoric when needed has almost always recovered its vitality and comprehensive scope, by reference to its classic sources. But that it should be ignored seems, as Dean Hunt suggests, hardly a compliment to education.

Rhetoric as a serious scholarly study I have treated in my former essay, and I shall not go over the same ground again. That there is a body of philosophy and principle worth scholarly effort in discovery, enlargement, and reinterpretation is beyond question, and fortunately more competent scholars each year are working at it. Rhetorical criticism and the study of rhetoric as a revealing social and cultural phenomenon are also gaining ground. New and interesting directions for research in these areas are being explored, or at least marked out; they are based on newly developed techniques and hitherto neglected kinds of data. One might mention, for example, those new approaches listed by Maloney:[36] the quantitative content analysis as developed by Lasswell; the qualitative content analysis as used by Lowenthal and Guterman; figurative analysis such as applied to Shakespeare by Caroline Spurgeon; and intonational analysis. Extensive and provocative suggestions are to be found in quantity in the text and bibliography of Brembeck and Howell's *Persuasion: A Means of Social Control*,[37] especially in Part VI. The section on rhetoric in the annual Haberman bibliography is convincing evidence of the vitality of current enterprise.[38]

Though new avenues, new techniques, new materials such as the foregoing are inviting to the increasing numbers of scholars whose interests and abilities—to say nothing of their

necessities—lie in rhetorical research, especially those new directions which lead to rhetoric as a cultural, a sociological, a social-psychiatric phenomenon, the older literary-historical-political studies are still neither too complete nor too good. In any event, each new generation probably needs to interpret afresh much of the relevant history of thought, especially the thought of the people as distinguished from what is commonly considered the history of ideas. For this the scholarship of rhetoric seems particularly adapted. Towards this purpose, I find no need to relocate the field of rhetorical scholarship as envisioned by Hudson and Wichelns, nor to recant from the considerations which I outlined in the *QJS* in 1937.[39] One may find it reassuring to observe, however, that much which was asked for in those essays has since then been undertaken and often accomplished with considerable success. Especially is this true of the study of public address in its bulk and day-to-day manifestations: in the movement studies, the "case" studies, the sectional and regional studies, the studies of "debates" and "campaigns" such as the debates on the League of Nations and the campaigns for conservation.

There remains much to do, nevertheless, and much to re-do in the more familiar and conventional areas of research and interpretation. The editing and translation of rhetorical texts is still far from complete or adequate. The canon of ancient rhetoric is, to be sure, in very good shape, and when Caplan's translation of the *Ad Herennium* is published in the Loeb Library there will hardly be a major deficiency. In post-classical, mediaeval, and renaissance rhetoric the situation is not so good, though it is improving. There are still too few works like Howell's *Rhetoric of Alcuin and Charlemagne* and Sister Therese Sullivan's commentary on and translation of the fourth book of St. Augustine's *De Doctrina.* Halm's *Rhetores Minores,* for example, is substantially unmolested so far.

English and continental rhetoric of the sixteenth, seventeenth, and eighteenth centuries is slowly appearing in modern editions by scholars who know rhetoric as the theory of public address. Our bibliographies show increasing numbers of these as doctoral dissertations, most of which, alas, seem to be abandoned almost as soon as finished. Only a few works of the sort, like Howell's *Fénelon,* represent mature, published work.

In the history and historical analysis of rhetoric, nothing of adequate range and scope yet exists. Thonssen and Baird's *Speech Criticism,* ambitious as it is, is only a beginning. The general history of rhetoric, and even most of the special histories, have yet to be written. Works now under way by Donald L. Clark and Wilbur S. Howell will make substantial contributions, but rhetoric from Corax to Whately needs far fuller and better treatment than it gets in the series of histories of criticism by the late J. W. H. Atkins.

Towards the study of the rhetorical principles and practice of individual speakers and writers the major part of our scholarly effort seems to have been directed. The convenience of this kind of study is beyond question and is hard to resist, either in public address or in literature. And this is as it should be. The tendency to write biographies of speakers, however, rather than rhetorico-critical studies of them, must be kept in check, or at least in proportion. Again for reasons of convenience, if not also of scholarly nationalism, the studies of American speakers are proportionately too numerous. British and foreign public address is still far too scantily noticed by competent rhetorical scholars.

Rhetoric and Poetic

This would not be the place, I think, even if Professor Thonssen's review of rhetorical works were not appearing in this same issue of the *QJS,* for a survey of rhetorical scholarship. The preceding paragraphs are intended only as a token of decent respect to accomplishment and progress in a discrete and important branch of humane scholarship. A further area where rhetorical scholarship may be very profitably pursued, however, perhaps deserves some special consideration.

Even if it were not for the contributions of Kenneth Burke, the study of rhetoric in literature and of the relation of the theory of rhetoric to the theory of poetic would be taking on renewed importance at the present time. The lively revival of rhetorical study in renaissance scholarship which I have mentioned is only one phase of the problem. A renewed or increased interest in satire, deriving in part, perhaps, from the excellent work which of late has been done on Swift, leads directly to rhetoric. The rhetorical mode is obviously at the center of satire, and any fundamental analysis of satire must depend upon the equipment for rhetorical analysis. Likewise, a complete dramatic criticism must draw upon rhetoric, both practically and philosophically. The internal rhetoric of the drama was specifically recognized by Aristotle when he referred readers of the *Poetics* to the *Rhetoric* for coverage of the element of *dianoia*, for the analysis of speeches in which agents try to convince or persuade each other. What, however, is the external rhetoric of the drama? What is the drama intended to do to an audience? Herein lies the question of the province of poetic as opposed to the province of rhetoric. When Antony addresses the Roman citizens in *Julius Caesar*, the existence of an internal rhetoric in the play is clear enough; the relation between Antony and his stage audience is unmistakably rhetorical. But what of the relation between Antony and the audience in the pit, or the Antony-stage-audience combination and the audience in the pit? The more we speculate about the effect of a play or any literary work on an audience, the more we become involved in metaphysical questions in which rhetoric must be involved.

Much contemporary poetry or pseudo-poetry in any generation is rhetorical in the most obvious sense—in the same sense as the epideictic oration. It "pleases" largely by rhetorical means or methods. It "reminds" us of experience instead of "organizing" or "creating" experience. It appeals to our satisfaction with what we are used to; it convinces us that what *was* still may be as it was, that old formulas are pleasantest if not best. It is not so much concerned with pointing up the old elements in the new, even, as establishing

the identity of the old and the contemporary. "What oft was thought, but ne'er so well expressed" is a distinctly rhetorical attainment, and it would not have occurred to Pope to suppose that the poetic and the rhetorical were antithetical, if indeed they were separable. Though sporadically the effort of critics and theorists has been to keep *rhetoric* and *poetic* apart, the two rationales have had an irresistible tendency to come together, and their similarities may well be more important than their differences. When the forming of attitude is admitted into the province of rhetoric, then, to Kenneth Burke, rhetoric becomes a method for the analysis of even lyric poetry. Hence a frequent term in certain kinds of literary analysis now is *poetic-rhetoric*, as for example in the first two sentences in Ruth Wallerstein's analysis of two elegies: "I want this paper to consider two poems, John Donne's elegy on Prince Henry and Milton's *Lycidas*, in the light that is shed on them by seventeenth-century rhetoric-poetic as I understand it. Both the significance of that rhetoric and the test of my view of it will reside in its power to illuminate the poems."[40]

Undoubtedly there are basic differences between *poetic* and *rhetoric*, both practical and philosophical, and probably these differences lie both in the kind of method which is the proper concern of each and the kind of effect on audiences to the study of which each is devoted. The purely poetic seeks the creation or organization of imaginative experience, probably providing for reader or audience some kind of satisfying spiritual or emotional therapy. The rhetorical seeks a predetermined channeling of the audience's understanding or attitude. Poetry works by representation; rhetoric by instigation. The poetic is fulfilled in creation, the rhetorical in illumination. "An image," wrote Longinus, "has one purpose with the orators and another with the poets; . . . the design of the poetic image is enthralment, of the rhetorical, vivid description. Both, however, seek to stir the passions and the emotions. . . . In oratorical imagery its best feature is always its reality and truth."[41] Poetry, declared Sir Philip Sidney, cannot lie because it affirms nothing; it merely presents. Rhetoric not only presents but affirms. That is its characteristic. Both poetic and rhetoric attain their effects through language. If the poet's highest skill lies in his power to make language do what it has never done before, to force from words and the conjunction of words meanings which are new and unique, perhaps it is the highest skill of the speaker to use words in their accepted senses in such a way as to make them carry their traditional meanings with a vividness and effectiveness which they have never known before.

Summary

In brief we may assign to rhetoric a fourfold status. So far as it is concerned with the management of discourse in specific situations for practical purposes, it is an instrumental discipline. It is a literary study, involving linguistics, critical theory, and semantics as it touches the art of informing ideas, and the functioning of language. It is a philosophical study so far as it is concerned with a method of investigation or inquiry. And finally, as it is akin to politics, drawing upon psychology and sociology, rhetoric is a social study, the study of a major force in the behavior of men in society.

Notes

1. Hoyt H. Hudson, "The Field of Rhetoric," *QJSE*, IX (April 1923), 167–180; Herbert A. Wichelns, "The Literary Criticism of Oratory," *Studies in Rhetoric and Public Speaking in Honor of James Albert Winans* (New York, 1925), pp. 181–216; Donald C. Bryant, "Some Problems of Scope and Method in Rhetorical Scholarship," *QJS*, XXIII (April 1937), 182–188, and "Aspects of the Rhetorical Tradition," *QJS*, XXXVI (April and October 1950), 169–176, 326–332.
2. *QJS*, XXXVII (October 1951), 281–298.
3. *Ibid.* (December 1951), 419–429.
4. *QJS*, XXXVIII (February 1952), 1–12.
5. *Ibid.* (April 1952), 133–144.
6. *Studies . . . in Honor of James Albert Winans*, pp. 3–60.
7. In his *The Ethics of Rhetoric* (Chicago: Henry Regnery, 1953), which has appeared since this article has been in proof, Richard M. Weaver of the College at the University of Chicago makes an interesting and useful effort to restore rhetoric to a central and respectable position among the arts of language and to assign it the function of giving effectiveness to truth.
8. *Ancient Rhetoric and Poetic* (New York, 1924), p. 5.
9. For example, Craig La Drière, "Rhetoric as 'Merely Verbal' Art," *English Institute Essays—1948*, ed. by D. A. Robertson, Jr. (New York, 1949), pp. 123–152.
10. Hudson, "Field of Rhetoric," *QJSE*, IX (April 1923), 177.
11. Book III, Chapter 7. Modern Library Edn., p. 97.
12. *Correspondence* (1844), I, 217.
13. *The Press and Society: A Book of Readings*, ed. by George L. Bird and Frederic E. Merwin (New York, 1951), preface, p. iv.
14. "Aspects of the Rhetorical Tradition" (1950), see above, note 1.
15. "Of Studies."
16. From *The Advancement of Learning*. See Karl R. Wallace, *Francis Bacon on Communication and Rhetoric* (Chapel Hill, 1943), p. 27.

17. *Educating Liberally* (Stanford University, 1945), pp. 10 ff.
18. Above, note 14.
19. See the very relevant analysis of some of the fictions of the ideology of American business in C. Wright Mills, *White Collar* (New York, 1951), Ch. 3, "The Rhetoric of Competition."
20. 7th edn. (London, 1823), pp. vii–viii.
21. *The Philosophy of Rhetoric* (New York, 1936).
22. (New York, 1952), pp. 18–19.
23. Observe the tradition of rhetoric as a systematic study, summarized in my "Aspects of Rhetorical Tradition," *QJS*, XXXVI. (April 1950), 169–172.
24. See, for example, Everett L. Hunt, "Ancient Rhetoric and Modern Propaganda," *QJS*, XXXVII (April 1951), 157–160.
25. Burke, *The Philosophy of Literary Form* (1941), 191–220; Scanlan, "The Nazi Party Speaker System, I & II," *SM*, XVI (August 1949), 82–97, XVII (June 1950), 134–148; "The Nazi Rhetorician," *QJS*, XXVII (December 1951), 430–440.
26. "Two Views of Propaganda," pp. 13–14; "Propaganda and Public Address," pp. 15–17.
27. See Richard McKeon, "Rhetoric in the Middle Ages," *Critics and Criticism, Ancient and Modern*, ed. R. S. Crane (Chicago, 1952), pp. 260–296, reprinted from *Speculum*, January, 1942; and Marvin T. Herrick, "The Place of Rhetoric in Poetic Theory," *QJS*, XXXIV (February 1948), 1–22.

28. *Isocrates*, trans. George Norlin (Loeb Classical Library, New York, 1929), II, 327.
29. From an original manuscript among the Wentworth-Fitzwilliam papers in the Sheffield City Library, used with the kind permission of Earl Fitzwilliam and the trustees of the Fitzwilliam settled estates.
30. See, for example, one of the latest, W. N. Brigance, "General Education in an Industrial Free Society," *QJS*, XXXVIII (April, 1952), esp. p. 181.
31. "Rhetoric and General Education," *QJS*, XXXV (October, 1949), 275, 277.
32. *Ibid.*, 279.
33. Herbert A. Wichelns, "Public Speaking and Dramatic Arts," in *On Going to College: A Symposium* (New York, Oxford University Press, 1938), p. 240.
34. Kenneth O. Myrick, *Sir Philip Sidney as a Literary Craftsman* (1935).
35. (2 vols., London, 1875), I, xxv.
36. "Some New Directions in Rhetorical Criticism," *Central States Speech Journal*, IV (February, 1953), 1–5.
37. (New York, 1952).
38. "A Bibliography of Rhetoric and Public Address," ed. F. W. Haberman, formerly appearing annually in the *QJS*, latterly in *SM*.
39. See above, note 1.
40. "Rhetoric in the English Renaisssance: Two Elegies," *English Institute Essays, 1948*, p. 153.
41. Trans. Rhys Roberts, sec. 15.

Herbert A. Wichelns

The Literary Criticism of Oratory

◊ *This pioneering essay, published in 1925, is generally regarded as a landmark study in twentieth-century rhetorical thought. Professor Wichelns' aim is to set out the parameters of literary and rhetorical criticism, showing wherein they conform to and deviate from each other. The analysis suggests that the primary goal of literary criticism is to discover and evaluate the permanent and universal values inherent in a discourse— either "uttered or written"—that has been preserved in print. The central purpose of rhetorical criticism, on the other hand, is to assess the effect of the speaker's "method of imparting his ideas to his audience." For the past six and one half decades, this essay has functioned as the starting point for critics interested in analyzing the impact of public discourse on modern society.* ◊

I

Samuel Johnson once projected a history of criticism "as it relates to judging of authors." Had the great eighteenth-century critic ever carried out his intention, he would have included some interesting comments on the orators and their judges. Histories of criticism, in whole or in part, we now have, and histories of orators. But that section of the history of criticism which deals with judging of orators is still unwritten. Yet the problem is an interesting one, and one which involves some important conceptions. Oratory—the waning influence of which is often discussed in current periodicals—has definitely lost the established place in literature that it once had. Demosthenes and Cicero, Bossuet and Burke, all hold their places in literary histories. But Webster inspires more than one modern critic to ponder the question whether oratory is literature; and if we may judge by the emphasis of literary historians generally, both in England and in America, oratory is either an outcast or a poor relation. What are the reasons for this change? It is a question not easily answered. Involved in it is some shift in the conception of oratory or of literature, or of both; nor can these conceptions have changed except in response to the life of which oratory, as well as literature, is part.

Herbert A. Wichelns, "The Literary Criticism of Oratory," *Studies in Rhetoric and Public Speaking in Honor of James Albert Winans* (New York: The Century Co., 1925): 181–216.

of both; nor can these conceptions have changed except in response to the life of which oratory, as well as literature, is part.

This essay, it should be said, is merely an attempt to spy out the land, to see what some critics have said of some orators, to discover what their mode of criticism has been. The discussion is limited in the main to Burke and a few nineteenth-century figures—Webster, Lincoln, Gladstone, Bright, Cobden—and to the verdicts on these found in the surveys of literary history, in critical essays, in histories of oratory, and in biographies.

Of course, we are not here concerned with the disparagement of oratory. With that, John Morley once dealt in a phrase: "Yet, after all, to disparage eloquence is to depreciate mankind."[1] Nor is the praise of eloquence of moment here. What interests us is the method of the critic: his standards, his categories of judgment, what he regards as important. These will show, not so much what he thinks of a great and ancient literary type, as how he thinks in dealing with that type. The chief aim is to know how critics have spoken of orators.

We have not much serious criticism of oratory. The reasons are patent. Oratory is intimately associated with statecraft; it is bound up with the things of the moment; its occasion, its terms, its background, can often be understood only by the careful student of history. Again, the publication of orations as pamphlets leaves us free to regard any speech merely as an essay, as a literary effort deposited at the shrine of the muses in hope of being blessed with immortality. This view is encouraged by the difficulty of reconstructing the conditions under which the speech was delivered; by the doubt, often, whether the printed text of the speech represents what was actually said, or what the orator elaborated afterwards. Burke's corrections are said to have been the despair of his printers.[2] Some of Chatham's speeches, by a paradox of fate, have been reported to us by Samuel Johnson, whose style is as remote as possible from that of the Great Commoner, and who wrote without even having heard the speeches pronounced.[3] Only in comparatively recent times has parliamentary reporting pretended to give full records of what was actually said; and even now speeches are published for literary or political purposes which justify the corrector's pencil in changes both great and small. Under such conditions the historical study of speech making is far from easy.

Yet the conditions of democracy necessitate both the making of speeches and the study of the art. It is true that other ways of influencing opinion have long been practised, that oratory is no longer the chief means of communicating ideas to the masses. And the change is emphasized by the fact that the newer methods are now beginning to be investigated, sometimes from the point of view of the political student, sometimes from that of the "publicity expert." But, human nature being what it is, there is no likelihood that face to face persuasion will cease to be a principal mode of exerting influence, whether in courts, in senate-houses, or on the platform. It follows that the critical study of oratorical method is the study, not of a mode outworn, but of a permanent and important human activity.

Upon the great figures of the past who have used the art of public address, countless judgments have been given. These judgments have varied with the bias and preoccupation of the critics, who have been historians, biographers, or literary men, and have written accordingly. The context in which we find criticism of speeches, we must, for the purposes of this essay at least, both note and set aside. For though the aim of the critic conditions his approach to our more limited problem—the method of dealing with oratory—still we find that an historian may view an orator in the same light as does a biographer or an essayist. The literary form in which criticism of oratory is set does not afford a classification of the critics.

"There are," says a critic of literary critics, "three definite points, on one of which, or all of which, criticism must base itself. There is the date, and the author, and the work."[4] The points on which writers base their judgments of orators do afford a classification. The man, his work, his times, are the necessary common topics of criticism; no one of them can be wholly disregarded by any critic. But mere difference in emphasis on one or another of them is important enough to suggest a rough grouping. The writers with whom this essay deals give but a subordinate position to the date; they are interested chiefly in the man or in his works. Accordingly, we have as the first type of criticism that which is predominantly personal or biographical, is occupied with the character and the mind of the orator, goes behind the work to the man. The second type attempts to hold the scales even between the biographical and the literary interest. The third is occupied with the work and tends to ignore the man. These three classes, then, seem to represent the practice of modern writers in dealing with orators. Each merits a more detailed examination.

II

We may begin with that type of critic whose interest is in personality, who seeks the man behind the work. Critics of this type furnish forth the appreciative essays and the occasional addresses on the orators. They are as the sands of the sea. Lord Rosebery's two speeches on Burke, Whitelaw Reid's on Lincoln and on Burke, may stand as examples of the character sketch.[5] The second part of Birrell's essay on Burke will serve for the mental character sketch (the first half of the essay is biographical); other examples are Sir Walter Raleigh's essay on Burke and that by Robert Lynd.[6] All these emphasize the concrete nature of Burke's thought, the realism of his imagination, his peculiar combination of breadth of vision with intensity; they pass to the guiding principles of his thought: his hatred of abstraction, his love of order and of settled ways. But they do not occupy themselves with Burke as a speaker, nor even with him as a writer; their first and their last concern is with the man rather than with his works; and their method is to fuse into a single impression whatever of knowledge or opinion they may have of the orator's life and works. These critics, in dealing with the public speaker, think of him as something other than a speaker. Since this type of writing makes but an indirect contribution to our judgment of the orator, there is no need of a more extended account of the method, expect as we find it combined with a discussion of the orator's works.

III

Embedded in biographies and histories of literature, we find another type of criticism, that which combines the sketch of mind and character with some discussion of style. Of the general interest of such essays there can be no doubt. Nine-tenths of so-called literary criticism deals with the lives and personalities of authors, and for the obvious reason, that every one is interested in them, whereas few will follow a technical study, however broadly based. At its best, the type of study that starts with the orator's mind and character is justified by the fact that nothing can better illuminate his work as a persuader of men. But when not at its best, the description of a man's general cast of mind stands utterly unrelated to his art: the critic fails to fuse his comment on the individual with his comment on the artist; and as a result we get some statements about the man, and some statements about the orator, but neither casts light on the other. Almost any of the literary histories will supply examples of the gulf that may yawn between a stylistic study and a study of personality.

The best example of the successful combination of the two strains is Grierson's essay on Burke in the *Cambridge History of English Literature*. In this, Burke's style, though in largest outline

only, is seen to emerge from the essential nature of the man. Yet of this essay, too, it must be said that the analysis of the orator is incomplete, being overshadowed by the treatment of Burke as a writer, though, as we shall see, the passages on style have the rare virtue of keeping to the high road of criticism. The majority of critics who use the mixed method, however, do not make their study of personality fruitful for a study of style, do not separate literary style from oratorical style even to the extent that Grierson does, and do conceive of literary style as a matter of details. In fact, most of the critics of this group tend to supply a discussion of style by jotting down what has occurred to them about the author's management of words; and in the main, they notice the lesser strokes of literary art, but not its broader aspects. They have an eye for tactics, but not for strategy. This is the more strange, as these same writers habitually take large views of the orator himself, considered as a personality, and because they often remark the speaker's great themes and his leading ideas. The management of ideas—what the Romans called invention and disposition—the critics do not observe; their practice is the *salto mortale* from the largest to the smallest considerations. And it needs no mention that a critic who does not observe the management of ideas even from the point of view of structure and arrangement can have nothing to say of the adaptation of ideas to the orator's audience.

It is thus with Professor McLaughlin in his chapter in the *Cambridge History of American Literature* on Clay and Calhoun and some lesser lights.

The pages are covered with such expressions as diffuse, florid, diction restrained and strong, neatly phrased, power of attack, invective, gracious persuasiveness. Of the structure of the speeches by which Clay and Calhoun exercised their influence—nothing. The drive of ideas is not represented. The background of habitual feeling which the orators at times appealed to and at times modified, is hinted at in a passage about Clay's awakening the spirit of nationalism, and in another passage contrasting the full-blooded oratory of Benton with the more polished speech of Quincy and Everett; but these are the merest hints. In the main, style for McLaughlin is neither the expression of personality nor the order and movement given to thought, but a thing of shreds and patches. It is thus, too, with Morley's pages on Burke's style in his life of the orator, and with Lodge's treatment of Webster in his life of the great American. A rather better analysis, though on the same plane of detail, may be used as an example. Oliver Elton says of Burke:

He embodies, more powerfully than any one, the mental tendencies and changes that are seen gathering force through the eighteenth century. A volume of positive knowledge, critically sifted and ascertained; a constructive vision of the past and its institutions; the imagination, under this guidance, everywhere at play; all these elements unite in Burke. His main field is political philosophy. . . . His favorite form is oratory, uttered or written. His medium is prose, and the work of his later years, alone, outweighs all contemporary prose in power. . . . His whole body of production has the unity of some large cathedral, whose successive accretions reveal the natural growth of a single mind, without any change or essential break. . . .

Already [in the *Thoughts* and in the *Observations*] the characteristics of Burke's thought and style appear, as well as his profound conversance with constitutional history, finance, and affairs. There is a constant reference to general principles, as in the famous defence of Party. The maxims that come into play go far beyond the occasion. There is a perpetual ground-swell of passion, embanked and held in check, but ever breaking out into sombre irony and sometimes into figure; but metaphors and other tropes are not yet very frequent. . . .

In the art of unfolding and amplifying, Burke is the rival of the ancients. . . .

In the speech on Conciliation the [oft-repeated] key-word is peace. . . . This iteration makes us see the stubborn faces on the opposite benches. There is contempt in it; their ears must be dinned, they must remember the word peace through the long intricate survey that is to follow. . . .

Often he has a turn that would have aroused the fervor of the great appreciator known to us by the name of Longinus. In his speech on Economical Reform (1780) Burke risks an appeal, in the face of the Commons, to the example of the enemy. He has described . . . the reforms of the French revenue. He says: "The French have imitated us; let us, through them, imitate ourselves, ourselves in our better and happier days." A speaker who was willing to offend for the sake of startling, and to defeat his purpose, would simply have said, "The French have imitated us; let us imitate them." Burke comes to the verge of this imprudence, but he sees the outcry on the lips of the adversary, and silences them by the word *ourselves;* and then, seizing the moment of bewilderment, repeats it and explains it by the noble past; he does not say when those days were; the days of Elizabeth or of Cromwell? Let the House choose! This is true oratory, honest diplomacy.[7]

Here, in some twenty pages, we have but two hints that Burke had to put his ideas in a form adapted to his audience; only the reiterated *peace* in all Burke's writings reminds the critic of Burke's hearers; only one stroke of tact draws his attention. Most of his account is devoted to Burke's style in the limited use of the term: to his power of amplification—his conduct of the paragraph, his use of clauses now long, now short—to his figures, comparisons, and metaphors, to his management of the sentence pattern, and to his rhythms. For Professor Elton, evidently, Burke was a man, and a mind, and an artist in prose; but he was not an orator. Interest in the minutiæ of style has kept Elton from bringing his view of Burke the man to bear on his view of Burke's writings. The fusing point evidently is in the strategic purpose of the works, in their function as speeches. By holding steadily to the conception of Burke as a public man, one could make the analysis of mind and the analysis of art more illuminating for each other than Elton does.

It cannot be said that in all respects Stephenson's chapter on Lincoln in the *Cambridge History of American Literature* is more successful than Elton's treatment of Burke; but it is a better interweaving of the biographical and the literary strands of interest. Stephenson's study of the personality of Lincoln is directly and persistently used in the study of Lincoln's style.

Is it fanciful to find a connection between the way in which his mysticism develops—its atmospheric, non-dogmatic pervasiveness—and the way in which his style develops? Certainly the literary part of him works into all the portions of his utterance with the gradualness of daylight through a shadowy wood. . . . And it is to be noted that the literary quality . . . is of the whole, not of the detail. It does not appear as a gift of phrases. Rather it is the slow unfolding of those two original characteristics, taste and rhythm. What is growing is the degree of both things. The man is becoming deeper,

and as he does so he imposes himself, in this atmospheric way, more steadily on his language.[8]

The psychology of mystical experience may appear a poor support for the study of style. It is but one factor of many, and Stephenson may justly be reproached for leaning too heavily upon it. Compared to Grierson's subtler analysis of Burke's mind and art, the essay of Stephenson seems forced and one-sided. Yet he illuminates his subject more than many of the writers so far mentioned, because he begins with a vigorous effort to bring his knowledge of the man to bear upon his interpretation of the work. But though we find in Stephenson's pages a suggestive study of Lincoln as literary man, we find no special regard for Lincoln as orator. The qualities of style that Stephenson mentions are the qualities of prose generally:

At last he has his second manner, a manner quite his own. It is not his final manner, the one that was to give him his assured place in literature. However, in a wonderful blend of simplicity, directness, candor, joined with a clearness beyond praise, and a delightful cadence, it has outstripped every other politician of the hour. And back of its words, subtly affecting its phrases, . . . is that brooding sadness which was to be with him to the end.[9]

The final manner, it appears, is a sublimation of the qualities of the earlier, which was "keen, powerful, full of character, melodious, impressive";[10] and it is a sublimation which has the power to awaken the imagination by its flexibility, directness, pregnancy, wealth.

In this we have nothing new, unless it be the choice of stylistic categories that emphasize the larger pattern of ideas rather than the minute pattern of grammatical units, such as we have found in Elton and to some extent shall find in Saintsbury; it must be granted, too, that Stephenson has dispensed with detail and gained his larger view at the cost of no little vagueness. "Two things," says Stephenson of the Lincoln of 1849–1858, "grew upon him. The first was his understanding of men, the generality of men. . . . The other thing that grew upon him was his power to reach and influence them through words."[11] We have here the text for any study of Lincoln as orator; but the study itself this critic does not give us.

Elton's characterization of Burke's style stands out from the usual run of superficial comment by the closeness of its analysis and its regard for the architectonic element. Stephenson's characterization of Lincoln's style is distinguished by a vigorous if forced effort to unite the study of the man and of the work. With both we may contrast a better essay, by a critic of greater insight. Grierson says of Burke:

What Burke has of the deeper spirit of that movement [the romantic revival] is seen not so much in the poetic imagery of his finest prose as in the philosophical imagination which informs his conception of the state, in virtue of which he transcends the rationalism of the century. . . . This temper of Burke's mind is reflected in his prose. . . . To the direct, conversational prose of Dryden and Swift, changed social circumstances and the influence of Johnson had given a more oratorical cast, more dignity and weight, but, also, more of heaviness and conventional elegance. From the latter faults, Burke is saved by his passionate temperament, his ardent imagination, and the fact that he was a speaker conscious always of his audience. . . . [Burke] could delight, astound, and convince an audience. He did not easily conciliate and win them over. He lacked the first essential and index of the conciliatory speaker, *lenitas vocis;* his voice was harsh and unmusical, his gesture ungainly. . . . And, even in the text of his speeches there is a strain of irony and scorn which is not well fitted to conciliate. . . . We have evidence that he could do both things on which Cicero lays stress—move his audience to tears and delight them by his wit. . . . Yet, neither pathos nor humor is Burke's *forte.* . . . Burke's unique power as an orator lies in the peculiar interpenetration of thought and passion. Like the poet and the prophet, he thinks most profoundly when he thinks most passionately. When he is not deeply moved, his oratory verges toward the turgid; when he indulges feeling for his own sake, as in parts of *Letters on a Regicide Peace,* it becomes hysterical. But, in his greatest speeches and pamphlets, the passion of Burke's mind shows itself in the luminous thoughts which it emits, in the imagery which at once moves *and* teaches, throwing a flood of light not only on the point in question, but on the whole neighboring sphere of man's moral and political nature.[12]

The most notable feature of these passages is not their recognition that Burke was a speaker, but their recognition that his being a speaker conditioned his style, and that he is to be judged in part at least as one who attempted to influence men by the spoken word. Grierson, like Elton, attends to the element of structure and has something to say of the nature of Burke's prose; but, unlike Elton, he distinguishes this from the description of Burke's oratory—although without maintaining the distinction: he illustrates Burke's peculiar oratorical power from a pamphlet as readily as from a speech. His categories seem less mechanical than those of Elton, who is more concerned with the development of the paragraph than with the general cast of Burke's style; nor is his judgment warped, as is Stephenson's, by having a theory to market. Each has suffered from the necessity of compression. Yet, all told, Grierson realizes better than the others that Burke's task was not merely to express his thoughts and his feelings in distinguished prose, but to communicate his thoughts and his feelings effectively. It is hardly true, however, that Grierson has in mind the actual audience of Burke; the audience of Grierson's vision seems to be universalized, to consist of the judicious listeners or readers of any age. Those judicious listeners have no practical interest in the situation; they have only a philosophical and æsthetic interest.

Of Taine in his description of Burke it cannot be said that he descends to the minutiæ of style. He deals with his author's character and ideas, as do all the critics of this group, but his comments on style are simply a single impression, vivid and picturesque:

Burke had one of those fertile and precise imaginations which believe that finished knowledge is an inner view, which never quits a subject without having clothed it in its colors and forms. . . . To all these powers of mind, which constitute a man of system, he added all those energies of heart which constitute an enthusiast. . . . He brought to politics a horror of crime, a vivacity and sincerity of conscience, a sensibility, which seem suitable only to a young man.

. . . The vast amount of his works rolls impetuously in a current of eloquence. Sometimes a spoken or written discourse needs a whole volume to unfold the train of his multiplied proofs and courageous anger. It is either the exposé of a ministry, or the whole history of British India, or the complete theory of revolutions . . . which comes down like a vast overflowing stream. . . . Doubtless there is foam on its eddies, mud

in its bed; thousands of strange creatures sport wildly on its surface: he does not select, he lavishes. . . . Nothing strikes him as in excess. . . . He continues half a barbarian, battening in exaggeration and violence; but his fire is so sustained, his conviction so strong, his emotion so warm and abundant, that we suffer him to go on, forget our repugnance, see in his irregularities and his trespasses only the outpourings of a great heart and a deep mind, too open and too full.[13]

This is brilliant writing, unencumbered by the subaltern's interest in tactics, but it is strategy as described by a war-correspondent, not by a general. We get from it little light on how Burke solved the problem that confronts every orator: so to present ideas as to bring them into the consciousness of his hearers.

Where the critic divides his interest between the man and the work, without allowing either interest to predominate, he is often compelled to consider the work *in toto*, and we get only observations so generalized as not to include consideration of the form of the work. The speech is not thought of as essentially a means of influence; it is regarded as a specimen of prose, or as an example of philosophic thought. The date, the historical interest, the orator's own intention, are often lost from view; and criticism suffers in consequence.

IV

We have seen that the critic who is occupied chiefly with the orator as a man can contribute, although indirectly, to the study of the orator as such, and that the critic who divides his attention between the man and the work must effect a fusion of the two interests if he is to help materially in the understanding of the orator. We come now to critics more distinctly literary in aim. Within this group several classes may be discriminated: the first comprises the judicial critics; the second includes the interpretative critics who take the point of view of literary style generally, regarding the speech as an essay, or as a specimen of prose; the third and last group is composed of the writers who tend to regard the speech as a special literary form.

The type of criticism that attempts a judicial evaluation of the literary merits of the work—of the orator's "literary remains"—tends to center the inquiry on the question: Is this literature? The futility of the question appears equally in the affirmative and in the negative replies to it. The fault is less with the query, however, than with the hastiness of the answers generally given. For the most part, the critics who raise this problem are not disposed really to consider it: they formulate no conception either of literature or of oratory; they will not consider their own literary standards critically and comprehensively. In short, the question is employed as a way to dispose briefly of the subject of a lecture or of a short essay in a survey of a national literature.

Thus Phelps, in his treatment of Webster and Lincoln in *Some Makers of American Literature*,[14] tells us that they have a place in literature by virtue of their style, gives us some excerpts from Lincoln and some comments on Webster's politics, but offers no reasoned criticism. St. Peter swings wide the gates of the literary heaven, but does not explain his action. We may suspect that the solemn award of a "place in literature" sometimes conceals the absence of any real principle of judgment.

Professor Trent is less easily satisfied that Webster deserves a "place in literature." He grants Webster's power to stimulate patriotism, his sonorous dignity and massiveness, his clearness and strength of style, his powers of dramatic description. But he finds only occasional splendor of imagination, discovers no soaring quality of intelligence, and is not dazzled by his philosophy or his grasp of history. Mr. Trent would like more vivacity and humor and color in Webster's style.[15] This mode of deciding Webster's place in or out of literature is important to us only as it reveals the critic's method of judging. Trent looks for clearness and strength, imagination, philosophic grasp, vivacity, humor, color in style. This is excellent so far as it goes, but goes no further than to suggest some qualities which are to be sought in any and all works of literary art: in dramas, in essays, in lyric poems, as well as in speeches.

Let us take a third judge. Gosse will not allow Burke to be a complete master of English prose: "Notwithstanding all its magnificence, it appears to me that the prose of Burke lacks the variety, the delicacy, the modulated music of the very finest writers."[16] Gosse adds that Burke lacks flexibility, humor, and pathos. As critical method, this is one with that of Trent.

Gosse, with his question about mastery of prose, does not directly ask, "Is this literature?" Henry Cabot Lodge does, and his treatment of Webster (in the *Cambridge History of American*

Literature) is curious. Lodge is concerned to show that Webster belongs to literature, and to explain the quality in his work that gives him a place among the best makers of literature. The test applied is permanence: Is Webster still read? The answer is, yes, for he is part of every schoolboy's education, and is the most quoted author in Congress. The sight of a literary critic resigning the judicial bench to the schoolmaster and the Congressman is an enjoyable one; as enjoyable as Mr. H. L. Mencken's reaction to it would be; but one could wish for grounds more relative than this. Mr. Lodge goes on to account for Webster's permanence: it lies in his power to impart to rhetoric the literary touch. The distinction between rhetoric and literature is not explained, but apparently the matter lies thus: rhetorical verse may be poetry; Byron is an example. Rhetorical prose is not literature until there is added the literary touch. We get a clue as to how the literary touch may be added: put in something imaginative, something that strikes the hearer at once. The example chosen by Lodge is a passage from Webster in which the imaginative or literary touch is given by the single word "mildew."[17] This method of criticism, too, we may reduce to that of Trent, with the exception that only one quality—imagination—is requisite for admission to the literary Valhalla.

Whether the critic's standards be imagination, or this together with other qualities such as intelligence, vivacity, humor, or whether it be merely "style," undefined and unexplained, the point of view is always that of the printed page. The oration is lost from view, and becomes an exercise in prose, musical,

colorful, varied, and delicate, but, so far as the critic is concerned, formless and purposeless. Distinctions of literary type or kind are erased; the architectonic element is neglected; and the speech is regarded as a musical meditation might be regarded: as a kind of harmonious musing that drifts pleasantly along, with little of inner form and nothing of objective purpose. This, it should be recognized, is not the result of judicial criticism so much as the result of the attempt to decide too hastily whether a given work is to be admitted into the canon of literature.

V

It is, perhaps, natural for the historian of literature to reduce all literary production to one standard, and thus to discuss only the common elements in all prose. One can understand also that the biographer, when in the course of his task he must turn literary critic, finds himself often inadequately equipped and his judgment of little value, except on the scale of literature generally rather than of oratory or of any given type. More is to be expected, however, of those who set up as literary critics in the first instance: those who deal directly with Webster's style, or with Lincoln as man of letters. We shall find such critics s Whipple, Hazlitt, and Saintsbury devoting themselves to the description of literary style in the orators whom they discuss. Like the summary judicial critics we have mentioned, their center of interest is the work; but they are less hurried than Gosse and Lodge and Phelps and Trent; and their aim is not judgment so much as understanding. Yet their interpretations, in the main, take the point of view of the printed page, of the prose essay. Only to a slight degree is there a shift to another point of view, that of the orator in relation to the audience on whom he exerts his influence; the immediate public begins to loom a little larger; the essential nature of the oration as a type begins to be suggested.

Saintsbury has a procedure which much resembles that of Elton, though we must note the fact that the former omits consideration of Burke as a personality and centers attention on his work. We saw that Elton, in his passages on Burke's style, attends both to the larger elements of structure and to such relatively minute points as the management of the sentence and the clause. In Saintsbury the range of considerations is the same. At times, indeed, the juxtaposition of large and small ideas is ludicrous, as when one sentence ends by awarding to Burke literary immortality, and the next describes the sentences of an early work as "short and crisp, arranged with succinct antithetic parallels, which seldom exceed a single pair of clauses."[18] The award of immortality is not, it should be said, based entirely on the shortness of Burke's sentences in his earliest works. Indeed much of Saintsbury's comment is of decided interest:

The style of Burke is necessarily to be considered throughout as conditioned by oratory. . . . In other words, he was first of all a rhetorician, and probably the greatest that modern times have ever produced. But his rhetoric always inclined much more to the written than to the spoken form, with results annoying perhaps to him at the time, but even to him satisfactory afterwards, and an inestimable gain to the world. . . .

The most important of these properties of Burke's style, in so far as it is possible to enumerate them here, are as follows. First of all, and most distinctive, so much so as to have escaped no competent critic, is a very curious and, until his example made it imitable, nearly unique faculty of building up an argument or a picture by a succession of complementary strokes, not added at haphazard but growing out of and onto one another. No one has ever been such a master of the best and grandest kind of the figure called . . . Amplification, and this . . . is the direct implement by which he achieves his greatest effects.

. . . The piece [*Present Discontents*] may be said to consist of a certain number of specially labored paragraphs in which the arguments or pictures just spoken of are put as forcibly as the author can put them, and as a rule in a succession of shortish sentences, built up and glued together with the strength and flexibility of a newly fashioned fishing-rod. In the intervals the texts thus given are turned about, commented on, justified, or discussed in detail, in a rhetoric for the most part, though not always, rather less serried, less evidently burnished, and in less full dress. And this general arrangement proceeds through the rest of his works.[19]

After a number of comments on Burke's skill in handling various kinds of ornament, such as humor, epigram, simile, Saintsbury returns to the idea that Burke's special and definite weapon was "imaginative argument, and the marshalling of vast masses of complicated detail into properly rhetorical battalions or (to alter the image) mosaic pictures of enduring beauty."[20] Saintsbury's attitude toward the communicative, impulsive nature of the orator's task is indicated in a passage on the well-known description of Windsor Castle. This description the critic terms "at once . . . a perfect harmonic chord, a complete visual picture, and a forcible argument.''[21] It is significant that he adds, ''The minor rhetoric, the suasive purpose [presumably the argumentative intent] must be kept in view; if it be left out the thing loses''; and holds Burke ''far below Browne, who had no need of purpose.''[22] It is less important that a critic think well of the suasive purpose than that he reckon with it, and of Saintsbury at least it must be said that he recognizes it, although grudgingly; but it cannot be said that Saintsbury has a clear conception of rhetoric as the art of communication: sometimes it means the art of prose, sometimes that of suasion.

Hazlitt's method of dealing with Burke resembles Taine's as Saintsbury's resembles that of Elton. In Hazlitt we have a critic who deals with style in the large; details of rhythm, of sentence pattern, of imagery, are ignored. His principal criticism of Burke as orator is contained in the well-known contrast with Chatham, really a contrast of mind and temperament in relation to oratorical style. He follows this with some excellent comment on Burke's prose style; nothing more is said of his oratory; only in a few passages do we get a flash of light on the relation of Burke to his audience, as in the remark about his eagerness to impress his reader, and in the description of his conversational quality. It is notable too that Hazlitt finds those works which never had the form of speeches the most significant and most typical of Burke's style.

Burke was so far from being a gaudy or flowery writer, that he was one of the severest writers we have. His words are the most like things; his style is the most strictly limited to the subject. He unites every extreme and every variety of composition; the lowest and the meanest words and descriptions with the highest. . . . He had no other object but to produce the strongest impression on his reader, by giving the truest, the most characteristic, the fullest, and most forcible description of things, trusting to the power of his own mind to mold them into grace and beauty. . . . Burke most frequently produced an effect by the remoteness and novelty of his combinations, by the force of contrast, by the striking manner in which the most opposite and unpromising materials were harmoniously blended together; not by laying his hands on all the fine things he could think of, but by bringing together those things which he knew would blaze out into glorious light by their collision.[23]

Twelve years after writing the essay from which we have quoted, Hazlitt had occasion to revise his estimate of Burke as a statesman; but his sketch of Burke's style is essentially unaltered.[24] In Hazlitt we find a sense of style as an instrument of communication; that sense is no stronger in dealing with Burke's speeches than in dealing with his pamphlets, but it gives to Hazlitt's criticisms a reality not often found. What is lacking is a clear sense of Burke's communicative impulse, of his persuasive purpose, as operating in a concrete situation. Hazlitt does not suggest the background of Burke's speeches, ignores the events that called them forth. He views his subject, in a sense, as Grierson does: as speaking to the judicious but disinterested hearer of any age other than Burke's own. But the problem of the speaker, as well as of the pamphleteer, is to interest men here and now; the understanding of that problem requires, on the part of the critic, a strong historical sense for the ideas and attitudes of the people (not merely of their leaders), and a full knowledge of the public opinion of the times in which the orator spoke. This we do not find in Hazlitt.

Two recent writers on Lincoln commit the opposite error: they devote themselves so completely to description of the situation in which Lincoln wrote as to leave no room for criticism. L. E. Robinson's *Lincoln as Man of Letters*[25] is a biography rewritten around Lincoln's writings. It is nothing more. Instead of giving us a criticism, Professor Robinson has furnished us with some of the materials of the critic; his own judgments are too largely laudatory to cast much light. The book, therefore, is not all that its title implies. A single chapter of accurate summary and evaluation would do much to increase our understanding of Lincoln as man of letters, even though it said nothing of Lincoln as speaker. A chapter or two on Lincoln's work in various kinds—letters, state papers, speeches—would help us to a finer discrimination than Professor Robinson's book offers. Again, the proper estimate of style in any satisfactory sense requires us to do more than to weigh the soundness of an author's thought and to notice the isolated beauties of his expression. Something should be said of structure, something of adaptation to the immediate audience, whose convictions and habits of thought, whose literary usages, and whose general cultural background all condition the work both of writer and speaker. Mr. Robinson has given us the political situation as a problem in controlling political forces, with little regard to the force even of public opinion, and with almost none to the cultural background. Lincoln's

works, therefore, emerge as items in a political sequence, but not as resultants of the life of his time.

Some of the deficiencies of Robinson's volume are supplied by Dodge's essay, *Lincoln as Master of Words*.[26] Dodge considers, more definitely than Robinson, the types in which Lincoln worked: he separates messages from campaign speeches, letters from occasional addresses. He has an eye on Lincoln's relation to his audience, but this manifests itself chiefly in an account of the immediate reception of a work. Reports of newspaper comments on the speeches may be a notable addition to Lincolniana; supported by more political information and more insight than Mr. Dodge's short book reveals, they might become an aid to the critical evaluation of the speeches. But in themselves they are neither a criticism nor an interpretation of Lincoln's mastery of words.

Robinson and Dodge, then, stand at opposite poles to Saintsbury and Hazlitt. The date is put in opposition to the work as a center of critical interest. If the two writers on Lincoln lack a full perception of their author's background, they do not lack a sense of its importance. If the critics of Burke do not produce a complete and rounded criticism, neither do they lose themselves in preparatory studies. Each method is incomplete; each should supplement the other.

We turn now to a critic who neglects the contribution of history to the study of oratory, but who has two compensating merits: the merit of recognizing the types in which his subject worked, and the merit of remembering that an

orator has as his audience, not pos-
terity, but certain classes of his own
contemporaries. Whipple's essay on
Webster is open to attack from various
directions: it is padded, it "dates," it is
overlaudatory, it is overpatriotic, it lacks
distinction of style. But there is wheat
in the chaff. Scattered through the customary discussion of Webster's choice
of words, his power of epithet, his compactness of statement, his images, the
development of his style, are definite
suggestions of a new point of view. It is
the point of view of the actual audience.
To Whipple, at times at least, Webster
was not a writer, but a speaker; the
critic tries to imagine the man, and also
his hearers; he thinks of the speech as
a communication to a certain body of
auditors. A phrase often betrays a
mental attitude; Whipple alone of the
critics we have mentioned would have
written of "the eloquence, the moral
power, he infused into his reasoning, so
as to make the dullest citation of legal
authority *tell* on the minds he addressed."[27] Nor would any other writer
of this group have attempted to distinguish the types of audience Webster
met. That Whipple's effort is a ram-
bling and incoherent one, is not here in
point. Nor is it pertinent that the critic
goes completely astray in explaining
why Webster's speeches have the
nature of "organic formations, or at
least of skilful engineering or architectural constructions"; though to say that
the art of giving objective reality to a
speech consists only of "a happy col-
location and combination of words"[28]
is certainly as far as possible from explaining Webster's sense of structure.
What is significant in Whipple's essay
is the occasional indication of a point of

view that includes the audience. Such
an indication is the passage in which
the critic explains the source of Webster's influence:

What gave Webster his immense influence over the opinions of the people of New
England, was first, his power of so "putting
things" that everybody could understand his
statements; secondly, his power of so
framing his arguments that all the steps,
from one point to another, in a logical series,
could be clearly apprehended by every intelligent farmer or mechanic who had a
thoughtful interest in the affairs of the
country; and thirdly, his power of inflaming
the sentiment of patriotism in all honest and
well-intentioned men by overwhelming appeals to that sentiment, so that after convincing their understandings, he clinched
the matter by sweeping away their wills.
Perhaps to these sources of influence may
be added . . . a genuine respect for the intellect, as well as for the manhood, of average men.[29]

In various ways the descriptive critics
recognize the orator's function. In some,
that recognition takes the form of a
regard to the background of the
speeches; in others, it takes the form of
a regard to the effectiveness of the work,
though that effectiveness is often con-
strued as for the reader rather than for
the listener. The "minor rhetoric, the
suasive purpose" is beginning to be felt,
though not always recognized and never
fully taken into account.

VI

The distinction involved in the presence of a persuasive purpose is clearly
recognized by some of those who have
written on oratory, and by some biographers and historians. The writers
now to be mentioned are aware, more

keenly than any of those we have so far met, of the speech as a literary form—or if not as a literary form, then as a form of power; they tend accordingly to deal with the orator's work as limited by the conditions of the platform and the occasion, and to summon history to the aid of criticism.

The method of approach of the critics of oratory as oratory is well put by Lord Curzon at the beginning of his essay, *Modern Parliamentary Eloquence*:

> In dealing with the Parliamentary speakers of our time I shall, accordingly, confine myself to those whom I have myself heard, or for whom I can quote the testimony of others who heard them; and I shall not regard them as prose writers or literary men, still less as purveyors of instruction to their own or to future generations, but as men who produced, by the exercise of certain talents of speech, a definite impression upon contemporary audiences, and whose reputation for eloquence must be judged by that test, and that test alone.[30]

The last phrase, "that test alone," would be scanned; the judgment of orators is not solely to be determined by the impression of contemporary audiences. For the present it will be enough to note the topics touched in Curzon's anecdotes and reminiscences—his lecture is far from a systematic or searching inquiry into the subject, and is of interest rather for its method of approach than for any considered study of an orator or of a period. We value him for his promises rather than for his performance. Curzon deals with the relative rank of speakers, with the comparative value of various speeches by a single man, with the orator's appearance and demeanor, with his mode of preparation and of delivery, with his mastery of epigram or image. Skill in seizing upon the dominant character-

istics of each of his subjects saves the author from the worst triviality of reminiscence. Throughout, the point of view is that of the man experienced in public life discussing the eloquence of other public men, most of whom he had known and actually heard. That this is not the point of view of criticism in any strict sense, is of course true; but the *naïveté* and directness of this observer correct forcibly some of the extravagances we have been examining.

The lecture on Chatham as an orator by H. M. Butler exemplifies a very different method arising from a different subject and purpose. The lecturer is thinking, he tells us, "of Oratory partly as an art, partly as a branch of literature, partly as a power of making history."[31] His method is first to touch lightly upon Chatham's early training and upon his mode of preparing and delivering his speeches; next, to present some of the general judgments upon the Great Commoner, whether of contemporaries or of later historians; then to re-create a few of the most important speeches, partly by picturing the historical setting, partly by quotation, partly by the comments of contemporary writers. The purpose of the essay is "to reawaken, however faintly, some echoes of the kingly voice of a genuine Patriot, of whom his country is still justly proud."[32] The patriotic purpose we may ignore, but the wish to reconstruct the *mise en scène* of Chatham's speeches, to put the modern Oxford audience at the point of view of those who listened to the voice of Pitt, saw the flash of his eye and felt the force of his noble bearing. This is a purpose different from that of the critics whom we have examined. It may be objected that Butler's lecture has the defects of its method: the amenities observed by a Cambridge don delivering a formal lecture at Oxford keep us from getting on with the subject; the brevity of the discourse prevents anything like a full treatment; the aim, revivification of the past, must be very broadly interpreted if it is to be really critical. Let us admit these things; it still is true that in a few pages the essential features of Pitt's eloquence are brought vividly before us, and that this is accomplished by thinking of the speech as originally delivered to its first audience rather than as read by the modern reader.

The same sense of the speaker in his relation to his audience appears in Lecky's account of Burke. This account, too, is marked by the use of contemporary witnesses, and of comparisons with Burke's great rivals. But let Lecky's method speak in part for itself:

He spoke too often, too vehemently, and much too long; and his eloquence, though in the highest degree intellectual, powerful, various, and original, was not well adapted to a popular audience. He had little or nothing of that fire and majesty of declamation with which Chatham thrilled his hearers, and often almost overawed opposition; and as a parliamentary debater he was far inferior to Charles Fox. . . . Burke was not inferior to Fox in readiness, and in the power of clear and cogent reasoning. His wit, though not of the highest order, was only equalled by that of Townshend, Sheridan, and perhaps North, and it rarely failed in its effect upon the House. He far surpassed every other speaker in the copiousness and correctness of his diction, in the range of knowledge he brought to bear on every subject of debate, in the richness and variety of his imagination, in the gorgeous beauty of his descriptive passages, in the depth of the philosophical reflections and the felicity of

the personal sketches which he delighted in scattering over his speeches. But these gifts were frequently marred by a strange want of judgment, measure, and self-control. His speeches were full of episodes and digressions, of excessive ornamentation and illustration, of dissertations on general principles of politics, which were invaluable in themselves, but very unpalatable to a tired or excited House waiting eagerly for a division.[33]

These sentences suggest, and the pages from which they are excerpted show, that historical imagination has led Lecky to regard Burke as primarily a speaker, both limited and formed by the conditions of his platform; and they exemplify, too, a happier use of stylistic categories than do the essays of Curzon and Butler. The requirements of the historian's art have fused the character sketch and the literary criticism; the fusing agent has been the conception of Burke as a public man, and of his work as public address. Both Lecky's biographical interpretation and his literary criticism are less subtle than that of Grierson; but Lecky is more definitely guided in his treatment of Burke by the conception of oratory as a special form of the literature of power and as a form molded always by the pressure of the time.

The merits of Lecky are contained, in ampler form, in Morley's biography of Gladstone. The long and varied career of the great parliamentarian makes a general summary and final judgment difficult and perhaps inadvisable; Morley does not attempt them. But his running account of Gladstone as orator, if assembled from his thousand pages, is an admirable example of what can be done by one who has the point of view of the public man, sympathy with his subject, and understanding of the speaker's art. Morley gives us much contemporary reporting: the descriptions and judgments of journalists at various stages in Gladstone's career, the impression made by the speeches upon delivery, comparison with other speakers of the time. Here history is contemporary: the biographer was himself the witness of much that he describes, and has the experienced parliamentarian's flair for the scene and the situation. Gladstone's temperament and physical equipment for the platform, his training in the art of speaking, the nature of his chief appeals, the factor of character and personality, these are some of the topics repeatedly touched. There is added a sense for the permanent results of Gladstone's speaking: not the votes in the House merely, but the changed state of public opinion brought about by the speeches.

Mr. Gladstone conquered the House, because he was saturated with a subject and its arguments; because he could state and enforce his case; because he plainly believed every word he said, and earnestly wished to press the same belief into the minds of his hearers; finally because he was from the first an eager and a powerful athlete. . . . Yet with this inborn readiness for combat, nobody was less addicted to aggression or provocation. . . .

In finance, the most important of all the many fields of his activity, Mr. Gladstone had the signal distinction of creating the public opinion by which he worked, and warming the climate in which his projects throve. . . . Nobody denies that he was often declamatory and discursive, that he often overargued and overrefined; [but] he nowhere exerted greater influence than in that department of affairs where words out of relation to fact are most surely exposed. If he often carried the proper rhetorical arts of amplification and development to excess, yet the basis of fact was both sound and

clear. . . . Just as Macaulay made thousands read history, who before had turned from it as dry and repulsive, so Mr. Gladstone made thousands eager to follow the public balance-sheet, and the whole nation became his audience. . . .

[In the Midlothian campaign] it was the orator of concrete detail, of inductive instances, of energetic and immediate object; the orator confidently and by sure touch startling into watchfulness the whole spirit of civil duty in man; elastic and supple, pressing fact and figure with a fervid insistence that was known from his career and character to be neither forced nor feigned, but to be himself. In a word, it was a man— a man impressing himself upon the kindled throngs by the breadth of his survey of great affairs of life and nations, by the depth of his vision, by the power of his stroke.[34]

Objections may be made to Morley's method, chiefly on the ground of omissions. Though much is done to re-create the scene, though ample use is made of the date and the man, there is little formal analysis of the work. It is as if one had come from the House of Commons after hearing the speeches, stirred to enthusiasm but a little confused by the wealth of argument; not as if one came from a calm study of the speeches; not even as if one had corrected personal impressions by such a study. Of the structure of the speeches, little is said; but a few perorations are quoted; the details of style, one feels, although noticed at too great length by some critics, might well receive a modicum of attention here.

Although these deficiencies of Morley's treatment are not supplied by Bryce in his short and popular sketch of Gladstone, there is a summary which well supplements the running account offered by Morley. It has the merit of dealing explicitly with the orator as orator, and it offers more analysis and an adequate judgment by a qualified critic.

Twenty years hence Mr. Gladstone's [speeches] will not be read, except of course by historians. They are too long, too diffuse, too minute in their handling of details, too elaborately qualified in their enunciation of general principles. They contain few epigrams and few . . . weighty thoughts put into telling phrases. . . . The style, in short, is not sufficiently rich or finished to give a perpetual interest to matters whose practical importance has vanished. . . .

If, on the other hand, Mr. Gladstone be judged by the impression he made on his own time, his place will be high in the front rank. . . . His oratory had many conspicuous merits. There was a lively imagination, which enabled him to relieve even dull matter by pleasing figures, together with a large command of quotations and illustrations. . . . There was admirable lucidity and accuracy in exposition. There was great skill in the disposition and marshalling of his arguments, and finally . . . there was a wonderful variety and grace of appropriate gesture. But above and beyond everything else which enthralled the listener, there were four qualities, two specially conspicuous in the substance of his eloquence—inventiveness and elevation; two not less remarkable in his manner—force in the delivery, expressive modulation in the voice.[35]

One is tempted to say that Morley has provided the historical setting, Bryce the critical verdict. The statement would be only partially true, for Morley does much more than set the scene. He enacts the drama; and thus he conveys his judgment—not, it is true, in the form of a critical estimate, but in the course of his narrative. The difference between these two excellent accounts is a difference in emphasis. The one lays stress on the setting; the other takes it for granted. The one tries to suggest his judgment by description; the other employs the formal categories of criticism.

Less full and rounded than either of these descriptions of an orator's style is Trevelyan's estimate of Bright. Yet in a few pages the biographer has indicated clearly the two distinguishing features of Bright's eloquence—the moral weight he carried with his audience, the persuasiveness of his visible earnestness and of his reputation for integrity, and his "sense for the value of words and for the rhythm of words and sentences";[36] has drawn a contrast between Bright and Gladstone; and has added a description of Bright's mode of work, together with some comments on the performance of the speeches and various examples of details of his style. Only the mass and weight of that style are not represented.

If we leave the biographers and return to those who, like Curzon and Butler, have written directly upon eloquence, we find little of importance. Of the two general histories of oratory that we have in English, Hardwicke's[37] is so ill organized and so ill written as to be negligible; that by Sears[38] may deserve mention. It is uneven and inaccurate. It is rather a popular handbook which strings together the great names than a history: the author does not seriously consider the evolution of oratory. His sketches are of unequal merit; some give way to the interest in mere anecdote; some yield too large a place to biographical detail; others are given over to moralizing. Sears touches most of the topics of rhetorical criticism without making the point of view of public address dominant; his work is too episodic for that. And any given criticism shows marked defects in execution. It would not be fair to compare Sear's show-piece, his chapter on Webster with Morley or Bryce on Gladstone; but compare it with Trevelyan's few pages on Bright. With far greater economy, Trevelyan tells us more of Bright as a speaker than Sears can of Webster. The *History of Oratory* gives us little more than hints and suggestions of a good method.

With a single exception, the collections of eloquence have no critical significance. The exception is *Select British Eloquence*,[39] edited by Chauncey A. Goodrich, who prefaced the works of each of his orators with a sketch partly biographical and partly critical. The criticisms of Goodrich, like those of Sears, are of unequal value; some are slight, yet none descends to mere anecdote, and at his best, as in the characterizations of the eloquence of Chatham, Fox, and Burke, Goodrich reveals a more powerful grasp and a more comprehensive view of his problem than does Sears, as well as a more consistent view of his subject as a speaker. Sears at times takes the point of view of the printed page; Goodrich consistently thinks of the speeches he discusses as intended for oral delivery.

Goodrich's topics of criticism are: the orator's training, mode of work, personal (physical) qualifications, character as known to his audience, range of powers, dominant traits as a speaker. He deals too, of course, with those topics to which certain of the critics we have noticed confine themselves: illustration, ornament, gift of phrase, diction, wit, imagination, arrangement. But these he does not over-emphasize, nor view as independent of their effect upon an audience. Thus he can say of Chath-am's sentence structure: "The sentences are not rounded or balanced periods, but are made up of short clauses, which flash themselves upon the mind with all the vividness of distinct ideas, and yet are closely connected together as tending to the same point, and uniting to form larger masses of thought."[40] Perhaps the best brief indication of Goodrich's quality is his statement of Fox's "leading peculiarities."[41] According to Goodrich, Fox had a luminous simplicity, which combined unity of impression with irregular arrangement; he took everything in the concrete; he struck instantly at the heart of his subject, going to the issue at once; he did not amplify, he repeated; he rarely employed preconceived order of argument; reasoning was his *forte*, but it was the reasoning of the debater; he abounded in *hits*—abrupt and startling turns of thought—and in side-blows delivered in passing; he was often dramatic; he had astonishing skill in turning the course of debate to his own advantage. Here is the point of view of public address, expressed as clearly as in Morley or in Curzon, though in a different idiom, and without the biographer's fulness of treatment.

But probably the best single specimen of the kind of criticism now under discussion is Morley's chapter on Cobden as an agitator. This is as admirable a summary sketch as the same writer's account of Gladstone is a detailed historical picture. Bryce's brief essay on Gladstone is inferior to it both in the range of its technical criticisms and in the extent to which the critic realizes the situation in which his subject was an actor. In a few pages Morley has drawn the physical characteristics of his subject, his bent of mind, temperament, idiosyncrasies; has compared and contrasted Cobden with his great associate, Bright; has given us contemporary judgments; has sketched out the dominant quality of his style, its variety and range; has noted Cobden's attitude to his hearers, his view of human nature; and has dealt with the impression given by Cobden's printed speeches and the total impression of his personality on the platform. The method, the angle of approach, the categories of description or of criticism, are the same as those employed in the great life of Gladstone; but we find them here condensed into twenty pages. It will be worth while to present the most interesting parts of Morley's criticism, if only for comparison with some of the passages already given:

I have asked many scores of those who knew him, Conservatives as well as Liberals, what this secret [of his oratorical success] was, and in no single case did my interlocutor fail to begin, and in nearly every case he ended as he had begun, with the word *persuasiveness*. Cobden made his way to men's hearts by the union which they saw in him of simplicity, earnestness, and conviction, with a singular facility of exposition. This facility consisted in a remarkable power of apt and homely illustration, and a curious ingenuity in framing the argument that happened to be wanted. Besides his skill in thus hitting on the right argument, Cobden had the oratorical art of presenting it in the way that made its admission to the understanding of a listener easy and undenied. He always seemed to have made exactly the right degree of allowance for the difficulty with which men follow a speech, as compared with the ease of following the same argument on a printed page. . . .

Though he abounded in matter, Cobden can hardly be described as copious. He is neat and pointed, nor is his argument ever left unclinched; but he permits himself no large excursions. What he was thinking of was the matter immediately in hand, the audience before his eyes, the point that would tell best then and there, and would be most likely to remain in men's recollections. . . . What is remarkable is, that while he kept close to the matter and substance of his case, and resorted comparatively little to sarcasm, humor, invective, pathos, or the other elements that are catalogued in manuals of rhetoric, yet no speaker was ever further removed from prosiness, or came into more real and sympathetic contact with his audience. . . .

After all, it is not tropes and perorations that make the popular speaker; it is the whole impression of his personality. We who only read them can discern certain admirable qualities in Cobden's speeches; aptness in choosing topics, lucidity in presenting them, buoyant confidence in pressing them home. But those who listened to them felt much more than all this. They were delighted by mingled vivacity and ease, by directness, by spontaneousness and reality, by the charm . . . of personal friendliness and undisguised cordiality.[42]

These passages are written in the spirit of the critic of public speaking. They have the point of view that is but faintly suggested in Elton and Grierson, that Saintsbury recognizes but does not use, and Hazlitt uses but does not recognize, and that Whipple, however irregularly, both understands and employs. But such critics as Curzon and Butler, Sears and Goodrich, Trevelyan and Bryce, think differently of their problem; they take the point of view of public address consistently and without question. Morley's superiority is not in conception, but in execution. In all the writers of this group, whether historians, biographers, or professed students of oratory, there is a consciousness that oratory is partly an art, partly a power of making history, and occasionally a branch of literature. Style is less considered for its own sake than for its effect in a given situation. The question of literary immortality is regarded as beside the mark, or else, as in Bryce, as a separate question requiring separate consideration. There are, of course, differences of emphasis. Some of the biographers may be thought to deal too lightly with style. Sears perhaps thinks too little of the time, of the drama of the situation, and too much of style. But we have arrived at a different attitude towards the orator; his function is recognized for what it is: the art of influencing men in some concrete situation. Neither the personal nor the literary evaluation is the primary object. The critic speaks of the orator as a public man whose function it is to exert his influence by speech.

VII

Any attempt to sum up the results of this casual survey of what some writers have said of some public speakers must deal with the differences between literary criticism as represented by Gosse and Trent, by Elton and Grierson, and rhetorical criticism as represented by Curzon, Morley, Bryce, and Trevelyan. The literary critics seem at first to have no common point of view and no agreement as to the categories of judgment or description. But by reading between their lines and searching for the main endeavor of these critics, one can discover at least a unity of purpose. Different in method as are Gosse, Elton, Saintsbury, Whipple, Hazlitt, the ends they have in view are not different.

Coupled with almost every description of the excellences of prose and with every attempt to describe the man in connection with his work, is the same effort as we find clearly and even arbitrarily expressed by those whom we have termed judicial critics. All the literary critics unite in the attempt to interpret the permanent value that they find in the work under consideration. That permanent value is not precisely indicated by the term beauty, but the two strands of æsthetic excellence and permanence are clearly found, not only in the avowed judicial criticism but in those writers who emphasize description rather than judgment. Thus Grierson says of Burke:

> His preoccupation at every juncture with the fundamental issues of wise government, and the splendor of the eloquence in which he set forth these principles, an eloquence in which the wisdom of his thought and the felicity of his language and imagery seem inseparable from one another . . . have made his speeches and pamphlets a source of perennial freshness and interest.[43]

Perhaps a critic of temper different from Grierson's—Saintsbury, for example—would turn from the wisdom of Burke's thought to the felicity of his language and imagery. But always there is implicit in the critic's mind the absolute standard of a timeless world: the wisdom of Burke's thought (found in the principles to which his mind always gravitates rather than in his decisions on points of policy) and the felicity of his language are not considered as of an age, but for all time. Whether the critic considers the technical excellence merely, or both technique and substance, his preoccupation is with that which age cannot wither nor custom stale. (From this point of view, the distinction between the speech and the pamphlet is of no moment, and Elton wisely speaks of Burke's favorite form as "oratory, uttered or written",[44] for a speech cannot be the subject of a permanent evaluation unless it is preserved in print.)

This is the implied attitude of all the literary critics. On this common ground their differences disappear or become merely differences of method or of competence. They are all, in various ways, interpreters of the permanent and universal values they find in the works of which they treat. Nor can there be any quarrel with this attitude—unless all standards be swept away. The impressionist and the historian of the evolution of literature as a self-contained activity may deny the utility or the possibility of a truly judicial criticism. But the human mind insists upon judgment *sub specie æternitatis.* The motive often appears as a merely practical one: the reader wishes to be apprised of the best that has been said and thought in all ages; he is less concerned with the descent of literary species or with the critic's adventures among masterpieces than with the perennial freshness and interest those masterpieces may hold for him. There is, of course, much more than a practical motive to justify the interest in permanent values; but this is not the place to raise a moot question of general critical theory. We wished only to note the common ground of literary criticism in its preoccupation with the thought and the eloquence which is permanent.

If now we turn to rhetorical criticism as we found it exemplified in the preceding section, we find that its point of view is patently single. It is not concerned with permanence, nor yet with beauty. It is concerned with effect. It regards a speech as a communication to a specific audience, and holds its business to be the analysis and appreciation of the orator's method of imparting his ideas to his hearers.

Rhetoric, however, is a word that requires explanation; its use in connection with criticism is neither general nor consistent. The merely depreciatory sense in which it is often applied to bombast or false ornament need not delay us. The limited meaning which confines the term to the devices of a correct and even of an elegant prose style—in the sense of manner of writing and speaking—may also be eliminated, as likewise the broad interpretation which makes rhetoric inclusive of all style whether in prose or in poetry. There remain some definitions which have greater promise. We may mention first that of Aristotle: "the faculty of observing in any given case the available means of persuasion";[45] this readily turns into the art of persuasion, as the editors of the *New English Dictionary* recognize when they define rhetoric as "the art of using language so as to persuade or influence others." The gloss on "persuade" afforded by the additional term "influence" is worthy of note. Jebb achieves the same result by defining rhetoric as "the art of using language in such a way as to produce a desired impression upon the hearer or reader."[46] There is yet a fourth definition, one which serves to illuminate the others as well as to emphasize their essential agreement: "taken broadly [rhetoric is] the science and art of communication in language";[47] the framers of this definition add that to throw the emphasis on communication is to emphasize prose, poetry being regarded as more distinctly expressive than communicative. A German writer has made a similar distinction between poetic as the art of poetry and rhetoric as the art of prose, but rather on the basis that prose is of the intellect, poetry of the imagination.[48] Wackernagel's basis for the distinction will hardly stand in face of the attitude of modern psychology to the "faculties"; yet the distinction itself is suggestive, and it does not contravene the more significant opposition of expression and communication. That opposition has been well stated, though with some exaggeration, by Professor Hudson:

> The writer in pure literature has his eye on his subject; his subject has filled his mind and engaged his interest, and he must tell about it; his task is expression; his form and style are organic with his subject. The writer of rhetorical discourse has his eye upon the audience and occasion; his task is persuasion; his form and style are organic with the occasion.[49]

The element of the author's personality should not be lost from sight in the case of the writer of pure literature; nor may the critic think of the audience and the occasion as alone conditioning the work of the composer of rhetorical discourse, unless indeed he include in the occasion both the personality of the speaker and the subject. The distinction is better put by Professor Baldwin:

> Rhetoric meant to the ancient world the art of instructing and moving men in their affairs; poetic the art of sharpening and expanding their vision. . . . The one is composition of ideas; the other, composition of images. In the one field life is discussed; in the other it is presented. The type of the one

is a public address, moving us to assent and action; the type of the other is a play, showing us [an] action moving to an end of character. The one argues and urges; the other represents. Though both appeal to imagination, the method of rhetoric is logical; the method of poetic, as well as its detail, is imaginative.[50]

It is noteworthy that in this passage there is nothing to oppose poetry, in its common acceptation of verse, to prose. Indeed, in discussing the four forms of discourse usually treated in textbooks, Baldwin explicitly classes exposition and argument under rhetoric, leaving narrative and description to the other field. But rhetoric has been applied to the art of prose by some who include under the term even nonmetrical works of fiction. This is the attitude of Wackernagel, already mentioned, and of Saintsbury, who observes that Aristotle's *Rhetoric* holds, "if not intentionally, yet actually, something of the same position towards Prose as that which the *Poetics* holds towards verse."[51] In Saintsbury's view, the *Rhetoric* achieves this position in virtue of its third book, that on style and arrangement: the first two books contain "a great deal of matter which has either the faintest connection with literary criticism or else no connection with it at all."[52] Saintsbury finds it objectionable in Aristotle that to him, "prose as prose is merely and avowedly a secondary consideration: it is always in the main, and sometimes wholly, a mere necessary instrument of divers practical purposes,"[53] and that "he does not *wish* to consider a piece of prose as a work of art destined, first of all, if not finally, to fulfil its own laws on the one hand, and to give pleasure on the other."[54] The distinction between verse and prose has often troubled the writers of criticism. The explanation is probably that the outer form of a work is more easily understood and more constantly present to the mind than is the real form. Yet it is strange that those who find the distinction between verse and prose important should parallel this with a distinction between imagination and intellect, as if a novel had more affinities with a speech than with an epic. It is strange, too, that Saintsbury's own phrase about the right way to consider a "piece of prose"—as a work of art destined "to fulfil its own laws"—did not suggest to him the fundamental importance of a distinction between what he terms the minor or suasive rhetoric on the one hand, and on the other poetic, whether or not in verse. For poetry always is free to fulfil its own law, but the writer of rhetorical discourse is, in a sense, perpetually in bondage to the occasion and the audience; and in that fact we find the line of cleavage between rhetoric and poetic.

The distinction between rhetoric as theory of public address and poetic as theory of pure literature, says Professor Baldwin, "seems not to have controlled any consecutive movement of modern criticism."[55] That it has not controlled the procedure of critics in dealing with orators is indicated in the foregoing pages; yet we have found, too, many suggestions of a better method, and some few critical performances against which the only charge is overcondensation.

Rhetorical criticism is necessarily analytical. The scheme of a rhetorical study includes the element of the speaker's personality as a conditioning factor; it includes also the public char-

acter of the man—not what he was, but what he was thought to be. It requires a description of the speaker's audience, and of the leading ideas with which he plied his hearers—his topics, the motives to which he appealed, the nature of the proofs he offered. These will reveal his own judgment of human nature in his audiences, and also his judgment on the questions which he discussed. Attention must be paid, too, to the relation of the surviving texts to what was actually uttered: in case the nature of the changes is known, there may be occasion to consider adaptation to two audiences—that which heard and that which read. Nor can rhetorical criticism omit the speaker's mode of arrangement and his mode of expression, nor his habit of preparation and his manner of delivery from the platform; though the last two are perhaps less significant. "Style"—in the sense which corresponds to diction and sentence movement—must receive attention, but only as one among various means that secure for the speaker ready access to the minds of his auditors. Finally, the effect of the discourse on its immediate hearers is not to be ignored, either in the testimony of witnesses, nor in the record of events. And throughout such a study one must conceive of the public man as influencing the men of his own times by the power of his discourse.

VIII

What is the relation of rhetorical criticism, so understood, to literary criticism? The latter is at once broader and more limited than rhetorical criticism.

It is broader because of its concern with permanent values: because it takes no account of special purpose nor of immediate effect; because it views a literary work as the voice of a human spirit addressing itself to men of all ages and times; because the critic speaks as the spectator of all time and all existence. But this universalizing of attitude brings its own limits with it: the influence of the period is necessarily relegated to the background; interpretation in the light of the writer's intention and of his situation may be ignored or slighted; and the speaker who directed his words to a definite and limited group of hearers may be made to address a universal audience. The result can only be confusion. In short, the point of view of literary criticism is proper only to its own objects, the permanent works. Upon such as are found to lie without the pale, the verdict of literary criticism is of negative value merely, and its interpretation is false and misleading because it proceeds upon a wrong assumption. If Henry Clay and Charles Fox are to be dealt with at all, it must not be on the assumption that their works, in respect of wisdom and eloquence, are or ought to be sources of perennial freshness and interest. Morley has put the matter well:

> The statesman who makes or dominates a crisis, who has to rouse and mold the mind of senate or nation, has something else to think about than the production of literary masterpieces. The great political speech, which for that matter is a sort of drama, is not made by passages for elegant extract or anthologies, but by personality, movement, climax, spectacle, and the action of the time.[56]

But we cannot always divorce rhetorical criticism from literary. In the case of Fox or Clay or Cobden, as opposed to Fielding or Addison or De Quincey, it is proper to do so; the fact that language is a common medium to the writer of rhetorical discourse and to the writer in pure literature will give to the critics of each a common vocabulary of stylistic terms, but not a common standard. In the case of Burke the relation of the two points of view is more complex. Burke belongs to literature; but in all his important works he was a practitioner of public address written or uttered. Since his approach to *belles-lettres* was through rhetoric, it follows that rhetorical criticism is at least a preliminary to literary criticism, for it will erect the factual basis for the understanding of the works: will not merely explain allusions and establish dates, but recall the setting, reconstruct the author's own intention, and analyze his method. But the rhetorical inquiry is more than a mere preliminary; it permeates and governs all subsequent interpretation and criticism. For the statesman in letters is a statesman still: compare Burke to Charles Lamb, or even to Montaigne, and it is clear that the public man is in a sense inseparable from his audience. A statesman's wisdom and eloquence are not to be read without some share of his own sense of the body politic, and of the body politic not merely as a construct of thought, but as a living human society. A speech, like a satire, like a comedy of manners, grows directly out of a social situation; it is a man's response to a condition in human affairs. However broadly typical the situation may be when its essential elements are laid bare, it never appears without its coverings. On no plane of thought— philosophical, literary, political—is

Burke to be understood without reference to the great events in America, India, France, which evoked his eloquence; nor is he to be understood without reference to the state of English society. (It is this last that is lacking in Grierson's essay: the page of comment on Burke's qualities in actual debate wants its supplement in some account of the House of Commons and the national life it represented. Perhaps the latter is the more needful to a full understanding of the abiding excellence in Burke's pages.) Something of the spirit of Morley's chapter on Cobden, and more of the spirit of the social historian (which Morley has in other parts of the biography) is necessary to the literary critic in dealing with the statesman who is also a man of letters.

In the case of Burke, then, one of the functions of rhetorical criticism is as a preliminary, but an essential and governing preliminary, to the literary criticism which occupies itself with the permanent values of wisdom and of eloquence, of thought and of beauty, that are found in the works of the orator.

Rhetorical criticism may also be regarded as an end in itself. Even Burke may be studied from that point of view alone. Fox and Cobden and the majority of public speakers are not to be regarded from any other. No one will offer Cobden's works a place in pure literature. Yet the method of the great agitator has a place in the history of his times. That place is not in the history of *belles-lettres*; nor is it in the literary history which is a "survey of the life of a people as expressed in their writings." The idea of "writings" is a merely mechanical one; it does not really provide a point of view or a method; it is a

book-maker's cloak for many and diverse points of view. Such a compilation as the *Cambridge History of American Literature*, for example, in spite of the excellence of single essays, may not unjustly be characterized as an uneven commentary on the literary life of the country and as a still more uneven commentary on its social and political life. It may be questioned whether the scant treatment of public men in such a compilation throws light either on the creators of pure literature, or on the makers of rhetorical discourse, or on the life of the times.

Rhetorical criticism lies at the boundary of politics (in the broadest sense) and literature; its atmosphere is that of the public life,[57] its tools are those of literature, its concern is with the ideas of the people as influenced by their leaders. The effective wielder of public discourse, like the military man, belongs to social and political history because he is one of its makers. Like the soldier, he has an art of his own which is the source of his power; but the soldier's art is distinct from the life which his conquests affect. The rhetorician's art represents a natural and normal process within that life. It includes the work of the speaker, of the pamphleteer, of the writer of editorials, and of the sermon maker. It is to be thought of as the art of popularization. Its practitioners are the Huxleys, not the Darwins, of science; the Jeffersons, not the Lockes and the Rousseaus, of politics.

Of late years the art of popularization has received a degree of attention: propaganda and publicity have been words much used; the influence of the press has been discussed; there have been some studies of public opinion.

Professor Robinson's *Humanizing of Knowledge*[58] is a cogent statement of the need for popularization by the instructed element in the state, and of the need for a technique in doing so. But the book indicates, too, how little is known of the methods its author so earnestly desires to see put to use. Yet ever since Homer's day men have woven the web of words and counsel in the face of all. And ever since Aristotle's day there has been a mode of analysis of public address. Perhaps the preoccupation of literary criticism with "style" rather than with composition in the large has diverted interest from the more significant problem. Perhaps the conventional categories of historical thought have helped to obscure the problem: the history of thought, for example, is generally interpreted as the history of invention and discovery, both physical and intellectual. Yet the history of the thought of the people is at least as potent a factor in the progress of the race. True, the popular thought may often represent a resisting force, and we need not marvel that the many movements of a poet's mind more readily capture the critic's attention than the few and uncertain movements of that Leviathan, the public mind. Nor is it surprising that the historians tend to be occupied with the acts and the motives of leaders. But those historians who find the spirit of an age in the total mass of its literary productions, as well as all who would tame Leviathan to the end that he shall not threaten civilization, must examine more thoroughly than they as yet have done the interactions of the inventive genius, the popularizing talent, and the public mind.

Notes

1. *Life of William Ewart Gladstone*, New York, 1903, II, 593.
2. *Select Works*, ed. E. J. Payne, Oxford, 1892, I, xxxviii.
3. Basil Williams, *Life of William Pitt*, New York, 1913, II, 335–337.
4. D. Nichol Smith, *Functions of Criticism*, Oxford, 1909, p. 15.
5. See Rosebery, *Appreciations and Addresses*, London, 1899, and Whitelaw Reid, *American and English Studies*, New York, 1913, II.
6. See Augustine Birrell, *Obiter Dicta*, New York, 1887, II; Walter Raleigh, *Some Authors*, Oxford, 1923; Robert Lynd, *Books and Authors*, London, 1922.
7. Oliver Elton, *Survey of English Literature, 1780–1830*, I, 234–53.
8. *Cambridge History of American Literature*, New York, 1921, III, 374–5.
9. *Cambridge History of American Literature*, III, 378.
10. *Ibid.*, pp. 381–2.
11. *Ibid.*, p. 377.
12. *Cambridge History of English Literature*, New York, 1914, XI, 30–5.
13. H. A. Taine, *History of English Literature*, tr. H. Van Laun, London, 1878, II, 81–3.
14. Boston, 1923.
15. W. P. Trent, *History of American Literature, 1607–1865*, New York, 1917, pp. 576–7.
16. Edmund Gosse, *History of Eighteenth Century English Literature, 1660–1780*, London, 1889, pp. 365–6.
17. *Cambridge History of American Literature*, New York, 1918, II, 101.
18. G. E. B. Saintsbury, *Short History of English Literature*, New York, 1915, p. 630.
19. *Ibid.*, pp. 629–30.
20. *Ibid.*, p. 631.
21. *Ibid.*
22. *Ibid.*
23. *Sketches and Essays*, ed. W. C. Hazlitt, London, 1872, II, 420–1.
24. *Political Essays with Sketches of Public Characters*, London, 1819, pp. 264–79.
25. New York, 1923.
26. New York, 1924.
27. E. P. Whipple, "Daniel Webster as a Master of English Style," in *American Literature*, Boston, 1887, p. 157.
28. *Ibid.*, p. 208.
29. *Ibid.*, p. 144.

30. London, 1914, p. 7.
31. *Lord Chatham as an Orator*, Oxford, 1912, p. 5.
32. *Ibid.*, pp. 39–40.
33. W. E. H. Lecky, *History of England in the Eighteenth Century*, New York, 1888, III, 203–4.
34. *Life of William Ewart Gladstone*, I, 193–4; II, 54–5, 593.
35. *Gladstone, his Characteristics as Man and Statesman*, New York, 1898, pp. 41–4.
36. G. M. Trevelyan, *Life of John Bright*, Boston, 1913, p. 384.
37. Henry Hardwicke, *History of Oratory and Orators*, New York, 1896.
38. Lorenzo Sears, *History of Oratory*, Chicago, 1896.
39. New York, 1852.
40. P. 75.
41. P. 461.
42. *Life of Richard Cobden*, Boston, 1881, pp. 130–2.
43. *Cambridge History of English Literature*, New York, 1914, XI, 8.
44. Oliver Elton, *Survey of English Literature, 1780–1830*, London, 1912, I, 234.
45. *Rhetoric*, ii, 2, tr. W. Rhys Roberts in *The Works of Aristotle*, XI, Oxford, 1924.
46. Article "Rhetoric" in the *Encyclopædia Britannica*, 9th and 11th editions.
47. J. L. Gerig and F. N. Scott, article "Rhetoric" in the *New International Encyclopædia*.
48. K. H. W. Wackernagel, *Poetik, Rhetorik und Stilistik*, ed. L. Sieber, Halle, 1873, p. II.
49. H. H. Hudson, "The Field of Rhetoric," *Quarterly Journal of Speech Education*, IX (1923), 177. See also the same writer's "Rhetoric and Poetry," *ibid.*, X (1924), 143 ff.
50. C. S. Baldwin, *Ancient Rhetoric and Poetic*, New York, 1924, p. 134.
51. C. E. B. Saintsbury, *History of Criticism and Literary Taste in Europe*, New York, 1900, I, 39.
52. *Ibid.*, p. 42.
53. *History of Criticism and Literary Taste in Europe*, p. 48.
54. *Ibid.*, p. 52.
55. *Op. cit.*, p. 4.
56. *Life of William Ewart Gladstone*, II, 589–90.
57. For a popular but suggestive presentation of the background of rhetorical discourse, see J. A. Spender, *The Public Life*, New York, 1925.
58. New York, 1923.

Walter J. Ong

The Province of Rhetoric and Poetic

◊ *This brief but important essay is an early modern attempt to draw the lines of demarcation that separate rhetoric from poetic. The author's primary contention is that the differences between these two genres of discourse are essentially matters of degree rather than of kind. Both arts, it is pointed out, utilize contingent propositions that lack the certitude of scientific writing. Moreover they share the common goal of striving to produce some type of persuasive effect. In doing its work, however, rhetoric is concerned with direct actions involving practical matters, and with strong logical connections in the use of enthymemes and examples. By contrast, poetic relies on indirect effects which are difficult to measure because of the individual nature of its appeals.* ◊

The literature of all ages is inextricably wound up with rhetorical and poetical theory. This is true even of a time like the present, when rhetorical theory often proceeds by a kind of negation of formal rhetoric. The conscious avoidance of certain devices not only is impossible without the substitution of others, but is itself based on a theory. We can avoid certain techniques, but not technique. Though we may have cultivated a horror of naming our tools, which earlier artists did not know, we still retain some knowledge of how to use them. Hence rhetoric and poetic remain with us.

But rhetorical and poetical theory has most often failed to find the location of the boundaries within which each of these two arts operate. Current studies in literary history have not placed the lines of demarcation any more accurately.[1] Although the literary historian's distinctions between rhetoric and poetic have been more or less sufficient for his immediate purposes, there is still need to settle more definitely how a poetical work differs from a rhetorical one. The investigation of this question falls rather to the lot of the philosopher than to that of the literary historian, and hence the present discussion will be properly philosophical.

Walter J. Ong, "The Province of Rhetoric and Poetic," *The Modern Schoolman*, (January 1942): 24–27. Reprinted with permission from *The Modern Schoolman*.

I

Those things in the world which are made by man, being artifacts and not as such possessed of any substantial forms of their own, are differentiated from one another in a variety of ways: in terms of a variety of accidents which they possess, as when I speak of square artifacts, or black artifacts; in terms of the material, that is to say, the second matter in which they have their being, as when I speak of works of stone or works of iron; and finally in terms of their final causality—and this is the way in which we most generally speak of them—as when I speak of a table or of a gun or of a fountain pen.

Differentiation of the works of man in terms of final causality will proceed according to the more or less perfect participation of these works in this principle.[2] Thus we have the division into works of non-servile or fine arts and works of servile arts. The former are more perfect in the order of final causality in that they are ordered directly to the speculative intellect, to man's enjoyment as things of beauty, and are therefore destined only indirectly for other use, although their contemplation is of course governed by prudence.

Over against these works of fine arts, we have the works of those arts such as the machinist's or the paint manufacturer's art, which works are not directly for contemplation but means to further ends.

Rhetoric Ordered to Action

Within this division of works of art in terms of final causality the division between works of rhetoric and works of poetic falls.[3] For, if we take rhetoric to signify what Aristotle took it to signify—"the ability to find the available means of persuasion with reference to any subject whatsoever"[4]—works of rhetoric must be ordered to the production of action in another individual and to action in the sense of something other than contemplation. Works of rhetoric have their finality, then, only in terms of that action to which they are ultimately directed. There is another art, which we call poetic, which produces works ordered to contemplation and to no other direct end, that is, works of beauty. Such works are produced simply to be enjoyed by the one contemplating them.

It is to be noted that this rhetoric and this poetic are logical arts directive of the acts of the intellect itself. It is true that there is what we may call a general poetic, an inclusive order of those arts directed to the production of works for contemplation, which has a kind of unity derived from the community of end realized in such works. This order of arts, or general poetic, breaks down into poetic in the ordinary sense, sculpture, music, painting, and so on.

To this general poetic there corresponds another order of arts which we may call a general rhetoric and which includes those arts which may produce action in others not only by intellectual persuasion but by means other than the significative use of words. The sales agent who installs fluorescent lighting to put his customers at ease and thus indirectly persuade them to buy an automobile is practicing this general rhetoric.

However, the rhetoric and poetic which govern the formal use of words

Figure 1

Ars logica directs the acts of the intellect itself (*actus rationis*).
Ars logica is diversified as are *actus rationis*:

		Treated by Aristotle in:	
I.	*Intelligentia indivisibilium*	*Praedicamenta (Catagoriae)*	
II.	*Compositio vel divisio*	*Perihermenias*	
III.	*Discursus*	Other logical treatises as follows:	

Art, like nature, acts in three ways, and the third act of the intellect has therefore a three-fold diversity, with corresponding arts:

A. *De necessitate (cum certitudine) ars logica judicativa*		*ex forma syllogismi: Analytica Priora cum forma ex materia syllogismi: Analytica Posteriora*	
B. *Frequentius*	*ars logica inventiva*		
1. *In pluribus*			
a. *Cum probabilitate*	*dialectica*		*Topica (Dialectica)*
b. *Cum suspicione*	*rhetorica*		*Rhetorica*
c. *Cum existimatione*	*poetica*		*Poetica*
2. *In paucioribus*	*sophistica*		*De Sophisticis Elenchis*

(as significative sounds) are both individual arts. They are logical arts, for each is not only a *habitus* of the intellect (all arts are this) but a *habitus* directive of the operations of the intellect itself. And yet they are not of the same species of logic as that according to which science (*scientia*) proceeds; for the connections in the logic of rhetoric and of poetic are not the necessary connections which exist in the logic of demonstration.

It will help to schematize a text from St. Thomas[5] (Fig. 1). Schematization of St. Thomas Aquinas *in I Anal. Post.,* Lect. 1. In the diagram[6] the connection between the members of the syllogism in *logica judicativa* (or *demonstrativa*) is a necessary one. As we proceed downwards, the connections are seen to become progressively looser. In dialectic (disputation) they require prob-

ability. The rhetorical syllogism, or "enthymeme," requires only suspicion—for this degree of certitude is sufficient to induce a man to act. In poetic, the logical connection is merely feigned, for the poet is *making* his connection. Certain and probable connections—more probably ("cum probabilitate") or less probable ("cum suspicione")—exist independently of the poet and hence are not his to make. The sophistical argument, of course, does not really conclude and resists conclusion, so that it is lower on the scale than even the merely assumed argument of poetic.

Rhetoric, then, and poetic both differ from the logic of the sciences in that neither requires certitude for its arguments.[7] Rhetoric must more closely approximate certitude in its conclusions. Poetic contents itself with a logic that is very thin: its argumentation is treated as though it concluded, and this assumption suffices. Furthermore, although rhetoric and poetic are distinct arts directive of the third operation of the intellect, no given work is the product of such an art alone. The works of these arts, as they stand concreted in matter, are erected by other arts as well, arts which are directive of the physical structure out of which such things are made, as, for instance, an art which directs the rhythmical use of words, and so on. It is the aggregate of all these arts necessary for the production of a work of rhetoric or poetic which is often meant by "rhetoric" or "poetic," and it is such an aggregate that we have called a "general rhetoric" or a "general poetic." A book professing to teach rhetoric may, then, treat of many things other than the enthymeme and the example, and thus present a composite of several arts. Quintilian's *Institutio Oratoria*, for instance, is a composite of this nature.[8]

II

An important phenomenon in literary history is the persistent confusion of poetic with rhetoric or with demonstrative logic.[9] Poetic and rhetoric are confused when, in an attempt to strengthen its logic, poetic is made to proceed by means of the rhetorical enthymeme and example. Such an attempt can only result in something neither fish nor flesh—a poetic whose works are ordered to the practical intellect. Nevertheless, this sort of monster can be fathered on every age since Plato's. It comes into being when poetry is taken to be a direct means of persuasion, either because the defense of an art which creates objects simply for contemplation is felt to be impossible, or because the common association of certain other arts with both poetic and rhetoric obscures the true position of these latter arts. Since the works of both poetic and rhetoric are concreted in matter which is words, these arts gather around themselves a system of satellitic arts which are often the same for both rhetoric and poetic, arts such as that which governs the production of oral sounds. The fact that these arts are found in connection with both rhetoric and poetic tends to obscure the fact that in each case they are serving a different purpose.

Judicative Logic and Poetic

The confusion which constantly tends to arise between poetic and the logic of demonstration which governs the sciences (including philosophy) is likewise of some importance. Clearly distinct from a work of rhetoric, a philosophical work, which proceeds according to *logica judicativa* and may be taken as typical of all scientific works, is not so easily distinguished from a poetical work. A philosophical treatise, like a poetical work, is directed to the speculative intellect. But in what way? The philosophical is concerned with the communication of something which has its existence independently of the words used to communicate it, and, while the poetic use of language communicates truth too, it is truth which does not exist in its totality as entirely independent of the language in which it is conveyed. The logical connections are made by the poet. They are fabricated (''cum existimatione''). Consequently, since they do not exist of themselves necessarily, assent to the argument of a poem must be induced by something other than the truths with which the poet deals, so that these truths are apprehended by the intellect with some special kind of cooperation on the part of the senses and emotions that is dependent on the very words in which the truths are presented. Insofar as a work acts independently of the words in which it is presented, it tends toward the scientific treatise.[10]

Now, in the confusion of poetic with rhetoric and with demonstrative logic, it is always poetic which tends to disappear. And the reason for this is not far to seek. The principal domestic struggle of Western culture has been between a philosophically centered and a rhetorically centered regimen. The forces engaged have been the champions of the speculative intellect versus the champions of the practical intellect. On this basis was waged the struggle between Socrates and the sophists, the struggle which led to John of Salisbury's *Metalogicus*, and the struggle which was echoed in Swift's *The Battle of the Books*. The victory has gone first to one side and then to another. Under the Roman Empire and until the eleventh century the rhetoricians were in the ascendency, but by the thirteenth century philosophy seemed destined to win out, only to receive a sharp set-back when rhetoric triumphed and made the Renaissance.[11]

Meanwhile poetic has had to eke out an existence in occupied territory. Philosophy is eminently speculative. It will do no work. Rhetoric is eminently practical. It will do a work which is itself productive of some work on the part of others. Poetic is practical, but its work is not. It runs shortly to a dead end. Its work is for the speculative intellect here and now, ordered further only indirectly by reason of prudence. Hence, tucked away in its tight little corner, poetical composition has never been accorded the prominence in any curriculum that either rhetoric or philosophy have, and even when rhetoric has fallen on evil days, as it had in the thirteenth century and as it more or less has now, it is still in a position to bestow largess on poetic, which, as an art, is consistently neglected in schools.

Poetry's Results—Indirect

The defense of poetry depends not on what its words do directly, but on what they do indirectly. Because so many well-meaning but unobserving persons insist on defending it for the direct results it produces—a line of defense which is untenable—neglecting the entirely valid argument that the organization which a schooled appreciation of poetry imposes upon the human being is something that cannot be attained independently of words of poetic (or of music, painting, and so on), we are continually having the wrong thing defended or the right thing defended for the wrong reasons. This difficulty is, of course, chronic, and will remain so, for the indirect results which works of poetic bring about in the human being are known only to those who have had experience of them.

It will be seen, then, that the contrast between poetic and scientific writing is a more basic one than that between verse and prose. In the one case the difference arises from final causality, while in the other it is merely of accidental origin, dependent upon and ordered to the purpose which the work is to serve.[12] This should be a commonplace. It has been said over and over again from Aristotle's time[13] on, even by persons whose discussions are critical rather than philosophical, as, for instance, Coleridge.[14] But it represents a stand which is continually being challenged.

There is, of course, a connection between verse and poetry, as there is between prose and scientific writing. Scientific writing, as has already been said, is concerned with the communication of something which has its existence independently of the words used to communicate it. Hence any configuration of those words lies outside the realm of such writing. If a scientific work is written in verse, the configuration is truly an ornament added to the scientific content of the writing. In poetry, however, the verse functions as an intimate part of the work itself. Apart from what special significative force verse rhythms may themselves exert (as in rhythmic onomatopoeia), they constitute a part of the object to be contemplated. Their relation to the "logical" content is close in a work where the connections in such content are, like the verse itself, of the author's own making.

Poetry in Prose

But this is not to identify verse with poetry, for prose, too, may be written to produce a work for contemplation. Such a work would be poetry in the sense in which this word is used here. No more is it to identify verse with one particular kind of rhythmic patterning (as, for example, with the syllable-counting systems of Homer, Vergil, and most English poets after the Conquest, as against the antithetical patterning of Hebrew poetry or the stress patterning of Old English or modern "free" verse).

Rhetoric, falling between *logica judicativa* and poetic, favors a prose development, for the rhetorician, although he deals with that which is not necessary (or certain), is not the "maker" that the poet is. His logic is not as intimately connected as the poet's is with the words in which it is concreted.

It is seen, then, that poetic is distinguished from rhetoric by the relative tenuousness of its logical connections. The logic of poetic and of rhetoric follows the end to which each of these arts is directed—the former to the making of a thing for contemplation, the latter to the production of action in another. Both poetic and rhetoric are distinct from the logic of the sciences in that their arguments do not proceed with necessity, although rhetoric approximates the necessary in a way that poetic does not.

However, as a matter of fact, most writing is a composite, not only in the sense that arts other than those which govern the operations of the intellect are needed in order that a given concrete piece of writing take form, but also in the sense that a given piece of writing will often partake of the nature of many kinds of writing at once. In most of what may be designated as poetry there is a considerable mixture of special pleading which is nothing more or less than dialectic or rhetoric. Again, what we would ordinarily call a poem may *de facto* convey scientific as well as poetic truth, although it is not as a poem that it does so. And a politician who should be practicing rhetoric may introduce a fact for its own sake. Finally, writing ostensibly scientific can and often does become a plea to take this attitude toward the subject, or that. Works of rhetoric, poetic, and science do not exist in the concrete in separate works. We must generally rest satisfied with calling a thing a poem because it is mostly a poem, or a political speech a work of rhetoric because it is nearer to that than it is to anything else.

Notes

1. Among the studies of rhetoric and poetic should be mentioned Charles Sears Baldwin's *Ancient Rhetoric and Poetic* (New York: The Macmillan Co., 1924), *Medieval Rhetoric and Poetic* (New York: The Macmillan Co., 1928), and *Renaissance Literary Theory and Practice* (New York: Columbia University Press, 1939), as well as Donald Lemen Clark's *Rhetoric and Poetry in the Renaissance* (New York: Columbia University Press, 1922). A bibliography which includes works on rhetoric and poetic is given by William G. Crane, *Wit and Rhetoric in the Renaissance* (New York: Columbia University Press, 1937), pp. 253–76. There are also bibliographies in Baldwin.
2. Final causality, form, accident, etc., are of course to be taken analogously when referring to artifacts.
3. There is no need to quibble over words. Rhetoric has some unpleasant meanings that interfere, but the meaning which is here attached to rhetoric is a traditional and accepted one. All that is asked is that the reader look to what is meant here by rhetoric—call it what he will.
4. *Rhetoric* i. 2. 1. 1355b.
5. *In I Anal. Post.*, lect. 1.
6. There are many points of difference among these arts which a scheme such as the one given here does not bring out. See, for example, Averroes *In Libros Rhetoricorum Aristotelis Paraphrasis*, lib. 1, praef. (ed. Venetiis: apud Iuntas, 1574, p. 65a): "Ars quidam Rhetoricae affinis est artis Topicae: quoniam ambae unum finem intendunt, qui est eloqui cum alio. et quo neutra istarum artium homo secum ipse utitur, sicut est Dispositio artis Demonstrationis: sed utitur eis cum alio."
7. Historical works occupy a special place by the side of science. History is not science, though it constantly approaches science, as a calculus to its term.
8. See, for instance, his treatment of gesture, xi. 3. 65 ff. Quintilian, who was a rhetorician without being a philosopher, defines rhetoric as "bene dicendi scientia." *Op. cit.* ii. 15. 34: "Huic eius substantiae maxime conveniet finitio, rhetoricem esse bene dicendi scientiam." Cf. *ibid.* ii. 15. 38. Not only is Quintilian's rhetoric a composite of many arts, but his "ars" and "scientia" are other things than St. Thomas'.
9. Baldwin, *Ancient Rhetoric and Poetic*, pp. 100, 229: *Medieval Rhetoric and Poetic*, pp. ix, 24, 39, etc. (see General Index under "poetic merged with rhetoric"). Clark, *op. cit.*, pp. 35–37.
10. Gerard Manley Hopkins, S. J., a poet highly conscious of technique, had an artist's characteristic awareness of this special mode of operation in poetry:
    "Poetry is speech framed for contemplation of the mind by way of hearing or speech framed to be heard for its own sake and interest even over and above its interest of meaning. Some matter and meaning is essential to it but only as an element necessary to support and employ the shape which is contemplated for its own sake." *The Note-Books and Papers of Gerard Manley Hopkins*, ed. by Humphrey House (London: Oxford University Press, 1937), p. 249.
    It should be noted, however, that what the poet makes is not independent of the truths he makes it of. The truths he employs are not the poetry, and he can use great truths to make poor poetry indeed, but he cannot make great poetry without great truths. Neither stone nor straw is of my making; nevertheless, although I can badly botch a piece of stone construction I attempt, a better house can be made of stone than of straw. For all

this, the poet can utilize any material, for he is not making houses but simply things: his art is in a way coextensive with being.

11. For a thorough and enlightening treatment of the conflict between philosophy and rhetoric that runs through the history of Western civilization, I am particularly indebted to some unpublished work of Professor Etienne Gilson made available in a course of lectures delivered recently by Dr. Bernard J. Muller-Thym at St. Louis University. Cf. also Charles Homer Haskins, *The Renaissance of the Twelfth Century* (Cambridge: Harvard University Press, 1927), pp. 93–126.

12. Cf. Hopkins again, *op. cit.*, pp. 249–51. This short section, headed "Poetry and Verse," is in reality a chapter on poetic, and directly pertinent to the present discussion.

13. *Poetics* i. 7–12. 1447b.

14. See *Biographia Literaria*, ed. by J. Shawcross (Oxford: The Clarendon Press, 1907), Ch. XIV (II, 5–13—esp. 10).

Robert J. Connors

Greek Rhetoric and the Transition from Orality

◊ *Robert J. Connors, of the English Department at the University of New Hampshire, bases this essay on the works of such twentieth-century scholars as Milman Parry, Rhys Carpenter, Eric Havelock, Julian Jaynes, and Walter Ong, all of whom have written about the period sometime in the late fifth and the early fourth century B.C. when the Greeks made the crucial transition from a primarily oral culture to a largely literate culture. Against the background of this cultural change, Connors gives us a new perspective on the origin and development of the art of rhetoric and on such important figures as Socrates, Plato, Gorgias of Leotini, and Aristotle, who played a part in the development of rhetoric at a time when, as Connors says, "it seems likely that every educated Greek could read and write from youth." ◊*

There is another art which has to do with words, by virtue of which it is possible to bewitch the young through their ears with words while they are still standing at a distance from the realities of truth, by exhibiting to them spoken images of all things, so to make it seem that they are true and that the speaker is the wisest of all men in all things.

—Plato, *Sophist*

The last fifty years have witnessed a revolution in the way that classical scholars view Homeric poetry, and indeed all of the works pre-dating the fifth century B.C. The writings of Milman Parry on the oral nature of the *Iliad* and the *Odyssey* and of Rhys Carpenter on the nature of early Greek alphabetical literacy have led later scholars to a sweeping reappraisal of the entire culture of pre-Socratic Greece. During the past two decades, questions of the effects of orality and literacy on the construction of a culture have been asked and answered anew. The theories of Eric A. Havelock, first proposed in 1963, have been in the vanguard of this reappraisal, and Havelock's insights have been deepened and extended by later scholars. This growing body of knowledge about ancient Greek culture and expression can, I believe, illuminate

Reprinted by permission of The Pennsylvania State University Press from *Philosophy and Rhetoric*, Vol. 19, No. 1, pp. 38–65. Copyright 1986 by The Pennsylvania State University.

some of the curious questions that traditional scholarship has left us concerning rhetorical practice in fifth and fourth-century Greece and give us insight into the fates and works of many of the figures, both major and minor, who shaped early Hellenic discourse. This essay will attempt to trace some of the outlines of such an application.

Havelock on Poetry and Orality

Eric Havelock posits a revolution in Greek thought and thinking processes that has three stages.[1] The first stage, that of an absolutely oral culture, is pre-Homeric, dating to before 700 B.C. when the works we now call Homeric were first written down in the newly invented alphabetical script. During this period, in which reading and writing of any sort were completely unknown to the vast majority of Greeks, all cultural tradition was passed on orally. The entirety of Hellenic culture, dating back to the Bronze Age and beyond, could only be transmitted by constant repetition and memorization by every citizen. Prose preservation of this tradition was not practicable: "The only possible verbal technology available to guarantee the preservation and fixity of transmission was that of the rhythmic word organized cunningly in verbal and metrical patterns which were unique enough to retain their shape. This is the historical genesis, the *fons et origo*, the moving cause of that phenomenon we still call 'poetry.' "[2]

Education in preliterate Greece involved nothing more or less than the memorization of the Greek cultural "book," enforced by constant repetition and recital and by constantly hearing others repeating the same rhythmically organized materials. The most central of these materials were presumably among the first to be written down when the Greek alphabet was devised: the works of "Homer" and "Hesiod." Once this alphabet was invented and put into limited use somewhere between 800 and 700 B.C., Greece entered a transitional period in which oral and literate elements were mixed within the culture. This is the period, especially that part of it after about 450 B.C., with which most of this essay is concerned. This transitional era was a time, especially during its early phase, of what Havelock calls "craft literacy," a period during which the ability to read and write was a specialized skill cultivated by only a few professionals. Not until the last few years of the fifth century B.C. is there evidence that reading was a skill taught to schoolboys, and we can assume that throughout this transitional period most people's consciousness was still shaped by the older tradition of oral recitation.

At some point during the fourth century B.C. Athenian culture as a whole shifted from a primarily oral to a primarily literate identity. At this time—and during the latter part of the transitional period, at least for some individuals—our modern literately fixed high consciousness came to full control of high culture and thought. Most of Havelock's *Preface to Plato* is concerned with showing how Plato announced and became the prime spokesman for the new, critical, individualistic, analytical form of human consciousness that replaced the older oral state of mind during this time. It was not, of course, a time of full literacy even for all franchised citizens, but after approximately 370 B.C. we see a state of affairs in Athens very different from that of even forty years earlier—a state of affairs in which analytical rationalism was essentially in control of the arts, the state mechanisms, and the means of information.

As a precondition for the oral transmission of Greek tradition, Havelock claims, there must have been an "oral state of mind," a mode of consciousness very different from that we take for granted in today's literate culture. How, he asks, could such feats of memorization—the memorization of the entire Homeric corpus, for instance—be possible for the average person? "Only, we suggest, by exploiting psychological resources latent and available in the consciousness of every individual, but which today are no longer necessary." These resources include "a state of total personal involvement and therefore of emotional identification with the substance of the poetised statement." Such powers of memory "could be purchased only at the cost of total loss of objectivity," says Havelock, and as a result the artist in the poetic experience that Plato calls *mimesis* had the power to "make his audience identify almost pathologically and certainly sympathetically with the content of what he is saying."³

The crux of Havelock's argument deals with Plato's opposition to the passive, communally oriented, non-critical oral consciousness that ruled the society in which he was born. Thus Plato refused in the *Republic* to admit poets and poetry into his ideal state, and thus,

I will argue, he opposed rhetoric, which began to take technical form during this period of oral-literate transition. I believe that oral rhetoric attained its great power and popularity among fifth and fourth-century Greek states by utilizing—in a quite conscious and "literate" fashion—the mechanisms of passive oral consciousness described by Havelock, mechanisms that still existed in most people and that made the Athenians of Socrates' and Plato's times peculiarly receptive to certain sorts of carefully wrought oral persuasion. Plato, I will argue, at the same time that he was fighting the effects of the poetic tradition, was also waging a battle against the power of the rhetorical movement which by nature attended on the decline of the old power of poetry. We can begin to explore this situation by examining certain aspects of the nature of early Greek rhetoric.

Prior to the first extant written speeches we have nothing but reportage and supposition. Thus our ideas about early rhetoric are automatically biased in a "literate" direction; we assume that early audiences heard discourse as we do, with critical detachment and rational analysis. But what is it that we in fact *know* about rhetoric—in the sense of affective public discourse as it was practiced and received—prior to 450 B.C., in a cultural milieu that was formed and controlled by the poetical educational process?

First, preliterate rhetoric was not "technical." The very fact that there is no mention of rhetoric as an art or teachable practice before Corax and Tisias in the mid-fifth century indicates that the ability to speak persuasively was considered a gift rather than a *techne.* All the evidence points to the fact that such a gift was closely related to the memoric and poetic abilities so carefully cultivated in the oral culture and that use of the art of speech depended on conscious or unconscious manipulation of the orally conditioned mental states of the audience.[4] It is impossible that such powerful forms and stimuli as dithyrambs and epic hexameters should not have some effect on the way that all public discourse is constructed in a society defining itself orally.[5]

We would naturally expect non-poetic public discourse in such a society to attempt to succeed by using the formulas that made the poetry successful, by using heavily rhythmic sentence patterns which concentrate on such devices as balance and antithesis, figures which would later be classified and called isocolon and homoeoteleuton. We would expect a heavy reliance upon common formulas; as Walter Ong points out in *Orality and Literacy,* oral thought is by nature formulaic, reliant upon set thoughts and expressions that are known to the auditors.[6] These formulas—"wine-dark sea," "wily Odysseus," and countless others known to all members of the culture—gave pleasure upon repetition, and certain classes of formulas must have been the bases of early rhetoric, as they would grow into the *topoi* and figures of later technical rhetoric.

This is *not* to say that the skills involved were the same or that early rhetoric *was* poetry. There must have been critical differences, the most important having to do with the purposive intent of the speaker and with the amount of rhythm and meter allowed. The pri-

mary aims of the bard or reciter of poetry were to entertain and those of the poetic teacher were to enforce the memorization of the poem. Persuasion to action had little place in the general purposes to which poetry was put; one recited or listened to poetry as both a pleasure and a duty, but affectively the acts were self-contained. Rhetorical acts were not, and that is the great difference. Some of the devices of rhetoric might have been similar to those of poetry, but behind every rhetorical utterance there was an agenda, a persuasive purpose. The poet or rhapsode sought to produce, as Gorgias put it, "fearful shuddering and tearful pity and grievous longing" in his hearers—but for their own sake. The rhetor sought to produce them for other motives—to press a point, gain adherence to a cause, win a case. The forms must have differed somewhat as well. When we look at the available evidence concerning the poetically based rhetoric of the Greek oral and early transitional periods, however, one characteristic of it comes through very clearly: It was a weapon far more powerful than we can easily imagine now.

The Power of Rhetoric in an Oral Culture

The accomplished rhetorician in a Greek polis before 450 B.C. was a figure to whom wealth and power came as a matter of course, a figure to be feared, admired—obeyed. One important reason why we get no word of rhetoricians as a class before 450 B.C. is that we know the great rhetoricians of this earlier period as the kings, nobles, leaders, and generals. A leader in such a culture had to be able to fight, but just as importantly, he had to be able to persuade *others* to fight. The abilities of the early Greek kings and leaders to shape actions through words attained and retained for them their power.

The earliest references we have to popular attitudes toward effective rhetoric illustrate this power of the *logos.* The *Iliad* refers to Nestor's "argument sweeter than honey," and it is he, the "orator" of the *Iliad*, whose speech convinces Patroclus to fight Hector—thus moving Achilles finally to go against Hector. The *Odyssey* contains a very telling passage describing how orators were viewed by their communities:

One man is rather insignificant in look;
But a god crowns his speech with grace, and men behold him
And are pleased. And he speaks without faltering,
With soothing deference, and he stands out in the gathering.
And they look upon him like a god as he goes through the city.[7]

This is rather a different picture of the reception of the rhetorician from that we see in a fully literate or even a later transitional culture. What Homer seems to be describing here is a non-critical, non-abstract, communally based, and essentially emotional response to the rhetorical discourse of Odysseus. It is a kind of response that gives the power of *logos* a depth and credibility we simply do not find in literate cultures, and there is much evidence that this passive, emotional, credential reception of rhetorical discourse was the rule down through the time of Socrates, Plato, and even Aristotle.

We only begin to catch direct glimpses of this orally based rhetorical power, of course, when written records begin to appear in some numbers during the mid-fifth century B.C. The first histories and extant orations support the idea of rhetorical power described by Homer. It seems clear, for instance, that the leaders of Athens during most of the fifth century were men relying on their powers of discourse at least as much as on their abilities. As such men arose, the practical danger was that the Athenian polity kept passing from the spell of one demagogue to that of another.[8] The midcentury tyrant Peisistratus, who convinced the Athenians to provide him with a bodyguard (actually a private army) which he then used to oppress them, is probably paradigmatic; in an oral or a transitional culture, any orator who had mastered the poetically based conventions that induced the passive, credulous oral mind-state could attain to great popular influence.

Modern commentators have been at a loss to explain why this pattern held, why the ancient Greeks, who have always been the western models for rationalism, so easily gave up their freedoms to so many glib-tongued demagogues. The pattern seems less mysterious, of course, when seen as one inevitable manifestation of the orality-literacy transition. The literate "modern" mind-state of rational calculation championed by Plato would of course appear in many forms other than those characterizing Platonic philosophy, and demagogy was no doubt one of them. In Plato's myth of the cave (which now appears much less fanciful than before—indeed, it is almost a straight analogy for the oral mind-state

Plato considered the enemy), the philosophers were those who had broken their chains, gone to the cave mouth, and tried to report the truth of what they had seen back to those still enchained. To use the same analogy, the demagogues were men who had broken their chains, gone to the cave mouth, and then returned to try to manipulate the shadows that still constituted everyone else's reality.

Demagogic oratory was the rule in Athenian politics (and to a lesser degree in Athenian law) so long as the majority of the population was unable or unwilling to subject oratory to the sort of critical analysis that is the natural literate response to persuasion. This seems not to have occurred until sometime in the fourth century B.C. Even the great Pericles was almost certainly a demagogic orator.[9] The story of Pericles' political career is the story of a man mastering tremendously difficult situations by the power of his speech, and though impressive and even glorious it is by no means unique. Masterful speech quite simply had a genuine power in early Greece that our critical sensibilities today have a hard time understanding. These early Greeks seem extremely credulous in many ways to us today—and indeed, they often seemed too credulous to each other.[10]

The Earliest Written Rhetorical Discourses

At the end of the fifth century B.C., we come to the early history of the "art" of rhetoric, which seems to develop concurrently with the widening of the literate mentality—at least to a certain point. The transitional rhetoricians appeared during these years, men who have left the first written speeches and who were also obvious masters of oral manipulation. These first written speeches have been problematical to scholars. It has been very difficult to understand how the extant fragments we have of the discourses of the early orators could possibly have been effective as persuasion, so rife are they with devices that today leave us cold. Indeed, their devices left critics cold a mere century after they were first delivered—and the reason for this, I would argue, is that after 330 B.C. all Greek writers (and remember that we hear no voices among the ancients but those of writers) existed within a paradigm of literate consciousness that could no longer understand the orally derived style of the earlier speakers.

The case of Antiphon of Rhamnus clearly illustrates this pattern, Antiphon whom Jebb calls the last of the "old orators." We have only a few of his works, but they all seem similar, and a modern reader of Antiphon's speeches would tend to agree with the judgment made by Dionysius in 60 A.D. that "Antiphon has nothing but his antique and stern dignity; a fighter of causes he is not."[11] Antiphon's oratory seems stiff, stuffy, vague, repetitive, larded with obvious general statements about the nature of life, containing very little evidence or factuality.

And yet, this is the same orator whose speeches brought the Four Hundred to power in the aristocratic coup of 411 B.C. This is the same Antiphon whose contemporary, Thucydides, described him as the ablest speaker in the Athenian legal system: "There was no man who could do more for any who consulted him, whether their business lay in the courts of justice or in the assembly."[12] Can this man, whose "great abilities" are so praised by his contemporaries, of whom Thucydides reports that his defense of himself was the best he (Thucydides) had ever heard, who quickly became a leader of his party and state, be the same orator condemned by Dionysius as possessing nothing more than "antique dignity"?

Yes. There is only one explanation for these differing views of Antiphon's rhetoric: the criteria of effective speaking had changed radically between Antiphon's time and Dionysius's. The sort of speech-art practiced by Antiphon seems strange to us, as it did to Dionysius, because it was formed so early—Antiphon is assumed to have been born around 480 B.C., and he was put to death in 411 B.C.—and formed to the needs of an orally attuned audience. The measured, cadenced dignity of Antiphon's style, "slow and majestic" as Jebb describes it, must have been one of the styles—it would be a mistake to think that there was only one—that could induce some version of the receptive, passive oral audience-state described by Havelock.[13] In fact, we can see in Antiphon's style and methods clear reflections of most of the characteristics that Ong ascribes to orally based expression: Antiphon is aggregative, not analytic; he relies on commonplaces, formulas, topics, sententious maxims; his speeches are repetitive and amplificatory; he narrates much of his position as an agonistic "story." An entire essay

could easily be devoted to exploring the orality inherent in Antiphon's presentations, but I think the point is made: Jebb's judgment that Antiphon is the last of the "old" orators and Lysias the first of the "new" is essentially correct; all it lacks is insight into *why*. Antiphon's basic orality and Lysias's basic literacy (Lysias was the first great *logographos*) tell us why.

Gorgias of Leontini has left for us more compelling mysteries than has Antiphon. Modern assessments of Gorgias's extant works, the *Encomium on Helen* and the *Palamedes*, have been less than kind. What, after all, are we to make of a style that has almost no parallels in modern prose?[14] Down through history runs the almost unanimous critical verdict that Gorgias's rhetoric is terrible stuff. Van Hook calls Gorgias's style "inartistic in the extreme . . . florid and frigid." Jebb is genuinely confused by Gorgias, calling him "an inventor whose originality it is hard for us to realize, but an artist whose faults are to us particularly glaring."[15]

Neither are the ancient critics much kinder to him. Dionysius in the first century A.D. excludes Gorgias from his list of great orators because he "exceeds the bounds of moderation, and frequently lapses into puerility."[16] Cicero in the first century B.C. accuses Gorgias of "immoderately abusing" devices of rhythm and figure.[17] Around the same time, Diodorus Siculus describes the Gorgianic style as once popular because it was exotic, "but," he reports, "it is now looked upon as labored and to be ridiculed when employed too frequently and tediously."[18] And even Aristotle, writing not more than forty-five years after Gorgias's death, condemns his style throughout Book III of the *Rhetoric*.[19] The Sicilian comes off poorly.

The long tradition of disparaging Gorgias's style seems to have begun with Aristotle, for we certainly see no such response to Gorgianic rhetoric before 350 B.C. or so. On the contrary, the few bits of evidence and testimony which have survived seem to indicate that Gorgias's rhetoric was effective and persuasive, that he was widely admired, that his popularity never waned during his life, and that he was wealthy and famous beyond all the other sophists. Gorgias visited Athens on numerous occasions and was invited to speak at the Olympic and Pythian games, a rare honor for a foreigner. He seems to have been in great demand throughout the Greek-speaking world as a teacher and a speaker, and he made a fortune during the last half of his life giving lessons and orations. Even his enemies respected his skill; Plato's attitude toward him in the dialogue that bears his name is critical, but not of Gorgias's style. Plato's whole presentation of the Sicilian shows that he is famous, well-liked, and a performer whose orations were eagerly sought treats. Plato's Gorgias may be wrong-headed, but he is not a fool or a buffoon.

How, once again, can we reconcile the marked wealth, success, and status of this orator with the obloquy heaped upon his works less than a century after his death? Traditional scholars have blamed "changing tastes," as if Gorgias's fall from popularity was similar to the Romantic poets' dismissal of the classical couplet form. But the change goes deeper than that, I think. I believe that Gorgias was the most successful manipulator of oral consciousness whose works the ancient world has left us, and that the condemnations of his style I have noted are all the works of men whose consciousnesses, like ours, were essentially shaped by alphabetical literacy and not by communal oral performance. Gorgias was the most popular speaker and most successful sophist of his time because he recognized more clearly than any other rhetor how to exploit the power of the *logos* in an oral culture.

Gorgias himself was not backward about describing the power of the *logos*; he seems, in fact, to revel in it. In the *Helen*, which was probably his trademark oration and central advertisement for himself, he ascribes to the *logos* a sort of power which sounds fantastic to the modern rhetorician. Traditional scholarship has assumed that Gorgias is being hyperbolic in these passages, inflating the power of speech, but I think we must consider the possibility that Gorgias is here offering a straight description of the effect that a master-speaker could have on an orally conditioned audience:

Speech is a powerful lord, which by means of the finest and most invisible body effects the divinest works; it can stop fear and banish grief and create joy and nurture pity . . . through the agency of words, the soul is wont to experience a suffering of its own. . . . Sacred incantations sung with words are bearers of pleasure and banishers of pain, for, merging with opinion [*doxa*] in the soul, the power of the incantation is wont to beguile it and persuade it and alter it by witchcraft. . . . The effect of speech upon the condition of the soul is comparable to the power of drugs over the nature of bodies. For just as different drugs dispel different secretions from the body, and some bring an end to disease and others to life, so also in the case of speeches, some distress, others delight, some cause fear, others make the hearers bold, and some drug and bewitch the soul with a kind of evil persuasion.[20]

This is not the only time we hear this analogy between speech and *pharmakein*, drugs; Plato uses it as well.

In the *Helen*, Gorgias's main argument is an attempt to clear Helen of blame for the Trojan War by claiming that if she were either forced *or* persuaded to go to Troy she is faultless; at the heart of his case is the claim that persuasion *equals* force, that under the spell of the *logos* one loses the will to resist the capable speaker. This sort of power goes far beyond what we think of as normal rhetorical suasion. What Gorgias is describing here is not the critical, analytical response of a literate audience, but rather what Havelock calls "submission to the paideutic spell," which involved the whole unconscious mind and probably the central nervous system, a total loss of objectivity as the audience gives itself up to identification with the speaker and his goals. Havelock, of course, was discussing the effects of epic and tragic poetry, not of rhetoric. But rhetoric for Gorgias was extremely poetical, as every commentator has noted; Gorgias's style has been so criticized because of its abundant use of every poetic device—antithesis, isocolon, parison, homoeoteleuton—except meter. These devices were not in Gorgias's work for mere show. His style is the result of his discovery of a *techne* by which he could most effectually tap the response of orally conditioned minds and provoke that poetic response through rhetoric.

Charles P. Segal, in what is probably the best essay on Gorgias's rhetoric that we have, recognizes this point. Segal wrote before Havelock's theories were widely known, but he clearly anticipates Havelock's ideas about the power of oral discourse in early Greece. Gorgias's equation of *logoi* and *pharmakein*, says Segal, means that "the force of the *logoi* thus works directly upon the *psyche*; they have an immediate, almost physical impact on it. . . . Gorgias regarded his rhetoric as having more than a superficial effect on the ear, as actually reaching and 'impressing' the *psyche* of the hearer."[21] Segal duly notes and brilliantly discourses on the psychology of Gorgianic rhetoric, but ultimately he reaches no conclusions about whether Gorgias's claims for the power of the logos were *true*. His unwillingness is understandable, for either Gorgias is talking through his hat or some tremendous change in human response has intervened between Gorgias and us. Jacqueline de Romilly has the same problem in her intriguing lectures on *Magic and Rhetoric in Ancient Greece:* she traces the power of rhetorical magic, but she cannot herself quite believe in it.[22]

My belief is that the magic, the references to *epadon* and *goeteia* that de Romilly finds in so many fourth and fifth-century sources, *did* exist, and that it is closely related to the effect of poetry and poetically based rhetorical *techne* on an oral culture. The persuasive powers of an accomplished orator during those transitional years must indeed have seemed magical to the majority of orally conditioned people. The power of poetry, related as it was to the sacred and to cultural continuity, had always been considered magical, but it was Gorgias, Thrasymachus, Antiphon, and others who learned to extend that "witchcraft," those poetic "spells" (*philtron*) into the realm of decision and non-poetic entertainment.

Plato's Struggle with Orally Based Rhetoric

As de Romilly notes, Gorgias's magic is *technical.* "He wants," she says, "to emulate the power of the magician by a scientific analysis of language and its influence. He is the theoretician of the magic spell of words."[23] In the *Helen* and the *Palamedes,* Gorgias explores the ways in which the *logos* "can effect the divinest works." For our purposes here, the important aspects of Gorgias's thought involve his belief in the extremely powerful—magical-seeming—influence that the rhetor's discourse has on the souls of his hearers and the claim that this manipulation of men's souls could be taught as a *techne.* It was on these two grounds that Gorgias encountered Plato, and while Plato clearly fought the Sicilian on the second point, he seems to have had no disagreement at all about the first. For Plato, rhetorical discourse *was* extremely powerful, even magical, and it is this rhetorical magic that Plato opposes as he opposes the poetic magic that spawned it. Against the *epadon* of poetic and rhetoric, which "charmed" and "enslaved" men, Plato opposed the rational, analytical power of dialectic, which was meant to break the spell, interrupt the charm, subvert the magic by questioning everything.

A great deal of worthy scholarship has, of course, been done on the Platonic response to rhetoric, but most of it has tended to concentrate on the content of Plato's writings. Most scholarship has also assumed a continuity in rhetorical practice that I am here deeply questioning.[24] In this section I want to examine a few issues that have been given less attention.

First of all, what sort of power does Plato consider the rhetorical logos to have? We are not here directly concerned with his judgment of the worthiness of that power, merely with its scope. And it is clear that Plato never underestimates the power of rhetoric. His famous definition of rhetoric as "an art which leads the soul by means of words"[25] echoes Gorgias's contention about the effect of the *logos* on the *psyche,* and Socrates admits in the *Menexenus* that the orators "bewitch our souls." "Every time I listen fascinated," says Socrates, "I am exalted and imagine myself to have become at once taller and nobler and more handsome . . . and this majestic feeling remains with me for over three days."[26]

Some idea of Plato's picture of the common response to oratory can be found in Socrates' joking around with Phaedrus when the latter reads him Lysias's speech in the *Phaedrus.* Humorously jabbing at Phaedrus's poor delivery, Socrates says that the reading produced in him a "divine frenzy," and later, when delivering his own oration, Socrates again jokes, "Do not be surprised if I seem to be in a frenzy as my discourse progresses, for I am already almost uttering dithyrambics," and later, "Do you not notice, my friend, that I am already speaking in hexameters [epic verse], not mere dithyrambics? . . . If I continue, what kind of hymn do you suppose I shall raise? I shall surely be possessed by the nymphs to whom you purposely exposed me."[27] What Socrates is jokingly describing here is the rhetorician's gradual approach to more and more powerful, "inspired" poetic techniques. From prose to dithyrambs to hexameter is a clear map of the journey to poetry, to that tapping of the poetic response mechanism that must have seemed magical. Thus, later in the same dialogue, Socrates may sneer at Gorgias and Tisias for elevating probabilities over truth, but he is also forced to agree that their techniques "have a very powerful force, especially in large assemblies."[28]

Plato presents the art of rhetorical witchery as a specialty of the sophists, Socrates' constant opponents in the dialogues. Protagoras, in the dialogue of the same name, was the first sophist, and Plato introduces him as a powerful rhetorical spellbinder with many followers and admirers, Protagoras "enchanting them with his voice like Orpheus, while they follow where his voice sounds, enchanted."[29] Socrates himself falls under Protagoras's influence after the old sophist is given a chance to make a long oration. "For a while" after the speech, says Socrates, "I was still under his spell and kept on looking at him as though he were going to say more, such was my eagerness to hear, but when I perceived that he had really come to a stop, I pulled myself together, as it were, with an effort."[30] This is Socrates speaking, the great rationalist. Throughout the dialogues Socrates admits that he is not immune to the blandishments of poetry and rhet-

oric; even as he condemns them, he is in danger of seduction by them. This danger raises the question: what sort of protective device might be found, what *pharmakon* or antidote could safeguard the mind from the corruptive rhetorical spell? For Socrates and Plato, this was a central question.

Let us not underestimate what they were up against. The spell of rhetoric, like the spell of poetry, was a powerful one, and the state of pleasurable receptive passivity that we have been describing was not only accepted, but eagerly sought after. Alcibiades' description of the common reaction to oratory in which the heart leaps, the tears gush forth, a whole audience shares a communal *ekplexis* and a spiritual tumult,[31] does not describe our response to oratory today. There seems to have been something intensely *pleasurable* in this oral reactivity that we completely miss.[32] A rhetorical performance by such an accomplished speaker as Gorgias was an occasion to be sought after, and Plato constantly refers to the pleasures involved in listening to rhetoric as analogous to the pleasure of eating or of makeup.[33]

This surrender to pleasure, to the hypnotic spell of the *logos* as it drew hearers into a state of non-analytic, compliant communality (and the analogy with hypnosis may be by no means misleading), is what Socrates in the dialogues had to contend with. Along with the natural attraction of others to the rhetorical *philtron*, Socrates also knew his own weakness: he, too, was likely to fall under the spell if a rhetorician was given the room to stretch out a speech, weave the spell. How to react to this, how to fight for the rational, analytical, individualistic thought that Socrates and Plato called philosophy, was the problem. Part of the solution is found, of course, in the contents of the dialogues, in those elements of the *Ion* and the *Republic* and the *Gorgias* and the *Phaedrus* that have been so well discussed by scholars. Just as important to the Socratic/ Platonic case, however, is the *form* of the dialogues.

Socratic Subversion of the Rhetorical Spell

Simply put, Socrates' answer to the danger of the rhetorical spell is to prevent it from being woven. Throughout all of the early dialogues, Socrates struggles hard to control the form that discourse will take. What he constantly tries to do is *subvert rhetorical magic by interrupting it with questions.* The very form of the dialectic method was the younger Plato's direct antidote to the spell of rhetoric as it was his indirect challenge to the power of poetic cultural transmission.[34] As Havelock says, dialectic in its simplest form merely asks a speaker to stop, repeat himself, explain what he meant. It was interruptive, disruptive:

But to say, "What do you mean? Say that again," abruptly disturbed the pleasurable complacency felt in the poetic formula or the image. It meant using different words and these equivalent words would fail to be poetic; they would be prosaic. As the question was asked, and the alternative prosaic formula was attempted, the imaginations of speaker and teacher were offended, and the dream so to speak was disrupted, and some unpleasant effort of calculative reflection

was substituted. In short, the dialectic . . . was a weapon for arousing the consciousness from its dream language and stimulating it to think abstractly.[35]

Havelock here characterizes dialectic as an offensive weapon, but clearly Socrates used it as a defensive tool as well.

This technique of interruptive question-and-answer, used as a subverter of one-way rhetorical address, runs through nearly all of the Socratic dialogues and most of the Platonic corpus; it is especially obvious in the earlier dialogues.[36] A great deal of the struggle in the *Protagoras,* for instance, is between Protagoras's desire to deliver his opinions in long speeches and Socrates' obdurate refusal to allow him to do it. Though Socrates treats Protagoras with respect, he continually works to head him off from speech-making—understandably, given Socrates' report of the hypnotic effect that Protagoras's long speeches have on him. The old sophist, however, is determined not to be robbed of his most potent weapon, and Socrates finally has to get up and threaten to leave if Protagoras won't submit to questions.[37] Protagoras is forced to back down.

The association of rhetoric with gustatory pleasure—with gluttonous entertainment—is found more notably in the *Gorgias,* where Socrates again refuses to hear a noted speaker declaim, though his companions consider Gorgias's oratory a treat, and in which he demands again that no "lengthy speeches" be used by his opponents. Socrates equates rhetoric with flattery in this dialogue because it consists of "giving people what they want . . . it aims at the pleasant and ignores the best," as does cookery.[38] Socrates' method throughout, of course, is to subvert Gorgias's and Polus's wishes to harangue the assembled people and thus control them, and he accomplishes this subversion by questioning the rhetors and forcing them to think abstractly and express prosaically (a process which Polus hates especially; see 475–76). Aware of where the rhetors' strengths lie, Polus tries to turn to the judgment of the (probably disappointed and frustrated) assembly for support, but Socrates slaps down this ploy: "The many I dismiss," he says firmly, acting out his conviction that one man's truth arrived at dialectically is more valuable than the opinions of any number of people swayed by the "dream language" of rhetoric.[39]

Socrates' questioning, his constant interruptions of his associates' desire to build a flow of discourse, must have been very annoying at times. Xenophon, in his "Memoirs of Socrates," tells that when Charicles, one of the Thirty Tyrants, commanded Socrates not to speak to the youth of Athens and met with questioning from him, he snapped, "It is so much your custom to ask questions when you are not ignorant of the matter in hand, that I do not wonder at your doing so now. Let us, however, have done for the present with your trifling interrogatories."[40] Xenophon describes Socrates' method thus: "His custom was to carry back the argument to the very first proposition; and from thence, set out in the search of truth."[41]

What all this evidence suggests is that Socrates and the younger Plato are retailing a method as well as a philosophy. Socrates has many truths to test, but finally what is most important to him is his form of investigating issues. The search for truth through analytical, rational, individualistic dialectical interchange is more central to Socrates' quest than any one doctrine. As he himself says in the *Lesser Hippias*, "I go astray, up and down, and never hold the same opinion" (346c). Presumably this is because the degree to which truth could be approximated in words was unknown. Rather than as the builder or progenitor of a unified, authoritarian, "Platonic" system of "idealistic" philosophy, I think it is more accurate to see Socrates as a radical iconoclast, constantly questioning those about him and trying to "awaken" them from what Havelock calls "the dream-language of the unconscious." This view is supported by Xenophon's testimony that Socrates eventually lost most of his followers because he gave them the impression that they knew nothing real.[42]

Given these facts, it seems likely that Plato's arguments against rhetoric, his charges that it was not an art and that it did not have a basis in the search for truth, were related to his argument against poetry. The danger that he saw from poetry—that it would perpetuate the older, non-rational oral consciousness—was different from the danger presented by rhetoric—that technical manipulation of oral consciousness by men unconcerned with truth could give some too great a power over others—but the younger Plato fought them both, as Socrates had, with the weapon of dialectic. The enemy, for both Socrates and the younger Plato, was the authoritarianism of one-way discourse, whether poetic or rhetorical. The philosophical reaction to such one-way spellbinding could only be to try to destroy the spell by interrupting, disrupting, subverting it with questions.

The Problem of Writing in Plato

The perspective I have been discussing can begin to explain, I think, one aspect of Plato's thought that Havelock seems deliberately to ignore: his open hostility toward writing. If, as Havelock claims, Plato "announced and became the prophet" of the literate revolution, it seems curious that in both the *Phaedrus* and the Seventh Epistle, Plato dismisses writing as unimportant at best, harmful at worst. Does this not undercut Havelock's (and my) position?

I think not, at least not if we try to imagine how writing might have looked to a philosopher whose entire commitment was to the give-and-take of small-group dialectic. To such a thinker, written documents—those closed-system, one-way discourses—could not be much better than poetic recitations or rhetorical harangues. Like recitations and speeches, written documents mean only to expose a passive audience to a product. They are the antithesis of dialectical process, which finds truth only in movement. Plato realized, of course, that written documents do not have the seductive, hypnotic, spell-

binding qualities that live rhapsodes and speakers had, and thus his arguments against writing are tinged more with contempt than with passion—but the arguments are the same: the truth cannot come from any one-way communication, for it is found in a shared process and nowhere else. "You might think that [written words] spoke as if they had intelligence," says Plato, "but if you question them, wishing to know about their sayings, they always say only one and the same thing."[43] Opposed to the dumb assertion of books is "the word which is written with intelligence in the psyche of the learner, which is able to defend itself. . . ."[44]

Plato makes this same complaint again and again about poetry, writing, and rhetoric: they cannot be questioned. Even the great orators and statesmen—Pericles in particular—come up short. Socrates denigrates them in the *Protagoras* as no better than the contemptible written word:

But suppose you put a question to one of them—they are just like books, incapable of either answering you or putting a question of their own. If you question even a small point in what has been said, just as brazen vessels ring a long time after they have been struck and prolong the note unless you put your hand on them, these orators too, on being asked a little question, extend their speech over a full-length course.[45]

All such one-way communications are related, and all are to be repudiated by a seeker of truth.[46]

In sum, Plato's attitude toward written discourse is negative because he saw his struggle very differently from the way we do now. From our perspective, Plato is the revolutionary prophet of a transforming literacy, and it is the orality-literacy division to which we pay most attention. To Plato, however, the revolution was dialectical, not literary; he fought for the process of analytical questioning, not for books. Books and writing were to him, if anything, part of the problem, as was any discourse that would not respond to questioning. In this, Plato was wrong, of course; the number of analytical rationalists made by dialectical conversion from orality—the "leaping spark"—was dwarfed by the numbers of young children being taught to read and write in the novel elementary schools of the late fifth and early fourth centuries B.C. It was this ever-larger number of literate souls and not the few trained thinkers produced by the Academy which transformed Greek culture during the fourth century. Plato may have been the prophet of this revolution, but he was never its strategist.

The Decline of Orally Based Rhetoric

At some point during Plato's life, at least so far as we can tell, the balance between orality and literacy shifted. A growing number of citizens of the polis were being trained in literate skills at an early age, and habits of individualistic thought and philosophical distancing were gnawing away at the old communality. Between 400 and 350 B.C., the Athenian policy ceased being an oral society which was manipulated by rhetors and "subverted" by dialecticians, and began to reorganize itself as a critical, disputatious, analytical community which applied more rational criteria to decisions. By 320 B.C., the execution of Socrates eighty years

earlier seemed inexplicable folly to Athenians; for them, Socrates was no longer a dangerous subverter of Athenian values but Plato's noble mentor as we see him today—through the medium of writing.

The modern technical development of rhetoric, from Aristotle onward, had been a product of this essentially literate post-Socratic culture. Aristotle's students were literate, though their potential audiences may not always have been, and thus his *Rhetoric* is a mixture of clearly modern techniques based on logical analysis and critical rationalism and of older terms of art that must have been more meaningful during the late transitional phase of Athens during which Aristotle wrote. Maxims, enthymemes, examples—the amount of scholarly wrangling over the meaning of these terms should tip us off that there is some essential key missing to our understanding of them. It is no coincidence that all three of these terms (and they are by no means the only unclear terms in the *Rhetoric*) have to do with the rhetor's relation with his audience, with what he can count on his hearers to know, believe, and feel in response to his cues. Aristotle may have been chagrined by "the uneducated" in his audience and by their uncritical responses, but he was too practical not to include rhetorical advice on how such an audience might be approached. The logical, analytical rhetoric he wished to recommend in a pure form (following Plato) simply did not serve every occasion. Cases should, he believed, "be fought on the strength of the facts alone, so that all besides demonstration of fact is superfluous. Nevertheless, as we have said, external matters do count for much, because of the sorry nature of an audience."[47] This is the voice, more common in Aristotle than one might expect, of a disappointed idealist.

Though the *Rhetoric* is a transitional work, it does contain the first clear rhetorical *techne*, explanations of techniques based on analysis, division, abstract thought. Such were rhetorical works to be ever after. There are oral residues in Demosthenes and in the later Isocrates (and it must be remembered that we have nothing of Isocrates except his later works, those written after he was sixty), but after around 350 B.C. rhetoric belonged more and more to the heirs of Lysias the logographer, not to those of Gorgias. With Isocrates' death in 338 B.C., the last man ever to have successfully practiced the old purely oral rhetoric was gone. The deaths of Aristotle and Demosthenes mark the latter edge of what I have been calling the period of transition; after 320 B.C. it seems likely that every educated Greek could read and write from youth. The older oral culture, with its unique modes of consciousness and response, was fast disappearing. Jebb dates the decline of Greek oratory from 320 B.C., and we can only wonder about the possible connections.

As I have tried to show, the close relationship of early rhetoric and poetic, when considered in the light of Havelock's theory of the "literate revolution" against poetic oral consciousness, may mean that we should reconsider our views of the nature of early Attic oratory. It may well be that Pericles and Gorgias were "spellbinders" in a far more literal sense than we had supposed, and Socrates' and Plato's struggle against rhetoric may have been a far more dangerous fight than it had first appeared. Aristotle's *Rhetoric*, which we think of as signalling the beginning of modern rhetorical history, may also signal the downfall of an older rhetoric—darker, more artistic, and far more coercive—that has survived only in fragments. More work needs to be done before we can understand all of the ramifications of the breakdown of oral consciousness and its meaning for rhetorical theory and practice. This essay has meant only to suggest some of the paths of investigation that may prove fruitful.

Notes

All translations, except where noted, have been taken from the editions published by the Loeb Classical Library.

1. This discussion is adapted from Eric A. Havelock, *Preface to Plato* (Cambridge. Harvard University Press, 1963), and from a later collection of Havelock's essays, *The Literate Revolution in Greece and its Cultural Consequences* (Princeton: Princeton University Press, 1982).
2. Havelock, *Preface to Plato*, 43–44.
3. Havelock, *Preface*, 44–45.
4. See Julian Jaynes' intriguing discussion of a possible physiological basis for this phenomenon in *The Origin of Consciousness in the Breakdown of the Bicameral Mind* (Boston: Houghton Mifflin, 1976), 365–70.
5. As George Kennedy points out, the earliest oratory must necessarily have shared many characteristics with the poetry that provided everyone's common cultural "book" (George Kennedy, *The Art of Persuasion in Greece* [Princeton: Princeton University Press, 1963], 5). Hesiod in the *Theogony* proclaims poetry and oratory to be sister-gifts from the Muses, (*Theogony*, trans. Richmond Lattimore [Ann Arbor: University of Michigan Press, 1959], vv. 90–99.) and Gorgias, the earliest orator from whom we have more than fragments, puts the case clearly: "All poetry I ordain and define to be discourse in meter" (*Encomium on Helen*, trans. LaRue Van Hook, *Classical Weekly* 6 [1913]: 9).

6. Walter J. Ong, S.J., *Orality and Literacy: The Technologizing of the Word* (New York: Methuen, 1982), 26. Ong lists a number of characteristics of orally based expression: it is additive rather than subordinative, tending to string out many "and" clauses; it is redundant and "copious," repeating and amplifying its materials; it remains close to the human lifeworld and does not much venture into abstract thought; it is agonistically toned, using struggle as a framework; it is empathetic and participatory rather than objectively distanced (36–56).

7. *Odyssey*, trans. Allen Cook (New York: Norton, 1967) VIII, 169, 73.

8. Jebb remarks on this phenomenon—the seeming inability of the Golden-Age Greeks to resist the blandishments of tyrants—with some chagrin. R. C. Jebb, *The Attic Orators* ([London: Macmillan, 1876], cix.)

9. Because Pericles left no writings, we cannot gather much about the devices he used in speaking (Thucydides' reportage of Pericles' speeches is probably substantially correct in terms of their content, but Thucydides was guided by literate constraints and thus could not report effectively on Pericles' style or methods, which presumably were developed to appeal to orally conditioned mentalities), but all the reports of his success indicate that he was a master at manipulation of the mass mind of his auditors.

10. Thucydides reports a debate on how Athens should deal with the rebellious city of Mitylene conducted in 427 B.C. by Cleon and Diodatus—who was known as a persuasive speaker. Cleon begins his speech with a plaint against the credulity of his audience:

    You estimate the possibility of future enterprises from the eloquence of an orator, but as to accomplished facts, instead of believing your eyes, you believe only what ingenious critics tell you. No men are better dupes. . . . In a word, you are at the mercy of your ears, and sit like spectators attending a performance of sophists, but very unlike counsellors of state (*Thucydides*, trans. Benjamin Jowett [Oxford: Clarendon Press, 1881], III, 38).

    This is the voice of a man who wishes his audience to wake from their orally conditioned trance state but does not see how the awakening can be accomplished except by sneering. Cleon lost the debate, and the inhabitants of Mitylene were spared.

11. Dionysius, *De Isaeo*, 20 (trans. in Jebb).

12. Thucydides, 8.6.

13. From Thucydides' reports, it seems possible that Pericles' style may have been similar to Antiphon's.

14. LaRue Van Hook is Gorgias's only English translator to try to capture the man's style as well as his content, and his version of the *Helen* begins to give us a feel for the Sicilian:

    But if by violence she was defeated and unlawfully she was treated and to her injustice was meted, clearly her violator as a terrifier was importunate, while she, translated and violated, was unfortunate. Therefore, the barbarian who verbally, legally, actually attempted the barbarous attempt, should meet with verbal accusation, legal reprobation, and actual condemnation. For Helen who was violated and from her fatherland separated and from her friends segregated should justly meet with commiseration rather than with defamation. For he was the victor and she was the victim. It is just therefore to sympathize with the latter and anathematize the former (*Helen*, 7).

    We should remember that Van Hook has not been able to capture the full flavor of the Gorgianic style even here.

15. *Attic Orators*, cxxi.

16. *De Isaeo*, 19.

17. *Orator*, 176.

18. *Historical Library*, 12. 53.

19. Aristotle comes close to sneering at Gorgias at times: "Since the poets were thought to have won their fame by their fine language, when their thoughts were not profound, so the language of prose first took on a poetical cast—for example, that of Gorgias. Even now the uneducated mostly think such discourses very fine. But it is not so" (*Rhetoric*, trans. Lane Cooper [New York: Appleton-Century-Crofts, 1931] 1403b). Aristotle is, of course, the first great champion of clarity in style, and throughout Book III of the *Rhetoric* he uses Gorgias as an example of "bad taste in style" for overuse of compound words, archaisms, and overly poetical metaphors.

20. *Encomium on Helen*, trans. George Kennedy, in *The Older Sophists*, ed. Rosamond Kent Sprague (Columbia: University of South Carolina Press, 1972), 8–14.

21. Charles P. Segal, "Gorgias and the Psychology of the Logos," *Harvard Studies in Classical Philology* 66 (1962): 105. See also Bruce E. Gronbeck, "Gorgias on Rhetoric and Poetic: A Rehabilitation," *Southern Speech Communication Journal* 38 (1972): "Persuasion (peitho) is therefore an art, an art of deception, which works through the medium of language to massage the psyche. The psyche, in turn, the seat of emotion (pathos), is almost a physical phenomenon, and certainly in contact with the physical body" (33).

22. Jacqueline de Romilly, *Magic and Rhetoric in Ancient Greece* (Cambridge: Harvard University Press, 1975). After showing how magic, poetry, and rhetoric were all linked and how terms of magic came to be linked first to poetic uses and then at last to rhetoric, de Romilly stops dead. She cannot believe in the magic she has so carefully traced; the best she can offer is a weak admission that there may be "a sort of spell attached to this artful arrangement of words" (20). Because the magic of the *logos* is gone now, de Romilly, rationalist that she is, must deny that it ever existed.

23. de Romilly, *Magic and Rhetoric*, 16.
24. Among the best of the available scholarly essay collections is *Plato's True and Sophistic Rhetoric*, ed. Keith V. Erickson (Amsterdam: Editions Rodopi, 1979).
25. *Phaedrus*, 261a.
26. *Menexenus*, 235a–b.
27. *Phaedrus*, 238–41.
28. *Phaedrus*, 268a.
29. *Protagoras*, 315a–b. Plato's conception of Protagoras must have come to him through Socrates, since Plato was only seven years old when Protagoras died.
30. *Protagoras*, 328d.
31. *Symposium*, 215e.
32. The connection between this pleasurable response to rhetoric and the epideictic genre of discourse needs to be looked at more closely. It may be that epideictic discourse is the vermiform appendix of rhetoric, an atrophy preserved by Aristotle from a time when oral discourse of praise or blame was an entertainment rather than a duty. For an excellent introduction to this genre, see Theodore C. Burgess, "Epideictic Literature," *Chicago Studies in Classical Philology* 3 (1902): 89–254.
33. Indeed, the whole argument of the *Gorgias* is that rhetoric is "ministry to the pleasure of body or soul without regard for the better and the worse . . . bent upon pleasure and the gratification of the spectators" (501–2).
34. In his fascinating essay, "The Cultural Role of Rhetoric," Richard Weaver makes the same case for dialectic as subversive, albeit from a different perspective. Weaver's essay is found in the collection *Language is Sermonic: Richard Weaver on the Nature of Rhetoric*, ed. Richard L. Johanneson, Rennard Strickland, and Ralph T. Eubanks (Baton Rouge: Louisiana State University Press, 1970), 163–70.
35. Havelock, *Preface*, 209.
36. My unprovable opinion is that many of the Platonic dialogues starring Socrates are indeed accurate reflections of Socrates' beliefs and methods, and that they were written by the younger Plato at least partly as a tribute to his dead mentor. The dialogue form evolved by Plato reflects Socrates' central belief that truth could not be pinned down or transmitted through any sort of one-way communication, that it must be attained through dialectical give-and-take. Only in later works, when Socrates is replaced as the main character, does the form of dialectic falter and finally all but disappear; in its place, we hear a droning lecture from a non-Socratic character—the voice, I would argue, of the older Plato himself.
37. *Protagoras*, 336b–c. "I had thought," says Socrates with some scorn, "that to hold a joint discussion and to make a long harangue were two distinct things." Prodicus, Protagoras's sophistic rival, sides with Socrates, saying that if Protagoras submits to dialectic, "we listeners would thus be most comforted, not pleased; for he is comforted who learns something . . . whereas he is pleased who eats something or has some pleasant sensation only in his body."
38. *Gorgias*, 465a.
39. Dialectic as subversion is also on clear display in the two Hippias dialogues, in which Socrates leads the poor sophist Hippias a merry dialectical chase while forbidding him use of his own favorite weapon. "Now if you choose to deliver a long speech," says Socrates in the *Lesser Hippias*, "I tell you now that you would not cure me [of ignorance]—for I could not follow you—but if you are willing to answer me, as you did just now, you will do me a great deal of good." (*Lesser Hippias*, 373a) Craftily, Socrates often pled his own thickheadedness as a reason to let him press questions.
40. "Memoirs of Socrates," trans. Sarah Fielding, in *Whole Works of Xenophon* (London: Jones and Co., 1832), 526.
41. "Memoirs of Socrates," 596. It also seems clear that while Socrates did have tremendous rhetorical power himself—see the *Meno* and the *Symposium*—he considered that its use for any but the highest ends was unworthy. His unwillingness to unlimber a rhetorical defense at his trial probably cost him his life, but he recognized that to have done so would have been a betrayal of all he believed in. To use rhetorical methods of emotional arousal, histrionics, "persuasion and supplication," would have been an admis-

sion of the worth and necessity of these techniques—and this Socrates would not do. His accusers had him caught in a truly exquisite vise. One of the most potent indications of a true "change of mind" in the fourth century B.C. is found in the Athenian crowd's reaction to Socrates' defense: they respond with outcries of anger and dissatisfaction to a speech that seems to us very moving and persuasive. The crowd was angry with him both because he would not recant his subversive rationalism *and because his discourse was not pleasurable to them.* Socrates knows this, of course, and after he is found guilty he makes a quiet admission that his refusal to play the courtroom "game" was deliberate:

Perhaps you think, gentlemen, that I have been convicted through lack of such words as would have moved you to acquit me, if I had thought it right to do and say everything to gain an acquittal. Far from it. And yet it is through a lack that I have been convicted, not however a lack of words, but of impudence and shamelessness, and of willingness to say to you such things as you would have liked best to hear. You would have liked to hear me wailing and lamenting, and doing and saying many things which are, as I maintain, unworthy of me—such things as you are accustomed to hear from others . . . nor do I now repent of having made my defense as I did, but I much prefer to die after such a defense than to live after a defense of the other sort (38–39).

Addressed to a disgruntled crowd that had come out for entertainment and instead gotten abstract instruction, this flat statement could only have made things worse. The jury proceeded to condemn Socrates to the death he seemed to want.

42. "Memoirs," 587.
43. *Phaedrus,* 275d.
44. Written words can really serve us "only as a reminder of what we know," says Plato; they cannot teach us anything new, because real knowledge can only be had in interchange with a teacher. At the heart of knowledge lies a quality that cannot possibly be transmitted in writing, an almost mystical illumination that Plato discusses in his Seventh Epistle: "I certainly have composed no work in regard to it, nor shall I ever do so in future; for there is no way of putting it in words like other studies. Acquaintance with it must come rather after a long period of attendance on instruction in the subject itself and of close companionship, when, suddenly, like a blaze kindled by a leaping spark, it is generated in the soul and at once becomes self-sustaining" (Seventh Epistle, in *Thirteen Epistles,* trans. L. A. Post [Oxford: Clarendon Press, 1925], 341c–d).
45. *Protagoras,* 275d.
46. See *Phaedrus,* 278 for a list of these related activities.
47. *Rhetoric,* 1404b. This is the voice of an Aristotle who wished to create a rhetoric that could live up to Plato's near-impossible *Phaedrus* definition.

Werner Jaeger

The Rhetoric of Isocrates
and Its Cultural Ideal

◊ *An eminent classicist, Jaeger reconstructs for us Isocrates' ideals of education and culture, ideals based on rhetorical training for civic leaders. In contrast to Plato's idealistic approach, Isocrates is very much the realist; his concern is with the immediate needs of the world about him. He is practical, political, and patriotic in his advocacy of pan-Hellenism. Plato, on the other hand, is other-worldly, philosophical, and rationalistic.*

While later admirers elevated Plato's approach to the sublime, in his own day Isocrates was the more influential instructor. And as Jaeger notes, "since the Renaissance, he [Isocrates] has exercised a far greater influence on the methods of humanism than any other Greek or Roman teacher." ◊

Greek literature of the fourth century reflects a widespread struggle to determine the character of true paideia; and within it Isocrates, the chief representative of rhetoric, personifies the classical opposition to Plato and his school. From this point on, the rivalry of philosophy and rhetoric, each claiming to be the better form of culture, runs like a leitmotiv throughout the history of ancient civilization. It is impossible to describe every phase of that rivalry: for one thing, it is rather repetitious, and the leaders of its opposing sides are not always very interesting personalities.

All the more important, therefore, is the conflict between Plato and Isocrates—the first battle in the centuries of war between philosophy and rhetoric. Later, that war was sometimes to degenerate into a mere academic squabble, in which neither side possessed any genuine vital force; but at its beginning the combatant parties represented the truly moving forces and needs of the Greek people. The field on which it was waged lay in the very centre of the political scene. That is what gives it the vivid colouring of a truly historical event, and the large sweep which keeps our in-

From *Paideia: The Ideals of Greek Culture,* Volume 3, by Werner Jaeger, translated by Gilbert Highet. Copyright © 1944, 1971 by Oxford University Press, Inc. Reprinted by permission.

terest in it permanently alive. In retrospect, we realize that in this conflict are symbolized the essential problems of that whole period of Greek history.

Today as of old, Isocrates has, like Plato, his admirers and exponents; and there is no doubt that since the Renaissance he has exercised a far greater influence on the educational methods of humanism than any other Greek or Roman teacher. Historically, it is perfectly correct to describe him (in the phrase used on the title-page of several modern books) as the father of 'humanistic culture'—inasmuch as the sophists cannot really claim that title, and from our own pedagogic methods and ideals a direct line runs back to him, as it does to Quintilian and Plutarch. But that point of view, dictated as it is by modern academic humanism, is vastly different from the attitude of this book—for our task here is to examine the whole development of Greek paideia and to study the complexities and antagonisms inherent in its problems and its meaning. It is important to notice that what is often regarded by contemporary educators as the essence of humanism is mainly a continuation of the rhetorical strain in classical culture; while the history of humanism is a far broader and richer thing than that, for it contains all the manifold survivals of Greek paideia—including the world-wide influence exercised by Greek philosophy and science. From this point of view, it is clear that an understanding of the true Greek paideia at once entails a criticism of modern academic humanism. On the other hand, the position and character of philosophy and science within Greek civilization as a whole cannot be properly estimated until they are seen striving against other types of intellectual activity in order to be accepted as the true form of culture. Ultimately, both the rivals, philosophy and rhetoric, spring from poetry, the oldest Greek paideia; and they cannot be understood without reference to their origin in it. But as the old rivalry for the primacy of culture gradually narrows to a dispute about the relative values of philosophy and rhetoric, it becomes clear enough that the ancient Hellenic partnership between gymnastic training and 'musical' culture has at last sunk to a much lower level.

To one who has just read Plato's *Protagoras* and *Gorgias* it seems obvious that the educational system of the sophists and rhetors was fundamentally an outworn ideal; and, if we compare it with the lofty claims advanced by philosophy—the claim that henceforth *all* education and *all* culture must be based on nothing but the knowledge of the highest values—it really was obsolete. And yet (as we have seen from our first glance over the later centuries of Greek history) the older type of education, the method of the sophists and the rhetoricians, remained unconquerably active and alive beside its rival, and in fact continued to hold a leading place as one of the greatest influences on the spiritual life of Greece. Perhaps the savage scorn with which Plato attacks and persecutes it may be partly explained by the victor's feeling that he is at war with an enemy who is, as long as he remains within his own frontiers, unconquerable. It is difficult for us to understand the violence of his detestation, if we think of his attacks as directed solely against the great sophists of Socrates' generation, considered as embodiments of the type of culture which he loathed: Protagoras, Gorgias, Hippias, Prodicus. When he wrote his dialogues, these men were dead, and, in that rapid century, half forgotten. It needed all Plato's art to call the strong personalities of the famous sophists out of the shadows to life once more. When he made his caricatures of them (caricatures which in their way are quite as immortal as his idealized portrait of Socrates), a new generation had grown up; and he was attacking them, his contemporaries, as well as his predecessors. We need not go so far as to see, in the opponents whom he describes, mere masks for notable men of his own age; and yet, in his presentment of the sophists, there are many contemporary traits. And there is one absolutely certain fact: Plato never argues with dead men, with historical fossils.

Nothing shows how strong and vital sophistry and rhetoric were, at the time when he began his struggle against them, more clearly than the personality of Isocrates, who actually entered on his career after *Protagoras* and *Gorgias* were written. It is particularly interesting that from the very outset he contested the claims of Plato and the Socratic circle, and defended sophistic education against their attacks. This means that he was writing from the firm conviction that such criticisms did not seriously shake his position. He was really a genuine sophist: indeed, it was he who brought the sophistic movement in education to its culminating point. Biographical tradition repre-

sents him as the pupil of Protagoras, of Prodicus, and especially of Gorgias; and archaeologists of the Hellenistic age found proof of the third of these connexions in his tombstone, which bore a figure they identified as Gorgias, pointing to a celestial globe. Another tradition asserted that Isocrates had studied with the great rhetor in Thessaly—doubtless during the last phase of the Peloponnesian war. Plato too, in his *Meno*, mentions that some part of Gorgias' career as a teacher was passed in Thessaly: an interesting proof of the fact that the new culture was penetrating even the frontier lands of Greece. Isocrates' first great book, the *Panegyricus*, which brought him fame almost overnight, closely resembles Gorgias' *Olympicus*; and the fact that he deliberately chose to compete with such a celebrated author in treating the same theme—a call to the Greeks to achieve national unity—is, according to Greek usage, a proof that he considered himself Gorgias' pupil. And the chief evidence for the fact is the dominant position he assigns to rhetoric— that is, to the most concrete, the least purely theoretical, type of sophistic culture. Throughout his life he aimed, like Gorgias, at teaching the art or craft of speaking (logòn technĕ); but he preferred to apply the title 'sophist' only to theorists, whatever their special interests might be. He used it, among others, for Socrates and his pupils, who had done so much to discredit the name. His own ideal he called 'philosophy'. Thus, he completely inverted the meanings given by Plato to the two words. Today, when Plato's definition of 'philosophy' has been universally accepted for centuries, Isocrates' procedure appears to have been a mere whim. But really it was not. In his time, those concepts were still developing, and had not yet finally hardened into their ultimate shapes. It was not Plato, but Isocrates, who followed the general idiom in calling Socrates and his pupils 'sophists' quite as much as Protagoras or Hippias; and in using 'philosophy' to mean intellectual culture in general, which is the sense it has in Thucydides, for example. He could well have said (as Pericles says in Thucydides) that the characteristic mark of the whole Athenian state was its interest in things of the mind, *philosophein*, and he does actually say something of the kind in the *Panegyricus*. Athens, he writes, invented culture (*philosophia*)—and he is obviously thinking of the whole community rather than of the small group of sharp-witted dialecticians gathered round Plato or Socrates. What he was aiming at was universal culture, contrasted with one definite creed or one particular method of attaining knowledge, as preached by the Platonists. Thus, in the opposing claims made by both sides to ownership of the title 'philosophy', and in the widely different meanings given to the word by the opponents, there is symbolized the rivalry of rhetoric and science for leadership in the realm of education and culture.

Isocrates, then, was the post-war representative of the sophistic and rhetorical culture which had flourished in the Periclean period. But he was much more. To think of him as nothing more than that is to ignore the best and most characteristic aspects of his personality. The particular way in which he distributes the emphasis, magnifying the importance of rhetoric and of prac-

tical politics, and pushing mere sophistry and theory into the background, shows his fine perception of the Athenian attitude to the new culture. It had, during his boyhood and youth, achieved an astonishing success in his native city of Athens; but it had also been violently opposed. Although he was far from being the first Athenian to declare himself its pupil and its champion, it was not really naturalized in Athens until he gave it a truly Athenian dress. In Plato the rhetors and sophists who argue with Socrates are always at a disadvantage, simply because they are foreigners, and do not understand the real problems of Athens and the Athenians. They always seem to be outsiders, as they enter the close, compact Athenian society, bringing with them their knowledge, 'imported ready-made', as it were. Of course they all speak the same international language, in which they can be understood by every educated man. But it never has the Athenian overtones. They lack the casual grace and the social ease without which they cannot achieve full success in the Athenian world. Their wide culture and their fabulous technical skill are admiringly welcomed, but in a deeper sense they remain ineffectual—at least for the time. Before it could become effective, the new element had to coalesce with the very special way of life which characterized the incomparable state of Athens; and none but an Athenian could bring about the coalition— an Athenian who, like Isocrates, was fully alive to the nature of his city and of the crisis which then confronted it. It was a full generation after its first appearance in Athens that rhetoric was naturalized there, under the influence of the tremendous events of the war and the post-war years—events which wrought a deep change in the very nature of rhetoric. At the same time it was profoundly affected by the moral reformation initiated by Socrates, and by the great social crises which had shaken the Athenian state throughout Isocrates' youth and early manhood. The new generation, heir to the Periclean system, found tasks of enormous difficulty confronting it. It was rhetoric, and not philosophy in the Platonic sense, that seemed to Isocrates to be the intellectual form which could best express the political and ethical ideas of his age, and make them part of the intellectual equipment of all contemporary Athenians. With this new conception of its purposes, Isocrates' rhetorical teaching emerged as part of the great post-war educational movement of Athens, into which all the efforts of his day to reform and rejuvenate the Athenian state were inevitably destined to flow.

The factors which brought this about were very various. Despite his mastery of language and of style, Isocrates was not a born orator. And yet, by its very nature, the Athenian democracy still held that no man could be an effective political force unless he was a master of oratory. He says himself that physically he had a weak constitution. His voice was not nearly powerful enough to reach large audiences; and he had an invincible fear of making a public appearance. Crowds terrified him. In speaking without embarrassment of this agoraphobia, Isocrates was not merely offering an excuse for his complete abstention from all political activity; besides that, he felt that his

strange condition was a very personal feature of his character, rooted far in its depths. As with Socrates, his refusal to enter politics was not a sign of lack of interest, but the result of a profound intellectual and spiritual conflict—a conflict which both hampered his activity and at the same time enlarged his understanding of the part he must play in the contemporary political crisis. Like the Platonic Socrates, he was convinced that he must initiate the much-needed reformation in some other way than by entering an active career as an orator in the assemblies and the law courts. Thus, he felt that the personal disabilities which made him unfit for normal political life summoned him to a higher vocation. His weakness was his destiny. But whereas Socrates, with his incessant questioning and examining, became an explorer in the sphere of morality, and found himself at last standing before the closed gates of a new world of knowledge, the more practical Isocrates, although for the time being he was deeply impressed by the personality of his great contemporary, and constantly strove to rival the lofty standard he set, felt nevertheless that his special gifts and his natural dislike for the mob predestined him to become within a small circle the teacher of a new type of political action.

Even the age in which he lived seemed to make this course inevitable. In the calm and concentration of his retirement, he wished to educate statesmen who could give new direction to the efforts of the misguided masses and to the politics of the Greek states, which had long been revolving hopelessly in a closed circle. He set out to inspire every pupil with a passion for the new aims which occupied his own mind. There was within him a political visionary whose thought moved in the same direction as that of the practical statesmen, and was led like them by such aspirations as Power, Glory, Prosperity, Progress. Gradually his experience led him to modify his aims; but from the very beginning he held that they could not be fulfilled by the outworn methods of the Periclean age—competitive diplomacy and exhausting wars between the separate Greek city-states. In that his thought is wholly a product of the weakness of Athens after the Peloponnesian war. Dreamer that he was, in his visions of the future he overleapt that weakness. He believed that Athens could play a leading part in Greek affairs only in peaceful agreement with Sparta and the other Greek states, with entire equality between victors and vanquished; for then the intellectual superiority of Athens to her coarser rivals would assure that she acquired the balance of power. Only such establishment of equality among the Greek states and their devotion to one great national purpose could arrest the dissolution of Greece, and therewith the total annihilation of the small separate states—which hitherto had striven only to destroy one another, although none of them had ever acquired a real superiority over all the rest, with the supreme power which would impose a lasting peace on the entire nation. To save Greece, a common national purpose must be found. And, after the bitter experiences of the Peloponnesian war, Isocrates considered that the essential duty of true statesmanship was to find it. True, there was an urgent preliminary: the political life of the Greek state

had to be purged of its deep corruption, and of the cause of that corruption—the poisonous mutual hatreds of the separate states and parties. It was exactly that selfish hatred of each for his neighbour which, according to Thucydides' tragic description, had during the Peloponnesian war served as a justification for every kind of monstrous crime, and had destroyed the foundations of all established moral codes. But Isocrates did not, like the Platonic Socrates, believe that the sorely needed reformation could be achieved by the creation of a new moral world, a state as it were within each man's soul. He held that the *nation*, the idea of Greece, was the point round which the new elements in the spiritual renaissance were to crystallize. Plato had accused rhetoric of being able only to teach men how to convince an audience, without pointing out any ideal to be pursued: and therefore of being only a practical means to provide intellectual instruments by which to achieve immoral ends. That weakness in the pretensions of rhetoric was undeniable; and, at a time when the conscience of the best of the Greeks was constantly becoming more sensitive, it was a real danger for the art. In the adoption of the Panhellenic ideal, Isocrates saw the way to solve this problem also. The essential was to find a mean, as it were, between the moral indifference which had previously characterized rhetorical education, and the Platonic resolution of all politics into morality, which from a practical point of view was certain to lead away from all politics. The new rhetoric had to find an ideal which could be ethically interpreted and which at the same time could be translated into practical political action. This ideal was a new moral code for Greece. It gave rhetoric an inexhaustible theme; in it the ultimate topic of all higher eloquence seemed to have been discovered once and for all. In an age when the old beliefs were losing their binding force and the long-established structure of the city-state was breaking up (the structure in which, till then, the individual had felt his own moral foundations securely embodied), the new dream of national achievement appeared to be a mighty inspiration. It gave life a new meaning.

In that critical time, therefore, Isocrates was, by his own choice of rhetoric as a career, driven to formulate the new ideals which we have described. It is entirely probable that he had been directly impelled towards them by Gorgias, whose *Olympicus* set forth the theme that was to be the centre of Isocrates' life-work. That happens often enough: in his last years a great master formulates an ideal, inspires his pupil with admiration for it, and through it shapes and directs his pupil's entire career. If Isocrates wanted to become a politician without being an orator, if he wished to assert himself as an educator and a rhetorical teacher against the competition of Socratic philosophy and of the earlier type of rhetoric, and to make head against their criticisms, he had found the only possible method of doing so in his concentration on the new ideal. That explains the doggedness with which he followed it to the end. His weaknesses make it easy enough to criticize him; but it is hard to find a man who fulfilled his self-imposed task more completely than Isocrates, and who was better suited to his own conception of his mission. That conception gave rhetoric the realistic content which it had long been accused of lacking. Through it the teacher of rhetoric at last achieved the dignity which put him on a level with the philosopher and made him independent of machine politicians— which actually gave him a higher rank than they possessed, inasmuch as he represented a higher interest than that of any separate state. The defects in Isocrates' own nature—not only his physical weakness, but the faults in his intellect and his character—and even the defects of rhetoric itself were, through his programme, almost converted into virtues; or so it seemed. The rhetor, the political pamphleteer and ideologist, has never since found himself in such a favourable situation or commanded such a widespread influence throughout an entire nation; and if his influence lacked something in richness, power, and genius, Isocrates partially compensated for that by an exceptionally long life of determined industry. Of course his determination does not affect the quality of his work; but still it was a vital element in the success of his mission, which, like that of the teacher, depended on his relation to living men.

For centuries past, historians have seen in Isocrates nothing more than a moralist, and have conceived him too exclusively as a writer and publicist, too little as a teacher. They did not fully realize that all his published writings, like those of Plato and Aristotle, were ancillary to the educational programme of his school. But the modern view of his career now does full justice to the political content of his books, and understands all their significance in the history of the fourth century. They were of course intended to produce an effect even outside the circle of his own pupils, and through them he often influenced men who had never heard him teach. But at the same time his political speeches were models of the new type of eloquence which he taught in his school. Later, in the *Antidosis,* he himself exemplified to a wider public the special character of his teaching, in a selection of passages taken from his most celebrated speeches. These speeches were intended to be models not only of content but of form, for in his teaching the two elements were inseparable. Whenever we try to re-create from the orations—which are our only evidence—the real character of the culture which he taught, we must always remember that dual purpose. Fortunately for us, he often expressed his views of his art and of his educational ideals; he often seized an opportunity to break off the thread of his argument, and to explain what he was saying, how he was saying it, and why. Indeed, at the beginning of his career he published several programme-works which clearly defined his position with reference to the other educational authorities of his time. We must start with them, if we are to comprehend the full extent of his activity, the true character of his paideia.

He had been a 'speech-writer', which in many respects corresponded to the profession of a barrister today; but we know nothing of the time when he abandoned that vocation for that of a teacher of rhetoric, or the reasons which led him to do so. Like Lysias, Isaeus, and Demosthenes, he had taken it up in order to make money—for his father's property had been largely de-

stroyed by the war. At a later time he was reluctant to mention that period of his career, although (as Aristotle humorously pointed out) volumes and volumes of the legal speeches he had written lay in the bookshops. Only a few of them survive: his pupils, who had charge of editing his works after his death, had no more interest in preserving them than the master himself. We can trace them no later than 390 or so. Therefore, the foundation of Isocrates' school roughly coincided with that of Plato's. In his introductory speech *Against the sophists*, it is clear that he has Plato's 'prospectuses', *Gorgias* and *Protagoras,* before him, and is deliberately trying to set up his own ideal of paideia in contrast to theirs. That takes us back to the same period. The incomparable value of that speech for us lies in the vividness with which it re-creates, blow upon blow, the first battle of the generation-long cultural war between the two great schools of education. And it is no less interesting for us to trace in it the immediate impression which Plato made on many of his contemporaries at his first appearance. Accustomed as we are to estimate his importance by the influence of his philosophy on more than twenty centuries of human history, we naturally imagine that he exercised the same powerful influence on the men of his own time. For that view Isocrates is a useful corrective.

He begins by saying that the representatives of paideia have a bad reputation, and he traces it to the excessive hopes which their self-advertisement excites among the public. Thereby he steps forth to oppose the exaggerated estimates of the power of education that were customary in his day. And, as a matter of fact, there must have been something very bizarre in the revolutionary change from Socrates' loudly expressed doubts whether such a thing as education really existed, to the passionate educational conviction of Plato's earlier dialogues. Here as elsewhere, Isocrates represents the happy mean. He himself, of course, wants to be a teacher too; but he 'very well understands' the laymen who would rather do nothing about education at all than believe the enormous promises of professing philosophers. How is it possible, he asks, to put any trust in their yearning for truth, when they themselves arouse so many false hopes? Isocrates names no names, but every word of his polemic is aimed straight at the Socratics, whom here and elsewhere he contemptuously calls 'disputers.' In *Protagoras* and *Gorgias* Plato had presented dialectic as an art far superior to the long-winded orations of rhetoricians. His opponent makes short work of dialectic: he couples it with eristic—namely, argument for argument's sake. True philosophy always endeavoured to keep itself free from eristic, although the methods of Plato's Socrates often seem to have much in common with it; and in fact there is a good deal of it in the earlier dialogues like *Protagoras* and *Gorgias*. No wonder then that Isocrates does not see dialectic in the same favourable light as the Socratics, who thought it was a perfect panacea for all spiritual ills. The infallible knowledge of values (*phonēsis*) which they promise as the result of their teaching must appear to ordinary reasonable people to be something too great for mankind to attain. Homer,

who knew so well the frontiers that separate men from gods, claims that only the gods have such unerring insight, and he is right. What mortal man has the audacity to promise to give his disciples infallible knowledge (*epistēmē*) of everything they ought to do or leave undone, and to lead them through that knowledge to supreme happiness (*eudaimonia*)?

In this criticism Isocrates has collected in a small space all the features which make Platonism repulsive to ordinary common sense: the peculiar technique of controversy by question-and-answer, the almost mythical importance which it attributes to phronésis (or knowledge of true values) as a special organ of reason, the apparently exaggerated intellectualism which holds knowledge to be the cure for everything, and the quasi-religious enthusiasm with which 'blessedness' is foretold to the philosopher. Obviously Isocrates is aiming some of his sharpest shafts at the terminological peculiarities of the new philosophical method: he tracks them down with the subtle instinct of the stylist for everything which seems odd or ludicrous to the average educated man; and by contrasting the Universal Virtue (*pasa aretē*) which is the putative aim of the Socratic knowledge of that which is 'good in itself', with the trifling fees for which the philosophers sell their wisdom, he really makes the man in the street doubt whether what the young student learns from the philosopher is worth very much more than he pays for it.

He adds that the philosophers themselves cannot believe very strongly in the perfect virtue which they say they wish to release in the souls of their pupils, because the regulations of their school betray a far-reaching distrust of its members. They demand that the fees be paid into an Athenian bank in advance, before the pupil can be admitted. They are justified, no doubt, in looking out for their own interests; but how can their attitude be reconciled with their claim to educate men to attain justice and self-mastery? This argument seems to us to be pitched rather too low; but it is not without wit. In *Gorgias* Plato had argued with just the same malice against the rhetors, who complain about the misuse their pupils make of the art of oratory, without seeing that they are accusing themselves—for if it were true that rhetoric improved its students, it would be impossible for those who had really learnt it to misuse it as they do. Actually, the amoral character of rhetoric was the principal charge against it. In several different contexts, Isocrates supports the view represented by Gorgias in Plato's dialogue: the view that the teacher imparts to his pupil the art of rhetoric in order that he may use it rightly, and is not to blame if the pupil misuses it. That is, he does not accept Plato's criticism, and maintains that Gorgias is wholly in the right. But he goes beyond that, and attacks the philosophers for distrusting their own pupils. That makes it probable that when he was writing the speech *Against the sophists* as an inaugural address, he knew Plato's *Gorgias* and deliberately set out to answer it.

Plato's dialogue must have seemed particularly offensive to him as a pupil of Gorgias, and he must have felt himself arraigned in the person of his master: for, as we have shown, it was

not only Gorgias himself but rhetoric in all its branches that Plato had impugned. All the typical doctrines of the 'eristics' which Isocrates ridicules in his inaugural speech *Against the sophists* had already been clearly enunciated in *Gorgias,* where they were analyzed with special reference to their significance for the new Platonic system of paideia. (*Paideia* II, 126f.) Plato and the Socratics are among the foremost of the opponents whom Isocrates attacks, and since he attacks them with special violence and completeness, it is clear that he fully understands the danger that threatens his ideal from their teaching. His invective is entirely realistic. He never makes it a theoretical refutation of his opponents' position, for he knows that if he did he would lose his case. The terrain he chooses is that of ordinary common sense. He appeals to the instincts of the man in the street—who, without comprehending the philosophers' technical secrets, sees that those who would lead their followers to wisdom and happiness have nothing themselves and get nothing from their students. Their poverty did not harmonize with the traditional Greek concept of *eudaimonia,* perfect happiness, and other sophists—Antiphon, for instance—had already derided Socrates for exalting it. The man in the street sees that those who expose the contradictions in people's speeches do not notice the contradictions in their own acts; and that, although they profess to teach their pupils how to make the right decision on every problem of the future, they cannot say anything at all or give any correct advice about the present. And when he further observes that the mob, whose conduct is based on nothing more than Opinion (*doxa*), find it easier to agree with one another and to hit the right course of action than those who pretend to be in full possession of Knowledge (*epistēmē*), he is bound to end by despising the study of philosophy—concluding it to be empty chatter, mere hair-splitting, and certainly not 'the care of the *soul*' (*psychēs epimeleia*).

This last point above all makes it certain that Isocrates is aiming his attacks at Plato and at the rest of the Socratics—Antisthenes in particular. He has deliberately—and in a way justifiably—mixed up their features into a composite portrait of 'the pupil of Socrates' which they all claimed to be. Nevertheless he knows very well that the pupils of Socrates are bitterly hostile to one another, and he converts their strife into another argument against professional philosophers—the favourite argument of common sense in every age. It was Antisthenes in particular who imitated his master's poverty and independence; while the abstract and theoretical aspects of Isocrates' portrait are principally drawn from Plato, and the description of philosophy as hair-splitting is obviously pointed at Plato's elaboration of dialectic into the art of logic. That was, as Isocrates rightly saw, a step into the sphere of theory and pure form. So he measures this new art of discovering contradictions—the art which attempts to conquer Opinion by Knowledge—against the old Socratic aim of 'caring for the soul,' and throws doubt on its ability to achieve that aim. Thereby he concludes his criticism precisely at the point where (as history shows) the real problem lies. And so, in the argument which we here witness between Plato and Isocrates, there is unfolded part of the long series of conflicts through which the ideal of culture has been developed—a dialectic process which still retains a deep and permanent value, independently of the small personal details of the dispute.

The second group of opponents attacked by Isocrates are described by him as teachers of politics. They do not, like the philosophers, search for the truth. They simply practise their techné—their craft, in the old sense of the word, whereby it implied no trace of moral responsibility. In *Gorgias*, Plato had asserted that true rhetoric ought, like the craft of the doctor, to entail such moral responsibility. Isocrates could not deny Plato's claim; and the moral factor is especially prominent in his treatment of the third group of his opponents, the teachers of forensic oratory. But he did not assert its validity simply in order to exalt Plato. His criticism of those who teach the craft of making political speeches introduces us to a type of education which was the absolute opposite of philosophy—the art of extempore speechmaking. As typical of the specialist in this subject we must think of Isocrates' own fellow-student in the school of Gorgias, Alcidamas—who like him published several model speeches, but whose forte was improvisation (*autoschediazein*). One of his speeches, which has been preserved, is significantly aimed against rhetors like Isocrates, who can write well enough but are incapable of seizing the critical moment to say the words demanded by the immediate situation. There can be no doubt that the constant practice of this technique was invaluable training for the student who intended to be an active public speaker, even although the actual teaching often degenerated into mere routine instruction, and grossly neglected the higher claims of art. This class of his opponents Isocrates charges with lack of taste: they have, he affirms, no aesthetic sense. In practice, their type of rhetoric turns out to be nothing more than a collection of formal devices which the pupil gets off by heart and can bring into play at any moment. It enlarges neither his intellect nor his experience, but merely teaches him the patterns of speechmaking as abstract forms to be learnt by rote, as the elementary teacher teaches little children the alphabet. This method is a fine example of the contemporary trend towards mechanizing both education and life itself as far as possible. Isocrates seizes the opportunity to distinguish his own artistry from this empty commercialized technique, and to clear himself from the charge which he might well have incurred through his distaste for the subtleties of philosophical education—the charge of being narrow-mindedly practical. What he is looking for is the middle way between high-flown theory and vulgar penny-chasing technical adroitness; and he finds it in artistically disciplined Form. In this he introduces a third principle. Here again we find that he explains himself and his ideal by contrast with another point of view. But by thus waging war on two fronts, he shows that his conflict with philosophical education, important as it is, expresses only half of his own ideal. He is just as far removed in the other direction from rhetoric in the accepted sense. For, in the sphere of rhetoric as well as in that of philosophy, Isocrates' paideia was something perfectly new.

More than any other sphere of life, the art of oratory resists the effort of systematic reason to reduce all individual facts to a number of established *schemata*, basic forms. In the realm of logic Plato calls these basic forms the Ideas. As we have seen, he took this three-dimensional mode of describing them from contemporary medical science, and applied it to the analysis of Being. In rhetoric we can see the same process in operation at the same time, though we cannot definitely say that it was directly influenced by Plato's use of the term *idea*. Medicine and rhetoric were by their very nature the spheres in which this conception of basic forms or Ideas could be developed—for medicine reduces a number of apparently different physiological events to a few fundamental types; and rhetoric likewise simplifies what seem to be separate and distinct political or legal situations. The essence of both skills is to analyse the individual case into its general aspects, so as to make it easier to treat in practice. The comparison of these general patterns to the letters of the alphabet (*stoicheia*)—which we find in Isocrates here, and later in Plato— was obvious enough. The act of reading is just the same as that of political or forensic or medical diagnosis: a large number of variously assembled shapes are reduced to a limited number of basic 'elements', and thus the meaning of each of the apparently manifold shapes is recognized. In science too, the 'elements' which make up physical nature were first called by that name in the same period, and the same analogy, drawn from language and the letters of the alphabet, lies behind it. Isocrates of course does not by any means reject the doctrine of a rhetorical system of Ideas. In fact, his writings show that he largely adopted that doctrine, and that he took as the foundation of his own teaching the mastery of the basic forms of oratory. But oratory which knew no more than these forms would be as sounding brass and a tinkling cymbal. The letters of the alphabet, immovable and unchangeable, are the most complete contrast to the fluid and manifold situations of human life, whose full and rich complexity can be brought under no rigid rule. Perfect eloquence must be the individual expression of a single critical moment, a *kairos*, and its highest law is that it should be wholly appropriate. Only by observing these two rules can it succeed in being new and original.

In a word, oratory is imaginative literary creation. Though it dare not dispense with technical skill, it must not stop short at that. Just as the sophists had believed themselves to be the true successors of the poets, whose special art they had transferred into prose, so Isocrates too feels that he is continuing the poets' work, and taking over the function which until a short time before him they had fulfilled in the life of his nation. His comparison between rhetoric and poetry is far more than a passing epigram. Throughout his speeches the influence of this point of view can be traced. The panegyric on a great man is adapted from the hymn, while the hortative speech follows the model of the protreptic elegy and the didactic epic. And, in these types, Isocrates copies even the order of his ideas from the well-established traditional order which was a rule in each of the corresponding poetic genera. More than

that: the position and prestige of the orator are determined by this parallel with the poet. The new vocation must support itself on an old and firmly-established one, and take its standards therefrom. The less Isocrates hopes or wishes to succeed as a practical statesman, the more he needs the prestige of poetry to set off his spiritual aims; and even in the educational spirit by which his rhetoric is inspired, he is deliberately emulating what the Greeks conceived to be the educational function of the poets of old. Later, indeed, he compares his work with that of the sculptor (as Pindar had done) and proudly puts himself on a level with Phidias; but that is more to illustrate the fact that there are still some who, despite the loftiness of his art, consider the rhetor's profession to be something second-rate. The classical Greeks had always tended to depreciate the sculptor's trade a little, as resembling the work of a common artisan—and that although the word *sculptor* could be applied to every worker in stone, from the ordinary mason to the creator of the Parthenon. But later, as the prestige of the plastic arts and their great masters gradually rose in the post-classical centuries, the comparison of oratory to sculpture and painting seems to become commoner. However, the dynastic succession of rhetoric to poetry remained the true image of the spiritual process in which rhetoric arose as a new cultural force: all late Greek poetry is simply the offspring of rhetoric.

Naturally, Iscorates' view of the educational value of rhetoric is defined by this conception of its true character. Being an act of creation, oratory in its highest ranges cannot possibly be taught like a school subject. And yet he holds that it can be employed to educate young men: because of his own peculiar view of the relation between the three factors which, according to the pedagogic theories of the sophists, are the foundation of all education. They are: (1) talent, (2) study, and (3) practice. The current enthusiasm for education and culture had helped to create and disseminate exaggerated views of their powers; but that enthusiasm had been succeeded by a certain disillusionment—due partly to Socrates' far-reaching criticisms of the limitations and pretensions of education, and partly to the discovery that many a young man whom the sophists had educated was no better than those who had never enjoyed such advantages. Isocrates explains the exact value of education with great care. He asserts that natural talent is the principal factor, and admits that great gifts, untrained, often achieve more than mere training without ability—if indeed it is possible to speak of training when there is nothing there to train. The element second in importance is experience, practice. It would appear that until then professional rhetors had theoretically recognized the trinity—talent, study, practice—but had in their own courses pushed study and training into the foreground. Isocrates modestly relegates training (*paideusis*) to the third rank. It can, he says, achieve much if it is helped by talent and experience. It makes speakers more clearly conscious of their art, stimulates their inventive faculty, and saves them much vague and unsuccessful searching. Even a less gifted pupil can be improved and intellectually developed by training, al-

though he can never be made into a distinguished orator or writer.

Rhetorical training, says Isocrates, can teach insight into the 'ideas' or basic patterns out of which every speech is built. He appears to mean that this phase of it, hitherto the only one which had been cultivated, was capable of far profounder development; and we would gladly hear more of his new doctrine of ideas, to be able to compare it with that of the older rhetors. But the real difficulty of the subject does not lie in that aspect of it—all the less so because it is taught so thoroughly. It lies in the right choice, commixture, and placing of the 'ideas' on each subject, in the selection of the correct moment, in the good taste and appropriateness with which the speech is decorated with enthymemes, and in the rhythmic and musical disposition of the words. To do all that correctly needs a powerful and sensitive mind. This, the highest stage of training, assumes in the pupil full knowledge of the 'ideas' of speech and skill in their employment; from the teacher it requires the ability to expound everything which can be rationally taught, and beyond that—i.e. in everything which cannot be taught—it demands that he should make himself a model for his pupils: so that those who can form themselves by imitating him may at once achieve a richer and more graceful style than any others.

Plato, in *The Republic*, later declared that the highest culture could be attained only if certain qualities which are rarely found together were to coincide. Similarly, Isocrates asserts that it is impossible for the teacher to succeed unless all the factors which we have mentioned are brought into play at once. Here the general Greek idea, that education is the process by which the whole man is shaped, is enunciated independently of Plato, and variously expounded in such imagery as 'model' or 'pattern' (*paradeigma*), 'stamp' (*ektypoun*) 'imitate' (*mimeisthai*). The real problem is how this process of 'shaping' can be converted from a beautiful image into a practical reality—that is, what is to be the *method* of forming the human character, and ultimately what is the *nature* of the human intellect. Plato seeks to form the soul through knowledge of the Ideas as absolute norms of the Good, the Just, the Beautiful, etc., and thus eventually to develop it into an intelligible cosmos which contains all being within itself. No such universe of knowledge exists for Isocrates. For him, rhetorical training is worked out simply by Opinion, not by Knowledge. But he frequently claims that the intellect possesses an aesthetic and practical faculty which, without claiming absolute knowledge, can still choose the right means and the right end. His whole conception of culture is based on that aesthetic power. Plato's dialectic guides the young student step by step towards the Ideas; but that still leaves it to him to employ them in his life and conduct, and the way in which he employs them cannot be rationally explained. In the same way Isocrates can describe only the elements and the separate stages of the educational act. The formative process itself remains a mystery. Nature can neither be wholly banished from it, nor be put wholly in control of it. Therefore, everything in education depends on the proper cooperation of nature and art. If we once decide that Isocrates' incompleteness (as Plato would call it) and

his reliance on mere Opinion (which Plato called the vital force of all rhetoric) were imposed on him by his subject, then we must conclude that his resolute self-limitation, and his deliberate renunciation of everything 'higher,' everything which he felt to be obscure and doubtful, were a sort of constitutional weakness converted by him into a strength. This, in the sphere of culture, is the same thing that assured Isocrates' own personal success: he has made a virtue of necessity. He recognizes the empirical character of rhetoric; and, whether or not it is right to call it a true techné or art—Plato in Gorgias had claimed that it was not—Isocrates holds fast to its empiricism. Therein he clings to the principle of imitation established by his predecessors—the principle which in the future was to play such an enormous part in rhetoric and (as literature came more and more under the influence of rhetoric) in every branch of literature. Here we know more of his method of teaching than we do of his attitude to the rhetorical doctrine of ideas; for all his great speeches were meant to be models in which his pupils could study the precepts of his art.

He spends little time on the third group of educators, the writers of forensic speeches. Obviously he considers them his weakest opponents—although Plato attacked them a good many years later in *Phaedrus*, and therefore thought them fairly important even then. It is clear that Isocrates believes their rivalry far less dangerous than that of the new philosophical culture, in which he recognizes the real threat to his own ideals. The forensic speechmakers were out to make money, and their product was meant for practical use. We know their technique from the sample speeches published by Antiphon, Lysias, Isaeus, Demosthenes, and even Isocrates himself at the outset of his career. This type of literature is one of the most remarkable plants in the garden of Greek literature—and a native Attic vegetable at that. The Athenian mania for litigation, so delightfully satirized by the comedians, is the obverse of the firm legality of the Athenian state: of that foundation in Law of which its citizens were so proud. It produced a universal interest in *agones*—lawsuits and prosecutions. The model speeches written by the logographers served both as advertisements for their authors, as patterns for their pupils to copy, and as interesting reading-matter for the public. Here too Isocrates manifests the more sensitive taste of the younger generation. Ironically he recommends that the logographers should leave it to the enemies of rhetoric (already numerous enough) to display this, its least attractive side, instead of proudly dragging it out into the glare of publicity; and he adds that anything that can be learnt in rhetoric is just as valuable in other spheres as in legal disputes. We need not question the sincerity of this attitude. It explains quite clearly why Isocrates abandoned the profession. He felt that the speechwriter was morally far below the philosopher. Clearly he is thinking not only of the men who write speeches for use in law courts, but of all kinds of rhetors, since he includes them all under the name of 'teachers of political oratory'. Doubtless the subjects investigated in philosophical education are not worth the trouble, and the arguers who 'wallow' in debates would get into serious danger if they applied their conclusions to real facts (here Isocrates is quoting Callicles in Plato's *Gorgias*, and taking his side too), but at least the fact that the rhetors talk about a better subject, politics, must not keep us from recognizing that in practice they generally misuse it and become interfering and ambitious busybodies. Thus Isocrates follows Plato in his criticism of the political orators, though he does not accept his positive conclusions. He does not believe that virtue can be taught, any more than the aesthetic sense. Plato refuses to grant the name of *techné* to any kind of education which does not teach virtue; and Isocrates frankly thinks it impossible to create such education. Nevertheless, he is inclined to concede that education of a political tendency might have some ethical influence if it were practised in the manner he recommends, not in the amoral way represented by earlier rhetoricians.

The striking thing about Isocrates' conception of Plato's paideia, as set forth in his speech *Against the sophists*, is that he entirely overlooks the political content of his opponent's theories. From Plato's early dialogues he must have got the same impression as they made, until a short time ago, on most modern readers—that their author's sole concern was moral reformation, an ideal which is somehow strangely connected with dialectic reasoning. The superiority of rhetoric, as Isocrates conceives it, is that it is entirely political culture. All that it has to do to attain spiritual leadership in the state is to find a new approach to life and its problems. The older type of rhetoric missed many important opportunities because it was content to serve day-to-day politics as an instrument, instead of rising above it. From this we can see that Isocrates believed he could inspire the political life of his nation with a higher moral creed. Unfortunately only a fragment of the speech on the sophists now survives, without the principal section, which doubtless explained his new ideal. Isocrates must have changed his attitude to Plato's cultural plans as soon as he understood the political aspect of his philosophy. Actually, he had already been warned by Plato's *Gorgias* that Socrates was the only real statesman of his age, because he alone tried to make his fellow-citizens better. That might well be interpreted as pure paradox—especially by Isocrates, who held that the moving impulse of all contemporary writers was to struggle for originality at all costs, hunting out hitherto unheard-of paradoxes on every subject, and who feared (with justice) that he could not rival Plato and the other philosophers in that exercise. But later, in his *Philip*, he reviews Plato's life-work not long after his death, and treats him as a very great political theorist, whose theories could unfortunately never be put into practice. When did he first change his view of Plato's character and philosophy?

We can find the answer in his *Helen*. Helen is a model encomium, addressed to a mythical personage, and paradoxically praising her although she was generally reviled. The exact date of its composition is unknown, but it was obviously written soon after the speech *Against the sophists*—namely, while Isocrates' school was yet new. A lower limit for its date is fixed by the singular

form which Isocrates, towards the end, gives to the praise of his heroine: it was she, he says, who first brought about national unity among the Greeks, in the war against Troy that resulted from her abduction. Thus he makes Helen a mythical symbol of the political aspirations which he expressed more fully soon after that, in the *Panegyricus* (380)—of the great struggle to unite the Greek states in a national crusade against the barbarians. In this first decade Isocrates is still moving in the paths beaten out by Gorgias. The relation between his *Panegyricus* and Gorgias' *Olympicus* is the same as that between his *Helen* and Gorgias' *Defence of Helen*. The little speech is (as he says) a first-fruits offering suitable for a man of paideia. It is interesting because of its renewed polemics against the Socratic school and its cultural ideal. Here again, as in the speech on the sophists, he blends the features of Plato and Antisthenes in a composite portrait. His attack is aimed, not at one particular person, but at the entire tendency of the new movement. Isocrates says he cannot interpret their utterances as anything more than attempts at paradoxical wit, when some of them (Antisthenes) teach that it is impossible to make a false statement, or to make two contradictory assertions about the same thing, while others (Plato) try to prove that courage, wisdom and justice are one and the same, and that none of these qualities is implanted in us by nature, but that they are all attained by one and the same knowledge ($\varepsilon\pi\iota\sigma\tau\eta\mu\eta$). Here Isocrates really does distinguish the Socratics from those who are mere arguers, who teach nobody, but only try to make difficulties for others. He objects that all of them try to refute others (*elegcheir*) or (*elenchein*), although they themselves have long since been refuted, and that their paradoxes are thrown into the shade by those of their predecessors the sophists: for instance, by Gorgias' statement that no existing thing exists, or Zeno's, that the same thing is both possible and impossible, or Melissus', that the apparently infinite multitude of things is really one.

With this pettifogging, Isocrates contrasts the simple effort to find out what is true: which he conceives to be the effort to get experience of reality and to educate oneself for political action. Philosophers are always chasing the phantom of pure knowledge, but no one can use their results. Is it not better to spend one's time on the things which people really need, even if we cannot achieve exact knowledge, but only approximate opinions about them? He reduces his own attitude towards Plato's ideal of scientific accuracy and thoroughness to the formula that the smallest advance in our knowledge of really important things is better than the greatest intellectual mastery of unimportant trifles which are irrelevant to our life. As a good psychologist, he evidently understands how much young men love dialectical disputation—for at their age, they have no interest in serious private or public problems, and the more futile a game, the more they enjoy it. But those who profess to teach them deserve reproach for allowing them to be charmed by it. They incur thereby the same guilt of which they accuse forensic orators—they corrupt the youth. They do not shrink from preaching the absurd doctrine that the life of beggars and exiles, deprived of all political rights and duties, is happier than that of others—namely, of the full citizens who remain peacefully in their native land. (This is clearly an allusion to the ethical individualism and cosmopolitanism of the radical wing in the Socratic school—Antisthenes, Aristippus, and their followers.) He finds the other philosophers to be even more ridiculous: those who think that their moral paradoxes really contribute something to the spiritual upbuilding of the state. This can only be a hit at Plato, who held that Socrates' moral evangel was true political science. If we are right in this identification, it was as early as the 'eighties, soon after he wrote his speech *Against the sophists*, that Isocrates changed his views of Plato's cultural ideal, and recognized that it too had political implications. Only he felt that its concentration on individual morality and on dialectical quibbles—which seemed to him the distinguishing tendency of Plato's educational system—was absolutely irreconcilable with the universally useful purpose which it professed to serve.

Thus, as Isocrates and Plato appear to approach nearer and nearer to each other in the practical aim of their cultural theories, Isocrates' disapproval for Plato's abstract 'roundabout way' becomes more and more pronounced. He knows only the direct route. There is in his system none of the inward tension that exists in the mind of Plato between the urgent will to action and the long philosophical preparation for action. True, he stands far enough away from the politics of his day and the activity of contemporary statesmen to understand Plato's objection to them. But, as stand Plato's objection to them. But, as a man who keeps to the middle way, he cannot appreciate the bold ethical claims of the Socratic system, which creates a gulf between the state and the individual. He does not look to Utopia for the improvement of political life. He embodies the rooted hatred of the propertied and cultured bourgeoisie both for the mad eccentricities of mob-rule and for the tyranny of individuals, and he has a strong admiration for respectability. But he has none of Plato's uncompromising passion for reformation, no thought of introducing such a terrific intensity into everyday life. Therefore, he does not realize the enormous educational power which lies in Plato's thought: he judges its value exclusively by its immediate utility for the particular political question which interests him. This is the internal condition of Greece, and the future relations of the Greek states to one another, after the great war. The Peloponnesian war had clearly demonstrated that the existing regime could not be permanent, and that the whole Greek world had to be rebuilt. When he wrote *Helen*, Isocrates was already at work on his great manifesto, the Panegyricus. Its purpose was to show the world that his school was able to state, in a new language, new ideals—not only for the moral life of the individual, but for the entire nation of the Hellenes.

Everett Lee Hunt

Plato and Aristotle on Rhetoric and Rhetoricians

◊ *Following Jaeger's method of explication from the extant writings of early Greek thinkers, Everett Lee Hunt contrasts the views of Plato and Aristotle on rhetoric and rhetoricians.*

While changing his interpretation somewhat over time, Plato's assessment of a rhetoric based on probability is essentially negative. For him, truth alone may serve as a basis for sound decision-making.

Aristotle, his protégé, is more concerned with classifying knowledge, with things as they are rather than things as they ought to be. Consequently, he produces an amoral, scientific analysis of persuasion, one which, Hunt tells us, "raises clearly the problem of the relation of rhetoric to psychology, ethics, politics, jurisprudence, and literary criticism." ◊

I

The art of rhetoric offered to the Athenian of the fifth century B.C. a method of higher education and, beyond that, a way of life. Plato attacked both. He gave rhetoric a conspicuous place in his dialogues because it represented in Athenian life that which he most disliked. His pictures of the rhetoricians are so broadly satirical that at times they become caricatures; but his literary power and philosophical originality have so impressed themselves upon succeeding ages that the sophists and rhetoricians of Athens have become

symbolical of false pretense of knowledge, overweening conceit, fallacious argument, cultivation of style for its own sake, demagoguery, corruption of youth through a skepticism which professed complete indifference to truth, and, in general, a ready substitution of appearance for reality.

We have the more readily accepted Plato's account because these faults have never been absent from civilization. If the sophists and rhetoricians of Plato's dialogues had not existed, it would have been necessary to invent

Everett Lee Hunt, "Plato and Aristotle on Rhetoric and Rhetoricians," reprinted from *Studies in Rhetoric and Public Speaking in Honor of James Albert Winans.* (New York: Century Co., 1925): 19–70. Pages 23–32 dealing with four sophists and Athenian criticism of them has been omitted from this version of Hunt's essay.

129

them. The qualities they typify are so universal that certain collective names for them have become a necessity for thought. Even Grote, the great defender of the historical sophists, when he desires to point out the fallacies of the Platonic Socrates, finds it convenient to accuse Plato of "sophistry." These qualities are not only objectively ever present, but we attribute them readily to any persons or arguments when for any reason our approval has not been won. An argument which we do not accept is sophistical, and the person who presents it a sophist. An appeal to the feelings of men which does not happen to warm our hearts is rhetorical, and its author a rhetorician. It was so in Plato's time, and it was no more safe then than now to take the words "sophistry" and "rhetoric" at their face value.

When we ask, who were the sophists, what did they teach, and what is the connection between sophistry and rhetoric, we have asked questions involving great historical and philosophical dispute. Generations of historians of philosophy, accepting Plato's account, have made the sophists the scapegoats for all intellectual—and, at times, moral—delinquencies. It is to Hegel that the sophists owe their rehabilitation in modern times. G. H. Lewes, five years before Grote published his famous defense of the sophists, characterized them as professors of rhetoric, and pointed out the bias which had caused their unfair treatment at the hands of Plato. Grote's classic treatment of the sophists in his *History of Greece* was termed by Henry Sidgwick "a historical discovery of the highest order." "Before it was written," says Professor Sidgwick, "the facts were all there, but the learned world could not draw the right inference." In two vigorous essays he defends Grote and makes some significant contributions to the controversy. John Stuart Mill, in an extended review of Grote's *Plato*, defends his interpretation in almost all points, and furnishes many additional arguments in defense of the sophists. E. M. Cope, in his essays on the sophistic rhetoric, rejects many of Grote's conclusions. Zeller is not inclined to look upon the sophists with favor. Chaignet, in his history of rhetoric, accepts the conventional contrast between Plato and the sophists. Jowett, Plato's translator, accepts many of Grote's conclusions, but rejects others. Gomperz, in his *Greek Thinkers*, written fifty years after Grote's history was published, says of his own contemporaries among historians of philosophy:

They still begin by handsomely acknowledging the ambiguity of the word "sophist," and the injustice done to the bearers of that name in the fifth century B.C. by the ugly sense in which the term came to be used, and they admit that restitution is due. But the debt is forgotten before it is paid; the debtor reverts to the old familiar usage, and speaks of the sophists once more as if they were really mere intellectual acrobats, unscrupulous tormentors of language, or the authors of pernicious teachings. The spirit may be willing, but the reason is helpless against the force of inveterate habits of thought. Verily the sophists were born under an evil star. Their one short hour of triumphant success was paid for by centuries of obloquy. Two invincible foes were banded against them—the caprice of language, and the genius of a great writer, if not the greatest writer of all times.

The itinerant sophists founded no schools, and most of their works have been lost. The evidence in the case is therefore of the kind which makes endless argument possible. A few conclusions may, however, be stated as generally agreed upon. The term sophist originally had no unfavorable connotation, and was applied to any man who was thought to be learned. Thus the seven sages of Greece, universally honored, were at times called sophists. In the time of Plato, the word carried with it something of reproach, but it was not a definitely understood term. Rival teachers employed it against each other. Thus Isocrates regarded speculative thinkers (Plato among them) as sophists, because he thought their speculations fruitless. He also attacked as sophists other teachers of rhetoric whose instruction he regarded as unintelligent, and whose promises to be their pupils he thought impossible of fulfillment. The general public used the term with almost no discrimination, and Aristophanes seized upon Socrates as the sophist who could be most effectively lampooned.

As to what they taught, it has been established that such terms as a sophistic mind, a sophistic morality, a sophistic skepticism, and others implying a common basis of doctrine are quite without justification. Their common characteristics were that they were professional teachers, that they accepted fees, and that rhetoric was a large element in the teaching of virtually all of them. The general emphasis upon rhetoric does not mean that, as scholars, all the sophists found their intellectual interests centered in rhetoric. But rhetoric was the one subject with which they could be sure to make a living. The conditions which made rhetorical training a universal necessity in Athens have been frequently set forth. The sophist who was a master of rhetoric had a number of possibilities before him. He could win power and repute by the delivery of eulogistic orations at public funerals, or deliberative addresses at times of political crises. He could appear at games, or upon occasions of his own making, with what we sometimes call occasional, or literary, addresses, expounding Homer or other works of Greek literature. He could write speeches for clients who were to appear in court. He was not allowed to appear in person as an advocate unless he could show that he had a direct connection with the case, but the profession of logographer was profitable. Finally, he was more certain of pupils in rhetoric than in any other subject. It is not strange, then, that with a wide range of individual interests, the sophists, with varying emphasis, should unite upon rhetoric as the indispensable part of their stock in trade.

The claim to impart virtue has at times been held to be the distinguishing mark of the sophist, and the attempt has been made to divide the sophists from the rhetoricians upon this basis. This cannot be done, for the two activities of making men virtuous and making them eloquent were inextricably intermingled. Hegel has pointed out what he regards as an essential difference between the sophists and modern professors. The professor makes no pretension to making men good or wise; he only presents to students his organized knowledge, realizing that knowledge comes but wisdom lingers. The sophists, on the other hand, laid claim to some actual effect from their teachings; they made men wise. This was at least in part due to the dominance of rhetoric. Aristotle might lecture upon the theoretical aspects of rhetoric—a procedure which seems to have been productive of little eloquence—but the prime purpose of the teaching of rhetoric was practical. Certain sophists made the payment of their fees dependent upon some proof that they had actually given to a pupil the ability to persuade an audience. With such a background, it is natural that the teaching of ethics as abstract knowledge would seem about as futile as the teaching of an abstract rhetoric. A man who taught ethics taught it practically, with injunctions and exhortations, and he expected practical consequences to follow. But one of the consequences always looked for was that the pupil should become such a person as to be persuasive when speaking in a public assembly. Ethics thus was often absorbed in rhetoric. The failures of many pupils to become either good or persuasive gave rise, then as now, to cynical reflections upon the futility of education, and there were many arguments as to whether virtue or rhetoric could be taught. In these arguments there were two extreme positions. Some inclined to believe that if you teach a man to be virtuous he will naturally be eloquent, and rhetorical instruction is unnecessary. Other sophists believed it quite impossible to teach virtue, but by constant attention to becoming a persuasive speaker virtue would be unconsciously acquired. The controversy over the relation of virtue to eloquence runs through the history of rhetoric, and may

be viewed as a technical question in that field. The attitude of sophists toward the teaching of virtue, then, cannot distinguish the sophists from the rhetoricians, and for the purposes of our study the two terms may be used almost synonymously—the word sophist, perhaps, being somewhat more inclusive.

IV

Turning to Plato, we have already noted that he shared the general dislike of fee-taking; but we should consider also those aspects of his thought which led him to dislike any persons who accepted Athenian life and institutions and participated actively in public affairs. Mill has pointed out:

> Plato, if he returned to life, would be to the full as contemptuous of our statesmen, lawyers, clergy, authors, and all others who lay claim to mental superiority as he ever was of the corresponding classes at Athens.

This would be true because Plato would find that our life bears a much closer resemblance to the Athens he knew, than to his *Republic*. We may cite the *Republic* and the *Laws* as sufficient evidence of Plato's discontent with the sorry scheme of things entire. He was not a reformer who could be contented with a gradual evolution in the direction of his ideals; nor did it disturb him that his Republic was not an earthly city; he was satisfied to believe that its pattern was laid up in the heavens. Scholars are becoming increasingly conscious, however, that his gaze was not exclusively heavenward as he wrote the *Republic*. He knew what he disliked in Athens, and his utopia owes at least as much to his dislikes as to his desires. Had the sophists and rhetoricians been the only objects of his scorn he might not have been driven to writing the *Republic*. But the politics, poetry, art, education, and religion of Athens were all wrong—so wrong that it was easier to paint a utopia than seriously to attempt the reformation of Athens. We may say in the beginning, then, that Plato's condemnation of rhetoric and rhetoricians is merely a small part of his condemnation of all contemporary civilization. We may note in passing, that rhetoric has its uses even for those who attack it; and that Plato's contrast between the rhetorician's world of appearance and the philosopher's world of reality was drawn with consummate rhetorical skill.

The supreme remedy for the ills of civilization, Plato believed, lay in the government of philosopher-kings. But until philosophers were kings, and could govern autocratically by their wisdom, without the necessity for persuading the multitude, they were to remain aloof from public affairs.

> The lords of philosophy have never, from their youth upwards, known their way to the Agora, or the dicastery, or the council, or any other political assembly; they neither see nor hear the laws or votes of the State written or spoken; the eagerness of political societies in the attainment of offices,—clubs, banquets, and revels, and singing maidens, do not even enter into their dreams.

In Plato's ideal realm, there was no place for rhetoric as a political agency. Large questions of policy were to be settled by the philosophers. Administration of routine affairs was to be in the hands of experts. There would be no litigation, for there would be no laws. Laws were as absurd and useless for philosopher-kings as decrees of the public assembly would be for pilots and physicians, whose actions were governed by their own arts. Later in life Plato despaired of finding philosophers, even in utopia, who could be trusted to govern without laws, or of inducing people to have confidence in them, even if they could be found, and his *Laws* is a concession to that feeling. But even in his later utopia there was no freedom of utterance, without which, of course, the development of rhetoric would be an impossibility. With the dogmatism of age upon him, he laid down laws which were to be permanent. The games of children, the restrictions upon foreign travel, the denial of freedom of speech, and the enforcement of ethical and theological dogmas, were all designed to protect the city against changes of any sort. The use of rhetoric in administering and interpreting the laws was also carefully guarded against.

Although rhetoric had no place in the courts or political assemblies of Plato's ideal realms, its scope in another field was to be greatly increased. All the literature and art of the Greeks was to be examined with a single eye to its effect upon the morals of the citizens. Truth and beauty were subordinated to goodness—to goodness as Plato conceived it. Whenever the attempt is made to govern the ideals of a people by censoring art in the interests of a dogmatic morality, all art tends to become rhetorical. To say that rhetoric was banished from the Republic, then, is not quite true. It was driven out the door only to fly in at the window. The unsympathetic interpreter of Plato would say that literature became part of the educator's rhetoric, with Plato as chief educator and chief rhetorician; a better Platonist, however, would hold that literature and education became philosophy, with Plato as chief philosopher.

One source of rhetoric and rhetoricians in any democracy is the continual and restless striving of the people to better their individual conditions. They perpetually seek to become what they are not, and in doing this they strive to bend the wills of others to their own ends. This state of affairs Plato avoided, in his *Republic*, by having a fixed and settled order of society, an order of experts, in which every man did his own work, and no man attempted the work of another. In this way ambitious, self-seeking demagoguery was to be eliminated.

There is no indication in the *Republic*, that even under philosopher-kings, with a scheme of education devised by Plato himself, and with art and literature revised in the interest of morals, the mass of the people were expected to rise to greater heights than a certain efficiency in minding their own routines. It is not particularly strange, then, that Plato had a great contempt for the people of Athens, who lived under a government so little influenced by Platonism. Plato adhered to the philosophic tradition in regarding public opinion as always wrong both because it was public and because it was merely opinion. Plato despised mere opinion almost as much as he did the public. He was never tired of contrasting the knowledge of the philosopher, who had attained real knowledge by dialectical investigation, and by contemplation of Ideas, with that shadow knowledge called opinion. Sometimes, of course, opinion would turn out to be right. And right opinion had a certain value as a guide to action in practical affairs; but even right opinion fell far short of philosophic knowledge. Plato never believed that probability was the guide of life. Education, for him, was a process of keeping the mass of people at their tasks with as few opinions as might be, and of enabling the few whose intelligence would permit, to attain philosophic knowledge. Those who knew were to abandon the pleasures of knowing, at stated intervals, and govern those who did not know. Thus opinion was largely to be eliminated from the State. The education given by the sophists and rhetoricians, on the other hand, was for the purpose of enabling a man to get on in a world of conjecture. Isocrates (whom we have not discussed, because, though he receives passing mention, he is hardly a figure in the Platonic pictures of contemporary rhetoricians) stated as his philosophy of education:

> It is impossible to attain absolute knowledge of what we ought or ought not to do; but the wise man is he who can make a successful guess as a general rule, and philosophers are those who study to attain this practical wisdom.

Akin to this is the educational aim of Protagoras—given us by Plato, but probably quite acceptable to Protagoras:

> If a young man comes to me he will learn prudence in affairs private as well as public, he will learn to order his own house in the best manner, and he will be best able to speak and act in affairs of state.

The education given by the sophists varied with individual teachers, but in general it aimed to enable the pupils to become leaders of men in a democracy.

It was practical in the sense in which all training for public affairs is practical; and it sought to enable the individual to use existing institutions rather than to overthrow them. The perversions of such education—half-knowledge, propaganda, demagoguery, philistinism, worship of the appearance of success—are probably even more prevalent now than then. Whether they are worse than the perversions of Platonism is too large a question to be argued here. But whether for good or ill, the conception of the aims and purposes of the American liberal college, as set forth by the most distinguished modern educators, is much closer to Isocrates and Protagoras than to Plato.

It is evident, from Plato's literary activities as an idealistic reformer and creator of utopias, from his conception of the philosopher as the true governor of mankind, and from his social, political, and educational philosophy, that he would have differed profoundly from the sophists and rhetoricians, even had all of them possessed the highest character and wisdom.

V

It will be convenient to discuss Plato's treatment of rhetoric and rhetoricians under four heads: the pictures he has given us of the individual rhetoricians, his general indictment of rhetoric in Athens, his suggestions for the creation of a nobler and better rhetoric, and his later attack upon the eristical rhetoricians who imitated the argumentative methods of Socrates.

The Platonic pictures of the sophists are scattered throughout the dialogues; but the most extended and vivid characterizations of them are in the *Protagoras,* the *Hippias Major* and *Hippias Minor,* the *Gorgias,* and the *Euthydemus.* Plato constantly contrasts them with the ironical Socrates. Socrates affects a great humility, the sophists are conceited and self-confident; Socrates is skilled in closely reasoned argument, the sophists are helpless in his hands; Socrates defines his terms, but the sophists, accustomed to haranguing uncritical audiences, use their terms with all the looseness and inaccuracy of common conversation.

Protagoras is pictured at the head of a group of admiring listeners, pleased at an opportunity to lecture in the presence of rival sophists. Although the reader feels that in the discussion with Socrates common sense is with Protagoras, he cannot but be amused at the spectacle of the eloquent, deep-voiced orator unable to defend even a sound argument against the dialectical attack of Socrates. Protagoras, with his popular lectures and his conventional morality, was too powerful a figure to please Plato, who was somewhat neglected in the Academy.

Hippias seems to have incurred the most vigorous enmity of Plato. In the *Hippias Minor* Socrates exposes the fallacies in the popular lecture on Homer that Hippias was accustomed to give before approving audiences. In the picture of Hippias at the Olympic games in garments, rings, and accoutrements of his own make, there is no suggestion that he was attempting to re-enforce his favorite doctrine of self-sufficiency; the

Platonic view is that Hippias was insufferably conceited over his versatility.

The references to Prodicus are scattered and incidental. He is described as a "taker to pieces of words," as "drawing useless distinctions about names," and as beginning his instruction with "initiation into the correct use of terms." In the *Cratylus* there is a satirical reference to the relationship between the fees of Prodicus and the amount of knowledge imparted.

Gorgias is portrayed in the dialogue bearing his name as professing to be able to answer any questions which may be asked him, and as being so familiar with all possible subjects of discussion that for many years he has heard no new question. He indulges in oratorical praise of the art of rhetoric, and is shown to be quite incapable of dialectical argument.

Polus, a young pupil of Gorgias, Callicles, a practical politician rather than a professional rhetorician, and Thrasymachus, the spokesman for doctrines that Plato wished to discredit, are described as being much like the better-known sophists.

Euthydemus and Dionysodorus, who belong to a later group of sophists, are caricatured in the *Euthydemus* with a dramatic vivacity and comic force which almost equals the *Clouds* of Aristophanes. They are characterized as "a new importation of sophists," who "will give lessons in speaking and pleading, and in writing speeches". This occupation is new to them, for they were previously teachers of the art of fighting in armor. They also profess to be teachers of virtue.

Although there are no formal charges made against any individual sophists in any of the dialogues, Plato has used all his literary resources to add to the effectiveness of his philosophical attack upon them.

VI

There is in the *Gorgias* a deeper purpose than an exhibition of the deficiencies of the predominant rhetorical technique. Plato here gives us a contrast between the true and the false life. The philosophic import of the dialogue has led some commentators to believe that the treatment of rhetoric is only incidental, or that rhetoric is used merely as introductory to the higher themes of philosophy. But Plato, for all his idealism, took as the point of departure for his reforms the weaknesses which he thought he saw in Athens, and rhetoric is, after all, a chief subject of the dialogue. Rhetoric, as philosophy, was a way of life. Rhetoric dealt not only with form and style; it also treated the matter and policy of public speaking. It offered something of a philosophy to the orator. It was almost indistinguishable from political science, and to the general public the orator was the statesman.

If there was anything which could pretend to dispute with philosophy the position of a master knowledge, or put forward a rival claim for the guidance of life and affairs, it was this art of rhetoric, which professed to train men for politics, and to make them able to act as well as speak efficiently. The teacher of philosophy had thus to be vindicated against the teacher of rhetoric; the philosophical statesman had also to be vindicated against the orator-statesman of actual Athenian politics.

In contrasting the philosopher and the rhetorician, Plato at times gives the impression of being on the defensive. This is not merely because rhetoric is more popular, but also because he had felt the reproaches of his friends for his inactivity in Athenian affairs. He was keenly conscious of the criticism of the philosopher which he put into the mouth of Callicles:

He [the philosopher] creeps into the corner for the rest of his life, and talks in a whisper with three or four admiring youths, but never speaks out like a freeman in a satisfactory manner.

One way to establish the supremacy of philosophy was to show that the claims of rhetoric as "the art of becoming great in the city," were not to be taken seriously. There must be an appeal to higher values. The belief that might makes right, the trust in things that are seen, must be replaced with a desire for the goods of the soul. The ignorance, prejudice, and selfishness of the rhetorician must be exposed; the most popular of arts must be shown to be no art at all when subjected to the scrutiny of a philosophical mind. The *Gorgias,* then, undertakes to refute the claims made for rhetoric by Gorgias, Polus, and Callicles. Socrates defeats each one in turn, so that we really have three dialogues in one, each antagonist advancing a somewhat different claim for rhetoric.

Gorgias, in the beginning, praises rhetoric for the power and influence it confers. He also defends it from the oft-repeated charge that it is frequently used wrongfully and works mischief in the state. But the definition of rhetoric is what Socrates seeks, and Gorgias appears to be as devoid of abstract ideas with which to frame a definition as the

other rhetoricians. The art of formal logic did not yet exist, and Socrates presses Gorgias with various analogies and ambiguities which both appear to mistake for valid arguments. Logic and rhetoric have not yet been clearly conceived as universal arts or sciences which admit of application to any subject matter; and it is not strange that Gorgias was unable to furnish the clear conception that Socrates sought. Socrates, then, had no great difficulty in establishing his own definition, that *rhetoric is the art of persuading an ignorant multitude about the justice or injustice of a matter, without importing any real instruction.* Rhetoric is most powerful with the ignorant many, because the rhetorician, as rhetorician, does not really know what he is talking about; he only appears to know, and the appearance is persuasive only with the ignorant. Plato here limits rhetoric to the discussion of matters concerning justice. He probably chose to discuss the forensic rather than the deliberative or epideictic rhetoric because the contemporary rhetoricians devoted most of their attention to it.

Socrates also compels Gorgias to admit that *rhetoricians do not really know their business,* for they do not teach their pupils about justice and injustice (an essential part of rhetoric, by the definition previously established). The actions of the pupils show that they have never learned to know justice—any rhetorician must admit that his pupils often act unjustly. Two things are to be noted about this argument. Gorgias and Socrates have different ideas of what it means to know justice. Gorgias means by it a sufficient practical knowledge of men and affairs to know what is conventionally moral in any given case. Socrates, on the other hand, means abstract, philosophical knowledge of the nature of justice. There is also underlying the argument the "vicious intellectualism" of Socrates. The Platonic Gorgias fails to object to the Socratic thesis that if students of rhetoric knew the nature of justice, they would never commit an injustice. To Gorgias, the teaching of justice was not a heavy responsibility, because the just or unjust actions of his pupils did not depend upon any ethical theories taught by him. The just rhetorician was just because he sought to live in a manner which his common sense told him would win the approval of his fellow men, and not because he had been taught to be virtuous. It is difficult to believe that the real Gorgias would have been so easily entrapped by the argument that the injustices committed by pupils of the rhetoricians proved the ignorance of the teachers.

Polus indignantly attempts to rescue his master, but he also falls an easy victim to the Socratic dialectic. Since both Gorgias and Polus have been more apt at praising rhetoric than at defining it, Socrates proceeds to attack their claims and to establish the point that *rhetoric is not of much use in the world*. There are four arguments to substantiate this: (1) Rhetoric is not an art; (2) rhetoric does not confer power; (3) rhetoric as a protection against suffering wrong is of little importance; and (4) rhetoric as a means of escaping a deserved punishment is not to be commended. The philosophy developed in support of these points loses little of its significance when separated from its immediate purpose of refuting the claims of rhetoric; but the unity of the dialogue is not perceived until it is understood that the philosophical theses are part of a consistent argumentative plan.

Rhetoric was not an art, Plato believed, because it did not rest on universal principles. It was really only a knack, a routine, or experience. Aiming at persuasion, it cared only for appearance. It did not aim at justice, but only at a semblance of justice. By an art, Plato meant more nearly what we should call a science, that is, a body of knowledge organized on universally valid principles. The dispute as to whether or not rhetoric was an art was of great practical significance to the rhetoricians. If it was not an art, and rested upon no principles, then the attempt to teach it must be futile. There has always been considerable skepticism as to the possibility of teaching rhetoric profitably. Its rules have often been multiplied in order to have something more to teach. Plato, in common with other writers of genius, was fond of minimizing the importance of technique, just as teachers as a class are fond of overemphasizing it.

Aside from the immediately practical effect upon the teaching of the subject, it was injurious to the prestige of rhetoric to deny it a scientific character. As Gomperz observes of the age:

All the business of mankind, from cooking a dinner to painting a picture, from going a walk to waging a war, was guided by rules and, wherever possible, reduced to principles.

Plato's charge that rhetoric was not an art, then, was somewhat analogous to the denial of a place among the sciences to sociology or psychology. Such a charge, even if unaccompanied by any implications concerning the doubtful morality of persuading ignorant multitudes, was enough to injure the subject.

In denying that rhetoric is an art, Plato gives it a place among the pseudo-arts. In the hierarchy of arts and pseudo-arts, the higher arts aim at the production, real or apparent, of permanent conditions; the lower, at the removal, real or apparent, of temporary derangements. Sophistry is distinguished from rhetoric and placed above it. Sophistry is an imitation of the statesman's art, which is higher than the art of the pleader, because the pleader only remedies miscarriages of justice, while the statesman has the opportunity to create permanent institutions which give society an organization based upon justice. We probably agree today in paying more honor to the statesman than to the trial lawyer. In the *Gorgias*, the sophist is the sham statesman; the rhetorician is the pleader who "makes the worse appear the better reason," and forgets justice in the winning of his case.

The second argument against rhetoric in the dialogue with Polus is that rhetoric, in spite of appearances, does not really confer power. People who do not know, in the philosophical sense (and Plato believed that very few could know anything in the philosophical sense), what is really good for them, have no power, for they are unable to do what they will. When they do evil, they are not doing what they will, for no one really wills to do evil; he only makes a mistake in the art of measuring. The Socratic belief that no man errs voluntarily is again the basis of the argument. The minor premise, that

rhetoricians have not the philosophical insight to know what is really good for them, Plato believes may safely be assumed.

The third and fourth assertions about rhetoric which Socrates established against Polus gain significance when considered in relation to the conditions of Athenian court procedure. With a jury of five hundred—somewhat predisposed to convict any wealthy man, since his goods would be at the disposal of the state—innocent persons were liable to be convicted on the flimsiest of charges. The size of the jury made oratory a much more important matter than evidence. This would make it quite as possible for the guilty to escape punishment, as for an innocent man to suffer at the hands of his enemies. Any practical-minded person would therefore conclude that rhetoric was of great importance to the innocent as a protection against injury, and to the guilty as a means of avoiding a just penalty. Socrates, however, denies both of these claims, and advances his famous paradoxes in support of his argument. Rhetoric is not of great importance as a protection against suffering wrong; the really important thing is to keep oneself from doing wrong, for doing wrong is a greater evil than suffering wrong. The dialectic by which Socrates establishes this is hardly as noble as the conclusion which he reaches, but Polus is not able to offer any effective opposition. Again, rhetoric as a means of escaping punishment is of no great service, for the man who is punished for his injustice is happier than he who is not punished. This Socratic thesis is a matter of feeling and belief rather than of logical proof, but against Polus it was not difficult to establish dialectically. If it is honorable to inflict punishment on a guilty person, then it must be honorable to receive it. Punishment, as a deliverance of the soul from evil, should be welcomed by the guilty as a medicine.

When Polus seems to be hopelessly defeated, Callicles takes up the argument. In the discussion with him the argument turns more directly to the contrast of philosophy and rhetoric as ways of life. In the words of Socrates:

> We are arguing about the way of human life; and what question can be more serious than this to a man who has any sense at all: whether he should follow after that way of life to which you exhort me, and truly fulfill what you call the manly part of speaking in the assembly, and cultivating rhetoric, and engaging in public affairs, after your manner; or whether he should pursue the life of philosophy, and in what this differs from the other.

Callicles vigorously attacks philosophy, upholds rhetoric, and offers in its support the doctrine that might makes right, that justice is but an artificial convention invented by the many weak to protect themselves against the few strong, that the law of nature decrees that the strong should take what they can get, and that in a society full of conventions, rhetoric offers the strong man the means of getting what he wants. The Socratic argument in reply to this passes into the realm of ethics, and deals with the self-seeker as such, rather than merely with the rhetorician.

Socrates is disposed to admit that there might conceivably be a true and noble art of rhetoric. The true rhetorician would attempt to improve the people, rather than to please them. He would attempt this, not only for the moral benefit of the people, but also because any process which does not improve souls is not really an art; it is an ignoble flattery. Among such flatteries are music, poetry, drama, and painting. They may occasionally improve the people, but for the most part they are to be viewed with distrust.

Although there might be a noble rhetoric, and true rhetoricians, none such have ever existed. All statesmen and rhetoricians of the past, even the best, such as Themistocles, Cimon, Miltiades, and Pericles, have failed to make the citizens any better. The proof of this is that the citizens treated these men very ungratefully and unjustly, which they would not have done if they had been taught justice by the statesmen. The professional teachers of rhetoric, even though the teaching of justice should be a part of the instruction in rhetoric, dare not trust their own pupils to treat them justly, for they exact a fee instead of leaving it to the pupil's sense of honor.

Socrates is further offended at the pretentiousness of rhetoric and rhetoricians. If rhetoric occasionally saves a life in courts of law, there are other life-saving arts which are equally important, and much more modest. A swimmer may save many lives, but he is not likely to boast that he practises the greatest of arts. Or a pilot, if swimming seems to be a contemptible example, is also a great life-saver. But he keeps his modesty. If he has any philosophy in him, he knows that some of the lives he has saved were probably not worth saving; but a rhetorician never seems to indulge himself in such sobering reflections.

Rhetoric destroys the integrity of a man's soul, for it involves conformity to the ways of the multitude. The philosopher, on the other hand, sees further:

The noble and the good may possibly be something different from saving and being saved, and that he who is truly a man ought not to care about living a certain time; he knows, as women say, that none can escape the day of destiny, and therefore he is not fond of life; he leaves all that with God, and considers in what way he can best spend his appointed term.

The dialogue closes with a myth of the after-world, in which the judgment that bestows rewards and punishments is not based upon appearances, as are the judgments won by the rhetoricians, but upon the true nature of the soul. The myth sums up the whole argument of the dialogue. The fundamental contrast is between appearances and reality; the rhetorician deals with appearances, the philosopher with reality.

In the *Gorgias*, the rhetoricians appear to be men bent upon getting on in the world. They seem to believe that an unjust man who escapes punishment, and practises his injustice on such a large scale that he is conspicuously successful, is a man to be envied and imitated. It is easy for us, made familiar with the doctrine that injustice is an evil, through the teachings of Plato, of the Stoics, and of Christianity, and accustomed at least to pay lip-service to it as a truism, to suppose that Plato was upholding the traditional righteousness against a peculiarly corrupt set of public teachers, the sophists and rhetoricians. It should be remembered, however, that public opinion in Athens was not with Plato. Instead of regarding

Gorgias and Polus and Callicles as especially corrupt, we should regard Plato as the reforming philosopher, attacking public opinion through its prominent representatives. That Plato himself took this view is shown by his remark in the *Republic* that the youth are not corrupted by individual sophists, but by the public.

It is also worthy of note that this attack upon rhetoric is itself a rhetorical triumph. The rhetoricians are ridiculed for their inability to reason closely, and to defend themselves against the dialectic of Socrates; but the triumph of the Platonic Socrates is not a triumph of logic over oratory. John Stuart Mill has put this clearly:

This great dialogue, full of just thoughts and fine observations on human nature, is, in mere argument, one of the weakest of Plato's works. It is not by its logic, but by its ēthos that it produces its effects; not by instructing the understanding, but by working on the feelings and imagination. Nor is this strange; for the disinterested love of virtue is an affair of feeling. It is impossible to prove to any one Plato's thesis, that justice is supreme happiness, unless he can be made to feel it as such. The external inducements which recommend it he may be taught to appreciate; the favorable regards and good offices of other people, and the rewards of another life. These considerations, however, though Plato has recourse to them in other places, are not available in the *Gorgias*. . . . It is the picture of the moral hero, still *tenax propositi* against the hostility and contempt of the world, which makes the splendor and power of the *Gorgias*. The Socrates of the dialogue makes us *feel* all other evils to be more tolerable than injustice in the soul, not by proving it, but by the sympathy he calls forth with his own intense feeling of it. He inspires heroism because he shows himself a hero. And his failures in logic do not prevent the step marked by the *Gorgias* from being one of the greatest ever made in moral culture.

VII

The *Phædrus*, which has been described as a dramatized treatise on rhetoric, contains three speeches upon the general subject of love; one of which Plato introduces as the work of Lysias, a noted rhetorician of the day, and two of which are put into the mouth of Socrates. It is in a comparison of these speeches that Plato's ideas about rhetoric are expressed. At the close of the final speech upon love, delivered by Socrates, Phædrus expresses his admiring approval; he fears that Lysias, whose speech he had just read to Socrates, could not produce anything as good; indeed, he had already been reproached for his speech writing. Socrates remarks that it is not writing speeches, but writing them badly, that is disgraceful. This opens the way for a discussion of the entire practice of speaking and writing.

Socrates enunciates as the first rule of good speaking:

> The mind of the speaker should know the truth of what he is going to say. . . . There never is nor ever will be a real art of speaking which is unconnected with the truth.

This rule of Socrates is contrasted with the prevalent conception of rhetoric. Rhetoric is usually considered to be an "art of enchanting the mind by arguments"; it has no concern with the nature of truth or justice, but only with opinions about them. Rhetoric draws its persuasive power, not from truth, but from harmony with public opinion. This conception of rhetoric, however, Plato thinks inadequate. The objection here is not, as is often stated, from high moral motives. In the *Gorgias* and elsewhere it is stated that the genuine rhetorician must be a true and just man. And from many sources we know how Plato abhorred the "lie in the soul." But here the ground is simple expediency. The art of persuasion is the art of winning the mind by resemblances. The speaker goes by degrees from that which is accepted to that which he wishes accepted, proceeding from one resemblance to another. If the difference between two resemblances is small, there is an excellent opportunity for making the audience believe that one is the other.

This rule, that "the mind of the speaker should know the truth of what he is going to say" and not "catch at appearances," may seem to be a commonplace. But it is not mere faithfulness to fact that Plato has in mind; it is that Truth which only philosophers know. All others dwell in a darkened cave. The moving figures they behold are not realities; they are shadows, phantoms. Only the philosopher has ascended into the clear light of day. Only he has beheld Ideas in their Absolute form. Only he it is who is able to see "unity and plurality in nature." Hence the exclamation of Socrates:

> Come out, children of my soul, and convince Phædrus, who is the father of similar beauties, that he will never be able to speak about anything unless he be trained in philosophy.

These Platonic conceptions are not new to Phædrus, and no time is wasted in explaining them. Having secured acceptance of the first rule of good speaking, Socrates proceeds to lay down two corollaries. First, rhetoric has greater power in discussions where men disagree and are most likely to be deceived. The rhetorician ought therefore to have in mind a clear distinction between debatable and nondebatable subjects. Secondly, particulars must be carefully observed, so that they may be properly classified. In other words, careful definitions must be drawn, and mere matters of opinion separated from matters of scientific knowledge.

A lack of any definition of the subject of love is the first criticism of the speech of Lysias. This is particularly reprehensible as love is used in two different senses. Socrates, however, was careful in both speeches to start from a definition of the love he was treating. Again, there is no principle of order in the speech of Lysias. He is accused of beginning at the end, and his topics follow one another in a random fashion.

I cannot help fancying that he wrote off freely just what came into his head. . . . Every discourse ought to be a living creature, having its own body and head and feet; there ought to be a middle, beginning, and end, which are in a manner agreeable to one another and to the whole.

From this study of the speeches on love, two fundamental principles of composition emerge:

First, the comprehension of scattered particulars in one idea; the speaker defines his several notions in order that he may make his meaning clear. . . . Secondly, there is the faculty of division according to the natural ideas or members, not breaking any part as a bad carver might.

But these processes of generalization and division, which the speech of the famous rhetorician failed to employ, are principles that Socrates has hitherto held to belong to dialectic, and not to rhetoric.

I am a great lover of these processes of division and generalization; they help me to speak and think. And if I find any man who is able to see unity and plurality in nature, him I follow, and walk in his steps as if he were a god. And those who have this art, I have hitherto been in the habit of calling dialecticians.

Phædrus acknowledges that these principles rightly belong to the dialecticians, but persists in inquiring about the principles of rhetoric; he mentions a number of prominent rhetoricians together with some characteristic elements of their systems. Socrates admits that in addition to the really fundamental principles of composition to be found in dialectic, there may be in rhetoric some "niceties of the art." Theodorus, Evenus, Tisias, Gorgias, Prodicus, Hippias, Polus, Protagoras, and the other rhetoricians spend much time upon proems, statements of fact, witnesses, proofs, probabilities, confirmations, superconfirmations, refutations, diplasiology, gnomolgy, and other technicalities. These theories and practices of the rhetoricians, however, are not really principles of the art of rhetoric. They are mere preliminaries, as the tuning of strings is preliminary to playing upon an instrument. But no one would call the tuning of strings the art of music. The contemporary rhetoricians have no more real claim to be practitioners of the art than a man who knows a few drugs, but does not know how to use them, could claim to be a physician. Since all these teachings of the rhetoricians are not true principles of the art, and are altogether useless except when used in conjunction with the principles of dialectic, Socrates proceeds to give what might be called an outline of a true art of rhetoric.

Oratory is the art of enchanting the soul, and therefore he who would be an orator has to learn the differences of human souls— they are of so many and of such a nature, and from them come the differences between man and man. He will then proceed to divide speeches into their several different classes. Such and such persons, he will say, are affected by this or that kind of speech in this or that way, and he will tell you why; he must have a theoretical notion of them first, and then he must see them in action, and be able to follow them with all his senses about him, or he will never get beyond the precepts of his masters. But when he is able to say what persons are persuaded by what arguments and recognize the individual about whom he used to theorize as actually present to himself, This is he and this is the sort of man who ought to have that argument applied to him in order to convince him of this; when he has attained the knowledge of all this, and knows also when he should speak and when he should abstain from speaking, when he should make use of pithy sayings, pathetic appeals, aggravated effects, and all the other figures of speech, when, I say, he knows the times and seasons of all these things, then, and not until then, is he perfect and a consummate master of his art.

Such an outline of rhetoric, Socrates feels, may be discouraging to the young Phædrus. The road to the mastery of such an art is obviously long and hard. The sophists, on the other hand, are represented by Plato as offering promises to impart culture quickly and easily. Here, then, is an opportunity for Socrates to compare the true way of mastering the art of rhetoric with the sophistic short cut. The rhetoricians succeed in imparting a certain skill in making plausible speeches because

they content themselves with creating an appearance of probability. They teach that "in speaking the orator should run after probability and say good-by to truth." The teaching of Tisias on the topic of probability, which enabled a man quickly to make a case either for the defense or the prosecution, regardless of the evidence, is cited as typical of the rhetoricians. To show the superiority of the true rhetoric over such trickery, Socrates repeats his former statement:

Probability is engendered in the minds of the many by the likeness of the truth, and he who knows the truth will always know best how to discover the resemblance of the truth.

The rhetoric of Tisias, then, is deficient in two respects. First, it is not even effective, for it is not quick at perceiving likenesses of truth; and secondly, such a rhetorician is as likely to deceive himself as his audience. Further, the true rhetorician masters his art after much labor:

Not for the sake of speaking and acting before men, but in order that he may be able to say what is acceptable to God and in all things to act acceptably to Him so far as in him lies.

Rhetoric, then, like all the arts, is to be an instrument of righteousness. After stating that enough has been said of the true and false art of rhetoric, Socrates feels that something remains to be said of the propriety and impropriety of writing. He proceeds to speak of writing, but only to condemn the practice. Concerning the invention of letters he cites a myth in which the prophecy is made that the art of writing will create forgetfulness and a pretense of wisdom. Contrasted with this futility of writing is "an intelligent writing which is graven in the soul of him who has learned, and can defend itself, and knows when to speak and when to be silent." This expression of opinion about writing concludes Plato's theory of rhetoric as found in the *Phædrus*.

That these suggestions of Plato for the organization of rhetoric into a scientific body of knowledge may be more clearly in mind when we come to contrast the *Phædrus* with Aristotle's *Rhetoric*, we shall here summarize them.

1. "The first rule of good speaking is that the mind of the speaker should know the truth of what he is going to say." This cannot be interpreted as an injunction to speak the truth at all times. It is rather to *know* the truth in order (a) to be persuasive by presenting to the audience something which at least resembles truth, and (b) to avoid being oneself deceived by probabilities. In order to know the truth, the rhetorician must be a philosopher.

2. The rhetorician must define his terms, and see clearly what subjects are debatable and what are not. He must also be able to classify particulars under a general head, so to break up universals into particulars. The rhetorician, then, must be a logician.

3. Principles of order and arrangement must be introduced. "Every discourse ought to be a living creature, having its own body and head and feet; there ought to be a middle, beginning, and end, which are in a manner agreeable to one another and to the whole."

4. The nature of the soul must be shown, and after having "arranged men and speeches, and their modes and affections in different classes, and fitted them into one another, he will point out the connection between them—he will show why one is naturally persuaded by a particular form of argument, and another not." In other words, the rhetorician must be a psychologist.

5. The rhetorician must "speak of the instruments by which the soul acts or is affected in any way." Here we have the division under which comes practically all of rhetoric when viewed more narrowly and technically. The "instruments" by which rhetoric affects the soul are style and delivery. Plato believed style to be acquired, however, as Pericles acquired it, by "much discussion and lofty contemplation of nature."

6. The art of writing will not be highly regarded; nor will continuous and uninterrupted discourse be regarded as equal to cross-examination as a means of instruction. This is Plato's way of saying that any method of attempting to persuade multitudes must suffer from the very fact that it is a multitude which is addressed, and that the best of rhetoric is unequal to philosophic discussion.

7. The rhetorician will have such a high moral purpose in all his work that he will ever be chiefly concerned about saying that which is "acceptable to God." Rhetoric, then, is not an instrument for the determination of scientific truth, nor for mere persuasion regardless of the cause; it is an instrument for making the will of God prevail. The perfect rhetorician, as a philosopher, knows the will of God.

VIII

De Quincey says that rhetoric has, in general, two connotations: one of ostentatious ornament, and the other of fallacious argument. That part of Plato's attack upon rhetoric which we have considered, largely concerns itself with rhetoric as "ostentatious ornament" (although the two aspects can seldom be completely separated). And it was this attack which led Plato to the constructive theory of the *Phædrus*. But there was a later assault upon the sophists which concerned rhetoric as an art of fallacious argument. The sophists of Plato's earlier dialogues are declaimers and rhetoricians who can overwhelm opponents with long speeches, but they are tyros in the art of argumentation. In the *Euthydemus, Sophist,* and *Statesman,* Plato caricatures the imitators of Socrates, who practise argumentation by question and answer, but who resemble Socrates as the wolf does the dog.

The *Euthydemus* is the earliest known attempt to exhibit a variety of fallacies. In it Plato desired to make clear the distinction between truly philosophical argumentation and the eristical disputation which served no purpose except to display a certain type of cleverness. A young man, Cleinias, is cross-examined by two sophistical teachers of argument, Euthydemus and Dionysodorus. They conduct their examination in a spirit of horse-play, and soon have the youth hopelessly confused. Socrates then rebukes them, and offers to examine Cleinias in a truly philosophical fashion. His kindly questions (much more kindly here than in other dialogues, but they serve Plato's purpose in emphasizing the contrast), which lead Cleinias to the conclusion that wisdom is the only good, and ignorance the only evil, are an example of the way in which a philosopher conducts an argument—for the enlightenment, and not the confusion, of youth.

Having distinguished the philosopher from the sophistical teachers of fallacious argument, Plato in an epilogue contrasts the philosopher and the orator-statesman. Here Plato is probably thinking of Isocrates and his "philosophy," which was a mixture of rhetoric and politics. Philosopher-politicians and speech writers, Socrates is made to say, imagine themselves to be a superior sort; they think they have a certain amount of philosophy, and a certain amount of political insight; thus they keep out of the way of all risks and conflicts and reap the fruit of their wisdom. Socrates asserts, however, that philosophy and political action tend to such different ends that one who participates in both achieves little in either. The Isocratean ideal of the orator-statesman, which had so great an influence upon Cicero, was objectionable to Plato for at least three reasons. In the first place, the true statesman was a philosopher rather than an orator; he ruled arbitrarily through his wisdom rather than through persuasion. Secondly, if the statesman was forced to stoop to the use of oratory, it was to be clearly understood that oratory was a subordinate instrument. The ideal of the orator-statesman only helped to confuse the superior art of politics with rhetoric. Thirdly, the orator-statesman falsely imagined that the ideas which he used in the persuasion of the public constituted his philosophy; whereas in reality he was so tied to particulars in all his speaking and thinking that he never approached the wisdom of the true philosopher.

In the *Euthydemus,* then, we have pictured a later development of the older sophists. Imitators of Socrates had appeared who taught the art of argumentation for pay: Isocrates had enlarged and dignified the instruction of the rhetoricians by allying it more closely with pan-Hellenic politics, and had become much more popular and successful than Plato. Plato insists that true philosophy is a different sort of thing, and indulges in caricature and satire to make it evident.

In the *Sophist,* we have an abstract and methodical discussion of that which is dramatically pictured in the *Euthydemus.* Plato planned a trilogy of dialogues, the *Sophist,* the *Statesman,* and the *Philosopher,* in which the man of the world and the man of wisdom should be contrasted. The *Philosopher* was never written, but from the *Sophist* and the *Statesman* we get the Platonic discussion of the false art of argumentation known as eristic.

The sophist, in the dialogue of that name, is discovered by a preliminary study of the angler, which suggests a method of search, and also furnishes an implied analogy, for the sophist is found to be a fisher of men who finally destroys them. By a series of homely figures the sophist is revealed in his various aspects. He is (1) a paid hunter after youth and wealth, (2) a retail merchant or trader in the goods of the soul, (3) he himself manufactures the learned wares which he sells, (4) he is a hero of

dispute, having distinctly the character of a disputant, (5) he is a purger of souls who clears away notions obstructive to knowledge. In the last-named characteristic, Plato seems about to admit that the sophist serves a great educational purpose, for he has previously admitted that "refutation is the greatest and chiefest purification." But the sophist, as the supposed minister of refutation, is related to the real purger of souls as "a wolf, who is the fiercest of animals, is to the dog, who is the gentlest." Here Plato does not seem to see that a given logical procedure is as a method essentially the same, whether used by a sophist or a philosopher. For Plato, even the *logical* nature of cross-examination seems to be changed by the *moral* nature of the examiner. No sophist ever employed greater fallacies than the Socrates of the Platonic dialogues; yet fallacies in the arguments of a philosopher seemed somehow elevated by their moral purpose. Aristotle followed Plato in this error. Probably no fallacy is more persistent than the judgment of logical method by the standard of moral purpose.

The eristical sophists, as the rhetorical, profess a knowledge which they do not have. They profess that the art of disputation is a power of disputing about all things. Plato puts the sophists in the position of teaching that a mastery of form gives also a mastery of substance. The sophists delight in the discovery that a certain facility in logical method, accompanied by entire unscrupulousness, can make almost any proposition appear to be plausible. With no standard of consistency looking farther than the immediate discussion, method can so arrange any small group of facts, or alleged facts, that any thesis may be made to appear tenable. The sophists *seem* to teach young men to argue about all things because "they make young men believe in their own supreme and universal wisdom." They are enabled to do this by their readiness in offering "conjectural or apparent knowledge of all things" as a substitute for truth. They are like painters who profess "by one art to make all things." What the sophist makes is a resemblance, but it is easy to deceive the less intelligent children, by showing his pictures at a distance, into believing that he has the absolute power of making what he likes. In the same way there is an imitative art of reasoning, and by the use of this art the sophist passes himself off as a philosopher. There are two types of these imitators: the popular orator, who makes long speeches to the multitude and who appears to be a statesman, and the sophist, who teaches argumentation and pretends to be a philosopher.

The *Statesman* is an attempt, by the same method of division used in the *Sophist,* to discover the true statesman. Here we have an introductory analogy concerning the weaver. As the weaver has the auxiliary arts of the fuller, the carder, and the maker of the warp and woof, so the statesman has the auxiliary arts of the rhetorician, the general, and the judge. There is always the danger, however, that the rhetorician may be mistaken for the statesman. Politics is the science that tells us when to persuade, and of what; rhetoric merely tells how to persuade. If the rhetoric be a noble rhetoric, however, and does really persuade men to love justice, it may be regarded as a useful instrument in our second-best state, where persuasion is an unfortunate necessity in government. Rhetoric, however, should never lose its instrumental character, and should never aspire to be more than one of the several subordinate arts which the statesman weaves together into the whole which is the state.

In these two dialogues, then, the *Sophist* and the *Statesman,* we are warned against the rhetorician, who appears in different guises. In the *Sophist,* he appears as the dialectician who purges the soul of false knowledge, but he is really an eristical disputant. In the *Statesman,* he appears as the persuader of the public who is quick to seize power as a demagogue unless he be kept strictly under the direction of the true statesman.

IX

To summarize briefly our whole discussion of Plato: we have shown that his treatment of rhetoric is based upon his feelings toward certain rhetoricians, and upon his dislike of the rhetorical tendency of all Athenian life. Plato never viewed rhetoric abstractly, as an art of composition, as an instrument that might be used or abused; he always considered it a false impulse in human thought. He therefore attacked in published dialogues the more prominent contemporary teachers and the art they professed to teach. The evidence seems to show that the sophists of the earlier attacks were intellectually respectable, and that they made significant contributions to the thought of their time. At the conclusion of his earlier attacks (if we may trust the attempts to arrange Plato's dialogues in approximately chronological order) Plato offers an outline of a reconstructed rhetoric. Here, too, he shows his inability to conceive of rhetoric as a tool; the ideal rhetoric sketched in the *Phædrus* is as far from the possibilities of mankind as his Republic was from Athens. In later life, a new generation of teachers that patterned its methods after Socrates, aroused the wrath of Plato, and he wrote other dialogues to distinguish the false art of argumentation from the dialectical processes of the true philosopher.

X

In turning to Aristotle, we shall be chiefly interested in his relation to Plato. To explain the relation of any one of Aristotle's treatises to Plato is, according to Sir Alexander Grant, almost a sufficient account of what it contains. Familiarity with the Platonic dialogues and their Athenian background, makes it possible to proceed more rapidly with the systematic work of Aristotle upon any particular subject under investigation. It is not our purpose here to present an exposition of the *Rhetoric*, and the preceding discussion should make it possible to condense the account of Aristotle, although his contribution to rhetoric is greater than that of Plato or the sophists.

It is obvious that as Plato's pupil, Aristotle must have had his attention called to those aspects of Athenian life which interested his master. As a reader of Plato's dialogues, Aristotle found a wealth of concretely pictured material ready for classification into various compartments of knowledge. Aside from the magnificent gesture of the *Phædrus*, Plato apparently gave little constructive thought to rhetoric. He did not teach its practice, nor lecture upon its theory. Aristotle, however, during the first period of residence at Athens, and while still a pupil of Plato at the Academy, opened a school of rhetoric in competition with Isocrates. We have here an instance of the way in which rhetoric in Athens, as in other times and places, has offered men whose minds could not be confined to a single field, an opportunity to establish themselves as teachers and thinkers. The works upon rhetoric which have been lost were probably composed during this earlier period. There seem to be adequate grounds for attributing three such works to Aristotle: a history of rhetoric, a dialogue upon the subject, named for Gryllus, a son of Xenophon, and the *Theodectea*, mainly devoted to style, composition, and arrangement, and which probably contained in greater detail the subject matter of the third book of the extant *Rhetoric*. It is not know when the *Rhetoric* was composed, but it was not published until Aristotle's second period of residence and teaching in Athens (336 B.C. is the most generally accepted date of publication). It is believed that the third book, which deals with style and arrangement, was not written until some time after the first two books. The *Poetics* was written before the third book of the *Rhetoric*, but probably after the earlier books. From this it is sometimes inferred that Aristotle's interest in style as a part of rhetoric was of late development. This is hardly consistent with his earlier treatment of the subject in the *Theodectea.* A more probable explanation of the greater interest which Aristotle seems to have felt in the subject of proofs and their sources is that this part of rhetoric represented most distinctly his own contribution to the subject. In writing of style and arrangement he was dealing with questions already fully treated by many writers, for most of whom he had little regard. In the first two books, however, he was organizing a new unity out of material drawn from logic, psychology, ethics, and politics. It may have been an additional source of pleasure to him to be able to draw from his own treatment of these special fields such material as was needed to give rhetoric a more philosophical character. It is significant that Aristotle, having taught rhetoric in his early youth, and having waged war with both preceding and contemporary rhetoricians, should, in his age, after having surveyed all the fields of knowledge, return to the treatment of the same subject. It seems to be one of the ironies of history that that portion of rhetoric which was most particularly his own, and which owed most to his previous work in other fields, should be forever slipping back into its component parts of logic, psychology, ethics, and politics; and that style and arrangement, regarded by both himself and Plato as mere preliminaries to the art, rather than the art itself, should fix more permanently the character of rhetoric.

XI

While Aristotle agreed with Plato in his contempt for the unscientific nature of the instruction given by other teachers of rhetoric, and in applying the term sophist to false pretenders to knowledge, his approach to rhetoric was affected by certain philosophical and temperamental divergences from Plato. It is an oft-quoted remark of Friedrich Schlegel's that every man is born either a Platonist or an Aristotelian. This is generally interpreted to mean that the tribe of Platonists are poets and mystics, seeking a truth above the truth of scientific knowledge, while the Aristotelians rely upon methodical experience and classified observations. It cannot be said that Aristotle paid greater attention than Plato to the facts of experience in the creation of a philosophical rhetoric, for he constructed the entire art from the general principles of dialectic, psychology, and ethics, referring to any existing examples of eloquence only most casually for the sake of illustration. But it is, perhaps, a safe generalization to say that Plato sought to reform life, while Aristotle was more interested in reorganizing theory about life. For this reason Aristotle's *Rhetoric* is largely detached from both morality and pedagogy. It is neither a manual of rules nor a collection of injunctions. It is an unmoral and scientific analysis of the means of persuasion.

We have seen that Plato was predisposed to feel a contempt for rhetoric and rhetoricians by certain of his political ideas—his belief in a government of philosophers, administered by experts; his desire for a permanent stratification of society, free from attempts of men to rise out of their class; and his profound contempt for public opinion. Aristotle had no enthusiasm for what has been called Plato's "pedantocracy." He realized that expert knowledge and professional training have their limitations, and that in political matters the judgment of the people may be superior to that of those who have special knowledge. Although Aristotle shared Plato's belief that a laborer could hardly possess a virtue which should entitle him to citizenship, he never expected ranks and classes to be permanently fixed, as in the *Republic.* In the *Politics* he suggests that final power should rest with the multitude, which, of course, would make rhetoric a universal political instrument. And Aristotle's attitude toward public opinion—the common sense of the majority—is distinctly different from that of Plato. This is most marked, perhaps, in his *Ethics,* although it is difficult to distinguish ethical from political thinking in the speculation of the period. But one impulse which set Plato to writing was his intense dissatisfaction with the empirical and prudential morality of his countrymen. The constant contrast in his dialogues is between unreflective, chaotic public opinion, and reasoned, philosophic knowledge. He did not care to organize public opinion, subject it to definitions, and extract from it its modicum of truth. The mind must not only reason about the good; it must contemplate the Idea of the Good in the heavens above until conformed to it. Aristotle attacked the Platonic doctrine of ideas, separated ethics from metaphysics, and took as his guiding principle a practical good, happiness. In discussing happiness, Aristotle did not limit himself to the doctrines of the philosophers; he often accepted generally received opinions, and where he rejected them he at least paid them the honor of refutation.

The lists and divisions of goods presented in the *Ethics* were largely derived from current Athenian discussion, and many ideas which Aristotle accepts as authoritative were common property. In the *Topics,* when he discusses the uses of dialectic, he explicitly recognizes the value of a wide acquaintance with public opinion. There was little danger that a Socrates, discoursing freely in the market place with anyone he chanced upon, would be unfamiliar with the beliefs of "the man in the street." But the growth of schools, the habit of scientific study, and the production of written compositions tended to make of the philosopher a man apart. Aristotle recognized the dangerous effect of this upon the public influence of the learned; he recommended the practice of dialectical discussion as a means of keeping in touch with the opinions of men. He himself drew up a collection of current proverbs. Even his more scientific works have been criticized for his willingness to accept common opinion where accurate observation was called for. We may say, then, that Aristotle approached the subject of rhetoric with a belief in its necessity as a political instrument and a conviction that both the trained thinker and the multitude would benefit by making a common stock of their wisdom for the guidance of the state.

XII

The effect of these philosophical divergences upon the treatment of rhetoric becomes clearly evident when we compare the Platonic discussion between

Gorgias and Socrates on the nature and functions of rhetoric with the statements upon the same subject in the early part of Aristotle's *Rhetoric*. Aristotle states clearly what Gorgias seemed to be groping for, and unmistakably sides with Gorgias against Plato in practically all controverted points. In the *Gorgias*, Socrates asserts that teachers of rhetoric know nothing of justice, and that the art of rhetoric is inimical to justice. Aristotle, in the first chapter of the *Rhetoric*, expresses his belief that rhetoric makes for the prevalence of truth and righteousness.

Rhetoric is useful because things that are true and things that are just have a natural tendency to prevail over their opposites, so that if the decisions of judges are not what they ought to be, the defeat must be due to the speakers themselves, and they must be blamed accordingly. . . . Further, we must be able to employ persuasion, just as strict reasoning can be employed, on opposite sides of a question, not in order that we may in practice employ it both ways (for we must not make people believe what is wrong), but in order that we may see clearly what the facts are, and that, if another man argues unfairly, we may on our part be able to confute him. No other of the arts draws opposite conclusions: dialectic and rhetoric alone do this. Both these arts draw opposite conclusions impartially. Nevertheless, the underlying facts do not lend themselves equally well to the contrary views. No; things that are true and things that are better are, by their nature, practically always easier to believe in.

It is worthy of note that Aristotle, although he does remark parenthetically that the rhetorician should not make people believe what is wrong, does not base his faith in the benefits of rhetoric upon the moral training of the rhetorician, but rather upon the nature of things. Rhetorical effectiveness does not add equally to the strength of a just and an unjust cause. To use an imperfect analogy, we may say, perhaps, that skilful presentation of a just cause strengthens its' appeal geometrically, while an unjust cause is aided only arithmetically. The inherent superiority of just and true things is thus increased by the universal use of rhetoric. This is a broader and sounder view than Plato was able to take. As a reformer Plato had no patience with the evils which inevitably accompany all good things. Aristotle is quite cognizant of the evils of rhetoric, but is content that the good shall, on the whole, outweigh it.

And if it be objected that one who uses such power of speech unjustly might do great harm, that is a charge which may be made in common against all good things except virtue, and above all against the things that are most useful, as strength, health, wealth, generalship.

In the *Gorgias*, Socrates establishes the point that the power of rhetoric is only an apparent power, because it rests upon the ignorance of the multitude addressed. The persuasion of the ignorant many is a rather unseemly occupation for a philosopher. As to the essentially popular function of rhetoric, Aristotle agrees, but without condescension.

Moreover, before some audiences not even the possession of the exactest knowledge will make it easy for what we say to produce conviction. For argument based on knowledge implies instruction, and there are people whom one cannot instruct. Here, then, we must use, as our modes of persuasion and argument, notions possessed by everybody, as we observed in the *Topics* when dealing with the way to handle a popular audience.

The Platonic Socrates argued against Gorgias and Polus that the persuasion of multitudes was not properly an art at all, but only a knack or routine or experience. The first claim that Aristotle makes for rhetoric is that it may properly be considered as an art.

All men attempt to discuss statements and to maintain them, to defend themselves and attack others. Ordinary people do this at random or through practice and from acquired habit. Both ways being possible, the subject can plainly be handled systematically, for it is possible to inquire the reason why some speakers succeed through practice and others spontaneously; and every one will at once agree that such an inquiry is the function of an art.

One of the Platonic reasons for refusing to admit that rhetoric was properly an art was the difficulty of discovering its proper subject matter. Gorgias is exhibited to us as struggling with this question, and as insisting that persuasive discourse is the proper subject-matter of rhetoric; but when Socrates presses him with analogies from the other arts, and asks him if instruction in music and geometry and arithmetic is not persuasive discourse, Gorgias is unable to make a satisfactory statement. This interested Aristotle; it led him to distinguish between rhetoric and the special sciences, but it did not lead him to deny that rhetoric was a discipline in itself.

Rhetoric may be defined as the faculty of observing in any given case the available means of persuasion. This is not the function of any other art. Every other subject can instruct or persuade about its own particular subject-matter; for instance, medicine about what is healthy and unhealthy, geometry about the properties of magnitudes, arithmetic about numbers, and the same is true of the other arts and sciences. But rhetoric we look upon as the power of observing the means of persuasion on almost any sub-

ject presented to us; and that is why we say that, in its technical character, it is not concerned with any special or definite class of subjects. . . . The duty of rhetoric is to deal with such matters as we deliberate on without arts or systems to guide us, in the hearing of persons who cannot take in at a glance a complicated argument, or follow a long chain of reasoning. . . . But the more we try to make either dialectic or rhetoric not, what they really are, practical faculties, but sciences, the more we shall inadvertently be destroying their true nature; for we shall be refashioning them and shall be passing into the region of sciences dealing with definite subjects rather than simply with words and forms of reasoning.

The argumentative purpose of the Socratic thesis in the *Gorgias*, that it is better to suffer wrong than to do it, was to disparage the claim made for rhetoric that it was useful for purposes of defense. Aristotle agrees that a man may well be eulogized for choosing to suffer wrong rather than to do it. Such a choice, however, is a *moral* problem for the individual, and is quite irrelevant to a consideration of the uses of any art— rhetoric or boxing or generalship. Aristotle insists that the use of speech and reason as a method of protection against injustice is distinctively human.

XIII

It is not surprising that Aristotle, as a writer on rhetoric, should disagree with the passionately hostile treatment of his subject in the *Gorgias*. Most writers who have compared the *Rhetoric* with Plato's sketch in the *Phædrus* content themselves with indicating the similarities of the two works. Aristotle's indebtedness to Plato is pointed out, and it is suggested that Plato, in lectures or conversation, may have given Aristotle a pretty complete outline for his work. When we consider the specific suggestions of the *Phædrus* for a philosophical rhetoric, however, the differences between the Platonic and the Aristotelian conception of the subject are at least as manifest as the likenesses.

Taking up first the relationship of rhetoric to Truth, we note a wide divergence. Plato held that the rhetorician must know the Truth, because probability was engendered by a likeness to Truth. Here Plato seems hardly consistent with himself, for a public so depraved as Plato felt all multitudes to be, would never care so much for a resemblance to Truth, as for a probability based upon a consonance with its own interests and tastes. Such a probability, however, could not, according to Plato, form the basis for any art.

For Aristotle, however, probability forms the very groundwork of rhetoric. Rhetoric is frankly an art of appearances. Its function is to enable a man to see quickly what are the available means of persuasion *on either side of any proposition.* The whole plan of the *Rhetoric* bears out this conclusion. Consider first the topics, or commonplaces, or, as Roberts translates the term, lines of argument. The topics, according to some critics, represent Aristotle's determined effort to classify the essentially unclassifiable. Aristotle himself seems hardly clear in his own mind whether the topics were to be regarded as premises or methods of argument, whether they were indicative or imperative. At any rate, they were collections of brief statements with which the rhetorician was to be familiar in order to call to mind immediately all the available arguments for either side of the case. If, for example, a written law is adverse to one's case, one can impugn its authority by an appeal to a higher and more universal law. On the other hand, if the law favors one's case, it can be urged that the attempt to be wiser than the law increases the bad habit of disobeying authority. It is noteworthy that as aids to invention the topics were not axioms, propositions universally true, but were often less than half-truths. For almost any Aristotelian topic, which was to serve as a reminder of or a basis for an argument, another topic could be found which would serve equally well for a contrary argument. The topics, then, constituted a sort of rhetoricians' first aid. They were to assist him in producing immediately, and perhaps without any special knowledge of the subject, a plausible argument upon either side of a debatable proposition.

Additional evidence of the merely contingent and probable nature of rhetoric, as opposed to the Platonic conception, is to be seen in the distinct method of reasoning which Aristotle elaborated for popular persuasion. Realizing, with Plato, that a general audience cannot be *instructed* by close reasoning, but must be *persuaded* by an easier procedure, he substitutes in rhetoric the enthymeme for the syllogism, and the example for the more careful induction of scientific reasoning. The enthymeme was a rhetorical syllogism; that is, a syllogism drawn, not from universal principles belonging to a particular science, but from probabilities in the sphere of human affairs. In proceeding hastily with a subject before an audience, it would usually happen that one of the three members of the formal syllogism would be omitted. Whether or not the essential distinction between the enthymeme and the syllogism is in the merely probable nature of the premises or in the suppression of one of the parts, the enthymeme is to be regarded as the principal method of popular presentation of thought. For the persuasive use of examples (less conclusive but more persuasive than a logical induction) Aristotle offers the astute advice, "If you put examples first, you must use many; if at the end, even one is enough."

A study of the topics, of enthymemes and examples, makes it evident that the rhetorical *processes* of invention and logical formulation were designed for quick plausibility. Turning from processes to *content*, this impression is heightened. For each of the three branches of rhetoric—deliberative, epideictic, and forensic—an outline of the usual subject-matter treated by the speaker is offered. A student of each of the special sciences represented would probably say that Aristotle has given us as the subject-matter of deliberative rhetoric a superficial political science; for epideictic rhetoric a conventional ethics; and for forensic rhetoric a very loose and inexact criminal jurisprudence.

The subjects suggested as the content of deliberative speeches are all much more fully treated in the *Politics.* The *Rhetoric* takes from the *Politics* a brief sketch of political matters upon which speakers must be persuasive. The rhetorician should be familiar with the various forms of government—democracy, oligarchy, aristocracy, monarchy—not that he shall determine which is best, or shall speak as a polit-

ical philosopher, but in order that he may gain persuasiveness by being able to adapt himself to the political beliefs of his audience. It is, of course, perfectly possible for the student of rhetoric to be a political scientist, as Aristotle himself was, but as a rhetorician his task is to use whatever political commonplaces are most likely to win approval. That Aristotle was fully conscious of the differences between his scientific and his rhetorical treatment of the same subject, is indicated by the statement with which he concludes his section on the forms of government in the *Rhetoric:*

> We have also briefly considered the means and methods by which we shall gain a good knowledge of the moral qualities and institutions peculiar to the various forms of government—only, however, to the extent demanded by the present occasion; a detailed account of the subject has been given in the *Politics.*

The epideictic speaker, as his function is to praise or blame, finds that his subject-matter lies largely in the field of ethics. We have in the *Rhetoric,* therefore, a summary view of the needed ethical material—happiness, goods, virtue and vice, wrong-doing and injustice, pleasure, equity, laws, and friendship. These subjects are given a much fuller exposition in the *Ethics,* and some of the rhetorical definitions, notably that of pleasure, are there repudiated. While neither ethics nor politics were exact sciences in Aristotle's eyes, and while he repeatedly insisted that the exactness of the physical sciences should not be expected in them, he nevertheless put forth a much greater effort in those fields than in rhetoric to arrive at conceptions that would bear searching criticism. The ethical conceptions of the *Rhetoric* are the conceptions of the man in the street—current popular notions that would supply the most plausible premises for persuasive speeches.

Aristotle remarks in the opening of the *Rhetoric* that forensic oratory, more than political, is given to unscrupulous practices. But the oratorical jurisprudence which he offers as the material of the forensic speaker would not go far to elevate the argumentation of the courtroom. This section of the rhetoric most clearly indicates that Aristotle's was a scientific and not a moral earnestness; the dialectician is here in the ascendant.

In dealing with the evidence of witnesses, the following are useful arguments. If you have no witnesses on your side, you will argue that the judges must decide from what is probable; that this is meant by "giving a verdict in accordance with one's honest opinion"; that probabilities cannot be bribed to mislead the court; and that probabilities are never convicted of perjury . If you *have* witnesses, and the other man has not, you will argue that probabilities cannot be put on their trial, and that we could do without the evidence of witnesses altogether if we need do no more than balance the pleas advanced on either side. . . . So, clearly, we need never be at a loss for useful evidence.

The entire section on forensic rhetoric recognizes that each pleader's loyalty is to his case, and that as a skilful rhetorician he must be quick to discern all the persuasive possibilities of any situation. Aristotle professed a dislike for the business, but once engaged in the classification of arguments he is concerned with rhetorical effectiveness and not with moral justifiability.

The explicit statement which shows that Aristotle regarded rhetoric as an instrument of persuasion quite de-

tached from the moral nature of the rhetorician, occurs in the third book, in connection with the discussion of delivery.

Besides, delivery is—very properly—not regarded as an elevated subject of inquiry. Still, *the whole business of rhetoric being concerned with appearances,* we must pay attention to the subject of delivery, unworthy though it is, because we cannot do without it.

Turning now from the general problem of the relationship of the *Rhetoric* to Platonic Truth, we take up the second of Plato's suggestions in the *Phædrus,* that the rhetorician must be a dialectician, a man who can distinguish between particulars and universals, who can define his terms, and who can distinguish debatable from undebatable questions. With this Aristotle seems to be in agreement. He opens his *Rhetoric* by declaring that it is the counterpart of dialectic. Elsewhere he refers to rhetoric as parallel to, an offshoot or branch of, dialectic. He also says that the master of dialectic will be the true master of rhetoric. But it is impossible to make clear the relation between dialectic and rhetoric without explaining the Platonic contrast between the two, and the great advance made by Aristotle in relating both of them to demonstrative science.

After all, the sum and substance of Plato's suggestions for rhetoric is that rhetoric, if it is really to be an art, must coincide with philosophy. When Plato said that the rhetorician must be a dialectician, he meant that he must be a philosopher. So far as he differs from the philosopher, he is an impostor; so far as he coincides with him, his art of rhetoric is superseded. But Aristotle gave to the term dialectic such a different significance that it is another thing entirely to say that the rhetorician should be a dialectician. For Plato, dialectic was the whole process of rational analysis by which the soul was led into the knowledge of Ideas. It had both a positive and a negative aspect. In the earlier dialogues the negative function was most prominent, and the principal contribution which the Socratic dialectic made to the wisdom of those who underwent his cross-examination was to disabuse them of their false knowledge. As Plato developed his own doctrine of Ideas, dialectic became the instrument of awakening by which the soul recollected the eternal Ideas which it had known in a pre-existent state. Dialectic became a means of positive instruction, as well as of refutation. As Plato grew old and became more dogmatic in exposition, he found the dialectical form somewhat inconvenient, but he did not develop a new form for didactic procedure. The teachings implanted by dialectic represented reasoned and tested conclusions, carrying with them the certainty of philosophical knowledge, as opposed to the superficial opinions which constituted the material of rhetoric, and which persuaded without giving any real instruction. In Plato's later life, mathematical reasoning came to represent the type of demonstrated knowledge, but at the time of the attacks upon the sophists and rhetoricians, certainty and exactitude were to be found through the dialectical process.

Aristotle had even more clearly in mind the antithesis between opinion or common sense and scientific knowledge or real instruction. He had, however, no sympathy with the Platonic doctrine of Ideas, and was free from any sense of a mystical significance for dialectic. Observing the didactic elements of the Platonic dialectic, he perfected the syllogism as the instrument of scientific knowledge and teaching. In the two books of the *Analytica Priora* he developed the functions and varieties of the syllogism and suggested that it could be applied both to scientific demonstration and to the process of argumentation in the realm of opinion. There is, however, such a difference of matter and purpose in scientific and nonscientific discussion that the use of the syllogism in the one and in the other is to be governed by a distinct body of theory. The *Analytica Posteriora* develops the use of the syllogism for demonstrative reasoning, and the *Topica*, together with the *Sophistici Elenchi*, for dialectic. The material for the *Topica* and the *Sophistici Elenchi*—which is really the last book of the *Topica*—is drawn from that type of argumentation pilloried by Plato in the *Euthydemus, Sophist*, and *Statesman*. Aristotle in his classification of fallacies cites the *Euthydemus* frequently. Plato drew a vivid picture of the fallacious disputers and excited the feelings of the reader against such arguments without really analyzing the fallacies. But Aristotle, in the *Sophistici Elenchi*, analyzed and classified fallacies with the purpose of enabling the reader to use them more skillfully. That type of disputation which Plato made a variety of false rhetoric, the very antithesis of true dialectic, is for Aristotle an integral part of dialectic. Thus it is evident that Aristotle has allowed dialectic to descend into that realm of

opinion inhabited by sophists and rhetoricians. Where Plato had been chiefly
impressed by the contrast between
rhetoric and dialectic, Aristotle noticed
the similarities. The realm of opinion,
which Plato had regarded as unworthy
the attention of the philosopher, is thus
accorded by Aristotle two distinct disciplines, dialectic and rhetoric. There
are differences between the two, but the
more fundamental contrast is between
rhetoric and dialectic, on the one hand,
and scientific reasoning, on the other.

Scientific procedure, for Aristotle,
starts with universal or necessary principles and proceeds to universal and
necessary conclusions. Both dialectic
and rhetoric, however, take as their
premises current popular opinions, or
perhaps the opinions of dissenters. Any
probable or plausible assertion will
serve. The fundamental principles of a
science cannot be proved within the
bounds of that science; they are therefore assumed. The only way of questioning them is in dialectical debate. A
few fundamental principles, as axioms,
are common to all or to several of the
sciences; but by far the larger part of the
principles employed are special to the
sciences concerned. As against this,
rhetoric and dialectic are not limited to
the propositions of any particular field.
They may regard the ultimate assumptions of any science as mere probabilities and discuss them as such. In
dialectic, the number of special propositions, corresponding to scientific laws
peculiar to one field, is small. On the
other hand, the number of general
propositions, called topics (corresponding to the comparatively few
axioms of science), is large. In science,
again, we do not have matter to be set-

tled by debate, but rather by impartial
investigation. Dialectic and rhetoric can
argue as easily upon one side of the
question as another. They may employ
any material conceded by an opponent.
They may be indifferent to the truth of
a conclusion if the form and method
have been accurately followed.

From all this it is evident that, as
contrasted with scientific knowledge,
dialectic and rhetoric are much alike.
There are certain differences, however,
which Aristotle regarded as sufficiently
fundamental to justify their treatment
as separate disciplines. The most obvious difference, and one which accounts for several others, is that
dialectic is an argument conducted by
two speakers with a small audience of
interested listeners who will see that the
argument is fairly conducted. Such a
method of argument is best fitted for
speculative questions, although it can
be applied to anything. It will be concerned with logical processes and not
with the feelings of an audience. It is
aimed not so much at persuading the
opponent as at defeating him by involving him in contradictions. The
method of reasoning employed is the
syllogistic or inductive, the only difference from genuinely scientific reasoning being that the materials are
taken from the realm of the merely
probable. Rhetoric, on the other hand,
because of the fact that one speaker is
continuously addressing a large audience of untrained hearers, cannot use
the form of scientific reasoning. In place
of the syllogism and induction it uses
the enthymeme and example. Since the
feelings of the hearers will probably be
more influential than the logic of the
speaker, rhetoric must include an ac-

count of the emotions and characters of men. While rhetoric is not necessary to the dialectician, the rhetorician will be better for a thorough knowledge of dialectic.

One additional contrast between rhetoric and dialectic is of significance. Theoretically, Aristotle regarded rhetoric and dialectic as applicable to the same range of subjects. Theoretically, anything could be discussed by either method. But practically, as we see when we compare the topics of the *Topica* and the *Rhetoric,* rhetorical discussion is limited to human actions and characters. The subject-matter of rhetoric is for practical purposes limited to ethics and politics. There is a mention of the popular exposition of scientific subjects as one of the uses of rhetoric, but the system as Aristotle develops it is much more limited than the system of dialectical argument.

Analytics (logic), dialectic, and rhetoric form the organon of thought and expression for the ancient world. Aristotle, as much indebted to the Platonic dialogues, perhaps, as to his own observations of Athenian life, observed scientific thought, systematized it, and gave us logic; observing the sport dear to all Athenians—argumentation by question and answer—and systematizing it, he gave us dialectic; observing and systematizing the art of persuading crowds, he gave us rhetoric. Thus, although Aristotle agrees with Plato that the rhetorician should also be a dialectician, it is evident that the dictum has a very different meaning for the two writers.

Another suggestion in the *Phædrus* concerned order and arrangement. This suggestion is developed by Aristotle in the second half of the third book of the *Rhetoric.* He attacks as unnecessarily complex the numerous divisions of the contemporary rhetoricians, and treats arrangement under the heads of Proem, Narrative, Proofs, and Epilogue. As our purpose is to compare Aristotle with Plato, rather than to give an exposition of his *Rhetoric,* we need observe only that this Platonic suggestion is carried out by Aristotle, although he was probably much more indebted to other rhetoricians than to Plato for his discussion of arrangement.

The Platonic requirement that the nature of the soul must be shown, and arguments adapted to the different kinds of people addressed by the speaker, is the basis of the oft-repeated assertion that the *Rhetoric* is an expanded *Phædrus.* There are two reasons for this. In the first place, that part of the second book of the *Rhetoric* which treats of the emotions and characters of men is the part which has the greatest interest and significance for the modern reader. Secondly, it is, perhaps, the most distinct addition Aristotle made to the work of his predecessors in the field. But even here, where Aristotle has apparently carried out the suggestions of his master most brilliantly, it must be observed that his treatment is only a popular and inexact discussion of the external manifestations of character and emotions, and not the sort of treatment he would have given the doctrine of the affections, had he developed it in his *De Anima.* It is also to be noted that while the classification of the emotions is as complete as the rhetorician would desire, Aristotle did not share Plato's notion that a true art of rhetoric would enable a speaker to adapt himself to each of the persons of an audience as the dialectician adjusts himself to one deuteragonist. He expressly disclaims such a belief.

The theory of rhetoric is concerned not with what seems probable to a given individual like Socrates or Hippias, but with what seems probable to men of a given type.

Nor does Aristotle suppose that even the best of rhetoricians will always succeed with his audience. The function of rhetoric is not simply to succeed in persuading, but rather to discover the means of coming as near such success as the circumstances of each particular case allow.

Style and delivery, Plato stated, were necessary preliminaries to the art of rhetoric. An elevated style, however, was to be attained, not by technique, but by contemplation of lofty subjects. Aristotle seems to have shared his master's feeling that style and delivery should be subordinate matters, as spectacle was the least artistic element of the drama. His classifying mind, however, was much better able than Plato's to resist the tendency to place all subjects in a hierarchical order of moral dignity and to slight all the lower orders. He dismisses delivery briefly with the explanation that not enough is yet known about it to treat it scientifically; but he does regard both delivery and diction as means of persuasive discourse.

Plato's dislike for wiring, which in our day would so limit the province of rhetoric, does not seem to have disturbed Aristotle. He wrote several times as much as Plato, and upon subjects which Plato would probably have regarded as unsuitable for literary presentation. It is only on the heights of learning that truth and beauty are always compatible, and for the most part Plato kept to the heights. Aristotle saw his own writing, not as moral truth to be graven on the soul of a reader, but as an instrument by which his thought was systematized and preserved. Had he agreed with the Socrates of the *Phædrus*, he would not have devoted twelve chapters of the *Rhetoric* to style.

XIV

In comparing Aristotle with Plato, we have seen that the *Rhetoric* discusses most of the questions of rhetorical theory raised by Plato in the *Gorgias*; it agrees with the rhetoricians that rhetoric is an art, that the universality of its applications does not mean that it has no subject matter of its own, that the evils arising from rhetoric are no greater than the evils that arise from the abuse of all good things, that truth and righteousness are, on the whole, more prevalent because of a general knowledge of rhetoric, and that the persuasion of multitudes of relatively ignorant people, instead of being merely a vulgar task, fit only for demagogues, is a necessary part of education and government in a stable society.

A contrast of the *Rhetoric* with the *Phædrus* makes it evident that even here Aristotle is closer to the rhetoricians than to Plato. Rhetoric *is* an art of appearance; and this fact prevents it neither from being an art nor from serving the ends of truth and righteousness. Rhetoric, instead of being a sham dialectic, is the *counterpart* of dialectic, a dialectic fundamentally different from the Platonic conception of it. The analysis of the emotions, which seems to follow Plato, is, after all, of a loose, inexact, and external character, as Aristotle thought was suitable for rhetoric. Aristotle agreed with Plato that the rhetorician should be virtuous and intelligent, that he should be a keen logician, that he should understand the ordering and arranging of material, and that he should know many things beyond the principles of rhetoric. They were also agreed that contemporary rhetoricians fell far short of these ideals. But the fact that Aristotle and Plato agreed upon the deficiencies of Athenian rhetoricians seems to have blinded us to the equally significant fact that Aristotle's rhetorical theory bears more resemblance to that of Protagoras and Gorgias than to that of Plato.

XV

The significance of a study of rhetoric in Athens is not entirely historical. However indifferent we may be to Protagoras and Gorgias, we live in a world of journalists, publicists, advertisers, politicians, diplomats, propagandists, reformers, educators, salesmen, preachers, lecturers, and popularizers. When in Platonic mood, we condemn them all as sophists and rhetoricians. And the Platonic attitude is supported by the growth of specialization and "research." To large classes of specialists, the rest of mankind is made up of ignorant laymen. These scholars and experts share Plato's contempt for the masses; they apparently are as blind as he to the limitations of the academic

mind; they dwell so securely in the well-mapped areas of knowledge that they decline to venture into the uncharted realms of opinion and probability. The modern sophists may justly be reproached for their habit of offering mere opinion when knowledge is obtainable; but it may be questioned whether theirs is a greater error than the specialists' habit of mistaking knowledge for wisdom. In the problem of the relation of Plato to Protagoras, of philosopher to sophist and rhetorician, are involved the issues which we debate when we discuss the aims of a liberal education, the desirability of government by experts, the relation of a university to the state, the duty of a scholar in a democracy, the function of public opinion in a popular government, the difference between a conventional and a rational morality, to say nothing of more speculative questions.

We cannot agree with Bishop Welldon's statement that Aristotle's *Rhetoric* is "a solitary instance of a book which not only begins a science, but completes it," but we do not regard the *Rhetoric* as of merely historical interest. It is the one treatment of the subject which raises clearly the problem of the relation of rhetoric to psychology, ethics, politics, jurisprudence, and literary criticism. If we have made any progress in these subjects since Aristotle, in so far his *Rhetoric* may be inadequate for modern needs. But for a sense of proportion and a grasp of relations, we do well to acquaint ourselves with the survey of the subject made by the great classifier of knowledge.

Edward P. J. Corbett

Introduction to the Rhetoric and Poetics of Aristotle

◊ *Anyone who wanted to get a basic idea of classical rhetoric from reading a primary text would do well to read Aristotle's* Rhetoric, *the fountain-head of all subsequent rhetorics in the classical tradition. And in order to get a firmer understanding of the* Rhetoric, *the reader should investigate some of Aristotle's philosophical works, such as the* Nicomachean Ethics *and the* Politics, *to which Aristotle frequently refers in his* Rhetoric, *and some of Aristotle's other contributions to the language arts, such as the* Poetics *and the six treatises on logic or dialectics in the* Organon. *In this Introduction from the Modern Library edition of* The Rhetoric and the Poetics of Aristotle, *keeping in mind the reader who is not yet very well acquainted with the works of Aristotle, Professor Corbett provides some biographical information about Aristotle, gives an overview of the contents and the organization of the* Rhetoric *and the* Poetics, *and explains the key concepts and terminology in both of these related and influential treatises. But this Introduction is no adequate substitute for the texts of the* Rhetoric *and the* Poetics *themselves.* ◊

The *Rhetoric* and the *Poetics* are two of Aristotle's contributions to the arts of language. His third contribution is the collection of treatises on logic known as the *Organon*.[1] One might say that the *Rhetoric*, the *Poetics*, and the *Organon* constitute the Aristotelian trivium. The third member of the medieval trivium, of course, was grammar, but in the Greco-Roman schools and even in the medieval schools, one of the areas of study under the heading of grammar was the sort of thing that Aristotle considers in the *Poetics*.

The Separate Provinces of Rhetoric and Poetics

Although all three texts occasionally discuss common topics, each of them has its distinctive province. The trea-

From *The Rhetoric and Poetics of Aristotle*. Introduction by Edward P. J. Corbett. Modern Library College Editions. New York: Random House, 1984. pp. v–xxvi. Reprinted with permission.

tises in the *Organon*, for instance, treat such subjects as the meaning of individual words, the formulation of propositions by putting individual words into subject-predicate relationships, strict logical reasoning in the form of the syllogism, and the art of dialectical discussion. The main province of the *Rhetoric* is the art of persuasive oratory. The *Poetics* deals primarily with the art of fiction—more particularly with the art of storytelling in the form of the drama and the epic. But in each of these treatises, there are implicit and explicit cross references to the other two, thus confirming the interrelationship of these arts of language.

There have been times, however, when the lines of demarcation between these allied but distinctive provinces have become blurred. The distinctions between the provinces of rhetoric and poetics have been especially liable to being confused. Starting with the Italian Renaissance in the sixteenth century, it was frequently difficult to tell whether a particular creative writer or literary critic was operating in the realm of rhetoric or the realm of poetics.

Wilbur Samuel Howell's collected essays, entitled *Poetics, Rhetoric, and Logic: Studies in the Basic Disciplines of Criticism* (1975),[2] try to correct the misconceptions that had developed about these three disciplines and to protest the exclusion of rhetoric and logic from modern literary theory. Howell may seem to want to have it both ways: to keep the distinctions between the three disciplines clear and yet to give rhetoric and logic as much of a place in literary theory as poetics has. But Howell is concerned that critics have not kept in mind the differences be-

tween mimetic or imitative discourse and nonmimetic discourse. Mimetic discourse, on the one hand, is a "literature of symbol"; nonmimetic discourse, on the other hand, is a "literature of statement." "The simplest way to describe this difference," Howell maintains, "is to say that the words which make up the rhetorical utterance lead the reader to states of reality, whereas the words making up the poetical utterance lead the reader to things which stand by deputy for states of reality."[3] Howell's main point is that the failure of critics to recognize the distinction between mimetic discourse and nonmimetic discourse and to give a place to logic and rhetoric along with poetics has prevented them from developing a literary theory comprehensive enough to deal with texts as different as Milton's *Paradise Lost*, an epic poem, and his *Areopagitica*, an essay in which he argues against censorship.

But if some critics have not been concerned about the differences between the provinces of poetics, rhetoric, and logic, Aristotle, with his lifelong passion for taxonomies, recognized and preserved the distinctions. The mere fact that he wrote treatises in all three areas suggests that he was aware of the distinctions. But philosophically too, he was committed to recognizing the differences. He classified the various arts and sciences into the theoretical, the practical, and the productive. Another way to put this classification is to say that he viewed the arts and sciences as being devoted to *knowing* (the theoretical) or to *doing* (the practical) or to *making* (the productive). What characterized theoretical sciences such as physics, mathematics, and meta-physics was that they dealt with things that could not be other than they were; they dealt with the necessary, not the contingent.

The difference between the necessary and the contingent was also the basis for the difference that Aristotle saw between science (*episteme̅*) and art (*techne̅*). The sciences dealt with the necessary, with the invariable, with what *had* to be; the arts dealt with the contingent, with the probable, with those areas where there were *choices* to be made. So those disciplines in the *Organon* dealing with strict demonstration or proof—that is, with reasoning or inference based on absolute premises leading to a necessary conclusion—were closer to being sciences than arts. But dialectical reasoning, which operated in the area of the contingent or the probable, was an art. If it was indulged in primarily for the sake of *knowing*, it was a theoretical art; if, on the other hand, it was indulged in for the sake of improved *doing* or *acting*, it was a practical art.

As Aristotle says in the very first sentence of his text on the subject, rhetoric is the counterpart of dialectic. As a way of *doing* or *acting*—specifically, as a way of arguing persuasively about contingent human affairs on the basis of mere probabilities—it is a practical art, like two other practical arts that Aristotle wrote treatises on, ethics and politics. Although a product usually results from rhetorical activity—namely, a speech—rhetoric is primarily an art of process. The art and the practice of rhetoric is even more prevalent today than it was in Aristotle's time. One can hardly get through a single day without being exposed dozens of times to some form of persuasive discourse, the main concern of the art of rhetoric. It is not too much to claim that rhetoric is the art that governs those human relationships that are conducted in the medium of spoken and written words.

Poetics, however, was primarily an art of product. It was indeed a productive art. The Greek words *poe̅sis* and poie̅tike̅ are derived from the verb poiein, "to make." Aristotle distinguishes *useful* arts, such as pottery, from *fine* arts, such as sculpturing. Poetics was a fine art, an art of composing imaginative literature—lyrics, plays, stories. The two kinds of imaginative literature that Aristotle ultimately focuses on in the *Poetics* are epic and tragedy. There is an indication, right in the text of the *Poetics*,[4] that Aristotle devoted a section of this treatise to a discussion of comedy, but that section is lost.[5] What has survived of the *Poetics*, however, has become the most influential—though not always the most revered—text in literary criticism.

Aristotle: The Man and His Works

What little is known about the life of Aristotle and about the circumstances surrounding the composition of his works has been gained (1) from remarks that Aristotle himself makes in his extant works, (2) from references to him and his works in the surviving texts of his contemporaries and of later classical authors (e.g., Cicero and Quintilian), and (3) from inferences and conjectures made on the basis of other surviving documentary evidence. Before we go on to consider the principal concepts and some of the key terminology of the *Rhetoric* and *Poetics,* we might review the generally accepted historical information about the man and his works.[6]

Aristotle was born in 384 B.C. in the little town of Stagira, in Macedonia, on the peninsula of Chalcidice, which juts into the Aegean Sea. His father, Nicomachus, was the court physician for Amyntas II, king of Macedonia and the father of Philip the Great. Aristotle's interest in the natural sciences and his penchant for classification may have been due to the early medical training he received from his father. In 367 B.C., at the age of seventeen, Aristotle went to Athens and enrolled as a student in Plato's Academy, remaining there for the next twenty years, as a student and a teacher, until Plato's death in 347 B.C. He left Athens at that time, largely because of the anti-Macedonian feeling that had sprung up there as a result of Philip's military victories, which weakened the Greek confederacy. He spent the next five years in Assos in Asia Minor and in Mitylene on the island of Lesbos, studying and teaching biology and zoology. In 342, Philip appointed Aristotle as tutor to his son Alexander, who was then only thirteen years old. It would be interesting to know what Aristotle taught this future military conqueror of the Middle East during the two years that he served as his teacher. In 335, on the death of Philip, Aristotle returned to Athens, where he entered on the most fruitful period of his life. He founded the famous Peripatetic School of philosophy at the Lyceum, where he lectured on a wide variety of subjects and wrote or revised most of his surviving works. With the death of Alexander the Great in 323, anti-Macedonian feeling again broke out in Athens, and Aristotle, after turning over his school to his pupil Theophrastus, retired to his native land, where he died a year later, in 322.

If the facts about Aristotle's life are meager and somewhat vague, the facts about the composition and publication of his works are even more scarce and uncertain. In Aristotle's time, there was no such thing as publication in the modern sense of that term. A manuscript culture prevailed at the time, and it was more likely that a literate slave enscribed the copy of a text than that the author laboriously wrote out the words. Very often, the students themselves made copies of the lectures delivered in the schools.

We do not know for certain when the text of the *Rhetoric* was written or "published," but classical scholars have made some educated guesses.[7] Because of a number of topical references in the text itself to Athenian events and concerns, one can feel quite secure in deducing that the *Rhetoric* was addressed to an Athenian audience. That inference in turn suggests that the *Rhetoric* was written either during Aristotle's first residence in Athens (367–347) or during his second residence (335–322). To determine which of these periods is the likelier one, one has to consider other textual and historical evidence. For instance, because of the many references in Book III of the *Rhetoric* to other Aristotelian works—the *Poetics* for one—about whose dates there is a fair degree of certainty, it seems safe to conjecture that Book III was written not only much later than Books I and II but also as late as the second period of residency. The latest historical reference in the *Rhetoric* occurs in Book II, Chapter 23, 1398a, where there is an allusion to the embassy that Philip sent to Thebes before the battle of Chaeronea, which it is known took place in 338 B.C. Ultimately, internal evidence of this kind supports the contention of E. M. Cope, perhaps the most learned of the nineteenth-century commentators on Aristotle's text, that although parts of the *Rhetoric* may have been conceived and even written quite early during Aristotle's first residency in Athens, the text that we have today was not finished and certainly not "published" until after 335, the beginning of his second and final residency in that Greek city.[8]

On the other hand, the available evidence confirms that all the lost rhetorical works of Aristotle were composed rather early in the period of the first residency. There is evidence that soon after he enrolled in Plato's Academy, Aristotle began to deliver afternoon lectures in rhetoric and that his earliest written composition was the dialogue *Gryllus*, which dealt with the nature of rhetoric.[9] Since the extant text of the *Rhetoric* creates the impression of being a tentative, unfinished set of lecture notes, it seems likely that Aristotle has incorporated some, if not most, of the notes he used in the elementary lectures that he was delivering in the years 360–353. Another of the lost rhetoric texts—part of which must have figured in those early lectures—was a text that bore the Greek title of *Synagōgē Technōn*, which can be translated as *A*

Collection of Rhetorical Handbooks. According to the testimony of his contemporaries who mentioned this text in their own works, this collection of excerpts from rhetoric textbooks past and present constituted a quick history of rhetoric from its origin, right up to the time when the anthology was compiled. Another text, which was questionably attributed to Aristotle, was entitled *Theodectea*, reputedly in honor of his friend and former pupil Theodectes. The *Rhetorica ad Alexandrum*, long thought to have been written by Aristotle, partly because he once tutored the young Alexander, was eventually rejected by classical scholars as being part of the Aristotelian canon and was attributed by some of them to a contemporary of Aristotle's, Anaximenes. What all of this history of the Aristotelian rhetorical texts indicates is that Aristotle became interested in rhetoric very early in his academic career and maintained an active interest in it throughout most of his life.

Most students of Aristotle's works regard the *Poetics* as being one of his later works. They assign it to the period of second residency in Athens and fix the completion date as falling somewhere in the range of 334–330 B.C. But throughout his voluminous commentary on the text, Gerald F. Else has presented suggestive, if not conclusive, evidence that "the basic stock of the *Poetics* text is early rather than late, i.e., belongs to the Assos-Mytilene period (347–342) or even to the time before Plato's death (347), rather than to Aristotle's last period in Athens (after 335)."[10] We may never be able to settle definitively the date of this influential text because, as John Gassner has pointed out, the oldest surviving Greek manuscript of the *Poetics* is dated about 1000 A.D.[11]

In any case, Aristotle's interest in the poetic branch of the language arts seems not to have developed until later in his professional career. In fact, one can no more read the *Poetics* in isolation from Aristotle's other works than one can read and adequately understand the *Rhetoric* apart from his other philosophic works. Richard McKeon has conveniently summarized how considerations of various aspects of the poetic art are interwoven through the fabric of some of the other famous texts of Aristotle:

Poetry is treated as such in the *Poetics*; its educational function is taken up in the *Politics*; the statements and arguments of poets and of characters in poetry are analyzed in the *Rhetoric*; the moral situations and moral aphorisms of poets are used in the *Nicomachean Ethics*; and poetry and mythology are quoted as evidence in the *Metaphysics*.[12]

Considering his honorific treatment of both rhetoric and poetics, Aristotle may well have developed very early in his student days in the Academy an interest in these two subjects and have resolved that some day he would counteract the derogatory treatment they had received from his mentor Plato. It is easy to find statements in the *Rhetoric* and the *Poetics* that seem to be direct contradictions of statements about rhetoric and poetics preserved in such Platonic dialogues as the *Phaedrus*, the *Gorgias*, the *Ion*, and the *Republic*.

Both the *Rhetoric* and the *Poetics* have been subjected to extensive and intensive analysis and interpretation. The very persistence of the commentary indicates the importance that scholars have attached to these two texts in the history of ideas. The very fact that learned scholars still argue with one another about many of the pregnant passages is evidence that these meticulously scrutinized texts do not readily yield their meaning. Part of the continuing difficulty with the texts is that one is dealing with translations from an ancient language. But even when the texts are read in their original language, it is difficult to get a secure grasp on the meaning because of the vagueness or ambiguity of many of the Greek words. Problems with the words are compounded by the fact that the texts that have come down to us represent sets of incomplete, unrefined lecture notes. Many of the statements in both texts that are now puzzling were undoubtedly elaborated on and illustrated in the classroom. Those oral glosses would be invaluable now if they could be recovered. Lacking them, one has to depend on one's own skill in reading, on the help to be had from astute classical scholars, and on the illumination offered by pertinent passages of other extant works by Aristotle.

The Rhetoric

The Aristotelian text known as the *Rhetoric* is concerned with the art of persuasive oratory. Partly in response to the negative views of rhetoric expressed by Plato in his dialogues called the *Gorgias* and the *Phædrus*, Aristotle wanted to give this art a more systematic, a more philosophical, treatment than it had received in previous handbooks (*technai*) of rhetoric. Although Aristotle was not as popular a teacher of rhetoric as his contemporary Isocrates, he did produce a seminal and, in many ways, an original treatise. Not

everything that is included in the following exposition of the Aristotelian
rhetorical system represents an original contribution to the Greek tradition
of rhetoric;[13] but even when he is repeating the commonplace concepts of
rhetoric, Aristotle manages somehow to
give them the stamp of his distinctive
authority.

There were three kinds of persuasive
oratory: (1) deliberative or political oratory—the oratory of the public forum;
(2) judicial or forensic oratory—the oratory of the law courts; and (3) epideictic
or demonstrative oratory—the oratory
of ceremonial occasions. With his great
penchant for symmetrical classifications, Aristotle worked out this neat
scheme for the three types of oratory
(see Chapter 2 of Book 1):

Forensic

1. Time province—the past
2. End or objective—the establishment of justice and injustice
3. Procedural means—accusation
   and defense

Epideictic

1. Time province—the present
2. End or objective—the establishment of honor and dishonor
3. Procedural means—praise and
   blame

Deliberative

1. Time province—the future
2. End or objective—the establishment of the expediency or the
   harmfulness of a proposed course
   of action
3. Procedural means—exhortation
   and dehortation

As in most classifications, the categories here occasionally "leak," but it is
surprising how often they remain firm.

Before we look in some detail at Aristotle's advice about how to manage the
arguments in these three types of oratory, we would do well to get an overview of the whole of the *Rhetoric*. One
way to get this overview is to look at the
contents pages of this edition, where W.
Rhys Roberts provides detailed annotations of each of the chapters. But
these annotations may be too detailed
to give the reader an easily comprehensible overview of the complete text. The
following brief outline of the main divisions of the three books of the *Rhetoric* may be easier to grasp:

Book I

General introduction to the art of rhetoric (Chapters 1–3)

2. The special topics (*eidē*) for each of
   the three types of oratory (Chapters 4–15)
3. The "non-artistic" (*atechnoi*)
   means of persuasion (Chapter 15)

Book II

1. The ethical appeal (*ēthos*) (Chapter
   1)
2. Analysis of contrasting pairs of
   emotions for the emotional appeal
   (*pathos*) (Chapters 2–11)
3. Analysis of types of human character according to age and fortune
   (Chapters 12–17)

A chapter of recapitulation and transition (Chapter 18)

4. The common topics (*koinoi topoi*)
   for inventing and refuting arguments (Chapters 19–26)

Book III

1. The style of persuasive speeches (Chapters 1–12)
2. The arrangement or organization of persuasive speeches (Chapters 13–19)

There are some questionable parts in this line-up of chapters. One wonders, for instance, why the common topics were not treated immediately after the special topics. Such mysteries lead one to conclude that Aristotle never finally edited his lecture notes before they were published. Overlooking questionable features of this sort, W. Rhys Roberts, the translator of the text of the *Rhetoric* used in this book, gives us this rather tidy outline of the text:

If we consider the work as a whole, the first Book may perhaps be described as mainly logical and political, the second as mainly ethical or psychological, the third as mainly literary or stylistic. The speaker perhaps counts most in Book I, the audience in Book II, and the speech itself in Book III. To the man who aspires to oratorical success, Book I seems to say: "Be logical. Think clearly. Reason cogently. Remember that *argument* is the life and soul of persuasion." Book II: "Study human nature. Observe the characters and emotions of your audience, as well as your own character and emotions." Book III: "Attend to delivery. Use language rightly. Arrange your material well. End crisply." And the whole treatise presupposes good wits and a fine general education.[14]

At the beginning of Chapter 2 of Book I, Aristotle gives his unique definition of rhetoric: "Rhetoric may be defined as the faculty (*dynamis*) of observing in any given case the available means of persuasion." There are a number of things to be noted about this definition. First of all, although the generic term that Aristotle uses here to define rhetoric is *dynamis* ("faculty" or "power" or "ability"), in most other places in the text, he speaks of rhetoric as being an *art* (*technē*). We can reconcile these two terms by taking the position that if one has mastered the *art* of rhetoric, one has the *faculty* or *ability* to discover the available means of persuasion. Aristotle does not designate persuasion as the end or function of rhetoric; rather, the function of rhetoric is to observe or discover the potentially persuasive arguments (*pisteis*) in a particular case. With this emphasis, Aristotle relieves rhetoric of the onus of having to achieve persuasion at any cost. He implies here and elsewhere that if one acquires the ability to discover the available arguments, one will be guided in making a choice of the most effective and legitimate arguments by one's intellectual and moral disposition. One final feature to note about the definition is that there is no mention that the act of persuasion is a verbal art. There is no such phrase as occurs in the definitions proposed by Cicero and Quintilian: "by means of speaking' (*in dicendo* or *scientia bene dicendi*). Aristotle probably felt that the verbal nature of rhetoric was so obvious that he did not need to be explicit about it in his famous definition.

Aristotle touches on virtually all of the key concepts and key terms of his system of rhetoric in the first three chapters of Book I. For that reason, these three chapters should be read very carefully, sentence by sentence. The remainder of the *Rhetoric* spells out in detail, and occasionally with illustrations, the general outline of Aristotle's rhetoric as it is laid out in these introductory chapters. Here we will review the main terms and concepts that figure in the *Rhetoric*.

One of Aristotle's innovative contributions to the art of rhetoric is his concept of the "available means of persuasion." The first division that he makes of these means is the dichotomy of "artistic proofs" (*entechnoi pisteis*) and "non-artistic proofs" or "non-technical proofs" (*atechnoi pisteis*). Basically, the distinction is made between those proofs that are produced in the art (*entechnoi*, literally, "in the art") of rhetoric and those proofs that are available from outside the art (*atechnoi*, literally, "not part of the art"). The non-artistic proofs are such substantiating data as laws, contracts, oaths, testimony of witnesses, and evidence given under torture (see Book I, Chapters 2 and 15). Speakers do not have to "invent" these proofs; they merely have to seek them out. These external proofs (except the last one perhaps) play a more prominent role in modern persuasive situations than they did in Aristotle's time.

But "the true constituents of the art"—by which Rhys Roberts in Chapter 1 means the essence of rhetoric—are the artistic proofs: the appeals to reason (*logos*), the appeals to the emotions of the audience (*pathos*), the appeals exerted by the character of the speaker (*ethos*). This tripartite division of the artistic proofs probably represents Aristotle's most original and most influential contribution to the art of rhetoric. These three species of proofs were picked up by virtually all subsequent rhetoricians and elaborated on and refined. Although all three of these kinds of proofs play a part in all three kinds of oratory, the logical proof is perhaps most prominent in judicial discourse, the ethical proof most prominent in deliberative discourse, and the emotional proof most prominent in epideictic discourse. And although the three proofs overlap somewhat, the ethical proof is most concerned with the speaker, the emotional proof with the audience, and the logical proof with the speech itself.

Aristotle observes in Chapter 2 of Book I that far from being the weakest of the means of persuasion, as some rhetoricians believed, the ethical appeal is probably the "most-effective." He is astute enough to recognize that if an audience does not admire or trust the speaker, all the skill in the world in managing the logical and emotional appeals will go for naught. He treats very briefly this most potent means of persuasion in the first chapter of Book II, telling the reader there that his previous analysis of virtue in Chapter 9 of Book I and his subsequent treatment of good will and friendliness under the emotions are pertinent to the ethical appeal. The most significant thing he says about *ethos* at the beginning of Book II is that a speaker will inspire the audience's confidence if he can create an image of himself as a person of good sense (*phronēsis*), goodwill (*eunoia*), and good moral character (*aretē*). Since Aristotle does not elaborate on these qualities in the *Rhetoric*, one has to consult some of his other philosophical works—especially the *Ethics*—in order to understand adequately everything that is encompassed in these three constituents of the speaker's ethical appeal.

Aristotle devotes ten chapters of Book II to a discussion of how to manipulate the emotions of the audience in argumentative situations, even though in the first chapter of the *Rhetoric*, he seems to deplore the use of emotional appeals. But what he really deplores in the first chapter is the stirring of emotions in inappropriate situations and the concentrating on emotional appeals to the utter exclusion of appeals to the rational faculties of the audience. Like Plato, Aristotle would prefer that people always made their choices and decisions on rational grounds; but realist that he is, he knows that people are creatures of passion and emotion as well as of reason. Far from believing that the stirring of human emotions is inherently immoral, Aristotle recognizes that if speakers do not responsibly rouse emotions, they will frequently not be able to persuade people to change their minds or be able to move them into action, even though the audience has been won over logically. Although subsequent rhetoricians acknowledged the importance of arousing or allaying the emotions of the audience, none of them devoted as much attention as Aristotle does in this book to an analysis of the basic emotions and of the way to stir them or calm them. Long before the development of a science of psychology, he gave us a remarkable analysis of the emotional mechanism of the human psyche.

Aristotle devotes considerable attention in the *Rhetoric* to the third mode of persuasion, the appeal to reason; but he expects his students to be familiar with what he has said about logical argument in the six treatises that constitute his *Organon*. He says in the very first sentence of the *Rhetoric* that "rhetoric is the counterpart of dialectic." One of the notions implicit in that pregnant first sentence is that there are some ways in which rhetoric and dialectic are similar. One similarity is that they both appeal to human reason but in a less formal and strict fashion than prevails in scientific demonstrations. The two basic ways in which the human mind reasons are induction (*epagōgē*) and deduction (*sullogismos*, "syllogism"). The rhetorical equivalent of induction is the example (*paradeigma*); the rhetorical equivalent of deduction is the enthymeme (*enthumēma*). As he says in Chapter 2, "When we base the proof of a proposition on a number of similar cases, this is induction in dialectic, example in rhetoric; when it is shown that, certain propositions being true, a further and quite distinct proposition must also be true in consequence, whether invariably or usually, this is called syllogism in dialectic, enthymeme in rhetoric."

The principles and rules and the fallacies of inductive and deductive reasoning are covered in the traditional logic course, but this is not the place to go into all the intricacies of that formalized system of reasoning. Suffice it to say here that whereas the enthymeme today denotes for many people a syllogism in which one of the premises is missing but clearly understood, it was for Aristotle a much more complex mode of reasoning. The differences might be summed up in this way: the Aristotelian enthymeme (1) often involved premises that were merely probable, thus leading to conclusions that were only generally or usually true; (2) allowed for the ethical and emotional dimensions of argument as well as for the logical; and (3) depended for its success in persuasion on the consensus that existed or was generated between the speaker and the audience.[15]

The topics (*topoi*) represented the system devised by the classical rhetoricians to aid the speaker in finding the available arguments in a particular case. Aristotle divides the topics into two kinds: the common topics (*koinoi topoi*) and the particular topics (*idia* or *eidē*). The particular topics are associated with the special subject or discipline that the discourse is considering. If, for instance, one was arguing a case at law, the particular topics resorted to would yield arguments or proofs pertinent to that legal case. Those same lines of argument would not be relevant, and therefore not effective, in a case of physics. In commenting in Chapter 2 on the particular topics, Aristotle observes that "most enthymemes are in fact based on these particular or special Lines of Argument" but that "the better the selection one makes of propositions suitable for special Lines of Argument, the nearer one comes, unconsciously, to setting up a science that is distinct from dialectic and rhetoric." As we saw in the outline on page xiv, Aristotle deals in Chapter 4–15 of Book I with the particular topics as they relate to the three types of oratory.

He first mentions the common topics in Chapter 2 of Book I and then treats them extensively in Chapters 19–26 of Book II. Because the common topics are not tied to any particular subject matter or to any specific type of oratory, they have wide applicability. For instance, the common topic of More or Less (or what might be called the topic of Degree) is usually applicable to discussions in the area of ethics or law or politics or the natural sciences—virtually to any and all subjects.

The four common topics that he mentions and discusses in Chapter 19 of Book II are (1) The Possible and the Impossible; (2) Past Fact; (3) Future Fact; and (4) Size (Big and Small; More and Less). But in Chapter 23 of Book II, he lays out twenty-eight general Lines of Argument. William M. A. Grimaldi demonstrates that these twenty-eight topics can be reduced to three inferential or logical patterns: (1) Antecedent-Consequent or Cause-Effect; (2) More-Less; and (3) some form of Relationship.[16] Interested readers can consult Grimaldi's article to find out to which of the three categories he assigns each of the twenty-eight topics. He has further argued that the particular topics (*eidē*) are *material topics* because they yield content or factual information on the subject being discussed and that the common topics (*koinoi topoi*) are *formal topics* because they are modes or forms of inference and are therefore more universal than the particular topics.[17]

There are some other technical terms in the *Rhetoric*, but readers can be left to discover and interpret those terms for themselves. The terms discussed here are the crucial ones for understanding Aristotle's system of rhetoric.

The Poetics

The *Poetics* considers the art of what might be called imaginative literature or, more specifically, the art of fiction—that is, made-up or invented narratives. But it is not a complete or a completed art of fiction. For one thing, it analyzes only one kind of fiction—imitative narratives—and only two species of those—tragedy and epic (the section on comedy was lost). For another thing, the *Poetics*, like the *Rhetoric*, is a fragmentary, unfinished treatise—probably a set of lecture notes. Yet despite its incompleteness, the *Poetics* has been unquestionably the most influential and the most discussed document of literary criticism in the Western world.

Because of the missing parts and the sometimes seemingly misplaced parts, scholars have studied the twenty-six chapters that constitute the extant text of the *Poetics* to see whether they could discern any tenable rationale for the organization of the book. On the contents pages preceding his translation of the *Poetics* in this book, Ingram Bywater has done some grouping of the twenty-six extant chapters into five larger categories, which he marks off with letters of the alphabet from A to E and with headings of his own devising. His designation of the major parts of this treatise has been generally accepted by later commentators on the text. Various critics, of course, might differ slightly about the number of the major parts and about the phrasing of the headings for the parts. For instance, it is defensible to combine Bywater's D and E and to end up with a four-part structure for the *Poetics* that would look like the following:

1. A general discussion of the art of imitative poetry (Chapters 1–5)
2. A discussion of the art of tragedy and its parts (Chapters 6–22)
3. A discussion of the art of epic poetry (Chapters 23–24)
4. A discussion of the problems of evaluating poetry, especially tragedy and epic (Chapters 25–26)

This structure is forecast in the very first sentence of the *Poetics*: "Our subject being Poetry, I propose to speak not only of the art in general but also of its species and their respective capacities; of the structure of the plot required for a good poem; and likewise of any other matters in the same line of inquiry." The discussion moves from the broad perspective of the imitative arts in general to a progressively narrowing focus on the species of imitative poetry (primarily tragedy). As we have seen, the discussion in the *Rhetoric* also moved in that broad-to-narrow way: from the general treatment of the art of rhetoric in the first three chapters to a discussion in the subsequent chapters of the specific means of achieving persuasion.

Elder Olson, one of the noted contemporary commentators on the *Poetics*, has pointed out that the way in which Aristotle has organized the *Poetics* is consonant with the rationale of any productive art.[18] When one is trying to figure out the principles governing any productive art, he says, one starts out by looking at a completed product of that art. One determines inductively or empirically what the governing principles of that completed whole is. This exploratory examination enables one to establish a formula for producing the whole. In the *Poetics*, the inductively derived formula is the definition, given at the beginning of Chapter 6, of one species of imitative poetry, tragedy. Using this definition or formula, one then proceeds deductively to determine what the constituent parts of such a whole must be, what the nature and the quality of those parts must be, and how those parts must be put together.

The *Poetics* starts out with a consideration of the imitative arts, such as music, dancing, painting, sculpture, and poetry. Aristotle seeks to determine inductively what the common and the differentiating principles of these arts are by looking at the objects they imitate, the means or medium they use in imitating, and the manner of their imitation. Even the brief history of poetry that Aristotle presents in Chapter 4 and carries over into Chapter 5 is part of his inductive quest for the formula of the kind of imitative poetry he will concentrate on. Once he has presented this formula in Chapter 6, he proceeds deductively from that point to the end, examining the nature and the structure of the six qualitative parts of a tragedy— plot, character, thought, diction, melody, and spectacle.

One might use this formula or definition as an entrée into a discussion of some of the key concepts and terms that figure in the *Poetics*. At the beginning of Chapter 6 of the *Poetics*, Ingram Bywater translates Aristotle's definition of tragedy into these words:

A tragedy, then, is the imitation of an action that is serious and also, as having magnitude, complete in itself; in language with pleasurable accessories, each kind brought in separately in the parts of the work; in a dramatic, not in a narrative form; with incidents arousing pity and fear, wherewith to accomplish its catharsis of such emotions.

As the classical scholar Gerald Else has pointed out,[19] all the concepts and terminology in this definition up to the final clause, which mentions the catharsis of pity and fear, were touched on in one of the first five chapters of the *Poetics*. Most of the commentary written about this treatise has centered on this definition, and most of it has been concerned with the meaning of the final clause.

At the beginning of Chapter 1, Aristotle observes that the various species of the imitative arts are characterized by the differences in the means, the manner, and the object of the imitation. In defining the imitative art that he is going to discuss for the next sixteen chapters. Aristotle assigns tragedy to the genus of imitation (*mimēsis*). In the subsequent parts of the definition, then, he differentiates tragedy from other kinds of imitative arts. For instance, he differentiates tragedy from comedy by pointing out that tragedy dramatizes a serious (*spoudaias*) action (its distinctive *object* of imitation). He differentiates tragedy from epic by saying that the action is dramatized rather than narrated (its distinctive *manner* of imitation). He distinguishes tragedy from some of the musical arts such as flute-playing and dancing by pointing out that tragedy is delivered in language (*logos*) embellished with rhythm and harmony (its distinctive *medium* or *means*).

Another way in which to view this definition is to see it as designating the four causes of a tragedy. According to Aristotle, the four causes of anything coming into existence are the *material* cause, the *formal* cause, the *efficient* cause, and the *final* cause. The four causes of a kitchen table, for instance, would be the carpenter (the efficient cause, the maker), who took wood (the material cause, the substance from which it is made) and shaped it in such a way (the formal cause, its form or structure) that it would be a suitable piece of furniture at which to sit and eat breakfast (its final cause, its purpose or use). Applying this formula to tragedy, we could say that the material cause would be what Aristotle calls the *object* of imitation (human actions); the formal cause would be a combination of the *means* (embellished language) and the *manner* (a dramatized presentation); the final cause, which is the one cause not discussed in the previous five chapter, would be the catharsis of the tragic emotions of pity and fear; the efficient cause, which is not explicitly mentioned in the definition but is implied, would be, immediately, the poet and, ultimately, the poetic art (the *poiētikē*).

The most troublesome term in the definition is *catharsis*. Curiously enough, the word *catharsis* in the sense that it has in the definition never appears again in the *Poetics*. In his *Politics* (Book VIII, Chapter 7, 1341b), where he is talking about the capacity of music to purge religious frenzy (*enthusiasmos*), Aristotle promises that he will speak more precisely about the term *katharsis* when he comes to talk about poetry (presumably in the *Poetics*); but he never does explain the term, and his failure to do so has encouraged countless critics and commentators to offer their interpretation of the term.

This is not the place to review the complex discussion of this puzzling term.[20] Suffice it to say that most interpreters have translated the Greek word *katharsis* in the medical sense of "purgation" or "purification." Most of them

agree that a *change* of some kind takes place in the spectators or the readers of the tragic play. What critics quarrel about is such questions as "Is it the audience that is purged of pity and fear, or is it the pity and fear themselves that are purged?" "Are the emotions of pity and fear in the audience for the play, or are they qualities of the incidents in the play itself?" "Are the tragic emotions of pity and fear removed (purged) altogether by the play, or are they merely refined (purified) by the experience of the play and rendered pleasurable?"

The definition leads into the long discussion, carried on over the next sixteen chapters, of tragic drama. This discussion is organized according to the six constituent parts of a tragedy: plot (*mythos*), character (*ēthos*), thought (*dianoia*), diction (*lexis*), song (*melos*), and spectacle (*opsis*). Plot, character, and thought are related to the *matter* of the play; diction and song are related to the *medium;* and spectacle is related to the *manner* of the presentation. In Chapter 6, Aristotle establishes a hierarchy for these parts, putting them in this order of decreasing importance: plot, character, thought, diction, song, and spectacle.

One of the ways in which Aristotle differs from later theorists of the narrative art is in arguing that plot, the structure of the action or the incidents, is for him the most important element in storytelling. Most modern theorists would rate character as the chief element. Aristotle argues for his position in this way (Chapter 6):

Tragedy is essentially an imitation not of persons but of action and life, of happiness and misery. All human happiness or misery takes the form of action; the end for which we live is a certain kind of activity, not a quality. Character gives us qualities, but it is in our actions—what we do—that we are happy or the reverse. In a play, accordingly, they do not act in order to portray the Characters; they include the Characters for the sake of the action. So that it is the action in it, i.e., its Fable or Plot, that is the end and purpose of the tragedy; and the end is everywhere the chief thing. Besides this, a tragedy is impossible without action, but there may be one without Characters.

In a creative-writing class or in a seminar on literary criticism, almost every sentence in that passage is liable to be challenged by someone in the class. Some people will contest even a basic philosophical principle such as the one in which Aristotle declares that "the end for which we live is a certain kind of activity, not a quality." It is partly because the *Poetics* provokes spirited assent or dissent that it has remained, to this day, one of the vital documents of literary aesthetics.

The *Poetics* has been the informing document for whole schools of literary criticism, such as the "Chicago school"—so called because many of its practitioners taught at the University of Chicago. The *Poetics* made it possible for critics to ask certain kinds of questions about the structure of a literary text that other methods of criticism did not allow. They did not deny, however, that other critical approaches are legitimate and useful if one has other sets of questions that one wants to ask of a literary text.

Furthermore, Aristotle laid down some principles about how to construct a story that are as sound today as they were in his day. He is talking in this document about one kind of story-telling—a tale of tragedy rendered in the dramatic form—and he is talking about the only kind of tragic drama that he is familiar with—the plays of such contemporary playwrights as Aeschylus, Euripides, and Sophocles. If he were alive today, he would be the first to admit that his *Poetics* is not broad enough to cover some of the tragic dramas that have been written since his time—Shakespeare's, for instance. But he probably would still maintain, and many modern critics and playwrights would agree with him, that a contemporary tragedy constructed according to his principles could be a powerful play, capable of stirring and ultimately purging emotions of pity and fear in a twentieth-century audience. For instance, plots in which the sequence of events is linked together in some kind of cause-and-effect way are more likely to be aesthetically satisfying than episodic plots, where the relationship between the successive incidents is simply arbitrary or at best merely temporal. And do we not still find those stories more lastingly satisfying in which the sequence of event has been made to seem not just possible but probable or, best of all, necessary?

Several other viable principles of this sort can be found in the *Poetics*, principles governing not just the construction of plots but the creation of characters, the establishment of the verbal style, and the management of the staging of the play. Those who are new to the *Poetics* are likely to meet with a number of surprising discoveries about the soundness and timelessness of the discussion and of the advice offered in this text. It is a treatise for all seasons.

Notes

1. The English titles often assigned to the six documents in this collection of logical treatises are the *Categories, On Interpretation,* the *Prior Analytics,* the *Posterior Analytics,* the *Topics,* and *On Sophistical Refutation.*
2. Wilbur Samuel Howell, *Poetics, Rhetoric, and Logic: Studies in the Basic Disciplines of Criticism* (Ithaca, N.Y.: Cornell University Press, 1975).
3. Ibid., pp. 223–224.
4. See the beginning of Chapter 6 of the *Poetics:* "Reserving hexameter poetry and Comedy for consideration hereafter, let us proceed now to the discussion of Tragedy." The promised treatment of hexameter poetry—that is, the treatment of epic poetry—is provided in Chapters 23 and 24, but we do not find the promised treatment of comedy in the extant text.
5. Lane Cooper has provided a hypothetical reconstruction of the lost section about comedy with his translation of the *Tractatus Coislinianus,* an anonymous Greek fragment, in his *An Aristotelian Theory of Comedy* (New York: Harcourt, Brace, 1922).
6. For a brief account of Aristotle's life and works, see W. D. Ross, *Aristotle: A Complete Exposition of His Works and Thought,* 5th ed. (New York: Meridian Books, 1959), Chapter 1.
7. A good account of the publishing history of Aristotle's text is to be found in Keith V. Erickson, "A Brief History of Aristotle's *Rhetoric*," pp. 1–18, which serves as an introduction to his bibliographic volume, *Aristotle's Rhetoric: Five Centuries of Philological Research* (Metuchen, N.J.: Scarecrow Press, 1975).
8. E. M. Cope, *An Introduction to Aristotle's Rhetoric* (London: Macmillan, 1867), p. 47.
9. See Anton-Hermann Chroust, "Aristotle's Earliest 'Course of Lectures on Rhetoric,'" *L'Antiquité classique* 33 (1964): 58–72, and by the same author, "Aristotle's First Literary Effort: The *Gryllus,* a Lost Dialogue on the Nature of Rhetoric," *Revue des Etudes Grecques* 78 (1965): 576–591. Both of these essays are reprinted in *Aristotle: The Classical Heritage of Rhetoric,* ed. Keith V. Erickson (Metuchen, N.J.: Scarecrow Press, 1974).
10. Gerald F. Else, *Aristotle's Poetics; The Argument* (Cambridge, Mass.: Harvard University Press, 1967), p. xi. See also p. 667 for the list of the additions that Else maintains Aristotle himself made to his own text.
11. See John Gassner, "Aristotelian Literary Criticism," Gassner's prefatory essay to the first American edition of S. H. Butcher *Aristotle's Theory of Poetry and Fine Arts with a Critical Text and Translation of the Poetics,* 4th ed. (New York: Dover Publications, 1951), p. xlvi.
12. Richard McKeon, "Aristotle's Conception of Language and the Arts of Language, Part II," *Classical Philology* 42 (1947): 37.
13. A convenient summary of Aristotle's original contributions to rhetoric can be found in Friedrich Solmsen's article "The Aristotelian Tradition in Ancient Rhetoric," *American Journal of Philology* 62 (1941): 35–50, 169–190. This article is reprinted in *Aristotle: The Classical Heritage of Rhetoric,* ed. Keith V. Erickson (Metuchen, N.J.: Scarecrow Press, 1974), pp. 278–309.
14. W. Rhys Roberts, *Greek Rhetoric and Literary Criticism* (New York: Longmans, Green, 1928), p. 50.
15. For a full and enlightened treatment of the Aristotelian enthymeme, consult the following sources: James H. Burney, "The Place of the Enthymeme in Rhetorical Theory," *Speech Monographs* 3 (1936): 49–74; Lloyd F. Bitzer, "Aristotle's Enthymeme Revisited," *Quarterly Journal of Speech* 45 (1959): 399–408; and William M. A. Grimaldi, "The Sources of Rhetorical Argumentation by Enthymeme, "*Studies in the Philosophy of Aristotle's Rhetoric* (Wiesbaden, Germany: Franz Steiner Verlag, 1972); Chapter 4: pp. 115–135. The first two articles are reprinted in *Aristotle: The Classical Heritage of Rhetoric,* ed. Keith V. Erickson (Metuchen, N.J.: Scarecrow Press, 1974), pp. 117–140 and 141–155, respectively.
16. William M. A. Grimaldi, "The Aristotelian *Topics,*" *Traditio,* 14 (1958): 1–16. This article has been reprinted in the above-mentioned Erickson anthology, *Aristotle: The Classical Heritage of Rhetoric, pp. 176–193.* See also the chapter of the Grimaldi monograph mentioned in the previous note.
17. Grimaldi, "The Aristotelian *Topics,*" in *Aristotle: The Classical Heritage of Rhetoric,* p. 186.
18. Elder Olson, "The Poetic Method of Aristotle: Its Powers and Limitations," in *Aristotle's Poetics and English Literature: A Collection of Critical Essays,* ed. Elder Olson (Chicago: University of Chicago Press, Gemini Books, 1965), p. 181.
19. Else, *Aristotle's Poetics,* p. 224.
20. Else has listed the seven points that are implied in most interpretations of *katharsis.* See his *Aristotle's Poetics,* p. 226.

Lester Thonssen and A. Craig Baird

Cicero and Quintilian on Rhetoric

◊ *If it can be said that the Greeks invented rhetoric, the Romans per-fected it. Cicero, Rome's foremost orator and a life-long student of phi-losophy and the liberal arts, provides us with more practical insights on speaking and writing than any of his predecessors or contemporaries. And he does so in such a way that his felicitous prose takes on "the character of finality." Cicero regarded Isocrates as "the father of eloquence"; con-sequently his varied writings on rhetoric sustain the Greek tradition in tact.*

A century later, the Roman teacher, Quintilian, solidified our store of rhetorical knowledge in a four volume compendium. He is perhaps best remembered for the definition of the perfect orator as "the good man skilled in speaking," a marriage of rhetoric and ethics particularly ap-pealing in the Christian era to follow. ◊

The Greeks gave us the basic principle of rhetoric. But the Romans and Graeco-Romans were highly skilled students whose penchant for organization and refinement of traditional lore asserted itself in their treatment of speechcraft. They may not have added much that was new, but they elaborated upon the previously determined tenets and placed them in patterns of somewhat sharper outline. Furthermore, the practical turn of the Roman mind in-sured the likelihood of certain depar-tures from the philosophical point of view regarding rhetoric, to a more purely pragmatic, pedagogical develop-ment. This is most clearly shown in the treatises of Cicero, the orator speaking on his art, and in the writings of Quin-tilian, the teacher discoursing on methods of instruction.

Despite certain differences in em-phasis and point of view between early Greek and Graeco-Roman writings on rhetoric, the latter quite naturally and uninterruptedly grows out of and blends with the former, so that the tradition of the subject is sustained in unbroken

Lester Thonssen and A. Craig Baird, "Cicero and Quintilian on Rhetoric," reprinted from *Speech Criticism: The Development of Standards for Rhetorical Appraisal.* New York: Ronald Press, 1948): 137–157.

continuity. The following sections show how the basic postulates of Greek inquiry served as the substructure of Roman thinking.

The ad Herennium

The *Rhetorica ad Herennium*, sometimes ascribed to Cicero (106–43 B.C.), provides a pattern of the rhetorical system taught at Rome during the early days of Cicero. Perhaps published about 86 B.C., this treatise in four books is, according to Atkins, "the first work of real significance belonging to the first century B.C. . . ."[1]

Book I deals with the kinds of oratory and the parts of rhetoric.[2] Demonstrative, deliberative, and judicial oratory represent the types of causes that a speaker may consider. In order to carry out his assignment, an orator must deal with five aspects or parts of rhetoric: *inventio, dispositio, elocutio, memoria,* and *pronuntiatio.* Each of these five parts can be acquired by an orator through art, imitation, and practice.

An orator's invention is revealed in six sections of an address: *exordium, narratio, divisio, confirmatio, confutatio,* and *conclusio.*

Three kinds of causes, or *constitutio causae,* are mentioned: those of fact (*coniecturalis*) interpretation (*legitima*) and right or wrong (*iuridicialis*). Under the heading of the status, or state, these concepts are discussed in a later section.

Book II treats of invention as it relates to forensic oratory; Book III, as it relates to deliberative and demonstrative speaking. *Dispositio, memoria,* and *pronuntiatio* also receive consideration.

The last book of the *ad Herennium* is devoted to *elocutio,* or style, and takes up about half of the entire treatise. A. S. Wilkins remarks that this section is of interest, not only because it is the first work on the subject in Latin, but also because it provides an abundance and excellence of illustration.

The author lists three kinds of style—*gravis, mediocris,* and *attenuata.* The general requirements of the speaker's language are elegance, or word choice; composition, or the union of words; and dignity, or adornment. To further the realization of the last requisite, the *ad Herennium* provides a long list of figures (*verborum exornatio and sententiarum exornatio*).

The Classical Divisions of Rhetoric

The parts or canons of rhetoric set forth in the *ad Herennium* represent the broad divisions of the whole subject; in many respects, they constitute the basic pattern of all theoretical and critical investigations into the art and practice of speaking.

According to the classical tradition, all rhetoric is divided into five parts: invention, disposition, elocution, memory, and delivery. This fivefold division is fairly standard in all major works after Aristotle until the eighteenth century. Minor changes in the meaning of the terms are developed in various treatises, but the pattern remains the same until the time of George Campbell, when *memory* practically drops out of the analysis.

These parts have distinctive functions. They are not only the concepts with which an orator must deal and which he must master in order to deliver an effective speech; they are also the aspects of the delivered oration which the critic, viewing the finished speech as a creative product, examines and evaluates.

The exact origin of the fivefold plan is in doubt. The first division of speech materials was probably into substance and form; next, into invention and arrangement. But the fivefold division is hard to trace.

The Inventive Aspect

Invention involves the attempt on the part of the orator, as Cicero says, "to find out what he should say. . . ." It is an investigative undertaking, embracing a survey and forecast of the subject and a search for the arguments suitable to the given rhetorical effort. As Baldwin remarks in his commentary, it refers to "the investigation, analysis, and grasp of the subject matter."[3] Thus certain writers—Aristotle among them—give more attention to invention than to the other parts of rhetoric. This is done on the ground, and perhaps properly, that the content is the most important part of a speech.

Without proposing to categorize the constituents of rhetorical theory, we may say in general that the concept of invention includes the entire investigative undertaking, the idea of the

status, and the modes of persuasion—logical, emotional, and ethical—in all of their complex interrelations.

Disposition of Materials

Disposition covers the concept of arrangement, of orderly planning and movement of the whole idea. Although the treatment of it differs within a narrow range among the several treatises, the general meaning is twofold: the appreciation of a plan for the speech as a whole, and the development of the specific parts of the speech, such as the exordium, narration, proof, peroration, and whatever other divisions the authors specify. Baldwin is correct in saying that what is noticeably missing, not only in Aristotle's treatment of disposition, but in the other works of the classical tradition as well, "is some definite inculcation of consecutiveness."[4]

In some treatises, ancient and modern, invention and disposition are treated under a common head—the assumption being that the orderly arrangement of the materials constitutes an essential part of the inventive process.

The Stylistic Feature

The third part of rhetoric was originally called *elocutio,* and it referred specifically to style. It embraced the concept of expression in language, resulting, basically, from the choice of words and their arrangement or composition. Among the ancient rhetoricians, the study of words and composition led to an analysis of the distinguishing marks of the kinds of style. Accordingly, in Cicero's *Orator*, to name but one treatise, the plain, the moderate, and the grand style are described and analyzed.

The Memory in Rhetoric

Memoria, the fourth part of rhetoric, does not receive systematic treatment in Aristotle's *Rhetoric*. Cicero, Quintilian, and other rhetoricians give it consideration. However, when we come to the major works of the eighteenth century, we note that this canon has been dropped. In recent volumes it receives only incidental treatment, although Lionel Crocker's *Public Speaking for College Students* devotes a complete chapter to "The Memory in Speech."

In the older sense, memory was a fairly comprehensive concept, embracing the speaker's mastery of all his material in sequential order. "Why should I remark," says Cicero,

. . . how excellent a thing it is to retain the instructions which you have received with the cause, and the opinion which you have formed upon it? to keep all your thoughts upon it fixed in your mind, all your arrangement of language marked out there? to listen to him from whom you receive any information, or to him to whom you have to reply, with such power of retention, that they seem not to have poured their discourse into your ears, but to have engraven it on your mental tablet?[5]

That Cicero regarded memory as an important part of the orator's equipment is further revealed in his criticism of the eminent speakers. He censures Curio for his "extremely treacherous" memory, saying

. . . after he had divided his subject into three general heads, he would sometimes,

in the course of speaking, either add a fourth, or omit the third. In a capital trial, in which I had pleaded for Titinia, the daughter of Cotta, when he attempted to reply to me in defense of Servius Naevius, he suddenly forgot every thing he intended to say, and attributed it to the pretended witchcraft and magic artifices of Titinia.[6]

In commenting on Hippias' contribution to rhetoric, and on the subsequent disappearance of the canon of memory, Bromley Smith says:

With the passing of the years . . . the notion that the memory of orators can be trained by systematic devices has almost disappeared. Memory itself remains and is highly esteemed, yet it has lost its ancient importance. Long ago Plato foresaw this when he remarked that the invention of writing by the Egyptian God, Theuth, caused learners to trust external written characters rather than themselves. That he was right may be judged from the number of speakers who read their addresses. Hippias, however, belonged to the old school; he believed he could train the memories of the future statesmen. His labors must have had a measure of success, sufficient indeed to encourage others. Since his days thousands have followed his idea, like a will-o'-the-wisp, through the bogs of discipline. At last sinking below their depth, they have disappeared, leaving only a few bubbles to remind the world that Memory, 'the warder of the mind,' was once a canon of rhetoric.[7]

Delivery

The last part of rhetoric—*pronuntiatio*—is the art of delivery. Its constituent elements are vocal utterance and bodily action. From Aristotle to the present day all systematic treatises on rhetoric have given some space to this canon.

A Great Orator's Conception of His Art

A Functional Approach to Speechmaking

"The Romans," said W. S. Teuffel, "were naturally well qualified for oratory by their acute intellect, their love of order and their Italian vivacity, tempered with Roman gravity."[8] They were practical people; so it is natural that their works on speaking should emphasize the functional aspects of the art, Cicero represented this practical inclination at its best. "The most eminent orator of Roman civilization, he wrote more than any other orator has ever written on rhetoric; and historically he has been more than any other an ideal and model."[9]

While discussing the efforts of the philosophers—Aristotle and Theophrastus included—as writers on rhetoric, Cicero inquires whether it would not be advantageous to consider the art of speaking from the point of view of the practicing orator *and* the philosopher. Surely the orator would be able to "set forth with full power and attraction" those same topics of virtue, equity, laws, and the like, with something more than the "tame and bloodless phraseology" of the philosophers. Accordingly, Cicero would interest himself in the development of an orator so "accomplished and complete" that he would be able to "speak on all subjects with variety and copiousness."[10]

Cicero tried, as his works show, to restore rhetoric to something of its earlier scope and vitality. As Atkins indicates,[11] he was "protesting against the narrowing of the province" of the speaking art, hoping to restore rhetoric as a "system of general culture" which would train men to write and speak competently on all possible subjects. In this effort Cicero was influenced and guided by the doctrines of Isocrates whom he regarded as the "father of eloquence."

Cicero was an eclectic. With the possible exception of the *Brutus*, the contents of all his works originate in the contributions of his predecessors and contemporaries. However, he embellished the old, saying it so much better that it took on a character of finality.

The Substance of the De Oratore

De Oratore is Cicero's most important book on rhetorical theory. Like many treatises of its kind, it is in dialogue form, with the celebrated orators Crassus and Antonius playing the major roles; and Scaevola, Catulus, Cotta, Sulpicius, Caesar, and Rufus serving in a minor way as interlocutors.

In Book I Crassus comments on the qualifications of the Ideal Orator, while in Book III he develops the Ciceronian conception of oratorical style. Antonius, serving as the protagonist in Book II, discourses on invention and disposition. Incidental remarks on humor are also introduced by Caesar.

Book I of De Oratore

In the first book we find, reminiscent of Isocrates and Aristotle, a development of the theme that to be successful the orator must conform to high and exacting qualifications. He must be a man of great learning.

A knowledge of a vast number of things is necessary, without which volubility of words is empty and ridiculous; speech itself is to be formed, not merely by choice, but by careful construction of words; and all the emotions of the mind, which nature has given to man, must be intimately known; for all the force and art of speaking must be employed in allaying or exciting the feelings of those who listen. To this must be added a certain portion of grace and wit, learning worthy of a well-bred man, and quickness and brevity in replying as well as attacking, accompanied with a refined decorum and urbanity. Besides, the whole of antiquity and a multitude of examples is to be kept in the memory; nor is the knowledge of laws in general, or of the civil law in particular, to be neglected. And why need I add any remarks on delivery itself, which is to be ordered by action of body, by gesture, by look, and by modulation and variation of the voice, the great power of which, alone and in itself, the comparatively trivial art of actors and the stage proves, on which though all bestow their utmost labor to form their look, voice, and gesture, who knows not how few there are, and have ever been, to whom we can attend with patience? What can I say of that repository for all things, the memory, which, unless it be the keeper of the matter and words that are the fruits of thought and invention, all the talents of the orator, we see, though they be of the highest degree of excellence, will be of no avail? Let us then cease to wonder what is the cause of the scarcity of good speakers, since eloquence results from all those qualifications. . . .[12]

Cicero shortly after sets forth his oft-quoted remark that the "proper concern of an orator, . . . is language of power and elegance accommodated to the feelings and understandings of mankind."[13]

We note, then, that Cicero, through his mouthpiece, Crassus, insists upon the orator's having virtually universal knowledge and skill. In the dialogue, Antonius holds that somewhat less learning is necessary, although he, too,

urges broad familiarity with the field of knowledge. But he insists upon a more *intensive* training leading to the acquisition of oratorical excellence. Antonius would develop the orator's natural talents and capacities for oratory, even if his intellectual control over the field of learning were somewhat more moderate than Crassus believed essential. Baldwin feels that, in a sense, both Crassus and Antonius are right. "Normally rhetoric is both extensive and intensive, both a comprehensive study of life and a specific art, even as the means of persuasion are both extrinsic and intrinsic."[14]

In this book Crassus also is made to delineate the five parts of rhetoric when he announces:

If, therefore, any one desires to define and comprehend the whole and peculiar power of an orator, that man, in my opinion, will be an orator, worthy of so great a name, who whatever subject comes before him, and requires rhetorical elucidation, can speak on it judiciously, in set form, elegantly, and from memory, and with a certain dignity of action.[15]

However, the principal reference at this point is to *invention*.

The Second Book

Book II treats mainly of invention and disposition, and with particular emphasis, of course, upon these concepts in their relation to forensic oratory. Care is taken to point out that the orator's painstaking investigation of the facts is indispensable to inventive skill. The accomplished orator will conduct research before taking the platform, will "take one time for premeditation, and another for speaking."

Though not original, Cicero's treatment of the *status*—determination of the character and issues of the case—is important to the study of rhetorical theory. He remarks:

There are in all, therefore, three sorts of matters, which may possibly fall under doubt and discussion; what is now done, what has been done, or what is to be done; what the nature of a thing is, or how it should be designated; for as to the question which some Greeks add, whether a thing be rightly done, it is wholly included in the inquiry, what the nature of the thing is.[16]

These are frequently called states of *conjecture, definition,* and *quality,* respectively. Cicero remarks that these considerations apply to all types of oratory in which dispute centers—forensic, deliberative, and panegyric.

The objects of discourse are said to be: "That we prove what we maintain to be true; that we conciliate those who hear; that we produce in their minds whatever feelings our cause may require."[17] The whole business of speaking, Cicero allows, rests upon these things for success in persuasion.

Cicero's treatment of pathetic and ethical proof adds little, if anything, that is new. He indicates that "mankind makes far more determinations through hatred, or love, or desire, or anger, or grief, or joy, or hope, or fear, or error, or some other affection of mind, than from regard to truth, or any settled maxim, or principle of right, or judicial form, or adherence to the laws."[18] He therefore comments on the way to make audience analyses, to move people to various emotional states, and to make the speaker's character aid in the persuasive undertaking.

As to arrangement of speech materials, Cicero offers little that is new. He indicates that two methods may be observed: "one, which the nature of causes dictates; the other, which is suggested by the orator's judgment and prudence."[19] The plan of organization he then describes is more detailed than Aristotle's, the difference resulting largely, however, from the fact that he is making an adjustment to forensic speaking.

Memory, as a distinct part of rhetoric, receives attention in Book II. Cicero opens his discourse by recalling the traditional incident which presumably prompted Simonides to "invent" the art of memory:

For they relate, that when Simonides was at Crannon in Thessaly, at an entertainment given by Scopas, a man of rank and fortune, and had recited a poem which he had composed in his praise, in which, for the sake of embellishment, after the manner of the poets, there were many particulars introduced concerning Castor and Pollux, Scopas told Simonides, with extraordinary meanness, that he would pay him half the sum which he had agreed to give for the poem, and that he might ask the remainder, if he thought proper, from his Tyndaridae, to whom he had given an equal share of praise. A short time after, they say that a message was brought in to Simonides, to desire him to go out, as two youths were waiting at the gate who earnestly wished him to come forth to them; when he arose, went forth, and found nobody. In the meantime the apartment in which Scopas was feasting fell down, and he himself, and his company, were overwhelmed and buried in the ruins; and when their friends were desirous to inter their remains, but could not possibly distinguish one from another, so much crushed were the bodies, Simonides is said, from his recollection of the place in which each had sat, to have given satisfactory direction for their interment. Admonished by this occurrence, he is reported to have discovered, that it is chiefly order that gives distinctness to memory; and that by those, therefore, who would improve this part of the understanding, certain places must be fixed upon, and that of the things which they desire to keep in memory, symbols must be conceived in the mind, and ranged, as it were, in those places; thus the order of places would preserve the order of things, and the symbols of the things would denote the things themselves; so that we should use the places as waxen tablets, and the symbols as letters.[20]

Cicero then observes that those things "are the most strongly fixed in our minds, which are communicated to them, and imprinted upon them, by the senses. . . ." And for the orator, the "memory of things is the proper business. . . ." "This we may be enabled to impress on our ourselves by the creation of imaginary figures, aptly arranged, to represent particular heads, so that we may recollect thoughts by images, and their order by place."[21]

The Third Book

In addition to restating the theme on the union of rhetoric and philosophy, the last book of *De Oratore* considers style and delivery.

The section on style deals chiefly with word choice, composition, and the various ornaments of speech. Cicero's point of view is clearly stated in this passage:

A speech, then, is to be made becoming in its kind, with a sort of complexion and substance of its own; for that it be weighty, agreeable, savoring of erudition and liberal knowledge, worthy of admiration, polished, having feeling and passion in it, as far as is

required, are qualities not confined to particular members, but are apparent in the whole body; but that it be, as it were, strewed with flowers of language and thought, is a property which ought not to be equally diffused throughout the whole speech, but at such intervals, that, as in the arrangement of ornaments, there may be certain remarkable and luminous objects disposed here and there.[22]

Baldwin looks upon Cicero's twenty chapters on style as a "brilliant instance of what the ancients meant by amplification. Logically they do little more than iterate the truism that style is inseparable from substance; but actually they make the truism live."[23]

Finally, Book III of the *De Oratore* sets forth a general theory of delivery, that phase of oratory which Cicero said had "the sole and supreme power." Without effective delivery, "a speaker of the highest mental capacity can be held in no esteem, while one of moderate abilities, with this qualification, may surpass even those of the highest talent."[24] Cicero comments on the use of gestures and bodily action, and on the necessity of varying the tones in vocal expression.

It may be said that, while constructing the pattern for the Ideal Orator, Cicero kept constantly in mind the practical requirements of one who proposed to play "the part of a true Roman citizen in the conflicts of the assembly and the law courts."

The Orator and a Conception of Style

Cicero's *Orator* is less comprehensive than the *De Oratore*, being devoted almost wholly to style. John E. Sandys says the purpose of it was to "meet the wishes of Brutus" and "to win over Brutus to his own side in the controversy with the Atticists. . . ." Another purpose, surely, was "to delineate the ideal orator." And it is evident that "the living image of his own oratorical greatness forms the foundation on which he builds his ideal fabric. His own speeches supply him with examples of every variety of oratorical excellence. . . ."[25] Baldwin remarks, apropos of the *Orator*, that few men "writing on style have shown in their own styles so much precision and charm."

The Doctrine of the Three Styles

In the *Orator*, which Sandys says belongs to the "aesthetics of oratory," Cicero classifies and describes the three kinds of style: the plain, the moderate, and the grand. These types arise from the orator's attempt to prove, to please, and to move; and the skilled orator should be able to do all three.

Regarding the plain style, Cicero says:

. . . we must give a sketch of the man whom some consider the only orator of the Attic style.

He is a gentle, moderate man, imitating the usual customs, differing from those who are not eloquent in fact rather than in any of his opinions. Therefore those who are his hearers, even though they themselves have no skill in speaking, still feel confident that they could speak in that manner. For the subtlety of his address appears easy of imitation to a person who ventures on an opinion, but nothing is less easy when he comes to try it; for although it is not a style of any extraordinary vigour, still it has some juice, so that even though it is not endowed with the most extreme power, it is still . . .

in perfect health. First of all, then, let us release it from the fetters of rhythm. For there is, as you know, a certain rhythm to be observed by an orator, proceeding on a regular system; but though it must be attended to in another kind of oratory, it must be entirely abandoned in this. This must be a sort of easy style, and yet not utterly without rules, so that it may seem to range at freedom, not to wander about licentiously. He should also guard against appearing to cement his words together; for the hiatus formed by a concourse of open vowels has something soft about it, and indicates a not unpleasing negligence, as if the speaker were anxious more about the matter than the manner of his speech. But as to other points, he must take care, specially as he is allowed more license in these two,—I mean the rounding of his periods, and the combination of his words; for those narrow and minute details are not to be dealt with carelessly. . . .

The language will be pure and Latin; it will be arranged plainly and clearly, and great care will be taken to see what is becoming. . . .

There will be a moderate use of what I may call oratorical furniture; for there is to a certain degree what I may call our furniture, consisting of ornaments partly of things and partly of words. . . .

He will have besides this, action, not tragic, nor suited to the stage, but he will move his body in a moderate degree, trusting a great deal to his countenance; not in such a way as people call making faces, but in a manner sufficient to show in a gentleman-like manner in what sense he means what he is saying to be understood.

Now in this kind of speech sallies of wit are admissible, and they carry perhaps only too much weight in an oration. Of them there are two kinds,—facetiousness and raillery,—and the orator will employ both; but he will use the one in relating anything neatly, and the other in darting ridicule on his adversaries.[26]

As for the moderate style, it is

. . . more fertile, and somewhat more forcible than this simple style of which we have been speaking; but nevertheless tamer than the highest class of oratory. . . . In this kind there is but little vigour, but there is the greatest possible quantity of sweetness; for it is fuller than the plain style, but more plain than that other which is highly ornamented and copious.

Every kind of ornament in speaking is suitable to this style; and in this kind of oratory there is a great deal of sweetness. It is a style in which many men among the Greeks have been eminent; but Demetrius Phalereus, in my opinion, has surpassed all the rest; and while his oratory proceeds in calm and tranquil flow, it receives brilliancy from numerous metaphors and borrowed expressions, like stars. . . .

The same kind of oratory (I am speaking of the moderate and temperate kind) admits of all sorts of figures of expressions, and of many also of ideas. Discussions of wide application and extensive learning are explained in it, and common topics are treated without any impetuosity. In a word, orators of this class usually come from the schools of philosophers, and unless the more vigorous orator, whom I am going to speak of presently, is at hand to be compared with them, the one whom I am now describing will be approved of.[27]

The orator who uses the grand style

. . . is the sublime, copious, dignified, ornate speaker, in whom there is the greatest amount of grace. For he it is, out of admiration for whose ornamented style and copiousness of language nations have allowed eloquence to obtain so much influence in states; but it was only this eloquence, which is borne along in an impetuous course, and with a mighty noise, which all men looked up to, and admired, and had no idea that they themselves could possibly attain to. It belongs to this eloquence to deal with men's minds, and to influence them in every imaginable way. This is the style which sometimes forces its way into and sometimes steals into the senses; which implants new opinions in men, and eradicates others which have been long established. But there is a vast difference between this kind of orator and the preceding ones. A man who

has laboured at the subtle and acute style, in order to speak cunningly and cleverly, and who has had no higher aim, if he has entirely attained his object, is a great orator, if not a very great one; he is far from standing on slippery ground, and if he once gets a firm footing, is in no danger of falling. But the middle kind of orator, whom I have called moderate and temperate, if he has only arranged all his own forces to his satisfaction, will have no fear of any doubtful or uncertain chances of oratory; and even if at any time he should not be completely successful, which may often be the case, still he will be in no great danger, for he cannot fall far. But this orator of ours, whom we consider the first of orators, dignified, vehement, and earnest, if this is the only thing for which he appears born, or if this is the only kind of oratory to which he applies himself, and if he does not combine his copiousness of diction with those other two kinds of oratory, is very much to be despised. For the one who speaks simply, inasmuch as he speaks with shrewdness and sense, is a wise man; the one who employs the middle style is agreeable; but this most copious speaker, if he is nothing else, appears scarcely in his senses. For a man who can say nothing with calmness, nothing with gentleness; who seems ignorant of all arrangement and definition and distinctness, and regardless of wit, especially when some of his causes require to be treated in that manner entirely, and others in a great degree; if he does not prepare the ears of his hearers before be begins to work up the case in an inflammatory style, he seems like a madman among people in their senses, or like a drunken man among sober men.[28]

Baldwin observes that the philosophy of such a classification, whatever its origin, "has been vicious as pedagogy." "Historically, the trail of the three styles has been baneful. For inculcating style perhaps the least fruitful means is classification."[29]

One of Aristotle's pupils, Theophrastus, is usually credited with being the formulator of the threefold classification of style. In Latin literature, the *ad Herennium* furnishes the first statement of the doctrine. That Aristotle recognized a distinction among types of literary expression is evident from several of his remarks in the *Rhetoric*. In the third book, he remarks that "to each kind of rhetoric is adapted a peculiar style," and goes on to show how written and oral style differ in that the former is more "precise" while the latter "partakes more of declamation."[30] Furthermore, he implies throughout that the different types of speaking deliberative, forensic, and epideictic call for different styles. However, he does not classify the styles according to the divisions which we have just discussed. Later theorists, it may be added, sometimes added a fourth kind. Philodemus evidently conceived of a fourfold classification; and Demetrius added the "forcible" type to the original three.

The doctrine of the three styles permeates the literature of rhetoric, either through open statement or through implication. "In the sphere of oratory," J. F. D'Alton remarks,

. . . the division became important, when it was adapted to the theory of the 'officia oratoris,' according to which it was the orator's duty to instruct, delight, and move his audience. The Plain style, with its predominant qualities of clearness and logical subtlety, was best suited to the purposes of instruction. When the Middle style became identified with the 'genus floridum,' with its characteristics of smoothness and charm, it was naturally assigned the task of giving pleasure to, or winning over an audience. The orator, however, could point to his greatest achievements as effected through the medium of the Grand style, which was calculated to play at will upon the feelings of an assembly. Cicero and Quintilian considered this style to be supreme, just as they considered that to stir the emotions was the highest function of the orator.[31]

The necessary qualities of a good style, as Cicero interpreted Theophrastus' teaching, were correctness, clearness, appropriateness, and ornament. Cicero did not, however, ascribe ornamentation to the Plain style, that being reserved in part for the Middle, and wholly for the Grand. Accordingly, we note that the so-called "virtues," or essential qualities, were not necessarily applied to all styles; instead, they were often assigned to particular styles for which they seemed uniquely suitable.

Cicero's Treatment of Rhythm

Cicero's theory of oratorical rhythm derives largely from Gorgias and Isocrates. Commenting on the nature of his doctrine, he says:

Let oratory then be, . . . mingled and regulated with regard to rhythm; not prosaic, nor on the other hand sacrificed wholly to rhythm; composed chiefly of the paeon, . . . with many of the other feet which he passes over intermingled with it.

But what feet ought to be mingled with others, like purple, must be now explained; and we must also show to what kind of speech each sort of foot and rhythm is the best adapted. For the iambic is most frequent in those orations which are composed in a humble and lowly style; but the paeon is suitable to a more dignified style; and the dactyl to both. Therefore, in a varied and long-continued speech these feet should be mingled together and combined. And in this way the fact of the orator aiming at pleasing the senses, and the careful attempt to round off the speech, will be the less visible, and they will at all times be less apparent if we employ dignified expressions and sentiments. For the hearers observe these two things, and think them agreeable: (I mean, expressions and sentiments.) And while they listen to them with admiring minds, the rhythm escapes their notice; and even if it were wholly wanting they would still be delighted with those other things. . . .

Accordingly, if the question is raised as to what is the rhythm of an oration, it is every sort of rhythm; but one sort is better and more suitable than another. If the question is, what is the place of this rhythm? it is in every portion of the words. If you ask where it has arisen; it has arisen from the pleasure of the ears. If the principle is sought on which the words are to be arranged; that will be explained in another place, because that relates to practice, . . . If the question is, when; always: if, in what place, it consists in the entire connexion of the words. If we are asked, What is the circumstance which causes pleasure? we reply, that it is the same as in verse; the method of which is determined by art; but the ears themselves define it by their own silent sensations, without any reference to principles of art.[32]

The observations on the preceding pages suggest that, all in all, the *Orator* is to be regarded as one of Cicero's important works. It is, in the opinion of Torsten Petersson, "Cicero's final statement not only of his oratorical idea but also of what he conceived himself to have attained."[33]

Other Rhetorical Treatises

Among Cicero's other rhetorical works, excluding the *Brutus* and *On the Best Style of Orators* which may more appropriately engage our attention later, are *On Topics, Dialogue Concerning Oratorical Partitions*, and *On Rhetorical Invention*.

On Topics is largely an abstract of Aristotle's treatment of the same subject. Cicero defines a topic as "the seat of an argument, and . . . an argument

is a reason which causes men to believe a thing which would otherwise be doubtful.[34] The sources and types of topics receive a fairly full measure of analysis.

A Dialogue Concerning Oratorical Partitions includes a brief and superficial discussion between Cicero and his son on the elements of the speaking situation—orator, speech, and subject—and on the parts of an oration—opening, narration, confirmation, and peroration.

On Rhetorical Invention, written when Cicero was about twenty-one years of age, demonstrates the truth of a remark found in the same work: "of those who are worthy of fame or recollection, there is no one who appears either to have said nothing well, or everything admirably."[35] Indeed, this is no consummate statement of the art of rhetoric, although it does reveal Cicero's early enthusiasm for oratory and, in a juvenile sort of way, his early mastery of many of its details. Only two of the four books remain. In later years, Cicero himself renounced the whole work as being "scarcely worthy of my present standing in life." His treatment of what Wilbur S. Howell calls the "Positions of Argument" is, however, important to rhetorical theory. Says Howell:

Both in *De Inventione* and the *Rhetorica ad Herennium*, analysis and synthesis are specific procedures designed on the one hand to yield, and on the other to employ, arguments and appeals which meet the severest tests of relevance and coherence. Each book is important to us because it gives expression to a precise intellectual method contrived to render purposeful the speaker's research for the natural divisions and the underlying unity of his speech.[36]

Cicero's contributions, in general, are less concise than Aristotle's *Rhetoric;* they are given more fully to the encouragement in the orator of copiousness in language; but they are developed more consistently from the point of view of the orator himself.

Pedagogical Inquiry into Rhetoric

". . . The premier teacher of imperial rhetoric and the greatest Latin authority upon education"—that is J. Wight Duff's[37] estimate of Quintilian who, about 95 A.D., brought out the truly monumental *Institutes of Oratory,* or the Teaching of Rhetoric. Like Cicero, Quintilian was erudite in an eclectic sort of way; in the *Institutes* he reveals a remarkably wide familiarity with and deep appreciation of the Greek and Latin writers. Living during the so-called Silver Age of Latin life, about 14 to 138 A.D., when, as Duff indicates, the "main clue to the literary qualities is to be found in education, and particularly in rhetorical education," Quintilian preserved much of the classical tradition and integrity of rhetoric. He did this at a time when rhetoric was no longer a powerful instrument in public affairs; when it was no longer a severe discipline, devoid of exhibitionism, for training the average man for active citizenship.

The Point of View in the Institutes

On the side of rhetorical theory, there is relatively little in the *Institutes* of an original character. Because most of what Quintilian sets down on the side

of systematic rhetoric has been said before, we shall confine our summary to those aspects of the *Institutes* which enlarge the conception of theoretical speechcraft; and we shall omit most of the pedagogical details which, though interesting and significant, are not germane to this inquiry.

Quintilian sets out to form the Perfect Orator who, in his words, "cannot exist unless as a good man." The orator conforming to his standards is, therefore, the good man speaking well.

Since an orator, then, is a good man, and a good man cannot be conceived to exist without virtuous inclinations, and virtue, though it receives certain impulses from nature, requires notwithstanding to be brought to maturity by instruction, the orator must above all things study *morality,* and must obtain a thorough knowledge of all that is just and honorourable, without which no one can either be a good man or an able speaker.[38]

Quintilian's conception of the orator as a good man would alone tend to refute the charge of insincerity against the *Institutes* voiced by a critic who called it a treatise on "Lying as a Fine Art for Those Fully Conscious of Their Own Rectitude."[39]

The formation of this perfect orator is not to be left to the philosophers; instead, the orator shall receive the necessary "excellence of mind" through rhetorical education. "I cannot admit," Quintilian observes, "that the principles of moral and honourable conduct are . . . to be left to the philosophers. . . ." Further in the discourse, he remarks:

As to the objection which some make, that it is the business of *philosophy* to discourse of what is good, useful, and just, it makes nothing against me; for when they say a philosopher, they mean a good man; and why then should I be surprised that an orator, whom I consider also to be a good man, should discourse upon the same subjects? especially when I have shown, . . . that philosophers have taken possession of this province because it was abandoned by the orators, a province which had always belonged to oratory, so that the philosophers are rather trespassing upon our ground.[40]

Hence, he voices what Colson calls "the age-long antithesis between rhetoric and philosophy." Colson also indicates that

Quintilian's view of the superiority of the 'rhetor' to the philosopher is clearly reflected in two events of the time. The first of these is the endowment of rhetoric by Vespasian. The other is the expulsion of the philosophers from Rome about A.D. 94. The latter, whatever its other causes may have been, was certainly from one point of view a triumph for Quintilian's educational views.[41]

The Use of Rules

While Quintilian respected rules in rhetoric, he did not allow them to interfere with the common-sense principles of speech preparation. He advocated a flexibility of usage, observing that "one great quality in an orator is discretion, because he must turn his thoughts in various directions, according to the different bearings of his subject."[42] A forensic orator, for instance, should, in his pleadings, "keep two things in view, *what is becoming,* and *what is expedient;* but it is frequently *expedient,* and sometimes *becoming,* to make some deviations from the regular and settled order. . . ."[43] Quintilian says "rhetoric would be a very easy and small matter, if it could be included in

one short body of rules, but rules must generally be altered to suit the nature of each individual case, the time, the occasion, and necessity itself. . . ."[44]

A Conception of the Status

The plan of the *Institutes* is based upon Quintilian's acceptance of the fivefold division of the art of rhetoric: invention, disposition, elocution, memory, and delivery;[45] of the threefold classification of the types of oratory: deliberative, forensic, and panegyric;[46] and of the threefold analysis of the speaker's object or purpose: to inform, to move, and to please.[47]

A feature of Quintilian's treatment of invention which differs in scope and detail from that of many of his predecessors is that of the *status,* or *state of a cause.* The concept of the *status,* or the location of a center of argument, finds its first formal embodiment in the *ad Herennium* and in Cicero's *On Invention.* This concept is among the most important contributions of the Latin writers to rhetorical theory. By elevating the study of invention, and by providing the speaker with methods by which to find, evaluate, and use his ideas on a given case, this doctrine exercised a profound influence upon subsequent theory and practice in public speaking and debating.

After examining the views adopted by previous writers on the subject, Quintilian thinks it best "to regard that as the *state of the cause* which is the strongest point in it, and on which the whole matter chiefly turns."[48] "Status," Baldwin comments, "meaning the essential character of the case as it appeared to preliminary survey of all the material and all the bearings, had come to denote a uniform system of determining that essential character by leading questions."[49] Through the medium of the status, therefore, the investigator or orator was able to find out what the body of material in the case meant.

Quintilian discusses two general states—the legal and the ratiocinatory. The former has many species, "as laws are numerous, and have various forms." The latter includes the status of conjecture or fact, the status of definition, and the status of quality.

These general states are, then, of two kinds: those depending upon legality, and those depending upon reasoning. The ratiocinatory states are simpler since they consist "merely in the contemplation of the nature of things. . . ." Briefly, they deal with these possible points in a case: whether a thing is—a matter of fact; what it is—a matter of definition; and of what species it is—a matter of quality. Thus, a case in the courtroom might center about the status of conjecture: Brown was either guilty or innocent of the charge of murder. Or, a case might deal with the status of definition: Brown killed a man but it was in self-defense, and hence was not murder. Or the status might concern quality: "Horatius committed a crime, for he killed his sister; he committed no crime, for he had a right to kill her who mourned at the death of an enemy."[50]

Style Treated Conventionally

Quintilian recommends that the greatest possible care be given to expression,

. . . provided we bear in mind that nothing is to be done for the sake of words, as words themselves were invented for the sake of things, and as those words are the most to be commended which express our thoughts best, and produce the impression which we desire on the minds of the judges. Such words undoubtedly must make a speech both worthy of admiration and productive pleasure; but not of that kind of *admiration* with which we wonder at monsters; or of that kind of *pleasure* which is attended with unnatural gratification, but such as is compatible with true merit and worth.[51]

Then follows a long and reasonably conventional discussion of style. The classifications and definitions of the figures and tropes are more systematically handled, however, than in any previous contribution.

Attitude Toward Delivery

It is of interest to note Quintilian's defense of "extempore" speaking:

But the richest fruit of all our study, and the most ample recompense for the extent of our labour, is *the faculty of speaking extempore;* and he who has not succeeded in acquiring it, will do well, in my opinion, to renounce the occupations of the forum, and devote his solitary talent of writing to some other employment; for it is scarcely consistent with the character of a man of honour to make a public profession of service to others which may fail in the most pressing emergencies, since it is of no more use than to point out a harbour to a vessel, to which it cannot approach unless it be borne along by the gentlest breezes. There arise indeed innumerable occasions where it is absolutely necessary to speak on the instant, as well before magistrates, as on trials that are brought on before the appointed time; and if any of these shall occur, I do not say to any one of our innocent fellow citizens, but to any of our own friends and relatives, is an advocate to stand dumb, and, while they are begging for a voice to save them, and are likely to be undone if succor be not instantly afforded them, is he to ask time for retirement and silent study, till his speech be formed and committed to memory, and his voice and lungs be put in tune?[52]

Practically, this manner of speaking requires a technique differing from the ordinary mode of address.

Yet if any chance shall give rise to such a sudden necessity for speaking extempore, we shall have need to exert our mind with more than its usual activity; we must fix our whole attention on our matter, and relax, for the time, something of our care about words, if we find it impossible to attend to both. A slower pronunciation, too, and a mode of speaking with suspense and doubt, as it were, gives time for consideration; yet we must manage so that we may seem to deliberate and not to hesitate.[53]

Final Estimate

Colson has pronounced the *Institutes* "one of the most remarkable and interesting products of Roman common sense."[54] At all points in the twelve books we are impressed by the sanity of the author in refusing to be bound by inflexible rules, and by his insistence upon shaping his doctrine to the varying demands of different speech situations. Eclectic as the treatment is, the contents take on new color and vitality at Quintilian's hands because he weaves his teaching experience and wise counsel into the fabric of the old theory.

Notes

1. J. W. H. Atkins. *Literary Criticism in Antiquity.* London, 1934. II, 16.
2. Cf. Augustus S. Wilkins. *M. Tulli Ciceronis De Oratore.* 3rd ed. Oxford, 1895. I, 56–64.
3. Charles Sears Baldwin. *Ancient Rhetoric and Poetic.* New York, 1924. p. 43.
4. *Ibid.,* p. 34.
5. *De Oratore.* Trans. by J. S. Watson. Philadelphia, 1897. II, lxxxvii.
6. *Brutus.* LX.
7. "Hippias and a Lost Canon of Rhetoric." *Quarterly Journal of Speech Education,* 12:144 (June, 1926).
8. *Teuffel's History of Roman Literature.* Trans. and ed. by George C. W. Warr. London, 1891. I, 64.
9. Baldwin. *Op. cit.,* p. 37.
10. *De Oratore.* I, xiii.
11. Atkins. *Op. cit.,* II, 23.
12. *De Oratore.* I, v.
13. *Ibid.,* I, xii.
14. *Op. cit.,* p. 46.
15. *De Oratore,* I, xv.
16. *Ibid.,* II, xxvi.
17. *Ibid.,* II, xxix.
18. *Ibid.,* II, xlii.
19. *Ibid.,* II, lxxvi.
20. *Ibid.,* II, lxxxvi.
21. *Ibid.,* II, lxxxviii.
22. *Ibid.,* III, xxv.
23. *Op. cit.,* p. 55.
24. *De Oratore.* III, lv.
25. John Edwin Sandys. *M. Tulli Ciceronis ad M. Brutum Orator.* Cambridge, 1885. pp. lviii, lxiv.
26. *Orator.* From *The Orations of Marcus Tullius Cicero.* Trans. by C. D. Yonge. London, 1852. IV, 403–407, *passim.*
27. *Ibid.,* IV, 407–409, *passim.*
28. *Ibid.,* IV, 409–410.
29. *Op. cit.,* pp. 56–57.
30. *Rhetoric.* Trans. by Theodore Buckley. London, 1883. pp. 246–247.
31. J. F. D'Alton. *Roman Literary Theory and Criticism.* London, 1931. pp. 74–75.
32. *Orator.* IV, 442–445, *passim.*
33. Torsten Petersson, *Cicero: A Biography.* Berkeley, Calif., 1919. p. 442.
34. *On Topics.* In *The Orations of Marcus Tullius Cicero.* Trans. by C. D. Yonge. London, 1919. IV, 460.
35. *On Rhetorical Invention.* In *Ibid.* IV, 309.
36. Wilbur Samuel Howell. "The Positions of Argument: An Historical Examination." In *Papers in Rhetoric.* Donald C. Bryant, ed. St. Louis, 1940. p. 9.
37. J. Wright Duff. *A Literary History of Rome in the Silver Age.* New York, 1927. p. 387.
38. *Institutes of Oratory.* Trans. by J. S. Watson. London, 1856. XII, ii, 1.
39. F. H. Colson. *M. Fabii Quintiliani Institutionis Oratoriae Liber I.* Cambridge, 1924. p. xxviii.
40. *Institutes.* II, xxi, 12–13.

41. *Op. cit.*, p. xxiv–xxv.
42. *Institutes.* II, xiii, 2.
43. *Ibid.*, II, xiii, 7.
44. *Ibid.*, II, xiii, 2.
45. *Ibid.*, III, iii.
46. *Ibid.*, III, iv.
47. *Ibid.*, III, v.
48. *Ibid.*, III, vi, 21.
49. *Op. cit.*, p. 74.
50. *Institutes.* III, vi, 76.
51. *Ibid.*, VIII, introd., 32–33.
52. *Ibid.*, X, vii, 1–2.
53. *Ibid.*, X, vii, 22.
54. *Op. cit.*, p. xxi.

Charles S. Baldwin

St. Augustine on Preaching

◊ *One of the new kinds of rhetoric that developed during the Middle Ages was the rhetoric of the sermon* (ars praedicandi). *Perhaps the most influential contributor to the rhetoric of preaching was St. Augustine (345–430 A.D.). In this excerpt from his book on* Medieval Rhetoric and Poetic, *Charles S. Baldwin gives us an overview of St. Augustine's rhetoric, as that is presented in Book IV of* De doctrina christiana, *and relates it to the rhetoric of the Sophists, which Augustine is rejecting, and to the rhetoric of Cicero, which he is appropriating and adapting for religious purposes. Two other illuminating essays about the rhetoric of preaching can be found in these two articles by James J. Murphy: "Saint Augustine and Rabanus Maurus: The Genesis of Medieval Rhetoric,"* Western Speech, *31 (Spring, 1967): 88–95 and "Saint Augustine and the Debate about Christian Rhetoric,"* Quarterly Journal of Speech, *46 (1960): 400–410.* ◊

With this elaborate pedagogical tradition [that of the Sophists] a clean break is made by St. Augustine. The fourth book of his *De doctrina christiana* has historical significance in the early years of the fifth century out of all proportion to its size; for it begins rhetoric anew. It not only ignores sophistic; it goes back over centuries of the lore of personal triumph to the ancient idea of moving men to truth; and it gives to the vital counsels of Cicero a new emphasis for the urgent tasks of preaching the word of God.

Abstractly and in retrospect the very character of Christian preaching seems necessarily to reject sophistic. But at the time this seemed anything but inevitable. Sophistic was almost the only lore of public speaking then active. It dominated criticism and education. The Greek fathers Gregory of Nyssa and Gregory Nazianzen might expose its falsity of conception; but they could not escape it. It had brought them up. Its stylistic habits were ingrained in their expression. Augustine too had been brought up on sophistic. Nor could he escape it. Again and again his style rings with its tradition.[1] Not only had he learned it for good; he had taught it. He had been himself, in Plutarch's sense

From *Medieval Rhetoric and Poetic*, The Macmillan Company, New York, 1928. Reprinted by permission of Marshall Baldwin.
*In the present volume, a small portion of material in the original essay has been omitted, as well as some of the original footnotes.

and Strabo's, a sophist. We must hasten to add that the great Christians of the fourth century, if they could not escape sophistic, at least redeemed it by curbing its extravagance and turning it to nobler uses. But Augustine did much more. He set about recovering for the new generation of Christian orators the true ancient rhetoric. He saw that for Christian preaching, sophistic must not only be curbed; it must be supplanted. Against the background of his day, his quiet, simple book, renouncing the balances and figures of his other works without renouncing their fervor, is seen to be a startling innovation.

Not the least striking trait of the innovation is its reserve. Augustine does not attack sophistic as the Gregorys do; he ignores it. In Chapter xxxi of Book II he had, indeed, mentioned it. Discussing there not style, but matter, he had contrasted the necessary training in argument with sophistic quibbling, and had then added, forecasting Book IV, that superfluous stylistic ornament also is sophistic.

> But training in argument on questions of all such kinds as are to be investigated and resolved in sacred literature is of the highest value; only we must beware of the lust for quarelling, and of the puerile display of skill in disappointing an opponent. . . . This sort of quibbling conclusion Scripture execrates, I think, in the text *Qui sophistice loquitur odibilis est.*[2] Even though not quibbling, a speech seeking verbal ornament beyond the bounds of responsibility to subject matter (*gravitas*) is called sophistic. II. xxxi.

But an uninformed modern reader of Book IV would hardly be aware that sophistic existed. No denunciation could be more scathing than this silence. In Augustine's view of Christian preach-

ing, sophistic simply has no place. A good debater, instead of parrying, he counters. He spends his time on his own case. A good teacher, he tells his neophytes not what to avoid, but what to do. He has so far renounced sophistic that he has no concern to triumph. He wishes simply to teach sound rhetorical doctrine. He achieves an extraordinary conciseness not so much by compression as by undeviating straightforwardness.

A reader familiar with the times, however, will be reminded of sophistic by many allusions. Single phrases or sentences some of them, a few more extended, they all serve to illuminate by contrast the true rhetoric.

> All these things, when they are taught by rhetors, are thought great, bought at a great price, sold with great boasting. Such boasting, I fear, I may suggest myself in speaking so; but I had to answer those ill-educated men who think that our authors are to be despised, not because they lack the eloquence which such critics love too much, but because they do not use it for display. vii.
>
> [But an audience of Christian sobriety] will not be pleased with that suave style in which though no wrong things are said, right things slight and frail are adorned with foamy circumlocution. xiv.
>
> I think I have accomplished something not when I hear them applauding, but when I see them weeping. xxiv.

Display, inflation, thirst for applause—every reader of Augustine's time would recognize in these allusions a repudiation of sophistic.

For Augustine thinks that Christian preaching is to be learned best from Christian preachers. As if in reply to Julian's scornful "Let them elucidate their Matthew and Luke," he recommends not only for doctrine, but for rhetoric, the Epistles, the Prophets, and the Fathers, and proceeds to analyze their style. The analysis, though based on the current Latin version, is generally transferable to the Greek, since it is much simpler than the classification set forth by sophistic. It exhibits sentence movement simply in climax, period, balance—those devices which are most easily appropriated and most useful. The general ancient counsels of aptness and variety are applied specifically to preaching. As to cadence (*clausula*), Augustine dispenses with all subdivisions, and even makes bold to assert that it must sometimes be sacrificed. Similarly omitting all classification of figures, he manages to suggest in a few words what figures are for. In a word, he shows how to learn from the Canon and the Fathers the rhetoric that is vital to homiletic.

This rhetoric, not only simpler than sophistic, but quite different in emphasis, is set forth in the terms of Cicero. Augustine has gone back four and a half centuries to the days before *declamatio*. The instruction that he draws from his analysis of Christian literature is planned upon the "instruct, win, move" (*docere, delectare, movere*) of *De oratore* and upon the corresponding three typical styles (*genus tenue—medium—grande*) of *Orator*. Evidently Augustine had the greater Cicero, not the lesser that sufficed for the Middle Age. He neither quotes nor cites any other rhetorician; and though his doctrine of aptness and of variety is common throughout the older rhetoric, for this too he had no need to go beyond the master's two great works. Nor have any others been more persuasive as to imitation, which is Augustine's controlling idea. This first Ciceronianism, too immediately aware of the perverted imitation of style taught by sophists to fall into the archaism and redundancy of later worship of Cicero, is a penetrative recovery of Cicero's larger meaning. Augustine's application of the three typical styles is more just and more practically distinct than Cicero's own. Would that all Ciceronians had been equally discerning!

Tabular View of St. Augustine's de Doctrina Christiana IV

A. For learning to preach, models are more fruitful than rules   i–v
B. Eminent models are offered by the literature of Christian eloquence vi–viii
   1. Christian eloquence not merely comparable with pagan, but distinctive.
   2. Analysis of *Romans* v. especially of climax, period, clauses, etc.
   3. Analysis of 2 *Corinth.* xi. 16, especially of variety.
   4. Analysis of *Amos* vi. especially of figures.
C. Christian preaching must fulfill all three typical tasks of oratory summarized in Cicero's *docere, delectare, movere*   ix–xix
   1. *docere*, subordinating even *integritas* to clearness   ix–xi
   2. *delectare*, necessary as a means, never an end   xii–xvii
   3. *movere*, to carry assent into action   xviii, xix
D. The three corresponding styles of oratory, Cicero's *tenue, medium, grande*, are exemplified in the Canon   xx
   1. *genus tenue* (*submissum*) in *Galatians* iv. 21 and iii. 15 as demanding trained reasoning and memory.
   2. *genus medium* (*temperatum*) in 1 *Timothy* v. *Romans* xii, xiii, as rhythmical, but with cadence often sacrificed.
   3. *genus grande* in 2 *Corinthians* vi. 2, *Romans* viii. 28, *Galatians* iv. 10, the last without the usual stylistic means.

E. They are also exemplified in St.
Cyprian *Ad Cæcilium* and *De habitu
virginum*, St. Ambrose *De Spiritu and
De virginibus*   xxii
F. No one of the three can effectively be
constant.   xxii, xxiii
G. Constancy is rather in the aim, which
is always persuasion   xxiv–xxvi
  1. The speaker's life is the greater
     means of persuasion in the third
     style   xxvii–xxviii
(Appended Note) The recital of borrowed
sermons is permissible   xxix
Conclusion, with reminder of prayer, in
thanksgiving   xxx, xxxi

The fourth book of the *De doctrina christiana* is specifically linked by its proem to the preceding three as setting forth presentation (*modus proferendi*). Books I–III have dealt with the study of the subject matter (*inventio*); Book IV is to deal with expression. Augustine thus makes the traditional fivefold division twofold. *Inventio*, which under sophistic had lapsed, he restores to its rightful place and gives it a new application to the exegesis of Scripture. Of the remaining four left to his second heading he discusses only style (*elocutio*). Delivery and memory are mentioned incidentally; plan is omitted. The omission is not negligent. The first chapter warns us not to expect a manual of rhetoric. Nevertheless a modern student cannot help wishing that so suggestive a treatise had both applied to preaching the ancient counsels as to plan and exhibited the New Testament in this aspect. Thus to analyze for imitation not only the style of the Pauline epistles, but their cogency of order, would doubtless have made the work unduly extensive. One hopes that seminarians of the fifth century were stimulated, and that seminarians of the

twentieth century will be stimulated, by the example of the treatise itself, to study *Romans* not only for appeal, but for cogency. Meantime Augustine's fourth book remains one of the most fruitful of all discussions of style in preaching.

Who dare say that the defenders of truth should be unarmed against falsehood? While the proponents of error know the art of winning an audience to good will, attention, and open mind, shall the proponents of truth remain ignorant? While the [sophist] states facts concisely, clearly, plausibly, shall the preacher state them so that they are tedious to hear, hard to understand, hard to believe? While the one attacks truth and insinuates falsehood by fallacious argument, shall the other have too little skill either to defend the true or to refute the false? Shall the one, stirring his hearers to error, urging them by the force of oratory, move them by terror, by pity, by joy, by encouragement, and the other slowly and coldly drowse for truth? ii.

But to learn such skill from rules, he goes on, is the way rather for boys than for men who have immediately before them the urgent tasks of preaching.

For eloquence will stick to such men, if they have the talent of keenness and ardor, more easily through their reading and hearing of the eloquent than through their following of the rules of eloquence. Nor does the Church lack literature, even outside the Canon established in the citadel of authority, to imbue a capable man with its eloquence, even though his mind be not on the manner but on the matter, provided he add practice in writing, in dictating, finally also in composing orally what he feels according to the rule of piety and faith. Besides, if such talent be lacking, either the rules of rhetoric will not be grasped, or if by great labor some few of them are partially grasped, they will be of no avail. . . . [Young preachers] must beware of letting slip what they have to say while they attend to saying it in good form. iii.

They must, indeed, know the principles of adaptation (iv), and develop their expression as far as they can; but they will do so best by imitation.

Whoever wishes to speak not only with wisdom, but with eloquence. . . . I rather direct to read or hear the eloquent and to imitate them by practise than advise to spend his time on teachers of the art of rhetoric. v.

Expressed in modern terms, Augustine's position is that rhetoric as a classified body of doctrine is properly an undergraduate study. It is not the best approach for seminarians because its method is analytical. The young preacher, needing rather promotion than revision, will advance more rapidly by imitation.

Starting from this principle, that the more fruitful study for learning to preach is imitation of Christian eloquence, Augustine proceeds to show (vi–viii) how distinctive is the eminence of such models and how repaying to analysis. His vindication should be pondered by those who still permit themselves to disparage without distinction the literary value of the New Testament, and by those who, granting poetic to Ambrose, remain unaware of his rhetoric.

At this point the question, perhaps, arises whether our authors, whose divinely inspired writings constitute for us a canon of most salutary authority, are to be called philosophers[3] only, or also orators. To me and to those who agree with what I am saying, the question is very easily answered. For where I comprehend them, nothing can seem to me either more philosophical or more eloquent. And all, I venture to say, who rightly comprehend what they speak, comprehend at the same time that they could not have spoken otherwise. For as there is an eloquence becoming to youth, another to age, nor can that be called eloquence which does not befit the character of the speaker, so there is an eloquence becoming to men most worthy of the highest authority and evidently inspired. Our authors have spoken with such eloquence. No other is becoming to them, nor theirs to others. For it is like themselves; and, the more it rejects display, the more it ranges above others not by inflation, but by cogency. Where on the other hand I do not comprehend them, though their eloquence is less apparent to me, I have no doubt that it is such as I find it where I do comprehend. The very obscurity of inspired and salutary utterances has been tinged with such eloquence that our minds should be stimulated not only in study [of their meaning], but in practise [of their art]. Indeed, if there were leisure, all the virtues and graces of eloquence with which those are inflated who put their style ahead of the style of our authors not by greatness, but by distension, could be exhibited in the sacred literature of those whom divine Providence has sent to instruct us and to draw us from this corrupt world to the world of happiness. But what delights me more than I can say in their eloquence is not what it has in common with pagan orators and poets. What I rather admire, what fills me with amazement, is that the eloquence which we hear around us has so been used, as it were through another eloquence of their own, as to be neither deficient nor conspicuous. For it should be neither condemned nor displayed; and they would have seemed to do the one if they shunned it, the other if it became noticeable. Even in those places where perhaps it is noticeable to experts, such is the message that the words in which it is expressed seem not to be sought by the speaker, but to subserve that message naturally, as if one saw philosophy issuing from her own home in the heart of the philosopher, and eloquence following as an inseparable servant even when not called.[4] vi.

The vindication of an eloquence distinctly Christian has the more weight because its doctrine of form and substance echoes from Cicero the best ancient tradition. The older tradition had in Augustine's time been so overlaid that he could do no better service to rhetoric than to recall it. In fact, Christian eloquence redeemed public speaking by reviving the true persuasion.

The insistence on the Ciceronian doctrine that style is not separable has a bearing more than historical. Not only for Augustine's time, but for any time, the truism must be reasserted. His iteration is more than preoccupation with Cicero, more than repudiation of sophistic. It springs from the cardinal importance of the truism for homiletic. In the pulpit the sophistic heresy of art for art's sake becomes intolerable.

Augustine's next step (vii) is to support his general claims for Christian eloquence, and to show how it may be studied, by analyzing briefly three typical passages. In the first, *Romans* v. 3–5, he analyzes prose rhythm under the familiar heads of classical sentence movement (*compositio*): phrases and subordinate clauses (*cæsa*), coordinate clauses (*membra*), period (*circuitus*), climax (*gradatio*), adding the equivalent Greek terms.

The passage is short enough, and the sentence movement simple enough, to be grasped readily. Its balance is striking without being monotonous, and is reinforced by a linking iteration that leads to a climax.[5] He is a wise teacher who begins with an instance so memorable. It must have seized even more quickly a generation familiar with both the terms and the method.

The next example, 2 *Corinthians* xi. 16–31, shows the same sentence devices carried through a much longer reach, and is therefore used both to reinforce the first and to add the impor-

tance of rhythmical variety. The counsel of variety, though a commonplace of the older rhetoric, had especial point by contrast with the sophistic fondness for trimming and prolonging balances. Incidental to the exhibition of variety is a reminder of aptness; and the analysis concludes:

> Finally all this breathless passage is closed with a period of two members. . . . But how after this impetus the brief statement interposed comes to rest, and rests the reader, how apt it is and how charming, can hardly be said. vii.

The analysis of the third example, *Amos* vi. 1–6, leads the study to longer and more sustained rhythmical reaches. Lest it seem the more difficult in the more figurative version of the Septuagint, Augustine quotes it "as translated from the Hebrew into Latin style through the interpretation of the priest Jerome, expert in both languages."

Much more urgent, leaping to attack, rising, prolonging, varying, subsiding to a pregnant close, the prophecy widens the conception of rhythmical range. Marking the rhythms briefly, Augustine uses it also to show the oratorical force of figures.[6] Thus a few pages of analysis are made to yield wide and definite suggestion. This, perhaps, is their outstanding merit; while they show the student what to look for, they invite him to go on for himself. But the pedagogical achievement does not stop there. The professor of rhetoric has seen that rhetorical analysis must be simplified, and that it must be made progressive. Where else shall we find so much drawn from three analyses? The first reduces the complicated lore of rhythm to its essentials. The second, reinforcing and extending these, dwells upon aptness as a corrective of rhetorical zeal, and as a constructive principle. The third, quoting rhythms still more urgent with emotion, passes to the emotional value of concrete words. To bring the over-classified lore of sophistic back to the simplicity of Aristotle was a service not only to homiletic, but to all rhetoric. A greater service was to substitute for the static and formalized pedagogy of the day a vital order. Augustine had been doubtless a popular professor; Christianity made him a great teacher.

Pedagogically, therefore, even his incidental definitions are worth noticing. That the function of grammar is traditionally to impart correctness of speech (iii) is used to support the contention that even this elementary skill comes best in fact from imitation. The period (vii) is defined so as to throw the emphasis on delivery. Its "clauses are suspended by the speaker's voice until it is concluded at the end." Therefore it "cannot have fewer than two clauses." So he points out in the passage from *Amos* that the rhythm is available for delivery (*in potestate pronuntiantis*) either as a series of six or as three pairs, and that the latter is more beautiful. So he suggests limiting analysis to give room for oral interpretation.

This same passage which we have set as an example can be used to show other things relevant to the rules of eloquence. But a good hearer is not so much instructed by discussion in detail as he is kindled by ardent delivery. vii.

The next and longest section (ix–xiv) is based on Cicero's "inform, please, move" (*docere, delectare, movere*). Distinguishing each of these tasks clearly, Augustine is at the same time careful to unite them, by progressively iterative transitions, in the single and constant task of persuasion. In exposition (*docere*) clearness may demand the use of popular expressions. What avails correctness in a diction that is not understood?

He who teaches will rather avoid all words that do not teach. If he can find correct words that are understood, he will choose those; if he cannot, whether because they do not exist or because they do not occur to him at the time, he will use even words that are less correct, provided only the thing itself be taught and learned correctly. ix.

The correctness (*integritas*) of diction boasted by the sophists, and carried by them even to the pedantry of archaism, is here faced squarely. The assertion that it must sometimes be sacrificed, the making of clearness absolutely paramount, is the bolder at a time when Christian preaching was not yet recognized as having secure command of elegance. Unmistakable clearness, Augustine goes on, is so much more important in preaching than in discussions permitting question and answer that the speaker must be quick to help unspoken difficulties.

For a crowd eager to grasp will show by its movement whether it has understood; and until it has given this signal the subject must be turned over and over by various ways of expressing it—a resource beyond the power of those who deliver speeches written out and memorized. x.

No warrant here, he adds (xi), for dilation beyond the demands of clearness, but good warrant for making instruction pleasant and appealing in order to hold attention. Passing thus to the two other tasks of oratory, he quotes

(xii) Cicero's "to instruct is of necessity, to please is for interest, to move is for victory." The three are then both carefully distinguished and shown to be a sort of geometrical progression. The first is first of necessity. It must be mastered; but it is rarely sufficient. To supply the lack, the second demands more rhetoric by demanding further adaptation to the audience; but it too must remain insufficient. So the third task, to move, is not merely the third item in a classification; it is the final stage in a progress. That progress is increasingly emotional. The last stage demands not only all the rhetoric of the preceding, but also the art of vivid imagery and of urgent application. So Augustine arrives at one of those linking summaries which constitute almost a refrain.

Therefore the eloquence of the Church, when it seeks to have something done, must not only explain to instruct and please to hold, but also move to win. xiii.

The next chapter (xiv) warns against resting in the second stage.[7] To make the pleasing of the audience an end in itself is the typical vice of sophistic. If preaching tolerates it, "the time will come when they will not endure sound doctrine; but after their own lusts shall they heap to themselves teachers, having itching ears." Augustine quotes, not these words of St. Paul, but Jeremiah, and rises to denunciation of mere pleasing. "Far from us be that madness." One of Cyprian's rare descriptive passages is adduced to show how "the wholesomeness of Christian preaching has recalled his diction from [sophistic] redundancy and held it to a graver eloquence of less display." As the ultimate objection to the sophistic ideal

is moral, so is the preacher's ultimate resource. Since his strength is derived from a source deeper than human skill, his best preparation is prayer. Augustine is not above enforcing this reminder by playing upon the words *orare, orator, oratio.* Nevertheless human skill is to be cultivated. Prayer itself proves the folly (xvi) of making no other preparation. He who abjures human lore of preaching because God gives us our messages might equally well abjure prayer because God knows us and our needs. The Pauline counsels specify how Timothy should preach. As God heals through doctors and medicines, so he gives the gospel to men by men and through man.

The transition (xvii) to the final task of moving men to action is another full and explicit iteration of all three, and at the same time a preparation for the next section on the corresponding three typical styles. Since the subject matter of preaching is always great, at least in implication (xviii), does it not always demand a great style? No; for a great matter (xix) may at the time rather demand exposition; and this in turn demands a restrained style. Again, a great matter may at the time rather demand praise or blame; and here enters the second task of so adapting the style as to win sympathy.

But when something ought to be done, and we are talking to those who ought to do it and will not, then the great subject is to be expressed greatly and in such wise as to bend their minds. . . . What subject is greater than God? Is it therefore not a subject for instruction? Or how can any one expounding the unity of the Trinity do it except by confining himself to exposition, that so difficult a distinction may as far as is possible be understood? Is ornament demanded here, and not rather argument? Is there here something that the audience is to be moved to do, and not rather something that it is to be taught to learn? Again, when God is praised in himself or in his works, what a vision of beautiful and splendid diction rises before any one praising as well as he can him whom no one praises aright and no one fails to praise in some way or other! But if God be not worshipped, or if idols be worshipped with him or even in his stead, whether dæmons or any other created being, then to meet so great an evil, and from this evil to save men, the preaching too must be great. xix.

Augustine has passed (xvii–xix) from Cicero's three tasks of oratory to his three typical styles by applying to the preacher Cicero's definition of the orator: "He, then, shall be called eloquent who can speak small things quietly, larger things proportionately, great things greatly."[8] Thus the three styles are *genus submissum* (or *tenue*), *genus temperatum* (or *medium*), and *genus grande*. As in Cicero, these correspond to *docere, delectare, movere,* and the second is connected with panegyric.

Augustine now proceeds to exemplify the first style (xx) from *Galatians* as calling for skill in reasoning and for a memory trained to bring in objections and difficulties where they can best be met. This debater's memory is precisely the ancient *memoria*, the fifth of the traditional parts of rhetoric. It seems to have fallen into abeyance under sophistic. What the sophists boasted was verbal memory, which Augustine merely mentions in his appendix as something quite different.

The same chapter (xx) exemplifies the second, or median style from *Timothy* and *Romans* as having the charm of

aptness. Here Augustine confronts squarely the sophistic habit of making rhythmical beauty paramount and the pagan disparagement of Christian style. Some one may find the cadence of *Romans* xiii. 14 defective. Certainly it would soothe the ear more rhythmically if the verb came last.

But a graver translator has preferred to keep the usual word-order [and, he might have added, the logical emphasis]. How this sounds in the Greek used by the apostle they may see whose expertness in that language goes so far. To me at least, the word-order, which is the same as in our version, does not seem there either to run rhythmically. Indeed, the stylistic beauty (*ornatum*) which consists of rhythmical cadences is defective, we must confess, in our authors. Whether this is due to our versions, or whether, as I incline to think, the authors deliberately avoided these occasions for applause, I do not venture to affirm, since I confess that I do not know. But this I know, that anyone who shall make their cadences regular in the same rhythms—and this is done very easily by shifting certain words that have equal force of meaning in the new order—will recognize that these inspired men lacked none of those things which he learned as great matters in the schools of the grammarians or rhetors. Moreover, he will discover many sorts of diction of so great beauty as to be beautiful even in our customary language, much more in theirs, and never found in the literature with which [the sophists] are inflated. But we must beware lest the addition of rhythm detract from the weight of inspired and grave sentences. Most learned Jerome does not carry over into his translation the musical skill in which rhythm is learned most fully, though our prophets did not lack even that, as he shows in the Hebrew meters of some of them; [and he gave this up] in order to keep truth to their words. . . . As in my own style, so far as I think I may do so modestly, I do not neglect rhythmical cadences,[9] so in our authors they please me the more because I find them there so rarely. xx.

The third, or great style, whether it be elegant or not, has for its distinguishing quality the force of emotional appeal. The instances are from 2 *Corinthians* vi and *Romans* viii. *Romans* is a long epistle, not a sermon. Though it was read aloud, of course, it is essentially a treatise, a philosophy of history. It is largely expository and argumentative. Since it is addressed primarily to reflection and reason, its main artistic reliance is on cogency of order. But even here presentation does not remain purely logical. For persuasion it must rise also emotionally. As we read in *Acts* xvii the outline of the apostle's Areopagus speech, we discern beyond the logical chain of propositions an expanding conception of the Life-giver. Who can doubt that the style too, as in *Romans,* rose to *grande?* The traditional doctrine of the peroration, easily as it may be abused, is only the expression in rhetoric of the audience's final demand and the speaker's final answer. That demand and that answer are emotional.

Although the whole epistle, except in the elegant last part, is written in the plain style, nevertheless the apostle inserts a certain passage of such moving force that it must be called great even though it has no such embellishments as those just cited. . . . Is there here either antithesis, or subordination for climax, or rhythm in phrase, clause, or period? None the less for that there is no cooling of the great emotion with which we feel the style to glow. xx.

After quoting without further comment examples from Cyprian and Ambrose, Augustine shows (xxii, xxiii) the need of variety. More even than other forms of oratory, preaching seems to suffer from a stylistic level. No one of the three styles, least of all the third, can effectively be prolonged; the change from style to style gives relief; and subordination of what might be heightened may enhance the emotion of what must be. What must be heightened is what is to rouse the audience to action. So the test of achievement in the third style is not applause, but tears and change of life (xxiv). So also the end of all eloquence, in whatever style, is persuasion (xxv).

In the restrained style the orator persuades of truth. In the great style he persuades to action. In the elegant style is he to persuade himself that he is speaking beautifully? With such an end what have we to do? Let them seek it who glory in language, who display themselves in panegyrics and such exercises, in which the hearer is neither to be instructed nor to be moved to any action, but merely to be pleased. But let us judge this end by another end. xxv.

Thus Augustine is more explicit than Cicero in showing that the three typical styles are but three ways (xxvi) of achieving a single end, even as the three corresponding tasks, though one of them absorbs attention at a time, are but three aspects of the single task. Nor can persuasion dispense with a means beyond art, the appeal of the speaker's life[10] (xxvii). Though the Church speaks not merely through a man, but through his office, persuasion needs for full effect his whole influence. Because his life is without shame, the preacher speaks not shamelessly (xxviii), not only with restraint and charm, but with power, to win obedience to the truth.

The historical significance of the *De doctrina christiana,* important as it is, should not obscure its value as a contribution to homiletic. The first homiletic, though one of the briefest, remains one of the most suggestive. It omits no essential; while it reminds us of the general principles of rhetoric, it emphasizes those applications to preaching which are distinctive; and it proceeds pedagogically. Though the *doctrina* of the title refers strictly to exposition, and this is amplified and iterated as a constant necessity, Augustine includes specifically and from the start both charm and appeal, and concludes by showing emotional appeal to be the final stage of the comprehensive task of persuasion. Homiletic is an application of rhetoric long established as permanent, consistent, and in both materials and conditions fairly constant. That it is also comprehensive, demanding all three typical styles, including argument in its exposition, winning sympathy in order to urge action, varying its art while holding to its single aim, is most suggestively established here in its first great monument.

Not only does Augustine forbid the arid and the tedious, not only does he insist on emotional appeal; he also vindicates for Christian eloquence the importance of charm. This was the more delicate because charm was both abused by contemporary sophists and still suspected by contemporary preachers. Augustine presents it at once frankly and with just discrimination. To make it an end in itself, he is careful to show, is indeed sophistic; but to ignore it is to forget that preaching is a form of the oratory of occasion.[11] The Areopagus speech of St. Paul, though it is only summarized in *Acts* xvii, is evidently occasional, and has clear indications of that adaptation to win sympathy which is Augustine's interpretation of Cicero's *delectare*. The speech on occasion, favorite form of oratory in Augustine's time, had been conventionalized to the point of recipe. The recipe, though he knew them all, Augustine simply ignores; the field he redeems. He shows Christian preaching how to cultivate it for real harvest. History has shown no other direction of rhetoric to be so peculiarly homiletic.

Already Christian eloquence had reached conspicuous achievement in panegyric and more widely in the field of occasional oratory. The pagan sophist must look to his laurels. But these very triumphs had brought the danger of lapsing into too familiar conventions. What in pagan oratory might be no worse than pretty or merely exciting, in Christian oratory would be meretricious. To hold his difficult course, the preacher, as Augustine reminds him again and again, must at every moment steer for his message. He must never deviate. Though sophistic lost its dominance centuries ago, it has never been quite dead, and it always besets preaching. Therefore a constant concern of homiletic is to exorcise it by a valid rhetoric; and no book has ever revealed this more succintly, more practically, or more suggestively than the *De doctrina christiana*.

Notes

1. For detailed analysis, see Barry (Sr. Inviolata), *St. Augustine the Orator*, Washington, D.C., 1924.
2. Even though the application of the text from *Ecclus.* xxxvii. 20 be questioned, the rebuke of sophistic display, whether in dialectic or in style, is none the less clear.
3. Thus I venture to translate *sapientes*, remembering the connotation of the word both for Augustine and for his master Cicero.

4. So toward the close "The Christian preacher prefers to appeal rather with matter than with manner, and thinks neither that anything is said better which is not said more truly, nor that the teacher must serve words, but words the teacher." xxviii.

5. The linking iteration is characteristic of climax as practised by sophistic.

6. Chapter xxix of Book III relegates the study of figures to *grammatica;* but there also Augustine reminds his readers that figures, without regard to books or teaching, are a natural expression of the imaginative impulse.

7. The warning is repeated where Augustine is gathering the three tasks into the final and constant idea of persuasion: "But that which is handled in the way of charm . . . is not to be made an end in itself (xxv) . . . nor does it seek merely to please." Nothing is more admirable in Augustine's exposition than this expert linking of his chain of progress.

8. *Orator,* xxix. 101.

9. For his cadences, see Barry, *op. cit.*

10. Aristotle, *Rhetoric* I. ii.

11. In the passage quoted above from Chapter xix, and in other places there are clear references to occasional oratory.

William G. Crane

English Rhetorics of the Sixteenth Century

◊ *The article reprinted here summarizes major representative works on rhetoric produced in England during the sixteenth century. Included in the survey is a description of two of the most popular and influential stylistic rhetorics—Richard Sherry's* A Treatise of Schemes and Tropes *and Henry Peacham's* The Garden of Eloquence—*and Thomas Wilson's comprehensive neo-classical volume on* The Arte of Rhetorique. ◊

The English rhetorics of the sixteenth century reflect the emphasis which the Renaissance placed on amplification and ornamentation. Prior to 1500 rhetoric had received only slight mention in *The Courte of Sapyence*, ca. 1480, attributed to Lydgate, and in Caxton's *Myrrour & Descrypcyon of the Worlde*, ca. 1480,[1] a translation of a French version of the *Speculum mundi*. That part of Stephen Hawes's *Pastime of Pleasure*, 1509, which deals with rhetoric places special stress upon the amplification of fables under the heading "invention" and upon certain stylistic devices which Hawes terms "the colouryng of sentences." Hawes has given much attention to the allegorical interpretation of fables, examples, and similitudes by poets. Leonard Cox's *The Arte or Crafte of Rhetoryke*, 1524 (?), the first book in English devoted exclusively to rhetoric, deals only with the first division of the subject, investigation, and with the closely allied matter of judgment. F. I. Carpenter demonstrated in the reprint which he edited for *University of Chicago Studies*, 1899, that the work was based upon and in part translated from Melanchthon's *Institutiones rhetoricae*, 1521. Some material was added from the rhetorical treatises of Cicero, who is named thirty times, and most of the illustrative matter came from his orations. Cox's interest is centered on the means of providing plenty of matter for the development of themes. The *Pro Milone*, one of the most ornate and copious of Cicero's orations, is cited as an example in which he "dyd brynge out of the placis of Rhetoryke arguments to prove his sayde theme or purpose." This oration was Cox's favorite and he never tired of quoting it. After Cicero, Erasmus

From "English Rhetoric of the 16th Century," *Wit and Rhetoric in the Renaissance* 97–112. Copyright © 1937 Columbia University Press. Used by permission.

is the authority most frequently appealed to by Cox. The *Moriae encomium, De conscribendis epistolis,* and *De copia* are mentioned, and the last furnishes illustrative material for several points. Throughout the work Cox's interest in amplification is evident. The use made of the processes of dialectical investigation by orators is stressed by him in his exposition of simple and compound "logical" themes. Regarding the first branch of rhetoric, investigation, he states,

Inuencyon is comprehended in certayn placys, as the Rhetoriciens call them, out of whom he that knoweth the facultye may fetche easyly suche thynges as be mete for the mater that he shal skepe of. . . . The theme proposed, we must after the rules of Rhetoryke go to oure placys that shal anone shew unto us what shalbe to oure purpose.[2]

The second book on rhetoric to appear in English was the compilation published by Richard Sherry in 1550, *A Treatise of Schemes and Tropes.* Though it professes to deal only with matters of styles, it is fairly representative of the rhetorical treatises which appeared in Latin during the Renaissance. The latter half of it is little more than an English version of the more important means of gaining plenty of matter set forth in the second part of Erasmus *De duplici copia verborum ac rerum.* Sherry names most of the sources from which he translated and merely claims for himself that he has given some pains to the section and arrangement of the definitions and that he has furnished some of the examples. He cites Cicero and Quintilian in support of the opinion that "eloqucion" is the principal part of rhetoric. For his definition of "eloqucion" as "wisdom speaking eloquently" he makes acknowledgment to Cicero's *De partitione oratoria.* The three kinds of style named by Cicero in the *De oratore*, the high, the low, and the mean are discussed. Sherry is particularly concerned with the first of these;

for it hathe wyth an ample maiestye verye garnyshed wordes, proper, translated, and graue sentences, whych ar handled in amplificacion and commiseracion, and it hath exornacions bothe of woordes and sentences, wherunro [sic] in oracions they ascribe very great strength and grauitie.[3]

Sherry's book may be considered in three sections corresponding to the sources from which each was particularly drawn. The definitions in the first part (B_5 recto to C_7 verso) of the tropes and figures depending upon diction and upon grammatical construction were translated from Mosellanus's *Tabulae de schematibus et tropis*, 1529, as were many of the examples. The section following (C_8 recto to D_7 recto) headed "The fyrst order of figures Rhetorical," came mainly from the last book of the *Rhetoricorum ad* C. *Herennium libri quatuor.* The third part of the treatise (D_7 verso to F_8 verso) deals with those devices for expanding a theme and obtaining variety of matter which today are called "figures of thought." In the sixteenth century they were generally known as "figures of sentence" or "figures of amplification." Sherry cites Cicero and Quintilian as authorities for designating them as "ornaments of sentence." He used the term "amplification" in the restricted sense of the exaggeration and extenuation of a matter, but he noted that the word might be used in a broader sense to include all the means of expanding a subject, as was pointed out in the commentary on Erasmus's *De duplici copia verborum ac rerum* by John Doelsch, known also under the names Weltkirch and Velcurio. The final section makes up half of Sherry's treatise and is little more than translation from the second part of the *De copia*, with some additions from Doelsch's commentary and from Erasmus's *Ecclesiastae sive de ratione concionandi libri quatuor*, 1535. Sherry also consulted the *Rhetoricorum ad C. Herennium libri quatuor* and Quintilian's *Institutio oratoria*, which were the main sources from which Erasmus drew in both of the works mentioned here. For instance, the discussion of "proues: a copious heaping of probacions" was extended considerably from what Erasmus had written in the *De copia*, by matter taken from the *Ecclesiastae* and, possibly, by some additions from Quintilian's treatise. Sherry directs the reader's attention to the extended treatment of the means of amplifying an oration set forth in the *Ecclesiastae*, where this subject occupies Chapters XXVIII to XLIII of Book III. The means of expanding a theme which Sherry presents are: (1) "particion called also diuision & distribucion rhetoricall,—when a thing that may be generally spoken, is more largely declared and diuided into partes;" (2) "enumeracion," of which there are three kinds; (3) "enargia, euidence or perspicuitie called also description rethoricall," of eleven varieties; (4) "amplificacion," in the restricted sense of exaggeration and extenuation; (5) "the inuencion of many proposicions"; (6) "proues, a copious heaping of probacions," under which the difference between circumstances peculiar to rhetoric and those which belong both to rhetoric and to dialectical investigation is pointed out; (7) "examples"; (8) "parable, which some call similitude, some comparacion"; (9) "icon" (vivid description by means of comparison); (10) "indicatio, or authoritie," of seven kinds, including moral sentences, *chria*, and proverbs; and (11) "exergasia" or "expolicion, when we tarye in one thynge, speakyne the same in diuerse wordes and fashions, as though it were not one matter but diuerse." Having set forth these means of expanding a theme Sherry abruptly closed his treatise with the following apology for omitting the remainder of the *De copia*.

And here me thynketh I maye ryghte well ende these Rhetoricall precepts, although I be not ignoraunt that much helpeth bothe to persuasions and copye, the proper handlyng of tales taken oute of the nature of beastes, dreames, fayned narracions, sumwhat lyke unto the truth, with allegories much used of diuines. But because they requyre a longer treatise, for this tyme I leaue them of, addynge unto these before written rules of oratory, a declamation bothe profitable and verye eloquente, written by Erasmus unto the moste noble Duke of Cleue, as here appereth after.

The *De copia* concluded with discussion of the topics which Sherry declared would "requyre a longer treatise." The declamation by Erasmus printed at the end of Sherry's work consists of a discourse of three and one-half pages on the education of children and "the selfe same matter enlarged by copye" to one hundred and twenty-nine pages. Both the tract and the epitome were printed at the end of some of the copies of the *De copia.* Leonard Cox stated in a letter to the printer Toye, in 1534, that he was making a translation of them. A better illustration could hardly be desired of the stress which Erasmus, Sherry, Cox, and many others in the sixteenth century placed upon amplification.

The only English rhetoric of the sixteenth century which goes beyond translation or close paraphrase is Thomas Wilson's *The Arte of Rhetorique,* 1553. Even it is in large part a compilation from easily recognized sources, particularly Erasmus's *Ecclesiastae sive de ratione concionandi libri quatuor,* Quintilian's *Institutio oratoria,* the *Rhetoricorum ad C. Herennium libri quatuor,* and various treatises of Cicero. For the time at which it appeared *The Arte of Rhetorique* displays an unusual amount of originality. At most points Wilson's sources are evident; yet he selected his materials with a view to the needs of his day and often restated them in words which bear his own stamp. The purpose for which the work was intended and the spirit in which it was written give it a measure of individuality. By reason of Wilson's own inclinations and the fact that one of his chief sources was Erasmus's *Ecclesiastae,* his treatise reflects the religious temper of mid-sixteenth-century England. In a number of ways it is connected with English wit of the sixteenth century. It appealed not only to those attracted by the ideal of Castiglione's *Courtier,* but also to the young men of the court who wished to be saved the trouble of studying rhetoric in the Latin texts. Of chief significance is the stress placed on

amplification throughout the volume. Two years before it appeared Wilson had published a treatise on logic in which the processes of dialectical investigation were treated in full. The usefulness of these means of analysis for obtaining variety of matter is emphasized in the first part of *The Arte of Rhetorique.* In connection with "the finding out of apt matter, called otherwise Inuention," Wilson states, "The places of *Logique,* giue good occasion to finde out plentifull matter. And therefore, they that will proue any cause, and seeke onely to teach thereby the trueth, must search out the places of *Logique,* and no doubt they shall finde much plentie."[4] Some pages beyond this he remarks again on the processes of dialectic as aids to amplification.[5]

Two-thirds of the second book of Wilson's *Arte of Rhetorique* is devoted to the discussion of amplification and the subject which Cicero had subjoined to it, "of delighting the hearers and stirring them to laughter." Wilson was not careful to distinguish between the broad and the narrow senses of the term "amplification." So far as this study is concerned his failure to do this is of no great consequence; all of the devices he considered there served for dilation of a theme. The treatment of amplification in the second book of his treatise came principally from Erasmus's *Ecclesiastae.* The long section on moving laughter, which follows, is nearly all from *The Courtier* of Castiglione, who had taken most of it from Cicero's *De oratore.* In *The Rise of English Literary Prose* Professor Krapp has remarked in connection with Wilson's treatment, "This whole passage on various methods of amplification reads like a description of Euphuism.''[6] It does present many, but not all, of the means used for amplification by Lyly and many other writers of his day. Some other devices are described in the last part of Wilson's treatise. Since this is readily accessible in the reprint of The Clarendon Press, only a few general comments need be made here. Translating from Erasmus's *Ecclesiastae* Wilson notes that moral sentences, similitudes, examples, and witty sayings are skillful devices with which to open a sermon or a speech.[7] At the beginning of his consideration of amplification, he remarks that it is of two sorts. ''The one resteth in wordes, the other in matter.''[8] Regarding the latter he states, ''Amplifying of the matter consisteth in heaping and enlarging of those places, which serueth for confirmation of a matter. As the definition, the cause, the consequent, the contrary, the example, and such other.'' In the course of fifteen pages, translated mainly from Erasmus's *Ecclesiastae,* he presents such means of amplification as comparison, moral sentences, proverbs, examples, comparison of examples, causes, and contraries. The heaping together of these devices receives special stress, and many examples are given. Some of Wilson's comparisons of humans with animals[9] are as fantastic as anything in the writings of John Lyly, who, it may be noted, drew many of his similes from the works of Erasmus, one of Wilson's authorities.

Amplification is mentioned several times in the discussion of the ornaments of style in the last book of *The Arte of Rhetorique.* The figures which Cicero called ''Exornation of sentences, or colours of Rhetorike'' are, according to Wilson, ''amplified by heaping examples, by dilating arguments, by comparing of things together, by similitudes, by contraries, and by diuers others like.''[10] Again, he notes in the course of his remarks on clear explanation and vivid description as means of developing a topic, ''Also similitudes, examples, comparisons, from one thing to another, apt translations, and heaping of Allegories, and all such figures as serue for amplification, doe much commend the lively setting forth of any matter.''[11] The bulk of Wilson's treatment of style is taken up by those devices which authorities, such as John Susenbrot and Henry Peacham, classed under the heading ''figures of amplification.'' Of particular interest in connection with amplification and the style of *Euphues* are the sections headed as follows: ''Wittie iesting,'' ''Digression,'' ''Asking other and answering our selfe,'' ''Doubtfulnesse,'' ''Distribution,'' ''A familiar talk or communication used,'' ''Description,'' ''A Similitude,'' ''Example,'' ''Of enlarging examples by copy,'' ''Of Fables,'' ''Contrarietie,'' ''Stomach greefe,'' ''Like ending and like falling,'' ''Egall members,'' ''Like among themselues,'' ''Gradation,'' ''Outcrying,'' ''Reckening,'' ''Reasoning a matter with our selues,'' ''Resembling of things,'' and ''Answering to our selfe.''[12] Wilson puts special stress upon various kinds of comparison and upon the heaping together of rhetorical devices. The four topics, ''Similitude,'' ''Example,'' ''Of enlarging examples by copy,'' and ''Of Fables'' take up more space than all of the others which have been mentioned. Regarding similitudes, Wilson notes, ''Therefore, those that delite to proue thinges by Similitudes, must learne to knowe the nature of diuers beastes, of mettales, of stones, and al such as haue any vertue in them, and be applied to man's life.'' John Heywood is named in connection with the remark that proverbs often involve comparison. An example of a "similitude enlarged" is preceded by the statement, "That if we purpose to dilate our cause hereby with poses & sentences, wee may with ease talke at large." The illustration which Wilson gives is remarkable for the amount of balance and antithesis which it involves. Following it he summarizes his discussion of similitudes as follows,

Thus similitudes might be enlarged by heaping good sentences, when one thing is compared with an other, and conclusion made thereupon. Among the learned men of the Church, no one vseth this figure more than *Chrisostome*, whose writings the rather seeme more pleasaunt and sweete. For similitudes are not onely vsed to amplifie a matter, but also to beautifie the same, to delite the hearers, to make the matter plaine, and to shewe a certaine maiestie with the report of such resembled things, but because I haue spoken of similitudes heretofore in the booke of *Logique*, I will surcease to talke any further of this matter.[13]

Brute beasts furnish most of the illustrations which Wilson gives under "Example."[14] They are all of the "unnatural natural history" type, which some critics have particularly associated with the writings of John Lyly. It may be noted in passing that Wilson not only presents devices of sentence structure, such as antithesis,[15] homoioteleuton,[16] parison,[17] and regression,[18] which some authorities have regarded as distinguishing marks of Lyly's style. He points out also that some of these,[19] particularly alliteration, had already been employed excessively before his day.

Henry Peacham's *The Garden of Eloquence, Conteyning the Figures of Grammer and Rhetorick,* 1577, is evidence of interest among English writers of the time in the rhetorical devices of amplification and ornamentation. The chief source of Peacham's material was John Susenbrot's *Epitome troporum ac schematum.* In 1593 a much revised edition of *The Garden of Eloquence* was published. Comparison of the two volumes reveals certain forces which had meanwhile been acting upon English prose. In the later edition, comments headed "the use" and "the caution" were appended to the discussions of most of the figures, and Peacham made an effort to bedeck his own language with "flowers" and "colours," especially with those ornamental devices which had been popularized by the group of writers of whom John Lyly is the best-known representative. It was Peacham, rather than they, who was the follower.

At the beginning of the earlier edition of *The Garden of Eloquence,* 1577, Peacham reproduced the diagrammatic division[20] of figures given in Susenbrot's *Epitome.* Half the book is taken up by the two sections at the close, "figures of sentences" and "figures of amplification." In the edition of 1593 these two parts have been reshuffled and divided into "figures of affection" and "figures of amplification." Neither classification is entirely consistent. Both serve to illustrate the difficulties which confronted rhetoricians in analzying the various kinds of figures. In particular they were undecided where to place such devices as exclamation, apostrophe, and prosopopoeia, which depend for their appeal upon arousing the emotions. Although useful for amplification, especially in the romances and sentimental novels, they were not, as were the figures of thought, based upon the processes of dialectical investigation. Various authorities grouped all, part, or none of them under the heading "figures of amplification." For the purposes of this study it is proper to consider both the figures of thought and the figures of emotion as devices of amplification. In the edition of 1593 Peacham has dealt with the figures of affection under four subheadings, "exclamation," "moderation," "consultation," and "permission," and he has also broken the figures of amplification up into four groups, "distribution," "description," "comparison," and "collection." A more consistent arrangement might have been to place the figures of "description" under the heading "affection." Whatever may be said of Peacham's classification, his interest in copiousness is evident throughout. He particularly recommends the figures of "distribution" as means of furnishing plenty and variety to a theme. Of the eleven devices named in this group, he states that "division," "partition," and "enumeration" serve most for expanding a subject. "Description" is set forth in glowing terms. The twenty figures considered under "comparison" begin with "comparison as it is usually and specially taken." Immediately after this come "similitudo," "dissimilitudo," and "antithesis." Whereas similes are highly commended, their misuse is not particularly stressed. Peacham justifies his term "collection" by assuming that all the figures under it "either leave the sense to be collected by the hearer, or do tend to the collection of proofes and conclusions." Under this heading "syllogismus," "aetiologia," "paradigma" (example), "gnome" (a moral sentence), and "expolition" are emphasized. The importance which Peacham attached to amplification is revealed by his discussion, by the illustrations he furnishes, by his own style, and by the fact that the larger part of his book is devoted to those two groups of figures which particularly serve for dilation. A list of the figures treated in his book is given in an appendix.[21] Many equivalent Latin, Greek, and English terms are given in his comments. The general remarks on amplification[22] in the later edition of his treatise illustrate both the importance which he attached to the means of expounding a theme and also his own efforts to achieve an ornate, copious style.

Aside from some remarks on delivery, Abraham Fraunce's *The Arcadian Rhetorike*, 1588, deals almost entirely with tropes and with figures of words. The explanatory discussions and some of the illustrations were taken either directly from the recension of Audomarus Talaeus's *Rhetorica* by Petrus Ramus or through the intermediary of *The Artes of Logike and Rhetorike*, 1584, usually attributed to Dudley Fenner. Both Talaeus and Ramus insisted that the figures of thought, those based on the processes of dialectical investigation, should be considered as belonging to logic. Hence none of these devices receives notice in Fraunce's treatise. Taking amplification in the broadest sense in which it was applied by sixteenth-century rhetoricians, the only figures in the book which fall under it are ten at the close based on appeal to the emotions—"exclamation," "epanorthosis," "aposiopesis," "apostrophe," "prosopopoeia," "addubitation," "communication," "praeoccupation," "sufferance," and "graunting." The greater part of the space in Fraunce's volume is given over to illustrative material from the writings of Sir Philip Sidney and the other authors named on the title page. So far as this study is concerned the significance of the work is chiefly in the attention which it directs to Sidney's partiality toward the figures which it treats. *The Arcadia* is profusely ornamented with tropes and with those figures, common to the romances, which attempt to arouse the feelings, whereas there are very few figures of the type upon which John Lyly mainly depended, those derived from the processes of dialectical investigation and directed to the reason.

The Arte of Englishe Poesie, 1589, attributed to George Puttenham, contains an extensive treatment of figures in the third book, entitled "Of Ornament." These pertain, the writer admits, mainly to oratory; yet he proceeds to demonstrate their application in poetry. An avowed intention of Puttenham's is to find English names for the Greek and Latin rhetorical terms which have occasioned so much confusion for over twenty centuries. Much information may be gleaned from his description of more than one hundred figures, from the English names he has invented, and from the poetical illustrations he has given. To the three groups of figures he has distinguished he has given the names "auricular," "sensable," and "sententious," which, he states, are equivalent, respectively,

to the terms "orthographicall," "syntactical," and "rhetorical."[23] Justification can hardly be found for all that he includes under these heads. In the first group fall twenty figures, such as zeugma, hysteron-proteron, homoioteleuton, alliteration, and asyndeton. The whole of the section labeled "sensable" is made up of tropes. The last division contains everything which is left. In his analysis Puttenham has described this group as follows,

your third sort serues as well th'eare as the conceit and may be called *sententious figures*, because not only they properly apperteine to full sentences, for bewtifying them with a currant and pleasant numerositie, but also giuing them effacacie, and enlarging the whole matter besides with copious amplifications.[24]

At the beginning of his discussion of this group of figures he has placed considerable stress on amplification. Under "antitheton"[25] he noted that Isocrates and Guevara, as well as some Englishmen, abused this figure. "Merismus, or the Distributer,"[26] "Orismus, or the Definer of difference,"[27] "Sinathrismus, or the Heaping figure,"[28] and "Exargasia"[29] are particularly noted as being valuable for the purposes of dilating a topic.

The English formularies of letter writing in the sixteenth century are, like the other books of rhetoric, based on the principles of ancient oratory.[30] The first to appear was William Fulwood's *The Enimie of Idlenesse*, 1568, which passed through seven editions before the end of the century. At the beginning Fulwood states,

And to describe the true definition of an Epistle or letter, it is nothing else but an Oration written, conteining the mynde of the

Orator or wryter, thereby to giue to understand to him or them that be absent, the same that should be declared if they were present.[31]

Dedicated to the "Maister, Wardens, and Company of the Marchant Tayllors of London," it was intended particularly for the merchant class, of which Fulwood was a member. Fulwood's volume is divided into four books. The first contains instructions with profuse illustrations; the other three consist entirely of model letters. The directions have to do mainly with externals of form and the proper language to use in writing to people in various stations of life. For those who may desire more complete treatment of "whether the matter that we write off bee honest, true or such like or whether it be slanderous, doubtfull, obscure, etc.," Fulwood recommends "the Rhetorike of Master Doctor Wilson, or Master Richard Rainolde." He mentions amplification, but in a way to suggest that his knowledge of it went no further than a casual acquaintance with Wilson's treatment.

Collections of epistles are much older than the formularies; and those who sought to provide instruction in the art depended more upon examples than upon precepts. Here, again, Cicero was acknowledged as the master. Yet the letters of Pliny, of Seneca, and of many Renaissance scholars circulated widely. According to John Donne, Montaigne mentions having seen four hundred volumes of epistles during his short tour in Italy. Model letters, as has been noted, make up the greater part of the first book of *The Enimie of Idlenesse* and the whole of the remaining three books. Fulwood seems to have been sincere in his desire to suit his work to the mer-

chant class. Still, out of fifty examples given in the first book, twelve are letters of Cicero, five are letters addressed to him or written by his contemporaries, and some others are translations of letters of state. Even business and domestic correspondence is exemplified from Cicero. Among the other illustrations in the first book many are suited rather to the scholar than to the busy man of affairs. One asks the loan of Cicero's *Paradoxes,* another for a book of rhetoric; a third accompanies a collection of moral sentences. In the first edition the second book contains twenty-three letters, all but one of which are from the popular Renaissance volume *Illustrium virorum epistolae,* made up principally of the correspondence of Angelo Poliziano. Later editions include three additional letters in this section, two of which are from *Amadis de Gaula.* Book three is made up of domestic and business correspondence, and book four of amatory epistles in prose and verse. The first among the love letters is from Aeneas Sylvius's *De duobus amantibus;* some others are from *Amadis.*

A Panoplie of Epistles, 1576, states on the title page that it is "Gathered and translated out of Latine into English by Abraham Flemming." Cicero's letters fill the first third of four hundred and fifty quarto pages; the second third is made up of epistles of Pliny and of selections attributed to Isocrates and others; the remainder of the volume contains correspondence of Renaissance scholars, such as Mantuan, Erasmus, Haddon, and Ascham. The letters are preceded by "An Epitome of Precepts," by way of a catechism of a student by his master. This is a translation of Christopher Hegendorff's *Methodus de conscribendis epistolis*, which deals mainly with the rhetorical commonplaces that serve to develop various kinds of letter. It was derived largely from Quintilian's *Institutio oratoria.* To the master's request for the sundry kinds of epistle, the scholar replies, "Of Epistles, some be demonstrative, some suasorie, and others some iudiciall." Called upon to give an example of the first, he delivers a long harangue in praise of Coriolanus, substituted for the one Hegendorff has on Hannibal. The master rewards him with the criticism, "I like well of your example, if it had bene breefer, and I commende your wit and inuention."[32] Shortly after, the following dialogue takes place.

Maister. Give me the common places of proofe and confirmation in this behalfe (the praise of a fact or deed of a person).

	Honest
	Profitable
Scholer. Places of	Not combersome
confirmation are	Religious
drawn from that	Just, etc.
which is	

Maister. Of a demonstratiue kinde of epistle, touching the thing, what be the places?

	Honest
	Profitable
Scholer. These and	Not tedious
such like be the	Hard and difficult
places, namely that	(Aiii recto)
which is	

In this manner the catechism proceeds, dwelling principally upon the places, or topics, of rhetorical investigation. Toward the close, the master asks, "How is a thing amplified or inlarged?"

The scholar replies:—

By circumstances	Of words	
	Sentences	
	Figures	Fab. lib 8. &
		Cic. in his
		particions.
	Places	
	Time	
	Maner, etc.	

We hardly need the gratuitious references to Quintilian and Cicero. In his copious marginal comments on the model letters, Flemming occasionally pointed out the figures of speech. A note on Cicero's "Epistle to Lucceio" calls attention to "how many wordes he bringeth together to beautifie his Metaphor or translation." The heading "D. Erasmus Roterodamus to Ilermo Burbanco" is followed by the conspicuous statement, "He beginneth his epistle with a [moral] sentence." Some space is devoted to explaining that the selection from Joannes Ravisius Textor on idleness, though addressed as a letter to a friend, is really a "theame." A letter of Ascham's to Queen Elizabeth is preceded by a long argument dwelling upon Ascham's skill in the use of rhetoric. It begins, "Writing to the Queenes maiestie, hee beginneth very Rhetorically, with a comparison of her highness, wherewith hee was discouraged, and her goodnesse whereby he was imboldened to write to her maiestie." The letter itself opens, "Most excellent Ladie Elizabeth, I haue laboured long in doubtfulnesse of mind, whether I should be more discouraged in consideration of your highnesse, or more imbouldened in respect of your goodnesse, to present you with an epistle." In the romances and sentimental novels the use of this device at the beginning of letters and speeches was a fixed convention. Flemming also called attention to Ascham's use of examples.

The Forrest of Fancy, 1579, by H. C., is merely a collection of letters, nearly all of which are amatory and in verse. From their quality it may be inferred that they are original compositions. Angel Day's *The English Secretorie,* 1587, deserves more attention. In it he discusses the methods of developing some thirty kinds of letters grouped under four main headings, "demonstrative," "deliberative," "judicial," and "familiar." For his explanatory matter Day was indebted in a general way to Erasmus's *De ratione conscribendis epistolas liber.* Most of the examples appear to be of Day's own composition. To the revised edition of 1592 he added a discussion of the duties of a secretary and a treatise of tropes and figures taken mainly from John Susenbrot's *Epitome troporum ac schematum.* In addition, marginal notes call attention, among other things, to all the devices of rhetoric serving for ornament and to the topics of rhetorical proof. Sometimes more than one dozen figures to a page are noted. From Day's statement that by a study of tropes and figures the reader may come to recognize them in his own letters one is inclined to suspect that, like a well-known gentleman who suddenly discovered he had been speaking prose, Day became aware that the letters he had written contained figures of rhetoric.

Thomas Blount's *Academie of Eloquence,* 1654, lies beyond the proper limits of this study. Yet it may serve to illustrate the direction in which rhetoric was proceeding at the close of Elizabeth's reign. It is divided into four sections. "The first part," Blount states, "contains a more exact *English Rhetorique,* then has been hitherto extant, comprehending all the most usefull Figures, exemplifi'd out of the *Arcadia* and other our choicest Authors." About twenty-five figures, roughly those treated in Talaeus's *Rhetorica,* are described. But in addition Blount attempts to give proper weight to amplification, which takes up thirty of the forty-six pages of the first book. Regarding the contents of the second part Blount may again be allowed to speak for himself:

You have [in this book] *formulae majores* or *Common-places,* upon the most usual subjects for stile and speech; The use and advantage whereof is asserted by my Lord Bacon, who (in his *Advancement of Learning*) sayes thus; "I hold the diligence and pain in collecting Common-places to be of great use and certainty in studying; as, that which aids the memory, sub-ministers copy to invention and contracts the sight of judgment to a strength."

This section occupies seventy pages. The third part consists of twenty pages of choice phrases, the fourth of some model letters. For a work which claims to contain "a more exact *English Rhetorique,* then has hitherto been extant," *The Academie of Eloquence* is in entirety an exceptionally feeble performance. It is evidence, however, of the emphasis placed on the devices of amplification in the first half of the seventeenth century and also an indication of the prevalent tendency to rely upon books of commonplaces and selected phrases as aids to composition.

218   *William G. Crane*

Notes

1. F. I. Carpenter has reprinted a section in *University of Chicago Studies*, No. 5, 1899.
2. Leonard Cox, *The Arte or Crafte of Rhetoryke*, Folio Aiiii verso.
3. Richard Sherry, *A Treatise of Schemes and Tropes*, Folio Biii verso.
4. Thomas Wilson, *The Arte of Rhetorique*, 1553. Reprint of the edition of 1585 by The Clarendon Press, 1909, p. 6.
5. *Ibid.*, p. 23.
6. George Philip Krapp, *The Rise of English Prose*, 1915, p. 331 n.
7. Thomas Wilson, *The Arte of Rhetorique*, p. 105.
8. *Ibid.*, p. 114.
9. "Againe, in young Storkes, we may take an example of loue towards their damme, for when she is old, and not able for her crooked bill to picke meate, the yong ones feede her. In yong Vipers there is a contrary example (for as *Plinie* saieth) they eate out their dammes wombe, and so come forth. In Hennes there is a care to bring vp their Chickens; in Egles the contrary, which cast out their Egges, if they haue any moe then three: and all because they would not be troubled with bringing vp of many."—*Ibid.*, p. 125.
10. *Ibid.*, p. 170.
11. "Illustris explanatio."—*Ibid.*, p. 178.
12. *Ibid.*, pp. 181–208.
13. *Ibid.*, p. 190.
14. *Ibid.*, pp. 191–94.
15. "Contrarietie."—*Ibid.*, p. 199.
16. "Like ending, and like falling."—*Ibid.*, p. 202.
17. "Egall members."—*Ibid.*, p. 204.
18. "Regression."—*Ibid.*, p. 205.
19. *Ibid.*, pp. 167–69 and 202–3.
20. *Cf.* Appendix VII, 1.
21. *Cf.* Appendix VII, 2.
22. *Cf.* Appendix VII, 3.
23. Puttenham, *The Arte of Englishe Poesie.* Arber's reprint, p. 171.
24. *Ibid.*, pp. 171–72.
25. *Ibid.*, p. 219.
26. *Ibid.*, p. 230.
27. *Ibid.*, p. 239.
28. *Ibid.*, p. 243.
29. *Ibid.*, p. 254.
30. *Cf.* E. N. S. Thompson, "The Familiar Letter," in *Literary Bypaths of the Renaissance*, 1924.
31. William Fulwood, *The Enimie of Idlenesse*, Folio A7 recto.
32. Abraham Flemming, *A Panoplie of Epistles*, 1576, Aii recto.

Edward P. J. Corbett

John Locke's Contributions to Rhetoric*

◊ *Although John Locke (1632–1704) served for a short time as a Lecturer in Rhetoric at Christ Church College, Oxford University, he was not enthusiastic about the study of rhetoric. Nevertheless, through his book* An Essay Concerning Human Understanding *(1690), he had a profound influence on the development of the "new rhetoric" in the eighteenth century. Professor Corbett organizes this essay on Locke around the six issues that Wilbur Samuel Howell saw as the main points of contention between the exponents of the old rhetoric and the exponents of the new rhetoric. Corbett restates each of the issues, indicates where Locke stood on that issue, and shows how Locke's views influenced the direction in which rhetoric went in the eighteenth century. For one thing, Locke's particular brand of epistemology, which became the foundation of empiricism, contended that the human mind derives all of its knowledge through experience.* ◊

For many twentieth-century teachers of English, John Locke (1632–1704) is a peripheral, rather than a mainstream, figure in the literary history of the late seventeenth and early eighteenth centuries. With some of those teachers, he merits mention only as the friend and physician of the first Earl of Shaftesbury, who served as the model for Achitophel in John Dryden's famous satire, and as the tutor for the third Earl of Shaftesbury, the author of the pre-Romantic manifesto *Characteristics*. Some teachers may have read Locke's *Second Treatise on Civil Government* in connection with an undergraduate course in political science, a great-books course in the humanities division, or a course on colonial American literature and learned that this document not only attempted to justify the Whig revolution of 1688 in England but also served our Founding Fathers as the rationale for our own revolution and democratic form of government. Even if they had not read snippets from Locke's *An Essay concerning Human Understanding* (1690) in anthologies of

*A slightly different version of this article was published in *The Rhetorical Tradition and Modern Writing*. Ed. James J. Murphy. New York: Modern Language Association, 1982. pp. 73–84.
From *College Composition and Communication*, "John Locke's Contributions to Rhetoric" by Edward P. J. Corbett. Copyright 1981 by the National Association of Teachers of English. Reprinted by permission of the publisher and Edward P. J. Corbett.

eighteenth-century literature, they could not escape the many references to that work in the literature and the literary histories of the period. If they were aware that the *Essay* was a philosophical work, they were not quite sure whether it should be classified primarily as a contribution to psychology or logic or metaphysics or epistemology. Virtually none of those twentieth-century teachers—including myself, until recently—were aware that Locke's *An Essay concerning Human Understanding* contributed to the development of rhetoric in the eighteenth century.

For those of us who regarded John Locke as only a subsidiary figure in the literary life of the eighteenth century, the following statement by Kenneth MacLean in his book *John Locke and English Literature of the Eighteenth Century* is an eye-opener: "The book that had most influence in the Eighteenth Century, the Bible excepted, was Locke's *Essay concerning Human Understanding* (1690)."[1] And this statement by Wilbur Samuel Howell comes as quite a shocker: "*The Conduct of the Understanding* and its parent work, *An Essay concerning Human Understanding*, were without question the most popular, the most widely read, the most frequently reprinted, and the most influential, of all English books of the eighteenth century."[2] There is enough testimony of that sort now available to make unquestionable John Locke's profound effect on the intellectual life of his time, and I should like to suggest to contemporary teachers of English, especially teachers of rhetoric and composition, that Locke can give

them insights into the human psyche that can enhance their teaching.

I am by no means the first one to note the rhetorical dimensions of Locke's famous *Essay,* but surprisingly little has been written about Locke as a contributor to the development of rhetorical theory. A ten-page bibliography of primary and secondary works at the back of the third edition of Richard I. Aaron's classic study contains not a single work concerning the rhetorical dimensions of Locke, if one can judge solely by the titles of the books and articles.[3] Wilbur Samuel Howell may be the first to note in a major journal that Locke influenced the development of rhetorical theory, and in a book published four years later, Howell clearly presents Locke as the dominant influence on the development of the "new logic" and the "new rhetoric" of the eighteenth century.[4]

I myself was prompted to take a look at Locke's *Essay* when I was investigating the rhetorical dimensions of John Henry Newman's *An Essay in Aid of a Grammar of Assent* (1870).[5] Newman frequently alluded to, or quoted from, Locke's *Essay,* and, while he clearly agreed with many of Locke's views on the processes of reasoning and assenting, he did disagree on a few points. So I decided to consult Locke's *Essay* to discover what might be useful for teachers in general and for teachers of writing in particular.

A convenient way for me to explore the rhetorical dimensions of the *Essay* is to make use of the six issues that Wilbur Samuel Howell saw as the main points of contention between the exponents of the old rhetoric and the exponents of the new rhetoric during the eighteenth century.[6] I will take up each issue in turn, indicate where Locke stood on the issue, and suggest some of the implications of that stand for teachers of rhetoric and composition.

(1) *Should rhetoric continue to concentrate on persuasive discourse or should it extend its province to include expository and didactic discourse?*

Rhetoric had its beginning in fifth-century Athens as the art of persuasive oratory. Throughout the next two thousand years or so, rhetoric continued to be preoccupied with persuasive discourse. Cicero and, later, Augustine tried to broaden the purview of rhetoric by positing for it a triple function: to teach *(docere)*, to delight *(delectare)*, and to persuade *(movere)*. But it was not until the scientific revolution, brought on by individuals like Descartes, Bacon, and Newton, that the notion of the expository and didactic functions of discourse really caught on.

John Locke was infected with the scientific spirit. Not only did his own studies at Oxford lead him to become a medical doctor, but two of his closest associates at Oxford were the medical scientist Thomas Sydenham and the chemist Robert Boyle. As a member of the Royal Society, he subscribed to its proposal for the creation of a verbal style that would be suitable for the transmission of the new scientific knowledge to the general public.

Locke's view of the proper function of discourse is epitomized in the following quotation from Book III of the *Essay,* in a chapter entitled "The Abuse of Words":

To conclude this consideration of the imperfection and abuse of language; the ends of language in our discourse with others being chiefly these three: first, to make known one man's thoughts or ideas to another; secondly, to do it with as much ease and quickness as is possible; and thirdly, thereby to convey the knowledge of things. Language is either abused or deficient when it fails in any of these three.[7]

This view of language as primarily an instrument of communication has prevailed in American composition courses in the twentieth century. Consequently, expository writing has been the dominant mode of discourse taught in the schools, although instructors have often treated argumentative writing as a species of expository writing. The notion that the language of expository discourse should be made easy to read was most recently espoused in E. D. Hirsch's plea for "relative readability."[8] The expansion of the province of rhetoric in the schools is probably due mainly to the influence of George Campbell, who proposed that the purposes of discourse were "to enlighten the understanding, to please the imagination, to move the passions, or to influence the will," or to the influence of Alexander Bain, who propagated the notion of the four modes of discourse—narration, description, exposition, and argumentation.[9] It is clear, however, that the impetus for that expansion comes from Locke's *Essay.*

(2) *Should rhetoric continue to concentrate on the so-called artistic proofs drawn from the use of the topics or should it also pursue the so-called inartistic proofs derived from outside sources?*

Locke's position on this issue is ultimately based on the thesis that he advances in Book I of the *Essay* and that becomes the major philosophical premise for his whole system of empiricism: the notion that people are born without any innate ideas.

If the human mind does not come equipped with ideas, how does it acquire knowledge? Locke answers that question in Book II. The human mind acquires all its knowledge through experience, and that experience takes two forms: sensation and reflection. The mind gets its ideas of particular, concrete objects through one of the five senses; it gets all other ideas by reflecting on its own operations. From such operations of the mind as "perception, thinking, doubting, believing, reasoning, knowing, willing," we receive into our understanding ideas as distinct as those we receive from "bodies affecting our senses" (II, i, 3–4, p. 105). To use the language of Wordsworth's "Immortality Ode," we do not come into this world "trailing clouds of glory" from some preexistent state. Rather, all our ideas come to us after birth, through the channels of our senses or through the operations of the mind on the images already perceived through the senses.

The analysis of the cognitive process as presented in Book II of the *Essay* has all kinds of implications for us as teachers. For one thing, Locke's heuristic system moves away from a reliance on classical topics and emphasizes external sources of data. Contemporary teachers have gained valuable insights into the psychology of knowing from the works of Jerome Bruner, Jean Piaget, lev Vygotsky, and others, but we must remember that before John Locke, there were very few, if any, analyses of the dynamics of how we come to know. Locke was not endowed with any special powers of divination about the cognitive process. He merely resorted to procedures that were available to anybody from the beginning of time, namely, circumspection, retrospection, and introspection. His rather crude psychology was as remarkable for his time as Aristotle's primitive analysis of the human emotions in the *Rhetoric* was to the ancients.

Locke's analysis of how human beings imprint images on the *tabula rasa* of their consciousness can enlighten us teachers of composition about the potentialities and the limitations of our students' heuristic capacities. Think of the implications of a situation that Locke describes in the first chapter of Book I: "If a child were kept in a place where he never saw any other but black and white, till he were a man, he would have no more ideas of scarlet or green than he that from his childhood never tasted an oyster or a pineapple has of those particular relishes" (I.i. 6; p. 107). If our students sometimes fail in doing our writing assignments, their failure may be due, not to the malfunctioning of whatever heuristic system they may have used, but rather to the narrowly circumscribed range of their experiences. The charges frequently made about the cultural bias of some of the national intelligence tests make more sense in the light of Locke's doctrine. If we dismiss our presumption that the range of our students' sensitive and reflective experiences is fairly uniform, we may recognize the need to devise some artificial ways of helping experience-starved students catch up.

One way we can help them is to expose them to situations that can factitiously expand their reservoir of ideas either through sense perceptions or through mental reflections. Just living in the world will, of course, provide students with the kind of experiences that could enlarge their fund of knowledge. But mere exposure to experiences will not automatically enlarge that fund. Locke makes it clear that, in a sense, we have to learn how to learn. We have to attune our senses so that they will absorb, at a maximum level, the data transmitted by the big, buzzing world out there. We have to be trained to observe keenly. And of course we also have to be trained in how to reflect fruitfully. Locke puts the matter this way:

For, though he that contemplates the operations of his mind cannot but have plain and clear ideas of them, yet unless he turn his thoughts that way and considers them *attentively,* he will no more have clear and distinct ideas of all the operations of his mind and all that may be observed therein than he will have all the particular ideas of any landscape or of the parts and motions of a clock who will not turn his eyes to it and with attention heed all the parts of it. (I.i.7; p. 107)

For that reason, as Locke observes, most children come very late to a perception of the operations of their own minds, and some never get any clear, solid ideas of these operations. The notion that our fund of ideas is dependent on the range of our experiences has at least one other implication for us teachers. If a profound disparity exists between the levels of knowledge that the speaker/writer and audience share, how can the speaker/writer achieve the kind of *identification* that Kenneth Burke says is vital for any communication and especially for persuasive discourse?[10] John H. Patton poses the problem in these words:

If the experience of the speaker, then, is fundamentally different from the experience of the audience, the Lockian approach would not allow for the possibility of genuine communication. By Locke's analysis, cross-cultural communication for example, while not being a completely meaningless term, would yet be limited to communication based upon common experience alone. (Patton, p. 21)

Patton derives his resolution of this dilemma from the essay "Of Eloquence," in which David Hume "recalls rhetoric to its classical activity as a persuasive art in stressing two elements which had been previously discarded by Locke: passion and imagination" (Patton, p. 23). Indeed, the common ground between the rhetor and the audience may lie more in the affective realm than in the cognitive realm.

(3) *Is the structure of most rhetorical proofs fundamentally deductive or fundamentally inductive?*

From the discussion in the previous section about the importance of experience as the source of knowledge, we could guess that Locke would favor the inductive approach, and indeed he does. He does not totally reject the deductive mode of reasoning. In fact, such a rejection would have been inconsistent with his view that mathematics is the appropriate model for scientific inquiry. But in chapter xvii of Book IV, entitled "Of Reason," he does discredit the syllogism, the Aristotelian paradigm of deductive reasoning.

His attack on the syllogism is grounded in his notion of the four degrees of reasoning:

the first and highest is the discovering and finding out of proofs; the second, the regular and methodical disposition of them and laying them in a clear and fit order to make their connexion and force be plainly and easily perceived; the third is the perceiving their connexion; and the fourth, the making a right conclusion. (IV.xvii.3; p. 669)

Fundamentally, he contends that the syllogism applies only to the third and fourth degrees and that, even there, the syllogism was not so much a means of establishing the connections between propositions as a device for testing the connections.[11]

If contemporary teachers of rhetoric and composition entertain an antipathy for syllogistic reasoning, they are more likely to have derived that attitude, if indirectly, from George Campbell's spirited attack on the syllogism in the sixth chapter of his *The Philosophy of Rhetoric* (1776) than from Locke's *Essay*. Regardless of the source of the current hostility or indifference to a systematic study of deductive reasoning, logic is now rarely studied formally in the composition classroom, and induction is unquestionably the reigning mode in current research and in reports on research. If any formal system of logic has replaced the scholastic logic of the syllogism in the modern composition classroom, it is symbolic logic or the claim/data/warrant system devised by Stephen Toulmin. Most college-level rhetoric texts omit any formal treatment of logic, and the few texts that do treat it devote three or four pages to a discussion of the formal and material fallacies only. In most forms of modern discourse, assertion and conclusions are most likely to be supported by empirically derived data than by deductive reasoning. Perhaps in no other area is the influence of Locke's *Essay* more evident in the modern classroom than in this shift from a reliance on deductive reasoning to a reliance on inductive reasoning.

(4) *Should rhetoric deal exclusively in probabilities or should it resort to certainties whenever they are available?*

In Book IV, Locke finally gets down to the main objective that he posed on the first page of the *Essay:* "to enquire into the original, certainty, and extent of human knowledge, together with the grounds and degrees of belief, opinion, and assent." In the first chapter of Book IV, he defined knowledge as "the perception of the connexion and agreement or disagreement and repugnancy of any of our ideas" (IV.i.2; p. 525). We come to knowledge, according to Locke, through one of three avenues: (1) through intuition, whereby we perceive the agreement or disagreement of ideas directly and immediately; (2) through demonstration, whereby we perceive their agreement or disagreement indirectly and mediately—that is, by the intervention of other ideas; and (3) through sensation (through the senses), whereby we come to an awareness of the existence of material objects. These three avenues of knowledge produce varying degrees of certainty, intuition producing the highest degree and sensation, the lowest.

In Chapter xiv of Book IV, Locke acknowledges that we would be at a great loss if we had to depend exclusively on certain knowledge in the conduct of everyday life. He recognized what Aristotle had recognized long before: that in the area of contingent human affairs, people frequently have to make practical decisions on the basis of what is only *probably* true; in fact, the situations in which our decisions can be guided by incontrovertible truths or evidence are extremely few in comparison with the many situations where we have to rely for guidance on mere probabilities.

Locke designated judgment as the faculty that helps us decide whether ideas agree or disagree when certain knowledge is not available (IV.xiv.3; p. 653). In the absence of absolute proofs, judgment relies on probabilities. Probability is the appearance of truth based on fallible proofs—that is, on proofs that lead to something less than absolute certainty (IV.xv.1; p. 564). Locke calls the acceptance that judgment accords to probable propositions "belief, assent, or opinion, which is the admitting or receiving any proposition for true upon arguments or proofs that are found to persuade us to receive it as true, without certain knowledge that it is so" (IV.xv.3; p. 655).

Up to this point, Locke does not tell us very much about probability that we could not have found in Aristotle's *Rhetoric.* For Aristotle, the area of the probable belonged to rhetoric, and the two rhetorical modes of proof, the enthymeme and the example, were distinct because they worked with probabilities and arrived at probable conclusions. In fact, the Greek word for rhetorical proofs, *pisteis,* derives from the Greek verb for "to believe." Locke made a special contribution to our views on probability by insisting on the resort to empirically verified data whenever those certainties were available, as they often are in the scientific realm. He also contributed to this matter by analyzing the psychology of assent much more extensively and intensively than Aris-

totle or anyone else had. Finally, he contributed to this area by proposing that there were degrees of assent, ranging "from the very neighborhood of certainty and demonstration quite down to improbability and unlikeliness, even to the confines of impossibility" (IV.xv.2; p. 655).

In the matter of degrees of assent, Locke may not have been right. Other thinkers, John Henry Newman among them, have argued that the act of assent is an all-or-nothing operation.[12] Nevertheless, Locke made a significant contribution to the teaching of rhetoric and composition by anatomizing the psychology of assent, thereby making us more conscious of the process by which assent is granted and better able to train our students in the rhetorical strategies that are likely to effect assent in a particular case.

(5) *Should discourse be organized in the six-part form recommended by Ciceronian rhetoric or could it be organized in simpler forms?*

One searches in vain in the *Essay* for any explicit pronouncement by Locke on the pattern Cicero formulated of an introduction, a narration, a partition, a proof, a refutation, and a peroration. Nor does he comment on the need for a simpler, more functional pattern of organization for modern discourse. Locke's brilliant argument in support of his thesis that we possess no innate ideas would not be difficult to analyze by means of Cicero's six-part structure. Yet from all we know about his pronouncements on other rhetorical matters, we can surmise that Locke would have approved of a simpler organizational structure, such as that recommended by Fénelon for the sermon in his *Dialogues sur l'eloquence* at the end of the seventeenth century or by Adam Smith for public addresses in his *Lectures on Rhetoric and Belles Lettres* in the mid-eighteenth century.[13] The thematic arrangement of the four books of his *Essay* is itself convincing evidence that he would not approve of the structure that the classical rhetoricians based on functions. This fifth issue is the only one requiring that we guess at the position Locke would take, but we can guess with some confidence that he would encourage the use of an organizational pattern that would facilitate the transmission of ideas to an audience of listeners or readers.

(6) *Should the rhetorical style be ornate and learned and heavily freighted with schemes and tropes or should it be plain and casual?*

As we might expect of a prominent member of the seventeenth-century Royal Society, Locke opposed the use of figurative language and other artifices of style in discourses designed to instruct and inform. In his view,

all the art of rhetoric, besides order and clearness, all the artificial and figurative application of words eloquence has invented, are for nothing else but to insinuate wrong ideas, move the passions, and thereby mislead the judgment; and so indeed are perfect cheat. And therefore however laudable or allowable oratory may render them in harangues and popular addresses, they are certainly, in all discourses that pretend to inform and instruct, wholly to be avoided; and where truth and knowledge are concerned, cannot but be thought a great fault, either of the language or person that makes use of them. (III.x.34; p. 508)

Locke is unequivocal here in his denigration of an ornate, tendentious, and ambiguous style for certain kinds of

discourse. Perry Miller has pointed out that the aim of the Royal Society, as stated in Bishop Sprat's *History of the Royal Society of London* (1667), was " 'to separate the knowledge of Nature, from the colours of Rhetorick, the devices of Fancy, or the delightful deceit of Fables.' In Locke, therefore," Miller goes on to say, "Sprat's ideal of style, freed from the domination of colors, devices, and deceits, maintaining an 'inviolable correspondence between the hand and the brain,' received at last a psychological and physiological justification."[14]

As students of English and American literature, we teachers have noted the evolution of the plain style, beginning in the eighteenth century with the casual, lucid, and graceful prose of such writers as Addison, Steele, and Swift and culminating in the twentieth century with the kind of spare, monosyllabic, short-sentence prose that Rudolf Flesch recommended highly in his *The Art of Readable Writing* (1949). We have also seen the eminently readable prose written by scientists and philosophers of the seventeenth and eighteenth centuries (Locke himself wrote that kind of prose) turn into the turgid, jargon-laden, and impersonal prose that appears in many of our professional journals. Locke can be said to have been on the winning side of this issue, and yet I think he would have agreed with those contemporary teachers of writing who deplore some of the developments in style that characterize much of the instructional and informative prose of the twentieth century.

It has been my purpose to alert teachers of rhetoric and composition to the potential usefulness of Locke's *An*

Essay concerning Human Understanding. I have not attempted to point out those instances in which his exposition and defense of his views on the cognitive process may be weak or inconsistent or downright wrong. Only a seasoned philosopher could detect the soft spots in Locke's position or presentation. One of the most judicious assessments of the strengths and weaknesses of Locke's views is provided by D. J. O'Connor, Professor of Philosophy at the University of Exeter, in his book entitled simply *John Locke.*[15] But on the chance that I have succeeded in arousing the interest of some teachers, I would hasten to add that Locke's *Essay* should not be made required reading for undergraduate students in our composition courses. Rather, we teachers should read and ponder it so that we can appropriate from it, and relay to our students, what could help them to understand how they come to know what they know and how they can effectively communicate to others what they have learned.

Locke himself would not approve of our using his book to teach rhetoric. Although he served in 1663 as Lecturer in Rhetoric at Christ Church, Oxford, he disapproved of formal classroom instruction in rhetoric, preferring instruction by example rather than by precept and by tutoring rather than by lecturing.[16] But he would approve of our consulting his book to learn something about how human beings think. In a paper, "Reading and Study," that he wrote in 1703, a year before his death, he said that it was imperative for us to acquire "a knowledge of men," and he strongly recommended the reading of "books that of purpose treat of human nature, which help to give an insight into it. Such are those treating of the passions, and how they are moved, whereof Aristotle in his second book of *Rhetoric* hath admirably discoursed, and that in a little compass."[17] Although Locke did not himself discourse in a "little compass," he did give us one of those books that supply the kind of knowledge about the cognitive behavior of men and women so vital to the rhetorician.

Notes

1. Kenneth MacLean, *John Locke and English Literature of the Eighteenth Century* (New Haven: Yale Univ. Press, 1936), p. v.
2. Wilbur Samuel Howell, *Eighteenth-Century British Logic and Rhetoric* (Princeton: Princeton Univ. Press, 1971), p. 277.
3. Richard I. Aaron, *John Locke* (Oxford: Clarendon, 1971).
4. Wilbur Samuel Howell, "John Locke and the New Rhetoric," *Quarterly Journal of Speech*, 53 (1967) 319–33. John B. O'Hara did a Ph.D. dissertation entitled "John Locke's Philosophy of Discourse" at the University of Oklahoma in 1963, and Jerry L. Weedon did a Ph.D. dissertation entitled "Philosophy as a Rationale for Rhetorical Systems: A Case Study Derivation of Rhetorical Cognates from the Philosophical Doctrine of John Locke" at UCLA in 1969. There have also been some additional articles published on Locke's contributions to rhetoric since Howell's article appeared in 1967: Jerry L. Weedon, "Locke on Rhetoric and Rational Man," *Quarterly Journal of Speech*, 56 (1970), 378–87; L. Brooks Hill, "Lockeian Influences in the Evolution of Rhetorical Theory," *Central States Speech Journal*, 26 (1975), 107–14; John H. Patton, "Experience and Imagination: Approaches to Rhetoric by John Locke and David Hume," *Southern Speech Communication Journal*, 41 (1975), 11–29.
5. See Edward P. J. Corbett, "Some Rhetorical Lessons from John Henry Newman," *College Composition and Communication*, 31 (1980), 402–12.

6. The six issues are listed and elaborated on in Howell's *Eighteenth-Century British Logic and Rhetoric,* pp. 441–47. I have paraphrased Howell's statements of the issues.

7. John Locke, *An Essay concerning Human Understanding,* ed. Peter H. Nidditch (Oxford: Clarendon, 1979), p. 504. Hereafter citations from the *Essay* will be documented parenthetically in the text with a notation like this: III.x.23; p. 504—that is, Book III, Chapter x, paragraph 23, on p. 504 of the Nidditch edition. I have made changes in Locke's style of capitalizing, italicizing, spelling, and punctuating whenever I felt that those features would puzzle or distract my readers.

8. E. D. Hirsch, *The Philosophy of Composition* (Chicago: Univ. of Chicago Press, 1977).

9. George Campbell, *The Philosophy of Rhetoric* (1776), ed. Lloyd F. Bitzer (Carbondale: Southern Illinois Univ. Press, 1963), p. 1; Alexander Bain, *English Composition and Rhetoric* (New York: Appleton, 1866).

10. Kenneth Burke, *A Rhetoric of Motives* (Berkeley: Univ. of California Press, 1969), p. 55.

11. Those who are interested in a more detailed summary of Locke's attack on the Syllogism can consult pp. 285–89 of Wilbur Samuel Howell's *Eighteenth-Century British Logic and Rhetoric.*

12. John Henry Newman, *An Essay in Aid of a Grammar of Assent,* ed. Charles Frederick Harrold (London: Longmans, 1947), pp. 131–33. In a lecture entitled "A Comparison of John Locke and John Henry Newman on the Rhetoric of Assent," given at the Speech Communication Association Convention, Anaheim, California, 12 November 1981, I argued that Newman was right and Locke wrong in the matter of degrees of assent.

13. For a convenient summary of Fénelon's and Adam Smith's recommendations about arrangement, see Howell, *Eighteenth-Century British Logic and Rhetoric,* pp. 446, 572.

14. Perry Miller, "The Rhetoric of Sensation," in *Perspectives of Criticism,* ed. Harry T. Levin (Cambridge: Harvard Univ. Press, 1950), p. 106.

15. O'Connor's book was originally published in 1952 in the Pelican Philosophy Series and was reissued with minor changes in 1967 in the Dover Publications Series on Philosophy.

16. See Maurice Cranston, *John Locke: A Biography* (London: Longmans, 1957), pp. 20–21, 25.

17. Cranston, p. 245.

Wilbur Samuel Howell

Renaissance Rhetoric and Modern Rhetoric: A Study in Change[1]

◊ *This essay advances the argument that five observable changes have occurred in our view of rhetoric since the onset of the Renaissance period which extended roughly from 1400 to 1700. These changes, as highlighted by the author, may be paraphrased as follows: (1) the study of logic has disassociated itself from the field of communication and formed an alliance with scientific investigation; (2) rhetoric has sought to elevate its status by focusing on learned as well as popular discourse; (3) the subject of invention has been expanded to include a strong stress on factual data or external realities; (4) arrangement patterns in discourse have moved in the direction of simpler organizational structures; and (5) the use of style, rather than featuring an almost exclusive concern with tropes and figures, has shifted its emphasis to a consideration of the language of "ordinary discourse" as characterized by the "business man's culture."* ◊

1

The Renaissance is a most convenient period with which to begin a discussion of the modern concept of rhetoric. That period, which may be roughly dated from 1450 to 1700, witnessed the last years of medieval civilization in Western Europe and the first years of modern civilization. Thus if we take our stand in the early Renaissance and examine the theory of communication which prevailed at that time, we are face to face with arrangements that counted almost two thousand years of history behind them and had changed only in detail in that double millennium. At the same time, as we look around in the Renaissance, we begin to see that things are changing in the theory of communication as in politics and theology and science, and that those changes have a

Reprinted from Wilbur Samuel Howell: *Poetics, Rhetoric and Logic: Studies in the Basic Disciplines of Criticism.* Copyright (©) 1975 by Cornell University. Used by the permission of the publisher, Cornell University Press.

familiar look, as if they would not be out of place among the similar arrangements of our twentieth-century world. In other words, the Renaissance is the one point in the history of Western Europe where the communication theory of ancient Greece and Rome and that of modern Europe and America are ranged side by side, the older one still alive but losing ground, the younger one still immature but growing. What better place could be found for the beginnings of a study of what rhetoric has lost and gained in the transition from medieval to modern times?

During the Renaissance, the theory of communication, exclusive of its poetical dimension, was made up of grammar, rhetoric, and dialectic or logic. These three liberal disciplines, which had been the trivium or lower group of liberal arts in the medieval universities, assumed most of the responsibility for training Renaissance students to speak and write. Latin was the language which those students were asked in grammar school and university to master as the universal basis for all kinds of communication, although as the seventeenth century drew to a close the emphasis upon vernacular languages became more and more pronounced.[2] That the trivium was actually regarded in the Renaissance as a group of studies expressly dedicated to the theory of communication is shown in Francis Bacon's great treatise, the *Advancement of Learning*, where Bacon, speaking of "the fourth kind of Rational Knowledge," proceeds not only to describe this knowledge as "transitive, concerning the expressing or transferring our knowledge to others," but also to term it "by the general name

of Tradition or Delivery" and later to analyze it as made up in large part of grammar, logic, and rhetoric.[3]

Bacon's discussion of these three basic liberal arts as three branches of the great science of transmitting knowledge from man to man, from place to place, and from age to age includes a more rational plan, a more fully developed overview, than one finds in the usual Renaissance treatise on education. But this does not mean that Bacon's ideas on the trivium were different from those of his time. On the contrary, although the precise content of any one member of the trivium was defined in different ways by different schools of thought during the Renaissance, Bacon's *Advancement of Learning* is in harmony with his era in treating the three liberal arts as offshoots of the theory of delivery or communication.[4] In all sectors of Renaissance opinion grammar was regarded as the study of the medium of communication, whether the medium was Latin for learned discourse or English for popular address. Similarly, dialectic or logic was for the most part regarded as the study of the means and methods of reaching the learned audience, whether in scholastic Latin sermons, lectures, and disputations, or in vernacular treatises like the *Advancement of Learning* itself. As for rhetoric, most segments of Renaissance opinion accepted it as the study of some or all of the means of making a discourse palatable and persuasive to the popular audience.

To be sure, the Ramists, whose system of dialectic and rhetoric became very popular in England between 1574 and 1620, did not divide dialectic from rhetoric by orienting the one predominantly toward the learned audience and the other predominantly toward the people.[5] But even they, in making rhetoric consist exclusively of style and delivery while dialectic assumed absolute control over invention and arrangement, tended in fact to relegate rhetoric to those crafts which popular discourse needs in more generous measure than does learned discourse. And it should be observed that dialectic and rhetoric were parts of the theory of communication in Ramus's scheme, as in the medieval synthesis, although Ramus explained the relation of these parts to each other in a different way from that used by scholastic logic or Ciceronian rhetoric.

Five changes in the ancient theory of communication began to appear during the Renaissance, and by and large these changes help to explain why modern rhetoric is as it is. I should like to mention these changes here and to indicate what seems to explain them. Then I should like to suggest some of the benefits or disadvantages they have brought to the modern academic study of communication.

2

Perhaps the most significant change that has come over the theory of communication during the last four hundred years is that logic has dissolved its alliance with the communication arts and has aligned itself instead with the theory of scientific investigation. Descartes in his famous *Discours de la méthode* indicated the need for a logic of inquiry to replace the older logic

of communication.[6] By and large, his summons proved to be prophetic. Logic has become the interpreter of scientific and philosophical method, whereas it had been the interpreter of the method of transmitting knowledge from expert to expert. In an academic sense, this means that logic has affiliated itself with the department of philosophy and has ceased to have any primary connection with the department of rhetoric. Of course, certain fragments of logic have continued to appear regularly in all treatises devoted by rhetoricians to argumentation and persuasion; but those fragments, which usually concern the forms of reasoning and fallacies, have not represented the full emphasis of the new logic and usually, indeed, have been conspicuous for their perfunctory character, their lack of originality, and their seeming dedication to the appearances rather than the essentials of the tradition they reflect. Meanwhile, logic has studied the sciences and mathematics, has formulated the canons of induction, has denied the priority of the syllogism, and has sought politely to disavow those who wanted to use the study of logic as a practical means of making themselves logical writers and speakers.

There can be little doubt that, since the Renaissance, the major intellectual energies in Western Europe have been devoted to the discovery of new truth, and the greatest reputations in the world of learning have been made by the scientists. At the same time, emphasis upon the communication of new truths across the barriers between persons, specialties, nations, language groups, and generations has been a diminishing study within the universities, although not a diminishing need in the practical world. Thus logic shifted its allegiance from communication to inquiry at an advantageous time. Higher academic rewards lay in the direction of an association with science, while communication could offer its academic devotees little more than a servant's wage. It may seem strange that rhetoric, contemptuously associated with the arts of promotion and self-aggrandizement, should have remained loyal to the unpopular and unprosperous cause of communication, while logic, the aristocratic disdainer of profitable enterprises, should have chosen to go where the academic profits were greatest. But so it was, at least within English and American universities of the late nineteenth and early twentieth centuries.

I do not mean to argue seriously that a shrewd self-interest was the real motive behind the attachment of logic to science. Instead, the attachment was a natural consequence of man's success in studying his physical environment. It has been more important since the Renaissance to devote oneself to the search for new knowledge than to the exposition of that knowledge to others, and logic has accepted this value as its guide. A few modern authors like Whately and Bain have continued to write on both logic and rhetoric after the example of Aristotle, Cicero, Thomas Wilson, Ramus, and others. But in the main the two disciplines have parted company, and the logicians have outclassed the rhetoricians in the eyes of the learned community, the favorable verdict for logic being decisive if not always founded upon an impartial examination of the evidence on both sides.

The renunciation by logic of its alliance with the theory of communication has been a serious blow to modern rhetoric. As I mentioned a moment ago, it has led to an obvious and fatal superficiality whenever rhetoricians have affixed to their own works an abbreviated version of traditional logical theory. It has also led to a counterrenunciation of logic by rhetoric, as in the elocutionary movement of the nineteenth century, where rhetoric became completely absorbed in delivery, not in the Baconian sense of the full act of communication but as the vocal and physical components of that act. Perhaps as philosophers and rhetoricians develop their present interest in semantics, a way will be found to create a new logic for the process of communication and to bring logic and rhetoric together in a more significant companionship than any they have enjoyed since the days of Thomas Wilson. Until this happens, however, rhetoric will be detached from some of the impulses that have accounted for its greatest past glories. When Aristotle began his *Rhetoric* by defining his subject as the counterpart of dialectic, he meant to ally his logical treatises, and in particular his *Topics*, with the work he was about to write. We might say that, until modern rhetoric helps to create a modern equivalent of Aristotelian dialectic and contributes vitally to its development, it will continue to lack what the best ancient rhetoric had—a sense of indissoluble kinship with the philosophical aspects of the enterprise of communication.

3

Another significant change that has occurred in the theory of communication since the Renaissance is that rhetoric has attempted to expand its interests so as to become the theory of learned discourse while remaining the theory of popular discourse. As I indicated above, logic had jurisdiction over the former theory in the ancient scheme as interpreted by the Renaissance. Indeed, Renaissance logicians and rhetoricians had a favorite image to describe the relation of logic to rhetoric, and that image associated logic with the closed fist, rhetoric with the open hand. According to Cicero and Quintilian, this image originated with Zeno the Stoic, and if you had asked a learned man of the Renaissance to explain it, he probably would have given you Cicero's interpretation as set forth in these words of the *Orator:*

> The man of perfect eloquence should, then, in my opinion possess not only the faculty of fluent and copious speech which is his proper province, but should also acquire that neighbouring borderland science of logic; although a speech is one thing and a debate another, and disputing is not the same as speaking, and yet both are concerned with discourse—debate and dispute are the function of the logicians; the orator's function is to speak ornately. Zeno, the founder of the Stoic school, used to give an object lesson of the difference between the two arts; clenching his fist he said logic was like that; relaxing and extending his hand, he said eloquence was like the open palm.[7]

Debate and disputation, as used in this passage, stand for all the types of philosophical or scholastic discourses that one finds in the world of learning; eloquence stands for the open, popular speech to political meetings, juries, and gatherings at public ceremonies and celebrations. As logic in the ancient scheme taught the young expert to communicate with his peers while rhetoric taught him to communicate with the populace, so in the modern scheme has rhetoric attempted to teach both functions, inasmuch as logic is no longer available for the purpose it once served.

The advantage of the ancient scheme was that it kept everybody reminded of the two worlds in which communication takes place, of the two types of discourses flowing from speaker to audience, and of the broad differences between the scholar and the popularizer. By his studies in logic and rhetoric a student would get an impression of the differences between dialectical and rhetorical invention, dialectical and rhetorical arrangement. He would also get a sense of the similarities between these procedures as dialectical and as rhetorical operations. Even the duplication between his classroom assignments in dialectic and those in rhetoric would have some value in reminding him of the essential unity of his various subjects. The same lesson studied from two points of view is often better than two lessons studied without reference to each other. And when the same lesson is studied under two teachers, one a rhetorician and the other a logician, the prestige of each increases that of the other, and the student feels a comfortable reassurance in the very fact that his teachers differ only in approach, not in aim.

Of course, when two subjects are adjusted to as narrow a distinction as that between the learned audience and the populace, there is danger that the distinction will seem relatively empty and that one of the two subjects will begin to appear nonessential. This danger was not acute in ancient Greece and Rome, where democratic political institutions and unhampered philosophical debate made rhetoric and logic necessary disciplines in the educational system. But later societies in Western Europe went through a long period of empire and monarchy, during which rhetoric and logic flourished as instruments inherited from the past, although the actual need for the functions discharged by rhetoric was not as pressing as was the need for ability in disputation and learned controversy.[8] Thus rhetoric occupied a somewhat uneasy position in the trivium during the Middle Ages, as grammar and logic were successively the dominant study.[9] It was partly to guarantee rhetoric a firmer standing in education and partly to prevent rhetoric and logic from repeating each other's doctrine that Ramus, as I said before, assigned the entire theory of invention and arrangement to logic and made rhetoric consist wholly of style and delivery. This reform tended to abandon the open emphasis upon the distinction between the learned and the popular audience and to substitute for it a more tangible means of differentiating logic and rhetoric. But neat and practical as it was, Ramism provies that rhetoric becomes a meaningless study unless it is sustained by its ancient concern for the popular audience, even as the Middle Ages show that rhetoric becomes the inferior discipline of communication in any society where the popular audience has no economic and political power.

Modern democratic society would appear to offer rhetoric a greater opportunity than it has had since ancient times; for the popular audience in a democracy is the true source of authority, and the learned community has great need for the technique of learned communication. Rhetoric has grasped that opportunity, so far as its concern for the popular audience goes. Departments of rhetoric and speech are the focus of study of the ways and means by which the modern speaker reaches the people. But rhetoric has not made much of a show in supplying a theory of learned communication that can compare with Renaissance dialectic. Where, for example, is there an attempt in modern rhetoric to provide a common vocabulary in which the learned men in one field can communicate with the learned men in another? Renaissance dialectic fashioned such a vocabulary from the ten categories of Aristotle and from the ten places of Ramus. Perhaps those vocabularies have completely lost their power to serve modern science. Still, a study of the circle of modern learning might reveal that the barriers between one specialized knowledge and another could be broken down by the use of certain common learned concepts. It would require great scholarship to develop those concepts, and great scholarship is one of the challenges that modern rhetoric has not met. Inspiration might come from the reflection that Aristotle developed his categories from a study of the circle of learning of his time and that a similar enterprise might be undertaken today, perhaps not by one individual scholar, but certainly by an interested group of specialists. Added inspiration might also come from our modern conviction that, unless our learned men can be taught to speak to each other and to the people, we shall create on the one hand a set of Balkanized knowledges and on the other a schism between the people and the intellectual classes. That sort of schism will make the demagogue our master, even as a Balkanized learning will destroy the unity of our culture and the meaning of our spiritual life.

4

A third great change in the theory of communication since the Renaissance concerns what I have been calling invention. To people untrained in the history of rhetoric, invention means either a mechanical device for the saving of labor or the act of discovering something new. In a contemptuous view of rhetoric, invention often means a falsehood, a deceit, an irresponsible utterance, a cynical departure from the truth for purposes of fraud. But invention to the rhetorical scholar means the devising of subject matter for a particular speech and, by extension, the providing of content in discourse. Lest this definition sound as if subject matter comes only from the speaker's mind, and not from the external realities of his environment, it should be emphasized that subject matter comes from external realities as seen and interpreted by the speaker and thus is not on the one hand the result of his fancy nor on the other the mere equivalent of bare facts. Inventional theory conceived in these

terms has greatly changed since the Renaissance.

Perhaps the best way to describe this change is to say that nowadays rhetoric in the quest for a theory of subject matter emphasizes external realities somewhat more than mental interpretation, whereas in the Renaissance, and for a thousand years before, mental interpretation was emphasized somewhat more, at times considerably more, than external realities.

Mental interpretation in the ancient scheme consisted in taking the basic facts in a given case and subjecting them to an armchair examination that had three main phases. The first phase supplied large elements of the speaker's actual arguments, and while in this phase he classified his case in relation to its standing or position in the world of cases. The world of cases was made up of positions of fact, of definition, of quality, and of procedure, according to the youthful Cicero's *De Inventione;* and these four positions were supplemented by five others that applied only to disputes involving written documents.[10] The second main phase of invention supplied materials for the ethical aspects of a discourse. These were found when the speaker classified his coming speech in relation to its kind in the world of speeches, there being three kinds, the deliberative, the forensic, and the epideictic, to which were respectively attached the ethical considerations of advantage, justice, and honor.[11] The third main phase of invention supplied materials for the structural parts of discourse, so far as these parts had not been stocked by the two other phases. Cicero listed these parts as six in number: exordium, narration, division, proof, refutation, conclusion. These six parts required various kinds of content, which Cicero describes at length.[12]

A similar explanation of the three main phases of rhetorical invention appeared in Thomas Wilson's *The Arte of Rhetorique* in 1553. In fact, Wilson used Cicero's *De Inventione* as one source of his treatment of invention, although the anonymous *Rhetorica ad Herennium*, which is almost as ancient as *De Inventione* and had for centuries been attributed to Cicero, was Wilson's more important source.[13] Now it must be conceded that *De Inventione* and the *Rhetorica ad Herennium* do not treat all details of inventional theory in the same way, but the differences between them are less significant historically than the similarities, and thus Wilson's special dependence upon the *Rhetorica ad Herennium* does not mean that he departs in any major way from the three phases just outlined.

Since Wilson's day, thanks to the influence of Bacon and Descartes, man has tended more and more to believe that his most important deliberations must be conducted in the light of all the particular facts that bear upon them. No longer does he feel that he can draw predominantly from common sense, general reason, or the wisdom that rests largely upon deductions from analogous past experience. When Descartes abandoned his belief in tradition and custom and decided to reconstitute his knowledge in terms of the direct observation of the great book of the world,[14] he not only took a decisive step toward the creation of modern science, but he

also represented in his own personal life the change that was coming over the whole intellectual life of Europe. And that change was too vast to leave rhetoric unaffected.

The modern speaker may be said to approach the problem of content by undertaking to study as many of the facts as he can possibly locate. "The really difficult problem in the preparation of the case," says a distinguished twentieth-century advocate, "is to learn what the facts are, and no matter how long or conscientiously you work, you will never know them all." He adds:

> The law seldom decides the issue, the facts do; and as contrasted with the ascertainment of the facts, the law is relatively easy to discover. There are a hundred good researchers of the law to one who has a genius, I may say a nose, for the discovery of the true facts.[15]

Later, when this same advocate is discussing the modern lawyer's closing speech to the jury, he likens the preparation of that speech to the preparation of a learned book:

> The trial, for the lawyer, is what research is for the author. Histories and biographies, letters, memoirs, diaries and the archives of great libraries are the material from which a book is made. The evidence, documents, and the demeanor of the witnesses are the stuff from which the advocate's summation must be constructed.[16]

These views emphasize that the modern speaker, whether in the law court or on the political platform, speaks less from the old method of armchair analysis than from the method of research into the realities of his case. Like Burke advocating conciliation with America, the modern speaker allows his speech to refer extensively and minutely to such concrete realities as population figures, trade statistics, and the amount of income from agriculture and fisheries. Like Webster answering Hayne, the modern speaker feels called upon to deal with such complex matters as the history of the federal land question, the tariff, consolidation of powers, internal improvements, and the issue of nullification. Like Lincoln at Cooper Union, he analyzes minutely such biographical and historical considerations as those relating to the individual attitudes of the constitutional Fathers toward slavery in the federal territories. Like Churchill in 1940, he discusses such facts as present military losses and gains on land, on the sea, and in the air. Today we consider such realities the building blocks of any serious and important speech, the grounds of any dependable induction; and our speakers, despite their frequent addiction to the trash and nonsense that clutter oratory no less than literature, adhere at their best to the principle that realities cannot be mastered except as speakers participate in the disciplines of the scholar and scientist.

In changing its predominant emphasis from mental interpretation to external realities, rhetorical invention has in our time simultaneously abandoned the historic distinction between artistic and nonartistic arguments. This distinction stemmed from Aristotle's *Rhetoric*, and upon it was based the concept of proof supplied by the classical system of invention as opposed to proof supplied by other means. Says Aristotle:

Of the modes of persuasion some belong strictly to the art of rhetoric and some do not.

By the latter I mean such things as are not supplied by the speaker but are there at the outset—witnesses, evidence given under torture, written contracts, and so on. By the former I mean such as we can ourselves construct by means of the principles of rhetoric. The one kind has merely to be used, the other has to be invented.[17]

It is doubtful that Aristotle meant this distinction to be as heavy a commitment to mental interpretation, and as light a commitment to external realities, as later classical rhetoricians assumed. In one of the most important chapters of the second book of his *Rhetoric* he lays great emphasis upon facts as the starting point for the construction of arguments on any subject.[18] But, even so, the passage just quoted seemed to identify external realities with nonartistic arguments and to put them both beyond the pale of the principles of rhetoric. Today the emphasis is almost exactly the reverse. The same external realities that have become the focus of scientific investigation claim the center of interest in the modern concept of rhetorical invention, while mental interpretation is accepted as the means of making those realities humanly important and of deciding how best to present and use them.

5

Still another change in the theory of communication since the Renaissance concerns the method of arranging ideas for public presentation. In this field, the change has been one in which complicated structures have been abandoned and simpler structures adopted.

If we were to wake up tomorrow in the England of 1625 and were interested in studying what that period thought of the problem of organizing discourses, we would find that two distinct practices were then in evidence.

One practice, which was applied to what I have been calling learned discourses, required such communications to be organized either in an ascending or a descending order of generality. The ascending order, called the compositive, required an author to proceed from the smallest units of a subject to the whole, as when a treatise on logic would treat first of words, then of propositions, and finally of syllogisms and arguments. The descending order, called the resolutive, required an author to proceed from the whole to smaller and smaller parts, until at length the indivisible units of the subject were reached.

The theory of learned presentation was not always treated in these two divisions by the logicians of the early seventeenth century. The Ramists, for example, believed that only the descending order was legitimate in the field of learned writing.[19] The Systematics believed in the ascending as well as the descending order, and occasionally one of them added a third method to these standard two.[20] Bacon, who did not belong to either of these schools, adhered to the theory that learned discourse had two other major divisions, "whereof the one may be termed Magistral, and the other of Probation."[21] Bacon means his divisions to represent the difference between elementary, dogmatic exposition and something more inquiring and philosophical; and

it must be admitted that this distinction, and his subsequent treatment of it, have greater range and caliber than did the standard distinction, although the latter was the more popular in its time.

The other practice of organizing discourses in the England of 1625 was applied to popular address, and it consisted in following the theory of the classical oration. Thus speakers were taught to arrange their ideas so that there was first an introduction, then a narration, and then a division or preview, these parts being forerunners of the proof, refutation, and conclusion, Cicero was, of course, the great authority behind this theory, although sixteenth-century England knew it also from Thomas Wilson's *The Arte of Rhetorique* and by 1625 from Thomas Vicars's *Manuductio ad Artem Rhetoricam* and Thomas Farnaby's popular *Index Rhetoricus*.

It is obvious that modern rhetoric advocates a simpler and more natural organization than that represented by Renaissance theory. Our learned discourses rarely adhere with regularity to an ascending or a descending pattern. Scholarship, history, biography, scientific exposition, organize themselves unobtrusively into sequences suggested by the relations of their units in space, time, logic, or causality. On many occasions serious arrangement appears to be in the class of things that an author must avoid, at least in outward appearance, as if the learned reader would be insulted by clarity of form, and the layman's delicate interest would not survive in the atmosphere of system and order.

As for our oratory, we organize it theoretically into fewer parts than did Cicero, and we strive in practice for the simplest possible structure. In fact, when Aristotle, long before Cicero, said that a speech needed to have only two parts, the statement and argument, to which on occasion the speaker might want to add an introduction and an epilogue, but no other divisions,[22] he was closer to our current practice than the Roman or medieval rhetoricians are. And why? Perhaps because his times were much like ours in preferring subject matter to form, inquiry to communication, individuality to convention, and democratic procedures to authoritarian rituals. At any rate, it cannot be denied that we have moved away from the ceremonial organization advocated by Cicero toward the simpler theory of Aristotle.

6

The fifth, and for my present purposes the final, change that has come over rhetoric since the Renaissance concerns the theory of style. Style is often conceived as the dress our thoughts wear when they have been made ready to appear in good society. "Elocution," said Thomas Wilson, "getteth words to set forth inuention, and with such beautie commendeth the matter, that reason semeth to be clad in Purple, walking afore both bare and naked."[23] We may elaborate this image a bit and say that the great change in the theory of rhetorical style since Wilson's day has been a change from the convention of imperial dress to the convention of the business suit.

In the sixteenth century rhetorical style was largely, sometimes exclusively, taught in terms of tropes and schemes.[24] Tropes were what we call today figures of speech, including such devices as metaphor, synecdoche, metonymy, irony, and allegory. Schemes were unusual arrangements of language. Thus language arranged in rhymed verses was one sort of scheme, called in Latin *similiter desinens* and in English *like-ending.* Other typical schemes involved saying the same thing in many different ways *(expolitio),* dividing a whole into parts *(partitio),* and changing suddenly from the third person to the second in order to speak as if directly to a person or thing (apostrophe). The list of schemes and tropes was long in sixteenth-century textbooks, as English schoolboys knew to their dismay.[25]

The theory behind tropes and schemes was that men have one language for ordinary intercourse and another for formal communication, and that the latter differs from the former by employing tropes and schemes throughout. Englishmen of the Renaissance did not believe the language of ordinary life to be suitable for formal discourse. They believed instead that formal discourse must be deliberately contrived to appear systematically unlike the language of ordinary life. The contrivances by which ordinary speech was transformed into proper oratorical or poetical speech were what the Renaissance understood tropes and schemes to be.

We all know that in present-day American education students no longer memorize tropes and schemes, nor do they use them as the official public language. Students are taught instead to speak a public language that corresponds to the best elements of the language of ordinary intercourse. Such public language is not unlike the poetic idiom identified by Wordsworth as "a selection of language really used by men."[26] Incidentally, Wordsworth's great contribution to English poetry has often been described as that in which poetry abandoned the stylistic conventions of the eighteenth century and learned to express itself in the speech of ordinary life. What could also be emphasized, however, is that Wordsworth's reforms in poetry were part of a great trend, begun in the Renaissance and constantly in evidence since, away from a contrived literary language and toward the idioms of everyday speech.

The tendency of modern rhetoric to recommend the speech of ordinary life as opposed to the artful and elaborate speech of the courtier reflects the change that has occurred since the Renaissance as political power and economic influence have been transferred from the aristocrat to the commoner. When the aristocrat was the final source of both of these forms of authority, ordinary language did not serve a decisive political or economic purpose, and tropes and schemes, as the antitheses of that language, were the preferred means of communication. But when the commoner became politically powerful, and wealth began to center in his commercial enterprises rather than as before in the aristocrats' estates, the tropes and the schemes passed into history, except as a way of expressing emotional overtones of meaning, while the idiom of ordinary life, purified of its

ordinary defects, assumed a new and growing importance. In support of this same trend, the new science found the fashions of aristocratic speech unsuited to the expression of scientific subject matter and unresponsive to the expectations of those seeking intellectual, humanitarian, or commercial profit from the publication of experiments and discoveries. Small wonder, then, that the scientists of the seventeenth century evolved their new vocabulary from "the language of Artizans, Countrymen, and Merchants, before that, of Wits, or Scholars."[27] Thus did the scientific, the economic, and the political forces in the pattern of Western European culture conspire to produce for the twentieth century a theory of rhetorical style quite different from that in vogue in the early Renaissance.

We should not say, however, that the rise of ordinary speech to a position of prominence in rhetorical style represents a gain for rhetoric, nor that the decline in the importance of tropes and figures represents a loss. What we should say is that ordinary speech as a medium of communication better reflects the needs of a businessman's culture and that tropes and figures were better for a culture of landed aristocrats. It is the business of rhetoric to react to the situation in which it is used and to reflect in its theory and needs that it serves. Rhetoric does not deserve praise for evolving its present theory of rhetorical style, for that is not praiseworthy which is done as a matter of normal obligation. But rhetoric would deserve blame if it still sought to elevate tropes and figures into the exclusive language of public discourse. That sort of attitude would be in effect a declaration that a given set of means is of greater value than its presumed end—that the way in which a communication is phrased counts more heavily than does the possibility that it will not reach its audience.

7

Other changes have taken place in the theory of rhetoric during the past four centuries. Some of them have come with the development of mass media of communication, some with the application of the concept of propaganda to the fields of commerce, public relations, and statecraft. Some have come as rhetoric has stated its problems in terms of the principles of modern psychology, some as means have been developed to explore the state of public opinion and to measure the effect of communications upon the audience. These changes are of course vitally important in the growth of modern rhetoric. I have not treated them here because the impulses which produced them have originated within the past half-century and thus cannot be said to have deep roots in the ancient world as well as in our own.

What I have tried to do here is to discuss five problems which rhetoric has faced in antiquity and in the period since the Renaissance; I have tried to indicate that the solutions of those problems have changed as needs have dictated. The emphasis upon the theory of communication during the Middle Ages gave rhetoric and its allied arts a central position in the academic curriculum. As a result of that emphasis, grammar, rhetoric, and logic shared the responsibility for teaching communication and intelligently divided that responsibility among them. Grammar became the study of the medium of communication, rhetoric and logic the study of the means of reaching the two types of audience. As emphasis has shifted from the theory of communication to the theory of inquiry, rhetoric has lost in certain directions but has held its own in others. It has lost its central position in the curriculum; it has lost its productive association with logic; and although it has extended its scope to include a concern for the learned audience, it has failed to develop for modern learning what ancient logic developed in its time—a vocabulary by which specialists in one field can communicate with specialists in other fields. Meanwhile, however, rhetoric has developed a theory of invention that fits modern requirements, and it has adapted itself to new conditions in respect to the theory of arrangement and style. Certainly its future will mean further change; and perhaps it can recover some of the ground it has lost in the last four hundred years, if it endeavors always to see its present problems in the light of its long and illustrious history.

Notes

1. This chapter represents a further development of ideas outlined in my *Logic and Rhetoric in England, 1500–1700*, and it foreshadows the major argument of Chapter 6 of my *Eighteenth-Century British Logic and Rhetoric*.
2. In 1660 Charles Hoole, a writer on education, reflected the classical orientation of the grammar school education of his century when he said that "*speaking Latine is the main end of Grammar.*" See "The Usher's Duty," in his *A New Discovery of the Old Art*

of Teaching Schoole, ed. E. T. Campagnac (London, 1913), p. 50. The italics are Hoole's. Some years later an educational reformer named John Newton in the Dedicatory Epistle and Preface to his *Introduction to the Art of Logick* (London, 1678) reflected the newer tendencies of the century in asserting that young people should be taught all the sciences in their own tongue and that Latin should be reserved only for those who wished to enter a learned profession.

3. *Works of Bacon*, VI, 282–303.
4. See my *Logic and Rhetoric in England*, chs. 2–5.
5. *Ibid.*, ch. 4.
6. René Descartes, *Discours de la méthode*, ed. Etienne Gilson (Paris, 1935), pp. 62–63.
7. *Orator*, 113, trans. H. M. Hubbell, p. 389. See also Quintilian, *Institutio Oratoria*, 2. 20. 7.
8. For a discussion of the effect of absolutism upon Roman eloquence of the early Empire, see Harry Caplan, "The Decay of Eloquence at Rome in the First Century," in *Studies in Speech and Drama in Honor of Alexander M. Drummond*, ed. Herbert A. Wichelns *et al.* (Ithaca, 1944), pp. 295–325.
9. See Baldwin, *Medieval Rhetoric and Poetic*, p. 151.
10. *De Inventione*, 1. 8. 10–18; 2. 4–51.
11. *Ibid.*, 1. 5. 7; 2. 4. 12; 2. 51–59.
12. *Ibid.*, 1. 14–56.
13. Russell Halderman Wagner, "Wilson and his Sources," *QJS*, XV (1929), 530–532. For an excellent discussion of the date, authorship, sources, and organization of the *Rhetorica ad Herennium* and its relation to *De Inventione*, see Harry Caplan, trans., *Ad C. Herennium de Ratione Dicendi*, Loeb Classical Library (Cambridge, Mass., 1954), pp. vii–xxxiv.
14. Gilson's ed., p. 51.
15. Lloyd Paul Stryker, *The Art of Advocacy* (New York, 1954), p. 11.
16. *Ibid.*, pp. 113–114.
17. *Rhetorica*, 1355[b] 36 ff., in *The Works of Aristotle*, ed. W. D. Ross, Vol. XI.
18. *Ibid.*, 1396[a]–1396[b].
19. For a discussion of this matter, see my *Logic and Rhetoric in England*, ch. 4.
20. *Ibid.*, ch. 5.
21. *Works of Bacon*, VI, 289.
22. *Rhetorica*, 1414[a]–1414[b].
23. Mair, p. 160.
24. See my *Logic and Rhetoric in England*, ch. 3.
25. Henry Peacham's *The Garden of Eloquence* (London, 1577, 1593) is one of the most complete of these lists. For a recent edition of this work, see William G. Crane's facsimile reproduction (Gainesville, Fla., 1954).
26. In his celebrated "Preface to the Second Edition of Several of the Foregoing Poems, Published, with an Additional Volume, under the title of 'Lyrical Ballads.' " See *The Complete Poetical Works of William Wordsworth*, ed. Andrew J. George (New York [1904]), p. 791.
27. See Thomas Sprat, *The History of the Royal Society of London* (London, 1667), p. 113.

James L. Golden and Edward P. J. Corbett

Introduction

◊ *The historical overview presented here provides a brief description of the principal elements of western rhetorical thought which were to have a profound influence on the theories developed by three celebrated British scholars—Hugh Blair, George Campbell, and Richard Whately. The first half of this introductory chapter summarizes the main ideas contained in Aristotle's* Rhetoric, *and the offices and canons of rhetoric, as well as pedagogical devices, emphasized by the Romans. This is followed by a sketch of what constituted the rhetorical training in the sixteenth and seventeenth centuries. The second half of the essay describes how Blair, Campbell, and Whately responded to four major rhetorical trends that were set into motion both by the classical rhetorical tradition and the emergence of modern scientific inquiry. These trends, as the authors point out, were neo-classicism, belles lettres, the Elocutionary Movement, and the Psychological-Philosophical approach.* ◊

Hugh Blair, George Campbell, and Richard Whately constituted the great triumvirate of British rhetoricians who came at the end of a long tradition of rhetoric which had its beginning in fifth-century Greece. But these men did not so much terminate a tradition as initiate the period of modern or new rhetoric. Space does not permit a survey here of the 2000-year history of rhetoric, a history which includes dozens of the most illustrious names associated with Western culture. Students interested in pursuing that history can turn to the surveys listed in the bibliography

at the end of this introduction. Here, however, we can put Blair, Campbell, and Whately into context by reviewing the main rhetorical doctrines and movements from the beginning in ancient Greece to the incipient decline of traditional rhetoric in early eighteenth-century England.

Although Aristotle, in a now lost history of rhetoric, named Empedocles of Agrigentum as the first teacher of rhetoric, Corax and his pupil Tisias are commonly accepted as having produced the first handbooks of rhetoric in Sicily during the first quarter of the fifth

From *The Rhetoric of Blair, Campbell, and Whately.* Edited by James L. Golden and Edward P. J. Corbett. Carbondale, IL: Southern Illinois University Press, 1990. Reprinted with permission from Southern Illinois University Press.

century B.C. Rhetoric began and for a long time remained exclusively the organon of oral, persuasive discourse of the courtroom. With the expulsion of a long line of tyrants, the citizens of Sicily rushed to court to plead their own cases for the recovery of their confiscated property, and in preparation for this special pleading before a jury of their peers they turned eagerly to anyone who could train them for this encounter. Gorgias of Leontini introduced rhetoric to Athens in 427, when he was sent on an embassy to that intellectually vibrant city. The Athenians were enthralled by Gorgias' eloquence, and soon numerous schools, taught by "rhetors" or "sophists," sprang up.

Not all Athenians, however, were impressed by this new art of persuasive oratory. The most prestigious opponent of the art was Plato, who echoed and reaffirmed the objections of his teacher, Socrates. As we learn from the *Gorgias* and the *Phaedrus*, Plato regarded rhetoric as a meretricious art, if indeed it was an art at all. For him, rhetoric was a mere "knack," a form of flattery, appealing to men's passions and emotions rather than reason; moreover, it based arguments on appearances and opinions rather than on reality and truth. Interestingly enough, Plato's strictures on rhetoric are the same objections that men of all ages have leveled against this seductive art. In the *Phaedrus*, however, Plato did admit that there could be such a thing as a "true rhetoric," but it would come about only if rhetoricians were to probe for the *truth* in all matters, attempt to formulate essential definitions of particulars, and study man's psychological dispositions so that they could adapt and ar-

range their arguments to suit the temper of an audience.

Aristotle responded to that challenge. His *Rhetoric,* composed over the period from 342 to 330 B.C., represents his efforts to compose a philosophical, scientific rhetoric, an eminently realistic rhetoric which took man as he was, not as Plato wished him to be. Since Aristotle's *Rhetoric* is the fountainhead of the system of rhetoric commonly labeled "classical," we can use his treatise as the basis of an exposition of the key doctrines and terminology of classical rhetoric. The reader should understand, however, that not all of the classical system is found in Aristotle's *Rhetoric* in a fully developed form. It was Quintilian's *Institutio Oratoria,* written in the first century A.D., that presented the fullest exposition of classical rhetoric, and it was Aristotle's contemporary, Isocrates, who, with his commitment to humanistic, moral, one-world ideals, proved to be the most popular and influential teacher of rhetoric in his era.

One of the key terms in the *Rhetoric* and a term which represents one of Aristotle's chief contributions to the development of "an art of rhetoric" was *probability.* Aristotle astutely recognized that many matters connected with human affairs were not susceptible to the kind of absolute, infallible proof that could be managed in logic or in a scientific demonstration. It is not always possible, for instance, to establish with absolute certainty that a man has committed the crime of which he is accused or that the passage of a proposed tax bill will inevitably produce the benefits its exponents claim for it. In such situations the lawyer or the statesman can produce only a high degree of probability; he must, in other words, *persuade* his audience that his claims are "true" or "beneficial." That notion of probability is implicit in Aristotle's definition of rhetoric as "the faculty of discovering the available means of persuasion in any given case."

What are the means of rhetorical proof, the means of winning assent to the probable truth of a proposition? Aristotle designed three modes of rhetorical proof: (1) *logos*—the appeal to the reason of the audience; (2) *pathos*—the appeal to the emotions of the audience; (3) *ethos*—the appeal that is exerted by the character and personality, by the "image," of the speaker or writer. In appealing to reason, we argue either inductively or deductively—"There is no other way," Aristotle says. The rhetorical equivalent of a full induction in logic is the *example,* a single instance of an analogous event or situation; the rhetorical equivalent of the syllogism in logic is the *enthymeme,* whose essential difference from the syllogism is not so much that one of the premises is left unstated as that the deductive argument is based on premises that are only probably or usually true rather than universally and infallibly true. The *topics* represented a system for probing any subject matter to discover something to say on that subject. Lines of argument, for instance, might be worked off from a *definition* of terms (what is the nature of the thing?); or from *comparison* (what is it like? what is it unlike? how does it differ in degree from something else?); or from *relationship* (what is the cause of this effect? what are the effects of this cause? if this antecedent condition exists, what conse-

quences follow?); or from *authority* (for these arguments one must go outside the subject matter for such supporting evidence as testimony, statistics, maxims, documents, laws, and so on).

These were the so-called common topics, sources of arguments on virtually any subject. There were special topics, too, which Aristotle designated in relation to the three kinds of persuasive discourse: (1) the *deliberative* or *political*—the kind of discourse in which we seek to induce an audience to adopt a particular point of view or a particular course of action, usually in matters concerning public affairs; (2) the *judicial* or *forensic*—in particular the persuasive discourse of the courtroom but in general any discourse which seeks to accuse or exonerate someone of crime, malfeasance, or misconduct; (3) the *epideictic* or *ceremonial*—discourse intent on praising or blaming some person or institution or event (for example, a funeral oration, a Fourth of July speech, "The Gettysburg Address"). In deliberative discourse, where we are seeking to win acceptance for a thesis or a course of action, we come down hard on the special topics of the *good* (something worthy of pursuit for its own sake) or the *advantageous* (something useful or beneficial); in judicial discourse, where we are seeking to indict or defend someone, we come down hard on the special topics of the *just* (the lawful) or the *unjust* (the illegal); in ceremonial discourse, where we are seeking to praise or blame someone, we come down hard on the special topics of *virtue* (moral good) or *vice* (moral evil).

To discover the available means of persuasion for an emotional or pathetic appeal, one must have a sense for the disposition of a particular audience, must be aware of the principal human emotions, and must know how to arouse or subdue those emotions. Aristotle devoted the major portion of Book II of his *Rhetoric* to an analysis of the basic human emotions and of the strategies for playing on those emotions. He was the only one of the classical rhetoricians to devote an extensive section of his rhetoric text to the strategies of emotional appeal. We shall see how in the eighteenth century, with the growth of interest in psychology, the British rhetoricians, especially George Campbell, made a significant contribution to the psychology of persuasion through the emotions.

Aristotle maintained that the ethical appeal could very well be the most significant of the appeals in the persuasive process, because if an audience did not trust or admire the speaker or writer, all of his logical and emotional appeals, however cogent they might be, would have little effect. Aristotle pointed out that the ethical appeal of a speaker or writer will be effective if in his discourse he creates an image of himself as being a man of good sense, good moral character, and good will toward his audience. The Latin rhetoricians, especially Quintilian, who defined an effective orator as "a good man speaking," reinforced this notion of the importance of the ethical appeal by insisting that to be an effective persuader one must give evidence of intelligence, learning, and moral integrity. This insistence on the *ethos* of the speaker was also Aristotle's way of answering Plato's charge that men skilled in the use

of words could use that power for nefarious purposes.

This process of finding all the available means of persuasion was treated by the ancient rhetoricians under the first of the five "offices" of rhetoric—*inventio* or invention, in the sense of "discovery" or "finding." The second "office" of rhetoric in the classical system was *dispositio* or arrangement, which was concerned with the selection of the arguments discovered through invention and their organization in the most effective order. Arrangement was commonly dealt with in terms of the parts of an oration: (1) the *exordium* or introduction, in which the speaker oriented, conciliated, and gained the attention of his audience; (2) the *narratio* or statement of the issue to be argued; (3) the *confirmatio* or proof, the main body of the discourse, in which the speaker presented his positive arguments for his thesis; (4) the *confutatio* or refutation of the opposing arguments; (5) the *epilogue* or conclusion, in which the speaker recapitulated his arguments, reinforced his ethical appeal, and perhaps made a final pitch to the emotions. Rhetoric texts gave general instructions about the kinds of strategy that might be employed, in a variety of circumstances, in each of these parts of the discourse. For instance, they would advise when it would be better to advance one's strong arguments first or when it would be better to refute the opposing arguments first before arguing one's own case.

The third "office" of traditional rhetoric was *elocutio* or style. This was concerned with the actual expression or verbalization of the arguments that had been discovered and judiciously selected and organized. Here students were instructed in the choice of apt, precise, decorous diction, in the disposition of words into perspicuous, graceful, arresting, rhythmical patterns, and in the use of figures of speech. Some of the rhetoricians, like Gorgias, and Demetrius in his *On Style*, and Dionysius of Halicarnassus in his *De Compositione Verborum*, and even Longinus in his great work *On the Sublime*, and several of the Renaissance rhetoricians, devoted their attention either predominantly or exclusively to style, and this preoccupation with style brought on the charge, at some time in every age, that rhetoric was more concerned with words than with matter, that it merely produced a lot of sound and fury signifying nothing. We shall see what careful attention Blair gave to style in his lectures on rhetoric.

The fourth and fifth "offices" of rhetoric were *memoria* or memorization and *pronuntiatio* or delivery. Although a great deal of attention seems to have been devoted to these two divisions of rhetoric in the classroom, little or no space was devoted to them in the rhetoric texts. Treatment of memorization consisted largely of suggested mnemonic devices to help students commit their prepared speech to memory so that it could be more spontaneously and vigorously delivered. Treatment of delivery consisted of training and frequent practice in the management of the voice and gestures. The second half of the eighteenth century saw a surge of interest in *elocution,* a term which by then had changed its meaning from "style" to "delivery," and, as we shall see, men like Thomas Sheridan, John Walker, and Richard Whately gave a

great impetus to the revived interest in the delivery aspects of rhetoric.

The system of rhetorical training outlined above was basically the one that prevailed in the schools throughout the Roman period, the Middle Ages, the Renaissance, and the seventeenth century. At different periods, of course, the system was subjected to retrenchments, amplifications, shifts of emphasis, revitalization, innovations, and changes in terminology, sometimes to suit the whim of a particular teacher or group, at other times to make the system more relevant to the needs and moods of the times. After the invention of printing, for instance, and during periods when a great deal of political and mercantile business was carried on through the medium of letters, the emphasis both in the classroom and in the rhetoric texts shifted more and more from oral to written discourse. In the Roman period, such pedagogical devices as the *progymnasmata* or elementary finger exercises in a variety of short written compositions and the declamatory exercises called *suasoriae* and *controversiae* had some value in that they enabled the student to learn by doing but often they became so artificial and fantastic that they lost their value as practical training for the real world of give-and-take that the student would enter. The Middle Ages saw a great growth of interest in the sermon, a species of discourse which did not exactly fit in with any of the kinds of oration—deliberative, forensic, or ceremonial—that the Greek and Roman rhetoricians had classified, and so medieval rhetoricians like St. Augustine, in his *De Doctrina Christiana*, adapted Ciceronian rhetoric so that it could serve as a means of expounding the Scriptures for the enlightenment of the laity and of inducing congregations to follow the straight and narrow path of virtue. When the humanists of the English Renaissance were preparing rhetoric courses for their schools, they turned mainly to the rhetorics of Cicero and Quintilian because those Roman rhetoricians had conceived of rhetorical training in terms of a liberal arts course rather than simply as an art for the composition of persuasive discourse; when clergymen took over as school-masters they looked with favor upon Quintilian's insistence that the rhetorician should be concerned with the moral, as well as the intellectual, development of his pupils. When the vernacular rhetorics, like Thomas Wilson's *Arte of Rhetorique* (1553), began to appear in the sixteenth century, some of the authors of those texts sought to replace the foreboding Greek and Latin terminology with simpler English words or coinages.

Two developments in the late sixteenth century threatened the preeminence of rhetoric in the curriculum and eventually effected profound changes in the rationale of rhetorical training offered in the schools. One of these was the revolution in rhetorical studies that the French scholar Peter Ramus promoted by fostering a realignment of the provinces of logic and rhetoric. He assigned invention and arrangement to logic, because he saw those activities as functions primarily of reason, and he relegated to rhetoric only the provinces of style and delivery, which he regarded as the peculiar functions of the imagination. This breakup of the traditional five-part structure of rhetorical training

was promoted in the schools through Ramus' influential logic text and the companion rhetoric text by his ardent disciple, Omer Talon. The effects of this Ramistic dichotomy are reflected in the titles of some of the most influential of the English vernacular texts: Dudley Fenner's *The Arts of Logic and Rhetoric* (1584), Abraham Fraunce's *The Lawyer's Logic* and *The Arcadian Rhetoric* (1588), Charles Butler's *The Two Books of Ramean Rhetoric* (1597), and Thomas Farnaby's *Index Rhetoricus* (1625). The most significant effect of this reassignment, however, was that the conceptualizing part of the composition process came to be regarded as an activity of private inquiry rather than one of the steps in the preparation for communicating with an audience.

This view of logic or dialectics as a tool for inquiry fitted in well with the growing interest in science, which was promoted by Francis Bacon early in the seventeenth century and by members of the Royal Society after 1660. In *The Advancement of Learning,* Francis Bacon proposed that the function of rhetoric was "to apply and recommend the dictates of reason to imagination in order to excite the appetite and will." In this distinctly Ramistic view, communication involves an interaction between reason and the imagination, but it is clear from Bacon's development of this notion that reason is the dominant faculty in the process. We are not surprised then to find Bacon and other men of science advocating that matter *(res)* should take precedence over words *(verba)* and eventually, through one of the programs of the Royal Society, the creation of a simple, unadorned prose style for the exposition of inductively derived discoveries. The ideal scientific style would be one as strictly denotative as mathematical symbols. Fortunately, the development of such a barren prose style was prevented by the development, in the Augustan Age, of an elegant middle style by such writers as John Dryden, Jonathan Swift, and Joseph Addison. The Royal Society's program to develop a "mathematical" style had at least one good effect therefore, in that it encouraged the development of a gracefully informal prose style that would counteract, on the one hand, the "barebones" prose of the scientist and, on the other hand, the kind of ornate, euphuistic prose that Thomas Hobbes dubbed a tissue of "windy blisters."

We are brought now, after a series of seven-league bounds through the long history of rhetoric, to the eve of the eighteenth century, when the future directions of rhetorical studies would be determined, for better or for worse.

From its beginning, the eighteenth century was virile and intellectually alive. It was a period characterized by intensive study of the classical tradition, a pervasive enthusiasm for the newly developing empirical method, a commitment to rationalism, a curiosity to understand human nature and man's relationship to God, a preoccupation with the origin and use of language, and an appreciation of the potentialities of persuasion as a force in a democracy and in a Christian society. These interests combined to create one of the most prolific eras in rhetorical history.

The eighteenth-century rhetoricians, most of whom were acquainted with the doctrines of the ancients, re-

ponded to these theories in different ways. Some writers, choosing to ignore contemporary ideas advanced in the natural and social sciences as well as in the humanities, held that there was no need to alter the teachings of Aristotle, Cicero, and Quintilian. Thus numerous continental classical works, such as Fènèlon's *Dialogues sur l' Eloquence* (1717), were translated into English. Of those British authors who produced volumes which strictly adhered to the classical framework, three were both representative and influential. These include John Holmes's *The Art of Rhetoric* (1739), John Lawson's *Lectures Concerning Oratory* (1752), and John Ward's *Systems of Oratory* (1759). The latter, which covers more than eight hundred pages, is, according to Douglas Ehninger, the most extensive restatement of ancient rhetorical theory in the English language. But despite the fact that *Systems of Oratory* contains a thorough and accurate interpretation of the classical rhetorical doctrines, and notwithstanding its immediate popularity, this work, like Holmes's *Art of Rhetoric* and Lawson's *Lectures Concerning Oratory*, was too sterile and unimaginative to constitute an important landmark in the evolution of rhetorical theory.

A second response to the classical rhetorical tradition was the development of the elocutionary movement. In theory the leaders of this movement accepted four of the five traditional canons of rhetoric: invention, disposition, style, and delivery. But, as Wilbur S. Howell has suggested, they were sensitive to the criticisms which science had leveled against the excessive preoccupation with style as expressed in such volumes as Leonard Cox's *The Arte or Crafte of Rhethoryke* (1530), Richard Sherry's *A Treastise of Schemes and Tropes* (1550), and Henry Peacham's *Garden of Eloquence* (1577). Moreover, they were aware of the unfavorable reaction produced by Peter Ramus when he sought to relegate invention and disposition to logic, and style and delivery to rhetoric. With enthusiasm, therefore, they turned to the one remaining canon which had not yet felt the full brunt of scientific criticism: delivery. In doing so, they expressed two rationalizations for explaining their decision to single out a particular rhetorical element. First, they had found ample support for emphasizing delivery in the celebrated, but apparently apocryphal, quotation of Demosthenes on the value of action, and in Quintilian's detailed analysis of voice control, eye contact, and bodily activity. Secondly, they shared Swift's and Chesterfield's concern with the carelessness in articulation, pronunciation, and action which all too often characterized the speaking of eighteenth-century Englishmen.

Among those treatises which best epitomize the elocutionary movement in England, perhaps the most significant were Thomas Sheridan's *Lectures on Elocution* (1763) and *Lectures on Reading* (1775), John Walker's *Elements of Elocution* (1781), and Gilbert Austin's *Chironomia, or a Treatise on Rhetorical Delivery* (1806). The principal merit of this movement found eloquent expression in Sheridan's recommendation that effective voice control and bodily activity utilize the conversational pattern of delivery. But the excesses, including Sheridan's de-

velopment of a complex marking system to be used in oral reading and Walker's absurd and ludicrous classification and description of the emotions, brought a charge of artificiality. The elocutionists, nevertheless, won many converts, including James Boswell, a former student of Love, the actor, and a close friend of Thomas Sheridan. Not even the barbs of Johnson could persuade Boswell that this form of speech training was artificial and impotent. He rejoiced when elocution, after several years of decline, was revived in London. In April 1781 with fifty men and twenty women, he went to hear Sheridan discuss his favorite subject. There, he tells us in his *Private Papers,* he was impressed with the apparatus which was used to "clear and smooth and mellow" the voice.

The rise of the belletristic movement in the eighteenth century constitutes a third response to the classical rhetorical tradition. This approach was based upon the concept that rhetoric and related polite arts, poetry, drama, art, history, biography, philology, and so on should be joined under the broad heading of rhetoric and belles lettres. Since these disciplines share a common interest in taste, style, criticism, and sublimity, they seek to instruct the student to become an effective practitioner and judge in written and oral communication. The belletristic scholar, therefore, was not content to construct a rhetorical theory limited to the subject matter covered by Aristotle in his *Rhetoric*. Instead he, consciously or unconsciously, gave equal emphasis to another tradition initiated by Aristotle's *Poetics,* Isocrates' theory of culture, Longinus' *On the Sublime,* and Horace's *Ars Poetica.*

This wedding of rhetoric and its companion art poetics took place in the modern era on the European continent in the later part of the sixteenth and early part of the seventeenth centuries. The principal works demonstrating this approach included Gerardus Vossius' *De Philosophia* (1658), Bernard Lami's *L'Art de Parler* (1675), and Charles Rollin's *De La Maniere d'Enseigner et d'Etudier les Belles-Lettres* (1726–1728). Two decades after the publication of Rollin's work, Adam Smith became the first Englishman to give impetus to the belletristic movement. In 1748, Smith, a native of Scotland and a graduate of Oxford University, began, under the sponsorship of Lord Kames, a series of public lectures in Edinburgh on rhetoric and belles lettres which were repeated during the following two years. Among the regular attendants who heard these discussions was a youthful minister of the Presbyterian Church at St. Giles, Hugh Blair. As the first public lecturer in the British Isles to unite rhetoric and belles lettres, Smith taught his audience to appreciate the nature of style, eloquence, and literary forms, and the pedagogically attractive method of using modern and classical models. The popularity of the lectures won for Smith a Chair at the University of Glasgow where, for more than a decade, he continued to teach rhetoric and belles lettres, even in his courses in moral philosophy and political economy.

Probably the most revolutionary response to the classical tradition was the emergence of the psychological-philosophical theories of public address. Many scholars, applying the principles of rationalism and the empirical method, saw the strengths and shortcomings of classicism. The more they studied ancient science, philosophy, and rhetoric, the more they realized man's lack of meaningful insight concerning his basic nature. Thus with a desire to advance knowledge in a crucial area which they had come to believe was either misunderstood or neglected by the ancients, they set for themselves the task of unraveling the mystery of the human mind and soul. Despite the fact that these philosophers and psychologists were essentially nonrhetoricians, they profoundly influenced the direction which rhetoric was to take during the latter half of the eighteenth century.

The writers who contributed the most elaborate theories describing man's mental and moral nature were John Locke, Francis Hutcheson, David Hume, David Hartley, Thomas Reid, and Adam Smith. In his celebrated *Essay on Human Understanding* (1689), Locke concluded that since the mind has the power to *perceive* and *prefer,* it must be comprised of two major faculties, the understanding and the will. In explaining the nature of the faculty of understanding, Locke developed his famous theory of ideas. Reflection upon sensory experience, he observed, produces ideas which are, in turn, held together in a meaningful pattern through the ability of the mind to trace relationships that show natural correspondence and connection. Similarly, reason enables us to unite ideas that are apparently unrelated by utilizing the laws of association. Here we may observe from past experiences that whenever a particular idea reaches the understanding an "associate appears with it."

Under such circumstances, the doctrine of association permits us to connect these concepts so that they will form an inseparable unit in our minds.

Locke's reflections led him to reject the syllogism on the grounds that it neither demonstrates nor strengthens the connection that two ideas may have with each other. Nor does it advance an argument or lead to moral truth. The power of inference, a talent given to man by God, makes it possible for us to perceive associations and to determine whether or not ideas are coherent or incoherent. Thus the understanding, concludes Locke, "is not taught to reason" by the "methods of syllogizing." The far-reaching significance of this thesis may be seen when we turn later to Campbell's theory of logical proof.

As one of the early proponents of faculty psychology, Locke came to believe that an idea which reaches the understanding does not necessarily have the power to motivate the will. The rational process, he held, must be reinforced by an emotional appeal that ultimately becomes the principal determinant of action. All of the emotions have one common element which Locke called "uneasiness," and described as the absence of some good. Whenever the mind experiences "uneasiness," it feels pain and generates the compelling desire to remove it. The will, in short, may be influenced when the passions are stirred, for the arousal of an emotion inevitably causes pain. There is little chance for persuasion, however, if the mind is at ease since the desire for happiness has already been achieved.

Locke's discussion of the nature of ideas, his tendency to compartmentalize the mind into faculties, his analysis of the doctrine of association, and his recognition that the emotions are the prime movers of the will profoundly influenced Hume. Few eighteenth-century thinkers were better qualified than Hume to follow the lead of Locke and probe into the mental characteristics of man in order to explain human knowledge. Impressed by the achievements of Newton in natural science and convinced that his success was due largely to the experimental method, Hume became the first writer to construct a solid empirical base upon which to build a science of human nature.

Probably the most important contribution Hume made to subsequent rhetorical theory was his extension of Locke's views on the laws of association. In his *Treatise on Human Nature* (1739), Hume observed that the mind moves freely from one idea to another through the three qualities of "resemblance, contiguity in time or place, and cause and effect." The imagination stimulates the mind to see the connection between ideas that are similar. Moreover, as the senses choose to change their focus from one object to another, they may proceed along a continuum of space and time. Ideas which are in juxtaposition naturally have strong associations with each other. There was little new in this concept of resemblance and contiguity. As Hume discussed the third quality of association, cause and effect, he was, however, original and influential. The mind, which he strangely held to be nothing more than a bundle of perceptions united by association, may be subdivided into two faculties, impressions and ideas. Although these elements differ from each other only in the degree of force and vivacity, impressions constitute the cause and ideas the effect. Past experience recalled by memory and reinforced by imagination enables us to make causal inferences. From these premises Hume suggested that a belief may be defined as "a lively idea related to or associated with a present impression."

Hume's willingness to give impressions a priority ranking over ideas prompted him further to develop the thesis that all human motivation stems from man's emotional nature. Standing squarely in the tradition of Locke, he argued that appeals to the passions, especially those which produce pleasure or pain, are necessary to induce the will to act. But he went far beyond Locke when he claimed that "reason is and ought only to be the slave of the passions, and can never pretend to any other office than to serve and obey them." Hume diminished the value of deductive reasoning not only because of his belief in the superior power of impressions, but also because of his devotion to the experimental method. He found it easy, therefore, to exclude the syllogism as an effective tool in exploring human knowledge. Similarly he distrusted elaborate chains of reasoning designed to prove the existence of God, and testimonials supporting the authenticity of the biblical miracles on the grounds that they could not be corroborated by present experience.

The interest which Locke and Hume displayed in faculty psychology and associationism was shared by David Hartley, a physician who wrote a detailed and cumbersome book entitled, *Observations on Man, His Frame, His Duty, and His Expectations* (1749). To the mental faculties of understanding and will outlined by Locke, Hartley added memory, imagination or fancy, and affection. He agreed with both Locke and Hume in asserting that reason and emotions are dependent upon the law of association. But unlike his predecessors, he introduced a new idea which he called "vibrations." "All human actions," he stated, "proceed from Vibrations in the Nerves of the muscles." Thus when a man experiences pain or pleasure, he is responding to sensations which take the form of muscular vibrations. In holding this position, Hartley veered in the direction of Hume's views on the power of impressions and away from Locke's commitment to reflective thinking. Hartley's elaborate and partially traditional, yet innovative approach contributed significantly to Joseph Priestley's *Course of Lectures on Oratory and Criticism* (1777). Moreover, it kept alive the growing concern of eighteenth-century scholars to root knowledge in human nature.

If Locke, Hume, and Hartley focused primarily, though not exclusively, on man's mental nature, it was Francis Hutcheson, a Scottish philosopher and professor, who gave the most penetrating insights into man's moral sense. In the second edition of his *Short Introduction to Moral Philosophy* (1753), he observed that human nature consists of soul and body, and that the soul, in turn, is comprised of two faculties, understanding and the will. Content to leave principles of the body to physicians like Hartley, he dealt only with the constituent elements of the soul. Hutcheson charged his students to use their conscience as a guide in analyzing their own sentiments, and then to employ the principle of sympathy in evaluating the actions of others. This twofold attack of self-analysis and fellow-feeling will bring man closer to God's intended purpose for his life, and help him share in the joys and sorrows of others.

Among those who were influenced by Hutcheson's doctrine of sympathy was Adam Smith, who used this thesis as the basis of his popular book, *The Theory of Moral Sentiments* (1759). "We must look at ourselves," argued Smith, "with the same eyes with which we look at others: we must imagine ourselves not the actors, but the spectators of our own character and conduct." Through this practice we will, as Hutcheson also stated, come to an understanding of our sentiments and an appreciation of the feelings of others.

Still another psychological and epistemological theme with eighteenth-century rhetorical implications attracted the attention of the students of human nature. This was the doctrine of "common sense," a theory advocated by the Scottish School of Philosophy in general, and crystallized in the major works of Thomas Reid—*Inquiry into the Human Mind, on the Principles of Common Sense* (1764), and *Essays on the Power of the Human Mind* (1812). Reid interpreted "common sense" as a science which could be coded in self-evident laws of nature recognized and understood by men of all cultures. Further, he held that since it is equated with good common judgment and is "the first-born of reason," it is the final arbiter of disputes that occur between experts on matters of taste and judgment.

We have traced four major responses to the classical rhetorical tradition that occurred in the first half of the eighteenth century: (1) the uncritical acceptance of ancient doctrines; (2) the singling out by the elocutionists of the canon of delivery as the most defensible and urgent need in speech training; (3) the uniting of rhetoric and belles lettres to form a broader view of written and oral communication; and (4) the grounding of all human knowledge, including rhetoric, in human nature. The question which as yet has not been answered is how did Campbell, Blair, and Whately respond to these rhetorical trends?

First, Campbell, Blair and Whately, applying the yardstick of critical judgment to the classical rhetorical theories, endorsed some ideas but modified and rejected others. As a basic premise, they argued that no one can succeed as a speaker, writer, or critic unless he is acquainted with the ancient authors. Of those who deserve special attention, Blair recommended Aristotle, Demetrius, Dionysius of Halicarnassus, Cicero, and, most importantly, Quintilian. Campbell, moreover, found it necessary to remind his theological students to immerse themselves in such specific works as Quintilian's *Institutio Oratoria*, Cicero's *De Inventione* and *De Oratore*, the *Ad Herennium*, Longinus' *On the Sublime*, and the critical essays of Dionysius. Nor was Whately less enthusiastic about the classical writers. He praised the systematic approach of Aristotle, the practical advice of Cicero, and the sound sense of Quintilian. Not to be overlooked is the fact that Blair, Campbell, and Whately gave force to these recommendations by turning freely to the works of the ancients for source material used for the purpose of illustrating their own rhetorical principles. Blair, for instance, repeatedly inserted quotations from his favorite author, Quintilian. On forty-nine separate occasions, Campbell alluded to the classical authors; similarly, Whately made seventy-one references. What they liked most of all was the classical emphasis on rules as an art form. In his *Lectures on Pulpit Eloquence*, Campbell taunted his contemporaries for their inability to extend the highly artistic approach to rhetoric developed by the ancients. "As to the rhetorical art itself," he said, "in the particular the moderns appear to me to have made hardly any advance or improvement upon the ancients. I can say, at least, of most of the performances in the way of institute, which I have had an opportunity of reading on the subject, either in French or English, every thing valuable is servilely copied from Aristotle, Cicero, and Quintilian."

Campbell, Blair, and Whately, in sum, endorsed at least five basic premises which constitute a major emphasis in classical rhetorical theory: (1) they accepted the classical communication model which focused on the speaker, the speech, and the audience; (2) they recognized that effective ethical, logical, and emotional proof are essential to persuasion; (3) they felt that a well-organized address should have interest, unity, coherence, and progression; (4) they held that style should be characterized by perspicuity and vividness; and (5) above all, they suggested that while nature endows the orator with special talents, nurture or

training is needed to improve and perfect these inborn traits.

Notwithstanding the fact that Campbell, Blair, and Whately borrowed heavily from the classical tradition, they deviated sharply from Aristotle, Cicero, and Quintilian in several important respects. Campbell, for example, did not attempt to present an elaborate analysis of each of the five canons of rhetoric containing practical rules for speech improvement. Convinced that this already had been achieved by the ancients, he concentrated instead on the task of formulating a philosophy of rhetoric which would answer Locke's celebrated indictment that rhetoric is a "powerful instrument of Error and Deceit." Blair likewise had a different aim, for he wanted to construct a rhetorical system which would not only help one become an effective speaker, but also a competent writer and critic in the broad field of literature. Whately, whose purpose was more narrow than that of both the ancients and of Campbell and Blair, chose to limit his discussion to "argumentative composition, *generally* and *exclusively*."

A second major modification of classical rhetorical theory occurs in the treatment of the ends of rhetoric. All of the ancient writers, with the possible exception of Cicero and Quintilian, restricted rhetoric to persuasion. But, as we shall note later, Campbell, Blair, and Whately gave equal emphasis to those speech purposes that appeal to the understanding.

A third and more significant alteration of the classical rhetorical tradition is seen in the handling of the canons of *inventio* and *dispositio*. The ancients had stressed the value of common-places or topics as useful aids in helping the speaker discover available means of persuasion. Blair's indictment of this practice is instructive. He rejected the doctrine of *loci communes* by pointing out that it has little effect on the improvement of invention. He supported the claim with the assertion that the inventive ability of a speaker is closely related to genius, and, therefore, cannot be materially affected by rhetorical rules. Then he posed the question: Can we imagine Demosthenes' use of artificial commonplaces in his eloquent attacks on Philip? This argument, echoed by Campbell and Whately, weakens a central position in classical inventional theory.

The ancient rhetoricians, further, had evolved a theory of proof which was compartmentalized into three distinctive forms: ethical, logical, and pathetic. Although these appeals may interact with one another, the boundaries are carefully delineated. Campbell, Blair, and Whately, as we have observed, recognized the persuasive power inherent in these forms of proof but chose, on the other hand, to blend them together, thereby blurring the lines of demarcation. Indeed, Whately goes so far as to treat the subject of "deference," which quite clearly belongs to ethos, as an aspect of the logical principle of presumption. In addition, Campbell's concept of sympathy is equally applicable to ethical and emotional proof.

These modifications of the canon of *inventio* could not help but affect the element of *dispositio*. By eliminating the role of discovery from *inventio*, Campbell, Blair, and Whately altered the starting point to be used in speech preparation. Speakers can assume that since arguments and proof are present from the outset, their principal challenge is to learn how to manage rather than invent or discover ideas. Blair illuminates this approach in his series of lectures entitled, "The Conduct of the Discourse in All Its Parts." Moreover, neither Campbell nor Whately deal with content and organization as separate entities. Thus the boundary lines between *inventio* and *dispositio*, as Ehninger has correctly observed, are blurred, just as they were in the forms of proof.

In dealing with the second rhetorical trend, the elocutionary movement, Campbell, Blair, and Whately supported the emphasis on the conversation pattern of delivery, but deplored the excesses of the elocutionists as a whole. In Blair's brief discussion of delivery, he acknowledged his debt to the movement by admitting that much of his material was taken from the writings of Thomas Sheridan who had stressed the importance of conversing with an audience in a geniune face-to-face manner. Campbell, who ignored delivery in his *Philosophy of Rhetoric*, presented practical rules on articulation and pronunciation in his *Lectures on Pulpit Eloquence* that were consistent with the recommendations of Sheridan. But while endorsing the suggestions of Sheridan, Blair, and Campbell could not condone the highly artificial teachings of other elocutionists such as Walker. Even less so could Whately, who felt constrained to devote Part IV of his *Elements of Rhetoric* to a stinging rebuke of the elocutionary movement for its violation of the natural method. Whately's attack, though not altogether discriminating or fair with respect to Sheridan, remains as the ablest critical analysis of one of the important trends in rhetorical history.

The belletristic movement, the third major rhetorical force operating in the eighteenth century, shaped the theories of Blair, but made little visible impact on the treatises of Campbell and Whately. Blair was impressed with the pedagogically attractive lectures of Adam Smith, which, in uniting the principles of rhetoric and belles lettres, relied on high-compulsion models drawn from classical and modern works. But, unlike Smith, Blair was not willing to limit his theory of criticism to the neoclassical doctrines of "refinement," "correctness," "strict unity," and "simple clarity." Indeed, he occasionally pushed aside these elements of decorum and propriety in order to make room in his system for some of the benchmarks of emerging romanticism, including disorder and irregularity as characteristics of the sublime, a belief that genius is a process in artistic creation, an acceptance of the supernatural elements in Shakespeare, and the general elevation of feeling and emotion. Blair's refusal to be identified with one school of thought contributed to the long-range effect of his work.

Campbell reacted cautiously to this tendency to combine rhetoric and polite literature in a single volume. Although he told his preministerial students to read "the lectures on eloquence lately published by the ingenious and truly eloquent Dr. Blair," he expressed concern about his friend Lord Kames's decision

to incorporate discussions of sculpture, painting, music, architecture, gardening, poetry, and eloquence in his *Elements of Criticism.* Campbell, however, was strikingly similar to Blair and other belletristic scholars in his attempt to amplify rhetorical doctrines with literary examples. In addition to the forty-nine classical references previously mentioned, he made forty-six allusions to Milton, Shakespeare, and Johnson, and 113 to the Augustan authors, Pope, Addison, Swift, and Dryden. Partly because of his own lack of interest in studying the broad range of literature and partly because of his belief that the belletristic school was too eclectic to be original and too superficial and wide in scope to be useful, Whately rejected it as he had the elocutionary movement.

The fourth rhetorical trend in the first half of the eighteenth century, the psychological-philosophical theory of human communication behavior, significantly influenced the principles of Campbell, and to a lesser degree, those of Blair and Whately. Campbell was intrigued by the prospects of letting nature provide the substance out of which rhetoric could be demonstrated and explained. In the preface to his *Philosophy,* he pointed out that his purpose was to exhibit, on the one hand "a tolerable sketch of the human mind," and, "on the other hand, from the science of human nature, to ascertain with greater precision the radical principles of that art, whose object it is, by the use of language, to operate on the soul of the hearer, in the way of informing, convincing, pleasing, moving, or persuading." In grounding rhetoric in human nature, Campbell accepted the following tenets advanced by Locke, Hume, and Hartley; (1) the mind is separated into faculties; (2) the experimental method is superior to syllogistic reasoning;; (3) ideas are held together by the laws of association; and (4) belief and persuasion are dependent upon the liveliness of an idea and the force of emotional appeals. From Hutcheson and Smith, Campbell borrowed the doctrine of sympathy and used it to explain the speaker's relationship with his hearers. Finally, he included Reid's philosophy of "common sense" as one of the three constituent elements of intuitive evidence.

Campbell's heavy reliance upon Locke, Hume, Hartley, and Reid did not prevent him from putting the stamp of his own original mind upon the psychological-epistemological theories of speech included in his text. He produced a new dimension to the faculties of the mind by inserting "imagination" and "passions" between "understanding" and the "will," and by arranging these faculties in an order of natural progression which culminates in the influencing of the will. Further, he attempted to fill in a gap created by Hume in his discussion of association by adding the quality of order in space and time to the other qualities of resemblance, contiguity, and causation. Lastly, he narrowed the meaning of "common sense" so that it would have greater relevance for rhetoric.

Some of the eighteenth-century views on the science of human nature are also present in the works of Blair and Whately. Both in his sermons and in his rhetorical lectures Blair expressed belief in the conviction-persuasion duality. In

his sermon, "On Devotion," preached several years before the publication of his lectures, he supported the claim of the faculty psychologists that enlightening the understanding is only the first step in persuasion.

That religion is essential to the welfare of man, can be proved by the most convincing arguments. But these, however demonstrative soever, are insufficient to support its authority over human conduct. For arguments may convince the understanding, when they cannot conquer the passions. Irresistible they seem in the calm hours of retreat; but, in the season of action, they often vanish into smoke. There are other and more powerful springs, which influence the great movements of the human frame. In order to operate with success on the active powers, the heart must be gained. Sentiment and affection must be brought to the aid of reason. It is not enough that men believe religion to be a wise and rational rule of conduct, unless they relish it as agreeable, and find it to carry its own reward.

Later in the same address Blair echoed the sentiments of Hume when he said: "It is not the sight, so much as the strong conception, or deep impression of an object, which affects the passions. . . . Look abroad in the world, and observe how few act upon deliberate and rational views of their true interest. The bulk of mankind are impelled by their feelings." Blair also gleaned from Smith's *Theory of Moral Sentiments* and Reid's "common sense" philosophy ideas which helped formulate his theories of taste and criticism. Evidence of Whately's indebtedness to the science of human nature may be seen in his discussion of the methods of inquiry and proof, his treatment of the managerial nature of invention, and his four references to Smith's *Moral Sentiments*.

Campbell, Blair, and Whately, it would appear, owed much to the rhetorical trends and psychological-philosophical ideas which flourished in the eighteenth century. But they were equally affected by another source of knowledge, the Judaeo-Christian tradition. By profession they were Protestant divines who believed in a moderate but orthodox interpretation of the Bible and in God's potential role in the affairs of men. As practicing ministers and theologians, they held that the doctrines of religion cope with the noblest subjects confronting man and that they provide the most revealing insights into human nature. Rhetoric at its highest, therefore, becomes the means of conveying sublime themes for the purpose of redeeming man from his degenerate state and of preparing the Christian preacher or layman to defend his faith.

Several important innovations give to the rhetorics of Campbell, Blair, and Whately an ecclesiastical emphasis. First, they drew heavily upon the Scriptures for illustrative material. Campbell, for instance, quotes from the Bible on seventy-six occasions, while Whately alludes to the Scriptures and to his own ecclesiastical writings forty-one times. Secondly, all three rhetorics contain practical advice for religious speakers. Blair developed a lecture on pulpit eloquence, and Campbell covered similar ground when describing types of persons addressed, different forms of discourse, and various speaking occasions. Even more religious instruction is found in Whately's *Elements of Rhetoric.* The most significant aspects of his logical proof, presumption, burden of proof, and refutation, are designed primarily to

help the Christian communicate his religious doctrines with precision and force.

Thirdly, the ecclesiastical nature of these rhetorics is evident in the extended discussions on testimony. In 1762, Campbell, with the approval of Blair, published his *Dissertation on Miracles* in response to Hume's treatise on the same subject which denied the authenticity of biblical testimony. Campbell sought to answer the scepticism of Hume by attempting to demonstrate that nothing in human nature, in recorded history, or in common sense has established a presumption which successfully negates the testimony of the Apostles concerning miracles. Campbell's arguments, later refined in numerous sermons before the Synod of Aberdeen and included in part in his *Philosophy of Rhetoric,* prompted Whately to write a pamphlet in 1819 entitled, *Historic Doubts to Napoleon Bonaparte.* In this popular and clever essay, Whately's purpose was to show how Hume's scepticism with respect to the value of testimony on miracles, if extended to its logical conclusion, could prove the premise that Napoleon Bonaparte never existed. This stress upon past fact rather than future fact elevated testimony to the level of artistic proof.

George Campbell, Hugh Blair, and Richard Whately then were the first rhetoricians of modern rhetoric. Anticipating present-day speech theory, they appreciated the multidisciplinary nature of communication. Thus they saw the relationships between rhetoric and literature, theology, psychology, philosophy, history, language, and natural science. What they borrowed from these and other related disciplines was modified to suit the needs of a developing, dynamic rhetoric with a strong ethical base. Although some of their conclusions can no longer be supported by recent scientific findings, the works of Campbell, Blair, and Whately have left their mark on twentieth-century rhetorical theory. Post-World War II courses combining units on reading, writing, speaking, and listening are directly traceable to Blair's lectures. The practice of assigning expository, persuasive, and entertaining speeches or themes adheres to Campbell's discussion on the ends of discourse. And current procedures in argumentation and in intercollegiate forensics are consistent with the recommendations of Whately. With such an influence, *The Lectures on Rhetoric and Belles Lettres*, the *Philosophy of Rhetoric*, and the *Elements of Rhetoric* can be profitably read by contemporary students of rhetorical theory.

Ronald F. Reid

The Boylston Professorship of Rhetoric and Oratory, 1806–1904: A Case Study in Changing Concepts of Rhetoric and Pedagogy

◊ *Ronald Reid indicates the theme of his essay in the first three paragraphs: he will show how the concept of rhetoric and of the teaching of rhetoric changed during the tenure of the first five holders of the Boylston Professor at Harvard University between 1806 and 1904. John Quincy Adams, the first holder of the Boylston chair, who was later to be the sixth president of the United States, adhered closely to the statutes set forth by Nicholas Boylston, the wealthy Boston merchant who endowed the chair: Adams concentrated on the kind of persuasive oratory that was taught by the Greek and Roman rhetoricians. Each of the four successors to Adams drifted in some measure from the specifications of the original commission. Some of the successors did not root their lectures exclusively or even primarily in the principles and practices of the classical rhetoricians; some began to emphasize written composition more than spoken oratory; others put increasing emphasis on the analysis and criticism of literary texts. Because of the prestige of Harvard, even in the nineteenth century when most of the colleges and universities in the United States were founded, the changes that the Boylston professors made in their curriculum profoundly affected how rhetoric was taught— or neglected—at other schools. ◊*

From the *Quarterly Journal of Speech* 45 (October 1959): 239–257. Reprinted with the permission of the Speech Communication Association and the author.

1.

The latter part of the eighteenth century saw a profound change in American university education: the system of class tutors was replaced by one in which each tutor specialized in an academic field. Philanthropists were then encouraged to endow specialized professorial chairs. One benefactor, Nicholas Boylston, a wealthy Boston merchant who died in 1771, willed Harvard College £1500 for the endowment of the Boylston Professorship of Rhetoric and Oratory. The professorship was one of the earliest to be endowed at Harvard, though insufficient income delayed its activation until 1806.

In the period under consideration, five men occupied the Boylston chair: John Quincy Adams, 1806–1809; Joseph McKean, 1809–1818; Edward T. Channing, 1819–1851; Francis James Child, 1851–1876; Adams Sherman Hill, 1876–1904. The purpose of this essay is not to discuss thoroughly each professor's rhetorical theory and pedagogical method, but to explore the changes in the basic concerns of rhetoric during the nineteenth century at Harvard. In 1806, rhetoric was concerned primarily with persuasive oratory and sunk its roots deeply in the classical tradition. By the time of Hill's retirement, what was called "rhetoric" was concerned not with oratory, but with written composition, expository and literary as well as persuasive, and made little direct reference to classical authors. And not even these new concerns were those of the Boylston professorship, which abandoned rhetoric for literature, oratory for poetry.

Such a dramatic shift of focus took place not only at Harvard, but in higher education generally. This paper, therefore, is a case study in changing concepts of rhetoric during the nineteenth century.

2.

In 1801, Ward Nicholas Boylston threatened to sue Harvard because no Boylston professor had yet been appointed. The lawsuit never materialized, but Harvard activated the professorship. A committee of the Corporation prepared statutes which required the professor (1) to meet the freshmen twice a week to discuss a classical text, portions of which students were to recite in English; (2) to meet the sophomores twice a week, devoting the first half-year to studying an English text, portions of which students were to recite from memory, and the second half to student delivery of non-original dialogues, speeches, and declamations and the writing of translations and original compositions;[1] (3) to meet the juniors fortnightly to instruct from the English text started the previous year and to correct written compositions; (4) to meet the seniors fortnightly to correct written compositions; (5) to assist students who were to speak at public exhibitions; (6) to deliver weekly public lectures to the two upper classes and resident graduates; (7) to preside at weekly declamations of the two upper classes.[2]

The statutes relied heavily upon classical pedagogical and rhetorical doctrines. Classical rhetorical pedagogy consisted of three fundamental parts: study of theory, practice, and exercises in imitation. The requirement of texts and public lectures gave theory an important role in the statutes' prescribed pedagogy. Practice in speaking and writing was demanded of all four classes. The requirement of as much written as oral practice did not mean that the statutes-writers were not primarily interested in oratory, for classical teachers considered written exercises as part of oratorical training.

Ancient teachers gave their students three exercises in imitation: memorization (of textbooks as well as literary and oratical models), translation, and paraphrase, all of which were preceded by the teacher's analysis of the model.[3] The statutes required only the first two exercises and did not demand analysis of models; but, albeit truncated, imitation was integral to the statutes' pedagogical prescription.

The statutes' outline of rhetorical theory, as it was to be developed in the public lectures, was rigidly classical. The professor was to begin his lectures with an historical and biographical account of ancient oratory and orators. He was to explain rhetoric's nature, object, and several kinds and to show its connection with the powers of the human mind. Rhetoric was to be divided into four parts, to be discussed in the following manner:

More particularly, under the head of *Invention* he shall treat of internal and external topics, the state of controversy, the different arguments, proper to demonstrative, deliberative, and judicial discourses; of the character and address of a finished orator, and of the use and excitation of the passions.

Under the head of *Disposition* he shall treat of the properties and uses of each of the parts of a regular discourse, such as Introduction, Narration, Proposition, Confirmation, Confutation, and Conclusion; adding suitable remarks on digression, transition, and amplification.

Under the head of *Elocution*, he shall treat generally and largely of Elegance, Composition, and Dignity, and of their respective requisites; and then particularly of the several species of style, as the low, middle, sublime &c. and of their distinguishing qualities, with respect both to thoughts and the words, illustrating the same by proper examples; and likewise of the various style [sic] of epistles, dialogues, history, poetry, and orations.

Under the head of *Pronunciation* he shall urge the immense importance of a good delivery, and treat particularly of the management of the voice and of gesture; interspersing due cautions against what is awkward or affected, with directions for the attainment of proper action, and incessantly pressing the superior excellence of a natural manner.[4]

Finally, the professor was to discuss the sermon, the methods of improving in eloquence (such as reading, writing, speaking, and imitation) and the "good orator" maxim. He was also to comment on characteristic features of celebrated speakers and writers throughout the lectures.

The second incumbent, Joseph McKean, stated explicitly that the statutes were modeled upon John Ward's *A System of Oratory,* an eighteenth century compendium of classical doctrine.[5] McKean's statement merits our belief, for he knew some of the statutes' writers. Furthermore, probability suggests Ward as the source. Ward was wisely used in America until about 1780;[6] the statutes were written by mature men a quarter-century later. Being laymen, they needed a source. Trained in the classical tradition, it would be natural for them to look to the major interpreter of that tradition.

Finally, comparison of Ward and the statutes reveals remarkable similarity. The organizational schemes are identical, not only in the over-all organization of material, but also in lower levels of subordination. Of special interest is the fact that the statutes required under disposition a lecture on transition, amplification, and digression and, under elocution, lectures on various literary forms, for these methods of synthesizing classical doctrine were unique to Ward in eighteenth century England. Without exception, both Ward and the statutes used the same classical author as the source of a given topic.[7]

3.

Ward Nicholas Boylston's abandonment of his threatened lawsuit was not without its *quid pro quo*, part of which was considerable voice in selecting the first professor. His favorite candidate was his friend, lawyer, and distant relative, John Quincy Adams.[8]

The offer of the professorship, officially tendered in the summer of 1805, tempted Adams. His support of Jefferson's foreign policy was alienating him from the Massachusetts Federalists, and his political future looked bleak.[9] However, he was unwilling to abandon public life. He answered the Corporation that his Senatorial duties "indeed may be temporary, and cease in the course of a few years, but they will be followed by others which would render a constant residence or attendance at Cambridge through the year alike impracticable for me."[10] So eager was the Corporation to obtain Adams's services that it offered the chair on a part-time

basis and allowed him to indicate which duties he would fulfill. He agreed to deliver the public lectures, preside at the declamations of the three upper classes, and help students prepare for exhibitions. He reserved the right to absent himself when Senatorial or other business necessitated.[11]

As a critic of declamation, Adams was concerned with the students' delivery, selection of pieces, and especially the "almost universal neglect of Memory [which] has crept on to such a degree, altogether from the indulgence in the College, which I am endeavouring to reform."[12] When presiding at declamations, he urged students to "discard their prompters, of their own choice, and advised them to let the Speaker always stand alone in the box." "The difficulty," he complained, "is to give them a taste for this exercise, which they now dislike more than any other that is required of them."[13]

As time passed, he became more pleased with the declamations, or at least complained about them less in his diary. A year after assuming the professorship, he was surprised when one speaker used a prompter.[14]

Early in the preparation of his public lectures, Adams objected to the rigidity of the Statutes: "I have also to remark that the minuteness of detail into which this same Article [the one prescribing the content of the lectures] enters, to prescribe the particulars of this Course, appears to me altogether unnecessary, and if to be adhered to, according to the letter, would impose upon me shackles, to which I am not inclined to submit. The divisions and subdivisions of the Science, and the proper means for pursuing its study might, I suppose in general be left to the Judgment of the Professor.''[15] As independent a man as Adams would no doubt have departed substantially from the statutes had he desired. But his modifications were minor, the only noteworthy ones being (1) restoration of memory as one of the five parts of rhetoric, (2) omission of the low-middle-grand stylistic classification, (3) failure to discuss the styles of various types of compositions, and (4) transfer of amplification from the lecture on digression and transition to the one on conclusion.

Adams's adherence to the statutes placed his lectures in the classical tradition. After a few lectures on the history of ancient rhetoric and oratory, he divided rhetoric into its five classical divisions. Invention was developed with lectures on the state of the controversy, topics, the arguments proper to each type of oration, the character of the speaker, and the passions. Disposition was discussed in terms of Cicero's six parts of an oration, with an additional lecture on digression and transition. Elocution was considered from a classical point of view, though he was not nearly so meticulous as the ancients in his catalogue of tropes and figures or in his stylistic classifications. Memory, to which Adams devoted only one lecture, was primarily a report of classical concepts. His lecture on delivery was drawn mostly from Quintilian and Cicero. He did not consider it appropriate to delve into detailed rules of voice and gesture but "The elements of criticism by Lord Kaimes, and the various writings of Sheridan and Walker upon elocution and the art of reading," he told his students, "will deserve your particular attention and study."[16]

On the rare occasions when Adams mentioned modern English rhetoricians, it was usually to disagree with them. Modern rhetoricians' objections to artificial inventional schemes were refuted and Blair's distinction between literal and figurative language pronounced unclear.[17]

Adams, though by his own admission a novice on rhetoric, did not allow his respect for classical writers to prevent him from disagreeing with them at times. For example, he thought Quintilian's "good man" concept not only unrealistic, but harmful; for it might cause students to think that a man was good merely because he happened to be an effective speaker.[18] He objected frequently to the minute divisions and subdivisions to which classical rhetoricians reduced the science. Disposition especially seemed to him to be meticulous beyond the point of endurance— even his own lectures on the subject seemed dull.[19]

More importantly, Adams recognized the need to modernize some aspects of classical theory. He sometimes reported parts of classical doctrine not for their applicability, but to give his students an historical overview of the subject. In his own words,

The purpose of my lectures . . . has been in the first instance to make you familiarly acquainted with the principles, transmitted in the writings of the ancient rhetorical masters; and in the next to discriminate those parts of their precepts, which were inseparably connected with the social institutions and manners of the ages and nations, for which they wrote, from those, which, being founded upon the broad and permanent basis of human nature, are still applicable, and will ever retain their force.[20]

This purpose often led Adams to discuss the relationship between social institutions and rhetoric. For example, although he reported the classical *status* system, he advised his students to use his own modified scheme; the modification was necessitated by the differences in the legal systems of the ancient world and the United States.[21] Similarly, Adams often illustrated principles of deliberative oratory with parliamentary rules and procedures of modern political assemblies.[22]

Basically, then, Adams's lectures were a mixture of instruction on composition and delivery, rhetorical criticism, and an historical sketch of rhetoric. In general, they were classical (though not slavishly so), not because he was afraid to violate the statutes, or because he lacked originality, but because he believed sincerely in classicism's vitality and usefulness in the nineteenth century.

Others shared Adams's belief. Prominent Bostonians often attended his lectures from time to time. The lower classmen also went to hear his public lectures until, as one reported, "requested by Mr. Adams not to do so as we were to hear the course in turn the following year."[23] After Adams resigned in the summer of 1809 to accept a diplomatic appointment, his students requested that he publish his lectures. He left the manuscript with two friends, Judge Davis and the Reverend Joseph Buckminster, who made only minor changes concerning capitalization and punctuation and omitted a few remarks relating to the opening or closing of a term and a few unfavorable comments on contemporaries, before sending it to the printer.

4.

The Corporation lost no time in replacing Adams, electing Joseph McKean on August 26, 1809. Interestingly, McKean, a former minister, was known primarily for his mathematical ability. He had previously declined the Hollis Professorship of Mathematics and Natural Philosophy because of ill health. But specialization was still only a budding phenomenon, and it was not unusual for a person to be offered chairs in different fields.

Inasmuch as McKean was a full-time professor, the Corporation outlined his duties much as they had originally been envisioned, except that he had no responsibility for teaching freshmen. He was required to deliver private lectures to the sophomores on Blair, to deliver public lectures to the upperclassmen, and to criticize various oral and written exercises.[24]

McKean's tenure resulted in no radical change in the concept of rhetoric. Less original than Adams, McKean organized his public lectures in strict accordance with the statutes. There is considerable internal evidence that he relied heavily upon John Ward in his classical treatment of rhetoric.[25]

Nevertheless, McKean's public lectures foreshadowed changes to come. There were traces of Blair and numerous references to Campbell, especially when treating emotional proof. Furthermore, although McKean defended the inventional schemes of status and topics against Blair's charge of pedantry, he was less enthusiastic about their utility than Adams. His frequent praise of Campbell and his occasional objections to the stringency of the statutes make one wonder whether his lectures might not have been modeled upon the creative English rhetorics if he had possessed a free hand. The statutes served as a dam to protect a rigidly-interpreted classicism from an English flood—but the dam was beginning to leak.

5.

The Corporation had difficulty in finding an acceptable replacement for McKean, largely because of the small income earned from the endowment. A year after McKean's death in 1818, the president of Harvard wrote George Bancroft that "Whether it will be vacant longer or be committed to Mr. Nicholls of Portland, Mr. Davis, Mr. Daniel Oliver of Salem, to Mr. Ed. T. Channing, to Mr. Frothingham [who had been McKean's assistant for several years], Mr. Brazer or Mr. Quincy, cannot be told."[26] In the fall of 1819, a decision was made. The Corporation elected Channing, a young lawyer who was spending more time editing the struggling young *North American Review* than he was on his meager law practice.

Channing's election aroused a storm of protest. Critics noted that he had been expelled from Harvard in the student rebellion of 1807, charged mediocrity, and whispered that his election was due only to the prominence of his brother, William Ellery Channing.

Channing also had defenders. Under the pen-name of *Popularis Aura* one Channing supporter suggested that his critics were evidently modest, for they wrote anonymously and had not been elected overseers.[27] If he is young, wrote *Fenelon,* so was Pitt when he became prime minister and so are many of the other professors.[28] *Justice,* after maintaining that college appointments were not fit subjects for public controversy, entered the debate by defending Channing's talents both as speaker and editor.[29]

The controversy would be merely a matter of interest, but not of significance, to historians of rhetoric were it not for the common argument that, regardless of the *degree* of Channing's talents, he did not have the *right kind.* *Alumnus,* singularly unimpressed with the fact that Channing was editor of a literary magazine, wrote a slashing attack in which he expressed surprise that the Corporation would elect anyone other than "an *able, practical orator*" and urged the appointment of someone "who had some acquaintance with public speaking in its various forms, and who had moreover some knowledge of mankind, and of nature & operations of our government, derived from actual observation and experience."[30]

Although explicitly acknowledging Channing's ability, *Harvard* made much the same point:

It cannot, however, be pretended that an editor of a Review need possess all those qualifications, which are deemed essential to a Professor of Rhetoric and Oratory. An acquaintance with the rules of criticism by no means implies a thorough knowledge of the principles of oratory. A person may be a good writer, and in the same time an indifferent speaker. Indeed, it is not a very difficult thing to write a tolerable essay; and to compose a decent oration, according to the rules of art, does not require superior powers of mind, and is not perhaps beyond the reach of ordinary talents. But to excel in public speaking, and to become an accomplished orator, has justly been considered among the highest efforts of human genius. In this Country, which opens a wide field for the display of eloquence, its importance will be duly estimated. The genius of our government, its popular character which pervades all its civil institutions, seems to invite the highest exercise of this sublime art. In short, here, as in the Republics of Greece and Rome, eloquence is power, and almost everything comes under its dominion.

Although agreeing that the policy of hiring young, studious men was good, *Harvard* continued:

But, we think the department of Rhetoric and Oratory furnishes an exception. Some experience and practice in the various forms of public speaking, as well as knowledge of books, are essential to a teacher of oratory. The art of persuasion, the power of producing conviction by addressing the passions, the feelings, the prejudices, and the understandings of men, cannot be thoroughly acquired in the closet. Besides, the Professor in that branch should be able to instruct by example, to rouse the genius and excite the emulation of youth by exhibiting before them a model for imitation.[31]

These critics may have been dreaming of the days when a United States Senator had caused considerable stir on the campus. But more than nostalgia was involved. Implicit in their views were some traditional ideas about rhetorical pedagogy: a teacher should be a good model; rhetorical doctrine must come from experience as well as from books; rhetoric and literature are separate disciplines; rhetoric is closely related to politics; oratory, not writing, is rhetoric's major concern.

6.

Although Channing's duties paralleled McKean's, his performance of them changed strikingly the nature of rhetoric. His public lectures, most of which were published after his death, bore little resemblance to those of Adams and McKean.[32]

First, Channing broadened the scope of rhetoric by his well-known definition of it as

a body of rules derived from experience and observation, extending to all communication by language and designed to make it efficient. It does not ask whether a man is to be a speaker or writer,—a poet, philosopher, or debater; but simply,—is it his wish to be put in the right way of communicating his mind with power to others, by words spoken or written. If so, rhetoric undertakes to show him rules or principles which will help to make the expression of his thoughts effective.[33]

Whereas McKean was primarily concerned with persuasion and distinguished rhetoric from poetic on the basis of the former having utility as its purpose and the latter having pleasure, Channing specifically objected to the "arbitrary and unwise" limitation of rhetoric to persuasion and broadened it to include poetry.[34] Persuasion, to affect the emotions, he argued,

appeals to man's imagination and taste,—to his sense of beauty and grandeur and moral excellence,—to his sense of wit and humor and irony and satire. . . . And surely the written book, the novel, the history, the fable and the acted play make their approaches to the heart in the same direction and by use of the same methods.[35]

Channing made one seemingly significant limitation on his broad definition:

It has nothing to do with the different departments of the Belles Lettres, as so many distinct forms of writing. It has nothing to do with an analysis of poetry, history, fiction, biography, the drama, &c., or with their laws or beauties. It leaves this whole field of criticism to other laborers, and limits its inspection of general literature to the purpose of ascertaining and illustrating the essentials of accurate and forcible expression in all good composition.[36]

In short, rhetoric was concerned with composition, not with criticism.

Despite his theoretical exclusion of criticism from rhetoric's domain, Channing did much to identify criticism with rhetoric. His public lectures, which by 1833 were entitled "Rhetoric and Criticism," were, as Wolff observes, "descriptive and critical rather than practical; he gives a student standards by which to judge existing discourse rather than assistance in producing his own."[37]

In the published version, almost half the lectures (eight of twenty) were devoted to demonstrative, deliberative, judicial, and pulpit oratory; but, unlike his predecessors' lectures, they gave no instruction in analysis or composition. His lecture on deliberative oratory, for example, was a critical discussion of the relationship of deliberative speaking to free institutions. There was no consideration of how a deliberative speech should be organized, nothing about the arguments to be employed or the emotions to be aroused.

Of the remaining lectures, three were clearly literary, as the titles—"Literary Tribunals," "Forms of Criticism," "Permanent Literary Fame"—suggest. Other lectures treated topics such as "The Orator and His Times," "The Study of Our Own Language," the writer's preparation and habits of reading.

Examination of the lecture notes of one of his students for 1833 reveals even more clearly the critical bias of the lectures. Of the twenty-one lectures,

probably the year's total, the first treated the four types of oratory, corresponding to the eight such lectures in the published version. The next five were on literary criticism: two on the forms of criticism, one on poetry, one on criticism of poems and novels, one an analysis of Scott's novels. The remaining lectures corresponded roughly to the latter lectures in the book.[38]

Channing's criticism in some respects was rhetorical, as when he analyzed the characteristics of American legal oratory and drew distinctions between legal and political oratory.[39] However, the criticism was mostly literary.

Channing made other significant departures from his predecessors' theories. He abandoned not only the classical pattern of organizing his lectures, but also the classical orientation of much of the theory. Invention was stripped of its analytical schemes. Regarding such aids, one student took the following notes:

The "Invention" of the ancients signifies the discovery of whatever belongs to the subject. To aid it they invented "Topics" or "Communes loci"—Though pedantic in their character, these Topics are founded on observation of the course of the mind—They are generalizations of the usual trains of thought—*They are of no practical use*—A great thinker needs no artificial aid. A superficial thinker would only become an endless talker, concealing his ignorance in the use of forms.[40]

Moreover, Channing's lectures contained no detailed accounts of emotional and ethical proof, which were integral to Adams's and McKean's classical doctrine.

Inasmuch as Channing disapproved of artificial aids in analysis, it is not surprising that he applied the same principle to synthesis. Disposition was almost completely ignored. Although there were some general statements about judgment, there was no detailed treatment of the functions and methods of the various parts of an oration.

Channing's discussion of style embodied some classical concepts; but there was nothing like McKean's detailed treatment of elocution, in which style was divided into elegance (consisting of perspicuity and purity), composition (consisting of period, order, juncture, and number) and dignity (consisting of tropes and figures). Instead, Channing discussed only general concepts, setting forth the view that precision (not persuasiveness) was the main ingredient of good style. Ornament was permissible—if it did not interfere with precision—but he urged caution in selecting tropes and figures.[41]

Channing departed from classical precept not in his rhetorical theory only; his pedagogical practice modified significantly the classical three-fold approach of theory, imitation, and practice. Channing taught theory; but, as set forth in his lectures, it was very general, devoid of detailed instructions. Only in part was this generality corrected by reliance on textbooks. Channing continued using Blair for a number of years but later discontinued it, and, after considerable experimentation, finally settled upon books II and III of Campbell's *Philosophy of Rhetoric,* together with Ebenezer Porter's *Analysis of Rhetorical Delivery* and Lowth's *Grammar,* for the sophomores; Whately's *Logic* for the juniors; and Whately's *Rhetoric* for the se-

niors.[42] Even *in toto* his selections from these texts were limited to grammar, style, delivery, and logical argumentation; there was little on non-logical rhetorical invention or disposition.

The doctrine of imitation was severely modified, for Channing objected to its fundamental premise, the use of models.[43] Furthermore, he believed that "Translations are difficult exercises for young writers, & are apt to give their styles the manner of a foreign idiom."[44] Memorization of texts, however, continued.

Practice also continued, though a subtle but significant shift of emphasis from speaking to writing took place. Although the statutes, like Channing, believed that the same rhetorical principles applied to both speaking and writing, it is nonetheless significant that in his lectures Channing usually used the word "writer." It was "A Writer's Preparation" and "A Writer's Habits," not a speaker's preparation or habits.

Furthermore, Channing, although a rigorous critic of themes, was an indifferent critic of declamation. Former students frequently remembered him as a theme-corrector, but there is a paucity of references to his oratorical teaching.[45] One of the few who did record something wrote: "Mr. Channing listened attentively to these declamations and marked them, I think, on a scale of twenty-four; but he never made any comment, unless it were to rebuke the choice of a piece offensively coarse, or some outrageous grotesqueness in delivery."[46]

However, Channing bemoaned the deficiencies in his students' delivery and believed that elocutionary instruction would help.[47] He therefore persuaded the overseers to employ an assistant to supervise additional exercises in declamation. His first assistant was a zealous elocutionist, Jonathan Barber, famous for his bamboo wheel, which enabled him to teach gestures in all 360 degrees to—alas—an unappreciative student body.[48] After Barber's departure, Channing had a number of assistants, most of them young graduates who stayed for a short time while engaging in further studies of their own.

Many of Channing's departures from classicism can be traced to British influence. With the entire intellectual atmosphere permeated with British thought, it was inevitable that British literary and rhetorical concepts would ultimately dominate American rhetoric.[49]

As Ehninger points out, all three major British rhetoricians—Blair, Whately, and Campbell—made significant departures from classical doctrine.[50] For example, none of them organized his book according to the standard classical pattern, all of them abandoned the inventional schemes of status and topics. Faculty psychology, literary concepts of genius and taste, the identification of rhetoric with belles lettres—all these movements were afoot in eighteenth-century English rhetoric and permeated Channing's theory and teaching. Furthermore, Channing was strongly influenced by the Common Sense doctrine.[51]

Channing's changes in the concept of rhetoric cannot be explained exclusively in terms of British influence. His own primary interest in literature was also a factor. In devoting almost a fourth of his public lectures to literary criti-

cism he had precedent in Blair, but not in Campbell or Whately. He could have assigned his sophomores book I of Campbell instead of just those parts relating to style. Nothing in Campbell or Whately inspired him to assign his students a preponderance of literary topics for themes. His occasional evening meetings in his study with students need not have been devoted to reading poets and novelists; they could have been spent studying political orations or rhetorical theory. Because of his own interests, Channing seriously weakened rhetoric's classic relation to politics. Perhaps *Harvard* and *Alumnus* had been right, after all.

7.

The literary concerns which Channing brought to the Boylston professorship never disappeared, Indeed, the trend to literary criticism became more pronounced during the tenure of Francis James Child, who was graduated as head of the class of 1846 and served as Channing's assistant from 1848 to 1850. It was, however, a different type of literary study, for Child was influenced profoundly by German scholarship, which he imbibed at Göttingen before succeeding to the Boylston professorship in 1851.[52]

Child found academic life in Germany radically different from that in his homeland. Instead of giving marks for schoolboy recitations, the German professor lectured or used the seminar method. Whereas the American student took a prescribed course of study, the Germans extended their ideal of Academic Freedom to the student, so that an unrestricted elective system pre-vailed. The American professor was almost exclusively a teacher; his German counterpart was a productive scholar. The Americans settled for a little knowledge; "A German scholar," as one German-trained American Ph.D. wrote, "sits and smokes and drinks coffee, and studies his sixteen hours a day, partly because it feels good."[53] The lecture and seminar methods, the elec-tive system, the concept of research and productive scholarship, the Ph.D. degree—all these are integral to Amer-ican universities today, but they were new to Child's generation.[54]

The German approach to rhetoric and literature was substantially dif-ferent from Harvard's. As early as the mid-seventeenth century, the German universities had begun to abandon Latin Humanism for a new type of Hu-manism. "Latin poetry and eloquence," Paulsen writes of the period, "were now as much despised as outward scho-lastic plunder by the 'moderns,' with Thomasius at their head, as the philos-ophy and theology of pseudo-philoso-phers and theologians had been two centuries before."[55] German scholar-ship soon thereafter abandoned the study of composition—written or spoken—and became preoccupied with criticism. Thus, Child was immersed in an environment which had a long tra-dition of criticism, but not of composi-tion.

German criticism did not ignore clas-sical rhetoric and oratory, though it ap-proached the subject as it did everything else—with a heavy-handed factual, "scientific," philological emphasis. But Child became more enchanted with its

researches in early English linguistics and literature.

Child returned to America inspired with German ideals of scholarship. He believed passionately in the concept of research, as one of Albert Bush-nell Hart's reminiscences illustrates: "Francis James Child used to say with a disarming twinkle that the University would never be perfect until we got rid of all the students. This was a hint at one of the strongest and most benefi-cent duties of the modern university, namely, to contribute to the world's stock of knowledge."[56] Putting his ideal into practice, Child acquired an inter-national reputation for his researches on Chaucer and Spenser and his collec-tions of Scottish and English ballads.

Because Child was one of the first American scholars to be trained in Ger-many, he occupied for many years an academically lonely position. René Wellek credits him with being the only productive scholar in the modern lan-guages in the United States during the 1850's.[57] With only limited support from other faculty members, his at-tempts to introduce advanced literary and linguistic studies were frustrated, just as the larger movement to intro-duce German methods was blocked time and again.

Perhaps because of these frustra-tions, the work of listening to decla-mations and correcting themes grew increasingly distasteful. Knowing that the German universities did not bother with such "elementary" things, he came to question their academic va-lidity. "Declamation," he wrote a friend, "we (I and a majority of the Faculty) ut-terly disapprove. We consider it perni-cious, and the abandonment of it as an 'advance' in the teaching of oratory, if,'' he added significantly, "such teaching is attempted." Themes, he concluded, deserve no more attention.[58] Writing of Child's years as Boylston professor, Barrett Wendell, a long-time colleague, wrote: "This work, as is well known, he never found congenial; and whatever the opinions with which he began it, he certainly relinquished it with grave doubts of its usefulness in the higher education."[59]

Regardless of his wishes, Child was obliged to continue the professorship along somewhat traditional lines. The public lectures continued to be required, and students continued to deliver declamations and to write themes. As in Channing's time, the sophomores studied Campbell while the juniors and seniors read Whately's *Logic* and *Rhetoric*.

However, Child made some substantial philological inroads into rhetoric's domain. The public lectures, which he entitled "English Language and Literature," completely ignored rhetoric in preference to linguistics and criticism. "I do not know that I can do anything better at present," he wrote a friend while preparing them, "than to select the age of Chaucer for my main subject & to group around old Jeffry & his time what I may have to say of earlier poetry."[60]

Child also introduced some linguistics and literature, especially the study of Anglo-Saxon, into the sophomore year, although that class continued to study Campbell. Limited success was achieved in getting languages taught as an elective. The Harvard *Catalogue* for 1853–54 announced that "The Gothic and Anglo-Sax Languages are taught (to those who desire to learn them), by Professor Child." Finally, in 1867, a credit-bearing elective course in Anglo-Saxon was authorized.

Child's victory over rhetoric came into sight in 1869, when Charles William Eliot became president of Harvard. During Eliot's presidency the ever-increasing pressures for change finally broke down all resistance and within twenty years Harvard resembled a German university more than the Harvard of Channing's time. A system of formal courses was established and in its wake came the elective system. "In 1874–75," Morison records, "President Eliot could announce that all required studies were now in Freshman year, except a few odd bits of Rhetoric, History, Philosophy, and Political Economy."[61] In 1883, the elective system was extended to the freshman year and "the President announced the 'practical completion of a development which began sixty years ago.' There were now no required courses save Freshman English and German (or French), Sophomore and Junior themes and forensics, and two easy half-year lecture courses, one on Chemistry and one on Physics."[62]

The rise of the system of courses resulted in some structural changes in the Boylston professorship. The public lectures were abandoned, inasmuch as all material was transmitted to students in "courses." "Rhetoric" and "elocution" became separate course titles, although they were given by the same department. Thus, Channing's partial abandonment of delivery to his assistant was now completed. Delivery was no longer part of rhetoric.

Eliot's strongly-held belief in the elective system was tempered by his belief in the importance of teaching students to express themselves clearly and effectively. In his famous *Atlantic* papers, written shortly before his election to the presidency, he wrote of the new scientific education:

No men have greater need of the power of expressing their ideas with clearness, conciseness, and vigor than those whose avocations require them to describe and discuss material resources, industrial processes, public works, mining enterprises, and the complicated problems of trade and finance. In such writings embellishment may be dispensed with, but the chief merits of style—precision, simplicity, perspicuity, and force—are never more necessary.[63]

All education should include "training in the power of expression—in clear, concise exposition, and in argument, or the logical setting forth of a process of reasoning."[64] Eliot, therefore, never permitted rhetoric to become an elective, though the advanced courses and elocution eventually lost their prescribed status.

Yet Eliot was sympathetic with Child's desire to introduce critical literary studies. In 1870, only a year after Eliot's inauguration, John Richard Dennett was made Assistant Professor of Rhetoric in order to give Child time for literature courses. Dennett was later replaced by Adams Sherman Hill, a Harvard graduate of 1853 and a lawyer-turned-journalist.[65]

A few years later, in 1876, Child was offered a professorship at The Johns Hopkins University, which began operation that same year. Johns Hopkins, the first American university founded on the German model, emphasized graduate study and productive scholarship. It would have been an excellent place for Child; but personal considerations as well as Eliot's reforms kept him at Harvard. The offer, however, was credited by Child with motivating Harvard to relieve him entirely of work in rhetoric.[66] The new arrangement was formalized by his being made "Professor of English"—the first such title at Harvard—and Hill's being promoted to the Boylston professorship.

Basically, Child did not change the concept of rhetoric. He simply avoided the subject as much as possible; and in the process he laid the foundations for the Department of English.

8.

Hill preserved the status quo for a short time. Elocution remained outside his realm. The sophomores continued to study part of Campbell and some English literature while the advanced classes read Whately. Themes and declamations continued.

Changes, however, were not long in coming. One was the incorporation of rhetoric into a new Department of English. The establishment of formal departments resulted from increasing specialization, enlarged course offerings, and a larger student body and staff. The courses taught by Child, Hill, and the elocutionist were considered closely enough related to be under one department. The name "English" was apt, inasmuch as either "rhetoric," "composition," "philology," "linguistics," or "literature" would have described only part of the department's work.

Partially as a result of the departmental name, the term "rhetoric" fell out of fashion. The old rhetoric courses came to be called "composition and rhetoric," "composition," or simply "English." The word "rhetoric," when used at all, eventually became limited to the required beginning course.

There was also considerable shifting of requirements. The sophomore course was put on the freshman level and the advanced courses reduced correspondingly. As the elective system obtained a firmer grip on the college, the two advanced courses were reduced to half-year requirements and ultimately were made electives. At the same time, as the number of courses offered by the college expanded, additional composition electives were added, including, in 1878, one in oral discussion for seniors.

The most significant change was rhetoric's abandonment of oratory. The advanced courses, commonly known during this period as "themes and forensics," consisted almost exclusively of written work. Writing in 1894, Barrett Wendell, who had joined the faculty as Hill's assistant in 1880, described the courses as follows:

In the half-course prescribed for Sophomores, lectures are given on Exposition, Argument, Description, and Narration; and during the year the students write twelve themes, of from five hundred to a thousand words. These are carefully criticised by teachers, and generally rewritten by the students, with this criticism in mind. In the half-course prescribed for Juniors there are lectures on Argument; and the students make one formal analysis of a masterpiece of argumentative composition, and write four arguments—known as "forensics"— of from a thousand to fifteen hundred words. Each of these is preceded by a brief, which is criticised by a teacher before the forensic is written. The forensics themselves are also carefully criticised, and frequently rewritten. All teachers engaged in these courses keep frequent office hours for personal conference with their pupils.[67]

The beginning course, too, gave much practice in writing, none in public speaking:

Lectures based . . . [on the text] are given, and also lectures dealing with some aspects of English Literature. Of these lectures students are required to write summaries. Besides this written work, every member of the class writes a composition in the classroom once a week; and these compositions are carefully criticised by the teachers.[68]

The reasons for rhetoric's abandonment of oratory were numerous. Perhaps one was Hill's interests; for he came to Harvard after almost two decades as a journalist. Second, Eliot's reforms, based on a radically new concept of education, brought a new type of student to the university. The first three Boylston professors taught in an age when almost every student was destined for one of two professions—the ministry or law, both of which involved the practice of public speaking. But the new trends, begun during Child's term and brought to completion during Hill's, brought budding chemists and physicians, engineers and technicians, businessmen and administrators, scholars and poets to the university. Many of these students would never give a speech in their lives. Students and faculty alike came increasingly to look upon composition as nothing more than a tool for help in getting through college; and, as the authors of the famous report of the overseers' committee on composition and rhetoric pointed out, writing became increasingly important to the student:

About the year 1870 a change began to make itself felt, first in numbers and then in the methods of the college, which gradually brought about what amounted to a revolution. The classes increased in size nearly fourfold, so as to become wholly unmanageable for oral recitation, and the elective system was greatly enlarged; step by step, the oral method of instruction was then abandoned, and a system of lectures, with periodic written examinations, took its place; so that at last the whole college work was practically done in writing. The need of facility in written expression was, of course, correspondingly increased. Without the power of writing his mother tongue readily and legibly, a college student was not equipped for the work he had to do, inasmuch as he did not have at his control an implement essential for doing that work.[69]

Even law and the ministry were undergoing changes which minimized the importance of oratorical ability. Law began to specialize, so that not all lawyers appeared in court to plead cases. Although no analagous change took place in the ministry, the German influence inspired new scholarly interests in such matters as ecclesiastical history and Biblical criticism, which occupied much of the future minister's time.

Finally, American society generally was less interested in oratory than it had been in ante-bellum days. It is beyond the scope of this paper to analyze the reasons; but the decline was a fact. Conversely, increasing mass literacy and a flood of popular magazines and newspapers increased the importance of the written word.

These factors influenced not only the curriculum-makers and teachers, but also the students. George Pierce Baker,

a student in the early 1880's and later a member of the faculty, testifies that there was a notable lack of student interest in public speaking during that decade. It was not until the advent of intercollegiate debate during the 1890's that interest in speaking revived and several courses in oral argumentation and debate were added to the curriculum at the request of students. Significantly, however, rhetoric had become so identified with writing that the new speech courses were neither called "rhetoric" nor made part of the Boylston professor's work. Instead, they were under Baker's jurisdiction.[70]

An equally profound change concerned the nature and pedagogical role of rhetorical theory. Its role was minimized, especially in the advanced courses, where textbooks were eventually abandoned. The underlying pedagogical principle was that a combination of practice and criticism, not theory, was the best way to learn to write. This view was explicitly acknowledged by Wendell: "In the courses in Composition, prescribed and elective alike, little importance is attached to theoretical knowledge of rhetoric as distinguished from constant practice in writing under the most minute practicable criticism. . . . It will be seen . . . that the use of text-books, as distinguished from personal instruction, is reduced to a minimum."[71] In the beginning course, there continued to be a text; but in 1878, Campbell was replaced by Adam Sherman Hill's own simplified *Principles of Rhetoric*.[72] Emphasis was on practice.

Another reason for the de-emphasis of theory was acceptance of the belief that students would learn much about composition by the study of literature. The study of literature in the freshman course, however, was not a return to the classical concept of imitation. On the contrary, Hill opposed imitation, per se, because "the best part of a good style is incommunicable."[73] "One may, however, get good from a master of English by unconscious absorption," he continued, "as one acquires good-manners by associating with gentlemen and ladies."[74]

Changes in pedagogical ideas about the importance of theory in relation to practice and literature were no more significant than changes in the nature of the theory itself. Although Hill's text was not original (indeed, it was eclectic, drawing on classical doctrines, Channing's definition of rhetoric, Herbert Spencer's principle of economy of style, Whately's concepts of argumentation, and Campbell's principles of style—to name only some of the more important sources), his selection of concepts, the emphasis he gave them, and his special method of organizing and simplifying them changed substantially the nature of rhetorical theory.

Defining rhetoric as "the art of efficient communication by language,"[75] Hill divided his text into two parts, "Composition in General" and "Kinds of Composition." The first part was divided into two books, the first on "Grammatical Purity." "The foundations of rhetoric," he wrote, "rest upon grammar; for grammatical purity is a requisite of good writing."[76] The test of purity was present use, not the origin of the language. Hill adopted Campbell's three rules of purity—precision, simplicity, and euphony—and devoted

many pages to violations of good usage—barbarisms, improprieties, solecisms.

The second book, "Rhetorical Excellence," was devoted largely to style, one chapter being devoted to "Choice of Words" and another to "Number of Words." The final chapter, "Arrangement," considered the arrangement of words in sentences, sentences in paragraphs, and paragraphs in whole compositions. The same principles of clearness, force, and ease were applied to all levels of arrangement.

The second part of Hill's text, "Kinds of Composition," was divided into description, narration, exposition, and argument.

Compared to earlier rhetorical theory, the book contained many unique features. First, whereas rhetoric had previously more or less presupposed grammar, Hill made grammar a major part of rhetoric. Somewhat given to pedantry, Hill, the "high priest of correctness and conformity to good usage,"[77] turned grammatical correctness into an ideal of composition—almost to the exclusion of other considerations.

Second, invention was completely abandoned. Channing had objected merely to inventional schemes, not invention, per se; but Hill explicitly excluded the most important branch of classical rhetoric: "the function of rhetoric is not to provide the student of composition with materials for thought . . . but to stimulate and train his powers of expression."[78]

Third, although Hill gave more attention to arrangement than Channing had, the application of the same general principles of clearness, force, and ease to all levels of arrangement blended *dispositio* with *elocutio*. Furthermore, very little attention was given to arrangement of the whole composition.

Fourth, the division of compositions into exposition, narration, description, and argument preserved Channing's broad definition of rhetoric while at the same time giving students more detailed instructions on composing each type than Channing's students had received.

Of particular interest is Hill's treatment of argument and persuasion; for it was far removed from that envisioned by the original statutes. The word "argument" was considered the broader term, and Hill's discussion of it, no doubt influenced by Whately, revolved around such concepts as presumption, burden of proof, evidence, and types of reasoning. "Persuasion" was restricted to appeals to the feelings; it was a useful "adjunct" to argument inasmuch as conviction (produced by argument) was sometimes insufficient to influence the will.

Hill's brief discussion of persuasion is a clear example of his reorganization and simplification of older doctrines. He reduced persuasion to five principles: (1) concreteness, (2) reserved force (Spencer's principle of economy), (3) climax, (4) variety, (5) adaptation. He also discussed the exordium and peroration and devoted a short special section to simplicity and sincerity.

Finally, the over-all tone of dogmatism which pervaded Hill's book was unlike that of any of his predecessors'. He reduced rhetoric to lists of principles and rules, set forth *ex cathedra*.

Various factors brought about these changes. Albert Kitzhaber, in an excellent discussion of the leading texts of this period, related the dogmatic tone of Hill's book to his personality. Hill seems not to have been a popular teacher and had a reputation as a dogmatic and biting theme-critic.[79]

Second, the intellectual life of the period was dominated by interest in science. Darwinism was the talk of the day, science courses were receiving considerable attention in the curriculum, the president of Harvard was a chemist, even literary scholarship was interested primarily in "scientific," philological fact-finding. Curiously, this scientific environment did not prompt rhetoric to emphasize its investigative and analytical aspects. But it is not curious that in an age when scientists talked of the "fundamental laws of nature," a rhetorician—even one who insisted that rhetoric was an art, not a science—would seek to reduce rhetoric to a few fundamental "rules." Nor is it curious that scientists often overestimated man's rationality, thereby creating an atmosphere more conducive to Whately's concepts of logical argument than to its "adjunct," persuasion.

Finally, rhetoric's immediate environment—the Department of English—needs to be considered. As enrollment increased, Hill's staff was enlarged; but the dividing line between composition and literature was increasingly blurred, so that it eventually disappeared. Hill himself taught several literature courses later in his career. With few exceptions, the new English teachers were more interested in literature than in traditional rhetoric. Small wonder that the literary forms of composition, description and narration, received attention at the expense of persuasion. Furthermore, the philological orientation of literary scholarship made it natural for rhetoric to concern itself with pedantic details of grammatical correctness at the expense of traditional rhetoric.

9.

Rhetoric's place in the university became increasingly insecure. Most English professors considered it a distraction from literary scholarship.

The sharpest attack came from a special committee of the overseers. After examining a mass of student themes, it pronounced them intolerable and, taking note of the tremendous amount of faculty time being expended on correcting simple grammatical errors, recommended that the dismal business of teaching fundamentals of composition be relegated to the high schools. If composition is to be taught in college, it concluded, let it be as an advanced elective.[80]

Yet rhetoric survived. In 1894, Wendell reported that of the nine full courses offered by the department, three were in composition; of the seventeen half-courses, four were in composition. In addition, elocution and oral discussion were available.[81] Within a few years after Wendell's report, several debate courses were inaugurated. When Bliss Perry joined the Harvard faculty in 1906, he was impressed—and, despite his earlier career as a teacher of oratory, somewhat puzzled—by the persistent faith in the value of composition courses.[82]

10.

By 1904, when Hill retired, the old endowed professorships were no longer independent departments; the university had grown too large for that. They were positions of honor, with old titles being maintained for tradition's sake, not because they necessarily described accurately the work of the professor.

LeBaron Russell Briggs was elected as Hill's successor. As an older, well-established professor, he taught advanced work, his main interest being literary composition on the graduate level. Thus the final proceedings were completed in the divorce of rhetoric and oratory from the Boylston Professorship of Rhetoric and Oratory.

11.

The history of the Boylston professorship might be summarized in terms of three influences: classical, English, German. The latter, coupled with the trend toward practical education, revolutionized the entire university in such a way that traditional rhetoric was thought to have little place in the curriculum. Philology flourished, rhetoric decayed.

These same trends occurred to a greater or lesser degree in all of American higher education. Thus, rhetoric underwent a marked decline, one which has been partially reversed only in the twentieth century. But although rhetoric declined, it served as the basis for departments in English language and literature.

Notes

1. Although the statutes do not state specifically that the dialogues, speeches, and declamations were to be non-original, the context implies it. Furthermore, *The Laws of Harvard College* (Cambridge, 1807) states that underclassmen are "to read, or deliver memoriter, *some celebrated orations, speeches, or dialogues,* [italics mine] in Latin or English, whereby they may be directed or assisted in their elocution and pronunciation." P. 6.
2. The statutes were adopted at a Corporation meeting, April 30, 1801; MS Harvard College Records, IV, gff., Harvard Archives.
3. See Donald Lemen Clark, *Rhetoric in Greco-Roman Education* (Morningside Heights, New York, 1957), esp. pp. 16gff; *John Milton at St. Paul's School* (New York, 1948), esp. pp.168ff.
4. Harvard College Records IV, 10ff.
5. Joseph McKean, Lectures on rhetoric and oratory delivered to his classes in Harvard College; MS in Harvard Archives.
6. Warren Guthrie, "The Development of Rhetorical Theory in America, 1635–1850," *Speech Monographs*, XIV (1917), 45.
7. Donald M. Goodfellow, in his "The First Boylston Professor of Rhetoric and Oratory," *New England Quarterly*, XIX (September 1946), 372–89, conjectures (p. 376) that the article on oratory in the third edition of the *Encyclopedia Brittanica* (1797) was the source of the statutes. Even if Goodfellow is correct, Ward is the model for the statutes, for the article not only refers the reader to Ward's *System*, but also is clearly a digest of that treatise. However, the article omits certain material which is in the *System* and which is called for by the statutes. Ward devoted several lectures to the styles of various types of composition, such as epistles and dialogues, but the *Encyclopedia* discusses only the style of the orator; similarly, there is nothing in the article about the methods of improving in eloquence (imitation, etc.), a subject which Ward considers at some length.

8. For additional details regarding the establishment of the professorship and Ward Nicholas Boylston's role in getting Adams elected, see Goodfellow, pp. 373ff. Adams's grandmother, Abagail, and Nicholas Boylston were cousins.
9. See Samuel Flagg Bemis, *John Quincy Adams and the Foundations of American Foreign Policy* (New York, 1949), p. 132.
10. To Samuel Dexter Exq.—Chairman of the Committee of the Corporation and Overseers of Harvard University, Quincy, 6 August 1805; John Quincy Adams, Letterbook, reel 135, Microfilms of the Adams Papers owned by the Adams Manuscript Trust and deposited in the Massachusetts Historical Society. This and subsequent quotations from the Adams Papers are used with the kind of permission of the Adams Manuscript Trust.
11. *Ibid.*
12. John Quincy Adams, Diary, August 27, 1806; reel 30, microfilms.
13. *Ibid.*, July 3, 1806.
14. *Ibid.*, July 10, 1807.
15. To the Corporation of Harvard University, Cambridge, 26 June 1806; Letterbook, reel 135, microfilms.
16. John Quincy Adams, *Lectures on Rhetoric and Oratory* (Cambridge, 1810), II, 384.
17. *Ibid.*, I, 208, 266ff; II, 256–7.
18. *Ibid.*, I, 157ff, 344ff.
19. After delivering his lecture on narration, he wrote in his diary: "It was the dullest I have yet delivered, and my only resource was to read it over as fast as possible. Though as long as any of those which have taken me from 40 minutes to three quarters of an hour, I went through it in 32 minutes."—June 19, 1807; reel 30, microfilms.
20. Adams, *Lectures*, I, 321; see also II, 140–1.
21. *Ibid.*, I, 297ff.
22. For example, Adams said that the classical deliberative argument of legality would have no weight in cases where the deliberating body had the power of changing the law, such as a town meeting. *Ibid.*, I, 260.
23. Edward Everett, MS Autobiography, chp. 5, p. 24; Everett Papers, Massachusetts Historical Society.
24. Corporation meeting, March 6, 1810; Harvard College Records, IV, 235.
25. My full discussion of Joseph McKean's public lectures and rhetoric and oratory is in preparation for a future article.

26. John T. Kirkland to George Bancroft, Cambridge, May 26, 1819; Bancroft Papers, Massachusetts Historical Society.

27. *Boston Daily Advertiser*, September 5, 1819, p. 2.

28. *Independent Chronicle & Boston Patriot*, September 29, 1819, p. 2.

29. *Boston Daily Advertiser*, September 29, 1819, p. 2; *Columbian Centinel*, October 2, 1819, p. 1.

30. *Independent Chronicle & Boston Patriot*, September 25, 1819, p. 1.

31. *Columbian Centinel*, September 22, 1819, p. 2.

32. Edwrd T. Channing, *Lectures Read to the Seniors in Harvard College* (Boston 1856). In the preface, he wrote that "I have taken but a part of the course for publication." (p. vi). Unfortunately, his lecture MSS have not been found.

33. *Ibid.*, p. 31. For further discussion of his definition, see Dorothy I. Anderson, "Edward T. Channing's Definition of Rhetoric," *Speech Monographs*, XIV (1947), 81–92.

34. Channing, pp. 32ff.

35. *Ibid.*, p. 33.

36. *Ibid.*, p. 41.

37. Samuel Lee Wolff, "Scholars," *The Cambridge History of American Literature* (New York, 1921), IV, 472.

38. H. Burroughs, Notes on the lectures of Professor Channing. On Rhetoric and Criticism—1833. . . . MS in Harvard Archives.

39. Channing, pp. 99ff.; 113ff.

40. Burroughs. Italics mine.

41. Channing, pp. 246ff.

42. For a more detailed discussion of Channing's experiments with texts, see Dorothy I. Anderson, "Edward T. Channing's Teaching of Rhetoric," *Speech Monographs*, XVI (August 1949), 70ff.

43. See [Edward T. Channing], "On Models in Literature," *North American Review*, III (July 1816), 202–209.

44. Burroughs.

45. George F. Hoar, for example, in his *Autobiography of Seventy Years* (New York, 1903), comments on Channing's criticism of themes (I, 87, 97, 123); but despite his deep interest in oratory, he is silent on Channing as a teacher of public speaking.

46. Andrew P. Peabody, *Harvard Reminiscences* (Boston, 1888), p. 89. Peabody also comments (p. 88) on Channing's own awkward delivery.

47. For his defense of elocution as a study, see Channing, pp. 46ff.

48. Barber, a disciple of Joshua Steele, came to America in 1823, taught elocution at Yale, wrote an elocution manual and taught at Harvard from 1830 to 1835. His bamboo wheel was the butt of many jokes, the ultimate indignity being its suspension on a *barber's* pole opposite the college yard.

49. For a discussion of British thought in America, see Merle Curti, *The Growth of American Thought*, 2nd. ed. (New York, 1951), pp. 233ff.

50. Douglas Ehninger, "Campbell, Blair, and Whately: Old Friends in a New Light," *Western Speech*, XIX (October 1955), 263–9.

51. Richard H. Dana, Jr., "Biographical Notice," in Channing, pp. xv–xvi.

52. There is no definitive biography of Child, but biographical details can be found in the following: "Francis James Child," *Harvard Graduates' Magazine*, V (December 1896), 209–10; C. E. Norton, "Francis James Child," *ibid.*, VI (December 1897) 161–9; Gamaliel Bradford, "Francis James Child," *Atlantic Monthly*, CXXXII (July 1923), 76–86.

53. Edward Everett, MS Diary, December 15, 1815; Everett Papers, Massachusetts Historical Society.

54. Among the numerous works which discuss the profound influence of German universities on American ones are the following: Charles Franklin Thwing, *The American and the German University, One Hundred Years of History* (New York, 1928); Abraham Flexner, *Universities: American, English, German* (New York, 1930); John A. Walz, *German Influence in American Education and Culture* (Philadelphia, 1936).

55. Friedrich Paulsen, *The German Universities and University Study*, trans. Frank Thilly and William W. Elwang (New York, 1906), pp. 40–1.

56. "Ten Years of Harvard," *Harvard Graduates Magazine*, XI (September 1902), 64.

57. "Literary Scholarship," *American Scholarship in the Twentieth Century*, ed. Merle Curti (Cambridge, 1953), p. 111.

58. F. J. Child to Richard H. Dana, Jr., Cambridge, Feb. 22, 1874; Dana Papers, Massachusetts Historical Society. In the same letter, Child indicated that he not only discouraged the Boylston declamations, but also attended against his will.

59. Signed letter in Boston *Evening Transcript*, September 17, 1896; clipping in Francis James Child: A selection of press cuttings &c., Harvard Archives.

60. F. J. [Child] to Charles [E. Norton], Cambridge, Sept. 28, 1851; Norton Papers, Houghton Library.

61. "Introduction," *The Development of Harvard University since the Inauguration of President Eliot, 1869–1929*, ed. Samuel Eliot Morison (Cambridge, 1930), pp. xlii–xliii.

62. *Ibid.*, p. xliii.

63. "The New Education, Its Organization—II," *Atlantic Monthly*, XXIII (March 1869), 359.

64. Charles William Eliot, *Educational Reforms, Essays and Addresses* (New York, 1898), pp. 321–2.

65. Very little readily-available biographical data on Hill exist. The most complete is "Adams Sherman Hill," *Report of the Harvard Class of 1853* (Cambridge, 1913), pp. 135–141.

66. John C. French, *A History of the University Founded by Johns Hopkins* (Baltimore, 1916) p. 89; Henry James, *Charles W. Eliot* (Boston, 1930), II, 14–5.

67. "English at Harvard," *The Dial*, XVI (March 1, 1894), 131–2.

68. *Ibid.*, p. 131.

69. Charles Francis Adams, E. L. Godkin, George R. Nutter, "Final Report on English Composition," *Harvard Graduates' Magazine*, VI (December 1897), 201.

70. See George P. Baker, "Debating at Harvard," *Harvard Graduates' Magazine*, VII (March 1899), esp. p. 363.

71. Wendell, p. 132.

72. New York, 1878.

73. Adams Sherman Hill, *Our English* (New York, 1888), p. 61.

74. *Ibid.*, p. 62.

75. Hill, *The Principles of Rhetoric*, p. v. This and subsequent quotations are from the second edition (1895).

76. *Ibid.*, p. 1.

77. Charles H. Grandgent, "The Modern Languages," Morison, p. 76.

78. Hill, *Principles*, p. vi.

79. Albert Raymond Kitzhaber, *Rhetoric in American Colleges, 1850–1900* (Ph.D. diss., Univ. of Washington, 1953), pp. 98ff.

80. Adams Godkin, Nutter, esp. 207ff.

81. Wendell, p. 131.

82. *And Gladly Teach* (Boston, 1935), pp. 253–4.

Andrea A. Lunsford

Alexander Bain's Contributions to Discourse Theory

◊ *Like so many others who have made a significant contribution to the theory and practice of rhetoric, Alexander Bain (1818–1903) was not primarily a rhetorician. Although he occupied the coveted chair of logic at the University of Aberdeen in 1860, he was recognized by his contemporaries principally as a psychologist. His foremost works in psychology* The Senses and the Intellect *(1855) and* The Emotions and the Will *(1859) were very influential and very much esteemed among contemporary professionals. But his enduring reputation in academic circles was achieved with his textbook* English Composition and Rhetoric *in 1866 and especially with the considerably expanded and revised edition of that work in 1888. In this essay, Andrea Lunsford, who is doing an edition of this text for the Southern Illinois University Press, gives us some biographical information about this talented Scotsman and assesses his contributions to discourse theory, both in his own time and in the first half of the twentieth century.* ◊

In 1977 Donald Stewart startled his audience at the National Council of Teachers of English Convention by giving them a test.[1] Not at all to his surprise, Professor Stewart found that although the teachers assembled devoted forty-five percent of their working time to teaching composition, hardly any of them recognized the names of twenty prominent rhetoricians or titles of works by those rhetoricians. Professor Stewart did not include Alexander Bain on his list, but had he done so, very few of the writing teachers in his audience would have heard of Bain. Almost certainly, none would have read his books on composition and rhetoric.

That such should be the case seems remarkable, for a great deal of what has been taught in traditional composition courses derives directly or indirectly from Bain's work. In an historical study of the paragraph written at the end of the nineteenth century, Edwin Lewis

From *College English* "Alexander Bain's Contributions to Discourse Theory by Andrea A. Lunsdford, March 1982. Copyright 1982 by the National Council of Teachers of English, Reprinted with permission.

describes Bain's influence as formative. Indeed, Lewis claims that Bain's analysis of the paragraph was presented and defended with the same acuteness and grasp that made him "perhaps the ablest writer on rhetoric since Aristotle."[2] Bain's stock, however, has plunged since Lewis wrote those words. The revival of interest in rhetoric occurring during the last three decades has led us to call into question what Richard Young calls the "current-traditional paradigm" in the teaching of composition.[3] For those challenging this paradigm and attempting to improve or replace it, Bain has become a popular whipping boy, identified with a rigidly prescriptive, product-centered system. Exactly who was Alexander Bain, and has his influence on our discipline been, on the whole, salutary or detrimental?

When Bain died at the age of eighty-six in 1903, major newspapers throughout Britain and North America carried the news. The headline in the New York *Times* read: "Professor Alexander Bain Dead: He rose from humble weaver to Rector of the University of Aberdeen" (19 September 1903, p. 7). In his autobiography Bain traces dispassionately the story of this rise: his lonely struggle to study mathematics and other subjects after leaving school at eleven to work as a weaver with his father; his attendance at evening school and at the local Mechanics' Institution; his introduction to a Marischal College professor who helped Bain improve his Latin and prepare to enter University. During his subsequent stay at Marischal, Bain distinguished himself in every subject, graduating with an MA at the head of his class in 1840.

Many young members of our profession will certainly identify with Bain during the next twenty years of his life: he was highly educated, he was publishing a number of influential works on psychology, he was the friend of John Stuart Mill and other leading thinkers of the day, and yet he couldn't find a suitable job.[4] Time after time, in fact, his applications for academic chairs were rejected, and he continued to work here and there—as a substitute teacher in Aberdeen, as an Examiner at the University of London, as a writer for the Chambers Information Series, even as a staunch reformer on the London Commission of Sewers. In his *Autobiography* (London: Longmans, Green, 1904) Bain gives what he believed to be the major reason for his failure to win a professorship: he never took the communion necessary to become an official member of the church.[5] In describing in the *Autobiography* the "failure of his religious conversion" he mentions one of his most marked intellectual traits:

the very early development of the tendency to take all statements of fact in their literal meaning, and to compare them with one another, and with the facts in their actual occurrence. Consequent on this tendency, or as an accompaniment of it, was the strong sense of contradictions when varying statements could not be reconciled. From my earliest consciousness, I had this peculiarity in a degree beyond what I could observe in those about me. (p. 12)

The strong tendency to minute observation and a dislike for contradictions are evident in Bain's work in what was then called "mental philosophy," and his work in psychology in turn strongly influenced his books on rhetoric.

Bain finally secured his fame with *The Senses and the Intellect* (1855) and *The Emotions and the Will* (1859). Bain is often referred to as a follower of Mill, a Utilitarian, an associationist.[6] His works, however, not only resist such easy, neat pigeon-holing but have been claimed by many to mark an epoch in British psychology. His criticisms of associationism stemmed from his distrust of the traditional associationist emphasis on introspection. Bain was much more inclined, in his study of the mind, to emphasize the relationship of observation (rather than introspection) to fact, in marked contrast to his contemporaries working in physiology. As a result Bain set out on a completely independent study of mental processes, which he pursued according to his formula of observation and comparison. To Bain the emotive, cognitive, and volitional aspects are not "compartments" of the mind; on the contrary, the mind is unified. Hence Bain dismisses the old faculty psychology. The very essence of all consciousness, he argues, lies in discrimination and retention. In his words:

no law of the intellect appears to be more certain than the law that connects our discriminating power with our retentive power. In whatever class of subjects our discrimination is great—colours, forms, tones, tastes—in that class our retention is great.[7]

Only on the basis of the mind's discriminative powers does association come into play.[8] We understand, then, and, by extension, we learn by virtue of our powers of discrimination, retentiveness, and similarity. In Bain's theory the mind is basically active, and the relation between thought and action and the great emphasis on discriminative powers are both relevant to Bain's later work in rhetoric.

The publication of *The Senses and the Intellect* and *The Emotions and the Will* secured the place in the history of philosophy that William James claimed for him when in 1876 he wrote that "The two philosophers of indubitably the widest influence in England and America since Mill's death are Bain and Spencer." Besides his long acquaintance with the two Mills and Bentham, Bain was now in touch with other leading scientists such as August Comte and Charles Darwin. In fact, his renown was such that a French reference book lists the following entry under Aberdeen: "A Scottish city somewhere on the North Sea. Birthplace of Bain."[9] In 1860, when the two Aberdeen Universities merged and a new Chair of Logic was created, Bain's application could no longer be ignored. After a bitter battle between the orthodox church and those of the more liberal scientific community, Bain, then forty-two, won the coveted academic chair in Aberdeen, which he held for the next twenty years.

At Aberdeen Bain came to rhetoric in a rather odd way. Through a curious revamping of the curriculum, the study of rhetoric was moved from the chair of moral philosophy to the new chair of logic. Henceforth, Bain controlled the teaching not only of logic, but of psychology or "mental philosophy" and of rhetoric as well, though Bain does not seem to have been particularly aware or appreciative of the reunion of subjects long since divorced by Ramus.

In fact, Bain divided the two subjects in practice, and his method of teaching suggests that he looked upon rhetoric primarily as an analytic study of style, its causes, and its effects. Forms of thought (inventional) would have been dealt with under the heading of logic. In spite of what appears to be an obvious extension of the romantic split between style and invention, a careful reading of Bain suggests the view that the mental skills he labored to develop in his students were the same for both logic and rhetoric classes. In both classes he aimed at developing "judgment and discernment" in his pupils, the skills Bain found most essential to all higher education.

For his mental philosophy classes, Bain lectured from his own books on psychology; for logic, he worked from a heavily emended copy of Mill. (He published his own *Logic* in 1870.) But for his large English class Bain could find no suitable text. He complains in the *Autobiography* (p. 175) that no existing grammar was sufficiently developed, and that those that were available were far too costly for his Scots thriftiness. Moreover, most recent rhetoric books were to his mind illogical and poorly thought out. It is characteristic of Bain that he set to work immediately to provide grammar and rhetoric texts for his class, and he spent a good deal of the next five years working intensively on these projects. His *English Grammar* appeared in 1862, and the first edition of his *English Composition and Rhetoric* in 1866. He revised both works as he used them; the most authoritative versions appeared in 1888.

In his textbooks and in his classroom teaching Bain was in many ways an educational reformer, intent on applying his considerable powers of observation, logical acumen, and knowledge of science to the study of grammar and rhet-

oric. First to go in his general academic housekeeping was the system of reading dictations and lectures from crumbling, decades-old notes to a class of utterly bored, almost stupefied boys. Out went the drumming into pupils, by rote, rules which they rarely understood.[10] Out also went the tradition of reading only those authors long since dead. In their places came Bain's system: the awakening of the pupils' own judgments through an appreciation of first principles; the steady practice and use of first principles; and the analysis of contemporary prose. Bain's classroom was a rhetorical field on which he demonstrated the art of analysis and exercised his young troops in its use. He would begin by introducing a principle of style and then go on to dissect it, examining pieces of prose or poetry in light of the principle. Bain's classroom procedure is, in fact, documented in many student reports. One writes, "His method was simple and thorough-going. He lectured on English Composition three times a week: on Mondays he cross-examined—and he *was* a cross-examiner—on the work of the preceding Friday."[11] Another student reports most emphatically what a number of other student accounts report:

We felt at once that we were now in a new world, in the region of clear exposition and critical analysis, as well as refined and elegant enunciation; and, as the lectures proceeded from grammar to rhetoric, . . . the wonder and the admiration grew, and by the end of the session we felt that there had been created in us a new faculty—that of appreciating and dissecting style.[12]

In all matters rhetorical, Bain followed the lead of his psychological works. That he clearly did so stands in contradiction to a charge laid against Bain by Albert Kitzhaber, who writes:

It is curious that Bain, one of the most advanced psychologists of his time, made so few applications of psychology to rhetoric. Associationism, with its emphasis on mental processes . . . would have had a very healthful influence on rhetorical theory in this period, and no one would have been better fitted to point out the relations than Bain. He failed to do so.[13]

In his bibliography Professor Kitzhaber cites only the 1866 American edition of Bain's *English Composition and Rhetoric*, and the format of that book does not reveal the influence of his psychology as clearly as does the revised and enlarged 1888 edition. Nevertheless, the major thrust of both editions is to exercise and enrich the discriminatory power of his pupils, and the relation of such exercises to Bain's psychological theory of mental discrimination is unmistakable, as is his relation of the qualities of style to various powers of the mind. If the influence is somewhat diffuse in the 1866 text, it is absolutely explicit in the 1888 revision. This expanded version appeared in two volumes, the first devoted to "Intellectual Qualities of Style" and the second to "Emotional Qualities of Style." Even the titles of the two volumes are thus closely related to the titles of Bain's psychological works. In the first volume, Bain's analysis of sentences and paragraphs is based on his psychological principles of similarity and contiguity. And in his treatment of the figures of speech in the second volume, Bain throws out the old distinction between tropes and schemes as artificial, insisting that the natural classification should be based on the three major aspects of mind: discrimination, similitude, and retentiveness. Bain's treatment of sympathy, also in the second volume, is directly related to his psychological work and, indeed, seems a clear if distant cousin of Kenneth Burke's concept of identification. While Bain's work is certainly superseded by advancements in our own century, he was ahead of his time in relating psychological theory to the theory of discourse.

A second charge laid against Bain in recent years is that his approach to rhetoric and composition was thoroughly anti-empirical and deductive. Paul Rodgers levels this charge in an important article, and it is elaborated and repeated by Arthur Stern in a 1976 essay.[14] A full reading of Bain's works indicates to me that these charges are partially wrong-headed. We should first recall that, at the time of Bain's major revision of the *Rhetoric*, empirical research in psychology was in its infancy; the application of empirical methods in fields outside the physical sciences was a novel concept only barely beginning to be explored by some of Bain's contemporaries. In spite of this fact, Bain's *Autobiography* (pp. 335–36, 378–79) shows that he was well aware of the work of leaders in the field. He traveled to Germany to visit the laboratories of Wilhelm Wundt and Hermann Helmholtz; in Paris he visited Ribot, founder of the *Revue Philosophique*.

Although I cannot be precisely certain of what Bain's critics mean by his being wholly "deductive," they do use the term in a pejorative way and seem to think that Bain *began* his exposition with a statement of first principles or axioms based on little or no empirical foundation. Such a reading of Bain seems to me to be extremely naive. In the first place, Bain was a professor of logic, the man who revised the manuscript of Mill's *Logic* and who went on to write a *Logic* of his own, including a critique of the syllogism as well as a thorough examination of induction. Given Bain's intensive study of logic, his familiarity with the latest experimental work of his day, and his life-long tendency to close observation of details, it seems highly unlikely that he was blindly tied to a simplified syllogistic method of reasoning. Furthermore, as a mental philosopher Bain stood in the tradition of the inductionist epistemology as articulated by Whewell and Mach. Certainly, the presentation in his texts proceeds from principle to example, but none of Bain's work, including his *Rhetoric*, should be viewed as deductive in any simple sense. Bain's investigation of written discourse takes account of what he believed to be the fundamental principles of human knowledge, but it proceeds from example to axiom and back again. That is, his procedure typifies the classical philosophical dyad—analysis/synthesis—much as it was practiced, for example, by Descartes. This process should not be confused with mere deduction.

Thus far, Bain's influence on our discipline seems not to have been overtly destructive: he associated discourse with mental processes, and he applied logical analysis and synthesis to rhetoric. But when it comes to Bain's work regarding paragraph and discourse analysis, critics are even more insistent that Bain's influence has been largely baneful. The six principles of paragraph construction that Bain listed are now fairly well known: what he called *explicit reference, parallel construction, unity, consecutive arrangement,* and *marking of subordination* eventually led to Barrett Wendell's triad of unity, mass, and coherence, and to our own long-familiar trinity of unity, coherence, and emphasis. Bain's third principle, which he called *indication of the theme* (*Rhetoric*, I, 94–122), soon reigned supreme as the topic-sentence law. The dogmatic way in which many modern texts have attempted to inculcate this "law" has come under severe attack in recent years, most memorably in Richard Braddock's "The Frequency and Placement of Topic Sentences in Expository Prose" (*Research in the Teaching of English,* 8 [1974], 287–302). In that study, Braddock examined twenty-five essays published in American magazines and concluded that topic sentences do not appear at the beginning of most paragraphs and that, in fact, a number of paragraphs have no topic sentence at all.

Paul Rodgers says that Bain put "paragraph rhetoric in a deductive cage" (p. 408), and Arthur Stern is even more critical of what he calls "hand-me-down Bainalities" (p. 255). Unfortunately, Bain nowhere describes exactly how he formulated the paragraph principles, although Rodgers, Stern, and others assume his method was some form of syllogistic reasoning. My reading of Bain suggests otherwise. In several passages of his *Autobiography,* he says he prepared to write his rhetoric texts by "extensive reading" of English authors and by careful analysis of their work. After the first edition of the *Rhetoric*, he continued to test his principles, and he asked colleagues to do so as well. Nowhere does he suggest that he simply dreamed up the paragraph principles and then searched for examples to shore up his rules. In fact, such a procedure would have gone against the grain of all Bain's other work. It seems much more plausible to suppose that Bain's intensive reading of prose, in particular the contemporary essayists, coupled with his intensely analytic turn of mind and the fact that he was working hard to prepare a practical and efficient course on rhetoric, led him to "discover" his principles empirically. Bain approached any subject by searching for first principles and definitions. In a later work he says, "The most obvious way to arrive at the definition of a general name is to survey the individual things denoted by the name; to compare them to one another, and to find out the points wherein they agree" (*On Teaching English*, p. 207).

I think, then, that we are safe in assuming that Bain followed just such a procedure in trying to find features characteristic of paragraphs in current nineteenth-century prose. I think we may also safely assume that Bain was familiar with *A Handbook of the English Tongue*, in which Joseph Angus discusses his empirical study of the paragraph and its characteristics, including unity of purpose and theme. Although Angus' book was published in 1861, five years before Bain's *Rhetoric*, Kitzhaber concludes that it "would be difficult to say" whether or not Bain drew on Angus' discussion (p. 245). But since Bain and Angus were both serving as examiners for the University of

London at the time Angus' book was published, Bain was almost certainly familiar with Angus' text. Most importantly, however, Bain's treatment is altogether more comprehensive than that of Angus—or of anyone else who had written to that date.

Nothing in Bain's work on composition shows his general method any more clearly than does his treatment of the paragraph. After stating the principles of the paragraph as general rules, he follows those rules immediately with a detailed analysis of extensive passages which exemplify them. We should note that Bain often examines long excerpts, even entire chapters, rather than isolated paragraphs which could certainly be produced to support almost any principle. Furthermore, his analysis of these passages allows him to introduce and explain exceptions to the rules. He notes, for instance, several occasions in which a series of paragraphs all relate to only one thematic unit or topic sentence. These analyses indicate that Bain looked on the paragraph principles not as hard and fast, immutable rules of composition, but as practical analytic tools for his pupils. They also indicate that Bain established his analytic principles on actual current practice.

While Bain was intent on giving his students some practical aid and exercise in discriminating among stylistic choices, he was also intent on relating the paragraph principles to one or more of the powers of the mind. In general, Bain places great emphasis on the reader or the audience in his analysis of the paragraph. More specifically, Bain shows that the most effective paragraphs are structured in such a way that they are easy to read or process, that they are memorable, and that they fulfill the psychological expectations of the reader.

Bain's treatment of the paragraph thus stands as an early and important attempt to describe the distinctive features of prose and to use the principles thus derived as analytic tools. In his classroom practice, however, descriptive features often became prescriptive judgments. We are unfortunate in that the prescriptivism latent in Bain's analysis soon became dominant in composition textbooks.

No discussion of Bain's *English Composition and Rhetoric* should fail to consider one other part of the "current-traditional paradigm" with which Bain is often linked. I refer, of course, to our own Four Horsemen, the forms of discourse. Most of us feel that the rigid adherence to these categories is theoretically insupportable, less than productive, and generally impossible; the categories are inadequate to our compositional needs. But is Bain responsible for our devotion to them? Is he responsible for putting discourse theory, as well as paragraph theory, into a cage?

We may profitably begin by asking ourselves why Bain is so strongly linked to the four forms and, indeed, where the forms originated. Kitzhaber notes that the terms associated with the forms or modes were in general use by mid-nineteenth century; and in a recent essay Robert J. Connors suggests that the "first definitive use" of our familiar modal terms occurred in Samuel P. Newman's 1827 text, *A Practical System of Rhetoric*.[15] I can find no evidence to suggest that Bain was familiar

with Newman's text. I wish to argue, however, that both writers derived their understanding of forms of discourse from earlier discussion of the *functions* of rhetoric, and most directly from George Campbell's *The Philosophy of Rhetoric* (1776). In that book Campbell lists the functions of rhetoric as to enlighten the understanding, to please the imagination, to move the passions, and to influence the will.[16] We can see Campbell's influence in Newman's description of didactic discourse as used to convey instruction, and persuasive or argumentative discourse as "designed to influence the will."[17] As a philosopher and psychologist, Bain was familiar with Campbell's work and, indeed, he cites Campbell's treatise in his preface to the first edition of the *English Composition and Rhetoric*. (Bain's successor at Aberdeen, William Leslie Davidson, followed Bain in most things, but he reverted to Campbell's descriptions of the functions of rhetoric almost word for word in his lectures.) Especially appealing to Bain would have been Campbell's effort to ground rhetoric in a theory of human nature and mind. Bain, in fact, attempts to do the same thing, an attempt that I believe led him eventually to discard the modes of discourse as taxonomic categories for his text.

In the first edition of *English Composition and Rhetoric* in 1866, Bain uses the modes as the organizing structure of his book. His introduction of the forms again reveals Campbell's influence: "Those [forms] that have for their object to inform the understanding fall under . . . *Description, Narration,* and *Exposition.* The means of influencing the will are given under . . .

Bain's Contributions to Discourse Theory **291**

Persuasion. The employing of language to excite pleasurable Feelings is . . . *Poetry*" (p. 19). Noting that he is the first to give extensive treatment to description, Bain sets forth guidelines designed to make descriptive passages readable and then goes on to relate principles of description to powers of the mind. Bain's subsequent treatment of narrative is particularly acute. In *On Teaching English* (1887) he deplores the tendency to look on narration as the "easiest" form of discourse, arguing that "Language is a single file; the subject matter may be double, triple, or any number of files. Or, to put it pedantically, so as to impress the memory, language is unilinear, matter may be bilinear, trilinear, or polylinear" (p. 10). The discussion of exposition, persuasion, and poetry proceeds along the same practical, common-sense lines, nowhere implying that these forms are fixed, separable entities. In fact, Bain continually points out the interrelationships among the forms, noting, for example, that "description is involved in all the other kinds of discourse," or that narration occurs in history, biography, science or exposition, and poetry (*English Composition and Rhetoric,* 1st ed., pp. 127, 146).

But Bain later dropped the forms of discourse as the organizing structure for his text, omitting the forms as separate headings in the 1888 revised edition of the *Composition and Rhetoric* and choosing instead to spread discussion of those forms throughout his analysis of discourse. As I noted above, Bain reorganized his text under the headings of "Intellectual Qualities of Style" and "Emotional Qualities of Style" and carefully related these elements to psy-chological or mental processes through which we understand and respond to discourse.[18] This organizational structure gave proper emphasis to Bain's major concern: relating discourse to mental processes.

If Bain's use of the modes of discourse derives from Campbell's concept of the functions of rhetoric as those functions relate to mental processes, Bain is nevertheless responsible for popularizing the modes as *categories of discourse.* The shift here is one from function (as used by Cicero, Augustine, and, in the eighteenth century, Campbell) to type of discourse, a shift we have failed to note. But I wish to make another point about Bain's use of the forms of discourse: put most simply, he uses the forms as analytic, not productive, tools. The distinction, I think, is crucial to a proper understanding of Bain's work. In *On Teaching English,* Bain sets out a rationale to accompany his two-volume textbook. "In Composition, as in Grammar," he argues, "we need two courses of instruction, running side by side. The first is, a systematic course of principles, with appropriate examples; the second, a critical examination of texts, passages, or writings" (p. 23). Notable for its omission is any mention of rules governing the production of discourse. Far from articulating such rules, Bain reiterates his goal: the development of discriminative judgment in his students through intensive and detailed analysis. In fact, Bain goes on to argue against the writing of essays in rhetoric classes on the grounds that composing essays calls on a multitude of skills other than analysis, skills which the rhetoric teacher, in fact, has failed to teach. What Bain goes on to do is to urge teachers to lead their students in analyzing prose, and to help out he offers a series of sample lessons. Each one offers a piece of discourse which Bain then analyzes in terms of the most effective order of words; the figures of speech and their relation to human understanding; the effectiveness of paragraph structure in relation to cohesion; and the forms he sees as most adaptive to intellectual qualities of style—description, narration, and exposition (persuasion is most adaptive to emotional qualities of style). Thus Bain clearly introduces the forms as analytic modes which can be used to trace the effects of a piece of discourse on the intellect and the emotions of the reader and the power or "energy" of the piece as a whole. As used in his revised work, the forms do not name discrete types of writing or aim at an exhaustive list of those types. Rather, they act as *forms through which we can understand and analyze writing,* much in the same way that the syllogism acts as a form through which we can understand and analyze logical argument.

Failing to understand Bain's use of the forms of discourse and apparently most familiar with the early 1866 edition of his textbook, later writers appropriated the forms as labels for types of writing rather than as forms through which we might come to analyze, understand, and appreciate writing. So I do not believe that Bain can stand convicted of "caging" discourse theory. What Bain constructed were patterns his students could use in analyzing writing and hence in exercising their intellectual judgment. It has been succeeding writers, including many of our contemporary authors, who turned Bain's analytic structure into a cage and twisted the key in the lock.

Bain made no exaggerated claim that his work was rigidly definitive, noting that his discussion of how particular compositions evoke various emotions would surely be vastly improved upon. In an 1892 speech Bain said, "In the philosophy of the mind, the displacement of one system by another is proverbial. All that we can count upon, when we have done our best, is that some stones may be found to fit into the structures of our successors. . . . It is enough to have helped a number of people to draw their own inferences."[19] Surely Bain would have been the first to say much the same about his work in rhetoric and composition. And he would have applauded those among us who are examining the evidence of discourse anew, using our own powers of observation to discover first principles and to ground composition theory in a general theory of mind. While I do not intend by any means to offer a blanket apologia for Bain, I do want to argue that we should try to see him clear and whole rather than piecemeal or in light of fragmentary attacks on only parts of his work. In the final analysis we could set no greater goal for ourselves than that Bain set for himself: the formulation of a theory of rhetoric comprehensive enough to draw upon experiential and theoretical results in half a dozen other, related disciplines, yet practical enough to provide us with characterizing features of discourse.

Notes

1. "Comp. vs. Lit.: Which Is Your Job and Which Is Your Strength?," *College English*, 40 (1978), 65–69.

2. *The History of the English Paragraph* (Chicago: University of Chicago Press, 1894), p. 29.

3. "Paradigms and Problems: Needed Research in Rhetorical Invention," *Research on Composing*, ed. Charles Cooper and Lee Odell (Urbana, Ill. NCTE, 1978). In this article, Young notes Daniel Fogarty's earlier use of the phrase "current-traditional rhetoric" in his *Roots for a New Rhetoric* (New York: Teacher's College, Columbia University, 1959), p. 118.

4. Manuscript letters held in various Scottish university archives chronicle the intense competition that took place whenever a university chair became available. Bain competed most often with John Veitch, translator and editor of Descartes, biographer of Dugald Stewart, and editor of Sir William Hamilton's *Lectures*. Only after Veitch took the post at St. Andrews did Bain finally win the chair at Aberdeen. See Edinburgh University Microfilm Manuscript #792.

5. Bain's acute awareness of the effects his refusal to take the communion had on his career is evidenced both in the *Autobiography* and in private correspondence. As late as 1875, in a letter to John Hill Burton, Bain muses on the consequences of his choice and says, "I have been reading again the 'Life of Hume' and going over that chapter on the attempt to have up Hume before the General Assembly, the question strongly occurred to me—why was Hume never dragged before the Civil Courts, under the statutes that make it penal to utter heretical opinions? Seeing that, in our own time, it has been possible to get convictions against atheists and profaners, surely in the last century . . . a prosecution before the Civil judges might have succeeded." Bain goes on to disparage "purely spiritual fulminating" and to note ironically that his personal views have caused him great difficulty. National Library of Scotland MS 9400, ff. 187.

6. In commenting on Bain's appointment at Aberdeen, A. C. Fraser calls Bain "an able man but rather too inclined to the school of Mill." Edinburgh University Microfilm MS #792.

7. *The Senses and the Intellect*, 4th ed. (London, 1894), pp. 354–56.

8. Bain's most complete efforts to define consciousness occur in *The Emotions and the Will*, 4th ed. (London, 1899).

9. Quoted in "Professor Bain," *Blackwood's*, 176 (1904), 95.

10. In *On Teaching English* (London: Longmans, Green, 1887), Bain criticizes the extreme emphasis on memory work, especially in teaching Shakespeare: "The Examination papers founded on the Shakespearian plays show memory at its maximum, judgment at its minimum. The teacher is made painfully aware, that his work consists in nearly unmitigated and uninteresting cram. . . . There is hardly anything contrived expressly to call the pupil's judgment into exercise" (p. 88).

11. *The Fusion of 1860: A Record of the Centenary Celebrations and a History of the University of Aberdeen, 1860–1960*, ed. W. Douglas Simpson (Edinburgh: Oliver and Boyd, 1963), p. 177.

12. *Records of the Arts Class 1864–68: University of Aberdeen*, ed. W. S. Bruce (Aberdeen: The Central Press, 1912), p. 15.

13. "Rhetoric in American Colleges, 1850–1900," unpublished doctoral dissertation, University of Washington, 1953, p. 193.

14. Paul C. Rodgers, Jr., "Alexander Bain and the Rise of the Organic Paragraph," *Quarterly Journal of Speech*, 51 (1965), 406; Arthur A. Stern, "When Is a Paragraph?," *College Composition and Communication*, 27 (1976), 254.

15. "The Rise and Fall of the Modes of Discourse," *College Composition and Communication*, 32 (1981), 444–455. I am indebted to Professor Connors for alerting me to Newman's discussion.

16. George Campbell, *The Philosophy of Rhetoric*, ed. Lloyd F. Bitzer (Carbondale: Southern Illinois University Press, 1963), p. 1. In his opening discussion, Campbell asserts that one function is primary in any given discourse, though other functions may serve subsidiary purposes. Cf. also Cicero, Quintilian, Augustine, and Bacon on the ends or functions of rhetoric.

17. *A Practical System of Rhetoric* (New York: Mark H. Newman, 1827), pp. 28–29.

18. Gerald Mulderig includes a careful discussion of the psychological bases of Bain's revised rhetoric in "Nineteenth-Century Psychology and the Shaping of Alexander Bain's *English Composition and Rhetoric*," paper presented at the MLA Convention, December, 1980.

19. Bain's speech on the occasion of the unveiling of his bust placed by the community of Aberdeen in the Public Library, quoted by William L. Davidson in "Professor Bain's Philosophy," *Mind*, n.s. 13 (1904), 178.

Edward J. P. Corbett

The Cornell School of Rhetoric

◊ *It was the Department of Speech and Drama at Cornell University in Ithaca, New York, that was mainly responsible for reintroducing the study of classical rhetoric into the curriculum of American universities in the second decade of the twentieth century. It was Everett Lee Hunt and Hoyt Hopewell Hudson, both of them sons of ministers and both of them graduates of Huron College in South Dakota, who proved to be the catalytic figures in this renaissance of classical rhetoric in the twentieth century. The list of the faculty and the graduates of the so-called Cornell School of Rhetoric is a veritable Who's Who in American Rhetoric, and the graduates of that program not only became leaders in the Speech Communication Association and writers of influential books and articles on rhetoric but also became prestigious members of the faculty at universities all over the country, where they introduced into the curriculum a component on classical rhetoric. The history of that movement constitutes one of the great success stories of higher education in this century.* ◊

The Cornell School of Rhetoric revived the teaching of classical rhetoric in American colleges and universities in the twentieth century and subsequently had a profound effect on rhetorical studies in this country. Most teachers and students in Speech/Communication departments are aware of that historical fact, and many of them know, in some detail, the history of the Cornell contribution because of several articles and books and convention talks that have been inspired by the movement.[1] But most teachers and students in English and other humanities disciplines, even those interested in rhetorical studies, are only vaguely aware—

if they are aware at all—of this important event in the history of ideas in this country. I want to acquaint interested members of this latter group with some of the details about the so-called Cornell School of Rhetoric.

I have used the word *so-called* because the title "Cornell School of Rhetoric" never had any official status. The department was originally designated as the Department of Public Speaking, and throughout most of its existence, it bore the title of Department of Speech and Drama. In the University catalogues, however, it was never referred to as the Department of Rhetoric. Yet

From the *Rhetoric Review* (September 1985): 4–14. Reprinted with permission.

the identity and impact of this department were so distinctive that it has commonly been referred to in professional circles as the Cornell School of Rhetoric.[2]

Interestingly enough, the emergence of the Cornell School of Rhetoric as a distinctive force in higher education occurred at the same time that the Speech Communication Association came into existence in 1914. In that year, a group of dissatisfied teachers of speech decided to break away from the National Council of Teachers of English and form their own professional organization. That divorce is itself an important milestone in the history of higher education in this country, but I do not want to be diverted into recounting the details of that rupture. The pertinent fact here is that this group of rebel teachers officially established an organization that they called the National Association of Academic Teachers of Public Speaking. They founded a journal too, entitled *Quarterly Journal of Public Speaking,* which began publication in 1915 under the editorship of James M. O'Neill of the University of Wisconsin, who also served as the first president of the Association. This journal was crucial to the welfare and future direction of the newly formed Association, because it was the channel through which the discipline could be shaped and the teachers of speech (at the time, mainly teachers of English) could be given a professional identity.

It is at this point that I want to introduce two remarkable young men from South Dakota, who became, in a sense, the catalytic figures in the Cornell movement and helped to shape a persistent, if not the predominant, strand

in the Speech Communication Association in America. They were Everett Lee Hunt and Hoyt Hopewell Hudson, recent graduates of an obscure denominational school, Huron College, in Huron, South Dakota, who stirred up some dust in those early years when the Association was trying to determine its mission and who helped shape the speech curriculum at Cornell. Both of them were sons of fundamentalist ministers, and both of them majored in the Greek and Latin classics.[3] Although Hudson was three years younger than Hunt, he took his B.A. two years earlier than Hunt, who did not graduate until 1913. After graduation, Hudson spent the next nine years in various activities: writing poetry, taking an M.A. degree at the University of Denver, and teaching high school in different parts of the country. After he graduated, Hunt spent the next five years as an instructor in Oratory and Debate at Huron College, a position for which he had had very little technical training during his undergraduate years.

The story of how these two young men from the Midwestern plains came to Cornell and made their mark in the academic world is a fascinating one. Hunt gained some national visibility just two years after taking his B.A. degree when he challenged some of the giants in the speech profession in the pages of the new journal, *Quarterly Journal of Public Speaking.* In the very first issue of that journal in 1915, James A. Winans, chairman of the speech department at Cornell and the author of the recently published textbook *Public Speaking,* which was to dominate the market for several years, published an article entitled "The Need for Research," in which he called for scientific studies in speech so that the newly formed Association could gain respectability along with the already established departments. In that same issue, the Research Committee, which President James M. O'Neill had appointed, also published an article in which they called for the same kind of research that Winans had called for. In the second issue of the journal, Everett Lee Hunt, the young, unknown instructor at a little private college in South Dakota, with only a B.A. degree and no formal training in speech, challenged both of those articles, maintaining that speech departments should head in a humanistic, not a scientific, direction. That challenge resulted in his subsequently engaging in a series of debates in print with some of the leading figures in the speech profession.

In the January 1916 issue of the journal, Charles H. Woolbert, an established professor of speech at the University of Illinois and one of the leaders of the break-away from English, proposed a curriculum for the speech sciences in the universities, a curriculum that was to set the basic pattern for the teaching of speech in this country for the twentieth century. Hunt published his vehement objection to that proposal, and Woolbert published his rebuttal to Hunt's objection, in the next issue (July, 1916) of the *Quarterly Journal of Public Speaking*. The battlelines between the humanists and the empiricists were clearly drawn.

Theodore Windt has summarized the position of the predominant and ultimately the prevailing group in the Speech Association, a group that he calls the "Midwesterners," composed primarily of the teachers at the large landgrant universities in the central part of the country ("Hoyt H. Hudson" 188–91). Since this position differed from that assumed by the Cornell School, it would be well to review the basic tenets of the Midwesterners:

(1) Speech, not the written language, was the defining feature of the new profession. [Increasingly during the nineteenth century, the focus of rhetorical studies had shifted to written discourse.]
(2) The curriculum should draw together all the subjects that rely primarily on spoken language—public speaking, speech science, speech correction, oral interpretation, and dramatics. [Many departments in those days were called "Speech and Drama."]
(3) The study of speech must be specialized and scientific. [For that reason, a Committee on Research was established in the first year of the Association.]
(4) The proper subject-matter for research and training was the techniques of how oral language is used—the mechanics of speaking. [This emphasis on the mechanics of speaking reflects the residual influence of the elocutionary movement, which had its beginnings in the late eighteenth century.]
(5) The study of speech can be divorced from English departments by adopting the objective of training graduate students to become experts in research on speaking. [The people in speech wanted to establish a distinct and respectable field of study.]

Professor Windt points out how Hunt opposed virtually every one of those basic tenets of the Midwesterners:

He stated that speech was a humane, not a scientific study. He opposed specialized training and advocated a liberal education. He said one could not separate ideas from techniques, content from form. He said rhetoric, not speech, was the center of the profession. But it was ideas in which he was not interested because the study of techniques or mechanics bored him. He wanted to prepare students for citizenship and life. ("Hoyt H. Hudson" 191)

Although James Winans, the chairman of the speech department at Cornell, had a scientific bent himself (he wanted to apply psychological principles to the study of speech) and although Hunt had attacked the position paper he had published in the first issue of the journal, he was so impressed by the brash young man that he invited Hunt to join his department at Cornell. At the time, Hunt was debating whether he would study for the ministry or go to graduate school. Finally, this twenty-eight-year-old instructor, with only a bachelor's degree, decided to accept the offer from the ivy-league school in the fingerlakes area of northern New York state. He began teaching there in the fall of 1918.

At the time, the notable faculty members involved in the program were, besides Winans, Lane Cooper, Alexander M. Drummond, Harry Caplan, and Herbert A. Wichelns. Lane Cooper had come to Cornell in 1902, and by 1918, having failed to convince the members of the English Department that their students should have a solid grounding in the Greek and Latin classics, he constituted a one-man department of Comparative Literature and Classics. Alexander Drummond, once a student of Lane Cooper's, was, like Winans, a graduate of Hamilton College, with a special interest in drama and the theater. Harry Caplan and Herbert A. Wichelns were doctoral students of Lane Cooper's and instructors of public speaking. In order to acquire academic credentials that would bring him abreast of his colleagues, Hunt attended graduate school at the University of Chicago for the next four summers, finally taking an M.A. degree

in philosophy, with a thesis on Plato's dialectical method. The next major event in this chronicle is the institution of the celebrated graduate seminar on classical rhetoric, but before we go into detail about that seminar, let us bring Hoyt Hudson to Cornell and briefly summarize his illustrious academic career.

When we last talked about Hoyt Hudson, he had taken an M.A. degree in literature at the University of Denver and had gone off to teach in high schools in various parts of the country.[4] In 1920, he was teaching high school in Cleveland, Ohio. Everett Hunt induced him to come to Cornell that fall to study for his doctorate. He took his Ph.D. in English just three years later in 1923, and from that point, he had a meteoric rise to national prominence in academia. His first job after graduation was at Swarthmore, where for two years he taught English and public speaking. For the next two years, from 1925 to 1927, he taught in the English Department at the University of Pittsburgh, where Raymond Howes, who had taken his B.A. degree at Cornell in 1924, did an M.A. thesis under him. In 1927, he left Pittsburgh to go to Princeton. In 1933, just ten years after taking his Ph.D., Hudson was made Professor of Rhetoric and Oratory and chairman of the English Department of Princeton, and also became editor of the *Quarterly Journal of Speech.* In 1942, he joined the faculty at Stanford University in Palo Alto. He died of a heart attack two years later on June 13, 1944, at age 50. Of all the books that he published in Renaissance literature during his career, the one that students of English are probably most familiar with is the anthology that he put together with J. W. Hebel in 1929, *Poetry of the English Renaissance.* His first love was literature, especially poetry, but we can look now at the significant contribution that he made to rhetorical studies in this country.

By the time Hudson came to Cornell in the fall of 1920, James Winans had moved to Dartmouth, and Alexander Drummond had taken over as the chair of the Department of Speech and Drama. Hudson, along with Harry Caplan and Herbert Wichelns, enrolled in the seminar on classical rhetoric that Everett Hunt and Alexander Drummond were offering that year. This seminar is reputed to be the first significant graduate seminar in classical rhetoric offered at a major American university in the twentieth century. Almost a quarter of a century later, Hoyt Hudson recalled that historic seminar:

Drummond took over the chairmanship that fall, and among other things, he wanted to build up the graduate work in rhetoric and public speaking. So he and Everett Hunt founded a seminar. They took a few of us through Aristotle's *Rhetoric* (it is quite possible that we were the only group in any American university then giving attention to what is now a perennial best-seller), Cicero's *De Oratore,* and Quintilian's *Institutions.* The three works occupied most of the academic year, though somewhere early in it we also polished off Plato's *Phaedrus* and picked up something about Isocrates and the Sophists. Things began to happen. We found that there were articles we wanted to write. We saw chances to apply classical dogmata to our dealings with modern material. (4)

In commenting fourteen years later on that recollection of Hudson's, Everett Hunt said.

This seminar might, perhaps, be taken as the beginning of a tradition at Cornell University that has grown continuously in breadth and depth. . . . The influence of the Cornell tradition in rhetoric has already extended far beyond the boundaries of any one university group, and rhetorical studies now flourish in many places. It is to be hoped that these diverse groups of students may have something of the sense of delight at the union of ancient traditions and modern practice which has been felt by the students of rhetoric at Cornell, and in particular by the associates of Herbert Wichelns. (1, 4)

Ironically, Hunt, who had done most of the planning and the teaching of that influential seminar, was never allowed to teach it again at Cornell because he did not have a Ph.D. But as Raymond Howes recalls, Hunt incorporated some of the material of that seminar into his undergraduate course in argumentation:

[Everett Hunt] was at Cornell during my undergraduate years, and as a junior, I took his course in Argumentation. We studied the Greek Sophists, the Roman orators, and the rhetorical treatises of Plato and Aristotle; Edmund Burke and other British orators, the debates over the American Constitution, and the Lincoln-Douglas debates over slavery and national unity. I remember writing a paper on Lysias, a Sophist who prepared speeches for clients who had to plead their own cases in the Greek courts; struggling through the *Federalist* papers; and impersonating Lincoln when we recreated a portion of one of the debates. (10)

Both of those descriptions of Hunt's courses indicate that in his own teaching, he practiced what he had preached in the journal articles that challenged the programs advocated by the leaders of the so-called Midwestern group of speech teachers. Although Hunt indicated in a general way what he thought the speech curriculum should be in the twentieth century, he never did lay out a specific curriculum for the kind of program he favored. Theodore Windt has pointed out what the challenges were at that time for those teachers who wanted to put a classical strand into the speech programs that were rapidly forming:

> To adapt classical rhetoric to modern times meant that the classical idea had to be refurbished, that invention had to be restored to its rightful place at the center of rhetoric, that some idea about how teachers and students should be educated had to be written and translations made and published, and that there be a recognition of the importance of rhetoric in the liberal arts curriculum. ("Hoyt H. Hudson" 192–93)

Windt maintains that Hoyt Hudson was "the first to outline the subjects that would define courses for graduate education in rhetoric and public address in America ("Hoyt H. Hudson" 197). Although Hudson had never published an article on rhetoric before coming to Cornell, he published four articles afterwards that helped to define the Cornell School of Rhetoric and to suggest a curriculum for graduate courses in rhetoric.[5]

Maybe the most influential of those articles was "The Field of Rhetoric," which was published in the year that he took his Ph.D. degree. The theme of those four articles and the crux of Hudson's and Hunt's opposition to the Midwesterners' view of what the speech curriculum should be are summed up in these two sentences from that article: "Rhetoric does not include all the work done by our present departments of public speaking: it does not include oral interpretation of literature, nor dramatics, nor studies designed to improve pronunciation and diction of or-

dinary conversation. But estimated historically and by its influence upon the affairs of the world, rhetorical discourse seems the most important subject with which we have to do" (Howes, *Historical Studies* 15). He said that the question of the relationship of rhetoric to the work of the English department was too complicated for him to explore in that article, but he cautioned English departments not to add rhetoric to the long list of other things they attempted to teach until they had acquired "complete knowledge of the breadth and importance of it and [complete awareness] of the distinction between rhetoric and other forms of literature" (Howes, *Historical Studies* 12–13).

Hudson attempted to draw that distinction in another of his influential essays, "Rhetoric and Poetry." Although he conceded that sometimes rhetoric and poetics are intermixed, he insisted that they were distinct disciplines. The essence of his distinction may be contained in his contention that "poetry is for the sake of expression; the impression on others is incidental. Rhetoric is for the sake of impression; the expression is secondary—an indispensable means" (Howes, *Historical Studies* 371). According to this criterion, George Bernard Shaw, Hudson maintains, is more of a rhetorician than he is a dramatic poet, and John Bunyan is a sterling example of a consummate rhetorician who, with his *Pilgrim's Progress*, became a poet.

We must bear in mind that Hudson was himself a published poet and that during most of his professional life, he was a teacher of literature in English departments. He must have had English teachers primarily in mind when he wrote the final paragraph of "Rhetoric and Poetry":

> To summarize, I have tried to emphasize the distinction between pure poetry and rhetoric, and then to suggest that rarely do we find them pure; that poetry in some of its most usual forms is more or less strongly tinged with a rhetorical element; that criticism will walk with surer feet if it can learn to isolate and analyze this rhetorical element. Hence it follows that a part of the equipment of a literary critic, and, we may add, of an interpreter of literature, must be a knowledge of the devices for getting and holding attention, the technique of adaptation of audience and occasion, which are the stock in trade of teachers of public speaking—in other words those "foolish little rhetorical tricks" which Shakespeare and Milton did not disdain to use. (Howes, *Historical Studies* 379)

Because Hudson believed so strongly in the value of humanistic learning, he, like Hunt, wanted English teachers and speech teachers to share the delights and the benefits of both rhetoric and poetics.

What lent a special cachet to the pioneering work of the Cornellians was the publication in 1925 of the first of the four *festschrifts* that I mentioned earlier: *Studies in Rhetoric and Public Speaking in Honor of James Albert Winans* (New York: Century Co., 1925). Windt said that this collection of essays "heralded, more than any other work by American scholars, the renaissance of classical rhetoric in modern times and marked the authors as twentieth-century conveyors of the legacy of Greece and Rome" (Everett Lee Hunt 186). The collection contained two of the most influential essays of the modern period: Everett Lee Hunt's "Plato and Aristotle on Rhetoric and Rhetori-

cians" and Herbert A. Wichelns' "The Literary Criticism of Oratory."[6] Hunt's essay was important because it perceptively summarized the main rhetorical doctrines of Plato, Aristotle, and the Sophists and posed the issues that divided them. Carroll Arnold said of this essay that it represented "the first inquiry into the validity of the classical tradition" (4). It is certainly one of the indispensable secondary works that every student of classical rhetoric has to read.

Wichelns' essay "The Literary Criticism of Oratory" surveyed the published criticism of such orators as Burke, Webster, Lincoln, Gladstone, Bright, and Cobden, and analyzed the authors' mode of criticism. Donald Bryant, one of the second-generation products of the Cornell School of Rhetoric, said of this essay that it "had a greater and more continuous influence upon the development of the scholarship of rhetoric and public address than any other single work published in this century" (Howes, *Notes on the Cornell School* 17). The influence of that seminal essay was diminished only when Edwin Black, one of the third-generation Cornellians and one of Wichelns' Ph.D. students, challenged the position of that essay in his book *Rhetorical Criticism: A Study in Method* (New York: Macmillan, 1965).

It is difficult to think of any other academic department in American universities in this century that had a more auspicious beginning than the Department of Speech and Drama at Cornell had. But very soon there was a shake-up of that department's illustrious personnel. Hoyt Hudson, as we have seen, left Cornell upon his graduation in

1923. Everett Lee Hunt moved on to Swarthmore College in 1926 and eventually became Dean there, a post he occupied for twenty years until his retirement in 1957. Harry Caplan moved out of the Department of Speech and Drama into the Department of Classics. Alexander Drummond gradually gravitated toward his first love, drama, and lost interest in rhetorical studies. Herbert Wichelns eventually returned to Cornell and became the mainstay of the department.

The list of the distinguished graduates of the Cornell School of Rhetoric over the next forty years reads like a Who's Who in Rhetoric. The mere recital of the litany of some of its graduates is testimony enough about the distinction and influence of that department: Hoyt H. Hudson, Herbert A. Wichelns, Harry Caplan, Raymond H. Howes, Wilbur Samuel Howell, Wayland Parrish, Russell H. Wagner, Karl R. Wallace, C. K. Thomas, Donald C. Bryant, Frederick W. Haberman, Ross Scanlan, Wilbur E. Gilman, Harold F. Harding, C. Harold King, Leland M. Griffin, William Utterback, Edwin Black, Lawrence W. Rosenfield. At least nine of those graduates served as editor of the *Quarterly Journal of Speech,* and at least that many Cornellians served as President of the Speech Communication Association. Many of them became chairs of speech departments at colleges and universities all over the country and saw to it that a classical component was added to the curricula of their departments. But the Cornell graduates probably exerted their greatest influence on the profession with their many convention talks and their published books and articles.

Raymond Howes observed that the eighteen Cornell people whose essays appeared in *Historical Studies of Rhetoric and Rhetoricians* had published forty-two books in the forty years since that celebrated first graduate seminar in classical rhetoric in 1920 (*Notes on the Cornell School* 5).

One of the great academic ironies of our time is that this once distinguished department has slipped into total eclipse. In 1963, the renowned Carroll Arnold, who had served as chairman of Cornell's speech department since 1957, left to join the speech department at Pennsylvania State. Sometime in 1964, the speech part of the Cornell department (but not the drama part) was voted out of existence by action of the College of Arts and Sciences. Some speech courses are now taught by adjunct professors in the College of Agriculture, but the illustrious department that was is no more.

What happened to this illustrious and influential department? The answer to that question is the subject for another article, and that article would have to be written by somebody who had an intimate knowledge of the state of affairs in the final years of the department.

Ultimately, the Midwesterners won. They were really the prevailing force right from the beginning in 1915, and they remain the dominating force in speech today. The Big Ten universities have been especially strong and influential. But other schools in various parts of the country have impressive programs too. Conspicuous by their absence have been the ivy-league schools. Even with its Boylston Professorship of Rhetoric in the nineteenth century, Harvard never had a graduate program in rhetoric. Although Princeton hired a number of Cornell graduates, including such giants as Hoyt Hudson and Wilbur Samuel Howell, it never had a graduate program in rhetoric. Cornell is the only ivy-league school that maintained a significant graduate program in rhetoric during the twentieth century. And a residual mark of its influence is the fact that virtually all the graduate speech programs in this country now have a classical-rhetoric component in them.

The most significant development in rhetorical studies in recent years is the growth in the number of graduate programs in rhetoric in English departments. I have always designated 1963 as the year when English teachers manifested a sudden upsurge of interest in rhetoric, especially as it related to the teaching of composition. That interest has built steadily since then, and already there are some strong graduate programs in rhetoric rooted in English departments, and there would be many more if there were available more English teachers qualified to teach graduate courses in rhetoric. It will be interesting to see whether any of these graduate programs become in the field of English what the graduate program at Cornell was in the field of speech.

Works Cited

Arnold, Carroll, "Rhetoric in America since 1900." *Re-Establishing the Speech Profession: The First Fifty Years.* Ed. Robert T. Oliver and Marvin G. Bauer. The Speech Association of the Eastern States, September 1959.

Howes, Raymond. *Notes on the Cornell School of Rhetoric.* Riverside, CA: Privately printed, 1976.

———. Ed. *Historical Studies of Rhetoric and Rhetoricians.* Ithaca: Cornell UP, 1961.

Hudson, Hoyt H. "Alexander M. Drummond." *Studies in Speech and Drama in Honor of A. M. Drummond.* Ithaca: Cornell UP, 1944. (This is one of the four *festschrifts* published in honor of the first generation of distinguished professors of rhetoric at Cornell.)

Hunt, Everett Lee. "Herbert A. Wichelns and the Cornell Tradition of Rhetoric as a Humane Subject." *The Rhetorical Idiom: Essays in Rhetoric, Oratory, Language and Drama Presented to Herbert August Wichelns.* Ed. Donald C. Bryant. Ithaca: Cornell UP, 1958. (This is another of the *festschrifts*.)

Windt, Theodore Otto, Jr. "Everett Lee Hunt on Rhetoric." *The Speech Teacher* 21 (September 1972): 177–92.

———. "Hoyt H. Hudson: Spokesman for the Cornell School of Rhetoric." *Quarterly Journal of Speech* 68 (May 1982): 186–200.

Notes

1. The unofficial chronicler of the Cornell School of Rhetoric has been Raymond F. Howes, who published a number of biographical sketches of the Cornell luminaries in the *Cornell Alumni News*, which he later collected and published in a privately printed pamphlet, *Notes on the Cornell School of Rhetoric* (Riverside, CA, 1976). Two of the most informative articles about the Cornell movement have been the articles that Theodore Otto

Windt, Jr. published in the *Quarterly Journal of Speech* on Everett Hunt and Hoyt Hudson: "Everett Lee Hunt on Rhetoric," *The Speech Teacher* 21 (September 1972): 177–92 and "Hoyt H. Hudson: Spokesman for the Cornell School of Rhetoric," *Quarterly Journal of Speech* 68 (May 1982): 186–200. Over a period of time, I exchanged correspondence about the Cornell School of Rhetoric with the following people: Carroll C. Arnold, Goodwin Berquist, Wilbur Samuel Howell, Raymond F. Howes, Everett Lee Hunt, James J. Murphy, and Theodore Otto Windt, Jr. The many *festschrifts* that were published in honor of several of the first generation of teachers in the Cornell School of Rhetoric and that contain information about the early years of the Cornell School will be cited below.

2. Raymond Howes says that Bower Aly of the University of Oregon was the first one to use the title "The Cornell School of Rhetoric" in print: "Origins of the Cornell School of Rhetoric," *Notes on the Cornell School of Rhetoric* (Riverside, CA: Privately printed, 1976). 1.

3. For the biographical details about Hunt and Hudson, I am indebted to the two articles by Theodore Windt listed in the first note: "Everett Lee Hunt on Rhetoric" and "Hoyt H. Hudson: Spokesman for the Cornell School of Rhetoric." For a complete bibliography of Everett Lee Hunt's works, see Theodore Otto Windt, Jr., "Bibliography of Works by Everett Lee Hunt," *Rhetoric Society Quarterly* 14 (Summer and Fall 1984): 163–72.

4. For the biographical details here, I am indebted to the aforementioned article by Theodore Windt, "Hoyt H. Hudson."

5. These are the four articles: "Can We Modernize the Theory of Invention?" *Quarterly Journal of Speech Education* 7 (Nov. 1921): 325–34: "The Field of Rhetoric," *Quarterly Journal of Speech Education* 9 (April 1923): 167–80, reprinted in *Historical Studies of Rhetoric and Rhetoricians*, ed. Raymond F. Howes (Ithaca, NY: Cornell UP, 1961), 3–15: "Rhetoric and Poetry," *Quarterly Journal of Speech Education* 10 (April 1924): 143–54, reprinted in *Historical Studies of Rhetoric and Rhetoricians*, 369–79; "The Tradition of Our Subject," *Quarterly Journal of Speech*, 17 (June 1931); 320–29.

6. Hunt's essay was first published in the *Quarterly Journal of Speech Education* 6 (June 1920): 35–36. Hunt's essay and an excerpt from Wichelns' essay were reprinted in *Historical Studies of Rhetoric and Rhetoricians*, ed. Raymond F. Howes (Ithaca, NY: Cornell UP, 1961).

Daniel Fogarty

I. A. Richards' Theory

◊ *Beginning with George Campbell's definition of rhetoric as "the art of adapting discourse to its end," I. A. Richards directs our attention to what people mean by the words they use. His thoughtful analysis embraces the concepts of abstracting, metaphor, definition, comprehension, and thought-word-thing relationships (elsewhere referred to as the semantic triangle). His goal is to identify the reasons why we sometimes experience difficulty comprehending a poem and the normal ways by which a message may be interpreted differently than its sender intended.* ◊

The work of Professor I. A. Richards presents a substantial departure from the traditional theory of rhetoric. He does not start his inquiry into rhetoric with a metaphysical methodology, as did Aristotle. He starts with the psycho-biological origins of man's drive to express himself in linguistic and other symbols. His method of inquiry, too, as he has explained it to the writer, is Platonic and dialectical, rather than Aristotelian and organizational. Plato's idea structure shows also in Richards' near-nominalistic relations between thoughts and things. There are three major additional differences that mark Richards' rhetoric as new. (1) He uses the findings of modern biology and psychology to help him explain the functions of rhetorical language. (2) He regards metaphor as a central aspect of rhetoric. (3) He deals with rhetoric not only as speech but as part of the communication process, whether a person is speaking, listening, writing, or reading to achieve efficient comprehension. These characteristics will, it is hoped, become clear in the delineation of Richards' theory that follows.

The treatment of Richards' theory is divided into six sections: his background and approach to rhetoric; his theory of abstraction; his approach to metaphor; his conception of thought–word–thing relationships; his theory of definition; and his theory of comprehending.

The Background and Approach to Rhetoric

Education at Cambridge University and five subsequent years there as a colleague of C. K. Ogden led to Richards'

Reprinted by permission of the publisher from Fogarty, Daniel, ROOTS FOR A NEW RHETORIC "I. A. Richards' Theory." (New York: Teachers College Press, © 1959 by Teachers College, Columbia University. All rights reserved.) pp. 28–55.

coauthorship with Ogden in his first important work connected with rhetorical theory, *The Meaning of Meaning* (1923). His research and reading since that time make him a recognized scholar in many relevant fields. Following *The Meaning of Meaning*, he published *Principles of Literary Criticism* (1924) and *Science and Poetry* (1925). Then, still at Cambridge, he published the results of his experiments with comprehension in *Practical Criticism* (1929). These works, all leaning toward a theory of interpretation, were written while Richards worked with Ogden on a basic English vocabulary that would simplify the problems of the translator and the beginner learning the English language. The next year, spent as visiting professor at Tsing Hua University in Peking, not only gave Richards experience with problems of interpretation, but seems to have confirmed his early theory. On his return from the East and while visiting Harvard, he published the results of his Peking studies in *Mencius on the Mind* (1931). The next four years saw three works into print. *Basic Rules of Reason* (1933) and *Coleridge on Imagination* (1934) testify to his persevering interest in the functions of the mind, relative to language. *The Philosophy of Rhetoric* (1936) is a series of lectures on Richards' new conception of rhetoric.

A second visit to Peking, from 1936 to 1938, as Director of the Orthological Institute of China, gave him time to get into publication the results of another set of experiments in interpretation. *Interpretation in Teaching* (1938), prepared for teachers, attempted to apply his theory of interpretation to the classroom. Subsequently he returned to Harvard University and served as Director of the Harvard Commission on English Language Studies, from 1939 to 1944, and from 1944 to the present as Director of Language Research. All this experience in the meaning aspects of language must have had a bearing on the final cast of his theory of rhetoric so directly aimed, as it is, at comprehension of meaning. These later years have provided educators and teachers with the most recent and mature formulation of Richards' work. In a letter commenting on the present analysis of his theory, he says:

I feel that my later work—with the deep indebtedness to Coleridge and Plato—is likely to be of far more permanent interest than the earlier (with its echoes, via Ogden mainly, of Bentham).[1]

Among other works, the most pertinent to rhetoric in these later years are *How to Read a Page* (1942) and *Speculative Instruments* (1955). The first makes much clearer the function of reason in the abstractive process. The latter contains one chapter that concisely explains what all the other works have been leading up to—his theory of comprehending.

In the wide range of his scholarly publications, the depth of his research in the many fields related to rhetoric stands out. He seems as familiar with Socrates as with Russell, as well read in logic and the mathematics of communication as in linguistics and psychology. Stanley Hyman says:

His learning in almost every area of knowledge is so tremendous, his significance so great in half a dozen fields besides criticism, and the brilliance and subtlety of at least his earlier books so overpowering, that any hit-and-run treatment of him in a few thousand words is bound to be laughably superficial.[2]

In conversation with the writer, Richards has revealed his deep roots in Plato and Coleridge, and the influence of other philosophers which is probably more prominent in his later works. He feels that whatever influence Kant and Bentham had on his work must have come through Ogden, and that a lot of his theory about thought–word–thing relationships might have come from the latter part of the ''Analytica Posteriora'' of Aristotle. Otherwise he acknowledges the help of G. F. Stout's psychology, Piaget's studies of children's language habits, and, for his first notions on primordial abstraction, William James's *Psychology*.[3] There are, however, strong Gestalt leanings[4] throughout his theory supplanting an admitted beginning in Associationism.[5] The preface to the first edition of *The Meaning of Meaning* testifies to the influence of Malinowski,[6] at least upon the contents of that early work.

It is important, for those interested in a practical teaching rhetoric, to remember that Richards is himself a teacher. Much of the research for his books was done in the classroom.[7] Whatever he may offer toward the improvement of courses in composition, speech, writing, and communication will be practical suggestions from a practicing teacher.

Richards' definition of rhetoric is borrowed from George Campbell's *The Philosophy of Rhetoric* (1835). For Campbell, rhetoric was the art of adapting discourse to its end.[8] The approach that brought Richards to this conception of a teaching rhetoric is Pla-

tonic rather than Aristotelian, as we have said. Richards does not build upon a foundation with logical blocks, from the ground up. His schematic idea of methodology is to start with whatever sticks up as the most urgent and pertinent element of a problem, and then work in any direction at all that has the scent of truth. The important thing, seemingly, to Richards, is to be free to seek in any direction at any time.[9] As he narrates the progressive steps in his early studies in rhetoric, this organismic rather than architectural method of inquiry becomes clear.

His point of departure was the most urgent and obvious question about man. What is the symbol-using power that is uniquely characteristic of him? Beginning with what was observable, Richards turned to the findings of biology and psychology. He could see that man shared with the most elemental types of animal the stimulus and response patterns of the merely nutritive and sense life. The response of an amoeba to prodding or the directional growing of a vine is not essentially different from the blinking of a man's eyes in a sudden strong light or the thrusting out of his hands as he begins to fall. Viewing such phenomena of response in the light of modern biology and psychology, Richards could describe them as fundamental sorting of the things they experienced.[10] Responses of organisms could be classified into two rough categories: acceptance and rejection. Repeated and multiplied experience conditioned the sortings into the habits of growth and feeding we observe.[11]

But man, besides the responses he shares with these elemental animals, has a unique kind of response to stimuli of all kinds, elemental or otherwise. He can use language symbols to express his feelings and needs. He even has a special way of assimilating and integrating with exterior stimuli.[12] He experiences what we call thoughts about these stimuli. Somehow, within his own organism, he can know what he is sorting from what, and make comparisons. Furthermore, he can store away residual traces of his sorting experiences in such a way that he can call them up again and again at will, without the original stimulus being there at all. So man is constantly comparing new experiences with old ones, in search of similarity.[13] At this point Richards seems to have seen that classifying with this conceptual sorting facility means distinguishing things from one another by abstract characteristics. Thus, out of primordial abstraction, or elementary animal sorting, he came to conceptual abstraction. As Richards explains:

A sensation would be something that was just *so*, on its own, a datum; as such we have none. Instead we have perceptions, responses whose character comes to them from the past as well as the present occasion. A perception is never just of an *it*; perception takes whatever it perceives as a thing of a certain sort. All thinking from the lowest to the highest—whatever else it may be—is sorting.[14]

It will help to remember, as we proceed with the discussion of abstraction and metaphor, thought–word–thing relationships and definition, that these four philosophical elements are probably equally basic and quite inseparable except for the purpose of discussion. Abstraction and epistemology and definition elements certainly do imply and include one another. Here we separate them only mentally,

and we begin with abstraction only because it follows so naturally from Richards' starting point in primordial sorting.

The Theory of Abstraction

In general, an abstraction is for Richards what it has been to philosophers for centuries: the selection of a characteristic attributable to many real objects, its segregation in the mind as an abstract idea, and its expression in symbols as an abstract word.[15]

But biology and psychology gave Richards insights into the process of abstracting. One of these insights involves his concept of the $\dot{\alpha}\rho\chi\acute{\eta}$ (reason). The other involves his notion of context.

The $\dot{\alpha}\rho\chi\acute{\eta}$ notion follows from primordial sorting. Since man possesses the characteristic abilities of each of the animal forms from the simplest to the most complex, he can put all these abilities to work in reaction to a given stimulus. His response can be, at one and the same time, biological, emotional, and conceptual.[16] When he does conceptualize a response, he can express it in language symbols. There is a complexity here, because the biological, emotional, and conceptual elements in the response fight for dominance at one another's expense.[17] There is a risk, then, of loss of real meaning in the expression of the real happening in language symbols. The organism sorts and compares the experience with other similar past experiences. When it conceptualizes the experience, when it abstracts the characteristic it selects (as it must do to classify it), it may be abstracting an emotional aspect and neglecting a very important conceptual meaning.[18] For example, catching a quick glimpse of a large red glow at the stage end of a theatre might call up past similar experiences of glowing red. One could recall the flame that once burned his finger, or a harrowing experience in a flaming building. He might, in instinctive panic, shout, "Fire!" If he did, he would have selected the emotionally frightening element of his own experience to interpret what might, on further examination, be only a red stage light for dramatic effect.

Richards' answer to this complexity of choice in the abstractive process is the $\alpha\rho\chi\eta$ (reason) whose function it is to control both the emotional and the conceptual elements in the process in a way that ensures the proper, realistic, and balanced whole meaning of the event. It is under the guidance and control of the reason that the process of abstraction can produce true and realistic abstract symbols.[19]

Richards' other important insight into the abstraction process is as closely connected with meaning as the first. He refers to the term "context" in a special sense. It includes not only all the concomitant surroundings of a thought and of the event the thought is about, but the whole complex of similar thoughts and events that might be compared with it in the mind's sortings. In short, a context embraces the whole field of experience that can be connected with an experienced event, or with the thought of that event.[20]

When we abstract, of course, we select some element from a very intricate maze of contexts, all classified under multiple aspects of past abstractions, like a complicated cross-reference index system.[21] When we abstract the characteristic "red" and apply it to the stage of a theatre, we have selected "red" from thousands of contexts, ranging through fire engines to the flush that accompanies embarrassment. The $\alpha\rho\chi\eta$ may have managed to control and balance the emotional elements in these contexts with the conceptual elements, and prevented our jumping to the untrue abstractive judgment that the stage is on fire. But there is another complexity here. The abstraction in any given event to be expressed has its own context, made up of the concomitant external and internal, real and remembered elements that connect with the thought and symbol "red" in this theatre, for this person, at this time.[22] Now the term "red" selects only the color characteristic and leaves out all the rest of the richness of the context. For the full meaning of "red," we have to look to the whole context of the symbol. From the concept of abstraction, Richards has come to the nature of meaning. In this connection he says:

In these contexts one item—typically a word—takes over the duties of parts which can then be omitted from the recurrence. There is thus an abridgement of the context only shown in the behavior of living things, and most extensively and drastically shown by man. When this abridgement happens, what the sign or word—the item with these delegated powers—means is the missing parts of the context.[23]

Richards' final admonition about abstraction is that we should remember it as a mental activity, and valid only in that sense.[24] In the discussion of parts of context and the conflict between emotion and intellect, we tend to think of these elements as really separate and distinct. This is one of the liabilities of abstraction. The parts of the context are one, and the desiring of the emotions is never quite separable from the thinking of the intellect. As Richards puts it, "We cannot, in fact, wholly leave off wanting. No thinking can be motiveless."[25]

We can proceed now, quite naturally, from Richards' general theory of abstraction to his most important application of it in the theory of metaphor.

An Approach to Metaphor

The analysis that Richards makes of metaphor harks back to his theory of abstraction. All metaphor does, after all, is abstract from one reference (thought) and attribute the abstracted quality of another reference for the purpose of clarifying or livening up its meaning.[26] Take, for example, the metaphor in the utterance "He was a lion in battle." Here are two symbols, "lion" and "man," and two references (thoughts), one for the lion and one for the man. The "lion" reference has been selected by the communicator as suitable to clarify or enliven his communicated reference of the man as a courageous fighter. Abstraction is the process used to select from the "lion" reference the characteristic of courage as being the most appropriate one among all the elements and characteristics in all the "lion" contexts usually known to people. Having eliminated all the other characteristics of "lion" and all the rest of their contexts, the communicator welded the abstracted quality of courage to the other refer-

ence, "man." It is this welding, this borrowing of a characteristic from one reference to attach it to another, that is essential to metaphor-making and distinguishes it from ordinary abstraction.[27] Richards sums up this theory in *The Philosophy of Rhetoric:*

In the simplest formulation, when we use a metaphor we have two thoughts of different things active together and supported by a single word, or phrase, whose meaning is a resultant of the interaction.[28]

For use in the discussion of metaphor, Richards has introduced two new terms, which, for him, avoid the ambiguity of the traditional terminology of metaphor. The term "tenor" he applies to the "underlying idea or principal subject which the vehicle or figure means."[29] This is the man in the example, "He was a lion in battle." The term "vehicle" is attached to the other reference—"lion"—that lends its selected characteristics to make the tenor clearer or more vivid.[30] For the basis of relationship between the two references or parts of the metaphor, he uses the traditional term "ground."[31]

Richards' most emphatic contention about metaphor, thus explained, is that language is naturally metaphoric. Since metaphor is just abstraction for the purpose of clearer and more vivid communication,[32] since it seems to be the nature of our thinking to be perpetually busy with sorting and classifying references and comparing contexts and their parts, and since our language symbolizes this thinking, it seems to Richards that our language must be highly, habitually, and even naturally metaphoric. He takes issue with Aristotle on this point in the early part of his treatment of metaphor in *The Philosophy of Rhetoric.*[33] Aristotle's contention seems to be that ability to use metaphor cannot be taught to another and that it is a sign of genius, inasmuch as it indicates an eye for resemblances. Richards' counter contention is, of course, that metaphor-making ability comes naturally to ordinary people. He remarks, in fact, that:

We cannot get through three sentences of ordinary fluid discourse without it. . . . Even in the rigid language of the settled sciences we do not eliminate or prevent it without great difficulty.[34]

Richards' theories of abstraction and metaphor have involved three elements of the thought process that need special examination. The next section will deal with Richards' concept of the relationships between thoughts, words, and things.

Thought–Word–Thing Relationships

Richards' epistemological theory concerns itself a good deal more with the operations of thoughts (references), words (symbols), and things (referents) than with their nature. As he states his aim, it is to find out "how words work."[35] The foregoing account of abstraction has shown how the thought process takes place, but has said nothing of the relationships between the three elements involved. The epistemological inquiry is, of course, not a distinct and different inquiry, but rather the same one viewed from a different angle.

At the outset there is need for a definition of Richards' terms. And possibly the best way to answer that need will be to cite his own description of the "match scrape" example of a mental operation and then cite his own definitions of all the elements in that exemplary operation:

The effects upon the organism due to any sign, which may be any stimulus from without, or any process taking place within, depend upon the past history of the organism, both generally and in more precise fashion. In a sense, no doubt, the whole past history is relevant; but there will be some among the past events in that history which will more directly determine the nature of the present agitation than others. Thus when we strike a match, the movements we make and the sound of the scrape are present stimuli. But the excitation which results is different from what it would be had we never struck matches before. Past strikings have left, in our organization, engrams, residual traces, which help to determine what the mental process will be. For instance the mental process is among other things an awareness that we are striking a *match.* Apart from the effects of similar previous situations we should have no such awareness. Suppose further that the awareness is accompanied by an expectation of a flame. The expectation again will be due to the effects of situations in which the striking of a match has been followed by a flame. The expectation is the excitation of part of an engram complex, which is called up by the stimulus (the scrape) similar to a part only of the original stimulus-situation.[36]

Here is a sign situation, a reference–symbol–referent unit—that is, a thought–word–thing unit—in which can be found all the elements for which Richards has specific terms. The *reference* is the thought about the scraping match and all its concomitant elements, together with similar groups of elements remembered as past similar experiences.[37] The *symbol* would of course be any language unit used to express what has gone on in the example.

"Match scrape," for instance, might express it in a given circumstance.[38] The *referent* is the actual event of the scraping of the match and the real concomitant motions, noises, sights, and so on, that happen independently of the subject's thought.[39] The *sign* is that one stimulus in the whole complex event which has the effect of reminding the subject of the rest of the details of the event as well as remembrances of past associable events—in this case, the scraping itself.[40] The *context* is the whole event with all its associations from the subject's past experience. Richards calls it a *psychological* context when referring to the event in thought process and linked with other, remembered, similar thought processes. He calls it an *external* context when referring to the actual event as happening outside the mind.[41] The movement of the fingers, the flash of light, and all the other concomitant real happenings of the match-scrape event are parts of the external context. The last important element in the sign situation is the *engram*. The term refers to the residual trace of some past excitation, either in the nerve tissue or in some other physiological function of a part of the organism.[42]

Richards' own definitions of these terms will serve to clarify the example and its explanation:

. . . for words, arrangements of words, images, gestures, and such representations as drawings or mimetic sounds we use the term symbols.[43]
. . . a reference . . . is a set of external and psychological contexts linking a mental process to a referent.[44]
. . . a referent . . . thing . . . object.[45]
A sign is always a stimulus similar to some part of an original stimulus and sufficient to call up the engram formed by that stimulus.[46]

A context is a set of entities (things or events) related in a certain way; these entities have each a character such that other sets of entities occur having the same characters and related by the same relation; and these occur "nearly uniformly."[47]
An engram is the residual trace of an adaption made by the organism to a stimulus.[48]

With the match-scrape example and a definition of terms, it becomes easier to understand Richards' diagram[49] of the relationships between thought, word, and thing; between reference, symbol, and referent:

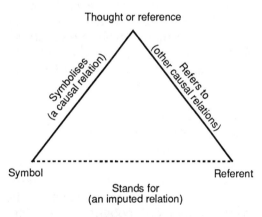

Figure 1. From *The Meaning of Meaning*, by C. K. Ogden and I. A. Richards (Routledge and Kegan Paul, Ltd., 1923), p. 11. Used by permission.

As can be seen in Richards' diagram, there is a causal relationship between the reference and the symbol. In other words, the communicator using a certain word or expression can cause his hearers to form a thought somewhat similar to his own. And, conversely, the thought or reference can cause, at least in part, the use of a certain symbol to express it.

The second relationship, between the reference and the referent, is also causal, inasmuch as the thing, or referent, which is or has been seen, felt, heard, and so on, has stimulated the organism and caused it to think about the source of the stimulation or have a reference about it. This causation can be directly from the present stimulation or indirectly from past stimulations or the memory of such stimulations.

But the last relationship—and this is the important one for Richards—is not directly causal, nor is the relationship a real one in the sense of the other two. This "imputed" relationship points to the key principle from which stems Richards' theory of propositional truth, his value norms, his theory of definition, and the validity of his criteria for accurate interpretation. It is the principle stating that there is no referential relation between the symbol and the referent, between the word and the thing. To phrase it differently, the symbol, or word, does not really "refer to" the thing or referent except indirectly through the thought or reference. The symbol merely "stands for" the thing referred to by the reference. Whereas it symbolizes the reference, it does not symbolize the thing.[50]

This key contention about the indirectness of the relationship between the symbol and the referent is of major importance to Richards, because a failure to understand and apply it is, for him, at the root of most of the problems of conceptual meaning.[51] The confusions of ambiguity and word shifts, multiple meaning, and out-of-place definitions are, in his theory, at least partly ascribable to the making of direct relationships between symbols and referents.[52]

Such a mistaken, direct, relationship would assume that the communicated content of a symbol is the same, or nearly the same, as the content of the thing it stands for, which is not usually or necessarily so.[53] It is easy to see a wide range of opportunity for ambiguity and inadequate definition in the atmosphere of such an assumption. But with this assumption denied, a word can mean many things to many people, can even mean different things to the same person at different times. It becomes necessary to check back to the referent if one is to understand the symbol. When a communicator uses a word he has so checked against the thing it stands for, he is much more likely to be clearly understood. It is for this reason that Richards so deplores any absolute doctrine of proper meaning[54] which assumes a direct, stable, and real relation between word and thing. Such a doctrine fails to take into account that the word stands for a host of different contexts, patterns, and associations for a different person or at a different time. If the reference is the pivot of the relation between symbol and referent, and if this pivotal reference is continually changing, enlarging, and enriching its contexts,[55] it is no wonder that the meaning of a symbol also undergoes change.

The psychological context of this pivotal reference is important, too. It explains the variability and ever-expanding breadth of the reference that goes with the symbol. For one word or symbol there can be as many references or thoughts as there are persons to think them. The communicator faces as many interpretations of his symbols as he has hearers, and even each of these is momentarily changing.[56] The hearer may be sure, when he hears a symbol, that it can mean something at least slightly different from any meaning it may have had at any other time in his hearing.

The contextual theory of signs clearly allows inferences that could be formulated as rules or laws, the obeying of which might prevent mistakes of comprehension. Richards does draw these inferences and does formulate six laws, which he calls the "Canons of Symbolism."[57] They simply state Richards' logic in the form of precepts, as based upon the principles of contradiction and identity.

The Theory of Definition

The concept of defining here proposed owes its simplicity and directness to the fact that its groundwork has just been laid in the immediately preceding theory of thought–word–thing relationships.

Richards begins by clearing away what he calls "the barren subtleties of Genus and Differentia"[58] in the traditional theory of definition. For him, they lead to four difficulties which a practical theory must avoid:

1. Confusion between real and merely verbal definition, the defining of words and of things.
2. Confusion of symbol and referent in casual conversation; that is, "saying 'chien means "dog" when we ought to say 'the word chien and the word "dog" both mean the same animal.'"
3. Forgetting that definitions are essentially "ad hoc"; in other words, "relevant to some purpose or situation

and consequently are applicable only over a restricted field or 'universe of discourse.'" . . . "Whenever a term is thus taken outside the universe of discourse for which it has been defined, it becomes a metaphor, and may be in need of fresh definition."

4. Confusing intensive with extensive definitions. According to Richards an intensive definition calls for no change in the sign situation that is common to the person defining (or his reference) and the thing defined. No change is required because the definer prefers to stick to this one sign situation and analyze it alone and more intensively. In the case of the extensive definition, the definer seeks outside this sign situation and its context so as to compare it with other signs and contexts and to distinguish it clearly.[59]

Richards' answer to these four problems is the principle of indirect relationship between the symbol and the referent. Whenever there is a difficulty about what a symbol means, when there is a question of definition, look for the referent.[60] A referent common to all concerned, in a discussion for instance, must be found. If agreement cannot be reached this way, then other referents must be found upon which there is agreement, and from these the required referent can be evolved through its connections with the other referents.[61] These relations between the referents known and the referents to be found are classified by Richards under ten heads that seem to define very well the range of the communicator's interest:

1. Symbolization
2. Similarity
3. Spatial relations

4. Temporal relations
5. Causal relations of the physical kinds
6. Causal relations of the psychological kinds
7. Causal relations of the psycho-physical kinds
8. Referent-reference relations (being the object of a mental state)
9. Common complex relations
10. Legal relations[62]

Clearly, one of the ways to find the referent for the term "cold war" would be to look for the well-known referents of the term "cold" and "war." Then, by Richards' similarity relation, a new symbol, "a kind of war with no firing," is found. And this, after all, is really a beginning definition of "cold war" which was found by seeking the known referents behind the unknown one.

Richards then proceeds to describe the range of definition. He regrets that this range is sometimes falsely limited because of the persistent tendency to think of words as having proper and unalterable meanings.[63] He explains how kinds of defining may grow out of purposes in their immediate use. A definition for speculative discussion may be quite different from a definition of the same referent with a view to a practical operation. The subterfuges, by which speakers and writers sometimes suggest unchangeable definition where there really is no such thing, are listed by Richards. The phonetic subterfuge groups a hazy or emotive word, like "discrimination," with others similar in sound but clear in meaning like "dirt" and "death."[64] The hypostatic subterfuge uses the most overloaded and confusing universal or abstract terms, like "liberty" and "glory."[65] The utraquistic

subterfuge uses words that have two meanings, such as the functional meaning of "knowledge" (knowing something), and the objective meaning (what is known).[66]

Up to this point Richards has been involved in highly speculative inquiry. While he has offered several practical rules of thumb, they were guides to efficient mental processes behind our rhetoric and communication rather than guides for immediate use in communicating.[67] At this point, however, he can take all this philosophy of rhetoric and apply it to what he feels is the most important single concern in an improved rhetoric or communication. He proposes that what needs thorough analysis, what needs to be adapted and applied to our symbol-using situation today, is comprehension, efficient interpretation.[68] Consequently, all his speculative inquiries culminate in his still speculative, but none-the-less practical, instruments of comprehending.

Toward a Theory of Comprehending

Although the clearest and most recent formulation of Richards' theory of comprehending is expressed in his latest book, *Speculative Instruments* (1955), the special research technique he uses to compile evidence for the theory is available only in *Practical Criticism* (1929) and *Interpretation in Teaching* (1938).

Faced with the emotive as well as the strictly referential content of language, Richards worked out a system which enabled him to give his students exercises in practical problems of interpretation and to gather evidence from these exercises about the roots of misunderstanding. The students, presented with identified passages of poetry and prose, voluntarily wrote protocols, or interpretations of the passages.[69] Richards' examination of these protocols revealed common patterns of frequently recurring kinds of mistakes, misinterpretations, meaning blocks, prejudices, preconceptions, and stock responses. From this information Richards developed a list of the ten difficulties readers generally have with poetry, and which also apply to prose:

1. Making out the plain sense
2. Sensuous apprehension
3. Imagery visualizing
4. Mnemonic irrelevances
5. Stock responses
6. Sentimentality
7. Inhibition
8. Doctrinal adhesions
9. Technical presuppositions
10. General critical preconceptions.[70]

Such is the material used to substantiate Richards' contentions with regard to the dangerously slippery subject of emotion and value.[71]

It was with these experimental findings that he approached the most recent form of his theory of comprehending. We will need to summarize what Richards intends by the terms "comprehending," "meaning," and "interpreting." A comprehending is, of course, an accurate and true understanding, but is described by Richards as the nexus or context, or the network of contexts, that connect a whole series of past occurrences of partially similar utterances in partially similar situations.[72] This comprehension is the seizing of a meaning. It is the birth in the comprehending organism of a ref-

erence or a feeling or a tendency or a purpose. The meaning itself, which is seized, is first described by Richards as "the missing parts of its context."[73] He means, of course, the missing parts of the psychological and external contexts referred to in his contextual theory of signs. He means the reference with its contexts. Interpretation is the process of seizing this meaning and having this comprehension.

By "instruments," in *Speculative Instruments,* Richards means the norms used to compare alternative meanings so as to arrive at accurate and true comprehension. These instruments are the elements common to all utterances and also the elements about which questions must be asked by the interpreter, lest he run the risk of misunderstanding the utterance. It is these instruments that Richards hopes will be at the center of the organization of a new rhetoric.[74] He was aiming at these instruments all along through what, in earlier stages, he called "tasks of rhetoric," "aims of discourse," "language function," and "kinds of meaning."[75]

The seven instruments in question are listed here with Richards' own diagram to show that, even though they are interdependent, purpose has a special place in any instance of comprehending.[76]

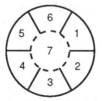

1. Indicating
2. Characterizing
3. Realizing
4. Valuing
5. Influencing
6. Controlling
7. Purposing

Figure 2. From *Speculative Instruments,* by I. A. Richards (University of Chicago Press, 1955), p. 26. Used by permission.

He labels this diagram "Comprehending," since these are the sorts of work the communication utterance does to make itself comprehensible. They are the functions of the message working to be understood, as well as the functions of the interpreting mind trying to understand.[77]

Indicating is simply pointing out the referent of the symbol situation. *Characterizing* goes further. It says something about the referent (or thing); sorts it out, to some extent, from other things; attaches characteristics to it; finds a context for it that has been put together by a nexus of other contexts of previously experienced, similar situations. In the utterance to be comprehended, indicating and characterizing merely point out and segregate the referent.[78]

Realizing is not meant in the allowable sense of accomplishing something or bringing something to fruition, but in the sense of understanding, "having before the mind more fully, more consciously, more vividly than on occasions of less realization."[79] It can overlap with characterizing, but it does not need to do so. In fact, as Richards says: "All my seven components can vary independently, though they usually don't."[80]

Valuing is the assessing of the utterance from the vantage point of worth, obligation, or justice. But the assessing must be as philosophically neutral as it can be without losing its truly evaluative function. To exercise this valuing properly, according to Richards' plan, the interpreter need not—and, of course, in this connection, cannot—be detached. But he must be as neutral as possible.[81]

Influencing marks the state of wanting to "change or preserve unchanged"[82] whatever the utterance in question concerns. It is the throwing of the interpreter's weight to the side of keeping the uttered situation as it is or changing it.

Controlling or administering is the instrument that measures interpretations inasmuch as they are making the decisions of stability or change mentioned in the paragraph on influencing. Here the claims of the other instruments of the utterance are objectively balanced and organized by the interpreting mind.[83]

Purposing is the measuring of the intention, the motive, the end, of the utterance. Richards puts this instrument in the central position in the diagram, not because purpose has a higher importance in any hierarchical sense, but because purpose is connected with that original drive of the organism to express itself. The purpose of the utterance is connected with that twofold cause of the use of language in all situations: the inner needs of the organism and the stimulations it receives from outside.[84]

While the first two of these instruments are usually primary, there is no need that they be so. The measuring and comparing that go on in each succeeding application of the seven instruments to the comprehending situation will be modified by the applications of the instruments that have been applied to it earlier.[85] Thus characterizing may be fuller and more detailed because it happens after realizing than if it were to happen before realizing. The seven instruments have no special order of application, no distinct sequence, no separation necessarily in time. But "they are all of them coactive together inextricably all the time."[86]

There is no necessary or set hierarchy in the interrelationships of these new instruments:

There is thus at the heart of any theory of meaning a principle of the instrument. The exploration of comprehension is the task of devising a system of instruments for comparing meanings. But these systems, these instruments, are themselves comparable. They belong with what they compare and are subject in the end to one another. Indeed this mutual subjection and control seems to be the αρχη for a doctrine of comprehension—that upon which all else depends.[87]

Thus the mutual control these instruments exercise over one another is the αρχη or first principle of the theory. The instruments are the yardsticks or calipers according to which the comparisons of meanings are to be made.[88] Nor does this system of instruments concern only the reader–hearer end of the communication unit. The writer–speaker can use these instruments too, to purify, clarify, and objectivize his communication.[89] But most important of all is the consideration that the education of efficient comprehenders amounts to the preparation of efficiently comprehending audiences which, presumably, would not long put up with the pervading and flagrant ambiguities and distortions of meaning to be found in so much of current spoken and printed material. Presumably, also, an exacting demand would be created for the type of communicator who has been educated to this kind of efficient comprehension, and has become accustomed to subjecting his utterances to a like efficient scrutiny with similar normative principles and instru-

ments.[90] He would, in other words, be behaving as his own first audience to pretest the offering of his own communication.

The sense of these seven instruments and their applicability becomes much clearer when Richards translates them into questions the interpreter may ask himself about different comparable interpretations he may see in any utterances. These questions correspond in number and order to the instruments themselves. Referring to such comparable interpretations, he asks:

1. How far do they pick out the same (or at least analogous) things to talk about?
2. How far do they say the same (or at least analogous) things about them?
3. How far do they present with equal vividness and/or actuality, weak or strong?
4. How far do they value in the same ways?
5. How far would they keep or change in the same ways?
6. How far are the dependencies and interplay between 1, 2, 3, 4, 5, and 6 itself the same in them both?
7. How widely would they serve the same purposes, playing the same parts, within the varying activities they might occur in?[91]

Richards also goes about the business of connecting his instruments with the sociology and psychology of communication. Taking the Shannon and Weaver diagram[92] of communication and making some small changes to suit his purposes better, he first inserts the

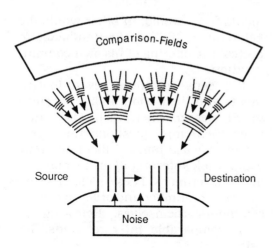

Figure 3. From *Speculative Instruments*, by
I. A. Richards (University of Chicago Press,
1955), p. 23. Used by permission.

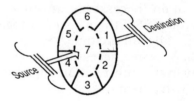

Figure 4.

These instruments as components of
his system of comprehension are the
heart and the head of Richards' proposed new rhetoric, the core of a discipline that will take the place of the old
rhetoric among the liberal arts.[95] A
grasp of such things and much practice
and exercising in them is Richards'
tentative answer to the rhetoric
problem. As we saw in the early pages
of this analysis of Richards' theory, he
is dissatisfied with the way current
rhetoric concentrates upon the mere
devices of persuasive composition and
speech. He wants a whole treatment of
man's symbol-using power in prose, its
philosophy as well as its practical application. He proposes that this wholeness should be reflected in a new
teaching rhetoric for classroom use.[96]

fields of comparison[93] so that the relation can be seen between the operation
of the principles of communication and
the operating fields of the instruments
(Fig. 3). Then, turning the diagram out
ninety degrees and looking down it as
one might aim down the length of a pole,
he shows the relational position of the
instruments themselves (Fig. 4). The
instrument diagram has now been fitted
on to the pole of the communication
diagram, much like a wheel upon an
axle. The fields of comparison in Figure
3 are, of course, represented as containing many different and comparable
readings or meanings or interpretations of the communicated utterance.
Consequently they are comparison
fields in the sense that it is here that the
interpreting mind will be making its
measurings and sortings according to
the seven instruments on the wheel
that encircles the fields at an angle of
ninety degrees in Figure 4.[94]

Notes

1. Letter from I. .A. Richards, Boston, December 7, 1956.
2. Stanley E. Hyman, *The Armed Vision* (New
York: Vintage Books, Inc., 1955), p. 278.
c1947, 1948, 1955, by Alfred Knopf, Inc.
3. Interview with I. A. Richards, Boston, October 5, 1956.
4. Richards' theory of context is clearly Gestal-
tist, as is his conception of comparison fields
in his more recent theory of comprehending.
5. I. A. Richards, *The Philosophy of Rhetoric*
(New York: Oxford University Press, c1936),
p. 15.

6. C. K. Ogden and I. A. Richards, *The Meaning of Meaning* (London: Routledge and Kegan Paul, Ltd., 1923), Preface to 1st ed., p. lx. Originally published by Harcourt, Brace & Co., Inc., New York.
7. Two of Richards' books are the direct result of classroom experiments: *Practical Criticism* (New York: Harcourt, Brace & Co., Inc., c1929) and *Interpretation in Teaching* (New York: Harcourt, Brace & Co., Inc., c1938).
8. George Campbell, *The Philosophy of Rhetoric* (Boston: J. H. Wilkins and Co., Hilliard, Gray, and Co., and Gould, Lincoln, and Kendall, 1835), p. 11.
9. Richards quotes from Plato's "Republic" to illustrate this dialectic seeking of the truth. He illustrates it himself in his inquiry steps from elemental biological abstraction to conceptual abstraction, to epistemology. For dialectic inquiry method, see *How to Read a Page* (New York: W. W. Norton & Company, Inc., 1942), pp. 215–222.
10. Ogden and Richards, *op. cit.*, p. 8; also Richards, *The Philosophy of Rhetoric*, pp. 29–31.
11. Richards, *The Philosophy of Rhetoric*, p. 30.
12. *Ibid.*
13. Ogden and Richards, *op. cit.*, p. 52.
14. Richards, *The Philosophy of Rhetoric*, p. 30.
15. Ogden and Richards, *op. cit.*, pp. 213–214; and Richards, *The Philosophy of Rhetoric*, p. 31.
16. Ogden and Richards, *op. cit.*, pp. 223–225; Richards, *The Philosophy of Rhetoric*, pp. 40–41; and *How to Read a Page*, pp. 98–99.
17. Richards, *How to Read a Page*, p. 75.
18. Ogden and Richards, *op. cit.*, pp. 124–125.
19. Richards, *How to Read a Page*, pp. 74–75 and 101–102.
20. Ogden and Richards, *op. cit.*, pp. 56–58; and Richards, *The Philosophy of Rhetoric*, pp. 34–37.
21. *Ibid.*, p. 35.
22. Ogden and Richards, *op. cit.*, p. 56.
23. Richards, *The Philosophy of Rhetoric*, p. 34.
24. Richards, *How to Read a Page*, pp. 98–99.
25. *Ibid.*, p. 99.
26. Ogden and Richards, *op. cit.*, p. 213.
27. *Ibid.*, pp. 213–214.
28. Richards, *The Philosophy of Rhetoric*, p. 93.
29. *Ibid.*, p. 97.
30. *Ibid.*, pp. 79 and 100.
31. *Ibid.*, p. 117.
32. Ogden and Richards, *op. cit.*, pp. 213–214.
33. Richards, *The Philosophy of Rhetoric*, pp. 89–93.
34. *Ibid.*, p. 92.
35. *Ibid.*, pp. 8 and 23.
36. Ogden and Richards, *op. cit.*, p. 52. Originally published by Harcourt, Brace & Co., Inc., New York, and quoted with their permission.
37. *Ibid.*, p. 90.
38. *Ibid.*, pp. 9 and 23.
39. *Ibid.*, p. 9, footnote.
40. *Ibid.*, p. 53.
41. *Ibid.*, pp. 58, 56–57, and 263–265.
42. *Ibid.*, p. 53.
43. *Ibid.*, p. 23.
44. *Ibid.*, p. 90.
45. *Ibid.*, p. 9, footnote.
46. *Ibid.*, p. 53.
47. *Ibid.*, p. 58.
48. *Ibid.*, p. 53.
49. *Ibid.*, p. 11.
50. *Ibid.*, pp. 10–12.
51. *Ibid.*, p. 12.
52. *Ibid.*, p. 2.
53. *Ibid.*, pp. 12 and 14–15.
54. Richards, *The Philosophy of Rhetoric*, p. 11.
55. Evidently, contexts must continually change, since fresh stimuli and responses are constantly being added to them as consciously remembered experience.
56. The "protocol" experiments, to be explained later in this chapter, and embodied in *Practical Criticism* and *Interpretation in Teaching*, will illustrate the varieties of interpretation.
57. Ogden and Richards, *op. cit.*, pp. 87–108.
58. *Ibid.*, p. 109.
59. *Ibid.*, pp. 111–112.
60. *Ibid.*, p .113.
61. *Ibid.*,
62. *Ibid.*, pp. 114–120.
63. *Ibid.*, p. 123.
64. *Ibid.*, p. 133.
65. *Ibid.*, pp. 133–134.
66. *Ibid.*, p. 134.
67. Richards, *The Philosophy of Rhetoric*, p. 23.
68. *Ibid.*, p. 3.
69. Richards, *Practical Criticism*, pp. 3–4.
70. *Ibid.*, pp. 12–15.
71. Richards, *Interpretation in Teaching*, pp. 23–25.
72. Richards, *Speculative Instruments* (Chicago: University of Chicago Press, 1955), pp. 23–24.
73. Richards, *The Philosophy of Rhetoric*, p. 37.
74. If, as we have seen, the theory of comprehension is the heart of Richards' new rhetoric, then his instruments of comprehending must also be central to it. See *Speculative Instruments*, p. 18, and *The Philosophy of Rhetoric*, p. 3.

75. Richards, *Interpretation in Teaching*, pp. 12 and 15; *Principles of Literary Criticism*, p. 2; and *Practical Criticism*, pp. 75–76.
76. Richards, *Speculative Instruments*, pp. 21 and 26.
77. *Ibid.*, pp. 26–27.
78. *Ibid.*, pp. 28–31.
79. From Richards' notes commenting on the first draft of the present study, Boston, December 7, 1956.
80. *Ibid.*
81. Richards, *Speculative Instruments*, pp. 34–35.
82. *Ibid.*, p. 35.
83. *Ibid.*, pp. 36–38.
84. *Ibid.*, pp. 19–22.
85. *Ibid.*, pp. 27–28.
86. From Richards' notes commenting on the first draft of the present study, Boston, December 7, 1956.

87. Richards, *Speculative Instruments*, pp. 18–19.
88. *Ibid.*, pp. 19 and 26.
89. Clearly, both the instruments and the parallel questions Richards derives from them (pages 52 and 53) are as workable for the communicator preparing his communication as for the interpreter comprehending a communication.
90. Richards, *The Philosophy of Rhetoric*, pp. 3, 8–11, 23–24, and 37.
91. Richards, *Speculative Instruments*, p. 27.
92. Claude E. Shannon and Warren Weaver, *The Mathematical Theory of Communication* (Urbana, Ill.: University of Illinois Press, 1949), p. 5.
93. Richards, *Speculative Instruments*, p. 23.
94. *Ibid.*, pp. 25–26.
95. Richards, *The Philosophy of Rhetoric*, p. 3.
96. *Ibid.*, p. 9.

Marie Hochmuth Nichols

Kenneth Burke and the "New Rhetoric"

◊ *Despite his difficult prose style, the work of Kenneth Burke merits careful study. For Burke provides his readers with a fresh new approach to rhetoric. For him, the key terms are identification and attitude rather than the neo-Aristotelean persuasion and proof. "You persuade a man," Burke declares, "only insofar as you can talk his language by speech, gesture, tonality, order, image, attitude, idea, identifying your ways with his."*

In the hands of Kenneth Burke, rhetorical criticism involves the application of a five part dramatistic model. Subjects for analysis run the gamut of popular culture, along with Shakespeare and Adolph Hitler. ◊

I

"We do not flatter ourselves that any one book can contribute much to counteract the torrents of ill will into which so many of our contemporaries have so avidly and sanctimoniously plunged," observes Kenneth Burke in introducing his latest book, *A Rhetoric of Motives,* but "the more strident our journalists, politicians, and alas! even many of our churchmen become, the more convinced we are that books should be written for tolerance and contemplation."[1] Burke has offered all his writings to these ends.

Burke's first work, *Counter-Statement,* published in 1931, was hailed as a work of "revolutionary importance," presenting "in essence, a new view of rhetoric."[2] Since that time, he has written a succession of books either centrally or peripherally concerned with rhetoric: *Permanence and Change,* 1935; *Attitudes toward History,* 1937; *The Philosophy of Literary Form,* 1941; *A Grammar of Motives,* 1945; and his latest, *A Rhetoric of Motives,* 1950. An unfinished work entitled *A*

From "Kenneth Burke and the 'New Rhetoric,' " *Quarterly Journal of Speech,* 38 (April 1952): 133–144. Reprinted with permission of Speech Communication Association.

Symbolic of Motives further indicates his concern with the problem of language.

Sometimes thought to be "one of the few truly speculative thinkers of our time,"[3] and "unquestionably the most brilliant and suggestive critic now writing in America,"[4] Burke deserves to be related to the great tradition of rhetoric.

Although we propose to examine particularly *A Rhetoric of Motives* we shall range freely over all his works in order to discover his principles. We propose to find first the point of departure and orientation from which he approaches rhetoric; next to examine his general concept of rhetoric; then to seek his method for the analysis of motivation; and finally, to discover his application of principles to specific literary works.

In 1931, in *Counter-Statement*, Burke noted, "The reader of modern prose is ever on guard against 'rhetoric,' yet the word, by lexicographer's definition, refers but to 'the use of language in such a way as to produce a desired impression upon the reader or hearer.' "[5] Hence, accepting the lexicographer's definition, he concluded that "effective literature could be nothing else but rhetoric."[6] In truth, "Eloquence is simply the end of art, and is thus its essence."[7]

As a literary critic, representing a minority view, Burke has persisted in his concern with rhetoric, believing that "rhetorical analysis throws light on literary texts and human relations generally."[8] Although Burke is primarily concerned with literature "as art,"[9] he gives no narrow interpretation to the conception of literature. He means simply works "designed for the express purpose of arousing emotions,"[10] going so far as to say, "But sometimes literature so designed fails to arouse emotions—and words said purely by way of explanation may have an unintended emotional effect of considerable magnitude."[11] Thus a discussion of "effectiveness" in literature "should be able to include unintended effects as well as intended ones."[12] By literature we mean written or spoken words.[13]

As has been observed, the breadth of Burke's concepts results "in a similar embracing of trash of every description. . . . For purposes of analysis or illustration Burke draws as readily on a popular movie, a radio quiz program, a *Herald Tribune* news item about the National Association of Manufacturers, or a Carter Glass speech on gold as on Sophocles or Shakespeare. Those things are a kind of poetry too, full of symbolic and rhetorical ingredients, and if they are bad poetry, it is a bad poetry of vital significance in our lives."[14]

Sometimes calling himself a pragmatist, sometimes a sociological critic, Burke believes that literature is designed to "do something"[15] for the writer and the reader or hearer. "Art is a means of communication. As such it is certainly designed to elicit a 'response' of some sort."[16] The most relevant observations are to be made about literature when it is considered as the embodiment of an "act."[17] or as "symbolic action."[18] Words must be thought of as "acts upon a scene,"[19] and a "symbolic act" is the "*dancing of an attitude,*"[20] or incipient action. Critical and imaginative works are "answers to questions posed by the situation in which they arose." Not merely "answers," they are *strategic* answers, or *stylized* answers,[21] Hence, a literary work is essentially a "strategy for *encompassing a situation.*"[22] And, as Burke observes, another name for strategies might be *attitudes.*[23] The United States Constitution, e.g., must be thought of as the "*answer*" or "*rejoinder*" to "assertions current in the situation in which it arose."[24]

Although Burke distinguishes between literature "for the express purpose of arousing emotions" and "literature for use," the distinction is flexible enough to permit him to see even in such a poem as Milton's *Samson Agonistes,* "moralistic prophecy" and thus to class it as "also a kind of 'literature for use,' use at one remove. . . ."[25]

In further support of his comprehensive notion of art is his conception that since "pure art makes for acceptance," it tends to "become a social menace in so far as it assists us in tolerating the intolerable."[26] Therefore, "under conditions of competitive capitalism there must necessarily be a large *corrective* or *propaganda* element in art."[27] Art must have a "hortatory function, an element of suasion or inducement of the educational variety; it must be partially *forensic.*"[28]

Burke thus approaches the subject of rhetoric through a comprehensive view of art in general. And it is this indirect approach that enables him to present what he believes to be a "New Rhetoric."[29] In part, he has as his object only to "rediscover rhetorical elements that had become obscured when rhetoric as a term fell into disuse, and other specialized disciplines such as esthetics,

anthropology, psychoanalysis, and sociology came to the fore (so that esthetics sought to outlaw rhetoric, while the other sciences . . . took over, each in its own terms, the rich rhetorical elements that esthetics would ban)."[30]

II

Sometimes thought to be "intuitive" and "idiosyncratic"[31] in his general theories, Burke might be expected to be so in his theory of rhetoric. "Strongly influenced by anthropological inquires,"[32] and finding Freud "suggestive almost to the point of bewilderment,"[33] Burke, essentially a classicist in his theory of rhetoric, has given the subject its most searching analysis in modern times.

According to Burke, "Rhetoric [comprises] both the use of persuasive resources (*rhetorica utens*, as with the Phillipics of Demosthenes) and the *study* of them (*rhetorica docens*, as with Aristotle's treatise on the 'art' of Rhetoric."[34] The "basic function of rhetoric" is the "use of words by human agents to form attitudes or to induce actions in other human agents. . . ."[35] It is "*rooted in an essential function of language itself, a function that is wholly realistic, and is continually born anew; the use of language as a symbolic means of inducing cooperation in beings that by nature respond to symbols.*"[36] The basis of rhetoric lies in "generic divisiveness which, being common to all men, is a universal fact about them, prior to any divisiveness caused by social classes." "Out of this emerge the motives for linguistic persuasion. Then, *secondarily,* we get the motives peculiar to particular economic situations. In parturition begins the centrality of the nervous system. The different nervous systems, through language and the ways of production, erect various communities of interests and insights, social communities varying in nature and scope. And out of the division and the community arises the 'universal' rhetorical situation.''[37]

Burke devotes 131 pages to a discussion of traditional principles of rhetoric, reviewing Aristotle, Cicero, Quintilian, St. Augustine, the Mediaevalists, and such more recent writers as De Quincey, De Gourmont, Bentham, Marx, Veblen, Freud, Mannheim, Mead, Richards and others,[38] noting the "wide range of meanings already associated with rhetoric, in ancient texts. . . .''[39] Thus he comes upon the concept of rhetoric as "persuasion"; the nature of rhetoric as "addressed" to an audience for a particular purpose; rhetoric as the art of "proving opposites"; rhetoric as an "appeal to emotions and prejudices"; rhetoric as "agonistic"; as an art of gaining "advantage"; rhetoric as "demonstration"; rhetoric as the verbal "counterpart" of dialectic; rhetoric, in the Stoic usage, as opposed to dialectic; rhetoric in the Marxist sense of persuasion "grounded in dialectic." Whereas he finds that these meanings are "often not consistent with one another, or even flatly at odds,"[40] he believes that they can all be derived from "persuasion" as the "Edenic" term, from which they have all "Babylonically" split, while persuasion, in turn "involves communication by the signs of consubstantiality, the appeal of *identification*."[41] As the "simplest case of persuasion,"

he notes that "You persuade a man only insofar as you can talk his language by speech, gesture, tonality, order, image, attitude, idea, *identifying* your ways with his.''[42]

In using *identification* as his key term, Burke notes, "Traditionally, the key term for rhetoric is not 'identification,' but 'persuasion.' . . . Our treatment, in terms of identification, is decidedly not meant as a substitute for the sound traditional approach. Rather, . . . it is but an accessory to the standard lore.''[43] He had noted that "when we come upon such aspects of persuasion as are found in 'mystification,' courtship, and the 'magic' of class relationships, the reader will see why the classical notion of clear persuasive intent is not an accurate fit, for describing the ways in which the members of a group promote social cohesion by acting rhetorically upon themselves and one another.''[44] Burke is completely aware that he is not introducing a totally new concept, observing that Aristotle had long ago commented, "It is not hard . . . to praise Athenians among Athenians,''[45] and that one persuades by "identifying" one's ways with those of his audience.[46] In an observation of W. C. Blum, Burke found additional support for his emphasis on *identification* as a key concept. "In identification lies the source of dedications and enslavements, in fact of cooperation."[47] As for the precise relationship between identification and persuasion as ends of rhetoric, Burke concludes, "we might well keep it in mind that a speaker persuades an audience by the use of stylistic identifications; his act of persuasion may be for the purpose of causing the audience to identify itself with the speaker's interests; and the speaker draws on identification of interests to establish rapport between himself and his audience. So, there is no chance of our keeping apart the meanings of persuasion, identification ('consubstantiality') and communication (the nature of rhetoric as 'addressed'). But, in given instances, one or another of these elements may serve best for extending a line of analysis in some particular direction."[48] "All told, persuasion ranges from the bluntest quest of advantage, as in sales promotion or propaganda, through courtship, social etiquette, education, and the sermon to a 'pure' form that delights in the process of appeal for itself alone, without ulterior purpose. And identification ranges from the politician who, addressing an audience of farmers, says, 'I was a farm boy myself,' through the mysteries of social status, to the mystic's devout identification with the source of all being."[49] The difference between the "old" rhetoric and the "new" rhetoric may be summed up in this manner: whereas the key term for the "old" rhetoric was *persuasion* and its stress was upon deliberate design, the key term for the "new" rhetoric is *identification* and this may include partially "unconscious" factors in its appeal. Identification, at its simplest level, may be a deliberate device, or a means, as when a speaker identifies his interests with those of his audience. But *identification* can also be an "end," as "when people earnestly yearn to identify themselves with some group or other." They are thus not necessarily acted upon by a conscious external agent, but may act upon themselves to this end. Identification

"includes the realm of transcendence."[50]

Burke affirms the significance of *identification* as a key concept because men are at odds with one another, or because there is "division." "Identification is compensatory to division. If men were not apart from one another, there would be no need for the rhetorician to proclaim their unity. If men were wholly and truly of one substance, absolute communication would be of man's very essence."[51] In pure identification there would be no strife. Likewise, there would be no strife in absolute separateness, since opponents can join battle only through a mediatory ground that makes their communication possible, thus providing the first condition necessary for their interchange of blows. But put identification and division ambiguously together . . . and you have the characteristic invitation to rhetoric. Here is a major reason why rhetoric, according to Aristotle, 'proves opposites.'[52]

As a philosopher and metaphysician Burke is impelled to give a philosophic treatment to the concept of unity or identity by an analysis of the nature of *substance* in general. In this respect he makes his most basic contribution to a philosophy of rhetoric. "Metaphysically, a thing is identified by its *properties*,"[53] he observes. "To call a man a friend or brother is to proclaim him consubstantial with oneself, one's values or purposes. To call a man a bastard is to attack him by attacking his whole line, his 'authorship,' his 'principle' or 'motive' (as expressed in terms of the familial). An epithet assigns substance doubly, for in stating the character of the object it . . . contains an implicit program of action with regard to the object, thus serving as motive."[54]

According to Burke, language of all things "is most public, most collective, in its substance."[55] Aware that modern thinkers have been skeptical about the utility of a doctrine of substance,[56] he nevertheless recalls that "substance, in the old philosophies, was an *act*; and a way of life is an *acting-together*; and in acting together, men have common sensations, concepts, images, ideas, attitudes that make them *consubstantial*."[57] "A doctrine of *consubstantiality* . . . may be necessary to any way of life."[58] Like Kant, Burke regards substance as a "necessary form of the mind." Instead of trying to exclude a doctrine of substance, he restores it to a central position and throws critical light upon it.

In so far as rhetoric is concerned, the "ambiguity of substance" affords a major resource. "What handier linguistic resource could a rhetorician want than an ambiguity whereby he can say 'The state of affairs is substantially such-and-such,' instead of having to say 'The state of affairs *is* and/or *is not* such-and-such.' "[59]

The "commonplaces" or "topics" of Aristotle's *Rhetoric* are a "quick survey of opinion" of "things that people generally consider persuasive." As such, they are means of proclaiming *substantial* unity with an audience and are clearly instances of identification.[60] In truth, *identification* is "hardly other than a name for the function of sociality."[61] Likewise, the many tropes and figures, and rhetorical form in the large as treated by the ancients are to be considered as modes of identification.[62] They are the "signs" by which the

speaker identifies himself with the reader or hearer. "In its simplest manifestation, style is ingratiation."[63] It is an attempt to "gain favor by the hypnotic or suggestive process of 'saying the right thing.' "[64] Burke discusses form in general as "the psychology of the *audience*,"[65] the "arousing and fulfillment of desires."[66] The exordium of a Greek oration is an instance of "conventional"[67] form, a form which is expected by the audience and therefore satisfies it. Other recognizable types of form are "syllogistic progression," "repetitive" form, and "minor or incidental" forms which include such devices as the metaphor, apostrophe, series, reversal, etc.[68] The proliferation and the variety of formal devices make a work eloquent.[69]

Reviewing *A Rhetoric of Motives*, Thomas W. Copeland observed, "It gradually appears that there is no form of action of men upon each other (or of individuals on themselves) which is really outside of rhetoric. But if so, we should certainly ask whether rhetoric as a *term* has any defining value."[70] The observation is probably not fair, for Burke does give rhetoric a defining value in terms of persuasion, identification, and address or communication to an audience of some sort, despite his observation, "Wherever there is persuasion, there is rhetoric. And wherever there is 'meaning' there is 'persuasion.' "[71]

It is true that in his effort to show "how a rhetorical motive is often present where it is not usually recognized, or thought to belong,"[72] Burke either points out linkages which have not been commonly stressed, or widens the scope of rhetoric. A twentieth-century orientation in social-psychological theory thus enables him to note that we may with "more accuracy speak of persuasion 'to attitude,' rather than persuasion to out-and-out action." For persuasion "involves choice, will; it is directed to a man only insofar as he is *free*." In so far as men "*must* do something, rhetoric is unnecessary, its work being done by the nature of things, though often these necessities are not of natural origin, but come from necessities imposed by man-made conditions,"[73] such as dictatorships or near-dictatorships. His notion of persuasion to "attitude" does not alter his generally classical view of rhetoric, for as he points out, in "Cicero and Augustine there is a shift between the words 'move' (*movere*) and 'bend' (*flectere*) to name the ultimate function of rhetoric." And he merely finds that this shift "corresponds to a distinction between act and attitude (attitude being an incipient act, a leaning or inclination)."[74] His notion of persuasion to "attitude" enables him to point out a linkage with poetry: "Thus the notion of persuasion to *attitude* would permit the application of rhetorical terms to purely *poetic* structures: the study of lyrical devices might be classed under the head of rhetoric, when these devices are considered for their power to induce or communicate states of mind to readers, even though the kinds of assent evoked have no overt, practical outcome."[75]

In his reading of classical texts, he had noted a stress "upon *teaching* as an 'office' of rhetoric." Such an observation enables him to link the fields of rhetoric and semantics. He concludes that "once you treat instruction as an aim of rhetoric you introduce a principle that can widen the scope of rhetoric beyond persuasion. It is on the way to include also works on the theory and practice of exposition, description, *communication* in general. Thus, finally, out of this principle, you can derive contemporary 'semantics' as an aspect of rhetoric."[76]

As he persists in "tracking down" the function of the term *rhetoric*, Burke notes an ingredient of rhetoric "lurking in such anthropologist's terms as 'magic' and 'witchcraft,' "[77] and concludes that one "comes closer to the true state of affairs if one treats the socializing aspects of magic as a 'primitive rhetoric' than if one sees modern rhetoric simply as a 'survival of primitive magic.' "[78] Whereas he does not believe that the term *rhetoric* is a "substitute" for such terms as *magic, witchcraft, socialization,* or *communication,* the term *rhetoric* "designates a *function* . . . present in the areas variously covered by those other terms."[79] Thus, one can place within the scope of rhetoric "all those statements by anthropologists, ethnologists, individual and social psychologists, and the like, that bear upon the *persuasive* aspects of language, the function of language as *addressed,* as direct or roundabout appeal to real or ideal audiences, without or within."[80] All these disciplines have made "good contributions to the New Rhetoric."[81]

In "individual psychology," particularly the Freudian concern with the neuroses of individual patients, "there is a strongly rhetorical ingredient."[82] Burke asks the question, "Indeed, what could be more profoundly rhetorical than Freud's notion of a dream that attains expression by stylistic subterfuges designed to evade the inhibitions of a moralistic censor? What is this but the exact analogue of the rhetorical devices of literature under political or theocratic censorship? The *ego* with its *id* confronts the *super-ego* much as an orator would confront a somewhat alien audience, whose susceptibilities he must flatter as a necessary step toward persuasion. The Freudian psyche is quite a parliament, with conflicting interests expressed in ways variously designed to take the claims of rival factions into account."[83]

By considering the individual self as "audience" Burke brings morals and ethics into the realm of rhetoric. He notes that "a modern 'post-Christian' rhetoric must also concern itself with the thought that, under the heading of appeal to audiences, would also be included any ideas or images privately addressed to the individual self for moralistic or incantatory purposes. For you become your own audience, in some respects a very lax one, in some respects very exacting, when you become involved in psychologically stylistic subterfuges for presenting your own case to yourself in sympathetic terms (and even terms that seem harsh can often be found on closer scrutiny to be flattering, as with neurotics who visit sufferings upon themselves in the name of very high-powered motives which, whatever this discomfiture, feed pride)." Therefore, the "individual person, striving to form himself in accordance with the communicative norms that match the cooperative ways of his society, is by the same token concerned with the rhetoric of identification."[84]

By considering style as essentially a mode of "ingratiation" or as a technique by which one gives the signs of identification and consubstantiality, Burke finds a rhetorical motive in clothes, pastoral, courtship, and the like.[85]

Burke links dialectics with rhetoric through a definition of dialectics in "its most general sense" as "linguistic transformation"[86] and through an analysis of three different levels of language, or linguistic terminology.[87] Grammatically, he discusses the subject from the point of view of linguistic merger and division, polarity, and transcendence, being aware that there are "other definitions of dialectics:"[88] "reasoning from opinion"; "the discovery of truth by the give and take of converse and redefinition"; "the art of disputation"; "the processes of 'interaction' between the verbal and the nonverbal"; "the competition of cooperation or the cooperation of competition"; "the spinning of terms out of terms"; "the internal dialogue of thought"; "any development . . . got by the interplay of various factors that mutually modify one another, and may be thought of as voices in a dialogue or roles in a play, with each voice or role in its partiality contributing to the development of the whole"; "the placement of one thought or thing in terms of its opposite"; "the progressive or successive development and reconciliation of opposites"; and "so putting questions to nature that nature can give unequivocal answer."[89] He considers all of these definitions as "variants or special applications of the functions"[90] of linguistic transformation conceived in terms of "Merger and division," "The three Major Pairs: action-passion, mind-body, being-nothing," and "Transcendence."[91]

Burke devotes 150 pages to the treatment of the dialectics of persuasion in the *Rhetoric*,[92] in addition to extensive treatment of it on the grammatical level.[93] Linguistic terminology is considered variously persuasive in its Positive, Dialectical, and Ultimate levels or orders.[94] "A positive term is most unambiguously itself when it names a visible and tangible thing which can be located in time and place."[95] Dialectical terms "have no such strict location."[96] Thus terms like "Elizabethanism" or "capitalism" having no positive referent may be called "dialectical."[97] Often called 'polar' terms,[98] they require an "opposite"[99] to define them and are on the level of "action," "principles," "ideas."[100] In an "ultimate order" of terminology, there is a "guiding idea" or "unitary principle."[101]

From the point of view of rhetoric, Burke believes that the "difference between a merely 'dialectical' confronting of parliamentary conflict and an 'ultimate' treatment of it would reside in this: The 'dialectical' order would leave the competing voices in a jangling relation with one another (a conflict solved *faute de mieux* by horsetrading'); but the 'ultimate' order would place these competing voices themselves in a *hierarchy*, or *sequence*, or *evaluating series*, so that, in some way, we went by a fixed and reasoned progression from one of these to another, the members of the entire group being arranged *developmentally* with relation to one another."[102] To Burke "much of the *rhetorical* strength in the Marxist dialectic comes from the fact that it is 'ultimate' in its order,"[103] for a

"spokesman for the proletariat can think of himself as representing not only the interests of that class alone, but the grand design of the entire historical sequence. . . ."[104]

In his concept of a "pure persuasion," Burke seems to be extending the area of rhetoric beyond its usual scope. As a metaphysician he attempts to carry the process of rhetorical appeal to its ultimate limits. He admits that what he means by "pure persuasion" in the "absolute sense" exists nowhere, but believes that it can be present as a motivational ingredient in any rhetoric, no matter how "advantage-seeking such a rhetoric may be."[105] Pure persuasion involves the saying of something, not for an extraverbal advantage to be got by the saying, but because of a satisfaction intrinsic to the saying. It summons because it likes the feel of a summons. It would be nonplused if the summons were answered. It attacks because it revels in the sheer syllables of vituperation. It would be horrified if, each time it finds a way of saying, 'Be damned,' it really did send a soul to rot in hell. It intuitively says, 'This is so,' purely and simply because this is so."[106] With such a concept Burke finds himself at the "borders of metaphysics, or perhaps better 'meta-rhetoric'. . . ."[107]

III

Of great significance to the rhetorician is Burke's consideration of the general problem of motivation. Concerned with the problem of motivation in literary strategy,[108] he nevertheless intends that his observations be considered pertinent to the social sphere in general.[109]

He had observed that people's conduct has been explained by an "endless variety of theories: ethnological, geographical, sociological, physiological, historical, endocrinological, economic, anatomical, mystical, pathological, and so on."[110] The assigning of motives, he concludes, is a "matter of *appeal*,"[111] and this depends upon one's general orientation. "A motive is not some fixed thing, like a table, which one can go to and look at. It is a term of interpretation, and being such it will naturally take its place within the framework of our *Weltanschauung* as a whole."[112] "To explain one's conduct by the vocabulary of motives current among one's group is about as self-deceptive as giving the area of a field in the accepted terms of measurement. One is simply interpreting with the only vocabulary he knows. One is stating his orientation, which involves a vocabulary of ought and ought-not, with attendant vocabulary of praiseworthy and blameworthy."[113] "We discern situational patterns by means of the particular vocabulary of the cultural group into which we are born."[114] Motives are "distinctly linguistic products."[115]

To Burke, the subject of motivation is a "philosophic one, not ultimately to be solved in terms of empirical science."[116] A motive is a "shorthand" term for "situation."[117] One may discuss motives on three levels, rhetorical, symbolic, and grammatical.[118] One is on the "grammatical" level when he concerns himself with the problem of the "intrinsic," or the problem of "substance."[119] "Men's conception of motive . . . is integrally related to their conception of substance. Hence, to deal with problems of motive is to deal with problems of substance."[120]

On the "grammatical" level Burke gives his most profound treatment of the problem of motivation. Strongly allied with the classicists throughout all his works in both his ideas and his methodology, Burke shows indebtedness to Aristotle for his treatment of motivation. Taking a clue from Aristotle's consideration of the "circumstances" of an action,[121] Burke concludes that "In a rounded statement about motives, you must have some word that names the *act* (names what took place, in thought or deed), and another that names the *scene* (the background of the act, the situation in which it occurred); also, you must indicate what person or kind of person (*agent*) performed the act, what means or instruments he used (*agency*), and the *purpose*."[122] Act, Scene, Agent, Agency, Purpose become the "pentad" for pondering the problem of human motivation.[123] Among these various terms grammatical "ratios" prevail which have rhetorical implications. One might illustrate by saying that, for instance, between scene and act a logic prevails which indicates that a certain quality of scene calls for an analogous quality of act. Hence, if a situation is said to be of a certain nature, a corresponding attitude toward it is implied. Burke explains by pointing to such an instance as that employed by a speaker who, in discussing Roosevelt's war-time power exhorted that Roosevelt should be granted "unusual powers" because the country was in an "unusual international situation." The scene-act "ratio" may be applied in two ways. "It can be applied deterministically in statements that a certain policy *had* to be adopted in a certain situation, or it may be applied in hortatory statements to the effect that a certain policy *should* be adopted in conformity with the situation."[124] These ratios are "principles of determination."[125] The pentad would allow for ten such ratios: scene-act, scene-agent, scene-agency, scene-purpose, act-purpose, act-agent, act-agency, agent-purpose, agent-agency, and agency-purpose.[126] Political commentators now generally use *situation* as their synonym for *scene*, "though often without any clear concept of its function as a statement about motives."[127]

Burke draws his key terms for the study of motivation from the analysis of drama. Being developed from the analysis of drama, his pentad "treats language and thought primarily as modes of action."[128] His method for handling motivation is designed to contrast with the methodology of the physical sciences which considers the subject of motivation in mechanistic terms of "flat cause-and-effect or stimulus-and-response."[129] Physicalist terminologies are proper to non-verbalizing entities, but man as a species should be approached through his specific trait, his use of symbols. Burke opposes the reduction of the human realm to terms that lack sufficient "coordinates"; he does not, however, question the fitness of physicalist terminologists for treating the physical realm. According to Burke, "Philosophy, like common sense, must think of human motivation dramatistically, in terms of action and its ends."[130] "Language being essentially human, we should view human relations in terms of the linguistic instru-

ment."[131] His "vocabulary" or "set of coordinates" serves "for the integration of all phenomena studied by the *social* sciences."[132] It also serves as a "perspective for the analysis of history which is a 'dramatic' process. . . ."[133]

One may wonder with Charles Morris whether "an analysis of man through his language provides us with a full account of human motives."[134] One strongly feels the absence of insights into motivation deriving from the psychologists and scientists.

IV

Burke is not only philosopher and theorist; he has applied his critical principles practically to a great number of literary works. Of these, three are of particular interest to the rhetorician. In two instances, Burke attempts to explain the communicative relationship between the writer and his audience. Taking the speech of Antony from Shakespeare's *Julius Caesar*,[135] Burke examines the speech from "the standpoint of the rhetorician, who is concerned with a work's processes of appeal."[136] A similar operation is performed on a scene from *Twelfth Night*.[137]

Undoubtedly one of his most straightforward attempts at analysis of a work of "literature for use," occurs in an essay on "The Rhetoric of Hitler's 'Battle' "[138] "The main ideal of criticism, as I conceive it," Burke has observed, "is to use all that there is to use."[139] "If there is any slogan that should reign among critical precepts, it is that 'circumstances alter occasions.' "[140] Considering *Mein Kampf* as "the well of Nazi magic,"[141] Burke brings his knowledge of sociology and anthropology to bear in order to "discover what kind of 'medicine' this medicine-man has concocted, that we may know, with greater accuracy, exactly what to guard against, if we are to forestall the concocting of similar medicine in America."[142] He considers Hitler's "centralizing hub of *ideas*"[143] and his selection of Munich as a "mecca geographically located"[144] as methods of recruiting followers "from among many discordant and divergent bands. . . ."[145] He examines the symbol of the "international Jew"[146] as that "of a *common enemy*,"[147] the " 'medicinal' appeal of the Jew as scapegoat. . . ."[148]

His knowledge of psychoanalysis is useful in the analysis of the "sexual symbolism" that runs through the book: "Germany in dispersion is the 'dehorned Siegfried.' The masses are 'feminine.' As such, they desire to be led by a dominating male. This male, as orator, woos them—and, when he has won them, he commands them. The rival male, the villainous Jew, would on the contrary 'seduce' them. If he succeeds, he poisons their blood by intermingling with them. Whereupon, by purely associative connections of ideas, we are moved into attacks upon syphilis, prostitution, incest, and other similar misfortunes, which are introduced as a kind of 'musical' argument when he is on the subject of 'blood poisoning' by intermarriage or, in its 'spiritual' equivalent, by the infection of 'Jewish' ideas. . . ."[149]

His knowledge of history and religion is employed to show that the "*materialization*" of a religious pattern" is "one terrifically effective weapon . . . in a period where religion has been progressively weakened by many centuries of capitalist materialism."[150]

Conventional rhetorical knowledge leads him to call attention to the "power of endless repetition"[151]; the appeal of a sense of "community"[152]; the appeal of security resulting from "a world view" for a people who had previously seen the world only "piecemeal";[153] and the appeal of Hitler's "inner voice"[154] which served as a technique of leader-people "identification."[155]

Burke's analysis is comprehensive and penetrating. It stands as a superb example of the fruitfulness of a method of comprehensive rhetorical analysis which goes far beyond conventional patterns.

Conclusion

Burke is difficult and often confusing. He cannot be understood by casual reading of his various volumes. In part the difficulty arises from the numerous vocabularies he employs. His words in isolation are usually simple enough, but he often uses them in new contexts. To read one of his volumes independently, without regard to the chronology of publication, makes the problem of comprehension even more difficult because of the specialized meanings attached to various words and phrases.

Burke is often criticized for "obscurity" in his writings. The charge may be justified. However, some of the difficulty of comprehension arises from the compactness of his writing, the uniqueness of his organizational patterns, the penetration of his thought, and the breadth of his endeavor. "In books like the

Grammar and the *Rhetoric*," observed Malcolm Cowley, "we begin to see the outlines of a philosophical system on the grand scale. . . . Already it has its own methodology (called 'dramatism'), its own esthetics (based on the principle that works of art are symbolic actions), its logic and dialectics, its ethics (or picture of the good life) and even its metaphysics, which Burke prefers to describe as meta-rhetoric."[156]

One cannot possibly compress the whole of Burke's thought into an article. The most that one can achieve is to signify his importance as a theorist and critic and to suggest the broad outlines of his work. Years of study and contemplation of the general idea of effectiveness in language have equipped him to deal competently with the subject of rhetoric from its beginning as a specialized discipline to the present time. To his thorough knowledge of classical tradition he has added rich insights gained from serious study of anthropology, sociology, history, psychology, philosophy, and the whole body of humane letters. With such equipment, he has become the most profound student of rhetoric now writing in America.

Notes

1. Kenneth Burke, *A Rhetoric of Motives* (New York: Prentice-Hall, Inc., 1950), p. xv. Reprinted with permission.
2. Isidor Schneider, "A New View of Rhetoric," *New York Herald Tribune Books*, VIII (December 13, 1931), 4.
3. Malcolm Cowley, "Prolegomena to Kenneth Burke," *The New Republic*, CXXI (June 5, 1950), 18, 19.
4. W. H. Auden, "A Grammar of Assent," *The New Republic*, CV (July 14, 1941), 59.
5. *Counter-Statement* (New York, 1931), p. 265.
6. *Ibid.*, p. 265.
7. *Ibid.*, p. 53.
8. *A Rhetoric of Motives*, pp. xiv, xv.
9. *Counter-Statement*, p. 156.
10. *Ibid.*
11. *Ibid.*
12. *Ibid.*
13. *Ibid.*
14. Stanley Edgar Hyman, *The Armed Vision* (New York, 1948), pp. 386, 387.
15. *The Philosophy of Literary Form* (Louisiana, 1941), p. 89.
16. *Ibid.*, pp. 235, 236.
17. *Ibid.*, p. 89.
18. *Ibid.*, p. 8.
19. *Ibid.*, p. vii.
20. *Ibid.*, p. 9.
21. *Ibid.*, p. 1.
22. *Ibid.*, p. 109.
23. *Ibid.*, p. 297.
24. *Ibid.*, p. 109.
25. *A Rhetoric of Motives*, p. 5.
26. *The Philosophy of Literary Form*, p. 321.
27. *Ibid.*
28. *Ibid.*
29. *A Rhetoric of Motives*, p. 40.
30. *Ibid.* pp. xiii, 40.
31. *The Philosophy of Literary Form*, p. 68.
32. *A Rhetoric of Motives*, p. 40.
33. *The Philosophy of Literary Form*, p. 258.
34. *A Rhetoric of Motives*, p. 36.
35. *Ibid.*, p. 41.
36. *Ibid.*, p. 43.
37. *Ibid.*, p. 146.
38. *Ibid.*, pp. 49–180.
39. *Ibid.*, p. 61.
40. *Ibid.*, p. 61, 62.
41. *Ibid.*, p. 62.
42. *Ibid.*, p. 55.
43. *Ibid.*, p. xiv.
44. *Ibid.*
45. *Ibid.*, p. 55.
46. *Ibid.*
47. *Ibid.*, p. xiv.
48. *Ibid.*, p. 46.
49. *Ibid.*, p. xiv.
50. Kenneth Burke, "Rhetoric—Old and New," *The Journal of General Education*, V (April 1951), 203.
51. *A Rhetoric of Motives*, p. 22.
52. *Ibid.*, p. 25.
53. *Ibid.*, p. 23.
54. *A Grammar of Motives* (New York, 1945), p. 57. For discussion of *substance* as a concept, see, *ibid.*, pp. 21–58; Aristotle, *Categoriae*, tr. by E. M. Edghill, *The Works of Aristotle*, ed. by W. D. Ross, I, Ch. 5; Aristotle, *Metaphysics*, tr. by W. D. Ross, Book, 8, 1017b, 10; Spinoza, *The Ethics* in *The Chief Works of Benedict De Spinoza*, tr.

by R. H. M. Elwes (London 1901), Rev. ed., II, 45 ff; John Locke, *An Essay Concerning Human Understanding* (London 1760), 15th ed., I, Bk. II. Chs. XXIII, XXIV.
55. *The Philosophy of Literary Form*, p. 44.
56. *A Rhetoric of Motives*, p. 21.
57. *Ibid.*
58. *Ibid.*
59. *A Grammar of Motives*, pp. 51, 52.
60. *A Rhetoric of Motives*, pp. 56, 57.
61. *Attitudes toward History* (New York, 1937), II, 144.
62. *A Rhetoric of Motives*, p. 59.
63. *Permanence and Change* (New York, 1935), p. 71.
64. *Ibid.*
65. *Counter-Statement*, pp. 38–57.
66. *Ibid.*, p. 157.
67. *Ibid.*, p. 159.
68. *Ibid.*, pp. 157–161.
69. *Ibid.*, pp. 209–211.
70. Thomas W. Copeland, "Critics at Work," *The Yale Review*, XL (Autumn 1950), 167–169.
71. *A Rhetoric of Motives*, p. 172.
72. *Ibid.*, p. xiii.
73. *Ibid.*, p. 50.
74. *Ibid.*
75. *Ibid.*
76. *Ibid.*, p. 77.
77. *Ibid.*, p. 44.
78. *Ibid.*, p. 43.
79. *Ibid.*, p. 44.
80. *Ibid.*, pp. 43–44.
81. *Ibid.*, p. 40.
82. *Ibid.*, p. 37.
83. *Ibid.*, pp. 37, 38.
84. *Ibid.*, pp. 38, 39.
85. *Ibid.*, pp. 115–127; see also, p. xiv.
86. *A Grammar of Motives*, p. 402.
87. *A Rhetoric of Motives*, p. 183.
88. *A Grammar of Motives*, pp. 402, 403.
89. *Ibid.*, p. 403.
90. *Ibid.*
91. *Ibid.*, p. 402.
92. *A Rhetoric of Motives*, pp. 183–333.
93. *A Grammar of Motives*, pp. 323–443.
94. *A Rhetoric of Motives*, p. 183.
95. *Ibid.*
96. *Ibid.*, p. 184.
97. *Ibid.*
98. *Ibid.*
99. *The Philosophy of Literary Form*, n. 26 p. 109.
100. *A Rhetoric of Motives*, p. 184.
101. *Ibid.*, p. 187.
102. *Ibid.*
103. *Ibid.*, p. 190.
104. *Ibid.*, pp. 190, 191.
105. *Ibid.*, p. 269.
106. *Ibid.*
107. *Ibid.*, p. 267.
108. *The Philosophy of Literary Forms*, n. 26. p. 109.
109. *Ibid.*, p. 105.
110. *Permanence and Change*, p. 47.
111. *Ibid.*, p. 38.
112. *Ibid.*
113. *Ibid.*, p. 33.
114. *Ibid.*, p. 52.
115. *Ibid.*
116. *A Grammar of Motives*, p. xxiii.
117. *Permanence and Change*, p. 44.
118. *A Grammar of Motives*, p. 465.
119. *Ibid.*
120. *Ibid.*, p. 337.
121. *Ethica Nicomachea*, tr. by W. D. Ross, III, i, 16.
122. *A Grammar of Motives*, p. xv.
123. *Ibid.*
124. *Ibid.*, p. 13.
125. *Ibid.*, p. 15.
126. *Ibid.*
127. *Ibid.*, p. 13.
128. *Ibid.*, p. xxii.
129. *The Philosophy of Literary Form*, pp. 103, 106.
130. *A Grammar of Motives*, pp. 55, 56.
131. *Ibid.*, p. 317.
132. *The Philosophy of Literary Form*, p. 105.
133. *Ibid.*, p. 317.
134. Charles Morris, "The Strategy of Kenneth Burke," *The Nation*, CLXIII (July 27, 1946), 106.
135. "Antony in Behalf of the Play," *Philosophy of Literary Form*, pp. 329–343.
136. *Ibid.*, p. 330.
137. "Trial Translation" (From *Twelfth Night*), *ibid.*, pp. 344–349.
138. *Ibid.*, pp. 191–220.
139. *Ibid.*, p. 23.
140. *Ibid.*
141. *Ibid.*, p. 192.
142. *Ibid.*, p. 191.
143. *Ibid.*, p. 192.
144. *Ibid.*
145. *Ibid.*
146. *Ibid.*, p. 194.
147. *Ibid.*, p. 193.
148. *Ibid.*, p. 195.
149. *Ibid.*
150. *Ibid.*, p. 194.
151. *Ibid.*, p. 217.
152. *Ibid.*
153. *Ibid.*, p. 218.
154. *Ibid.*, p. 207.
155. *Ibid.*
156. Malcolm Cowley, "Prolegomena to Kenneth Burke," *The New Republic*. CXXII (June 5, 1950), 18, 19.

Richard L. Johannesen, Rennard Strickland, and Ralph T. Eubanks

Richard M. Weaver on the Nature of Rhetoric: An Interpretation

◊ Richard Weaver, late of the University of Chicago, was a Platonic idealist and a Southern conservative. He believed that the purpose of rhetoric was to gain adherence to first principles, to the traditional values which underlie the structure of society. All rhetoric, Weaver contended, was advisory; indeed the very words we use to express our ideas are suasory in nature.

The special relationship of rhetoric and dialectic was Weaver's focus. He held that the way one argued revealed the quality of his rhetoric, and that argument from principle and definition took precedence over argument from similitude (i.e. analogy), cause and effect, and circumstance. He favored order in all things and found much to criticize in postwar social science, general semantics, and modern advertising. ◊

Modern philosopher Eliseo Vivas uses the ancient term "rhetor" to describe the late Richard M. Weaver. Vivas contends that Weaver saw the importance of rhetoric, in its classical sense, as "no other thinker among us . . . has seen it."[1] Weaver remains, no doubt, one of the most stimulating and controversial rhetorical theorists of our time. From the outset of his career he has provided, as Paul Tillich observes of his first work, "philosophical shock—the beginning of wisdom." Over the years, Weaver's views on the nature of rhetoric have had increasing influence among rhetorical scholars.[2]

Weaver as a social critic has sought to clarify the role of rhetoric in improving a declining modern culture. At one point in *Visions of Order* he described a "kind of doctor of culture," a description which could also serve as a virtual self-portrait of his own function. Even though a member of the culture, this "doctor" in some degree had estranged himself from his culture through study and reflection. He had "acquired knowledge and developed habits of thought which enable him to see it in perspective and to gauge it."[3]

Although he wrote a large number of articles, essays, lectures, books, and

Reprinted by permission of Louisiana State University Press from *Language Is Sermonic: Richard M. Weaver on the Nature of Rhetoric*, edited by Richard L. Johannesen, Rennard Strickland, and Ralph T. Eubanks. Copyright © 1970 by Louisiana State University Press.

book reviews both on academic and political subjects,[4] Weaver's views on rhetoric can be gleaned primarily from the following published sources: *Ideas Have Consequences,* a post-World War II critique of American society; *The Ethics of Rhetoric; Composition,* a college textbook; "Language is Sermonic," a lecture delivered to a graduate speech seminar at the University of Oklahoma; *Visions of Order,* a posthumously published critique of our present society; *Life Without Prejudice and Other Essays,* a collection of previously published essays; "Relativism and the Use of Language"; "Concealed Rhetoric in Scientistic Sociology"; and "To Write the Truth."[5]

Weaver held two basic orientations that are of prime importance to an understanding of his rhetorical views.[6] First, politically he was a conservative of some note. Leading conservatives such as Russell Kirk and Willmoore Kendall held him in esteem.[7] Weaver was, for example, an associate editor of the conservative *Modern Age,* a contributor to *National Review,* a trustee of the Intercollegiate Society of Individualists, and a recipient in 1962 of a national award from the Young Americans for Freedom. In his public lectures, such as "How to Argue the Conservative Cause," he actively advocated rational conservatism.

In his mid-twenties Weaver had moved from arch-socialist to ardent conservative.[8] A product of southern upbringing and education in North Carolina, Kentucky, Tennessee, and Louisiana, he defended Southern Agrarian traditions.[9] At Vanderbilt University he was exposed to the Southern Agrarian ideas of John Crowe Ransom, Robert Penn Warren, Donald Davidson, and Allen Tate.[10] Kendall contends that Weaver was more a commentator *on* Southern Agrarianism than a devotee of its ideals.[11] Weaver himself admitted that at Vanderbilt he felt a "powerful pull" toward the Agrarian ideals of the individual in contact with nature, the necessity of the small-property-holding class, and a pluralistic society.[12] He left Vanderbilt poised between the opposites of socialism and Southern Agrarianism and by the early 1940's had firmly opted for conservatism generally and some particular facets of Southern Agrarianism.[13] For example, Weaver championed the Agrarian ideal of individual ownership of private property and disdain of science as inadequate to deal with values.[14] He desired in society law, order, and cohesive diversity. The just and ideal society, he believed, must reflect real hierarchy and essential distinctions. An orderly society following the vision of a Good Purpose, with men harmoniously functioning in their proper stations in the structure, constituted Weaver's goal.[15]

Secondly, Weaver was a devoted Platonic idealist.[16] Belief in the reality of transcendentals the primacy of ideas, and the view that form is prior to substance constituted his philosophical foundation.[17] While not a Platonist in all matters, he yet looked for societal and personal salvation to ideals, essences, and principles rather than to the transitory, the changing, and the expedient. His view was antipragmatic and antiutilitarian. While general semanticist S. I. Hayakawa attacks Weaver's Platonic idealism, Russell Kirk praises Weaver as a "powerful mind given to meditation upon universals."[18]

The ultimate "goods" in society were of central concern to Weaver.[19] Reality for him was a hierarchy in which the ultimate Idea of the Good constituted the value standard by which all other existents could be appraised for degree of goodness and truth. Truth to him was the degree to which things and ideas in the material world conform to their ideals, archetypes, and essences. He contended that "the thing is not true and the act is not just unless these conform to a conceptual ideal."[20] What *the* ultimate Good was and how it is known through intuition, Weaver never really made clear. What comprised *his* ultimate Good was likewise unclear. But he viewed freedom, justice, and order as ideals toward which men and cultures must strive. The reality of nature he saw as a dualistic paradox of essences and transformations. "Whatever the field we gaze upon," he observed, "we see things maintaining their identity while changing. Things both *are* and *are becoming.* They are because the idea or general configuration of them persists; and they are becoming because with the flowing of time, they inevitably slough off old substance and take on new."[21]

Weaver held a complex conception of the nature of knowledge. He partially agreed with Mortimer Adler that there are three "orders" of knowledge. First is the level of particulars and individual facts, the simple data of science. Second is the level of theories, propositions, and generalizations about these facts. Third is the level of philosophic evaluations and value judgments about such theories.[22] At this third level, ideas, universals, and first principles function as judgmental standards. Knowledge based on particulars alone and on raw physical sensations is suspect since it is incomplete knowledge. True knowledge is of universals and first principles. Weaver adopted at one point the absolute position that "there is no knowledge at the level of sensation, and that therefore knowledge is of universals . . . the fewer particulars we require in order to arrive at our generalization, the more apt pupils we are in the school of wisdom."[23] In two other books he suggested that "Knowledge of universals comes through dialectic, the ability to differentiate existents into categories, and through intuition, the ability to grasp 'essential correspondences.' "[24]

Weaver believed man's essential nature encompasses fixed elements, yet for him the good man seemed more an ideal than an actuality. He held that man's fundamental humanness is founded in four faculties, capacities, or modes of apprehension.[25] Man possesses a rational or cognitive capacity which gives him knowledge; an emotional or aesthetic capacity which allows him to experience pleasure, pain, and beauty; an ethical capacity which determines orders of goods and judges between right and wrong; and a religious capacity which provides yearning for something infinite and gives man a glimpse of his destiny and ultimate nature.

Weaver used a tripartite division of body, mind, and soul to further explain man's essential nature. The body, man's physical being, houses the mind and soul during life but extracts its due through a constant downward pull toward indiscriminate and excessive satisfaction of sensory pleasure. The body is self-centered and disdainful of worthy goals.[26] Man's mind or intellect provides him with the potential to apprehend the structure of reality, define concepts, and rationally order ideas. While giving man the capacity for knowledge and order, the mind is guided toward good or evil by the disposition of the soul.[27] Man's soul or spirit—depending upon whether it has been trained well or ill—guides the mind and body toward love of the good or toward love of physical pleasure. Weaver found the concept of soul difficult to explain; it seemed for him to encompass man's ethical and religious capacities.[28] The elements of man's essential nature he viewed as fixed. Yet he implied that the dominance of one component over others is determined by man's training, environment, and culture.

Weaver underscored two additional concepts in his analysis of man's uniquely human characteristics.[29] Man's capacity for choice-making affords him his dignity—if judiciously exercised in selecting means and ends. And as the symbol-using animal—although the definition is a partial one—man rises above the sensate and can communicate knowledge, feeling, and values.

In readily accepting the label of conservative, Weaver emphasized that a conservative believes there is a structure of reality independent of his own will and desire and accepts some principles as given, lasting, and good.[30] The true conservative for Weaver was one "who sees the universe as a paradigm of essences, of which the phenomenology of the world is a sort of continuing approximation. Or, to put it another way, he sees it as a set of definitions which are struggling to get themselves defined in the real world."[31]

These two fundamental orientations, political conservatism and Platonic idealism, led Weaver in *Ideas Have Consequences* and *Visions of Order* to indict contemporary Western culture for having lost faith in an order of "goods." Among the societal weaknesses and vices he condemned were the following: scientism, nominalism, semantic positivism, doctrinaire democracy, uncritical homage to the theory of evolution, radical egalitarianism, pragmatism, cultural relativism, materialism, emphasis on techniques at the expense of goals, idolization of youth, progressive education, disparagement of historical consciousness, deleterious effects of the mass media, and degenerate literature, music, and art.

Weaver outlined the program he thought necessary for the restoration of health to Western culture. Among his positive suggestions were the development of a sense of history; balance between permanence and change; reestablishment of faith in ideas, ideals, and principles; maintenance of the "metaphysical right" of private property; education in literature, rhetoric, logic, and dialectic; respect for nature, the individual, and the ideals of the past; reemphasis on traditional education; and control (but not elimination) of war.[32]

From this vantage point Weaver expounded his view of the nature, function, and scope of rhetoric. As his writings on rhetoric show, he was familiar with the ancient theories of Plato, Aristotle, Cicero, and Quintilian.[33] And Plato's views on the subject held a special attraction for him. The influence of Kenneth Burke is also clearly reflected in Weaver's writings on rhetoric.[34] At one point Weaver views rhetoric as a process of making identifications and he widens the scope of rhetoric beyond linguistic forms to include a rhetoric of "matter or scene," as in the instance of a bank's erecting an imposing office building to strengthen its image.[35]

In Weaver's view, rhetoric makes convictions compelling by showing them in the contexts of reality and human values. Rhetoric, he wrote, is "persuasive speech in the service of truth"; it should "create an informed appetition for the good."[36] It affects us "primarily by setting forth images which inform and attract." And generally, rhetoric involves questions of policy. It operates formally at the point "where literary values and political urgencies" can be combined. "The rhetorician," he observed, "makes use of the moving power of literary presentation to induce in his hearers an attitude or decision which is political in the very broadest sense."[37]

Weaver explained the "office" of rhetoric at some length: "Rhetoric seen in the whole conspectus of its function is an art of emphasis embodying an order of desire. Rhetoric is advisory; it has the office of advising men with reference to an independent order of goods and with reference to their particular situation as it relates to these. The honest rhetorician therefore has two things in mind: a vision of how matters should go ideally and ethically and a consideration of the special circumstances of his auditors. Toward both of these he has a responsibility."[38] The duty of rhetoric, then, is to combine "action and understanding into a whole that is greater than scientific perception." Weaver the Platonic idealist believed that "rhetoric at its truest seeks to perfect men by showing them better versions of themselves, links in that chain extending up toward the ideal which only the intellect can apprehend and only the soul have affection for."[39]

Rhetoric, held Weaver, is axiological; it kneads values into our lives.[40] Rhetoric is the cohesive force that molds persons into a community or culture. Because man is "drawn forward by some conception of what he should be," a proper order of values is the "ultimate sanction of rhetoric." Rhetoric involves the making and presenting of choices among "goods" and a striving toward some ultimate Good. By its very nature, he emphasized, "language is sermonic"; it reflects choices and urges a particular "ought." The "noble rhetorician," in Weaver's view, functions to provide a better vision of what we can become. The true rhetorician attempts to actualize an "ideal good" for a particular audience in a specific situation primarily through "poetic or analogical association." He demonstrates, for instance, how an action, urged as just, partakes of ideal justice.

Weaver, therefore, condemned most social scientists for pretending to avoid value judgments in their writings while actually making such judgments.[41] He particularly attacked general semantics for its relativistic "truth" and its attempt to denude language of all reflections of value tendencies.[42] He also realized that rhetoric can be perverted to employ base techniques and to serve base ends. Such perversion, he believed, occurs in much modern advertising. Against these possibilities Weaver strove in all his writings on rhetoric. For he was certain that "all things considered, rhetoric, noble or base, is a great power in the world."[43]

Like Aristotle, Weaver perceived a close relationship between dialectic and rhetoric.[44] Dialectic, he maintained, is a "method of investigation whose object is the establishment of truth about doubtful propositions." It is "abstract reasoning" upon the basis of propositions through categorization, definition, drawing out of implications, and exposure of contradictions. Dialectic involves analysis and synthesis of fundamental terms in controversial questions. Both dialectic and rhetoric operate in the realm of probability. Rhetoric is joined with "that branch of dialectic which contributes to choice or avoidance"—that branch of dialectic which examines ethical and political questions. Good rhetoric presupposes sound dialectic. A successful dialectic secures not actuality but possibility; "what rhetoric thereafter accomplishes is to take any dialectically secured position . . . and show its relationship to the world of prudential conduct."[45] Weaver's criticism of the semantic positivists suggests that dialectic alone, without a succeeding rhetoric, is "social agnosticism." With dialectic unaided by rhetoric, man "knows" only in a vacuum. Thus, as earlier noted, "the duty of rhetoric is to bring together action and understanding into a whole that is greater than scientific perception." Rhetoric seeks actualization of a dialectically secured position in the existential world.

Weaver knew that logos, pathos, and ethos must combine in sound rhetoric.[46] For him "the most obvious truth about rhetoric is that its object is the whole man." It presents its arguments first to the rational aspect of man. Yet a complete rhetoric goes beyond man's cognitive capacity and appeals to other facets of his nature, especially to his nature as an emotional being, "a being of feeling and suffering." In addition, he realized that a "significant part of every speech situation is the character of the speaker." For Richard Weaver, then, the function of rhetoric was to make men both feel and believe and to perceive order, first principles, and fundamental values.

He seemed committed to the proposition that as a man speaks, so he is— or that style is the man. A person's typical modes of argument and his stylistic characteristics Weaver saw as keys to that person's philosophical orientation. An analysis of a person's rhetorical style, for example, illuminated his world view.[47] Frequent use of the conjunction "but" indicates, for example, a "balanced view" as a habit of mind. Again: A person's level of generality in word choice tells us something about his approach to a subject.

"A man's method of argument is a truer index of his beliefs than his explicit profession of principles," Weaver held as a basic axiom.[48] "A much surer index to a man's political philosophy," he felt, "is his characteristic way of thinking, inevitably expressed in the type of argument he prefers." Nowhere does a man's rhetoric catch up with him more completely than in "the topics he chooses to win other men's assent." At one point Weaver elaborated his fundamental view at some length:

In other words, the rhetorical content of the major premise which the speaker habitually uses is the key to his primary view of existence. We are of course excluding artful choices which have in view only *ad hoc* persuasions. Putting the matter now figuratively, we may say that no man escapes being branded by the premise that he regards as most efficacious in argument. The general importance of this is that major premises, in addition to their logical function as a part of a deductive argument, are expressive of values, and a characteristic major premise characterizes the user.[49]

From the Aristotelian *topoi* Weaver selected and ranked certain "topics" or regions of experience to which an advocate could turn for the substance of persuasive argument. These "topics" are the "sources of content for speeches that are designed to influence."[50] By ranking them from the most to least ethically desirable, based on his philosophic conception of reality and knowledge, he outlined a hierarchy of topics which a persuader might use and which a critic could employ to assess the rhetoric of others.[51]

A speaker would make the highest order of appeal by basing his argument on genus or definition.[52] Argument from genus involves arguing from the nature or essence of things. It assumes that there are fixed classes and that what is true of a given class may be imputed to every member of that class. In the argument from genus the classification already is established, or it is one of the fixed concepts in the mind of the audience to which the argument is addressed. In argument from definition, the work of establishing the classification must be done during the course of the argument, after which the defined term will be used as would a genus. Further: Definitions should be rationally rather than empirically sustained. Good definitions should be stipulative, emphasizing what-ought-to-be, rather than operative, emphasizing what-is. Under argument from genus or definition, Weaver also included argument

from fundamental principles and argument from example. An example, he felt, always implies a general class. He believed that arguments from genus or definition ascribe "to the highest reality qualities of stasis, immutability, eternal perdurance."

He admitted that his preference for this mode of argument derived from his Platonic idealism. This mode of argument, he felt, was also a mark of the true conservative. To argue from genus or definition was to get people "to see what is most permanent in existence, or what transcends the world of change and accident. The realm of essence is the realm above the flux of phenomena; and definitions are of essences and genera."[53]

Weaver applied this viewpoint in his evaluation of the rhetoric of Abraham Lincoln.[54] He explicitly cited over a dozen examples of Lincoln's rhetoric. Yet unfortunately he did not indicate whether he based his generalizations on a careful examination of the entire corpus of the martyred President's oratory. Weaver's analysis led him to conclude that, although sometimes arguing from similitude, as in the Gettysburg Address, and again from consequence and circumstance, Lincoln characteristically argued from genus, definition, and principle. His greatest utterances, for example, were "chiefly arguments from definition." And in Weaver's view, therefore, Lincoln was a true conservative.[55] In contrast, many of Lincoln's contemporary Whigs were conservative, Weaver argued, only in the negative sense that they opposed Democratic proposals. Naturally Weaver praised Lincoln's rhetoric and his philosophical position.

As second in rank among the topics Weaver placed argument from similitude.[56] In this mode of argument are embraced analogy, metaphor, figuration, comparison, and contrast. Metaphor received focused attention from Weaver; to him it was often central to the rhetorical process.[57] Some of our profoundest intuitions concerning the world around us, he noted, are expressed in the form of comparisons. His Platonic idealism again helped him rank this topic. The user of an analogy hints at an essence he cannot at the moment produce. Weaver asserted that "behind every analogy lurks the possibility of a general term."

Argument from cause and effect stands third in Weaver's hierarchy of topics, and includes argument from consequences.[58] Although causal reasoning is a "less exalted" source of argument, we "all have to use it because we are historical men." This method of argument and its subvarieties, he felt, characterized the radical and the pragmatist. Causal argument operates in the realm of "becoming" and thus in the realm of flux. Argument from consequences attempts to forecast results of some course of action, either very desirable or very undesirable. These results are a determining factor for one in deciding whether or not to adopt a proposed action. Arguments from consequences, Weaver observed, usually are completely "devoid of reference to principle or defined ideas."

At the very bottom of Weaver's hierarchy stands argument from circumstances, another subvariety of causal reasoning.[59] This mode of argument, in his view, is the least "philosophical" of the topics because it admits of the least perspicaciousness and theoretically stops at the level of perception of fact. Argument from circumstances characterizes those who are easily impressed by existing tangibles, and such argument marks, he believed, the true liberal.[60] The arguers from circumstance, concerned not with "conceptions of verities but qualities of perceptions," lack moral vision and possess only the illusion of reality. We are driven back upon this method of argument when a course of action cannot be vindicated by principle or when effects cannot be demonstrated. The argument simply cites brute circumstance; it suggests expediency. "Actually," he explains, "this argument amounts to a surrender of reason. Maybe it expresses an instinctive feeling that in this situation reason is powerless. Either you change fast or you get crushed. But surely it would be a counsel of desperation to try only this argument in a world suffering from aimlessness and threatened with destruction."[61]

Weaver employed this topic to analyze the rhetoric of Edmund Burke, commonly classified as a conservative.[62] He conceded that many of Burke's observations on society have a conservative basis. On the other hand, he contended that when Burke came to grips with concrete policies, his rhetoric reflected "a strong addiction to the argument from circumstance." Weaver concluded, "When judged by what we are calling aspect of argument," Burke was "very far from being a conservative."[63] Burke was at his best, Weaver argued, when defending immediate circumstances and "reigning" circumstances. And until the time of the

French Revolution when he felt the need for "deeper anchorage," Burke's habitual argument from circumstances marked him philosophically as a liberal.[64] Weaver held Burke in low esteem as a conservative.

Again, while Weaver cited some dozen examples of Burke's rhetoric, he failed to indicate whether his generalizations rested on a scrutiny of all Burke's speeches, letters, and essays. It is in this connection also worthy of note that Russell Kirk has levied several objections to Weaver's evaluation of Burke.[65] First, the true conservative described by Weaver, contends Kirk, represents Weaver's *ideal* and ignores the historical fact that a true conservative is a follower of Edmund Burke, no matter what his typical mode of argument. Second, Kirk alludes to one of Burke's speeches to indicate that while Burke disdained "abstraction," he did praise genuine "principle." Here Kirk ignores Weaver's axiom that the important index is not what one says, but how one characteristically argues. Third, Kirk claims that although Abraham Lincoln often may have argued from principles and definition, he also often acted from circumstances and consequences. Finally, Kirk sees Burke's prosecution of Warren Hastings, and his attack on French errors during the Revolution as "instances of argument and action from definition."

Weaver's central premise of a typical pattern of argument for a speaker implies simple frequency of usage, as reflected in his use of the terms "characteristic" and "habitual." But some speakers may not have a clearly predominant mode of argument; they may blend a number of types of argu-

ment mentioned by Weaver. Judgment of the speaker is then more difficult. More important, some speakers may use arguments from consequences and circumstances more frequently than other types and yet use a few arguments from genus or principle as the fundamental arguments underlying all others.[66] Finally, Weaver fails to explain how a critic may determine whether a given line of argument is a metaphysical choice reflecting a speaker's philosophical stance or an "artful" choice necessitated by the practicalities of audience adaptation.

The use of characteristic mode of argument as the prime standard for rhetorical criticism represents an overly simplistic approach to evaluation of rhetorical practice. Such analysis promotes the slighting of other relevant factors in the rhetorical process. In the dramatistic terms proposed by Kenneth Burke, Weaver overemphasizes "agency" at the expense of "agent," "act," "scene," and "purpose." His typology of the "aspect" of argument can afford valuable insights, but it must not be taken as a well-rounded critical system. Yet in fairness to him it must be admitted that he did not intend his system to serve as the universal criterion for rhetorical criticism.

In addition to the hierarchy of "internal" sources of argument is the "external topic" of argument from authority and testimony.[67] Statements made by observers and experts take the place of direct or logical interpretation of evidence. Such testimony often embodies arguments from genus or definition, cause-effect, consequences, and circumstances, and thus can be judged by the standards appropriate to such arguments. But also involved is the more general question of the status of the authority. Thus a sound criterion, wrote Weaver, is that an argument from authority is only as good as the authority itself.

In his writing and teaching Weaver constantly strove to train his students in ethical rhetoric. Hence knowledge of rhetoric and skill in its use provided a defense against base rhetoric and propaganda.[68] In rhetorical education he placed prime emphasis on invention and style. Argumentation, including induction, deduction, and a modernized set of *topoi* adapted from Aristotle, formed a crucial part of rhetorical education.[69] The enthymeme received focused attention in Weaver's philosophy of rhetoric.[70] The rhetorician, he observed, enters into a oneness with his audience by tacitly agreeing with one of its perceptions of reality. Weaver noted further that the enthymeme functions only when the "audience is willing to supply the missing proposition."[71]

In *Composition*, a college textbook, Weaver treated the following "topics": genus or definition, cause and effect, similitude, comparison, contraries, circumstance, testimony, and authority. As could be expected, a major part of Weaver's text was devoted to style, including grammar and composition. His persistent efforts stimulated introduction of units on logic and the revitalized "topics" into the freshman English course in the College of the University of Chicago.[72]

Edward P. J. Corbett credits the article by Bilsky, Weaver, and others in *College English* (in 1953)—"Looking for an Argument"—with providing "perhaps the first suggestion of the value of classical rhetoric for the Freshman Composition course." Corbett claims that the treatment of the *topoi* in Weaver's *Composition* "represented the first instance of the use of the topics in a freshman rhetoric since the appearance of Francis P. Donnelly's books in the 1930's."[73]

Weaver's writings on rhetoric emphasize the processes and techniques of invention and the elements of effective style, giving minor place to organization and none to the classical canons of delivery and memory. He aims indeed at revitalizing invention and argumentation. To Weaver true rhetoric involves choices among values and courses of action; it aims at showing men "better versions of themselves" and better visions of an ultimate Good. As Platonic idealist and political conservative, he praised the ideal, the essence, the unchangeable, and condemned the particular, the transitory, and the expedient. A speaker's characteristic use of argument from genus, definition, principle, similitude, cause and effect, consequences, and circumstances, Weaver regarded as an index to the speaker's philosophical viewpoint and ethical stature.

By reaffirming and refining the essential connection between dialectic and rhetoric, Weaver illuminated the true province of rhetoric. Indeed, Weaver's theory pointed the way to the current rapproachement between philosophy and rhetoric.[74] Some of Weaver's political, philosophical, and rhetorical assumptions may be questioned in whole or in part. Still, there is little doubt that Weaver's theory, rooted as it was in a dialectic of the "true nature of things," has helped to reestablish rhetoric as a substantive discipline—a discipline concerned with matters of "the real world" and with the preservation of "the permanent things."

Notes

1. Eliseo Vivas, "The Mind of Richard Weaver," *Modern Age*, VIII (Summer, 1964), 309; Vivas, "Introduction," in Weaver, *Life Without Prejudice and Other Essays* (Chicago: Regnery, 1965), xiii–xiv. When Weaver died at age fifty-three, April 3, 1963, he was professor of English in the College of the University of Chicago.

2. For the influence of Weaver's ideas on other rhetorical theorists see Maurice Natanson, "The Limits of Rhetoric," *Quarterly Journal of Speech*, XLI (April, 1955), 133–39; Virgil Baker and Ralph Eubanks, *Speech in Personal and Public Affairs* (New York: David McKay, 1965), viii, 74, 80, 113; Ralph Eubanks and Virgil Baker, "Toward an Axiology of Rhetoric," *Quarterly Journal of Speech*, XLVIII (April, 1962), 157–68; Walter R. Fisher, "Advisory Rhetoric: Implications for Forensic Debate," *Western Speech*, XXIX (Spring, 1965), 114–19; Donald Davidson, "Grammar and Rhetoric: The Teacher's Problem," *Quarterly Journal of Speech*, XXXIX (December, 1953), 424–36; Ralph T. Eubanks, "Nihilism and the Problem of a Worthy Rhetoric," *Southern Speech Journal*, XXXIII (Spring, 1968), 187–99; W. Ross Winterowd, *Rhetoric: A Synthesis* (New York: Holt, Rinehart and Winston, 1968), 9–10, 13. Some of Weaver's essays now are being reprinted in anthologies on rhetoric. See, for example, Joseph Schwartz and John Rycenga (eds.), *The Province of Rhetoric* (New York: Ronald Press, 1965), 275–92, 311–29; Dudley Bailey (ed.), *Essays on Rhetoric* (New York: Oxford University Press, 1965), 234–49; Maurice Natanson and Henry W. Johnstone (eds.), *Philosophy, Rhetoric, and Argumentation* (University Park: Pennsylvania State University Press, 1965), 63–79.

3. Although most of his writings on rhetoric have this thrust, one of his most clearly focused essays was "The Cultural Role of Rhetoric," in *Visions of Order* (Baton Rouge: Louisiana State University Press, 1964), Chap. 4. See also page 7.

4. The editors wish to acknowledge the cooperation of Louis Dehmlow, compiler of Weaver's papers, and the late Kendall Beaton, literary executor, in securing a bibliography of Weaver's writings and copies of some of Weaver's unpublished manuscripts. A complete bibliography of Weaver's published writings appears in his *The Southern Tradition at Bay*, edited by George Core and M. E. Bradford (New York: Arlington House, 1968), 401–18.

5. *Ideas Have Consequences* (Chicago: University of Chicago Press, 1948); *The Ethics of Rhetoric* (Chicago: Regnery, 1953); *Composition: A Course in Writing and Rhetoric* (New York: Holt, Rinehart and Winston, 1957); "Language Is Sermonic," in Roger E. Nebergall (ed.), *Dimensions of Rhetorical Scholarship* (Norman: University of Oklahoma Department of Speech, 1963); *Visions of Order; Life Without Prejudice and Other Essays;* "Relativism and the Use of Language," in H. Schoeck and J. W. Wiggins (eds.), *Relativism and the Study of Man* (New York: Van Nostrand, 1961), 236–54; "Concealed Rhetoric in Scientistic Sociology," *Georgia Review*, XIII (Spring, 1959), 19–32; "To Write the Truth," *College English*, X (October, 1948), 25–30.

6. James Powell, "The Foundations of Weaver's Traditionalism," *New Individualist Review*, III (1964), 3–7; E. Victor Milione, "The Uniqueness of Richard M. Weaver," *Intercollegiate Review*, II (September, 1965), 67.

7. Russell, Kirk "Richard Weaver, R I P," *National Review*, XIV (April 23, 1963), 308; Willmoore Kendall, "How to Read Richard Weaver," *Intercollegiate Review*, II (September, 1965), 77–86. In fact Kendall argues that Weaver was so unique that he was virtually the only true American conservative on the contemporary scene.

8. Weaver discusses this transition in his autobiographical article "Up from Liberalism," *Modern Age*, III (Winter, 1958–59), 21–32. Starting in 1932 he was a formal member of the American Socialist Party for at least two years.

9. Weaver, "The Southern Tradition," *New Individualist Review*, III (1964), 7–17. Born in Weaverville, North Carolina, in 1910, he received his B.A. from the University of Kentucky in 1932, M.A. from Vanderbilt University in 1934, and Ph.D. from Louisiana State University in 1943.

10. For statements of Southern Agrarian precepts, including those of Ransom, Warren, Davidson, and Tate, see *I'll Take My Stand: The South and the Agrarian Tradition*, by

Twelve Southerners (New York: Harper, 1930); see also Herbert Agar and Allen Tate, *Who Owns America? A New Declaration of Independence* (Boston: Houghton Mifflin, 1936). Ransom, Warren, Davidson, and Tate, who led the influential literary group known as the "Nashville Fugitives," reflect on their participation in the Southern Agrarian movement in Rob Roy Purdy (ed.), *Fugitives' Reunion: Conversations at Vanderbilt* (Nashville: Vanderbilt University Press, 1959), 177–218. Ransom directed Weaver's M.A. thesis on "The Revolt Against Humanism." A recent analysis of the Southern Agrarian philosophy is Alexander Karanikas, *Tillers of a Myth: Southern Agrarians as Social and Literary Critics* (Madison: University of Wisconsin Press, 1966).

11. Kendall, "How to Read Richard Weaver," 78.
12. "Up from Liberalism," 23; Weaver, "The Confederate South, 1865–1910: A Study in the Survival of a Mind and Culture" (Ph.D. dissertation, Louisiana State University, 1943), 517. In a slightly revised form this dissertation has been published as *The Southern Tradition at Bay*.
13. "Up from Liberalism," 23–24; Weaver, "The Tennessee Agrarians," *Shenandoah*, III (Summer, 1952), 3–10.
14. *Who Owns America?*, 182–83, 325–26; *Ideas Have Consequences*, Chap. 7.
15. *Ideas Have Consequences*, 20, 35–51, 74–75; *Visions of Order*, 13, 22–39.
16. *Ideas Have Consequences*, 3–5, 12–17, 22–23, 34, 52, 60, 73, 119, 130–32, 146–47, 154; *Visions of Order*, 20–21, 38, 134–35; "Language Is Sermonic," 55; *Ethics of Rhetoric*, 3–26.
17. Weaver, Foreword to *Ideas Have Consequences* (paperback, 1959), v; Weaver, *New York Times Book Review* (March 21, 1948), 29.
18. S. I. Hayakawa, *Symbol, Status, and Personality* (New York: Harcourt, Brace, and World, 1963), 154–70, 182–85; Russell Kirk, "Ethical Labors," *Sewanee Review*, LXII (July–Sept., 1954), 489.
19. *Ideas Have Consequences*, 17, 51–52; *Ethics of Rhetoric*, 211–32.
20. *Ideas Have Consequences*, 130, 4. For many of the insights in the following paragraphs concerning Weaver's philosophy of reality and knowledge, the authors wish to acknowledge the research of Thomas D. Clark. See Thomas D. Clark, "The Philosophical Bases of Richard M. Weaver's View of Rhetoric" (M.A. thesis, Indiana University, 1969).
21. *Visions of Order*, 23.

22. *Ethics of Rhetoric*, 30–31; *Ideas Have Consequences*, 18.
23. *Ideas Have Consequences*, 12–13, 3, 27.
24. *Visions of Order*, 12; *Ethics of Rhetoric*, 49–54, 56–57, 203–204.
25. *Visions of Order*, 85; "Language Is Sermonic," 50–51; *Life Without Prejudice*, 146.
26. *Visions of Order*, 9, 144; *Life Without Prejudice*, 146; *Ideas Have Consequences*, 18.
27. *Visions of Order*, 24, 50, 85; *Ideas Have Consequences*, 19–20; *Life Without Prejudice*, 45–46.
28. *Visions of Order*, 43–44, 47, 85, 144; *Ideas Have Consequences*, 19–20; *Ethics of Rhetoric*, 17, 23.
29. *Visions of Order*, 135; *Ideas Have Consequences*, 167; *Life Without Prejudice*, 46–47. For Kenneth Burke's analysis of man as the symbol-using animal, see Burke, *Language as Symbolic Action* (Berkeley: University of California Press, 1966), 3–24.
30. *Life Without Prejudice*, 157–59.
31. *Ethics of Rhetoric*, 112.
32. Some of Weaver's positive suggestions were propounded in *Ideas Have Consequences* and *Visions of Order*; others were presented in some of his articles such as "The Humanities in a Century of Common Man," *New Individualist Review*, III (1964), 17–24. See also *Life Without Prejudice*, 15–64, 99–120; *The Southern Tradition at Bay*, 29–44, 388–96.
33. Wilma R. Ebbitt, "Richard M. Weaver, Teacher of Rhetoric," *Georgia Review*, XVIII (Winter, 1963), 417. These ancient sources are reflected, for example, in *Ethics of Rhetoric*, 128, 174, 203; *Composition*, 212; and "Language Is Sermonic," 62. Chapter one of *Ethics of Rhetoric* is a perceptive analysis of Plato's *Phaedrus*.
34. Weaver, "Concealed Rhetoric in Scientistic Sociology," 20–24, 28–30; *Ethics of Rhetoric*, 12, 22, 128, 225; "Language Is Sermonic," 60–61; *Composition*, 43; *Visions of Order*, 105; *Life Without Prejudice*, 46–47.
35. "Concealed Rhetoric in Scientistic Sociology," 20, 22.
36. *Life Without Prejudice*, 116–18.
37. *Ethics of Rhetoric*, 16, 17, 115; "Language Is Sermonic," 63.
38. "Language Is Sermonic," 54. Rhetoric must integrate the realms of Ideas and Particulars, of Being and Becoming.
39. *Ethics of Rhetoric*, 24–25. The infusion of Weaver's philosophy into his view of rhetoric bears out his premise that our "conception of metaphysical reality finally governs our conception of everything else." *Ideas Have Consequences*, 51.

40. *Ethics of Rhetoric*, 18, 23, 24, 211; "Language Is Sermonic," 58, 60–63; *Ideas Have Consequences*, 3, 19–20, 153, 167; *Visions of Order*, 67–69, 135; *Life Without Prejudice*, 118. Weaver made a detailed analysis of ultimate "god terms" and "devil terms" which have potency in contemporary American discourse. See *Ethics of Rhetoric*, 211–32.

41. "Concealed Rhetoric in Scientistic Sociology," 19–32. Weaver also analyzed the "sources of pervasive vices" in the rhetoric of social scientists, sources which make their prose difficult to understand and seemingly divorced from reality. See *Ethics of Rhetoric*, Chap. 8.

42. *Ideas Have Consequences*, 4–5, 150–60; *Visions of Order*, 67–70; "Relativism and the Use of Language," 236–54; Weaver, "To Write the Truth," 25–30.

43. *Ethics of Rhetoric*, 11–12, 18–24, 217, 232; *Ideas Have Consequences*, 153; *Life Without Prejudice*, 121–28.

44. *Ethics of Rhetoric*, 15–22, 25, 27–29; *Composition*, 120–23; *Visions of Order*, 55–72. For an example of Weaver's use of dialectic see *Visions of Order*, 92–112. As a rhetorical critic, he analyzed the use of rhetoric and dialectic by John Randolph of Roanoke, Henry David Thoreau, and by Bryan and Darrow in the Scopes Trial. See *Life Without Prejudice*, 65–97; *Ethics of Rhetoric*, Chap. 2.

45. *Ethics of Rhetoric*, 27–28.

46. "Language Is Sermonic," 51, 59–60; *Ethics of Rhetoric*, 134; *Ideas Have Consequences*, 19, 21, 165–67; *Visions of Order*, 70–72.

47. *Ethics of Rhetoric*, 115–42, 167. As a rhetorical critic, Weaver used a stylistic analysis to probe the "heroic" prose of John Milton and to illuminate the "spaciousness" of American oratory in the 1840's, and 1850's. See *Ethics of Rhetoric*, Chaps. 5 and 6.

48. This and the following quotations are from *Ethics of Rhetoric*, 58, 112, 114, 55.

49. *Ibid.*, 55–56. Although Weaver excludes "artful choices," the point can be raised that rhetoric by definition is artful in its adaptation to audience and situation and in its conscious effort at success. For an interesting attempt to test Weaver's axiom, without prior knowledge of Weaver's view, see Edwin S. Schneidmann, "The Logic of Politics," in Leon Arons and Mark May (eds.), *Television and Human Behavior* (New York: Appleton-Century-Crofts, 1963), 177–99.

50. "Language Is Sermonic," 53; *Composition*, 124.

51. "Language Is Sermonic," 55.

52. *Ibid.*, 53, 55–56; *Composition*, 124–27; *Ethics of Rhetoric*, 27, 56, 112–14; *Visions of Order*, 6. For Weaver's own extensive use of argument from genus or definition see, for example, *Ideas Have Consequences*, 43–44, 101, 129, 172; *Visions of Order*, Chaps. 1, 2, and 8.

53. "Language Is Sermonic," 55; *Life Without Prejudice*, 158–59.

54. *Ethics of Rhetoric*, 85–114. The user of arguments from genus, principle, and definition often realizes that on some issues there is no middle ground, only right and wrong. Lincoln, for instance, knew that honesty and long-run political success on the slavery issue depended upon avoiding major middle-road positions. But the failure of Stephen Douglas on the slavery question, believed Weaver, was that he chose an untenable position in the "excluded middle." See *Ethics of Rhetoric*, 94–95, 105–107.

55. Weaver saw George Washington as the "archetypal American conservative." *Life Without Prejudice*, 165.

56. "Language Is Sermonic," 53, 56; *Ethics of Rhetoric*, 56–57; *Composition*, 129–32. For examples of Weaver's own use of argument from similitude see *Visions of Order*, Chaps. 2 and 7.

57. *Ethics of Rhetoric*, 18, 23, 127–35, 150–52, 202–206; *Composition*, 248–58; *Visions of Order*, 142.

58. "Language Is Sermonic," 53, 56; *Composition*, 127–28; *Ethics of Rhetoric*, 57; *Life Without Prejudice*, 142, 145; Weaver, "A Responsible Rhetoric," (Address delivered March 29, 1955, to a Great Issues Forum of students at Purdue University), 4. See *Visions of Order*, Chaps. 1 and 2, for examples of his use of causal reasoning. And to a degree his *Ideas Have Consequences* is an argument from consequences; violation of certain ideals, values, and principles has led to destructive consequences.

59. "Language Is Sermonic," 57; *Ethics of Rhetoric*, 57–58; *Composition*, 128–29; *Ideas Have Consequences*, 151. An example of Weaver's infrequent personal usage is in *Ideas Have Consequences*, 134.

60. Weaver's major redefinition of the terms "liberal" and "conservative" seems to violate the type of linguistic covenant which he espouses as necessary in "Relativism and the Use of Language," 247–53.

61. "Language Is Sermonic," 57.

62. *Ethics of Rhetoric*, 55–84; Weaver, "The People of the Excluded Middle" (unpublished and undated manuscript), 12. Weaver felt that

although circumstance was no more than a retarding factor in Lincoln's considerations, circumstance was for Burke the deciding factor. See *Ethics of Rhetoric*, 95.

63. *Ethics of Rhetoric*, 58.
64. "The People of the Excluded Middle," 12.
65. Russell Kirk, "Ethical Labor," 485–503.
66. See, for example, Richard L. Johannesen, "John Quincy Adams' Speaking on Territorial Expansion, 1836–1848" (Ph.D. dissertation: University of Kansas, 1964), 304–50.
67. "Language Is Sermonic," 54, 57; *Composition*, 132–34.
68. *Composition*, iii–iv; *Ethics of Rhetoric*, 232; "To Write the Truth," 25–30.
69. *Composition*, 90–120, 123–34.
70. *Ethics of Rhetoric*, 173–74; *Visions of Order*, 63–64; *Composition*, 118–20; "Concealed Rhetoric in Scientistic Sociology," 29–31.
71. For a similar view see Lloyd Bitzer, "Aristotle's Enthymeme Revisited," *Quarterly Journal of Speech*, XLV (December, 1959), 399–408. American oratory in the 1840's and 1850's was characterized by the use of "uncontested terms" and ideas "fixed by universal consensus" as unstated premises already accepted by audiences. This characteristic marked the "spaciousness" of the rhetoric of that era. See *Ethics of Rhetoric*, 164–74.
72. Ebbitt, "Richard M. Weaver, Teacher of Rhetoric," 417. Insight into argumentation and the *topoi* as taught to the freshman is gained from Manuel Bilsky, McCrea Hazlett, Robert Streeter, and Richard Weaver, "Looking for an Argument," *College English*, XIV (January, 1953), 210–16. Many of Weaver's personal classroom concerns are reflected in an unpublished paper, "The Place of Logic in the English Curriculum."
73. Edward P. J. Corbett, "Rhetoric and Teachers of English," *Quarterly Journal of Speech*, LI (December, 1965), 380.
74. Natanson, "The Limits of Rhetoric," 136–37. Witness the increased recent interest in scholarly scrutiny of philosophical-rhetorical issues. See, for example, Otis Walter, "On Views of Rhetoric, Whether Conservative or Progressive," *Quarterly Journal of Speech*, XLIX (December, 1963), 367–82, and the journal, *Philosophy and Rhetoric*, published by the Pennsylvania State University Press.

Ray D. Dearin

The Philosophical Basis of Chaim Perelman's Theory of Rhetoric

◊ *This 1969 essay introduces contemporary students of argumentation to the teachings of Chaim Perelman of the University of Brussels whose training was in law, philosophy, and rhetoric. The author describes how Perelman, like Toulmin, is at the forefront of those who hold that practical reasoning, not formal or rationalistic logic, is the method of argument employed in human affairs. Among those points emphasized in this study are Perelman's commitment to such ideas as the need to identify rhetoric with the "methodology of the sociology of knowledge," with the process of the type of informal logic used in jurisprudence, and with the role that decision-making plays in our daily lives. Although Perelman, as the study suggests, uses the term "new rhetoric" to define his approach, he feels that one of his principal missions is to revitalize classical rhetoric for the modern student. ◊*

To think philosophically about any subject is to approach it rationally. As Henry W. Johnstone, Jr. puts the matter, "Philosophy is just the use of reason to examine each mode of human experience."[1] There are times when a close rational examination of a subject such as rhetoric becomes especially necessary. Johnstone continues:

The need for a philosophical examination of rhetoric is most acute and the examination most welcome when the orderly processes through which people are normally able to persuade one another suddenly go awry and can no longer be counted on. Aristotle's examination of rhetoric was carried out in just such a period of reversal. Individuals claiming to be able for a fee to persuade anyone of anything were making a mockery of the art of persuading. In so doing, they unwittingly called attention to the need for a philosophical scrutiny of the foundations of rhetoric. Aristotle supplied such a scrutiny, disengaging persuasiveness from dialectical shenanigans and associating it firmly with virtue.[2]

In addition to a disruption or perversion of normal communication processes, other crises have called forth reexaminations of rhetoric. The problems of integrating the contributions of the pagan writers on rhetoric into the pedagogy of Christian theology occupied the atten-

Mr. Dearin is Assistant Professor of Speech at Iowa State University.
Ray D. Dearin, "The Philosophical Basis of Chaim Perelman's Theory of Rhetoric," *Quarterly Journal of Speech*, 55 (October 1969): 213–224. Reprinted with permission from the Speech Communication Association.

tion of Augustine. In the eighteenth century, current views about psychology and epistemology led George Campbell to write *The Philosophy of Rhetoric.* Today modern science, with its concomitant effects on every field of learning, provokes new inquiries into the nature of rhetoric and into its relevance to present-day man and his problems.

Among the contributions of modern theoreticians of rhetoric, none stresses the interrelationship of philosophy and rhetoric more strongly nor reveals more clearly the relevance of rhetoric to twentieth-century man than does the theory espoused by the modern Belgian philosopher Chaim Perelman. The seeds of thought scattered throughout Perelman's numerous writings on such diverse topics as law, ethics, epistemology, philosophy, sociology, and argumentation over a period of more than three decades have already borne fruit in his *nouvelle rhétorique,* a theory whose fullest explication is found in the *Traité de l'argumentation,* which was written in collaboration with Madame L. Olbrechts-Tyteca in 1958. Since the publication of that treatise, Perelman has amplified and refined his theory of rhetoric in many books and articles. Doubtless, further extensions and refinements remain to be made.

Although future modifications may be expected, the uniqueness of Perelman's contributions and their obvious importance as specimens of modern rhetorical scholarship justify a close analytical scrutiny by students of rhetoric. Before one makes such an examination, however, he should ferret out the postulates and philosophical assumptions underlying Perelman's theory of rhetoric. To conduct such an investigation is the purpose of this article.

Stated most generally, the philosophic thought of M. Perelman represents a quest for a nonformal logic, one which may play a role in the behavioral sciences and philosophy analogous to that of modern formal logic and empiricism in the exact sciences. Moreover, the presuppositions behind his theory of rhetoric are foundational to his philosophical goal. I propose to show that in opposition to classical rationalism, which sought unique truth and certitude about its conclusions, Perelman enlarges the domain of reason to encompass a rhetorical rationalism that allows for a pluralism of values and a multiplicity of ways of being reasonable.

In my attempt to clarify Perelman's philosophical assumptions, I shall present four aspects of his thought: his conception of the nature of philosophy; his epistemology, which forms the substructure of the *nouvelle rhétorique;* his search for a nonformal logic that led him to the judicial model; and, finally, the concept of rhetorical reason, the culmination of his philosophic efforts.

1

One of Perelman's central concerns is to establish the philosophical method as a necessary mode of viewing man and his problems. For him, philosophy plays a role in the clarification of the human condition which science can never usurp. To be sure, at an early stage in his career, Perelman recognized certain similarities between the scientific method and philosophy. Thus, he wrote in 1940 that "the philosophical method has the same logical structure as that of science. It consists of deducing from certain principles and from certain definitions . . . a set of consequences, and of comparing, as far as possible, these consequences with the facts."[3] But the limitations of science in dealing with human problems are clearly set forth in Perelman's recent work, *An Historical Introduction to Philosophical Thinking.* In a critique of Auguste Comte's positivism, for example, he writes:

It cannot be denied that Comte's analysis is correct regarding certain areas of knowledge where scientific answers have completely replaced theological or philosophical concepts. But that is quite another thing from saying that *all* human problems can be solved by calling on the experimental or deductive methods of science alone. The study not of what is but of what ought to be, what has the greater value, what is preferable, and what should determine our choices and our conduct can be abandoned to scientific methods only when we are dealing with purely technical problems. But that is far from being the case. Not only does the solution of our fundamental problems elude science and technology; the very hypothesis that philosophy can be dispensed with is itself a philosophical hypothesis.[4]

So Perelman believes in the meaningfulness and importance of philosophy. His conception of the aim of philosophy, however, differs markedly from the views of earlier philosophers who attempted to base their systems on necessary or self-evident theses. In fact, whereas traditional metaphysics has always sought to discover eternal and immutable principles, Perelman believes that philosophy should "elaborate principles of being, thought, and action that are humanly *reasonable*."[5] He maintains that the proverbial controversies and interminable discussions that mark the whole history of philosophic thought are due not to the

lack of lucidity or the positive errors of philosophers, but to the very nature of the enterprise itself.[6] Moreover, philosophy cannot rightly employ the methods of formal logic. "The goal of philosophy," he writes, "is to influence the mind and win its agreement, rather than to perform purely formal transformations of propositions."[7] In effect, "whoever develops a philosophical system undertakes to address everyone and to convince everyone."[8] In Perelman's fundamental conception of philosophy, therefore, the contingent nature of the axioms of every metaphysical system necessitates a recourse to rhetoric. This reliance upon argument is obligatory. Even those philosophers who have despised rhetoric have been compelled to use it: "The metaphysical rationalists, who strive to eliminate every conflict of values from their vision of the universe, which explains their scorn for rhetoric, arrive at their ends only after having imposed, thanks to rhetoric, their fundamental principles. . . . Every metaphysician must furnish reasons for the superiority of his system and, so long as his system is not admitted, he can only resort to the processes of rhetorical argumentation."[9]

Just as the philosopher resorts to argumentation in his presentation of a defensible world view, he also employs it in making ethical judgments. In his recent treatise, *Justice,* Perelman states:

The specific role of philosophy is, in effect, to propose to humanity objective principles of action that will be valid for the will of all reasonable men. This objectivity . . . envisages . . . an attempt to formulate norms and values such as could be proposed to every reasonable being. But to *propose* does not mean to *impose*. This distinction must be maintained at all cost. Otherwise we run

Ray D. Dearin

the risk of a philosopher-king who would use the political authority and power of the State to ensure the supremacy of his convictions, his values, and his norms.[10]

The problems involved in the "ideal of universality" and the notion of "all reasonable men" will be set aside for subsequent consideration in connection with Perelman's conception of reason. At present, it is sufficient to note that in proposing ethical values, as in elaborating a world view, every philosopher employs postulates whose contingent nature excludes them from the realm of scientific demonstration or from the domain of formal logic.

Even if the principles of a philosophical system are granted by everyone, its conclusions may possibly be accepted by only a certain number of men. Because proof in philosophy is not simply a transposition in the order of axioms and theorems as in the deductive sciences of mathematics or geometry, the "conclusions are quite different from the original premises, and the process of arriving at them can only be explained by a difference in the nature of the proof."[11] Hence, Spinoza's ideal of a geometric, deductive, rationalistic philosophy can never be attained. As Perelman says, "A philosophical system cannot be proved like a treatise in geometry."[12]

The direction of Perelman's own thought concerning the nature of philosophy is revealed most clearly in his distinction between primary philosophies and regressive philosophy. Most traditional systems have been of the former type. Each has attempted to construct an edifice of universal, immutable truths. No provision has been made for future modifications. Conse-

quently, when a crack appears in its foundation, the philosopher has been forced to admit that he has been mistaken, to attribute his error to spurious evidence or to a fallacious view of necessity, and then, after making the required modifications, to rebuild the structure as solidly as possible, and to proceed again to defend it to the last assault.[13] Regressive philosophy, on the other hand, affirms that from the time the philosopher begins his reflection, he starts with "a set of facts which he considers neither necessary, nor absolute, nor definitive, but as sufficiently assured to permit him to ground his thought."[14] Unlike the primary philosophy, "every crisis in its foundations constitutes, for regressive philosophy, a confirmation, a deepening of thought, for which it can only rejoice."[15] When he must modify his system, the philosopher will choose from among alternative possibilities the modification he deems best. Of course, he then must justify his choice by presenting reasons why it seems preferable to him, if he wishes to obtain the agreement of his peers.[16] Perelman's preference for regressive philosophy may be explained succinctly in these words: Philosophizing is a *human* endeavor. He states: "It is man, in the final analysis, who is the judge of his choice, and other men, his collaborators and his adversaries, judge, at the same time, this choice and the man who has chosen."[17]

This brief account of Perelman's views about philosophy reveals his beliefs that philosophy is an essential activity whose function cannot be replaced by science, that its methods are rhetorical and argumentative, rather than deductive and mathematical, and that the philosopher should entertain no delusion that his premises and conclusions are necessary or irrefragable. Not surprisingly, this attitude toward philosophy engenders a distinctive theory of knowledge.

2

In 1950 Perelman and Olbrechts-Tyteca suggested that a revival of rhetoric ought to accompany the formulation of a modern epistemology: "We believe that a theory of knowledge which corresponds to this climate of contemporary philosophy needs to integrate into its structure the processes of argumentation utilized in every domain of human culture and that . . . a renewal of rhetoric would conform to the humanist aspect of the aspirations of our age."[18] The form a modern view of knowledge should take can be better understood when the deficiencies in earlier theories are pointed out.

In the first place, the nationalists, empiricists, and positivists all failed to understand that, unlike physical phenomena, mental phenomena are not susceptible to quantification. A new insight came when Immanuel Kant observed that intensive magnitude is of an entirely different order from extensive magnitude. Perelman says, "This distinction of Kant's blazed the trail for Bergson's analysis. Bergson showed that psychological phenomena are qualitatively different from each other and that we cannot apply calculation or measure to them."[19]

A second flaw in traditional epistemologies, especially those inspired by the Cartesian model of an eternal and unchanging reason, is their failure to account for historical and social conditions. According to Perelman, "The concrete problem of the theory of knowledge is to study the means which make it possible to describe and explain phenomena and to determine the influence which the objects of our knowledge exercise on the processes that make knowledge possible."[20] A study of the *means* used to describe and explain phenomena will doubtless entail a consideration of the role of language in the acquisition of knowledge. That possibility will be considered presently. But it is the other aspect of the problem, the influence exerted by the *objects* of our knowledge, that suggests the relevance of social and cultural factors in the theory of knowledge. These factors led Perelman to assign to rhetoric a fundamental role in epistemology. In effect, for him rhetoric becomes the methodology of the sociology of knowledge. He writes:

To determine the field of application of the sociology of knowledge, it would be necessary to study most closely this strange logic [rhetoric] and the reasons which make it undergo the influence of social and cultural factors. One would see upon analysis that the proofs which govern it are neither the evidence of calculus nor experimental evidence, but those which Aristotle called "dialectical proofs," and which he studied in his *Topics* and his *Rhetoric*. In effect, socially conditional knowledge concerns the beliefs, the agreements, the adhesions of men. . . . Only a detailed examination of rhetorical argumentation will permit the founding of the sociology of knowledge upon the most solid bases.[21]

Thus, Perelman believes that modern epistemology should deal with all the factors, including social and cultural elements, which condition the acquisition of ideas and beliefs.

As stated earlier, a study of the means used to describe and explain phenomena introduces the element of language into any modern theory of knowledge. Perelman has long been aware of the problems involved in the communication of "meaning" through linguistic symbols.[22] In recent years he has shown that a weakness in classical rationalism was its belief that self-evidence founded on the identity of subject and object can lay claim to the truth. "Every assertion," he says, "before it can be judged true or false, must first be meaningful. Linguistic statements are made up of symbols which, by definition, cannot coincide with what they designate. In this case, how is it possible to identify the truth of a judgment with the self-evidence of an intuition?"[23] The best that rationalists can do is to "make the intervention of languages inoffensive as possible in order to render perfectly transparent the veil that it cannot help but be."[24] Perelman states his own view flatly: "The choice of a linguistic form is neither purely arbitrary nor simply a carbon copy of reality. The reasons that induce us to prefer one conception of experience, one analogy, to another, are a function of our vision of the world. The form is not separable from the content; language is not a veil which one need only discard or render transparent in order to perceive the real as such; it is inextricably bound up with a point of view, with the taking of a position."[25]

These foregoing weaknesses in earlier epistemologies are most pronounced in classical rationalism, and Perelman's work is, in large part, devoted to the overthrow of the Cartesian theory of knowledge. The Cartesian view of science as a collection of facts that have been established and definitively remain so "is, in the end, a theory of knowledge which is not human, but divine; of knowledge acquired by a unique and perfect Being, without initiation, training, tradition or need to learn. On this view, the history of knowledge, on its positive side, becomes uniquely that of additions, not that of successive modifications."[26] Such a notion is, of course, antithetical to Perelman's conception of a regressive philosophy. In contrast to the *results* of the scientific method, the Belgian philosopher would stress the *process* by which scientific theories come to be accepted:

If we assume that the sciences develop on the basis of opinions previously accepted— and replaced by others either when difficulty results from some contradiction or in order to allow of new elements of knowledge being integrated in the theory—then the understanding of scientific methodology requires us to be concerned not with building the scientific edifice on the foundation of self-evident truths, but with indicating why and how certain accepted opinions come to be no longer regarded as the most probable and the most suitable to express our beliefs, and are replaced by others. The history of the evolution of scientific ideas would be highly revealing in this regard.[27]

In Perelman's way of looking at scientific activity, "neither the self-evident principles of the rationalists nor the irrefragable facts of the empiricists constitute clear and distinct elements of knowledge which no subsequent progress would later modify or make more specific."[28] Not only have the rationalistic and empiricist ideas "generated misconceptions about the role of language and the methodology of the sciences," but by conceiving knowledge as "a structure at the base of which is an indubitable experience of sense-given data," they have led to an altogether "misleading contrast between knowledge and opinion."[29] As will be observed, Perelman attempts to remove this unnecessary distinction in his enlarged concept of reason.

Perelman stresses the importance of the problem of justifying one's fundamental postulates. He writes:

For centuries logicians have been able to neglect the problem of the justification of one's choice of axioms, by considering the latter either as self-evident or as arbitrary. In the first case, since we must bow to the evidence, we have no choice and therefore no need to justify our acceptance. In the second case, since all choices are considered equally arbitrary, it is impossible to justify any one by showing it to be preferable to any other. When we reject both of these extremes, so reminiscent of realism and nominalism, when we admit that a choice of axioms is possible and that it is not entirely arbitrary, then the justification of choice ceases to be a negligible problem.[30]

By rejecting the idea of a self-evident intuition and its opposite extreme, Perelman thus conceives of an epistemology that is not only the antithesis of the Cartesian view, but one that also blurs the dubious distinction between knowledge and opinion. He states plainly: "I shall grant the status of knowledge to a tested opinion, to an opinion, that is, which has survived all objections and criticisms and with regard to which we have a certain confidence, though no certainty, that it will resist all such future attacks."[31]

The whole effect of Perelman's theory of knowledge, it should be clear by now, is to assert the role of decision in the working out of our ideas. This point of view emphasizes the *reasons* we have for deciding in a particular way as well as the *techniques of reasoning* by which we arrive at those decisions. Perelman believes, then, that an epistemology should be "founded on what a theory of the nature of argumentation, as it actually is, can teach us."[32] The next stage of our investigation chronicles his search for a nonformal logic that can explain how decisions are actually made.

3

For over twenty-five years, Perelman has been intrigued by the idea of justice, and, if one does not miss the connection between justice and "justification," then the relevance of this aspect of the philosopher's thought to his theory of rhetorical argumentation is obvious. To begin with, Perelman sought to clear away from the concept of justice the extraordinary confusion surrounding the multiplicity of meanings that have been attached to the idea throughout history. He found at first that the varied meanings of the word "justice" appear irreconcilable. Currently, the term is used to designate at least six different ideas:

1. To each the same thing.
2. To each according to his merits.
3. To each according to his works.
4. To each according to his needs.
5. To each according to his rank.
6. To each according to his legal entitlement.[33]

As Julius Stone correctly observes, when Perelman is confronted with these multifarious conceptions of justice, his method is to seek "a kind of nucleus of justice, which shall be independent of varying usage-associations, and of the ideological implications of such usage."[34] Indeed, Perelman finds that beneath all the various systems of concrete justice and running throughout all the various conceptions of justice is one formal, abstract principle. Stated simply, formal justice consists of "*a principle of action in accordance with which beings of one and the same essential category must be treated in the same way.*"[35] This principle, being purely formal and abstract, is never realized in any normative system of justice. As will be seen, an arbitrary element always intervenes to flout formal justice. But the utility of this general principle extends beyond the field of ethics to the problem of justification in general. "Justification," writes Perelman, "can deal with legality, morality, regularity (in the widest sense of the word), usefulness or expediency."[36] Moreover, since the idea of justification implies the "possibility of an unfavorable appraisal of what you are trying to justify,"[37] it follows that the matter under consideration is debatable. Under such conditions, rational argument ensues, and here Perelman's abstract principle becomes a *rule of justice* that may be applied, he thinks, to determine the relative strength of arguments: "It is useless to try to define rational argumentation the way we define a demonstrative technique, namely, by its conformity to certain prescribed rules. Unlike demonstrative reasoning, arguments are never correct or incorrect; they are either strong or weak, relevant or irrelevant. The strength or weakness is judged according to the Rule of Justice, which

requires that essentially similar situations be treated in the same manner."[38] Thus, a principle derived from Perelman's analysis of justice constitutes a yardstick for determining the strength of arguments which, by their very nature, cannot be judged according to the rules of formal logic.

Doubtless, a principal reason for Perelman's preoccupation with the notion of justice is that it lies in an area where value judgments abound. As indicated earlier, there can be no perfect justice because an arbitrary element enters into every normative system. Indeed, that element is the *value* affirmed by the principles of the system which are themselves not justified. For example, the decision to follow the principle, "to each according to his works," rather than "to each according to his needs" affirms a value judgment that is not itself obviously justified. Says Perelman, "This latter touch of the arbitrary it is logically impossible to avoid."[39] The implications of Perelman's rejection of the notion of unique truth are felt most strongly in the realm of values. From his own pluralistic perspective, two different decisions about the same object can both be reasonable as long as they express coherent and philosophically founded points of view.[40] If statements of value can be neither true nor false, then how are we to reason concerning values? Clearly, some way is needed: "The need for a logic of value judgments has been felt in philosophic thought from the day when it was realized that truth or falsity is not a property that can be attributed to every proposition."[41] In a sense, Perelman's analysis of justice has led him to formulate his philosophical goal. Max

Loreau, in a critical exposition of his philosophy, identifies this objective which colors all of Perelman's work: "*to produce an instrument capable of achieving in the realm of values results exactly analogous to those pursued by analytical reasoning in the domain of the exact sciences.*"[42]

The search for a nonformal logic and the results of that endeavor are best reported in the philosopher's own words:

Ten years after the beginning of our project, we had not found the logic of value judgments that we were looking for. We did, however, rediscover a long-neglected logic which had been completely forgotten by contemporary logicians, although it had been treated at length in the ancient treatises on rhetoric and in the *Topics* of Aristotle. This was the study of what Aristotle called dialectical proofs in contrast to the analytical proofs that interest modern logicians exclusively. In an extended empirical and analytical study called *Traité de l'argumentation* Mme. Olbrechts-Tyteca and I were able to put forward this nonformal logic as a theory of argumentation, complementary to the theory of demonstration that is the object of formal logic. . . . The same techniques of reasoning which we use to criticize and to justify opinions, choices, claims, and decisions, are also used when it comes to criticizing and justifying statements that are usually qualified as value judgments. That is why the practical use of reason cannot be understood without first integrating it into a general theory of argumentation.[43]

Before considering this "practical use of reason," which is central in Perelman's thought, it is instructive to notice the model he uses to exemplify the nonformal mode of reasoning. That model is drawn from jurisprudence. He says, "A thorough investigation of proof in law, of its variations and evolution, can, more than any other study, acquaint us with the relations existing between thought and action."[44] In resorting to the judicial model, Perelman makes a choice similar to that of the English philosopher and logician, Stephen Toulmin. Toulmin, whose search for a "working logic" applicable to human decision-making closely parallels Perelman's quest, also turns to law for his paradigm. Toulmin remarks: "Logic (we may say) is generalised jurisprudence. Arguments can be compared with lawsuits, and the claims we make and argue for in extra-legal contexts with claims made in the courts, while the cases we present in making good each kind of claim can be compared with each other."[45] Julius Stone points out that both Perelman and Toulmin use the judicial model as an aid for their philosophical tasks, rather than to make judicial tasks easier.[46] However, Perelman, who is trained in law as well as in philosophy, has more than an ordinary interest in the legal process.

The selection of courtroom reasoning as a model of nonformal logic offers certain advantages. First, the judge, under penalty of law in most legal systems, cannot avoid rendering and justifying a decision. Perelman says: "The techniques peculiar to the reasoning of jurists . . . all go hand in hand with the obligation laid on the judge to decide and to give reasons for his decision. His business is to draw up a judgment as consistent as possible with the provisions of the law, and such consistency cannot be determined by the criteria of formal logic alone. The obligation to take a reasoned decision is an essential element in the constitution of juridical knowledge."[47] Secondly, the logic of jurisprudence is completely ignored by modern formal logicians: "When the advocates accuse each other of not respecting *logic*, the word 'logic' does not designate . . . formal logic, the only logic practiced by the majority of professional logicians, but juridical logic, which modern logicians entirely ignore."[48] Thirdly, legal reasoning ordinarily recognizes that presumption favors the *status quo:* "Law teaches us . . . to abandon existing rules only if good reasons justify their replacement: Only change requires justification, presumption playing in favor of what exists, just as the burden of proof falls upon him who wants to change an established state of affairs."[49] A fourth advantage of the judicial model, closely allied with the third, is that law recognizes the role of precedent in human reasoning and conduct. And here we see how the generalized "rule of justice" is made to play a key role in all rational argumentation. Perelman states:

The historicity of reason is always closely connected with its becoming part of a tradition, in which innovation must always produce its letters of credence. That is why so often the best justification of a course of conduct . . . consists in showing that that course is in conformity with the recognized order, that it can avail itself of unquestioned precedents. Precedent plays a quite primary role in argumentation, the rationality of which is linked with the observance of the *rule of justice*, which demands equal treatment for similar situations. Now, the application of the rule of justice assumes the existence of precedents to teach us how situations similar to the one confronting us now have been dealt with in the past. These precedents, just like the models by which a society is inspired, make part of its cultural tradition, which can be reconstructed on the basis of the argumentations in which they have been employed.[50]

We see, then, how Perelman's analysis of justice reveals a principle of action, formalized as the rule of justice,

which serves as a common element in all rational activity. Although Perelman and his colleague, Olbrechts-Tyteca, could find no special logic of value judgments, their rediscovery of the dialectical proofs of Aristotle, together with a thorough understanding of the juridical patterns of argument, leads to an enlarged view of reason.

4

In setting forth his vision of an enlarged reason, Perelman hopes to counteract the pernicious influence of two groups: the Cartesian rationalists and the modern mathematical logicians. Both groups share the responsibility for the narrow concept of reason that exists today. Perelman and Olbrechts-Tyteca say: "The logician, inspired by the Cartesian ideal, feels at home only in the study of the proofs that Aristotle qualified as analytic. . . . And this tendency is all the more strongly marked after a period in which, under the influence of the mathematical logicians, logic was reduced to formal logic, to a study of the means of proof used in the mathematical sciences. As a result, reasoning which is foreign to the purely formal domain escapes logic, and consequently escapes reason too."[51] Elsewhere Perelman expresses his disappointment over the reduction of logic to the study of formal reasoning: "We feel that this narrowing of the field of logic is disastrous for the methodology of the human sciences, for law and for all branches of philosophy."[52] Again, Toulmin's thought runs in a similar direction. Toulmin writes: "In logic as in morals, the real problem of rational assessment—telling sound arguments from untrustworthy ones, rather than consistent from inconsistent ones—requires experience, insight and judgment, and mathematical calculations (in the form of statistics and the like) can never be more than one tool among others of use in this task."[53] Both Perelman and Toulmin believe, then, that formal logic has unduly restricted the concept of reason.

A study of Perelman's philosophy must be aware of the philosopher's distinction between two types of reason—the logical and the rhetorical. A logical system, for Perelman, is a set of propositions and rules that manages to remove itself from time, isolating its data from every context except itself and fixing the instruments which it uses. Those instruments are correct expressions and rules of inference. Rhetoric, on the other hand, explores the domain of concrete and situated reason. Concerning this rhetorical reason, Loreau writes: "Its investigation bears upon discourse which allows a place to the non-conventional, to the implicit, to the indeterminate; it aspires to the explication and to the structuration of the systems of reasoning used implicitly in the discursive exploitation of the margin of indetermination which affects ideas and which is manifested when the meaning attributed to these latter finds itself contested, either by a new truth or by a new situation."[54] Perelman hopes to reassert this second kind of reasoning, the rhetorical. He believes that reason serves not only to discover truth and error, in the narrow logical sense, but also to justify and to argue:

Besides demonstrative and calculating reason, there exists a reason that deliberates and argues. Without a broadened vision of reason, which would enable us to understand what is meant by deciding and making an enlightened choice, a rational concept of liberty and human responsibility remains impossible. Besides the Cartesian conception of liberty, adherence to evidence, there is room for a concept of liberty-responsibility where, being face to face with arguments pro and con, neither of which is compelling, we decide that one side has more weight, and in doing so we take a final step. . . .

This broadening of our concept of reason, which no longer limits the rational to the analytical, opens a new field of study to the investigations of the logicians; it is the field of those reasons which, according to Pascal and according to contemporary logicians, reason does not know.[55]

When the full implications of this broadened idea of reason are felt, the traditional distinction between the will and the understanding, reminiscent of faculty psychology, will disappear. Along with it will go the conviction-persuasion dichotomy which has plagued rhetorical theory for so long. Perelman and Olbrechts-Tyteca suggest that this unhappy distinction may be traced back to Aristotle, who devoted his *Topics* to the theoretical discussion of theses and his *Rhetoric* to the peculiarities of audiences.[56] At any rate, the philosophers following Descartes, whether rationalist or antirationalist, have, for the most part, fallen into the same fundamental error. Pascal opposed will to understanding, insight to geometry, the heart to reason, and the art of persuading to that of convincing. In a similar fashion, Kant opposed faith to science, and Bergson opposed intuition to reason. As for Perelman, he believes that these dichotomies constitute a dilemma and are based on an egregious error: "The error is to conceive man as made up of completely separated faculties."[57] In an article reporting the results of their survey of the fields of logic and rhetoric, Perelman and Olbrechts-Tyteca conclude that "the conviction-persuasion opposition cannot suffice when one leaves the bounds of a strict rationalism and examines the diverse means of obtaining the adherence of minds."[58]

By extending the domain of reason, Perelman hopes, of course, to give a rational basis to law, ethics, philosophy, political debate, and other areas of human endeavor that "cannot be considered relevant to logic in the strict sense."[59] Thus, when he and his collaborator examine the processes of actual argument in their *Traité*, they avow their intention to examine "arguments presented by publicists in their newspapers, by politicians in their speeches, by advocates in their pleadings, by judges in their deliberations, by philosophers in their treatises."[60] Only a reason broad enough to manifest itself in all the areas of human activity where justifications have to be made can be a truly practical reason. Perelman asks: "Must we abandon all philosophical use of practical reason and limit ourselves to the technical use of reason in the domain of action? Must we use our reason only to adjust our means to totally irrational ends? Affirmative answers to these questions form the position of all positivist philosophers, from Hume to Ayer. . . . Are the search for a rational foundation for our individual and collective actions and the desire to elaborate an ethic, a philosophy of law, and a political philosophy nourished only on illusion and illogic."[61] As we have seen, the whole tenor of Perelman's philosophic thought provides a negative answer to such questions. For him, there exists a reason whose function is not merely to verify and to demonstrate, but also to deliberate, to criticize, and to justify, to give reasons for and against. In short, the function of reason is also to argue.

5

The philosophical basis upon which Chaim Perelman develops his theory of rhetoric should now be tolerably clear. His predisposition to reject the Cartesian notions of self-evidence and the uniqueness of truth leads him to conceive the aim of philosophy to be the elaboration and the justification of a defensible world view. Perelman believes that since one's fundamental axioms are neither self-evident nor necessary, a philosopher must resort to rational argumentation in order to supply such justification.

As we have seen, the epistemology that results from these presuppositions emphasizes the role of decision in the acquisition and transmission of knowledge. The idea that our knowledge constitutes an edifice of immutable truths, an idea stemming from the erroneous doctrines of classical rationalism and empiricism, is shattered by the realization that the truth of our beliefs cannot be guaranteed once and for all. As Perelman maintains, such truths "are worked out, made specific and refined—and these truths constitute no more than the best tested of our opinions."[62] The principal effect of this revelation is to remove the misleading distinction between knowledge and opinion.

Further, in search of a principle of justification that can lay claim to being rational, Perelman finds in his analysis of justice a common, abstract element at the base of the various conceptions of justice—the principle that beings of the same essential category must be treated alike. The arbitrariness inherent in the selection of the "essential categories' renders absolute justice impossible and highlights the need for a logic of value judgments. Perelman's search for such a logic merely leads him back to a consideration of the techniques of argument analyzed by Aristotle in his *Topics* and his *Rhetoric*. Thus, the philosopher concludes that a general theory of argumentation inspired by classical rhetoric is needed.

Finally, Perelman's view of rationality greatly enlarges the concept of reason inherited from Descartes and his successors. This "rhetorical reason" operates in the realm of the probable, the contingent, and the plausible; in brief, it seems especially adaptable to the behavioral sciences, to law, and to philosophy. It is in the light of Perelman's entire philosophical enterprise, then, that one should approach his theory of rhetoric.

Notes

1. "The Relevance of Rhetoric to Philosophy and of Philosophy to Rhetoric," *QJS*, LII (February 1966), 42.
2. *Ibid.*, 44.
3. Ch. Perelman, "Une conception de la philosophie," *Revue de l'Institut de Sociologie*, XX (1940), 46. [Translation mine.]
4. Trans. Kenneth A. Brown (New York, 1965), pp. 5–6.
5. Ch. Perelman, "On Self-Evidence in Metaphysics," *International Philosophical Quarterly*, IV (February 1964), 5–6.
6. *Ibid.*
7. Perelman, *An Historical Introduction to Philosophical Thinking*, p. 101.
8. *Ibid.*, p. 99.
9. Ch. Perelman, "Réflexions sur la justice," *Revue de l'Institut de Sociologie*, XXIV (1951), 280–281. [Translation mine.]
10. (New York, 1967), p. 78.
11. Perelman, *An Historical Introduction to Philosophical Thinking*, p. 101.
12. *Ibid.*, p. 140.
13. Ch. Perelman, "Philosophies premières et philosophie régressive," *Dialectica*, III (1949), 190.
14. *Ibid.*, 185–186. [Translation mine.]
15. *Ibid.*, 190.
16. *Ibid.*, 184–185.
17. *Ibid.*
18. Ch. Perelman and L. Olbrechts-Tyteca, "Logique et rhétorique," *Revue philosophique*, CXL (January 1950), 35. [Translation mine.]
19. Perelman, *An Historical Introduction to Philosophical Thinking*, p. 186.
20. *Ibid.*, p. 205.
21. Ch. Perelman, "Sociologie de la connaissance et Philosophie de la connaissance," *Revue internationale de philosophie*, IV (July 1950), 315. [Translation mine.]
22. In 1940 Perelman was concerned to show that philosophy could deal just as objectively with the emotive meanings of words as with their conceptual meanings. ["Une conception de la philosophie," p. 41.] He was familiar with these distinctions made by C. K. Ogden and I. A. Richards in *The Meaning of Meaning* (London, 1923).
23. Perelman, "On Self-Evidence in Metaphysics," 13.
24. *Ibid.*, 16–17.
25. Chaim Perelman, "Rhetoric and Philosophy," trans. Henry W. Johnstone, Jr., *Philosophy and Rhetoric*, I (January 1968), 17–18. Elsewhere M. Perelman amplifies the idea that language is neither a simple copy of preestablished structures nor an arbitrary creation of man: "Although language is a human artefact, it is not produced by any irrational decision of a single individual. It develops, normally, in the midst of a community, the members of which can modify it by the use they make of it as soon as they consider there are any reasons for promoting any change." [Ch. Perelman, *The Idea of Justice and the Problem of Argument*, trans. John Petrie (London, 1963), p.123.]
26. Perelman, *The Idea of Justice and the Problem of Argument*, pp. 116–117.
27. *Ibid.*, p. 94.
28. *Ibid.*, p. 95.

362   *Ray D. Dearin*

29. H. L. A. Hart, Introduction to *ibid.*, p. xi. Professor Hart also remarks that "in this part of his work M. Perelman has reached, by an independent route, conclusions similar to those of contemporary English philosophers who have also been critical of both the rationalism and the empiricism of the past."
30. Perelman, *Justice*, p. 60.
31. Perelman, *The Idea of Justice and the Problem of Argument*, p. 117.
32. *Ibid.*, p. 122.
33. *Ibid.*, p. 7. [This section of the book originally appeared in 1945 as *De la justice.*]
34. *Human Law and Human Justice* (Stanford, Calif., 1965), p. 302.
35. Perelman, *The Idea of Justice and the Problem of Argument*, p. 16.
36. Ch. Perelman, "Value Judgments, Justifications and Argumentation," trans. Francis B. Sullivan, *Philosophy Today*, VI (Spring 1962), 46.
37. *Ibid.*
38. Perelman, *Justice*, p. 83. He goes on to say that "relevance and irrelevance are to be examined according to the rules and criteria recognized by the various disciplines and their particular methodologies."
39. Perelman, *The Idea of Justice and the Problem of Argument*, p. 60.
40. See Ch. Perelman, "Désaccord et rationalité de décisions," *Logica e Analist: Archivio di Filosofia* (1960), 93.
41. Perelman, "Réflexions sur la justice," 269.
42. "Rhetoric as the Logic of the Behavioral Sciences," trans. Lloyd I. Watkins and Paul D. Brandes, *QJS*, LI (December 1965), 456.
43. Perelman, *Justice*, pp. 58–59.
44. Perelman, *The Idea of Justice and the Problem of Argument*, p. 108.
45. *The Uses of Argument* (Cambridge, 1964), p. 7.
46. *Legal System and Lawyers' Reasonings* (Stanford, Calif., 1964), p. 335.
47. Perelman, *The Idea of Justice and the Problem of Argument*, p. 90.
48. Ch. Perelman, Preface to *Introduction à la logique juridique*, by Georges Kalinowski (Paris, 1965), p. v. [Translation mine.]
49. Perelman, *Justice*, p. 104.
50. Perelman, *The Idea of Justice and the Problem of Argument*, p. 157.
51. Ch. Perelman and L. Olbrechts-Tyteca, *Traité de l'argumentation*, 2 vols. (Paris, 1958), I, 3. [From a translation of the introduction of this work by Francis B. Sullivan, which appeared as "The New Rhetoric," *Philosophy Today*, I (March 1957), 5.]
52. Ch. Perelman, "Reply to Henry W. Johnstone, Jr.," *Philosophy and Phenomenological Research*, XVI (December 1955), 245.
53. Toulmin, p. 188.
54. Loreau, "Rhetoric as the Logic of the Behavioral Sciences," 457–458; see also Max Loreau, "Pour situer la nouvelle rhétorique," *Logique et analyse*, VI (December 1963), 104.
55. Chaim Perelman, "How Do We Apply Reason to Values?" *Journal of Philosophy*, LII (December 22, 1955), 802.
56. Perelman and Olbrechts-Tyteca, *Traité de l'argumentation*, I, 62. [Translation mine.]
57. *Ibid.*
58. Perelman and Olbrechts-Tyteca, "Logique et rhétorique," 7. [Translation mine.]
59. Ch. Perelman and L. Olbrechts-Tyteca, "Act and Person in Argument," *Ethics*, LXI (July 1951), 251.
60. Perelman and Olbrechts-Tyteca, *Traité de l'argumentation*, I, 13.
61. Perelman, *Justice*, pp. 57–58.
62. Perelman, *The Idea of Justice and the Problem of Argument*, p. 133.

Wayne Brockriede and Douglas Ehninger

Toulmin on Argument: An Interpretation and Application

◊ *In this essay, written in early 1960, Wayne Brockriede and Douglas Ehninger discuss the nature and significance of Stephen Toulmin's important work on* The Uses of Argument *which appeared in England in 1958. As can be seen the authors, in endorsing Toulmin's six-step model of argument as a system of reasoning which conforms closely to communication patterns in human affairs, present six advantages which this approach has over the traditional enthymematic structure. The essay also modifies and extends the model so that a new means of classifying artistic proofs could be developed. The terms that are used to designate these arguments are "substantive," "authoritative," and "motivational." These counterparts of Aristotle's notions on logical, ethical, and pathetic proof are, according to the authors, "the possible routes which the warrant may travel." Overall, the article establishes a strong preference for "substantive" or logical appeals as the most desirable means of persuasion.* ◊

During the period 1917–1932 several books, a series of articles, and many Letters to the Editor of *QJS* gave serious attention to exploring the nature of argument as it is characteristically employed in rhetorical proofs.[1] Since that time, however, students of public address have shown comparatively little interest in the subject, leaving to philosophers, psychologists, and sociologists the principal contributions which have more recently been made toward an improved understanding of argument.[2]

Among the contributions offered by "outsiders" to our field, one in particular deserves more attention than it has so far received from rhetoricians. We refer to some of the formulations of the English logician Stephen Toulmin in his *The Uses of Argument*, published in 1958.[3]

Mr. Brockriede is Assistant Professor of Speech and Supervisor of Forensics at the University of Illinois. Mr. Ehninger is Associate Professor of Speech at the University of Florida.
Wayne E. Brockriede and Douglas Ehninger, "Toulmin on Argument: An Interpretation and Application," *Quarterly Journal of Speech*, 46 (February 1960): 44–53. Reprinted with permission from the Speech Communication Association.

Toulmin's analysis and terminology are important to the rhetorician for two different but related reasons. First, they provide an appropriate structural model by means of which rhetorical arguments may be laid out for analysis and criticism; and, second, they suggest a system for classifying artistic proofs which employs argument as a central and unifying construct. Let us consider these propositions in order.

1

As described by Toulmin, an argument is *movement* from accepted *data*, through a *warrant*, to a *claim*.

Data (D) answer the question, "What have you got to go on?" Thus *data* correspond to materials of fact or opinion which in our textbooks are commonly called *evidence*. Data may report historical or contemporary events, take the form of a statistical compilation or of citations from authority, or they may consist of one or more general declarative sentences established by a prior proof of an artistic nature. Without data clearly present or strongly implied, an argument has no informative or substantive component, no factual point of departure.

Claim (C) is the term Toulmin applies to what we normally speak of as a *conclusion*. It is the explicit appeal produced by the argument, and is always of a potentially controversial nature. A claim may stand as the final proposition in an argument, or it may be an intermediate statement which serves as data for a subsequent inference.

Data and claim taken together represent the specific contention advanced by an argument, and therefore constitute what may be regarded as its *main proof line*. The usual order is *data* first, and then *claim*. In this sequence the *claim* contains or implies "therefore." When the order is reversed, the *claim* contains or implies "because."

Warrant (W) is the operational name Toulmin gives to that part of an argument which authorizes the mental "leap" involved in advancing from data to claim. As distinguished from data which answer the question "What have you got to go on," the warrant answers the question "How do you get there." Its function is to *carry* the accepted data to the doubted or disbelieved proposition which constitutes the claim, thereby certifying this claim as true or acceptable.

The relations existing among these three basic components of an argument, Toulmin suggests, may be represented diagrammatically:

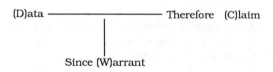

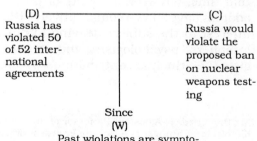

In addition to the three indispensable elements of *data, claim,* and *warrant,* Toulmin recognizes a second triad of components, any or all of which may, but need not necessarily, be present in an argument. These he calls (1) *backing,* (2) *rebuttal,* and (3) *qualifier.*

Backing (B) consists of credentials designed to certify the assumption expressed in the warrant. Such credentials may consist of a single item, or of an entire argument in itself complete with data and claim. Backing must be introduced when readers or listeners are not willing to accept a warrant at its face value.

The rebuttal (R) performs the function of a safety valve or escape hatch, and is, as a rule, appended to the claim statement. It recognizes certain conditions under which the claim will not hold good or will hold good only in a qualified and restricted way. By limiting the area to which the claim may legitimately be applied, the rebuttal anticipates certain objections which might otherwise be advanced against the argument.

The function of the qualifier (Q) is to register the degree of force which the maker believes his claim to possess. The qualification may be expressed by a quantifying term such as "possibly," "probably," "to the five per cent level of confidence," etc., or it may make specific reference to an anticipated refutation. When the author of a claim regards it as incontrovertible no qualifier is appended.

These additional elements may be superimposed on the first diagram:

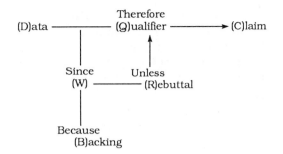

We may illustrate the model as follows:

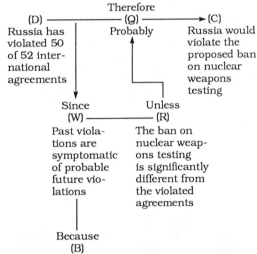

Other nations which had such a record of violations contined such action/Expert X states that nations which have been chronic violators nearly always continued such acts/etc.

2

With Toulmin's structural model now set forth, let us inquire into its suitability as a means of describing and testing arguments. Let us compare Toulmin's method with the analysis offered in traditional logic, the logic commonly used as a basic theory of argumentation in current textbooks. We conceive of arguments in the customary fashion as (1) deriving from probable causes and signs, (2) proceeding more often by relational than implicative principles, (3) emphasizing material as well as formal validity, (4) employing premises which are often contestable, and (5) eventuating in claims which are by nature contingent and variable.

The superiority of the Toulmin model in describing and testing arguments may be claimed for seven reasons:

1. Whereas traditional logic is characteristically concerned with *warrant-using* arguments (i.e., arguments in which the validity of the assumption underlying the inference "leap" is uncontested), Toulmin's model specifically provides for *warrant-establishing* arguments (i.e., arguments in which the validity of the assumption underlying the inference must be established—through backing—as part of the proof pattern itself).[4]

2. Whereas traditional logic, based as it is upon the general principle of implication, always treats proof more or less as a matter of classification or compartmentalization, Toulmin's analysis stresses the inferential and relational nature of argument, providing a context within which all factors—both formal and material—bearing upon a disputed claim may be organized into a series of discrete steps.

3. Whereas in traditional logic arguments are especially designed to produce universal propositions, Toulmin's second triad of backing, rebuttal, and qualifier provide, within the framework of his basic structural model, for the establishment of claims which are no more than probable. The model directs attention to the ways in which each of these additional elements may operate to limit or condition a claim.

4. Whereas traditional logic, with its governing principle of implication, necessarily results in an essentially static conception of argument, Toulmin by emphasizing *movement* from data, through warrant, to claim produces a conception of argument as dynamic. From his structural model we derive a picture of arguments "working" to establish and certify claims, and as a result of his functional terminology we are able to understand the role each part of an argument plays in this process.

5. Whereas the modes based on the traditional analysis—enthymeme, example, and the like—often suppress a step in proof, Toulmin's model lays an argument out in such a way that each step may be examined critically.

6. Whereas in the traditional analysis the division of arguments into premises and conclusions (as in the syllogism, for example) often tends to obscure deficiencies in proof, Toulmin's model assigns each part of an argument a specific geographical or spatial position in relation to the others, thus rendering it more likely that weak points will be detected.

7. Whereas traditional logic is imperfectly equipped to deal with the problem of material validity, Toulmin makes such validity an integral part of his system, indicating clearly the role which factual elements play in producing acceptable claims.

In short, without denying that Toulmin's formulations are open to serious criticism at several points[5]—and allowing for any peculiarities in our interpretations of the character of traditional logic—one conclusion emerges. Toulmin has provided a structural model which promises to be of greater use in laying out rhetorical arguments for dissection and testing than the methods of traditional logic. For although most teachers and writers in the field of argumentation have discussed the syllogism in general terms, they have made no serious attempt to explore the complexities of the moods and figures of the syllogism, nor have they been very successful in applying the terms and principles of traditional logic to the arguments of real controversies. Toulmin's model provides a practical replacement.

3

Our second proposition is that Toulmin's structural model and the vocabulary he has developed to describe it are suggestive of a system for classifying artistic proofs, using argument (defined as *movement* from data, through warrant, to claim) as a unifying construct.[6]

In extending Toulmin's analysis to develop a simplified classification of arguments, we may begin by restating in Toulmin's terms the traditional difference between *inartistic* and *artistic* proof. Thus, conceiving of an argument as a movement by means of which accepted data are carried through a certifying warrant to a controversial claim, we may say that in some cases the data themselves are conclusive. They approach the claim without aid from a warrant—are tantamount to the claim in the sense that to accept them is automatically to endorse the claim they are designed to support. In such cases the proof may be regarded as *inartistic*. In another class of arguments, however, the situation is quite different. Here the data are not immediately conclusive, so that the role of the warrant in carrying them to the claim becomes of crucial importance. In this sort of argument the proof is directly dependent upon the inventive powers of the arguer and may be regarded as *artistic*.

If, then, the warrant is the crucial element in an artistic proof, and if its function is to carry the data to the claim, we may classify artistic arguments by recognizing the possible routes which the warrant may travel in performing its function.

So far as rhetorical proofs are concerned, as men have for centuries recognized, these routes are three in number: (1) an arguer may carry data to claim by means of an assumption concerning the relationship existing among phenomena in the external world; (2) by means of an assumption concerning the quality of the source from which the data are derived; and (3) by means of an assumption concerning the inner drives, values, or aspirations which impel the behavior of those persons to whom the argument is addressed.

Arguments of the first sort (traditionally called *logical*) may be called *substantive;* those of the second sort (traditionally called *ethical*) may be described as *authoritative;* and those of the third sort (traditionally called *pathetic*) as *motivational.*

Substantive Arguments

The warrant of a substantive argument reflects an assumption concerning the way in which things are related in the world about us. Although other orderings are possible, one commonly recognized, and the one used here, is sixfold. Phenomena may be related as cause to effect (or as effect to cause), as attribute to substance, as some to more, as intrinsically similar, as bearing common relations, or as more to some. Upon the first of these relationships is based what is commonly called argument from *cause;* on the second, argument from *sign;* on the third, argument from *generalization;* on the fourth, argument from *parallel case;* on the fifth, argument from *analogy;* and on the sixth, argument from *classification.*

Cause. In argument from cause the data consist of one or more accepted facts about a person, object, event, or condition. The warrant attributes to these facts a creative or generative power and specifies the nature of the effect they will produce. The claim relates these results to the person, object, event, or condition named in the data. An illustration, from cause to effect, at the top of the page. When the reasoning process is reversed and the argument is from effect to cause, the data again consist of one or more facts about a person, object, event, or condition; the warrant

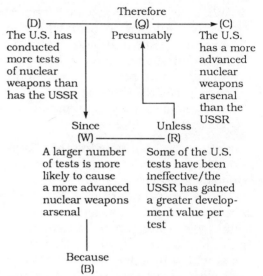

asserts that a particular causal force is sufficient to have accounted for these facts; and the claim relates this cause to the person, object, event, or condition named in the data.

Sign. In argument from sign the data consist of clues or symptoms. The warrant interprets the meaning or significance of these symptoms. The claim affirms that some person, object, event, or condition possesses the attributes of which the clues have been declared symptomatic. Our first example concerning Russia's violation of international agreements illustrates the argument from sign.

Generalization. In argument from generalization the data consist of information about a number of persons, objects, events, or conditions, taken as constituting a representative and adequate sample of a given class of phenomena. The warrant assumes that what is true of the items constituting the sample will also be true of additional members of the class not represented in the sample. The claim makes explicit the assumption embodied in the warrant. The form can be diagrammed so:

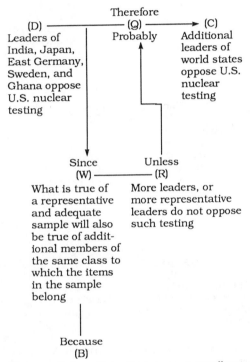

The sample is sufficiently representative/large enough/etc.

Parallel Case. In argument from parallel case the data consist of one or more statements about a single object, event, or condition. The warrant asserts that the instance reported in the data bears an essential similarity to a second instance in the same category. The claim affirms about the new instance what has already been accepted concerning the first. Here is an illustration:

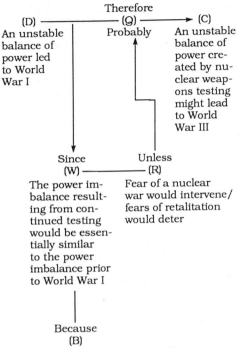

Both situations are characterized by an arms race, dynamic power blocs, etc.

In argument from parallel cases a rebuttal will be required in either of two situations: (1) if another parallel case bears a stronger similarity to the case under consideration; or (2) if in spite of some essential similarities an essential dissimilarity negates or reduces the force of the warrant. The example illustrates the second of these possibilities.

Analogy. In argument from analogy the data report that a relationship of a certain nature exists between two items. The warrant assumes that a similar relationship exists between a second pair of items. The claim makes explicit the relationship assumed in the warrant. Whereas the argument from parallel case assumes a resemblance between two *cases*, the analogy assumes only a similarity of *relationship*. Analogy may be illustrated so:

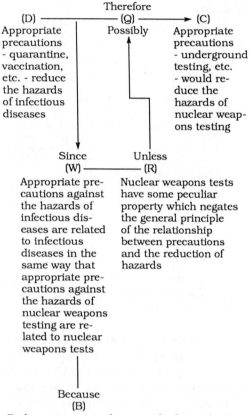

In most cases the analogical relation expressed in an argument from analogy will require a strongly qualifying "possibly."

Classification. In argument from classification the statement of the data is a generalized conclusion about known members of a class of persons, objects, events, or conditions. The warrant assumes that what is true of the items reported in the data will also be true of a hitherto unexamined item which is known (or thought) to fall within the class there described. The claim then

transfers the general statement which has been made in the data to the particular item under consideration. As illustrated, the form would appear:

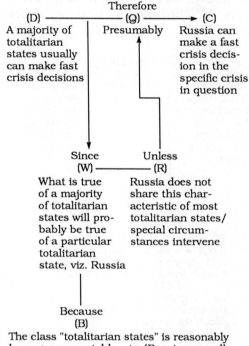

Two kinds of reservations may be applicable in an argument from classification: (1) a class member may not share the particular attribute cited in the data, although it does share enough other attributes to deserve delineation as a member of the class; and (2) special circumstances may prevent a specific class member from sharing at some particular time or place the attributes general to the class.

Authoritative Arguments

In authoritative arguments the data consist of one or more factual reports or statements of opinion. The warrant affirms the reliability of the source from which these are derived. The claim reiterates the statement which appeared in the data, as now certified by the warrant. An illustration follows:

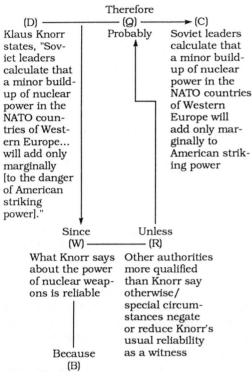

Knorr is a professor at Princeton's Center of International Studies/is unbiased/has made reliable statements on similar matters in the past/etc.

The structure and function of an authoritative argument remains basically the same when the source of the data is the speaker or writer himself. The data is carried to claim status by the same sort of assumption embodied in the warrant. We may infer a claim from what Knorr says about nuclear weapons whether he is himself the speaker, or whether another speaker is quoting what Knorr has said. Thus the *ethos* of a speaker may be studied by means of

the Toulmin structure under the heading of authoritative argument.

Motivational Arguments

In motivational arguments the data consist of one or more statements which may have been established as claims in a previous argument or series of arguments. The warrant provides a motive for accepting the claim by associating it with some inner drive, value, desire, emotion, or aspiration, or with a combination of such forces. The claim as so warranted is that the person, object, event, or condition referred to in the data should be accepted as valuable or rejected as worthless, or that the policy there described should or should not be adopted, or the action there named should or should not be performed. Illustrated the form would appear:

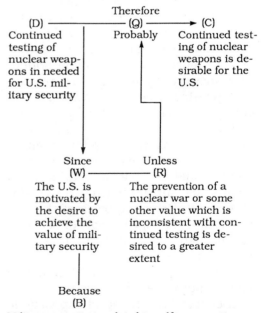

Military security is related to self-preservation, the maintenance of our high standard of living, patriotism, the preservation of democracy, etc.

4

We have exhibited the structural unity of the three modes of artistic proof by showing how they may be reduced to a single invariant pattern using argument as a unifying construct. Let us as a final step explore this unity further by inquiring how artistic proofs, so reduced, may conveniently be correlated with the various types of disputable questions and the claim appropriate to each.

Let us begin by recognizing the four categories into which disputable questions have customarily been classified: (1) Whether something is? (2) What it is? (3) Of what worth it is? (4) What course of action should be pursued? The first of these queries gives rise to a question of *fact*, and is to be answered by what can be called a *designative claim*; the second, to a question of *definition*, to be answered by a *definitive claim*; the third, to a question of *value*, to be answered by an *evaluative claim*; and the fourth, to a question of *policy*, to be answered by an *advocative claim*.

Supposing, then, that an arguer is confronted with a question of fact, calling for a designative claim; or a question of policy, calling for an advocative claim, etc., what types of argument would be available to him as means of substantiating his claim statement? Upon the basis of the formulations developed in earlier sections of this paper, it is possible to supply rather precise answers.

Designative Claims. A designative claim, appropriate to answering a question of fact, will be found supportable by any of the six forms of substantive argument, or by authoritative argu-

ment, but not by motivational argument. That is, whether something exists or is so may be determined: (1) by isolating its cause or its effect (argument from cause); (2) by reasoning from the presence of symptoms to the claim that a substance exists or is so (argument from sign); (3) by inferring that because some members of a given class exist or are so, more members of the same class also exist or are so (argument from generalization); (4) by inferring because one item exists or is so, that a closely similar item exists or is so (argument from parallel case); (5) by reasoning that D exists or is so because it stands in the same relation to C that B does to A, when C, B, and A are known to exist or to be so (argument from analogy); and (6) by concluding that an unexamined item known or thought to fall within a given class exists or is so because all known members of the class exist or are so (argument from classification). Moreover, we may argue that something exists or is so because a reputable authority declares this to be the case. Motivational argument, on the other hand, may not be critically employed in designative claims, because values, desires, and feelings are irrelevant where questions of fact are concerned.

Definitive Claims. The possibilities for establishing definitive claims are more limited. Only two of the forms of substantive argument and authoritative argument are applicable. We may support a claim as to what something is: (1) by comparing it with a closely similar phenomenon (argument from parallel case); or (2) by reasoning that because it stands in the same relation to C as B does to A it will be analogous to C, where the nature of C, B, and A are known (argument from analogy). In addition, we may support a definition or interpretation by citing an acceptable authority. Among the substantive arguments, cause, sign, generalization, and classification are inapplicable; and once again motivational argument is irrelevant since emotions, wishes, and values cannot legitimately determine the nature of phenomena.

Evaluative Claims. Evaluative claims may be supported by generalization, parallel case, analogy, and classification, and by authoritative and motivational arguments. By generalization a class of phenomena may be declared valuable or worthless on the ground that a typical and adequate sample of the members of that class is so. By classification, in contrast, we infer from the worth of known members of a class the probable worth of some previously unexamined item known or thought to belong to that class. By parallel case, we infer goodness or badness from the quality of an item closely similar. By analogy, however, we infer value on the basis of a ratio of resemblances rather than a direct parallel. In authoritative argument our qualitative judgment is authorized by a recognized expert. In motivational argument, however, an item is assigned a value in accordance with its usefulness in satisfying human drives, needs, and aspirations. Arguments from cause and sign, on the other hand, are inapplicable.

Advocative Claims. Advocative claims may legitimately be established in only four ways. We may argue that some policy should be adopted or some action undertaken because a closely similar policy or action has brought desirable results in the past (argument from parallel case). We may support a proposed policy or action because it bears the same relation to C that B does to A, where B is known to have brought desirable results (argument from analogy). Or, of course, we may support our claim by testimony (authoritative argument), or by associating it with men's wishes, values, and aspirations (motivational argument).

This analysis concerning the types of arguments applicable to various sorts of claims may be summarized in tabular form:

	Designative	Definitive	Evaluative	Advocative
Substantive				
A. Cause	x			
B. Sign	x			
C. Generalization	x		x	
D. Parallel Case	x	x	x	x
E. Analogy	x	x	x	x
F. Classification	x		x	
Authoritative	x	x	x	x
Motivational			x	x

The world of argument is vast, one seemingly without end. Arguments arise in one realm, are resolved, and appear and reappear in others; and new arguments appear. If one assumes some rationality among men, a system of logical treatment of argument is imperative. The traditional logical system of syllogisms, of enthymemes, of middles distributed and undistributed, may have had its attraction in medieval times. The inadequacies of such a logic, however, have been described by experts; for example, see J. S. Mill on the syllogism and *petitio principii*.[7] The modern search has been for a method which would have some application in the dynamics of contemporary affairs.

Toulmin has supplied us with a contemporary methodology, which in many respects makes the traditional unnecessary. The basic theory has herein been amplified, some extensions have been made, and illustrations of workability have been supplied. All this is not meant to be the end, but rather the beginning of an inquiry into a new, contemporary, dynamic, and usable logic for argument.

Notes

1. E.g., such books as James M. O'Neill, Craven Laycock, and Robert L. Scales, *Argumentation and Debate* (New York, 1917); William T. Foster, *Argumentation and Debating* (Boston, 1917); and A. Craig Baird, *Public Discussion and Debate* (Boston, 1928); such articles as Mary Yost, "Argument from the Point of View of Sociology," *QJS*, III (1917), 109–24; Charles H. Woolbert, "The Place of Logic in a System of Persuasion," *QJS*, IV, (1918), 19–39; Gladys Murphy Graham, "Logic and Argumentation," *QJS*, X (1924), 350–363; William E. Utterback, "Aristotle's Contribution to the Psychology of Argument," *QJS*, XI (1925), 218–225; Herbert A. Wichelns, "Analysis and Synthesis in Argumentation," *QJS*, XI (1925), 266–272; and Edward Z. Rowell, "Prolegomena to Argumentation," *QJS*, XVIII (1932), 1–13, 224–248, 381–405, 585–606; such Letters to the Editor as those by Utterback, XI (1925), 175–177; Wichelns, XI (1925), 286–288; Ralph C. Ringwalt, XII (1926), 66–68; and Graham, XII (1925), 196–197.

2. See, for example, Mortimer Adler, *Dialectic* (New York, 1927); Paul Edwards, *The Logic of Moral Discourse* (Glencoe, Ill., 1955); Carl I. Hovland, Irving L. Janis, and Harold W. Kelley, *Communication and Persuasion* (New Haven, Conn., 1953); Chaim Perelman, *Traité de l'argumentation*, 2 vols. (Paris, 1958), and *La nouvelle rhétorique* (Paris, 1952); and John Cohen, "Subjective Probability," *Scientific American*, MCMVII (1957), 128–38.

3. (Cambridge, Cambridge University Press). See especially the third of the five essays in the book. *Cf.* J. C. Cooley, "On Mr. Toulmin's Revolution in Logic," *The Journal of Philosophy*, LVI (1959), 297–319.

4. In traditional logic only the epicheirema provides comparable backing for premises.

5. It may be charged that his structural model is merely "a syllogism lying on its side," that it makes little or no provision to insure the formal validity of claims, etc.

6. Our suggestion as to the structural unity of artistic proofs is by no means novel. The ancients regularly spoke of *pathetic* and *ethical* enthymemes, and envisioned the *topoi* as applicable beyond the *pistis*. (See in this connection James H. McBurney, "The Place of the Enthymeme in Rhetorical Theory," *SM*, III [1936], 63.) At the same time, however, it must be recognized that especially since the advent of the faculty psychology of the seventeenth and eighteenth centuries, rhetorical thought has been profoundly and persistently influenced by the doctrine of a dichotomy between pathetic and logical appeals. (For significant efforts to combat this doctrine see Charles H. Woolbert, "Conviction and Persuasion: Some Considerations of Theory," *QJS*, III [1917], 249–264; Mary Yost, "Argument from the Point of View of Sociology," *QJS*, III [1917], 109–124; and W. Norwood Brigance, "Can We Redefine the James-Winans Theory of Persuasion?" *QJS*, XXI [1935], 19–26.)

7. *A System of Logic*, I, Chap. 3, Sec. 2.

James L. Golden, Goodwin F. Berquist, William E. Coleman

Emerging European Perspectives on Rhetoric

◊ *This essay seeks to show that among the authors in Europe, in addition to Toulmin and Perelman, who have contributed significantly to rhetorical thought, three contemporary scholars stand out. They are the Italian philosopher Ernesto Grassi, the German social critic Jurgen Habermas, and the French Theorist Michel Foucault. Influenced by Plato, Cicero, and Vico, Grassi, we are told, seeks to elevate rhetoric by uniting content and form, and by showing how discourse at its highest appeals to the whole person. Similarly, as this study demonstrates, Habermas, with his concern for the "ideal speech situation," highlights the elements of communication competence, including speech act utterances that conform to the criteria of sound reasoning. Finally, the essay notes that Foucault covers new ground in his provocative analysis of epistemes or discursive formations, the archaeological or genealogical method of inquiry, power, and the nature of an author.* ◊

In the preceding chapters on contemporary rhetorical thought, we have sought to provide an overview of the major communication perspectives advanced by representative scholars from the United States, Canada, Great Britain, and Belgium. Such authors as Burke, Richards, McLuhan, Perelman, Toulmin, and Weaver, as observed in this section, have had a profound influence on current thinking during the past several decades. They by no means, however, are the only significant theorists in the last half of the twentieth century who have turned their attention to at least some of the important aspects of rhetorical theory. Of these numerous writers who have done so, three European scholars stand out as major synthesizers and innovators of western thought. All have in their own way contributed significantly to our understanding of the nature and potentialities of rhetoric. They are the Italian humanist Ernesto Grassi, the French philosopher and historian

James L. Golden, Goodwin F. Berquist, and William E. Coleman, "Emerging European Perspectives on Rhetoric," *The Rhetoric of Western Thought*, 4th ed. (Dubuque, IA: Kendall/Hunt Publishing Company, 1989): 428–446. Reprinted with permission.

Michel Foucault, and the German critical theorist Jurgen Habermas.[1] It will be our purpose in this chapter not to discuss their broad-ranging theories as a whole, but to highlight some of their most crucial ideas that have relevance for contemporary students of rhetoric.

Our analysis will begin with Grassi whose primary intellectual concern is rhetoric as grounded in the philosophy of humanism.

Ernesto Grassi

Grassi relies heavily, as we shall see, upon the writings of such authors as Plato, Aristotle, Cicero, and Quintilian. But the principal source and inspiration for his ideas are the works of Giambattista Vico and the Italian humanists. Grassi, however, is far more than a summarizer or synthesizer of the contributions of others. Instead, as we are now ready to note, he takes their premises and through his own observations of life and sense of values is able to apply them to contemporary rhetorical situations. What gives freshness and an enduring thrust to Grassi's approach is the vocabulary he uses and the arguments he develops to show that rhetoric is essential to the doing of philosophy and science; and, as a result, is on a comparable level as a worthy field of study.

In examining the principal elements of Grassi's perspectives on rhetoric, we will divide our discussion into two parts: (1) an analysis of his views on the general nature of rhetoric; and (2) a consideration of three essential faculties that are available to the rhetor who is interested in a humanistic-based theory of communication.

The Nature of Rhetoric

An important starting point in gaining an understanding of Grassi's description of the nature of rhetoric is to summarize the distinction he draws between critical or rational discourse and topical discourse. In making this differentiation, he takes the side of Vico who, as earlier pointed out, developed his stance as a response to Descartes' critical method. What Vico and Grassi find unacceptable in a strictly rationalistic approach is its emphasis on truth derived from logical demonstration: its rejection of probable knowledge; its dismissal of history, metaphysics, and politics; its relegation of rhetoric to a nonphilosophical and non-scientific category; and its tendency to ignore human problems as a legitimate field of study for scientific inquiry.[2]

Topical philosophy, on the other hand, is an initial step in a relevant scientific investigation. As in the case of Vico, Grassi equates the canon of invention with the topical method. Through this process the rhetor creates arguments that generate hypotheses which must be tested in the subsequent phases of any scientific analysis. When viewed from this vantage point, topics which ultimately lead to a discovery of first principles, take priority over pure rationalism.[3]

Grassi's enthusiasm for Vico's notion of topical philosophy, with its stress on probability, verisimilitude, and creativity; and his distrust of the Cartesian doctrine of truth and certainty, with its focus on mathematical logic, helped form his concept of the nature of rhetoric. A human being, he concluded, cannot be expected to respond to rational appeals alone. All persons have affective as well as cognitive components in their nature which are related to the emotions. It follows, therefore, that unless the passions are stirred, genuine persuasion will not occur.[4]

On this point Plato served as a model to Grassi. In the third speech delivered in the *Phaedrus*, for example, Socrates made it clear that arguments based on strong reasoning must be enforced by those designed to arouse the emotions and elevate the soul. Thus, in keeping with Plato's intention the reader of this dialogue on true rhetoric can experience the feeling of eros or love as a powerful motivating force.[5]

In detailing approvingly Plato's strong interest in uniting content and form, knowledge and the passions, Grassi had in mind another purpose— to place rhetoric on an equal plane with that of philosophy. Whereas philosophy sets for itself the goal of stimulating the intellect, he argues, rhetoric seeks to appeal to the whole person.[6] In extending this idea, Grassi follows a pattern similar to that which we noted in Weaver's essay on the "Phaedrus and the Nature of Rhetoric." We recall that Weaver sought to show that the three speeches set forth in this dialogue represent addresses that may be called specimens of evil, neuter, and noble rhetoric respectively. Grassi, as can be seen from the ensuing excerpt drawn from his essay on "Rhetoric and Philosophy," uses a different vocabulary to reach a similar conclusion concerning what he perceives to be three types of discourse:

To sum up, we are forced to distinguish between three kinds of speech: (1) The *external, 'rhetorical speech,'* in the common meaning of the expression, which only refers to images because they affect the passions. But since these images do not stem from insight, they remain an object of opinion. This is the case of the purely emotive, false speech: 'rhetoric' in the usual negative sense. (2) The *speech which arises exclusively from a rational proceeding.* It is true that this is of a demonstrative character but it cannot have a rhetorical effect, because purely rational arguments do not attain to the passions, i.e., 'theoretical' speech in the usual sense. (3) The *true rhetorical speech.* This springs from the *archai,* non-deducible, moving, and indicative, due to its original images. The original speech is that of the wise man, of the *sophos* who is not only *episthetai* but the man who with insight leads, guides, and attracts.[7]

In demonstrating that meaningful rhetoric contains a happy blending of eloquence and wisdom, of rational and emotional appeals, Grassi is also striving to illustrate that "true philosophy is rhetoric and . . . true rhetoric is philosophy, a philosophy which does not need an 'external' rhetoric to convince, and a rhetoric that does not need an 'external' content of verity."[8] What he is arguing for, in short, is the adoption of a type of rhetoric that is both epistemic and persuasive. At the point where this occurs rhetoric and philosophy become one.

Three Primary Faculties of True Rhetoric

The preceding discussion suggests the broad outline used by Grassi to sketch the general nature of his theory of rhetoric. In order to understand more fully how a rhetor may achieve this high level discourse, we need to shift our focus to three vitally significant faculties that are crucial parts of "true rhetorical speech." Influenced by Cicero and Vico in particular and the renaissance scholars in general, Grassi labels two of these faculties *ingenium* and work. The third concept, which is a more traditional one, he refers to as metaphor. Quite clearly these three faculties, as will be seen, are interrelated and integrated elements which depend upon each other for their effectiveness. Despite the fact that they are interdependent and often overlap, we will analyze each as a separate notion that performs a special task in a rhetorical enterprise.

Ingenium. Of the three faculties we are ready to discuss, *ingenium* appears to be the most important; for it is the concept which forms the foundation of the other two and, in effect, constitutes the essence of the humanistic tradition. Since Cicero was the first western author who dealt with *ingenium* in depth, Grassi uses him as a point of departure, praising him as he does so for his Latin originality. What Cicero saw when he contemplated nature, Grassi observes, was a mysterious notion which can never reveal itself fully to a human being. Those who lack discernment, therefore, are incapable of rising above sensory data or experiences—a condition which significantly limits their knowledge and understanding. To offset this fact, one needs to possess the necessary virtues to exercise *ingenium*. This suggests an ability to "catch sight of relationships of *similitudes* among things. . . ."[9] When this is realized, a person has succeeded in transcending a sensory awareness and in constructing "a world of his own."[10] In holding such a favorable attitude toward the idea of *ingenium*, Grassi argues, Cicero came to believe that rhetoric assumes a position of primacy

in helping an individual cope with the complexities of nature.

Cicero's ideas on *ingenium* as a central aspect of rhetoric had a noticeable influence on the thinking of Renaissance scholars. Not the least of these was Gracian—a Spanish philosopher and critic. To Gracian *ingenium* is an "act of insight," a process which reveals divinity, and a "sphere of acuteness and wit" which enables one to "decipher the world" through the power of recognizing resemblances between objects.[11]

Additionally, as in the case of his ideas on rhetoric in general, Grassi found Vico's description of *ingenium* to have special significance because of its connection with topical philosophy. By contrasting *ingenium* with rational reasoning, Vico was able to point out that genius as a faculty of comprehension is prior to a system of deduction which is unable to go beyond original premises. To put it another way, "the ingenious faculty assumes the important function of supplying arguments which the rational process itself" cannot discover.[12]

The ideas expressed by Cicero, Gracian, and Vico led Grassi to conclude that *ingenium* is the major source responsible for our image of the world. Moreover it is this faculty which gives purpose and direction to a speaker's use of *inventio* which, in turn, enables him/her to demonstrate creativity in uniting diverse as well as similar aspects of nature.[13]

Work. If *ingenium* is the virtue that enables a rhetor to create and establish the climate for shared meaning through discourse, the domain of work, according to Grassi, is the energizing force which helps make this possible. The function of work is to fulfill human needs by stimulating the development of language and by bringing about the transfer of meaning. Work, in sum, is the activity that gives birth and thrust to human history and society.[14] Perceived in this light, it is an important handmaiden of *ingenium*.

Metaphor. In our discussion of the first two faculties, we have seen that *ingenium* is a creative talent that enables one to see similitudes in nature and to apply work in an imaginative manner for the purpose of assisting human beings to fulfill their desire to gain new knowledge. The principal method by which this can be done is in the use of language—primarily the metaphor. The humanistic tradition, Grassi forcefully argues, emphasizes the limitations of a "purely rational" language which seeks to prove the validity and reliability of a proposition by using objective language that crosses the boundaries of time. Such language, he adds, is non-rhetorical and, therefore, non-persuasive.[15]

In making the above claims, Grassi's purpose is not to show that rational thought and language have no utility for one who seeks a deeper appreciation of the intricacies of nature; rather his aim is to demonstrate that there is an initial step that is necessary in the production of knowledge. That step consists of the utilization of analogical or metaphorical language "whereby the soul transfers meaning to appearances."[16] Since imagistic statements outline "the basis or framework of rational argument," they come "before and provide that which deduction can never discover."[17]

Grassi reminds us that the metaphor, which has its roots in the Classical period and finds eloquent expression in the form of parables nd allegories in the Old and New Testaments, gains its strength through the process of "showing" or revealing important relationships in nature. Convinced that the essence of rhetoric is persuasion and that the metaphor is a powerful instrument to stimulate a reader or hearer, Grassi uses the catch phrase "poet as orator." As a practitioner in the art of using symbols in a graphic manner, the poet relies on "figurative expressions" that convey impressions of "color, sounds, smells, tangibles" which open the doors to the mind.[18]

The fact that poetry often utilizes fantasy and occasionally takes the form of "divine madness" in no way diminishes its effectiveness or soundness as a legitimate rhetorical genre. For the poet-orator performs a highly valuable function. By using words that are vivid images revealing relationships, he/she "calls the human world into being," and, therefore, provides "the possibility of mankind liberating itself from the immediate structures of nature."[19]

Grassi, it is clear, has detailed a theory of rhetoric that is humanistic in its outlook. Quite clearly much of what he says is not new. As an admirer of Plato, Cicero, Quintilian, Vico, and a group of Renaissance authors, he makes extensive use of their ideas in forging his own philosophy. His contributions, nevertheless, are significant. In recognizing the oratorical function of the poet, he reaffirms in a telling way the relevance of Blair's practice of combining rhetoric and belles lettres, and in Burke's belief that rhetoric and poetics share similar forms. In addition, by stressing the need to appeal to the whole person in order to produce persuasion that is value-laden, he lends force to Weaver's refutation of those semanticists who in their attempt to reduce language to a scientific expression depreciate the worth of tropes as a stylistic form. Similarly in stating that rhetorical language precedes the articulation of rational claims, he gives fresh emphasis to the current trend we have described as "rhetoric as a way of knowing." With Toulmin and Perelman he is stating anew that rhetoric's principal ally is informal or practical reasoning that strives to generate understanding and gain an adherence of minds.

Jurgen Habermas

As we move now to a consideration of some of the leading perspectives on rhetoric developed by Habermas, we will be confronted with a scholar whose range of knowledge is broad and whose critical skills are sufficiently well honed to enable him to help us glimpse the nature of a rhetoric of the future.

Habermas has been appropriately described as "the most promising latter-day descendant of what has come to be known as the 'Frankfurt School' of social theory."[20] Along with other members of this group, he is a Marxist whose non-orthodox perspective prompts him to attempt to modify Marxism in order to help this world view become more relevant in contemporary society. Since he is motivated by a desire to "reunite theory and practice in the twentieth-century world," he has achieved the

important status of a "grand theorist."[21] Perceiving natural science as an inadequate means of studying human behavior, he focuses on communication and informal reasoning as areas of study which are central to his philosophy.[22] And herein lies his significance to contemporary students of rhetoric.

Habermas' ideas on rhetoric fall neatly within several carefully delineated categories which move in an order of progression that gives his thoughts strong unity, coherence, and emphasis. Thus we will adhere to the following pattern that seems to characterize his writings on communication theory. First we will discuss briefly his overall ideas on communicative competence or, as he describes it, universal pragmatics. Next we will analyze how competence is achieved through speech act utterances and soundly conceived arguments. Our final step will strive to demonstrate how a level of communicative competence which epitomizes the effective use of speech acts and persuasive reasons has the potential to produce an ideal speech situation. What we will note as our discussion proceeds is that each of these concepts is closely integrated with the others.

Communication Competence or Universal Pragmatics

In introducing his first theme, Habermas notes: "I have proposed the name Universal Pragmatics for the research program aimed at reconstructing the universal basis of speech."[23] Within this context the word "universal" refers to that type of communication practiced in normal speech. Unlike distorted communication patterns, normal speech conforms to public, "intersubjectively recognized rules" in which "the communicated meanings are identical for all members of the language-community."[24] Any person engaged in normal speech is aware of the distinction between a "subject and object" and can "differentiate between outer and inner speech and separate the private from the public world."[25]

Normal speech occurs, moreover, when a speaker takes cognizance of the fact that as conversation takes place, he/she not only focuses on the propositional subject at hand but on the self. This type of discourse, therefore, combines communication on an object with "a meta-communication on the level of intersubjectivity."[26] Unless it can be assumed by a participant in a rhetorical setting that each speaker is a competent communicator who has knowledge of the topic, an awareness of the role of self, and an interest in shared meaning, there is no opportunity for the fulfillment of rational communication goals. It is for this reason that Habermas, influenced in part by Freud's ideas on psychoanalysis, spends so much time discussing the nature of distorted communication.

Even though we will now discuss speech act utterances and argumentation theory and practices as separate units, it should be remembered that they play a fundamental role in Habermas' theory of communication competence or Universal Pragmatics.

Speech Act Utterances

We were first introduced to the notion of speech act theory in the section on Rhetoric as Meaning. Some of the ideas discussed in that chapter, particularly those advanced by the linguistic philosophers Austin and Searle, serve as a basis or a launching point for Habermas' analysis of speech utterances. But, as in the case of most of Habermas' summaries and formulations, he utilizes his talent as a critic to modify some of the basic beliefs that have influenced him. In keeping with this practice, he points out the limitations as well as the strengths of Austin and Searle, and then extends some of their main ideas with the help of a fresh vocabulary that is uniquely his own.

"A general theory of speech actions," according to Habermas, "would thus describe exactly that fundamental system of rules that adult subjects master to the extent that they can fulfill the conditions for a happy employment of sentences and utterances."[27] These rules, for the most part, center on the dual problem of normative expectations as they pertain to the meaning of the content of a message and the successful forming of an intended relationship between the speaker and the listener.[28]

Habermas adheres to a traditional approach in drawing a distinction between locutionary and illocutionary speech acts. The first of these components, which is concerned with propositional content, is of little long range interest to him. Here he is satisfied to say that such action "says something" by expressing "states of affairs." The major criterion used to evaluate a locutionary act is comprehensibility. This suggests that in assessing the effectiveness of this type of utterance, the following question must be answered: "Is the content of the proposition clear?"

Where Habermas places his greatest emphasis is on the illocutionary component which features performative or action-centered utterances. These statements may contain, for example, a promise, request, command, assertion, or avowal on the part of the speaker; and they generally make use of the first person pronoun. The following typical illustration is listed by Habermas: "I hereby promise you [command you, confess to you] that p. . . ."[29] Such claims, in short, constitute an offer that presumably will be carried out at a specified time within a specific situation. If the author of the utterance appears to be sincere and if the content of the message makes a reasonable appeal, the illocutionary or persuasive force is strengthened.

One of Habermas' most original contributions to speech act theory is his five-fold classification of performative acts. The terms he uses to describe these acts are "imperatives," "constatives," "regulatives," "expressives," and "communicatives." "Imperatives" or "perlocutions" are used when a speaker, who has come to believe that a particular action is needed in order to bring about a desired state in the future, attempts to persuade a specific listener to take on this challenge. This expression of a will is designed to influence another person in an objective manner. The end goal of this strategic action is to produce success.[30]

The purpose of "constatives" is to explain the meaning contained in a statement. As Habermas puts it: "Constative speech acts . . . not only embody knowledge," they "represent it,"[31] and they do so by stating, asserting, describing, and explaining.

Whether or not "constatives" are viewed as productive depends on the degree of understanding reached and conformity of the claim to the criterion of truth.[32]

In contrast to the first two speech act components, "regulatives" operate within the sphere of accepted moral standards. A speaker who utilizes this act may issue a command or use such words as "forbid," "allow," or "warn" in an effort to establish a relationship with another person and to implement a moral or legal rule. The ensuing criteria are used to measure the worth of this type of statement: (1) To what extent does an act conform to a normative regulation; and (2) How desirable is the norm itself?[33] Notwithstanding the fact that "regulatives" are concerned with the generation of a shared meaning among participants who, it is hoped, will have a mutually respectful relationship with each other, these speech acts gain their distinctive quality by focusing primarily on "what ought to be."[34]

The term "expressives" is used by Habermas to depict a fourth category of speech acts. This form of statement has as its major purpose the revelation of a speaker's self—his/her subjective thoughts concerning a personal experience involving an emotional attitude, the interpretation of a desire or need, or the commitment to a value. In this sense, as Habermas observes, it represents a dramaturgical action that embodies "a knowledge of the agent's own subjectivity." If such self-representation is to be taken seriously, it must meet the test of "truthfulness."[35]

The final speech act that is rhetorically significant, according to Habermas, is labeled "communicatives."

This concept appears to be more comprehensive than are the other four types because of the fact that they perform some of the functions of regulative speech acts. Through the activity of "questioning and answering, addressing, objecting, admitting, and the like," for instance, they "serve the organization of speech, its arrangement into themes and contributions, the distribution of conversational roles," and "the regulation of turn-taking in conversation."[36] But, as Habermas is careful to point out, "communicatives" should be treated "as a separate class because of *their reflexive relation to the process of communication.*" This reflexivity empowers "communicatives" to include within their scope such argumentative utterances as "affirming," "denying," "assuring," and "confirming."[37]

The foregoing analysis has sought to show how Habermas took the ideas of Austin and Searle, and then modified, refined, and extended them by creating a fresh vocabulary and by instituting an instructive classification system. More importantly for our purposes in this chapter, his discussion of speech act theory is vitally relevant for the development of his ideas on communication competence. It is further significant to note that speech act theory as detailed here lays the groundwork for Habermas' philosophy of argument.

Theory of Argument

To see how Habermas' theory of argument unfolds and to understand the crucial part that it plays in his discussion of communication competence, we will begin this section with a brief description of the importance of argumentation and then proceed to a consideration of the analytical aspects of argumentative speech, the nature of validity claims, and the notion of truth.

Habermas makes the point that all speech act utterances have as an end to achieve an agreement that is based on good reasons. This means that whenever an expression is articulated by a rhetor, the reasons for delivering it should be evident to the hearer. To highlight this position, Habermas makes the following claim: "Thus the rationality proper to the communicative practice of everyday life points to the practice of argumentation as the court of appeal."[38] This statement, which is strikingly similar to the belief of Toulmin—a scholar whose ideas have doubtless influenced Habermas' thinking—sets the stage for the additional claim that an argument is a systematic expression that "contains reason or grounds that are connected . . . with the *validity claim*" of a problematic utterance.[39]

A final point concerning Habermas' description of the importance of argumentation is his conviction, shared by both Toulmin and Perelman, that a rhetor engaged in the presentation of reasons in supporting a position must be willing to expose his claims to criticism by others. It follows, therefore, that if the criticism is perceived as sound, the original claim should be altered so as to gain an adherence of minds. Viewed from this perspective, "argumentation," it seems clear, "plays an important role in learning processes."[40]

Habermas is more innovative as he next moves to a consideration of the three aspects of argumentative speech.

These he defines as "process," "procedures," and "product." Since the latter two aspects are not basically rhetorical, we will touch on these first, and then amplify the central concept of "process."

When we treat argumentation as a "procedure," states Habermas, we are focusing on an interaction method that is "subject to specific rules." The communication genre that is used here is dialectic which tends to be outside of rhetoric because of its preoccupation with a "ritualized competition" and "pragmatic procedures of argumentation."[41]

Similarly non-rhetorical is argumentation that is concerned with "product." Such argumentation is designed "to produce cogent arguments that are convincing in virtue of their intrinsic properties and with which validity claims can be redeemed or rejected."[42] This type of reasoning falls within the realm of logic, and has as its ends to reach a level of validity that is certain.

We are now prepared to see how argument as "process" is rhetorical and, at the same time, crucial to Habermas' belief that it is a cornerstone to achieving communication competence. A "process" view suggests that argumentation, which is informal and practical in nature, is based on contingent statements that must be negotiated between the rhetor and the listener. This perspective exemplifies a reflective enterprise that excludes the use of force and stresses the value of a cooperative search for knowledge.[43]

In his development of the "process" view of argument, Habermas introduces Perelman's notion of the universal audience. This form of argument, he says, implies the existence of a universal audience that, it is hoped, will give its assent to a particular utterance. If it does, the soundness of the argument has been upheld even by the most insightful hearer.[44]

Two other elements of Habermas' treatment of argument are essential aspects of his theory of practical reasoning. They are his ideas on the nature of validity and truth. To be valid a claim, he asserts, should be comprehensible, truthful, right, and appropriate. For the purpose of illustrating how these criteria work, let us examine the following seven statements which are similar to the ones used by Habermas in his work on *Reason and the Rationalization of Society:*

1. The Washington Redskins are a certainty for winning the Super Bowl in January, 1989.
2. AIDS may be caused by intravenous needles and by sexual intercourse.
3. The best way to reduce the federal government budget deficit is to raise personal income taxes.
4. Universities should make greater efforts to recruit minority students.
5. A student is entitled to see letters of recommendation that are in his/her file.
6. The movie *Cry for Freedom* spends too little time in discussing the role played by black South Africans in their struggle for human rights.
7. A whale is a mammal.

In each of these instances, the hearer, according to Habermas, is confronted with three choices: to agree, to disagree, or to abstain. Statements 1, 2, and 3—which deal with prediction, explanation, and efficacy respectively—are to be evaluated from the standpoint of truth. Utterances 4 and 5, which contain an admonition and an expression of justification, are to be tested by the standard of normative rightness. Claim 6 is a value judgment that is to be measured against the criterion of appropriateness. Finally, statement 7 is expected to meet the dual test of truth and comprehensibility.[45]

In view of the fact that the notion of truth is so vital in assessing the soundness of a speech act utterance that sets forth an argument, it is desirable at this juncture for us to see more clearly the stance Habermas takes on this subject. He upholds the premise that truth is not something which necessarily conforms to scientific verifiability. Nor does it consist of a relationship between an individual and the external world. It is instead a shared conclusion that is reached through the process of sound reasoning. Since it refers to an agreement resulting from the use of warrants, it may be described as "a consensus theory of truth."[46]

One critic has observed that "Habermas' theory of truth has been quite widely influential in the philosophical literature, and leads directly to his concept of the ideal speech situation."[47] This latter theme, which will now be analyzed, is the ultimate point in a philosophy that emphasizes communication competence.

Ideal Speech Situation

What has been said thus far about Habermas' ideas on the subject of communication competence or Universal Pragmatics, speech act theory, and argument as "process" are essential elements of his famous concept of the ideal speech situation. This speech situation, first of all, presupposes the existence of a normal, rather than distorted, communication pattern by each of the participants. Each person taking part in a conversation is expected to use symbols that are to be understood in a comparable manner by all of those who are present.

Secondly, an ideal speech situation is one in which each participant has full freedom to make use of the five types of speech act utterances. That is, the speaker has the privilege of using "imperatives" for the purpose of influencing, in an objective manner, the will of another; of using "constatives" to explain what a statement means; of using "regulatives" to establish an interpersonal relationship concerning a moral code; of using "expressives" to reveal his/her subjective thought or identity; and of using "communicatives" not only to regulate such matters as turn-taking but to assure, affirm, or deny.

An ideal speech situation, thirdly, suggests the need to make certain that all of the speech act utterances fulfill the requirements of sound reasoning. This includes the four validity tests of comprehensibility, truthfulness, rightness, and appropriateness. Of similar importance it embraces the notion that when one develops an argumentative claim, the position that is being advanced is open to criticism by others with the expectation that the claim may have to be modified.

The ideal speech situation, then, is one that features the following elements: (1) each person participating in a rhetorical situation has the freedom to express his/her ideas openly and to critique the utterances of others; (2) the concepts of force and power, which are inclined to inhibit the contributions of lower status discussants, are to be eliminated; (3) arguments primarily based on an appeal to tradition, because of their tendency to superimpose the past on the present, are to be exposed; and (4) truth is to be obtained by gaining a consensus or an adherence of minds.

Not a few critics have tried to suggest that Habermas' ideal speech situation, like Perelman's notion of the universal audience which Habermas endorses, is an "arbitrarily constructed ideal" that can never be achieved in a real life setting. This view, we feel, would not disturb Habermas. For what he is arguing is that if all the speakers engaged in a dialogue presuppose the presence of an ideal speech situation, the quality of the discourse will be significantly improved.[48]

As we think about a rhetoric of the future, we are convinced that Habermas' theories will play a fundamental role. His abiding belief that communication competence resulting from an instructive and persuasive use of speech act utterances and sound reasoning, occurring within an ideal speech situation, place him in the forefront of those who are interested in the theme of how rhetoric may perform the task of producing knowledge.

Michel Foucault

The last of the European scholars to be considered in this chapter, Michel Foucault, is unlike any of the authors we have analyzed in this volume. He has not developed, for example, a well organized theory of rhetoric or system of argumentation; nor do his numerous works contain, except in an incidental way, any references to the ideas of the leading rhetoricians of western thought. Yet despite this approach, Foucault is an important figure for any student interested in a rhetoric of the future.

Some observers have ranked Foucault as a "grand theorist";[49] others have described him as "the thinker who wedded philosophy and history and in so doing developed a dazzling critique of modern civilization."[50] These tributes are consistent with the enthusiasm shown by the educated populace who have read his works. Translations of his writings have appeared in sixteen different languages. Moreover, between the period from 1966 to 1984, the *Social Sciences Citation Index* and the *Arts and Humanities Citation Index* contain 4,385 references to his journal articles alone. Overall, he ranks twenty fourth among the sixty most heavily cited authors in the field of the Arts and Humanities in the twentieth century.[51]

What is present in the works of Foucault which account for his current popularity and influence? More specifically for our purposes, what does he say about the subject of communication theory that warrants his inclusion in this textbook on rhetorical theory? The answer to these queries, we hope, will be made clear as we summarize some of Foucault's major perspectives on language and discourse. Our analysis will center on three main themes which tend to be treated, with varying degrees of emphasis, in most of his works. They are as follows: (1) his theory of *epistemes* or discursive formations; (2) his archaeological/genealogical method of inquiry; and (3) his notion of power. It will soon be evident that these three subjects will be united under Foucault's strong concern for language structure and usage.[52]

Epistemes or Discursive Formations

As a historian Foucault is interested in knowing what constitutes knowledge in a given period in history. He seeks to ascertain this by examining the nature of the discourse that is used which proves to be acceptable to society at the time of its utterance. This discourse "is made up of a limited number of statements for which a group of conditions can be defined," and it features "particular modes of existence."[53] When these statements or groups of signs adhere to a consistent, repeatable pattern and employ similar rules, they may be classified as *epistemes* or discursive formations which represent the shared knowledge of an historical era.

What Foucault is suggesting is that the expression of knowledge is an articulation of propositional statements that conform to widely accepted rules. Often, however, these rules of discourse, while operative, "are not rules which individuals consciously follow."[54] But even though the rules may be only on a subconscious level, they nevertheless are the dominant influence in the making of knowledge claims.

To study a particular discursive formation, therefore, a theorist needs to ask specific questions designed to discover the rules that undergird the statements that are employed. The following sample of questions listed by Philip illustrates the types of interrogatives that are relevant for an understanding of Foucault's position:

1. What rules permit certain statements to be made?
2. What rules order these statements?
3. What rules permit us to identify some statements as true and some as false?
4. What rules allow the construction of a . . . classificatory system?
5. What rules are revealed when an object of discourse is modified or transformed?
6. What rules allow us to identify certain individuals as authors?[55]

To these might be added two other questions raised by Foucault: (1) What rules give a discourse "value and practical application as scientific discourse?" (2) Why "is it that one particular statement appeared rather than another?"[56] Such questions, it should be noted, "provide necessary pre-conditions for the formation of statements."[57]

Throughout Foucault's writings answers to the foregoing rule-related questions may be found. Our end here, however, is not to discuss each of these queries but to analyze two or three that are uniquely important. We will phrase them as follows: (1) What rules allow specific statements to be made, while other possible statements are excluded or silenced? (2) What rules enable us to determine whether or not a statement may be viewed as true or false? (3) What rules make it possible to decide who or what an author is? A discussion of these questions, it is hoped, will give us a clearer understanding of what is involved in the concept of an *episteme* or discursive formation.

Foucault's answer to the first question above, dealing with the making and the prohibiting of certain statements, has far reaching significance for a student of contemporary rhetorical theory. For in his discussion of the "rules of exclusion," whereby possible knowledge claims are not permitted to be expressed, he is covering ground that all of the authors we have analyzed to date have left largely unexplored. He does so with the rationale that what is excluded or silenced may be as important as what is accepted as knowledge.

Foucault's career-long interest in the subjects of madness or insanity and of sexuality, which he felt were taboos in discourse for centuries, doubtless played a part in motivating him to examine the "rules of exclusion." In his "Discourse on Language," he tells us that every society has a system of rules for controlling what is to be said and for disseminating what is to be regarded as knowledge. This control may take the form of exclusion or prohibition. "We know perfectly well," he notes, "that we are not free to say just anything, that we simply cannot speak of anything, when we like, or where we like. . . ."[58] This prohibition may extend to objects, to rituals, or to specific subjects.

But exclusion is not limited to external rules; it may also involve internal rules that govern "the principles of classification, ordering and distribution."[59] Finally, there are rules of exclusion which prevent certain people from entering discourse if they are perceived as lacking specific qualifications or as failing to meet a series of preconditions. One of the implications of Foucault's notion of the "rules of exclusion" is that when one studies an *episteme* that existed in any period, it is desirable to know how certain possibilities for discourse were never realized.

Foucault appears to be on more controversial ground when he seeks to answer the question about the truth and the falsity of a claim. The rule which he embraces is a discourse-centered one in which he argues that truth is what is accepted as being true within a discursive formation. He held that since there can be no perfect relationship between a symbol and its referent, and since the human sciences can be traced back primarily to non-rational origins, then truth is at all times dependent upon discourse.[60] One critic expresses the following strong reservations about what he concludes is a relativistic theory of truth: "If what Foucault says is true then truth is always relative to discourse; there cannot be any statements which are true in all discourses, nor can there be any statements which are true for all discourses. . . ."[61]

In his discussion of the third question, which focuses on the rules characterizing the nature of an author, Foucault is both innovative and insightful. The title of his provocative essay on this subject is "What Is an Author?" In providing an answer to his own question. Foucault refutes the traditional view that an author automatically holds a superior position to that of the text. The argument that he propounds instead is that the author is a product of the discursive formation that is prevalent. Thus the role and function of an author vary from period to period according to the dominant *episteme* that is in operation. This means that at times it is necessary to identify an author; at other times the name is suppressed or pushed aside. All that counts in such instances are the meanings inherent in the statements or propositions that are uttered.

There are two other problems, Foucault adds, associated with the idea of elevating the status of an author. First, an author's published works only reveal what was stated for public consumption. They do not give a full picture of all his/her ideas. For instance, they do not show what was said in conversations, or in unpublished writings, or in marginal notations on manuscripts— all of which are also fundamental aspects of the author's philosophy or beliefs.

Secondly, Foucault points out, author one is not author two. Many authors of the first type, such as creators of novels or another communication genre, may develop an approach that is worthy of emulation. But in the end this level of writer is never more than the author of a particular text. The second type author, however, performs a more vital function. It is one who initiates a new discursive practice that has the power to generate a completely different kind of discourse that will be influential over a long period of time. Included in this category are Freud and Marx whose works "established the endless possibility of discourse."[62]

Our task in examining the nature and role of an author, therefore, is to discover the rules that account for the author's function and position in a specific discourse. What Foucault most earnestly wished to happen in the future is the initiation of a culture in which we do not need to raise questions about the identity of an author or the nature of the self revelation through language. Instead of wondering who is speaking, our attention should be centered on the more important questions such as these:

What are the modes of existence of this discourse?
Where does it come from; how is it circulated; what controls it?
Who can fulfill these diverse functions of the subject?
What placements are determined for possible subjects (authors)?[63]

It seems clear that by upgrading the value of the content of discourse and by depreciating the worth of an author's role in the production of discourse, Foucault offers a compelling challenge to the traditional theory of ethos or ethical proof as an essential factor in rhetoric.

The Archaeological/Genealogical Method of Inquiry

Foucault gave two names to his method of inquiry for examining the discursive formations of a historical era. He used the words "archaeological" and "genealogical." These metaphors were carefully chosen so that they could depict in a graphic manner the nature of his investigative procedure. Just as an archaeologist digs into the earth in order to discover physical artifacts that shed light on a particular age, Foucault's archaeologist is one who similarly follows a path of descent in an effort to unearth the rules responsible for a discursive formation.

Before we make the slight distinction that may be drawn with respect to the meaning of the terms genealogy and archaeology, let us see in a general way what the method entails. Earlier we noted Foucault's concern about how a particular discursive formation tended to present a limited view of the possibilities for knowledge within a historical period. This occurred for the most part, as we have seen, because of the "rules of exclusion" or the practice of silencing certain potential statements that could have been made. As a result, history has passed on to us a unitary view of what knowledge was at a given time. All too often it was a view based on fragments and presumed continuities of thought which failed to take into consideration the notion of discontinuity.

Archaeology, in sum, is a special method of research which seeks "to emancipate historical knowledges" that have been suppressed or ignored; to give a history to sentiments and instincts that have been motivating; and to cast doubt on traditional conclusions that have been presented with unchallenged finality. In the doing of its work, archaeology would give attention to local as well as to more widely circulated claims. As Foucault elaborates on this point, he draws a distinction between the related terms of archaeology and genealogy:

Archaeology would be the appropriate methodology of this analysis of local discursivities, and genealogy would be the tactics whereby, on the basis of the descriptions of these local discursivities, the subjected knowledges which were thus released would be brought into play.[64]

It is highly instructive to observe that this method of inquiry, from Foucault's perspective, is not merely an exercise in recreating a more accurate picture of the past. It also serves the essential function of gaining an access to knowledge that might be used in a tactical way for the benefit of members of society today—especially that group of people who have been excluded from participating in discourse on a subject that is of significance to them.

Foucault applies his archaeological/genealogical method in his most influential book *The Order of Things*.[65] His research on the period beginning with the sixteenth century and extending to the current period led him to conclude that there were four eras that exemplify well delineated *epistemes*. He identifies them as the pre-Classical era (approximately 1500 to 1620 or 1630); the Classical period (about 1630 to 1775 or 1780); the Modern age (roughly 1800 to 1950); and the Contemporary era (from 1950 to the present). A brief summary of the first two *epistemes* will be given here for the purpose of seeing how the archaeological method does its work. Regrettably, Foucault did not develop the *episteme* that has been paramount in the last four decades.

Foucault argues that the pre-Classical *episteme* derived force from the single theme of resemblance. Consequently, all of the statements that were accepted as knowledge in this era were grounded in the unifying notion of comparisons or similitudes. Man, nature, the stars, and the divine, for example, were merely reflections of each other. The world, according to this view, "must fold in upon itself, duplicate itself, or form a chain with itself so that things can resemble one another."[66]

Gradually, Foucault asserts, scholars in the seventeenth century began to see the inherent limitations of this *episteme*. They came eventually to believe that knowledge based on resemblances was incapable of enlarging our understanding. Indeed, a statement expressing a so-called knowledge claim did no more than affirm what was already recognized as being true. Among the first to see this major shortcoming, observes Foucault, was Francis Bacon whose concept of the fallacies of the idols—Tribe, Cave, Marketplace, and Theatre—was a critique of resemblances. Since the idols as conceived by Bacon were errors in perception, those who were led astray by these faulty judgments tended to see resemblances where resemblances did not exist.

Later when Descartes also saw weaknesses in the pre-Classical interpretation of resemblances, he joined Bacon and other scientific thinkers in initiating a discontinuity that ushered in a new discursive formation that Foucault describes as Classical. This episteme drew heavily upon reasoning, representation, and order, and remained dominant until the end of the eighteenth century.[67]

Power

The last element to be analyzed in our brief description of Foucault's principal perspectives on discourse is the subject of power. As one whose most active years occurred in the volatile decade of the 1960s, Foucault saw power from many different angles. He saw it as an apparatus of the state, as a means of influence enforced by the judicial system, and as an economic function which, in the view of many Marxist scholars, had a relationship to production and domination. These personal observations, in conjunction with his in depth studies of the past, turned him in a different direction as he sought to discover the role that power played in the development

and perpetuation of a discursive formation, and in the eventual creation of a discontinuity that resulted in the initiation of a new *episteme*.

Foucault's probes led him to infer that power focuses on social relations and persuasive strategies. Commenting on this point, Philip notes: "Foucault (in the latter part of his career) sees power as a relationship between individuals where one agent acts in a manner which affects another's actions."[68] Individuals, according to this interpretation, serve the dual function of being the targets of power and the exercisers of it. "Because of this, power relations are always potentially unstable and potentially reversible—I may limit your choice of actions, but your actions may equally limit mine."[69]

If power utilizes persuasive strategies in order to influence the actions of others, what is its relationship to knowledge and truth? Foucault's answer to this question is unequivocal. Power produces that which is judged to be knowledge and truth. A practitioner is able to do this by stimulating a hearer to put his/her received knowledge into use in such a way that further knowledge may be generated. An ethical issue arises, Foucault implies, from this concept of power. If one persuades another to adopt a particular claim, ordering, or classification that is only partial in scope, then we may be endorsing a discursive formation that has excluded vital points of view. Although the resulting formation will constitute what is regarded as truth at a given moment in history, it will be flawed.[70]

Because power makes use of persuasion that affects social relations, thereby determining what is to be viewed as knowledge and truth, Foucault draws this conclusion:

The longer I continue, the more it seems to me that the formation of discourses and the genealogy of knowledge need to be analysed, not in terms of consciousness, modes of perception and forms of ideology, but in terms of tactics and strategies of power.[71]

It is appropriate, we feel, that our study of the rhetoric of western thought conclude with this analysis of representative perspectives of Foucault's theory of discourse. As can be readily seen, many of his ideas challenge some of the basic assumptions that have been made by other rhetoricians and by historians. Regardless of what we think about the merits of some of his most provocative claims, he has presented to us a challenge that we cannot easily ignore. In effect, he is saying that if we want a viable rhetoric of the future, we need to reexamine the past again and again to see what possibilities we have overlooked, or what potentially rich ideas have been silenced or excluded. Equally important, he has outlined an archaeological method of inquiry that may serve as a guide in performing this task.

Notes

1. We would like to congratulate Sonya K. Foss, Karen A. Foss, and Robert Trapp for their inclusion of chapters on these three scholars in their volume entitled: *Contemporary Perspectives on Rhetoric* (Prospect Heights, Ill., 1985).

2. Ernesto Grassi, "Critical Philosophy or Topical Philosophy?", in George Tagliacozzo and Hayden V. White, eds., *Giambattista Vico: An International Symposium* (Baltimore: The Johns Hopkins University Press, 1969), pp. 39–44.

3. "Critical Philosophy or Topical Philosophy?", 45–49.

4. Grassi, "Rhetoric and Philosophy," *Philosophy and Rhetoric*, 9 (1976), 208–209.

5. "Rhetoric and Philosophy," 210–212.

6. "Rhetoric and Philosophy," 214.

7. "Rhetoric and Philosophy," 214.

8. "Rhetoric and Philosophy," 214.

9. Grassi, *Rhetoric as Philosophy: The Humanist Tradition* (University Park: The Pennsylvania State University Press, 1980). Hereafter cited as *Rhetoric as Philosophy*.

10. *Rhetoric as Philosophy*, p. 10.

11. *Rhetoric as Philosophy*, p. 16.

12. Grassi, "The Priority of Common Sense and Imagination: Vico's Philosophical Relevance Today," In George Tagliacozzo, Michael Mooney, and Donald P. Verene, eds., *Vico and Contemporary Thought* (Atlantic Highlands, N.J.: Humanities Press, 1976), p. 172.

13. *Rhetoric as Philosophy*, p. 51.

14. See *Rhetoric as Philosophy*, pp. 86, 100; and "The Priority of Common Sense," pp. 174–183.

15. *Rhetoric as Philosophy*, p. 96.

16. *Rhetoric as Philosophy*, p. 100.

17. *Rhetoric as Philosophy*, p. 97.

18. *Rhetoric as Philosophy*, p. 113.

19. *Rhetoric as Philosophy*, p. 75.

20. Anthony Giddens, "Jurgen Habermas," in Quentin Skinner, ed., *The Return of Grand Theory in the Human Sciences* (Cambridge: Cambridge University Press, 1985). p. 124.

21. Giddens, p. 123.

22. See Thomas McCarthy's "Introduction," in Jurgen Habermas, *Communication and the Evolution of Society* (Boston: Beacon Press, 1979), xvii.

23. *Communication and the Evolution of Society*, p. 5.

24. Habermas, "Toward a Theory of Communicative Competence," *Recent Sociology*, No. 2, Hans Peter Dreitzel, ed. (London: Collier-MacMillan, 1970), p. 122.

25. *Recent Sociology*, p. 122.

26. *Recent Sociology*, p. 143.

27. Habermas, *Communication and the Evolution of Society*, p. 26.

28. *Communication and the Evolution of Society*, p. 35.

29. Habermas, *Reason and the Rationalization of Society*, p. 289.

30. *Reason and the Rationalization of Society*, pp. 325, 329.

31. *Reason and the Rationalization of Society*, p. 333. On this point McCarthy notes: "The employment of constatives makes possible the distinction between a public world (being, that which really is) and a public world (appearance)." "A Theory of Communicative Competence," *Phil. Soc. Sci.* 3 (1973), 138.

32. *Reason and the Rationalization of Society,* p. 329.

33. *Reason and the Rationalization of Society,* p. 334.

34. McCarthy, "A Theory of Communicative Competence," 138.

35. *Reason and the Rationalization of Society,* pp. 326, 329, and 334.

36. *Reason and the Rationalization of Society,* p. 326.

37. *Reason and the Rationalization of Society,* p. 326.

38. *Reason and the Rationalization of Society,* p. 17–18.

39. *Reason and the Rationalization of Society,* p. 18.

40. *Reason and the Rationalization of Society,* p. 18.

41. *Reason and the Rationalization of Society,* p. 26.

42. *Reason and the Rationalization of Society,* p. 25.

43. *Reason and the Rationalization of Society,* p. 25.

44. *Reason and the Rationalization of Society,* p. 26.

45. See *Reason and the Rationalization of Society,* pp. 36–40.

46. McCarthy, "A Theory of Communicative Competence," 141.

47. Giddens, 130.

48. For an excellent analysis of Habermas' ideas on the ideal speech situation, see Giddens, 131, and McCarthy, "A Theory of Communicative Competence," 137–148.

49. See Mark Philip, "Michel Foucault," in *The Return of Grand Theory in the Human Sciences.*

50. J. G. Merquior, *Foucault* (Berkeley: University of California Press, 1985), p. 16.

51. See Allan Megill, "The Reception of Foucault by Historians," *Journal of the History of Ideas,* XLVIII (Jan.–Mar., 1987), 135–141.

52. See "Preface" of Donald F. Bouchard, ed., *Language, Counter-Memory, Practice* (Ithaca: Cornell University Press, 1977).

53. Foucault, *The Archaeology of Knowledge* (New York: Pantheon Books, 1972), p. 117.

54. Philip, 70. Also see Foucault's "Foreward to the English Translation of *The Order of Things* (New York: Vintage Books, 1970).

55. Philip, 69–70.

56. *The Archaeology of Knowledge,* p. 27.

57. Philip, 69.

58. *The Archaeology of Knowledge,* p. 216.

59. *The Archaeology of Knowledge,* p. 220.

60. In his essay on Nietzsche, he observed: "Truth is undoubtedly the sort of error that cannot be refuted because it was hardened into an unalterable form in the long baking process of history. "Nietzsche, Genealogy, History," in *Language, Counter-Memory, Practice,* p. 144.

61. Philip, 70.

62. "What is an Author?", in Bouchard, pp. 131–136. Foucault also makes the following interesting point: "A study of Galileo's works would alter our knowledge of the history, but not the science of mechanics; whereas, a reexamination of the books of Freud or Marx can transform our understanding of psychoanalysis or Marxism," "What is an Author?", p. 136.

63. "What is an Author?", 138.

64. *Power/Knowledge,* Colin Gordon, ed. (New York: Pantheon Books, 1980), p. 87.

65. Merquior calls this work Foucault's "masterpiece," *Foucault,* p. 35.

66. *The Order of Things,* pp. 25–26.

67. See in particular the chapter on "Representing," *The Order of Things,* pp. 46–77.

68. Philip, 74. Foucault noted: "In reality, power means relations, a more-or-less organized, hierarchical coordinated cluster of relations," *Power/Knowledge,* p. 199.

69. Philip, 75.

70. Consider, for example, the following statement describing the end of the pre-Classical *episteme:* "And it was also in the nature of things that the knowledge of the sixteenth century should leave behind it the distorted memory of a muddled and disordered body of learning in which all the things in the world could be linked indiscriminately to men's experiences, traditions, or credulities." *The Order of Things,* p. 51.

71. *Power/Knowledge,* p. 77.